Volkswagen
Rabbit
Scirocco

Service Manual
1975, 1976, 1977

Complete Service Manuals published by Robert Bentley, Inc.

Volkswagen Beetle and Karmann Ghia Official Service Manual Type 1, Model Years 1966–1969. Volkswagen of America, Inc.

Volkswagen Super Beetle, Beetle and Karmann Ghia Official Service Manual Type 1, Model Years 1970–1977. Volkswagen of America, Inc.

Volkswagen Station Wagon/Bus Official Service Manual Type 2, Model Years 1968–1977. Volkswagen of America, Inc.

Volkswagen Fastback and Squareback Official Service manual Type 3, Model Years 1968–1973. Volkswagen of America, Inc.

Volkswagen Dasher Service Manual, Model Years 1974–1977. Robert Bentley, Inc.

Volkswagen Rabbit/Scirocco Service Manual, Model Years 1975–1977. Robert Bentley, Inc.

Audi Fox Service Manual, Model Years 1973–1977. Robert Bentley, Inc.

Capri Complete Service Manual, Model Years 1970–1975. Robert Bentley, Inc.

Complete Official Triumph TR2 & TR3, 1953–1961 — includes Driver's Instruction Book and Service Instruction Manual. British Leyland Motors

Complete Official Triumph TR4 & TR4A, 1961–1968 — includes Driver's Handbook, Workshop Manual, Competition Preparation Manual. British Leyland Motors

Complete Official Triumph GT6, GT6+ & GT6 Mk III, 1967–1973 — includes Driver's Handbook and Workshop Manual. British Leyland Motors

Complete Official Triumph TR6 & TR250, 1967–1975 — includes Driver's Handbook and Workshop Manual. British Leyland Motors

Complete Official Triumph Spitfire Mk III, Mk IV & 1500, 1968–1974 — includes Driver's Handbook and Workshop Manual. British Leyland Motors

Complete Official Triumph Spitfire 1500, 1975–1977 — includes Driver's Handbook and Workshop Manual. British-Leyland Motors

Complete Official Triumph TR7, 1975–1977 — includes Driver's Handbook and Workshop Manual. British Leyland Motors

Complete Official Austin-Healey 100-Six and 3000, 1956–1968. British Leyland Motors

MG Workshop Manual: Complete Tuning and Maintenance for All Models from "M"–Type to TF 1500. W. E. Blower

Complete Official MGB, 1962–1974 — includes Driver's Handbook, Workshop Manual, Special Tuning Manual. British Leyland Motors

Complete Official MGB, 1975–1977 — includes Driver's Handbook, and Workshop Manual. British Leyland Motors

Complete Official Jaguar "E" — includes Driver's Handbook, Workshop Manual, Special Tuning Manual. British Leyland Motors

Complete Official 948cc & 1098cc Sprite/Midget — includes Driver's Handbook, Workshop Manual, Special Tuning Manual. British Leyland Motors

Complete Official 1275cc Sprite/Midget, 1967–1974 — includes Driver's Handbook, Workshop Manual, Emission Control Supplement. British Leyland Motors

Complete Official MG Midget 1500, 1975–1977 — includes Driver's Handbook and Workshop Manual. British Leyland Motors

Volkswagen
Rabbit
Scirocco

Service Manual
1975, 1976, 1977

Robert Bentley, Inc.

Published and distributed by:

ROBERT BENTLEY, INC.
872 Massachusetts Avenue
Cambridge, Massachusetts 02139

This Manual may be purchased at authorized Volkswagen dealers, at selected bookstores and automotive accessories and parts dealers or directly by mail from the Publisher, Robert Bentley, Inc. at the above address.

NOTE TO USERS OF THIS MANUAL

The Publisher encourages comments from readers of this Manual. These communications have been and will be carefully considered in preparation of this and other Manuals. Please write to Robert Bentley, Inc., at the address on this page.

This Manual is published by Robert Bentley, Inc., which has sole responsibility for its content. Volkswagen has not reviewed and does not vouch for the accuracy of the technical specifications and procedures described in this Manual.

Library of Congress Catalog Card No. 77-79890
ISBN 0-8376-0088-X
Second Revised Edition
10 9 8 7 6 5 4 3 2

LPV 997 171

Manufactured in the United States of America

FOREWORD

The VW Rabbit and the VW Scirocco are thoroughly modern automobiles that have set new standards world-wide for outstanding economy and performance. Though their exceptional handling and responsive engines have made the Rabbit and the Scirocco great favorites with automobile enthusiasts, their sportiness has been achieved without sacrificing economical operation. Consequently, the Rabbit and the Scirocco have also received broad acceptance among every-day drivers who are primarily interested in practical and efficient transportation.

This VW Rabbit/Scirocco Service Manual covers the Rabbit two-door sedans, the Rabbit four-door sedans, and the Sciroccos sold in the United States and Canada for the Model Years 1975, 1976 and 1977. The chassis numbers assigned to the Rabbits and Sciroccos during these model years are:

Rabbit Two-door Sedan/Four-door Sedan	Scirocco
1975: 175 3000 001 to 175 3500 000	1975: 535 2000 001 to 535 2500 000
1976: 176 3000 001 to 176 3500 000	1976: 536 2000 001 to 536 2500 000
1977: 177 3000 001 to 177 3500 000	1977: 537 2000 001 to 537 2500 000

The chassis number of your VW is found in the engine compartment, atop the suspension strut mounting of the right-hand front wheel housing. This Manual is organized so that changes from model year to model year are noted, and if a change within one model year is made, the chassis number of the first Rabbit or Scirocco with this change is given.

For the VW owner with mechanical skills and for independent garages, this Manual gives all the specifications that are available in a VW workshop. In addition, a VW owner who has no intention of working on his or her car will find that reading and owning this Manual will make it possible to discuss repairs intelligently with a professional mechanic.

The aim throughout has been simplicity, clarity, and completeness with step-by-step procedures and accurate specifications. Every human effort has been made to ensure the highest degree of accuracy possible. When the vast array of data presented in this Manual is taken into account, however, no claim to infallibility can be made.

We, therefore, cannot be responsible for the result of any errors that may have crept into the text. The Publisher encourages comments from the readers of this Manual in regard to any errors and, also, suggestions for improvement in the presentation of the technical material. These communications have been and will be carefully considered in the preparation of this and other manuals. Please write to Robert Bentley, Inc., 872 Massachusetts Ave., Cambridge, Massachusetts 02139.

The VW owner intending to do maintenance and repairs should have a set of metric wrenches, a torque wrench, screwdrivers, and feeler gauges, since these basic hand tools will be used in accomplishing a majority of the repairs described in this Manual. Usually, there will be a caution in the text when a repair requires special tools or special skills.

If you are a professional mechanic already working on imported cars, you may have some VW special tools that are shown in some of the illustrations in this Manual. If you have previously worked only on American-manufactured cars, you will not have to replace your expensive micrometers, vernier calipers, and other precision tools because specifications are given both in millimeters and in inches, except when special VW metric tools are indispensable (these measurements are given only in millimeters).

Volkswagens are constantly being improved and sometimes these changes—both in parts and specifications—are made applicable to older VWs. Thus, a replacement part to be used on an older VW may not be the same as the part used in the original installation. These changes are noted in this Manual. If a specification given in this Manual differs from one in an earlier source, disregard the earlier specification. The specifications in this Volkswagen Service Manual are accurate as of the publication date of this Manual.

Volkswagen offers an extensive warranty. Therefore, before deciding to repair a VW that is covered by the new-car warranty, consult your Authorized VW Dealer. You may find that he can make the repair either free or at minimum cost.

The Volkswagen is both an easy car to service and an easy car to get serviced. If you should have difficulty determining what needs to be done, the VW Computer Analysis and Maintenance service, available at almost all VW dealerships, can pinpoint many problems in one rapid check. This service is available for all models, and you can use it even if you intend to do your own maintenance and repairs. When a repair is needed that you feel is too difficult to do yourself, a trained VW mechanic is ready to do the job for you.

Robert Bentley, Inc.

Please read these warnings and cautions
before proceeding with maintenance and repair work.

Directions for using torque wrenches calibrated in newton meters

In adopting the SI *(Systeme International)* units of measure, which constitute the Modernized Metric System, tool manufacturers are beginning to introduce torque wrenches that are calibrated in newton meters. As metrication proceeds, torque specifications given in foot pounds (ft. lb.) and meter kilograms (mkg) will eventually be replaced by torque specifications given in newton meters (N·m or Nm).

At present, there are in use too few torque wrenches calibrated in newton meters to justify the inclusion of newton meter torque specifications in this Manual. Nevertheless, if you purchase a new torque wrench, we recommend that you try to obtain one that is calibrated in newton meters. Such a tool can easily be used with this Manual by converting the meter kilogram specifications to newton meters.

To convert meter kilograms (mkg) to newton meters, simply disregard the decimal point. For example, 3.5 mkg would become 35 Nm. To convert centimeter kilograms (cmkg) to newton meters, point-off the one place with a decimal. For example, 50 cmkg would become 5.0 Nm. These conversions are not mathematically precise (3.5 mkg actually equals 34.3 Nm) but they are adequate for normal workshop purposes.

BRAKES AND WHEELS

Contents

1

Brakes and Wheels

The diagonal dual-circuit hydraulic foot brakes operate on all four wheels. The foot pressure required to operate the brakes is reduced by a vacuum powered servo installed between the pedal and the master cylinder. Early Rabbit models imported into the U.S. have drum brakes at all four wheels. However, all Scirocco models and many Rabbits—particularly the latest models—have floating caliper front disc brakes and rear drum brakes. On Rabbit models, there is a pressure regulator in the hydraulic lines to the rear brakes. The regulator prevents the rear brakes from locking when the brakes are being used to their maximum.

A dual-chamber master cylinder provides operating pressure to both brake circuits. The system is so designed that leaks in one circuit cannot affect the other. One circuit operates on the right front wheel and the left rear wheel. The other circuit operates on the left front wheel and the right rear wheel. An electrical warning system in the master cylinder causes a red warning indicator in the instrument panel to light up if hydraulic pressure is too low in either brake circuit. If you see this light while you are driving, it is imperative that the brake system be given a thorough check, even though braking action may still seem satisfactory. Complete loss of pressure in one of the brake circuits will cause the pedal to fall closer to the floor during braking and will result in abnormally long stopping distances.

Because safe vehicle operation depends very heavily on the brakes, all brake system service and repair work must be carried out with extreme cleanliness, careful attention to specifications, and proper working procedures. All necessary information is given here, although some of the operations that are described may be of practical value only to professional mechanics. If you lack the skills, the special tools, or a clean workshop for servicing the brake system, we suggest you leave these repairs to an Authorized Dealer or other qualified shop. We especially urge you to consult your Authorized Dealer before attempting repairs on a car still covered by the new-car warranty.

The pages devoted to wheels and tires should have practical interest to all drivers, whether they service their own cars or not. A great many cases of abnormal tire wear or poor vehicle handling are the direct result of improperly fitted tires, incorrectly inflated tires, or driving practices that damage the tires. It is our belief that following the advice offered here will not only save you money but also make your driving safer.

1. GENERAL DESCRIPTION

Fig. 1-1 is a simplified schematic diagram of the diagonal dual-circuit brake system. Each chamber of the dual-chamber master cylinder is connected to one of the circuits. The front chamber of the master cylinder operates the brakes on the right front wheel and the left rear wheel. The rear chamber of the master cylinder operates the brakes on the left front wheel and the right rear wheel. Each circuit is capable of operating independently of the other.

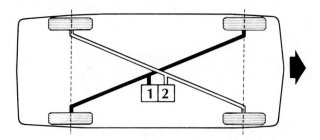

Fig. 1-1. Simplified schematic diagram of the diagonal dual-circuit brake system. Arrow indicates front of car.

Master Cylinder and Hydraulic Lines

The master cylinder generates the hydraulic pressure needed to operate the brakes and is connected to the wheel cylinders by the brake lines and hoses. When the driver depresses the brake pedal, the movement is transmitted by a rod to a valve inside the vacuum powered brake servo. Depending on the movement of the valve, engine vacuum acts upon the servo piston. The piston is connected to a pushrod that moves the master cylinder pistons. The system fails safe so, if the servo ceases to function, the foot brakes can still be applied. However, the pedal pressure required will be somewhat greater than normal.

Calipers and Wheel Cylinders

The drum brake wheel cylinders are of the rigidly-mounted, dual opposed piston type. When hyraulic pressure is applied to the cylinder, the pistons move outward, applying mechanical pressure to the brake shoes.

Two kinds of front disc brake calipers have been used on the cars covered by this manual. Both kinds are of the floating caliper type. One kind of caliper, manufactured by Teves (ATE), has a single piston. The other kind of caliper, manufactured by Girling, has two opposed pis-

tons that move outward through opposite ends of the same cylinder. Both kinds of calipers use identical brake pads, though no other parts are interchangeable.

Pressure Regulator

Rabbit models have pressure regulated rear brakes. The pressure regulator is located beneath the car, near the left-hand side of the rear axle. The regulator is connected by a coil spring to the rear axle beam. Thus, axle beam deflection is transmitted to the pressure regulator. When the rear wheels are lightly loaded, less hydraulic pressure is supplied to the rear brakes in order to keep the rear wheels from locking up.

Parking Brakes

The cable-operated parking brake works on the rear wheels only. The hand lever is held or released by a ratchet and is centrally located between the front seats.

2. MAINTENANCE

The following routine maintenance operations should be performed at the times or mileages listed in **LUBRICATION AND MAINTENANCE.** Instructions for doing these jobs can be found in this section under the headings listed after each maintenance check.

1. Checking and changing brake fluid. **9.1**
2. Checking brake linings. **8.2**
3. Checking brakes for correct adjustment. **8.1**
4. Checking parking brake adjustment. **10.1**
5. Checking brake lines and hoses for leaks and damage. **6**
6. Checking brake lights. **4.1**
7. Checking operation of brake warning system. **4.1**
8. Checking brake pressure regulator pressures (Rabbit models only). **4.4**
9. Checking tires for wear, damage, and correct inflation pressures. **11.**

3. BRAKE TROUBLESHOOTING

Table a lists brake problems, probable causes, and suggested remedies. The numbers in bold type in the Remedy column refer to the numbered headings in this section of the Manual under which the suggested repairs are described.

Table a. Brake Troubleshooting

Problem	Probable Cause	Remedy
1. Pedal goes all the way to floor in braking	a. Linings worn b. No fluid, low fluid	a. Adjust brake shoes (never adjust at pedal.) See **8.1.** b. Find and repair leaks. Fill and bleed system. See **9.**
2. Low pedal even after adjustment and bleeding	Master cylinder defective	Replace or rebuild master cylinder. See **4.2, 4.3.**
3. Pedal spongy or brakes work only after pedal is pumped	a. Insufficient fluid in reservoir b. Air in system c. Spring weak in master cylinder	a. Top up fluid and bleed system. See **9.** b. Check for leaks and bleed system. See **9.** c. Replace or rebuild master cylinder. See **4.2, 4.3.**
4. Braking action decreases after shoes have been adjusted	a. Brake lines leaking b. Defective master or wheel cylinders	a. Tighten connections or fit new lines and hoses. See **6.** b. Replace or rebuild faulty cylinder. See **4.2, 4.3, 7.2, 7.3, 8.4, 8.5.**
5. Brakes overheat	a. Compensating port blocked b. Pushrod misadjusted c. Brake shoe return springs weak d. Rubber parts swollen	a. Clean master cylinder. See **4.2, 4.3.** b. Adjust pushrod length. See **5.2.** c. Fit new return springs. See **8.2, 8.3.** d. Flush system, replace fluid and all rubber parts. See **9.**
6. Brakes inefficient despite high pedal pressure	a. Linings oiled up b. Unsuitable brake linings c. Loose or leaking vacuum hose to power brake servo d. Servo diaphragm leaking e. Poor seal between servo and master cylinder f. Check valve in vacuum line not working properly	a. Clean drums. Replace linings and oil seals. See **8.2, 8.3.** b. Fit new linings. See **7.1, 8.3.** c. Replace leaking vacuum hoses or tighten hose clamps. See **5.3.** d. Replace the servo. See **5.3.** e. Replace large sealing ring. Check piston rod for damage and, if necessary, replace it. See **4.2.** f. Replace faulty valve. See **5.1.**
7. Brakes bind while car is in motion	a. Compensating port blocked b. Brake fluid unsuitable c. Pushrod misadjusted	a. Disassemble master cylinder and clear port. See **4.2, 4.3.** b. Flush system and refill. See **9.** c. Adjust pushrod length. See **5.2.**
8. Brakes chatter and tend to grab	a. Linings worn b. Drums out-of-round	a. Fit new linings. See **7.1, 8.3.** b. Recondition or replace drums. See **8.2, 8.7.**
9. Drum brakes squeak	a. Unsuitable or badly fitted linings b. Brake linings dirty c. Backing plates distorted d. Brake shoe return springs weak e. Poor lining contact pattern due to shoe distortion	a. Fit new linings properly. See **8.3.** b. Clean brakes. See **8.2.** c. Check backing plates for distortion and fit new parts if necessary. See **8.2, 8.6.** d. Fit new return springs. See **8.3.** e. Align shoes with backing plate with 0.20 mm (.008 inch) clearance at lining ends and contact across full width. See **8.3.**
10. Disc brakes squeak	a. Unsuitable pads b. Spreader spring faulty or missing c. Pad guide surfaces dirty or rusted d. Pads dirty or glazed e. Lining loose on pad	a. Fit new pads. See **7.1.** b. Install new spreader spring. See **7.1.** c. Clean pads and calipers. See **7.1.** d. Clean and replace pads. See **7.1.** e. Replace pads. See **7.1.**

(continued on next page)

Table a. Brake Troubleshooting (continued)

Problem	Probable Cause	Remedy
11. Brakes give uneven braking	a. Oil or grease on linings	a. Clean drums. Fit new linings and seals or wheel cylinders if necessary. See **8.2, 8.3, 8.4.**
	b. Brake pressure regulator defective	b. Adjust or replace brake pressure regulator. See **4.4.**
	c. Poor contact between lining and drum due to brake shoe distortion	c. Shape shoes to leave 0.20 mm (.008 inch) clearance at lining ends. See **8.3.**
	d. Brake shoes too tight in the adjusting screw slots or in wheel cylinder pistons	d. Free up shoes. See **8.3.**
	e. Different types of linings on same axle	e. Fit new shoes or pads. See **7.1, 8.3.**
	f. Incorrect tire pressures or unevenly worn tires	f. Correct pressures or replace worn tires. See **11.2, 11.6.**
	g. Drums or discs out-of-round or scored	g. Recondition or replace discs or drums. See **7.4, 8.2.**
	h. Disc brake pads sticking in caliper	h. Clean caliper and pads. See **7.1.**
	i. Disc brake pads reinstalled in wrong location	i. Install new pads. See **7.1**
	j. Brake shoes not in contact with backing plate	j. Reposition shoes or align or replace backing plate. See **8.3, 8.6.**
	k. Pistons tight in wheel cylinders	k. Free up pistons. See **8.5.**
	l. Dirt in brake lines or hoses	l. Clean system and replace defective parts. See **6, 9.**
12. Brakes pulsate	a. Drums out-of-round (drum brakes only)	a. Recondition or replace drums. See **8.2.**
	b. Excessive disc runout or thickness variations (disc brakes only)	b. Recondition or replace discs. See **7.4.**
	c. Mating surface between disc or drum and hubs dirty	c. Clean surface. Reinstall disc or drum. See **7.4.**
	d. Brake pads worn out	d. Fit new pads. See **7.1.**
13. Foot pressure on brake pedal must be increased when the pedal reaches a certain position	Groove worn in piston rod that allows air from ventilation drilling to enter servo as groove goes past sealing cup	Replace or rebuild master cylinder. See **4.2, 4.3.**

4. MASTER CYLINDER AND PRESSURE REGULATOR

The master cylinder is mounted on the vacuum powered brake servo, inside the engine compartment. A translucent plastic brake fluid reservoir is mounted atop the brake master cylinder.

4.1 Testing and Replacing Brake Light/Warning Light Switches

The brake light/warning light electrical connections are shown in Fig. 4-1. The dashboard-mounted brake warning light should light up when the engine is being started (key position 3). This is a functional check to show whether or not the bulb is burned out. The light goes off when the key has been released to position 2. If the light comes on during braking, it indicates either a leak or a pressure loss in one of the brake circuits.

To test brake light switch contacts:

1. Check the brake light bulbs. Replace if necessary.

2. Disconnect the outside wires from the front brake light/warning light switch (**81** and **81a**, black-red and blue-brown wires; see Fig. 4-1).

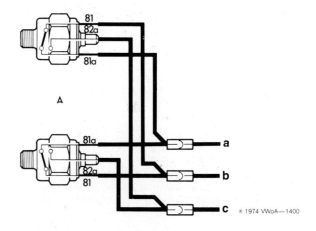

A. Brake light/warning light switches
a. Blue-brown wire to terminal K on dual-circuit brake warning and safety belt warning system control light
b. Black-red wire to brake lights
c. Yellow-red wire to terminal 30d on fuse box

Fig. 4-1. Electrical wiring and terminals of brake light/warning light switches.

3. Switch the ignition on and depress the brake pedal. The brake lights should go on. If they do, reconnect the wires to the front switch and remove the wires

(81 and **81a)** from the rear switch. Repeat the test. The brake lights should go on.

4. If the brake lights do not work in one of the tests, replace the defective switch (the one that remained connected during the test).

To replace switch:

1. Disconnect all wires from the defective switch.

2. Unscrew the switch from the master cylinder. Keep the sealing washer.

3. Install the sealing washer and the new switch. Torque to 2.0 mkg (14 ft. lb.). Then connect the wires as indicated in Fig. 4-1.

> **NOTE** ——
> For additional information about the electrical circuits, consult the wiring diagrams in **ELECTRICAL SYSTEM.**

To test brake warning light contact:

1. Check the socket and the light bulb. If necessary, replace them.

2. Operate the starter. The warning light should come on.

3. Open the bleeder valve at the left rear wheel. (See **9. Bleeding Brakes.**)

4. Start the engine and depress the brake pedal. The brake warning light should come on.

5. Close the bleeder valve of the left rear brake and open the bleeder valve at the right rear wheel. Repeat the test described in step 4.

6. Close the bleeder valve. Check the fluid level in the brake fluid reservoir. If necessary, add fluid.

> **CAUTION** ——
> Use only new, unused brake fluid that meets SAE recommendation J 1703 and conforms to Motor Vehicle Safety Standard 116 DOT 3.

4.2 Removing and Installing Master Cylinder

The master cylinder is mounted on two studs on the vacuum powered brake servo. In removing or installing the master cylinder, be careful not to bend any of the brake lines or damage the union nuts that hold the lines to the master cylinder.

To remove:

1. Using a clean syringe, remove the brake fluid from the reservoir. Discard the fluid.

> **WARNING** ——
> Do not start a siphon with your mouth or spill fluid onto the car. Brake fluid is both poisonous and damaging to paint.

2. Disconnect the battery ground strap. Then disconnect the wires from the brake light/warning light switches. If necessary, attach tags to the wires so that later you can reinstall the wires in their original positions.

3. Disconnect the brake lines from the master cylinder.

4. Remove the two nuts that hold the master cylinder to the vacuum powered brake servo. Then remove the master cylinder from the car. Discard the old vacuum seal O-ring that is between the master cylinder and the servo.

To install:

1. Install a new vacuum seal O-ring in the annular groove of the master cylinder.

> **NOTE** ——
> The master cylinder pushrod inside the vacuum powered brake servo is factory-machined to precise tolerances and does not require adjustment prior to installation of the master cylinder—even if a new servo has been installed.

2. Position the master cylinder on the servo and, while you hold the cylinder in position, screw the brake line union nuts into the master cylinder by a few turns.

3. Install the nuts that hold the master cylinder to the brake servo. Torque the nuts to a maximum of 1.3 mkg (9.4 ft. lb.). Over-tightening the nuts may damage the servo.

4. Torque the brake line unions to 1.5 to 2.0 mkg (11 to 14 ft. lb.).

5. Reconnect the wires to the brake light/warning light switches. If necessary, refer to the wiring diagram given in **4.1 Testing and Replacing Brake Light Warning Light Switches.**

6. Fill the brake fluid reservoir with new, unused brake fluid that meets SAE recommendation J 1703 and conforms to Motor Vehicle Safety Standard 116 DOT 3. Then bleed the entire brake system as described in **9. Bleeding Brakes.**

7. Reconnect the battery ground strap. Then check the brake operation with a road test. Make sure that pedal travel is not excessive and that the pedal does not feel spongy—which could indicate that the bleeding operation needs to be repeated. The brake warning light should not come on during braking.

4.3 Rebuilding Master Cylinder

In rebuilding the brake master cylinder, always use all of the parts that are included in the repair kit. To prevent wear and leakage, use the lubricants specified in the following procedure.

> **WARNING** ——
>
> *Rebuilding the master cylinder requires skill, special tools, and perfectly clean working conditions. Because the master cylinder has a vital influence on safe vehicle operation, you should not attempt to repair a master cylinder that has a worn cylinder bore or other physical damage.*

To disassemble:

1. Remove the master cylinder as described in **4.2 Removing and Installing Master Cylinder.** Remove the residual pressure valves and the brake light/warning light switches.

2. Carefully remove the fluid reservoir from the master cylinder by pulling its outlet pipes out of the rubber plugs. Then remove the rubber plugs from the master cylinder.

3. Remove the stop screw and its seal from the top center part of the master cylinder. Push the pistons slightly in, then use snap ring pliers to remove the circlip. See Fig. 4-2.

47-032

Fig. 4-2. Circlip being removed from master cylinder.

4. Withdraw the stop washer/primary piston assembly from the rear chamber of the master cylinder. Then,

by tapping the cylinder on a piece of soft wood, or by injecting compressed air, remove the secondary piston assembly from the front chamber of the master cylinder.

5. Carefully inspect the bore of the master cylinder. If the bore surface is scored, corroded, or in any way damaged, replace the entire master cylinder.

Minor scratches and hardened deposits can be removed from the cylinder with a brake cylinder hone. When using a brake cylinder hone, lubricate the stones with brake fluid only, never with mineral oil or kerosene. While the hone is spinning, move it in and out of the bore rapidly in order to achieve an even polish over the entire cylinder wall.

After honing, check the fit between the new pistons and the cylinder bore. If the clearance exceeds 0.10 mm (.004 in.), the entire master cylinder should be replaced. The clearance can be measured by inserting a feeler gauge between the piston and the cylinder wall. However, a brake cylinder bore measuring tool or a snap (telescope) gauge and micrometer are preferable tools.

> **WARNING** ——
>
> *After honing the master cylinder, clean any burrs from the compensating ports. Otherwise, the burrs may damage the rubber cups.*

To assemble:

1. Thoroughly clean the master cylinder with new unused brake fluid that meets SAE recommendation J 1703 and conforms to Motor Vehicle Safety Standard 116 DOT 3.

> **WARNING** ——
>
> *Never wash brake parts in gasoline or other petroleum-based solvents since they are damaging to rubber parts in the system.*

2. Check the repair kit to make sure that it contains all the necessary new seals, cups, and pistons. Fig. 4-3 is an exploded view that shows all the master cylinder components.

3. Check that there is no foreign matter on the new parts. If necessary, wash the parts in new, unused brake fluid that meets SAE recommendation J 1703 and conforms to Motor Vehicle Safety Standard 116 DOT 3.

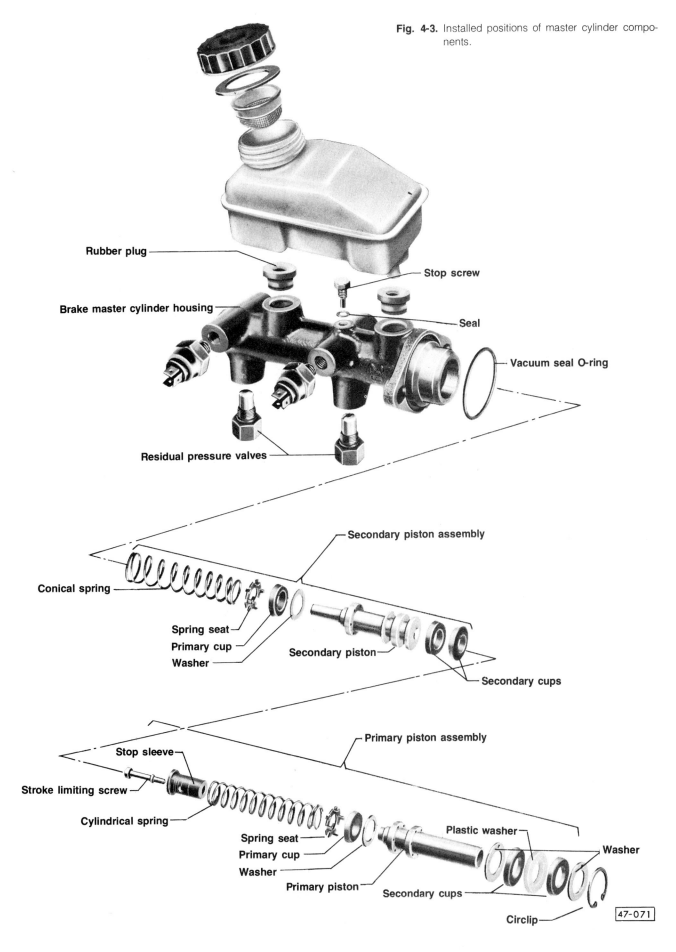

Fig. 4-3. Installed positions of master cylinder components.

Rubber plug

Stop screw

Brake master cylinder housing

Seal

Vacuum seal O-ring

Residual pressure valves

Conical spring

Secondary piston assembly

Spring seat

Primary cup

Washer

Secondary piston

Secondary cups

Primary piston assembly

Stop sleeve

Stroke limiting screw

Cylindrical spring

Spring seat

Primary cup

Washer

Primary piston

Plastic washer

Washer

Secondary cups

Circlip

47-071

4. Install the new small-diameter cups, washers, and spring seats on the new pistons. In installing the small-diameter cups, it is helpful to have a conical cup sleeve such as the one shown in Fig. 4-4. If this tool is unavailable, liberally lubricate the new cups with new, unused brake fluid and be careful not to cut or tear the cups when you pass them over the piston lands.

NOTE ——

The lips of the cups must point in the direction shown earlier in Fig. 4-3.

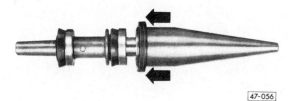

Fig. 4-4. Cup being installed on piston. The cup has been slipped over the conical sleeve from the small end. The sleeve is then placed over the piston, and the cup slipped off the sleeve (arrows) into its groove.

5. Lightly coat the pistons and the installed cups with VW brake cylinder paste. Alternatively, you can fully lubricate the cylinder bore, the pistons, and the cups with new, unused brake fluid that meets SAE recommendation J 1703 and conforms to Motor Vehicle Safety Standard 116 DOT 3.

NOTE ——

Brake cylinder paste is available from your Authorized Dealer and should be the preferred form of lubrication when brake cylinders are repaired. Brake fluid should be considered a satisfactory substitute only if you are unable to reach an Authorized Dealer. Brake cylinders will give longer service when lubricated with VW brake cylinder paste than when lubricated by brake fluid alone.

6. Hold the master cylinder with its closed end down. Install the conical spring—large end first. Then install the secondary piston assembly, pushing it as far as possible into the cylinder.

7. Lubricate the shaft of the primary piston with a light coat of silicone grease (provided in the repair kit). Also fill the annular grooves in the large-diameter secondary cups with silicone grease.

8. Install the metal washers, the large-diameter secondary cups, and the plastic washer on the shaft of the primary piston. The lips of both the large-diameter secondary cups should point into the cylinder, and the radial hole in the plastic washer should point upward when the master cylinder is installed on the car.

9. Start the secondary piston into the cylinder. While holding the cylinder with its open end down, fully install the secondary piston assembly as indicated in Fig. 4-5. Then install the circlip.

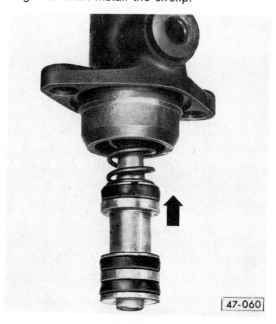

Fig. 4-5. Secondary piston assembly being installed (arrow).

10. Install the stop screw and a new seal. Torque to 0.5 to 1.0 mkg (3.5 to 7.0 ft. lb.).

CAUTION ——

Be sure the stop screw hole is clear. If it is blocked by the piston, damage will result as the screw is installed.

11. Screw the brake light/warning light switches and the residual pressure valves into the master cylinder. Torque to 2.0 mkg (14 ft. lb.).

12. Coat the rubber plugs with new, unused brake fluid. Then press them into the cylinder. Lubricate the fluid reservoir outlet pipes with new, unused brake fluid and install the reservoir on the master cylinder.

13. Install the master cylinder as described in **4.2 Removing and Installing Master Cylinder.**

4.4 Testing and Replacing Rear Brake Pressure Regulator (Rabbit only)

The brake pressure regulator is beneath the car, located on the body just ahead of the rear axle. The regulator is operated mechanically by a coil spring attached to the rear axle beam. The pressure regulator cannot be repaired and must be replaced as a unit if it is faulty. However, the regulator can be adjusted if the front and rear brake pressures are not correctly proportioned.

To pressure-test the brake pressure regulator, you must install two pressure gauges as shown in Fig. 4-6 and Fig. 4-7. The pressure gauges should have a capacity of 160 kg/cm² (2300 psi) and have hoses equipped with threaded ends that can be installed in place of the brake bleeder valves.

Fig. 4-6. Pressure gauge hose attached to bleeder valve hole of front brake caliper.

Fig. 4-7. Pressure gauge hose attached to bleeder valve hole of rear wheel cylinder.

To test regulator:

1. Remove all luggage and other cargo from the car. Fill the fuel tank.

2. Have one person, approximately 75 kg (165 lb.), sit in the driver's seat. Jounce the car several times at the rear and allow it to settle into its natural attitude.

3. Without having the person leave the driver's seat, install spring tensioners as shown in Fig. 4-8 and Fig. 4-9. Tighten the wing nuts until the tensioner hooks just make contact. The object of installing

the tensioners is to keep the rear springs in exactly the positions they assumed after you carried out step 2.

WARNING ——

Be sure that the tensioners are firmly attached to the lower spring supports. Otherwise, when the person gets out of the driver's seat, a tensioner may fly off and cause injury.

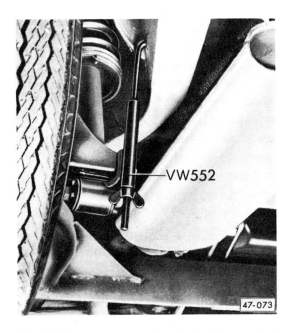

Fig. 4-8. Tensioner correctly installed on left rear shock absorber mounting.

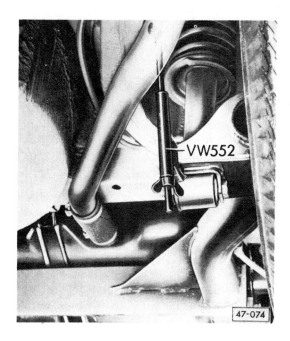

Fig. 4-9. Tensioner correctly installed on right rear shock absorber mounting.

4. Remove the brake bleeder valve from the right rear wheel cylinder. Then connect a pressure gauge. Remove the brake bleeder valve from the left front brake caliper and connect a second pressure gauge.

5. Using the bleeder valves on the gauges, bleed both hoses and gauges. See **9. Bleeding Brakes.**

6. Firmly depress the brake pedal several times. Then depress the brake pedal until the gauge on the left front brake caliper reads 50 kg/cm² (710 psi). The gauge on the right rear wheel cylinder should then read 31 to 35 kg/cm² (440 to 497 psi).

7. Depress the pedal further until the gauge on the left front brake caliper reads 100 kg/cm² (1422 psi). The gauge on the right rear wheel cylinder should then read 53 to 57 kg/cm² (753 to 810 psi).

8. If the rear wheel pressures measured in the two preceeding steps are too high, loosen the clamp bolt at the regulator and reduce the spring tension by moving the bolt in the direction of the black arrow in Fig. 4-10. If the rear wheel pressures were too low, increase the spring tension by moving the bolt in the direction indicated by the white arrow in Fig. 4-10. Tighten the clamp bolt when the correct pressures have been obtained.

CAUTION —

Do not adjust the spring tension with the brake pedal depressed. Doing this could damage the pressure regulator.

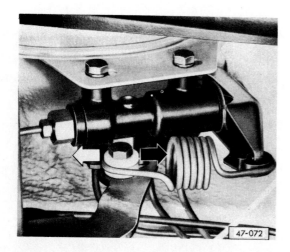

Fig. 4-10. Brake pressure regulator operating spring tension adjustments. Arrows are explained in preceding text.

9. Repeat the pressure comparisons and adjustments until the correct rear brake pressures

are indicated. If the correct rear brake pressures cannot be obtained by adjusting the spring tension, replace the pressure regulator.

10. When the correct pressures have been obtained, remove the gauges and bleed the brake system as described in **9. Bleeding Brakes.** Remove the spring tensioners.

NOTE —

It is unnecessary to repeat the pressure tests at the oppostie wheel on each side.

Replacing Brake Pressure Regulator

The brake pressure regulator is held to the car body by two bolts, as shown previously in Fig. 4-10. After disconnecting the spring from the operating lever and disconnecting the brake lines from the regulator, you can remove the regulator from the car by taking out the two bolts. Installation is the reverse of removal. Torque the mounting bolts to 1.5 mkg (11 ft. lb.). Torque the brake line unions to 1.5 to 2.0 mkg (11 to 14 ft. lb.). Following installation, bleed the entire brake system as described in **9. Bleeding Brakes.** Then adjust the pressure regulator as previously described.

5. BRAKE PEDAL AND BRAKE SERVO

Two kinds of vacuum powered brake servos (Fig. 5-1 and Fig. 5-2) have been used in the cars covered by this Manual. Both kinds have the same specifications and can be interchanged with no modification.

5.1 Servicing Vacuum Powered Brake Servo

There is a filter in the rear of the vacuum powered brake servo. This filter does not need to be replaced unless the adaptor housing has been removed. Nevertheless, it is wise to replace the filter any time that the servo is removed from the car. Instructions for replacing the filter are given in **5.3 Removing and Installing Vacuum Powered Brake Servo.**

If the vacuum powered brake servo is faulty, it must be replaced; no repairs are possible. The troubleshooting table given in **3. Brake Troubleshooting** will help you to determine troubles that can be caused by a faulty servo.

Before you assume that there is trouble in the master cylinder or the vacuum powered brake servo, check the vacuum hoses carefully. If they are disconnected from either the engine or the servo, or if they are cracked and leaking, the servo will not operate. Also test the vacuum check valve as described under the next heading.

1

47-157

Fig. 5-1. Brake servo and master cylinder manufactured by Bendix.

47-152

Fig. 5-2. Brake servo and master cylinder manufactured by Teves (ATE).

Testing Vacuum Check Valve

There is a check valve installed in the vacuum line from the engine to the brake servo. The purpose of this valve is to prevent an engine backfire from producing pressure rather than vacuum in the brake servo vacuum chamber.

To test the vacuum check valve, remove it from the vacuum line. Blow into the valve in the direction indicated by the arrow. The valve should lift from its seat and permit pressure to escape from the top. The valve must seal if you blow into its opposite end. Install the valve with the arrow toward the brake servo.

5.2 Removing and Installing Brake Pedal and Clutch Pedal

A longer steering column was introduced on the 1976 models. At the same time, the pedals, the brake servo, and the pedal mounting were changed. These parts of 1975 cars are not interchangeable with corresponding parts of 1976 and later cars. Nevertheless, the removal, adjustment, and installation procedures for the pedals is the same for all the cars covered by this Manual.

The brake pedal used on cars with automatic transmissions is different from the brake pedal used on cars with manual transmissions (Fig. 5-3). In addition, on cars with manual transmissions, the clutch pedal is mounted on the same shaft as the brake pedal. If you wish to remove the clutch pedal as well as the brake pedal, disconnect the clutch cable from the clutch pedal. It may be necessary to slacken the clutch cable adjustment beforehand. If so, see **ENGINE AND CLUTCH.**

Fig. 5-3. Exploded view of brake pedal and related components.

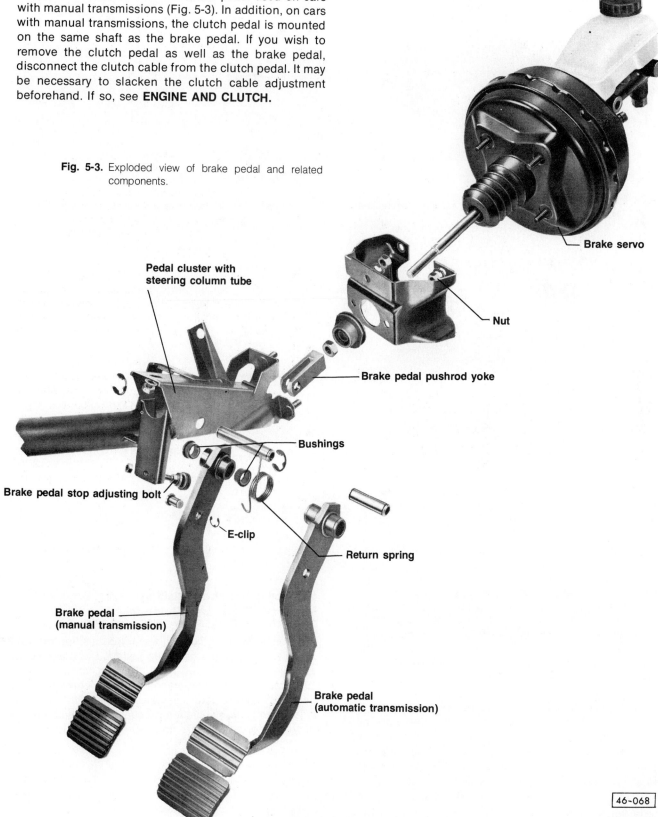

Pedal cluster with steering column tube

Brake servo

Nut

Brake pedal pushrod yoke

Bushings

Brake pedal stop adjusting bolt

E-clip

Return spring

Brake pedal (manual transmission)

Brake pedal (automatic transmission)

46-068

To remove:

1. Remove the left-hand under-dash panel. On cars with automatic transmissions, carefully measure the distance between the brake pedal foot pad and the steering wheel. Write down the measurement for use during installation.

2. Using pliers or a screwdriver, remove the clevis pin retainer and clevis pin from the brake pedal pushrod yoke. See Fig. 5-4 and Fig. 5-5.

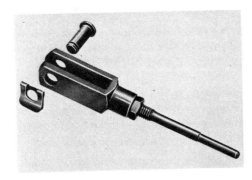

Fig. 5-4. Clevis pin with separate retainer used until early in the 1976 model year. Some early cars may have an E-clip retainer, as previously shown in Fig. 5-3.

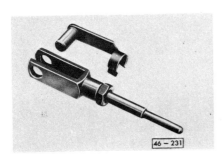

Fig. 5-5. Clevis pin with integral retainer used on most 1976 and all later cars.

3. Unhook the pedal return spring from the pedal.

4. Carefully pry off the E-clip or the spring retainer that is on the right-hand end of the pedal cross shaft.

5. Slide the cross shaft out to the left until it is possible to remove the brake pedal and, if necessary, the clutch pedal.

Installation is the reverse of removal. Before you install the brake pedal pushrod yoke clevis pin, check the pedal pushrod adjustment. On cars with manual transmissions, the brake pedal must be at the same height as the clutch pedal; on cars with automatic transmissions, the brake pedal must be at the same distance from the steering wheel as it was before removal. If necessary, adjust the pushrod as described under the next heading.

Adjusting Brake Pedal Pushrod

Unlike some other cars, there should be no clearance between the pedal pushrod and the internal parts of the servo. In installing the brake pedal, installing a new servo, or correcting the pedal pushrod adjustment, first disconnect the pedal pushrod yoke from the brake pedal. To do this, use pliers or a screwdriver to remove the E-clip, the spring clip, or the clip on the late-type clevis pin with integral retainer. See Fig. 5-3, Fig. 5-4, and Fig. 5-5 given earlier. Withdraw the clevis pin from the yoke and the pedal.

> **CAUTION ——**
>
> *If you have not already done so, measure the distance from the brake pedal foot pad to the steering wheel on cars with automatic transmissions. You will need this measurement in order to adjust the pushrod.*

Loosen the locknut on the brake pedal pushrod and the locknut on the brake pedal stop adjusting bolt, which was shown earlier in Fig. 5-3. Turn the stop adjusting bolt until its rubber buffer is as far as possible away from the brake pedal.

Lift the pedal out of the pushrod yoke, then turn the yoke on the threaded end of the pushrod until, with the clevis pin installed in the yoke and the pedal, the brake pedal foot pad is at the same height as the clutch pedal on cars with manual transmissions or, on cars with automatic transmissions, is at the same distance from the steering wheel as you measured prior to the removal of the clevis pin. Install the E-clip or the retainer for the clevis pin when the pushrod adjustment is correct, then tighten the yoke's locknut.

Adjust the position of the pedal stop adjusting bolt until the rubber buffer just contacts the brake pedal. Then tighten the locknut.

> **CAUTION ——**
>
> *Never adjust the pedal stop bolt so that the rubber buffer presses down the brake pedal. This will cause the brakes to drag, resulting in damage to the brake system.*

5.3 Removing and Installing Vacuum Powered Brake Servo

You should not attempt to remove the vacuum powered brake servo without also removing the master cylinder. Even when the master cylinder is unbolted from the servo, the attached brake lines will not permit the master cylinder to be moved far enough aside for removal of the servo. Attempting to force it aside will damage the brake lines.

To remove servo:

1. Using a clean syringe, remove the brake fluid from the master cylinder reservoir. Discard the fluid.

> **WARNING** —
>
> *Do not start a siphon with your mouth or spill fluid onto the car. Brake fluid is both poisonous and damaging to paint.*

2. Disconnect the battery ground strap. Then disconnect the wires from the brake light/warning light switches. If necessary, attach tags to the wires so that later you can reinstall the wires in their original positions.

3. Disconnect the brake lines from the master cylinder. Disconnect the vacuum hose from the servo.

4. Working inside the passenger compartment, remove the left-hand under-dash panel. On cars with automatic transmissions, carefully measure the distance between the brake pedal foot pad and the steering wheel. Write down the measurement for use during installation.

5. Using pliers or a screwdriver, remove the clevis pin retainer and clevis pin from the brake pedal pushrod. If necessary, consult the illustrations given in **5.2 Removing and Installing Brake Pedal and Clutch Pedal.**

6. Working under the hood, remove the four nuts that hold the vacuum powered brake servo to the mounting bracket. Then remove the servo and the master cylinder as a unit.

7. If necessary, remove the master cylinder from the servo and discard the vacuum seal O-ring that is between the master cylinder and the servo.

8. To service the filter, remove the rubber boot. Take the cap off the end of the servo, then withdraw the damping ring and the filter. See Fig. 5-6.

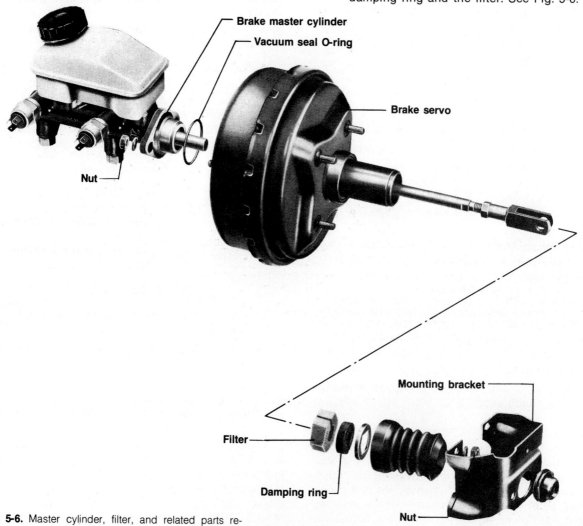

Fig. 5-6. Master cylinder, filter, and related parts removed from vacuum powered brake servo.

47-077

To install:

1. Install a new filter and a new damping ring. The slot in the filter must be offset 180° from the slot in the damping ring. Then install the cap and the rubber boot.

   NOTE ——

   The filter and the damping ring for the Teves (ATE) servo are not the same as corresponding parts for the Bendix servo.

2. Install a new vacuum seal O-ring in the annular groove of the master cylinder. Then install the master cylinder on the servo. Torque the nuts to a maximum of 1.3 mkg (9.4 ft. lb.). Over-tightening the nuts may damage the servo.

3. Position the servo and master cylinder in the car. Loosely install the nuts and washers that hold the servo to the mounting bracket.

4. While you hold the master cylinder and servo in position, screw the brake line union nuts into the master cylinder by a few turns.

5. Torque the nuts that hold the servo to the mounting bracket to a maximum of 1.3 mkg (9.4 ft. lb.). Over-tightening the nuts may damage the servo.

6. Torque the brake line unions to 1.5 to 2.0 mkg (11 to 14 ft. lb.). Reconnect the vacuum hose to the servo.

7. Working beneath the dashboard, adjust the brake pedal pushrod with careful reference to the instructions given in **5.2 Removing and Installing Brake Pedal and Clutch Pedal.** Then install the under-dash panel.

8. Reconnect the wires to the brake light/warning light switches. If necessary, refer to the wiring diagram given in **4.1 Testing and Replacing Brake Light/Warning Light Switches.**

9. Fill the brake fluid reservoir with new, unused brake fluid that meets SAE recommendation J 1703 and conforms to Motor Vehicle Safety Standard 116 DOT 3. Then bleed the entire brake system as described in **9. Bleeding Brakes.**

10. Reconnect the battery ground strap. Then check the brake operation with a road test. Make sure that pedal travel is not excessive and that the pedal does not feel spongy—which could indicate that the bleeding operation needs to be repeated. The brake warning light should not come on during braking.

6. BRAKE LINES AND HOSES

The brake lines are steel tubes mounted on the car's body. They carry brake fluid from the master cylinder to the flexible brake hoses that serve the wheel cylinders.

The brake lines are so routed that they are not exposed to moisture and to the hazard of flying stones. The steel clips that secure the lines to the body at short intervals prevent vibration and chafing that might weaken the tubing.

6.1 Removing and Installing Brake Lines

The brake lines should be inspected regularly, certainly whenever there is brake trouble or the brakes are being serviced. Look for signs of corrosion, leaks around the unions, leaks in the lines themselves, and dents or cracks that may soon cause trouble.

Replacement lines can be obtained from your Authorized Dealer. The unions are factory-installed on the replacement lines, and the lines themselves are preformed to the correct shape for immediate installation.

To remove brake line:

1. Unscrew the unions on the line ends (Fig. 6-1).

2. Remove the spring steel clips that hold the line to the body.

3. Remove the brake line from the vehicle.

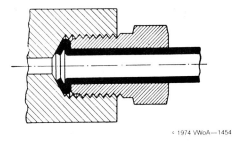

© 1974 VWoA—1454

Fig. 6-1. Cross section of brake line union. Notice the double flare that holds the union on the tubing.

To install brake lines:

1. Route the new line so that it follows the routing of the old line.

2. Lubricate the flared ends of the brake lines with brake fluid, then insert the unions and torque them to 1.5 to 2.0 mkg (11 to 14 ft. lb.).

NOTE ——

Use a properly fitting wrench to avoid rounding off the union.

3. Carefully install the clips to hold the new line.

4. Bleed the brakes as described in **9. Bleeding Brakes.**

WARNING ——

When installing brake lines, be very careful not to dent, flatten, or bend the tubing enough to collapse it. The resulting restriction can upset brake balance and will create stress points in the tubing that may later cause it to crack. Never attempt to straighten a bent or dented brake line.

6.2 Removing and Installing Brake Hoses

Being flexible, brake hoses are much more subject to wear than brake lines. The hoses should, therefore, be inspected very carefully every time routine maintenance is being carried out.

To remove brake hose:

1. Remove the road wheel.

2. Unscrew the union that holds the hose to the brake line.

3. Remove the spring steel hose clip from the bracket on the frame or axle.

4. Pull the hose off the line and plug the line with a new brake bleeder dust cap.

5. Unscrew the hose from the brake caliper or wheel cylinder.

NOTE ——

Girling brake caliper hose connections have a left-hand thread.

To install brake hose:

1. Obtain a new hose of the correct length. See Fig. 6-2.

WARNING ——

If the hose is too long, it may rub the wheel or moving suspension parts. If too short, it could break when drawn tight by wheel travel or steering movements. In either case, partial brake failure could result. Hoses must never be painted, and they can be damaged by grease, oil, gasoline, or kerosene. Brake hoses that bulge or appear oil-soaked or cracked must be replaced immediately.

2. Install the hose, following the removal steps in reverse. The hose must hang down and be free of twists.

3. Torque the hose ends to 1.5 mkg (11 ft. lb.) in disc brake calipers and to 1.5 to 2.0 mkg (11 to 14 ft. lb.) in other locations.

4. Check the hose position and the routing in all steering and suspension travel positions.

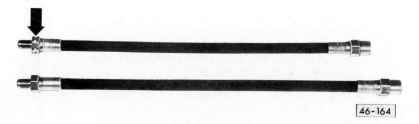

46-164

Fig. 6-2. Hoses for front brake calipers. Hoses for Girling caliper (top) are shorter than hoses for Teves (ATE) calipers (bottom) and have a left-hand thread on the connection to the caliper. Girling hose is identified by groove (arrow).

7. DISC BRAKES

The brake calipers are mounted at the leading edges of the discs and may be of either Girling or Teves (ATE) manufacture. See Fig. 7-1 and Fig. 7-2. Each make of caliper has its own kind of brake hose, as described in **6. Brake Lines and Hoses,** and faulty calipers must always be replaced with calipers of the same manufacture. The brake pads for both kinds of calipers are, however, identical.

Fig. 7-2. Girling caliper.

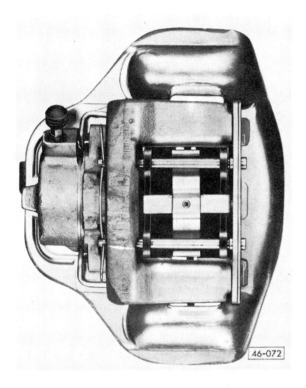

Fig. 7-1. Teves (ATE) caliper.

7.1 Removing and Installing Brake Pads

Some of the cars covered by this Manual have a built-in brake pad wear indicator system (Fig. 7-3). When the lug on the disc contacts the extension on the pad, the driver feels a pulsation in the brakes. If the car is not equipped with the brake pad wear indicator system, you should replace the pads when the friction material has worn to a remaining thickness of 2.00 mm (.080 in.).

Though the pads for Girling calipers are the same as the pads for Teves (ATE) calipers, the procedure for replacing the pads is different for each kind of caliper. Each caliper will be covered separately.

Fig. 7-3. Brake pad wear indicator system. Extension of pad's lining material is at **A;** lug on brake disc friction surface is at **B.**

To remove Girling caliper pads:

1. Remove the front wheel. Then carefully pry off the spreader spring (Fig. 7-4).

Fig. 7-4. Girling caliper spreader spring being pried off. Notice screwdriver blade position.

2. Remove the bolt that holds the clip for the U-shaped pad retainer to the caliper frame. Then pull out the retainer as indicated in Fig. 7-5.

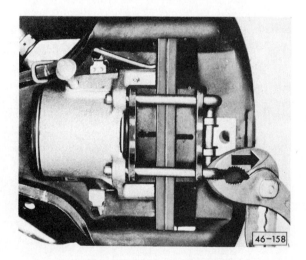

Fig. 7-5. Pad retainer being removed. Use pliers to pull retainer out in direction indicated by arrow.

3. Pull the brake pads out of the caliper as shown in Fig. 7-6.

NOTE ——

If the discs are deeply scored, it may be necessary to press the pistons slightly into the caliper in order to free the pad.

WARNING ——

If the pads are to be reused, mark each pad and its original position in the caliper. Changing the location of used pads will result in uneven braking.

Fig. 7-6. Brake pad being removed with T-handled puller. Tool is convenient, but not necessary.

To install:

1. Inspect the spreader spring and the retainer. If either part is worn, cracked, deformed, or badly corroded, replace both parts, which are included in repair kit Part No. 171 689 445.

2. Scrape clean the pad seating and sliding surfaces in the caliper, then blow out the dirt with compressed air. Make sure that the floating part of the caliper moves smoothly in the frame.

3. Check the rubber dust seals for the pistons. They must not be cracked, hard, or swollen. If necessary, remove the caliper from the car as described in **7.2 Removing and Installing Brake Caliper.** Then replace the seals as described in **7.3 Brake Caliper Repair.**

4. Check the brake disc for wear as described in **7.4 Brake Disc.** If necessary, replace or recondition the disc.

5. Push both pistons into the cylinder with a piston retracting device as shown in Fig. 7-7.

NOTE ——

As you push in the pistons, brake fluid will be forced back into the reservoir. So first remove some fluid to prevent the reservoir from overflowing.

WARNING ——

Do not start a siphon with your mouth or spill fluid on the car. Brake fluid is both poisonous and damaging to paint.

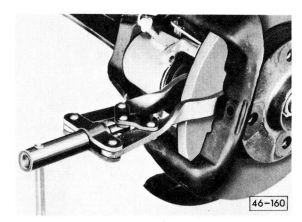

Fig. 7-7. Pistons being pushed into cylinder bore.

6. Install the pads in the caliper.

> **WARNING** ——
>
> *Install used pads in the positions you marked for them during removal. If the pads are in the wrong locations, or bind in the caliper, uneven braking will result.*

7. Install the silencer shims, where applicable, and the U-shaped pad retainer.

> **WARNING** ——
>
> *Do not grease the retainer. Heat produced by braking can melt the lubricant and cause it to flow onto the pads or the disc. To help eliminate squeaking brakes, you can apply a thin coating of Plastilube® to the points indicated by the arrows and the shading in Fig. 7-8. Do not use any other lubricants and be careful not to get the Plastilube® on the friction surfaces of the pads or the disc.*

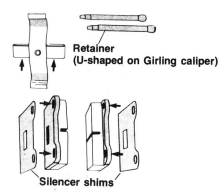

Retainer
(U-shaped on Girling caliper)

Silencer shims

Fig. 7-8. Arrows and shaded areas that indicate where Plastilube® can be applied to brake parts. The silencer shims shown can be obtained from Authorized Dealers and will help prevent brake squeaking.

8. Install the clip and the bolt indicated in Fig. 7-9. Torque the bolt to 2.0 mkg (14 ft. lb.).

Fig. 7-9. Bolt (arrow) that holds clip for U-shaped retainer.

9. Install the spreader spring as shown in Fig. 7-10. The arrow must point in the direction of forward wheel rotation (point down).

Fig. 7-10. Spreader spring being installed.

10. Check the level of the brake fluid in the reservoir. If necessary, add fresh fluid.

> **CAUTION** ——
>
> *Use only new, unused brake fluid that meets SAE recommendation J 1703 and conforms to Motor Vehicle Safety Standard 116 DOT 3.*

To remove Teves (ATE) caliper pads:

1. Remove the retaining pin spring clip. Using a punch and a hammer, drive out the pad retaining pins. Take out the cross-shaped spreader spring. Then pull out the inner pad as shown in Fig. 7-11. The pins on the removing tool engage the retaining pin holes in the pad.

   NOTE ——

   If the discs are deeply scored, it may be necessary to press the piston slightly into the caliper in order to free the pad.

Fig. 7-11. Inner brake pad being removed with T-handled puller. Tool is convenient, but not necessary.

2. The outer brake pad is positioned in a notch (Fig. 7-12). To disengage the pad from the notch, press the floating frame and brake cylinder inward. Then pull the pad out of the caliper.

   WARNING ——

   If the pads are to be reused, mark each pad and its original position in the caliper. Changing the locations of used pads will result in uneven braking.

Fig. 7-12. Outer brake pad being removed. Floating frame must be pressed inward to disengage pad from notch (arrow).

To install:

1. Inspect the spreader spring, the retaining pins, and the retaining pin spring clip. If any part is worn, cracked, deformed, or badly corroded, replace it.

2. Scrape clean the pad seating and sliding surfaces in the caliper, then blow out the dirt with compressed air. Make sure that the floating part of the caliper moves smoothly in the frame.

3. Check the rubber dust seal for the piston. It must not be cracked, hard, or swollen. If necessary, remove the caliper from the car as described in **7.2 Removing and Installing Brake Caliper.** Then replace the seals as described in **7.3 Brake Caliper Repair.**

4. Check the brake disc for wear as described in **7.4 Brake Disc.** If necessary, replace or recondition the disc.

5. Push the piston into the cylinder with a piston retracting device as shown in Fig. 7-13.

   NOTE ——

   As you push in the piston, brake fluid will be forced back into the reservoir. So first remove some fluid to prevent the reservoir from overflowing.

   WARNING ——

   Do not start a siphon with your mouth or spill fluid on the car. Brake fluid is both poisonous and damaging to paint.

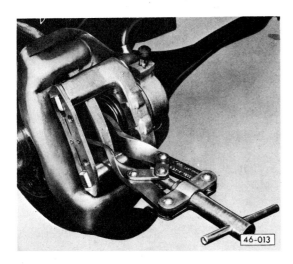

Fig. 7-13. Piston being pushed into cylinder bore.

6. Check the 20° angle of the piston face recess as shown in Fig. 7-14. If necessary, rotate the piston to obtain the correct angle as shown in Fig. 7-15.

Fig. 7-14. Gauge with 20° angle being used to check piston position.

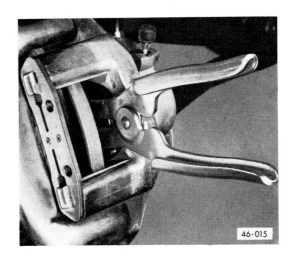

Fig. 7-15. Piston-rotating pliers being used to correct piston position.

7. Install the pads in the caliper.

> **WARNING ——**
>
> *Install used pads in the positions you marked for them during removal. If the pads are in the wrong locations, or bind in the caliper, uneven braking will result.*

8. Where applicable, install the silencer shims.

> **NOTE ——**
>
> To help eliminate squeaking brakes, you can apply a thin coating of Plastilube® to the points indicated by the arrows and the shading in Fig. 7-16.

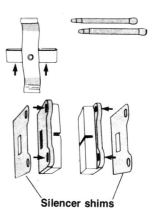

Silencer shims

Fig. 7-16. Arrows and shaded areas that indicate where Plastilube® can be applied to brake parts. The silencer shims shown can be obtained from Authorized Dealers and will help prevent brake squeaking.

9. Install a retaining pin, the cross-shaped spreader spring, and then the second retaining pin as shown in Fig. 7-17. Install the retaining pin spring clip as shown in Fig. 7-18.

WARNING ——

Do not grease the retaining pins or other parts with any lubricant other than Plastilube®. Heat produced by braking can melt ordinary greases and cause them to flow onto the pads or the disc. Be careful, however, not to get Plastilube® on the pad or the disc friction surfaces.

Fig. 7-17. Retaining pin being installed (arrow).

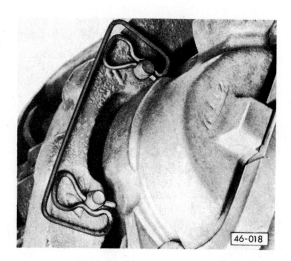

Fig. 7-18. Retaining pin spring clip correctly installed.

10. Check the level of the brake fluid in the reservoir. If necessary, add fresh fluid.

CAUTION ——

Use only new, unused brake fluid that meets SAE recommendation J 1703 and conforms to Motor Vehicle Safety Standard 116 DOT 3.

7.2 Removing and Installing Brake Caliper

Before you can remove the caliper, you must remove the brake pads as described in **7.1 Removing and Installing Brake Pads.** Never attempt to remove a brake caliper until it has cooled.

If the brake caliper is to be completely removed from the car, unscrew the brake hose from the caliper and seal the hose with a clean bleeder valve dust cap. If the caliper is only being partially removed, for example to obtain clearance for removal of the brake disc, the brake line need not be disconnected. Simply hang the partially removed caliper from one of the steering tie rods with a stiff wire hook. Doing this will eliminate the need for bleeding the brakes, which is necessary if the hose is disconnected. Never allow the caliper to hang by its hose.

To remove the caliper, take out the two bolts shown in Fig. 7-19. You must use a 15-mm wrench to remove or install the brake caliper mounting bolts. There is no suitable U.S. standard wrench size. A ⅝-in. wrench will fit too loosely and round off the corners of the bolt head.

When you install the caliper, make sure that the bleeder valves are uppermost. Though there may originally be spring washers on the mounting bolts, install the bolts without washers. Torque the bolts to 6.0 mkg (43 ft. lb.). Consult **6. Brake Lines and Hoses** before you replace a brake hose. The hoses for Girling calipers are shorter than those for Teves (ATE) calipers and have a left-hand thread at the caliper end.

After you have installed the brake pads and related parts, as described in **7.1 Removing and Installing Brake Pads,** depress the brake pedal several times while the car is stationary to ensure that the pads are seated against the disc. If the hose has been disconnected, bleed the brakes as described in **9. Bleeding Brakes.**

Fig. 7-19. Exploded view of front brake assembly showing removal of brake caliper and related
components.

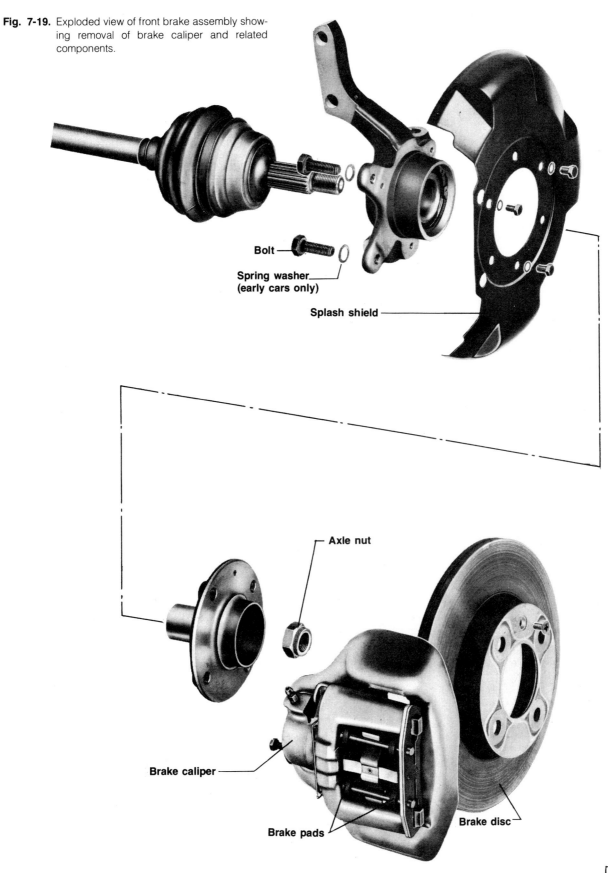

Bolt

Spring washer
(early cars only)

Splash shield

Axle nut

Brake caliper

Brake pads

Brake disc

46-067

7.3 Brake Caliper Repair

The procedure for disassembling and assembling Girling brake calipers is different from the procedure for disassembling and assembling Teves (ATE) calipers. Though pads for the two kinds of calipers are identical, no other parts are interchangeable.

CAUTION —

If you lack the skills, tools, or a clean workshop for servicing the brake calipers, we suggest you leave these repairs to an Authorized Dealer or other qualified shop. We especially urge you to consult your Authorized Dealer before attempting repairs on a car still covered by the new-car warranty.

To disassemble Girling caliper:

1. Remove the caliper from the car as described in **7.2 Removing and Installing Brake Caliper.** Thoroughly clean the exterior of the caliper using a wire brush and compressed air.

2. Hand-press the cylinder assembly out of the frame as indicated in Fig. 7-20.

Fig. 7-20. Cylinder assembly being removed (arrow) from caliper frame.

3. Remove the retaining rings from the dust seals. Then remove the dust seals. Using compressed air, as shown in Fig. 7-21, blow the pistons out of the cylinder.

4. If necessary, remove the bleeder valve from the cylinder or remove the retaining springs and locating spring from the caliper frame.

5. Remove the piston seals from the inside of the cylinder.

Fig. 7-21. Pistons being removed from cylinder. Soft jaws on vise prevent pistons from being blown completely out of cylinder.

To assemble:

1. Clean all parts with brake fluid only. Check the parts for wear. If the cylinder is damaged, replace the entire brake caliper. Do not hone the cylinder.

2. Lightly coat the pistons and the new piston seals with VW brake cylinder paste. Alternatively, you can fully lubricate the cylinder bore, the pistons, and the seals with new, unused brake fluid that meets SAE recommendation J 1703 and conforms to Motor Vehicle Safety Standard 116 DOT 3.

NOTE —

Brake cylinder paste is available from your Authorized Dealer and should be the preferred form of lubrication when brake cylinders are repaired. Brake fluid should be considered a satisfactory substitute only if you are unable to reach an Authorized Dealer. Brake cylinders will give longer service when lubricated with VW brake cylinder paste than when lubricated by brake fluid alone.

3. With soft jaws installed on the vise, install the pistons and seals in the cylinder as shown in Fig. 7-22.

4. Lightly rub VW brake cylinder paste into the inside of the rubber dust seal. Install the dust seal and lock it in place with the retaining ring. See Fig. 7-23.

1

Fig. 7-22. Pistons and piston seals being pressed into cylinder.

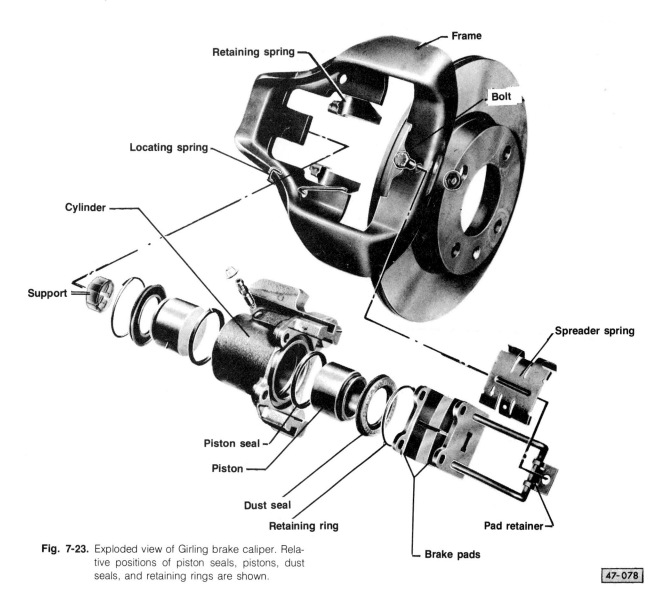

Fig. 7-23. Exploded view of Girling brake caliper. Relative positions of piston seals, pistons, dust seals, and retaining rings are shown.

5. Install the support in the hollow of the piston that presses against the caliper frame. Slide the cylinder assembly into the caliper frame as shown in Fig. 7-24. The retaining springs must be between the sliding surfaces of the frame and the cylinder. The locating spring must exert pressure against the upper edge of the cylinder assembly.

NOTE ——

The cylinder assembly must not bind in the frame. If possible, lightly lubricate all sliding surfaces with Plastilube®, but do not use any other kind of lubricant.

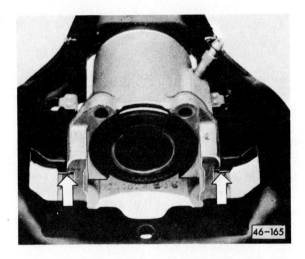

Fig. 7-24. Cylinder assembly being slid into frame. Retaining springs are indicated by the arrows.

6. If necessary, install the bleeder valve. Then install the caliper on the car.

To disassemble Teves (ATE) caliper:

1. Remove the caliper from the car as described in **7.2 Removing and Installing Brake Caliper.** Thoroughly clean the exterior of the caliper using a wire brush and compressed air.

2. Hand-press the cylinder sideways so that its closed end is against the floating frame. Push the mounting frame away from the cylinder as shown in Fig. 7-25. Then lift the mounting frame out of the floating frame.

3. To avoid damaging the piston, place a hardwood block in the floating frame as shown in Fig. 7-26. Then press the cylinder assembly out of the floating frame. Remove the guide spring.

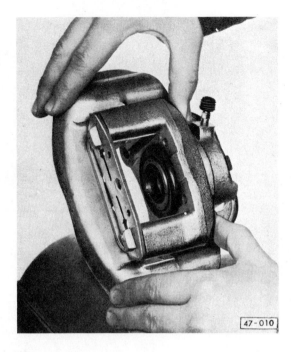

Fig. 7-25. Mounting frame being pushed away from cylinder.

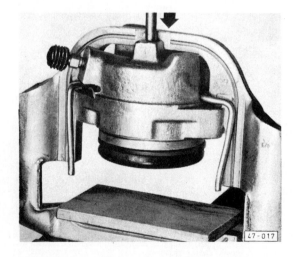

Fig. 7-26. Hardwood block installed in floating frame. Push cylinder assembly out of frame as indicated by the arrow.

4. Remove the retaining ring from the dust seal. Then remove the dust seal. Using compressed air, as shown in Fig. 7-27, blow the piston out of the cylinder.

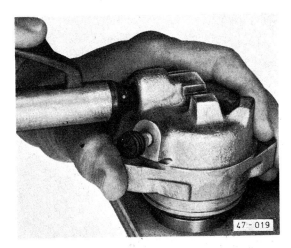

Fig. 7-27. Piston being removed from cylinder. Place piston against wooden block so that it is not blown completely out of cylinder.

5. Remove the piston seal from the cylinder with a plastic rod as shown in Fig. 7-28.

Fig. 7-28. Piston seal being removed from groove in the cylinder bore.

6. If necessary, remove the bleeder valve from the cylinder.

To assemble:

1. Clean all parts with brake fluid only. Check the parts for wear. If the cylinder is damaged, replace the entire brake caliper. Do not hone the cylinder.

2. Lightly coat the piston and the new piston seal with VW brake cylinder paste. Then install the seal. Alternatively, you can fully lubricate the cylinder bore, the piston, and the seal with new, unused brake fluid that meets SAE recommendation J 1703 and conforms to Motor Vehicle Safety Standard 116 DOT 3.

NOTE ——

Brake cylinder paste is available from your Authorized Dealer and should be the preferred form of lubrication when brake cylinders are repaired. Brake fluid should be considered a satisfactory substitute only if you are unable to reach an Authorized Dealer. Brake cylinders will give longer service when lubricated with VW brake cylinder paste than when lubricated by brake fluid alone.

3. With soft jaws installed on the vise, install the piston in the cylinder as shown in Fig. 7-29.

Fig. 7-29. Piston being pressed into cylinder.

4. Lightly rub VW brake cylinder paste into the inside of the rubber dust seal. Install the dust seal and lock it in place with the retaining ring. See Fig. 7-30.

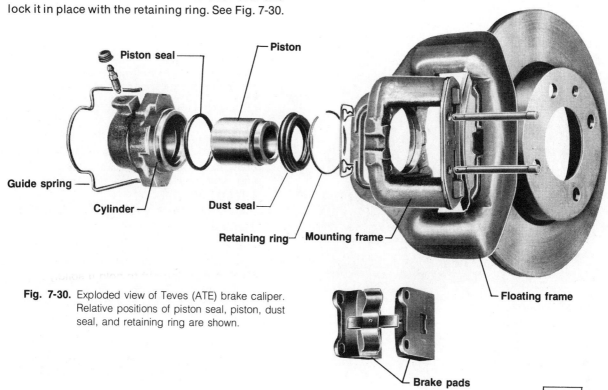

Fig. 7-30. Exploded view of Teves (ATE) brake caliper. Relative positions of piston seal, piston, dust seal, and retaining ring are shown.

5. Install the guide spring on the cylinder. Working on alternate sides of the cylinder assembly (Fig. 7-31), use a brass drift and a hammer to drive the cylinder fully onto the floating frame.

NOTE ——

The cylinder assembly must not bind in the frame. If possible, lubricate all sliding surfaces with Plastilube®, but do not use any other kind of lubricant.

Fig. 7-31. Cylinder assembly being driven onto floating frame. Apply drift alternately to the two surfaces indicated by arrows.

6. Place the mounting frame in the guide spring and push the mounting frame onto the floating frame. There are two grooves (Fig. 7-32) in the mounting frame that must be pushed over the ribs on the floating frame.

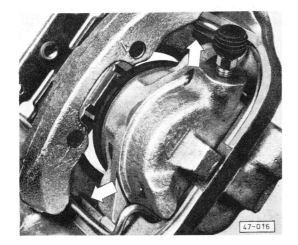

Fig. 7-32. Mounting frame being installed in floating frame. Grooves in mounting frame are indicated by the arrows.

7. Check the 20° angle of the piston face recess as shown in Fig. 7-33. If necessary, rotate the piston to obtain the correct angle.

8. If necessary, install the bleeder valve. Then install the caliper on the car.

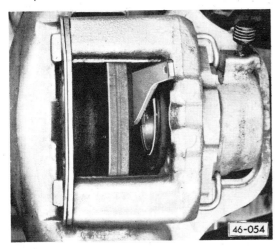

Fig. 7-33. Gauge with 20° angle being used to check piston position.

7.4 Brake Disc

Cars with Girling brake calipers have the same discs as cars with Teves (ATE) brake calipers. The brake discs are separate from the front wheel hub and are easily removable once the caliper is off the suspension strut.

Checking Brake Disc

The brake discs should be checked for wear each time repair work is done on the front brakes. Replace the discs if they are worn, scored with sharp ridges or cracked. Also replace brake discs that have worn down, or have been machined, to a thickness of 10.50 mm (.413 in.) or less.

Check the discs for excessive runout. If a low-speed front end shimmy goes away when you release the brakes, excessive brake disc runout is probably the cause of the shimmy.

To measure runout:

1. Remove the front wheel. Put the transmission in neutral.

2. Install the measuring appliance on the pad retaining pins or pad retainer as shown in Fig. 7-34. Tighten the wing nut to hold it solidly in position.

3. Install the dial indicator on the appliance with its gauge pin against the disc surface. Then zero the gauge.

© 1974 VWoA—1461

Fig. 7-34. Brake disc runout being measured. A dial indicator on a magnetic base can also be used. Brake assembly shown here is not for a car covered by this Manual.

4. Slowly hand-turn the brake disc to check the runout. The maximum allowable runout is 0.10 mm (.004 in.).

5. If the brake disc runout exceeds specifications, replace or recondition the brake disc.

Removing and Installing Brake Disc

The brake caliper must be removed from the suspension strut before the brake disc can be taken off. Hang the caliper from the steering tie rod with a stiff wire hook. Leaving the brake hose attached will save you the job of bleeding the brakes.

CAUTION ——

Always remove the brake caliper. Never try to remove the disc by using force. Force may cause the caliper mounting frame to crack or break.

To remove the brake disc from the front wheel hub, remove the countersunk flathead screw that is located midway between two of the wheel bolt holes. Then pull the disc off the wheel hub. Installation is the reverse of removal.

CAUTION ——

Normally, the disc can be easily pulled off the hub. However, you should not use a steel hammer to drive off the disc if it is rusted tight. Doing this could ruin the disc. Instead, use a rubber hammer or a large three-arm wheel puller.

Reconditioning Brake Discs

Discs that have not worn to a thickness of 11.00 mm (.433 in.) or less can be reconditioned by an Authorized Dealer or a qualified automotive machine shop—if the following restrictions are observed:

1. The minimum allowable thickness after rework is 10.50 mm (.413 in.). (New brake discs are 12.00 mm (.472 in.) thick.)

CAUTION ——

Never rework brake discs to a lesser thickness. Doing this will allow the pistons to travel farther out in their cylinders. This may severely damage the calipers and the pistons.

2. After reworking a brake disc, its thickness should not vary by more than 0.02 mm (.0008 in.) measured at several locations on the disc.

3. The brake disc must be reworked equally on both sides to prevent squeaking, chattering, or brake pedal pulsation. The maximum amount removable per side is 0.50 mm (.020 in.).

4. The maximum allowable runout of a reworked brake disc is 0.10 mm (.004 in.).

7.5 Removing and Installing Brake Disc Splash Shield

The brake disc splash shield must be removed whenever the wheel hub or front wheel bearing is serviced or replaced—or if the splash shield itself is damaged. Minor changes have been made to the shape of the splash shield in order to accommodate the two different kinds of brake calipers. Replace damaged splash shields with splash shields that are suitable to the brake calipers on the car. Left and right splash shields are different.

The splash shield cannot be removed until the wheel hub has been pressed out of the front wheel bearing housing. In doing this, the wheel bearing is ruined and must be replaced. To remove the splash shield, follow the instructions given in conjunction with removal and installation of front wheel bearings in **SUSPENSION AND STEERING.**

8. DRUM BRAKES

All of the cars covered by this Manual have drum-type rear brakes. In addition, most of the Rabbit models sold in 1975 and 1976 have drum-type front brakes. The parking brake lever, which is connected by cables to the drum-type rear brakes, is covered in **10. Parking Brake.**

8.1 Adjusting Drum Brakes

The clearance between the brake linings and the drums gradually increases owing to normal wear. This change is indicated by increasing pedal travel in applying the brakes. When pedal travel becomes excessive, the brake shoes must be adjusted to position the linings nearer the drums. These adjustments are made at the individual wheels. The disc brakes used on the front of all Scirocco models and some Rabbit models require no adjustment. On cars with front disc brakes, adjust the rear brakes only.

To adjust:

1. Raise the car and fully release the parking brake.

2. Depress the brake pedal as far as it will go several times. This centers the brake shoes in the drums.

NOTE ——

If the brakes are far out of adjustment, it may be necessary to recenter the shoes once or twice during the course of adjustments.

3. Remove the rubber plugs from the holes in the brake backing plates.

4. By looking through the hole near the edge of each backing plate, check the remaining thickness of the brake linings (Fig. 8-1). If the linings are worn excessively, replace the brake linings as described in **8.3 Removing and Installing Brake Shoes.**

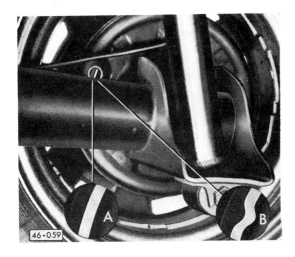

Fig. 8-1. Brake lining thicknesses being checked. Riveted linings indicated by smoothly-radiused shoes (**A**), should be replaced when worn to a remaining thickness of 2.50 mm (.100 in.) or less. Bonded linings, indicated by kinked shoes (**B**), should be replaced when worn to a remaining thickness of 1.50 mm (.060 in.) or less.

5. To adjust drum-type rear brakes, use a screwdriver as shown in Fig. 8-2 to turn the star wheel of the adjuster. Turn the adjuster until a slight drag is noted when the wheel is turned by hand. Then back off the adjuster three or four clicks so that the wheel turns freely.

NOTE ——

On Rabbit models, residual pressure in the brake pressure regulator may make turning the right rear wheel difficult. If so, press the lever of the pressure regulator in the direction indicated in Fig. 8-3. Do not back off the brake adjuster unnecessarily.

Fig. 8-2. Rear drum-type brake being adjusted (arrows). Levering the adjuster star wheel upward will advance the brake shoes toward the drum.

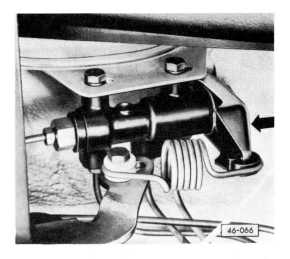

Fig. 8-3. Residual pressure being relieved from pressure regulator. Press lever in direction indicated by arrow.

6. To adjust drum-type front brakes, use a screwdriver as shown in Fig. 8-4 to turn the star wheel of the adjuster. Turn the adjuster until the brake shoes are in firm contact with the brake drum. Then back off the adjuster until the wheel can be turned by hand (a slight lining rubbing noise is permissible). From this position, back off the adjuster two clicks.

Fig. 8-4. Front drum-type brake being adjusted (arrows). Turning the adjuster clockwise will advance the brake shoes toward the drum.

8.2 Removing and Installing Brake Drum

On cars with drum-type front brakes, the front brake drums can be removed and installed without disturbing the wheel bearings. Simply remove the road wheel, then remove the countersunk flat-head screw and pull the brake drum off the hub (Fig. 8-5). If the brake drum is badly worn, it may be necessary to back off the brake adjuster before you can pull off the drum.

Installation is the reverse of removal. Torque the road wheel lug bolts to 9.0 mkg (65 ft. lb.). Following installation, adjust the brakes as described in **8.1 Adjusting Drum Brakes.**

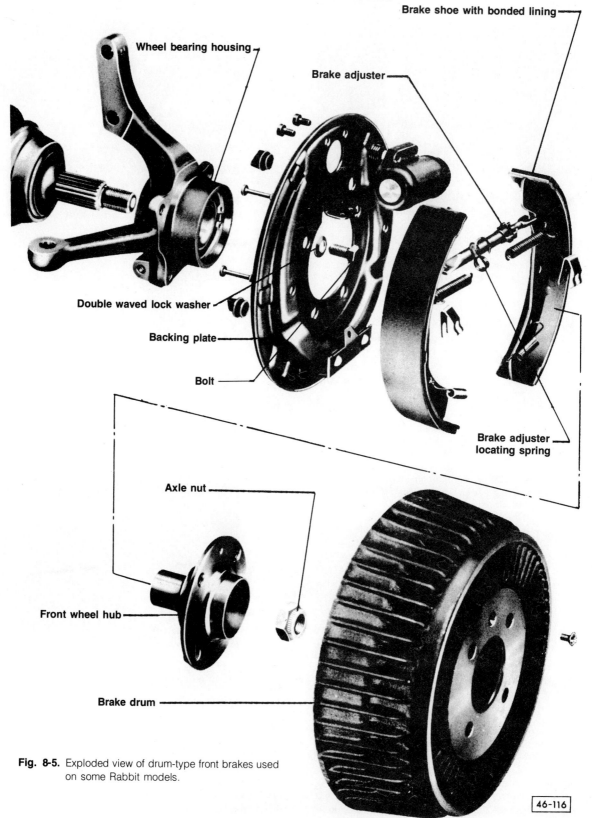

Fig. 8-5. Exploded view of drum-type front brakes used on some Rabbit models.

46-116

The rear brake drums can be removed without contaminating the lubricant in the hub. However, dirt usually gets onto the stub axle, which must be cleaned and lubricated before you reinstall the brake drum. If you wish to clean and repack the wheel bearings, use the procedure given in **SUSPENSION AND STEERING** instead of the procedure given here.

To remove:

1. Fully back off the brake adjuster as described in **8.1 Adjusting Drum Brakes.** Pry off the dust cover.

2. Remove the cotter pin and the nut lock. Remove the nut from the stub axle. See Fig. 8-6.

3. Pull off the brake drum, being careful not to let the thrust washer and the outer tapered-roller bearing inner race fall out and onto the floor.

Fig. 8-6. Exploded view of drum-type rear brake.

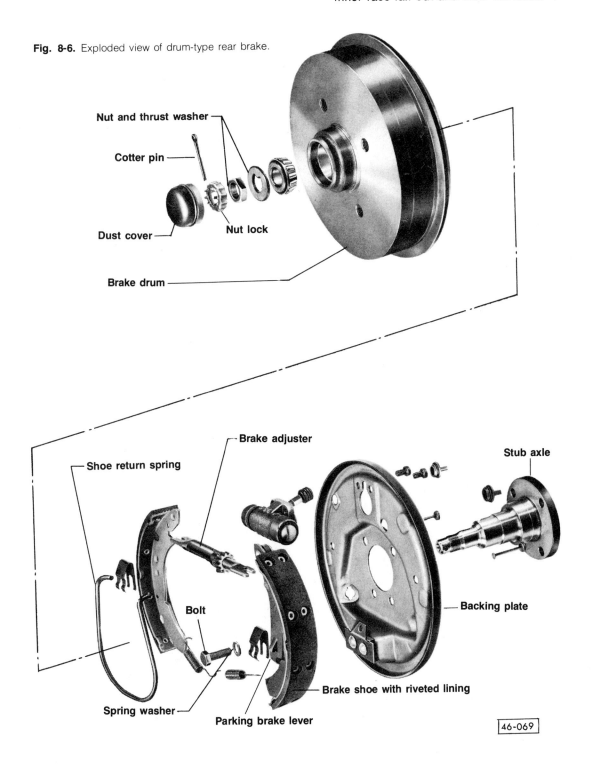

Nut and thrust washer

Cotter pin

Dust cover

Nut lock

Brake drum

Brake adjuster

Shoe return spring

Stub axle

Bolt

Backing plate

Spring washer

Parking brake lever

Brake shoe with riveted lining

46-069

4. Store the brake drum in a clean place. Cover the hub with a clean cloth so that dirt cannot enter.

To install:

1. Wipe clean the stub axle. Then coat it lightly with multipurpose grease.

> **NOTE——**
>
> If you are unsure of the kind of grease that is in the wheel bearings, or if you cannot obtain the same kind of grease, either repack the bearings with the new kind of grease or lightly coat the stub axle with some of the original grease obtained from inside the dust cover. Mixing two different kinds of grease will sometimes cause a chemical reaction that reduces the effectiveness of the lubricant.

2. Carefully slide the brake drum onto the stub axle so that the grease seal or bearing races are not accidentally damaged by the sharp threads.

3. Install the thrust washer and the nut. Tighten the nut until the bearings just contact their outer races.

4. Adjust the position of the nut until you can just move the thrust washer sideways with the tip of a screwdriver as shown in Fig. 8-7.

Fig. 8-7. Friction on thrust washer being checked by moving thrust washer with screwdriver.

5. Install the nut lock so that its projections do not cover the cotter pin hole. Then install a new cotter pin.

6. Install the dust cover and the road wheel. Torque the road wheel lug bolts to 9.0 mkg (65 ft. lb.).

8.3 Removing and Installing Brake Shoes

Removal and installation of the rear brake shoes requires a somewhat different procedure from that used in removing and installing the front brake shoes of cars that have drum-type front brakes. The two procedures will be given separately. You can identify the components mentioned in these procedures by referring to Fig. 8-5 or Fig. 8-6, which were given earlier.

To remove rear brake shoes:

1. Remove the brake drum as described in **8.2 Removing and Installing Brake Drum.**

2. Pull forward the parking brake lever that is on the rear brake shoe, then disconnect the cable from the lever.

3. Check the wheel cylinder for sticking pistons by having someone slowly depress the brake pedal while you watch to see whether the brake shoes move out the same distance at a uniform rate.

> **NOTE——**
>
> Insert two screwdrivers behind the backing plate flange. Press them against the shoes to limit their travel. Also lift the wheel cylinder boot to check for fluid leakage. If the cylinder is sticking, leaking, or if the bleeder valve is rusted tight, rebuild or replace the cylinder.

4. Remove the shoe retaining spring clips and the shoe retaining pins.

5. Using pliers, remove the brake shoe return spring, which is under tension.

6. Pull the shoes outward, then remove the adjuster. Remove the shoes and the coil-type return springs by disengaging the shoes from the lower support.

To install rear brake shoes:

1. Inspect the brake drum and compare it to the specifications given in **8.7 Reconditioning Brake Drums.** Make sure that the same type linings are used at both rear wheels.

WARNING ——

Using linings of different size or composition on opposite sides of the car can cause dangerously uneven braking.

2. Disassemble the adjuster and clean the threads. Lubricate the threads with molybdenum grease or zinc oxide grease and reassemble the adjuster.

3. Install the coil-type return spring on each brake shoe. Then attach each shoe and its spring to the lower support on the backing plate.

NOTE ——

The brake shoe with the parking brake lever on it must be installed at the edge of the backing plate that is toward the rear of the car.

4. After both shoes have been loosely installed, move one shoe out at the top so that you can install the adjuster. The adjuster should be in its fully backed-off position.

5. Install the shoe retaining pins and the shoe retaining spring clips.

6. Using pliers, install the brake shoe return spring.

7. Install the brake drum as described in **8.2 Removing and Installing Brake Drum.** Then adjust the brakes as described in **8.1 Adjusting Drum Brakes.**

To remove front brake shoes:

1. Remove the brake drum as described in **8.2 Removing and Installing Brake Drum.**

2. Check the wheel cylinder for sticking pistons by having someone slowly depress the brake pedal while you watch to see whether the brake shoes move out the same distance at a uniform rate.

NOTE ——

Insert two screwdrivers behind the backing plate flange. Press them against the shoes to limit their travel. Also lift the wheel cylinder boot to check for fluid leakage. If the cylinder is sticking, leaking, or if the bleeder valve is rusted tight, rebuild or replace the cylinder.

3. Using brake spring pliers, remove the lower return spring. See Fig. 8-8.

4. Remove the shoe retaining spring clips and the shoe retaining pins. See Fig. 8-9.

Fig. 8-8. Brake shoe being dismounted from backing plate. Shoe retaining spring clips are at arrows **A**; lower return springs are at arrows **B**.

5. Pull the lower ends of the shoes over the wheel hub as indicated in Fig. 8-9. Then unhook the upper return springs and take off the brake shoes.

6. Remove the adjuster, carefully unhooking its locating spring from the bracket.

Fig. 8-9. Brake shoes being removed.

To install front brake shoes:

1. Inspect the brake drum and compare it to the specifications given in **8.7 Reconditioning Brake Drums.** Make sure that the same type linings are used at both front wheels.

WARNING ——

Using linings of differents size or composition on opposite sides of the car can cause dangerously uneven braking.

2. Disassemble the adjuster and clean the threads. Lubricate the threads with molybdenum grease or zinc oxide grease and reassemble the adjuster.

3. If previously removed, hook the upper return springs onto the bracket on the backing plate. Install the brake adjuster and its locating spring. See Fig. 8-10. Fig. 8-11 shows the correct position for the adjuster locating spring.

Fig. 8-10. Upper return springs and adjuster installed on backing plate.

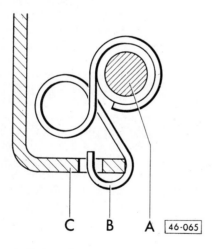

A. Brake adjuster
B. Brake adjuster locating spring
C. Bracket on backing plate

Fig. 8-11. Brake adjuster locating spring correctly installed.

4. Hook the upper return springs to the shoes and engage the shoes in the ends of the adjuster. See Fig. 8-12.

Fig. 8-12. Brake shoes being installed.

5. Pass the lower ends of the brake shoes over the wheel hub and engage them in the lower support on the backing plate. Then install the lower return springs using brake spring pliers.

6. Install the shoe retaining pins and the shoe retaining spring clips.

7. Install the brake drum as described in **8.2 Removing and Installing Brake Drum.** Then adjust the brakes as described in **8.1 Adjusting Drum Brakes.**

8.4 Removing and Installing Wheel Cylinder

To remove a wheel cylinder, first carry out the procedure for removing the brake shoes as given in **8.3 Removing and Installing Brake Shoes.** Disconnect the brake hose from the rear of the brake assembly and seal it with a clean bleeder valve dust cap. Working behind the backing plate, remove the two bolts that hold the wheel cylinder to the backing plate. Then take the wheel cylinder off the front of the backing plate.

Installation is the reverse of removal. Torque the mounting screws to 1.0 mkg (7 ft. lb.). Torque the brake hose to 1.5 mkg (11 ft. lb.). Install the brake shoes as described in **8.3 Removing and Installing Brake Shoes.** Then bleed the brakes as described in **9. Bleeding Brakes.**

8.5 Wheel Cylinder Repair

Because replacement wheel cylinders are inexpensive, it is usually more economical to replace them as a unit. However, repair kits are available. Other than a very light honing to remove tarnish or gummy deposits, no machine work should be done.

At least two different kinds of wheel cylinders have been used on the cars covered by this Manual. So, when you buy replacement parts, take the old cylinder with you for comparison. Fig. 8-13 shows the components of a rear wheel cylinder. Front wheel cylinders, on cars that have them, are similar.

The internal parts can be hand-pressed out of the housing once the boots are removed. Prior to assembly, clean all parts with brake fluid only.

Fig. 8-13. Exploded view of rear wheel cylinder.

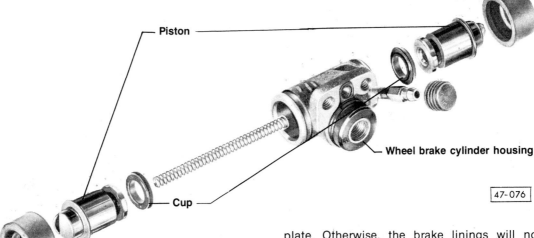

Check the cylinder for wear. Do not machine or hone metal from the cylinder bore. A new, lubricated piston must be an airtight fit. If it is not, replace the cylinder.

> **NOTE ——**
>
> Vacuum should keep a new piston (lubricated with brake fluid) from falling out of the cylinder when the bleeder valve and brake hose holes are sealed, and when you cover the opposite end of the cylinder with your thumb.

Lubricate the cups with brake fluid during installation. Coat the pistons with VW brake cylinder paste and insert them in the cylinder. Install the remaining parts.

> **NOTE ——**
>
> Brake cylinder paste is available from your Authorized Dealer and should be the preferred form of lubrication when brake cylinders are repaired. Brake fluid should be considered a satisfactory substitute only if you are unable to reach an Authorized Dealer. Brake cylinders will give longer service when lubricated with VW brake cylinder paste than when lubricated by brake fluid alone.

8.6 Removing and Installing Backing Plate

On cars with drum-type front brakes, you cannot remove the backing plate without first pressing out the wheel hub. Follow the instructions given in conjunction with front wheel bearing replacement in **SUSPENSION AND STEERING.**

If the backing plate is bent, or if the raised areas that the brake shoes ride against are badly worn, replace the plate. Otherwise, the brake linings will not line up properly with the drum and will wear to a taper.

Remove the brake shoes as described in **8.3 Removing and Installing Brake Shoes.** Remove the wheel cylinder as described in **8.4 Removing and Installing Wheel Cylinder.** Detach the parking brake cable conduit from the rear wheel brake backing plate. Then take out the four bolts that hold the backing plate and the rear stub axle to the axle beam. Remove both the backing plate and the stub axle.

Installation is the reverse of removal. Prior to installation, make sure that the mating surfaces on the backing plate and the stub axle are completely clean. Torque the four mounting bolts to 6.0 mkg (43 ft. lb.). Then install the wheel cylinder, the brake shoes, and the brake drum as described under preceding headings.

8.7 Reconditioning Brake Drums

Check the brake drums whenever new linings are installed. Taper, scoring, or other wear must, if possible, be corrected on a special machine by an Authorized Dealer or a qualified automotive machine shop. Both rear drums or both front drums must be machined to the same dimensions. The linings should be ground to the new radius with a special machine by an Authorized Dealer or other qualified shop. Unless the linings are radiused to fit the reconditioned drums, uneven or ineffective braking may result.

Table b. Brake Drum Specifications

Drum-type front brakes (certain Rabbit models only)	Maximum permissible radial runout or out-of-round for used or reconditioned drums	0.05 mm (.002 in.)
	Inside diameter of new brake drum	230.10 mm ±0.20 mm (9.059 in. ±.008 in.)
	Maximum permissible diameter after reconditioning	230.60 mm ±0.20 mm (9.079 in. ±.008 in.)
	Inside diameter wear limit	231.10 mm ±0.20 mm (9.098 in. ±.008 in.)
Rear brake drums (all models)	Maximum permissible radial runout or out-of-round for used or reconditioned drums	0.05 mm (.002 in.)
	Inside diameter of new brake drum	180.00 mm (7.086 in.)
	Maximum permissible diameter after reconditioning	180.50 mm (7.105 in.)
	Inside diameter wear limit	181.00 mm (7.125 in.)

The accuracy of the machine work will be improved on rear brake drums if the road wheel can be mounted on the brake drum during machining and the wheel bolts tightened to 9.0 mkg (65 ft. lb.). The specified brake drum dimensions and wear limits are given in **Table b.**

9. BLEEDING BRAKES

Bleeding the brakes removes air from the hydraulic system. This task must be performed whenever the brake lines have been disconnected or after a brake cylinder has been replaced or repaired. If the brake pedal feels spongy when you apply the brakes, it is an indication that air has entered the system. If bleeding fails to correct the problem, there are probably leaks to be fixed.

Brake Fluids

Additional fluid must be added to the system when it is bled. The quality of the new brake fluid is important. All VW brake fluids have similar chemical and performance characteristics and may be mixed regardless of differences in color. Using a brake fluid that does not conform with SAE recommendation J 1703 and Motor Vehicle Safety Standard 116 DOT 3 can cause brake failure, premature wear, or erratic operation.

9.1 Changing Brake Fluid

Change the brake fluid in your VW every two years. Brake fluid tends to absorb moisture from the air, and water can initiate corrosion. Water can also cause the fluid to boil when the brakes are used very hard.

It is particularly important that the brake systems of vehicles with disc brakes have a fluid with a high boiling point. Since the brake calipers surround the friction linings, they pick up a great deal of heat from them.

NOTE ——
Whenever you change brake fluid, you should at the same time test the brake light/warning light switches as described in **4.1 Testing and Replacing Brake Light/ Warning Light Switches.**

To change fluid:

1. Attach suitable hoses to the bleeder valves for draining the fluid into containers.

2. Open the left rear and the right front bleeder valves and pump the brake pedal until fluid ceases to flow out of them.

3. Open the right rear and the left front bleeder valves and pump the brake pedal until fluid ceases to flow out of them.

4. Close all bleeder valves.

5. Fill the fluid reservoir with new, unused brake fluid that meets SAE recommendation J 1703 and conforms to Motor Vehicle Safety Standard 116 DOT 3. Then bleed the system by either of the methods described.

9.2 Bleeding with Pressure Bleeder

Whenever possible, brake bleeding should be done with a pneumatic pressure bleeder similar to that shown in Fig. 9-1. Connect this device to the brake fluid reservoir. The bleeder fills the system with fluid under pressure and will complete the job in a very short time. Simply open the bleeder valve, quickly depress and slowly release the pedal several times, and then close the bleeder valve. A fluid receptacle supplied with the bleeding device must be fitted to the wheel being bled.

Fig. 9-1. Pressure bleeder for bleeding brake system.

9.3 Bleeding by Pumping

For car owners, the pumping method of bleeding the brakes is usually more practical, even though it requires two persons. Have your helper sit in the car to pump the brake pedal. You will then be free to move from wheel to wheel to perform the actual bleeding.

To bleed:

1. Fully fill the fluid reservoir with brake fluid that meets SAE recommendation J 1703 and conforms to Motor Vehicle Safety Standard 116 DOT 3.

2. Take the dust cap off the bleeder valve at the right-hand rear wheel. Slip a 4-mm ($^{5}/_{32}$-in.) I.D. hose over the bleeder valve and submerge the other end in a clear glass jar partially filled with clean brake fluid. The jar must be clear so that you can see air bubbles coming out of the hose.

3. Open the bleeder valve a half turn. Have your helper slowly depress the brake pedal until it reaches the floor and keep it there while you close the bleeder valve.

4. Have your helper slowly release the pedal until it is completely up. Repeat the preceding step until no more air bubbles emerge from the hose.

5. Repeat the entire bleeding procedure on the other three wheels in the sequence given in Fig. 9-2.

> **NOTE ——**
>
> Refill the reservoir after bleeding each wheel cylinder. If the system contains a great deal of air or if the brake fluid is being changed, it will be necessary to add more fluid once or twice while bleeding each wheel cylinder. Never let the reservoir be emptied completely, or you will have to start bleeding the brakes all over again.

> **CAUTION ——**
>
> *Do not allow brake fluid to come in contact with painted surfaces. Brake fluid contains a solvent damaging to most finishes.*

> **WARNING ——**
>
> *Do not use soft drink bottles or other food containers to store brake fluid or to bleed the brakes. Brake fluid is poisonous.*

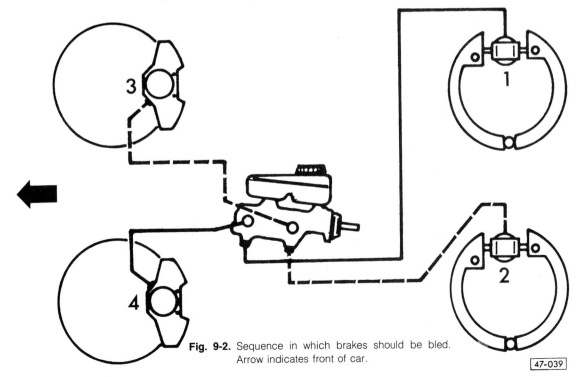

Fig. 9-2. Sequence in which brakes should be bled. Arrow indicates front of car.

47-039

9.4 Flushing Brake System

Never use anything but brake fluid to flush the brake system. Alcohol must not be used since it will destroy residual lubrication and will encourage the accumulation of water in the system.

> **NOTE ——**
> Do not rely on flushing alone to clean a brake system contaminated by dirt or rust. To remove all foreign matter, you must disassemble the system and clean the parts individually.

10. PARKING BRAKE

The components of the parking brake lever are shown in Fig. 10-1.

Fig. 10-1. Components of parking brake lever.

The parking brake operates only on the rear wheels. It is completely mechanical and independent of the hydraulic brake system. Once the parking brake handle has been pulled up, it is held in position by a ratchet. The lever will remain in the same position until the ratchet is released by pressing in the button on the end of the handle and allowing the parking brake lever to move down.

Two individual cables extend from the parking brake lever—one going to each rear wheel. The cables are attached to a compensator bar at the lever. Pulling the parking brake handle upward tightens the cables and moves the rear brake shoes into contact with the rear brake drums. Each cable operates on a lever attached to the rear brake shoe of each rear brake. The movement of the lever is transmitted to the front shoe of each rear brake by the brake adjuster assembly.

10.1 Adjusting Parking Brake

The parking brake should be adjusted whenever the rear brake linings have worn enough so that it is possible to raise the brake handle three clicks without noticeable braking action.

To adjust:

1. Raise the car on a hoist or support the rear of the car on jack stands placed beneath the welded flange of the body side member/floor plate. (There is a triangular mark on the side member at this point, located approximately below the rear edge of the front door.)

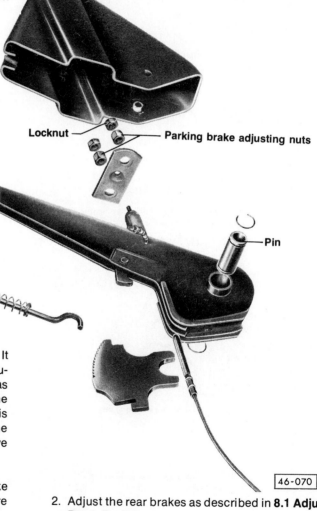

Locknut — Parking brake adjusting nuts

Pin

46-070

2. Adjust the rear brakes as described in **8.1 Adjusting Drum Brakes.**

3. Take out the screws, then remove the cover from the parking brake lever in the passenger compartment.

4. Pull the parking brake lever up two clicks. Then loosen the locknuts as indicated in Fig. 10-2.

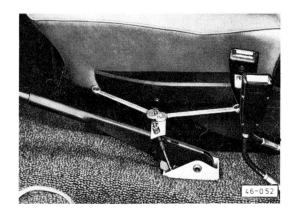

Fig. 10-2. Locknut being loosened while adjusting nut is held stationary with a second wrench.

5. Working alternately, tighten each adjusting nut a little at a time until it just becomes impossible to turn either rear wheel by hand.

6. Release the parking brake and check that both rear wheels rotate freely. If so, tighten the locknuts.

> **NOTE ——**
>
> The compensating bar should be horizontal following adjustment. If it is not, you can tighten one adjusting nut more than the other in order to level the bar. If, however, after leveling the bar, one cable end projects noticeably farther above its locknut than the other, that cable is probably stretching. If so, replace it as described in **10.3 Removing and Installing Brake Cable.**

7. Install the cover on the parking brake lever.

10.2 Removing and Installing Parking Brake Lever

To remove the parking brake lever, remove the cover by taking out the screws. Remove the locknuts, the adjusting nuts, and the compensating bar. These parts were illustrated earlier in Fig. 10-1. Take out the pin and remove the lever. Do not press the release button or the ratchet segment will fall out.

Before installation, disassemble the lever and clean the internal parts. Grease the parts before assembling them in the lever. Installation is the reverse of removal. Grease the lever pin before inserting it and refitting the circlip. Adjust the parking brake during installation of the cables in the compensating bar.

10.3 Removing and Installing Brake Cable

If the rear wheel brake shoes are correctly adjusted, but the compensating bar is not horizontal after adjusting the parking brake, one cable may be stretching. Left in service, the cable will eventually break.

To replace a parking brake cable, take off the locknut and the adjusting nut that hold the cable in the compensating bar. Remove the rear brake drum. Then unhook the cable from the lever on the rear brake shoe. Unbolt the bracket that holds the cable in the backing plate and take the cable and its flexible conduit out of the backing plate.

> **CAUTION ——**
>
> If the bolt that holds the parking brake cable is locked in place by corrosion, treat it with rust solvent or penetrating oil before attempting to force it loose. If the bracket is allowed to turn with the bolt, the flexible cable conduit may be damaged.

Pull the old cable out of the conduit to the rear. Then grease the new cable and insert it. Use a long screwdriver or a stiff wire hook to loop the cable around the curved guide channel on the parking brake lever. Adjust the parking brakes as you attach the cable. Check the adjustment again after about 300 mi. (500 km).

Cable Conduit and Mounting

On early cars, the cable conduit is attached to a bracket welded to the rear axle beam, as shown in Fig. 10-3. Later cars have a wire clip on the axle beam, as shown in Fig. 10-4.

Fig. 10-3. Early parking brake cable conduit mounting.

Fig. 10-4. Late parking brake cable conduit mounting.

If the parking brake cable makes squeaking or grinding noises (which may occur even when the parking brake is not applied and the car is being driven), apply water resistant grease at the point indicated in Fig. 10-5.

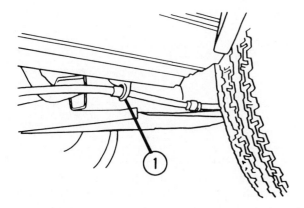

Fig. 10-5. Cable conduit mounting on body (**1**).

If the noise persists after lubricating the body mounting, check whether the car has the early-type mounting on the axle, as previously shown in Fig. 10-3. If so, modify the mounting on the axle as follows: cut open the bracket and remove the cable conduit, then chisel the mounting off the axle beam. Drill a 4.5-mm (³/₁₆-in.) hole in the axle's trailing arm as indicated in Fig. 10-6. Install the cable conduit as shown, using the following parts:

> Clamp—Part No. 411 201 189
> Bolt—Part No. N 10 697.1
> Nut—Part No. N 11 004.2
> Washer—Part No. N 12 097.1

NOTE ——

In modifying the right-side cable, you should glue a strip of felt or foam rubber to the bottom of the fuel tank at the point where there is a possibility that the conduit may contact the tank. On some cars you may also need to grind a piece out of the axle beam extension, as indicated by arrow **A** in Fig. 10-6.

Fig. 10-6. Cable conduit bracket modification. Bolt hole location dimensions **a** are 18 mm (¾ in.). Arrow **A** indicates where a piece may need to be ground out of the axle beam extension of some cars, in order to prevent damage to the cable conduit.

11. WHEELS AND TIRES

Tires are subject to many stresses. If they are to perform as intended, they must be inflated to specifications and correctly balanced. Properly maintained, the factory-installed tires will provide long service with comfort and safety. But they must never be kept in service when worn out or damaged by accidents or careless driving.

11.1 Wheels

The Rabbit model is equipped with 4½J X 13 rims. An optional 5J X 13 rim is also available for the Rabbit and is standard on the Scirocco. Both kinds of wheels have an offset of 45 mm (1 ⁴⁹/₆₄ in.).

Offset is the difference between the center of rim width and the mounting face that bolts to the brake drum or brake disc. The use of wheels other than those standard for a given year and model is discouraged. Many of the wider wheels sold by accessory companies do not have the correct offset dimension. This may impose excessive stress on the wheel bearings or alter steering behavior.

The wheels on all models covered by this Manual are suitable for use with tube or tubeless tires of the correct size, including radials. Tires of nonstandard size may be used only if the tire manufacturer specifies them for your particular make and model VW.

11.2 Tire Types and Pressures

Radial ply tires are factory-installed on all cars covered by this Manual. It is recommended that replacement tires also be of radial ply construction. Use 145 X 13 tires with

4½J X 13 wheels; use 155 SR 13 tires on Rabbit models with 5J X 13 wheels and 175/70 SR 13 tires on Scirocco models with 5J X 13 wheels.

Conventional Tires

Conventional bias ply tires offer very good riding characteristics and are well suited to highways and rough roads alike. Bias-constructed tires can be made extremely strong through the use of an almost infinite number of plies. The basic simplicity of bias ply design also results in lower construction costs.

Radial Tires

There is less friction between the fabric layers in radial ply tires, so they generate less heat. This makes them especially suitable for long-distance, high-speed driving. They also do not heat up so much when carrying heavy loads. Their rigid tread improves wet-weather traction, but tends to produce a harsher ride and increased road noise on some kinds of surfaces.

Winter Tires

Although inferior to regular tires for dry-road wear and handling, winter (mud and snow) tires can greatly improve operation on snowy or slushy roads. Studded winter tires improve traction on icy surfaces, but can be damaged by fast driving on dry roads and may damage some road surfaces. They should be used only if icy conditions predominate throughout the winter months. Also check your local vehicle laws. The use of studded tires may be restricted in your area.

CAUTION ——

If you install winter tires on only two of the four wheels, the winter tires should be installed on the front wheels. Also, to prevent dangerous handling, your winter tires must be of radial ply construction if the normal radial tires are kept on the rear wheels. If you install winter tires on all four wheels, the tires should all have the same kind of construction.

Tire Pressures

The inflation pressures given in **Table c** apply to the standard radial tire sizes that are installed at the factory. If you install tires of another kind, follow the inflation recommendation made by the tire manufacturer for your particular car and tire combination.

Because steel and textile cord radial tires have different traction characteristics, it is important that all four tires on the car have the same cord material. Tire effectiveness under various road conditions is shown in the following chart:

Operating conditions	Dry	Wet	Snow	Ice
Snow w/studs radial ply	0	–	X	X
Snow w/studs bias ply	0	–	X	X
Snow radial ply	X	X	X	0
Snow bias ply	X	X	X	0
Standard radial ply	X	X	0	0
Standard bias ply	X	X	0	–

X = Effective   0 = Restricted effectiveness   – = Noneffective

Table c. Standard Radial Tire Pressures

Wheel size	Tire size	Car model	Loads	Front pressure	Rear pressure
4½J × 13 with a 45-mm offset	145 × 13	1975 and 1976 Rabbit	All	27 psi	27 psi
		1977 and later Rabbit	Half load	27 psi	27 psi
			Full load	27 psi	31 psi
5J × 13 with a 45-mm offset	155 SR × 13	1975 and 1976 Rabbit	All	27 psi	27 psi
		1977 and later Rabbit	Half load	27 psi	27 psi
	175/70 SR × 13	1975 and 1976 Scirocco	All	27 psi	27 psi
		1977 and later Rabbit and Scirocco	Half load	27 psi	27 psi
			Full load	27 psi	31 psi

11.3 Normal Tire Wear

The original equipment tires on your VW have built-in tread wear indicators. These indicators are molded into the bottom of the tire tread grooves. The indicators eventually appear as the result of normal wear. They are about 13 mm (½ in.) wide in visible bands when the tire tread depth gets down to 1.5 mm (¹/₁₆ in.).

When these indicators appear in two or more adjacent grooves of a tire tread, as shown in Fig. 11-1, the tire must be replaced. It is recommended that tires be replaced well before the indicators are as visible as shown. Worn tires cannot grip even a dry road surface properly and are almost completely ineffective on a wet road surface.

WARNING ——

Do not assume that a tire is sound merely because the tread wear indicators have not yet appeared. Always check for cuts, cracks, rubber separation, and internal damage. Normal wear is only one factor in determining tire serviceability.

B2-928

Fig. 11-1. Indicator showing on worn-out tire.

For best all-round handling, always replace all four tires at the same time. If this is not possible, replace both tires on one axle. Do not combine tires of different ply construction, size, or tread pattern.

WARNING ——

Break in new tires by driving at moderate speeds for the first 60 to 100 mi. (100 to 160 km). New tires do not have full traction when first installed.

Normal tire wear is accelerated by higher speeds. Wear at a constant 35 mph (56 kph) is only about a third of that produced at a constant 70 mph (112 kph)—not half, as might seem logical.

Weather also affects normal tire wear. Hot weather is the most damaging and when heat is combined with high speeds and underinflation, tire structure is seriously endangered. Cold weather prolongs tire life; so does wet weather, which reduces the friction between tire and road.

11.4 Removing and Installing Wheels

The VW Owner's Manual supplied with the car lists the proper procedures for this job. The following points, however, deserve mention to mechanics not familiar with the VW Owner's Manual or with VW cars.

First, use the hubcap remover on cars with hubcaps. This is a wire hook that can be slipped into holes in the edges of the hubcaps. It prevents scratches on the painted wheel and makes the job quicker and easier.

Next, use only the VW jack supplied with the vehicle. Never attempt to lift a VW with an ordinary bumper jack. The cross section of VW bumpers is not contoured for the lifting hook on such jacks, and the vehicle cannot be lifted safely by them. If a hydraulic-type floor jack is used, be certain to position it carefully. Place blocks ahead and behind the wheels that remain on the ground to prevent the vehicle from rolling.

CAUTION ——

Under no circumstances must the car be lifted by placing a jack under the engine, transmission, the middle of the rear axle, or floor pan. Serious damage can result from these practices.

All wheel bolts are removed by turning them counterclockwise. When tightening the wheel bolts, torque them to 9.0 mkg (65 ft. lb.). Use a torque wrench. Pneumatic tools are seldom capable of attaining the prescribed torque with accuracy.

11.5 Wheel Rotation

Although the tires will develop a normal wear pattern under most conditions, abnormal road surfaces or variations in driving technicque may produce unequal wear of the four tires on a car. If, after a period of service, the tires on your vehicle show uneven wear, all four wheels can be rotated as shown in Fig. 11-2.

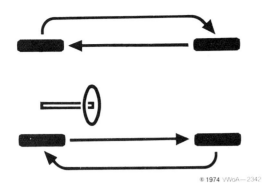

Fig. 11-2. Pattern of recommended wheel rotation. Wheel rotation is not required but may be desirable if tires are wearing unevenly.

11.6 Changing Tires

Dismounting or mounting tires on the rims requires a tire appliance with power enough to force the tire bead over the inner hump on the rim. When carrying out these operations, be sure that the rubber lining on the inner wall of the tire and tire beads is not damaged.

To dismount tire:

1. Take off the valve cap, carefully unscrew the valve core, and let the air out of the tire. Then press the tire bead off the rim as shown in Fig. 11-3.

Fig. 11-3. Pressing tire bead off rim.

2. Pry the tire sidewalls, one after the other, over the rim edges as shown in Fig. 11-4.

Fig. 11-4. Prying tire sidewalls over rim edges.

3. Check the airtight lining inside the tire for damage and bruises between the lining and casing. Carefully inspect the outside of the tire for embedded stones, cuts, grease, and signs of uneven wear.

4. Check the rubber part of the valve for cracks and damage. If the valve is faulty, remove it from the rim. Lubricate a new valve with soapy water. Then install the new valve as shown in Fig. 11-5.

Fig. 11-5. A valve tool being used to install a new valve in the rim.

To mount tire:

1. Check the rim for damage. Radial runout must not exceed 1.25 mm (.050 in.); lateral runout must not exceed 1.50 mm (.060 in.).

2. Using a wire brush, remove any dirt from the rim shoulders and flanges. Smooth any sharp edges before mounting the tire on the wheel.

3. Insert the valve with the valve installing tool.

NOTE ——

Use inner tubes with radial tires if the vehicle will be used on rough roads or off road.

4. Mount the tire on the rim as shown in Fig. 11-6. If there is a red dot on the sidewall, position it toward the valve.

© 1972 VWoA—491

Fig. 11-6. Tire being mounted on rim. Use soft soap or a special rubber lubricant on the rim for safe, easy mounting.

5. Remove the valve core, if not already removed.

6. Inflate the tire to at least 43 psi (3 kg/cm²).

NOTE ——

Use a bead expander strap, if necessary, to obtain an airtight seal. When inflating the tire you should hear the bead snap over the inner hump on the rim.

7. Install the valve core and inflate the tire to the correct running pressure, as listed earlier in **11.2 Tire Types and Pressures.**

8. Immerse the wheel in water. Check for leaks.

9. Balance the wheel and install it on the car.

11.7 Abnormal Wear

Following are the six most common causes of abnormal tire wear (extra wear):

1. Underinflation or overinflation

2. Hard driving (high speed driving, violent braking, sudden cornering)

3. Rough or abrasive road surfaces, high crown roads, and very uneven road surfaces

4. Poorly aligned wheels (front or rear)

5. Poorly balanced wheels (front or rear)

6. Vehicle overloading or carrying too much weight for tire capacity.

Improper Inflation

Tire life depends greatly on correct inflation. Unfortunately, there are many ways for a tire to lose air. Every tire normally loses some air pressure due to the diffusion of air molecules through the rubber. Although tubeless tires hold air pressure longer than tires with inner tubes, it is recommended that you check the pressure even of tubeless tires once a week.

Tire pressures should be checked before driving, when the tires are still cold. If tire pressures are checked after driving, the pressures will have increased from the heat of road friction and internal flexing. If air is bled from a warm tire to obtain the pressure recommended for a cold tire, the tire will actually be underinflated. A tire that is driven while underinflated will overheat because of increased tire flexing and will rapidly lose its road-holding ability as tire strength begins to diminish.

There is always a reason when a tire loses a significant amount of air in a short period of time. Aside from a hole in the tire, the possible causes are a leaky rim or valve, loose-fitting tire beads, foreign matter in the rim, or an uneven surface between the rim shoulder and the tire.

Fig. 11-7 shows three tire inflation conditions. The shape of the tire is changed by the degree of inflation. This can cause abnormal wear. An underinflated tire wears at its edges; an overinflated tire wears at its center. The profile of an underflated tire is similar to that of an overloaded tire. The same kind of wear will result from overloading, with the added possibility of severe heat damage and possible structural failure.

© 1974 VWoA—1435

Fig. 11-9. Underinflation wear. Tire worn out by running it with too low an air pressure.

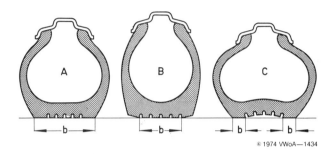

© 1974 VWoA—1434

Fig. 11-7. Tire inflation. Condition **A**, normal inflation condition **B**, overinflation; condition **C**, underinflation. Dimension **b** is the width of the tire tread in contact with the road.

Hard Driving

Tires may wear abnormally because of excessive speed, heavy braking (see Fig. 11-10), high speed cornering, and similar violent or abrupt maneuvers. Conservative driving preserves tire life.

Fig. 11-8 shows typical tire wear due to overinflation. Because a narrower portion of the tread is in contact with the road, wear occurs faster than normal. This tire is worn out despite the good tread remaining at the edges.

© 1974 VWoA—1438

Fig. 11-8. Overinflation wear. Tire worn out by running it with excessive air pressure.

© 1974 VWoA—1439

Fig. 11-10. Abnormal tire wear due to locking the brakes. Uneven braking forces can also cause heavy tire wear.

Road Surfaces

Some road surfaces tend to increase tire wear. Rough, anti-skid surfacing materials abrade the tread and accelerate normal wear. Roadways with high crowns necessitate constant steering correction to keep the car headed parallel to the highway. This will eventually produce the kind of abnormal wear usually associated with improper front wheel alignment. Obstructions and road hazards

Fig. 11-9 shows the tread wear pattern of an underinflated tire. This worn-out tire still has deep tread in its center, although the edges are completely bald. Such tires should be removed from service immediately. As with tires worn unevenly by overinflation, they provide very limited adhesion in wet weather and almost no traction in deep snow. In addition, side grip for cornering is seriously impaired.

can cause severe tire damage and can even break the casing internally, as shown in Fig. 11-11.

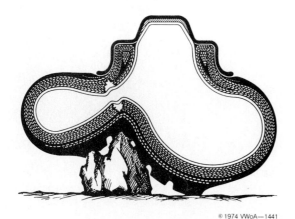

© 1974 VWoA—1441

Fig. 11-11. Internal damage. Striking an obstacle in the road may tear the ply layers. Such damage renders the tire unfit for use. You may have to take the tire off its rim to see such defects.

Faulty Wheel Alignment

Excessive tire wear will result from misalignment of any of the four wheels on the car. If irregular tire wear appears, check the front wheel track, the front wheel angles at full steering lock, the ride height and rear wheel track, the position of the axles relative to each other, the wheelbase on both sides of the car, the front and rear wheel camber, the setting of the rear spring plates, and the condition of the shock absorbers. The abnormal wear caused by misalignment usually takes the form of greater wear at one edge of the tread than on the other. Alignment specifications are given in **SUSPENSION AND STEERING.**

Wheels Out of Balance

Wheels that are out of balance cause abnormal tire wear and constitute a driving hazard. Unbalanced wheels bounce, tramp, and wobble. The faster you drive, the more dangerous these wheel vibrations are.

Wheel imbalance is always more evident on the front wheels, and usually more dangerous. Fig. 11-12 shows the condition that static balancing of the wheel and tire can detect. The effect of such imbalance is shown in the right-hand part of the illustration.

Fig. 11-13 shows the type of imbalance that only dynamic balancing can detect. Although in perfect static balance, the concentrations of mass are not in line with one another or with the tire centerline. The wheel wobbles sideways when it spins, as shown on the right-hand side of the illustration. This causes deep wear in the form of cupped areas on the tread. Check that wheel runout does not exceed 1.25 mm (.050 in.) either radially or laterally before dynamic balancing the wheel. Replace the wheel if it does.

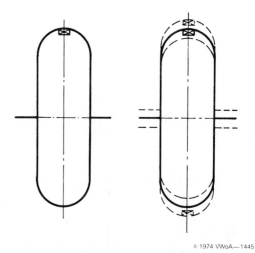

© 1974 VWoA—1445

Fig. 11-12. Imbalance that can be cured by static balancing. Vibration of the spinning wheel is shown at the right.

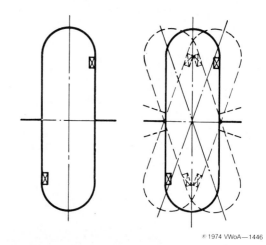

© 1974 VWoA—1446

Fig. 11-13. Imbalance that can be cured only by dynamic balancing. Vibration of the spinning wheel is shown at the right.

Overloading

Overloading the tires causes damage similar to that produced by underinflation. The excessive heat generated by an overloaded tire weakens the tire and causes difficult vehicle handling. The maximum load capacity (given in the Owner's Manual), added to the weight of the vehicle, must never exceed the total load capacity of the four tires (marked on their sidewalls).

12. BRAKES AND WHEELS TECHNICAL DATA

The following tables give all specifications related to the brake system, tires, and wheels. Wheel alignment specifications are given in **SUSPENSION AND STEERING.**

I. Tightening Torques

Location	Designation	mkg	ft. lb.
Stop screw in master cylinder housing	special screw	1.5 to 2.0	11 to 14
Residual pressure valve in master cylinder	—	2.0	14
Brake light/warning light switch in master cylinder	—	2.0	14
Brake line to master cylinder	union nut	1.5 to 2.0	11 to 14
Master cylinder to vacuum powered brake servo	nut	1.3 maximum	9.4 maximum
Vacuum powered brake servo to mounting bracket	nut	1.3 maximum	9.4 maximum
Brake caliper to front suspension strut	bolt	6.0	43
Brake hose in brake caliper	—	1.5	11
Girling caliper pad retainer clip to caliper frame	bolt	2.0	14
Brake disc splash shield to front suspension strut	bolt	1.0	7
Rear wheel brake cylinder to backing plate	bolt	1.0	7
Brake hose in rear wheel brake cylinder	—	1.5	11
Rear brake backing plate and stub axle to axle beam	bolt	6.0	43
Pressure regulator to car underbody	bolt	1.5	11
Brake line unions	union nut	1.5 to 2.0	11 to 14
Brake hoses—except in caliper or wheel cylinder		1.5 to 2.0	11 to 14
Road wheel to brake disc or brake drum	lug bolt	9.0	65

II. Tolerances, Wear Limits, and Settings

Designation	New Part	Wear Limit
A. Disc Brakes		
1. Front wheel discs ....thickness	12.00 mm (.472 in.)	—
...............minimum thickness before machining	—	11.00 mm (.434 in.)
...............maximum amount removable per side (disc must be reworked equally on both sides)	0.50 mm (.020 in.)	—
........................minimum permissible thickness	—	10.50 mm (.413 in.)
...............minimum thickness after machining	—	10.50 mm (.413 in.)
..................maximum permissible runout	—	0.10 mm (.004 in.)
...........maximum permissible thickness variation	—	0.02 mm (.0008 in.)
2. Brake pad linings ....remaining thickness	—	2.00 mm (.080 in.)
B. Drum Brakes		
1. Front wheel drums ....inside diameter of new drum	230.10 mm ±0.20 mm (9.059 in ±.008 in.)	—
.............maximum permissible inside diameter	—	231.10 mm ±0.20 mm (9.098 in. ±.008 in.)
.............maximum inside diameter after machining	—	230.60 mm ±0.20 mm (9.079 in. ±.008 in.)
.............maximum radial runout or out-of-round	—	0.05 mm (.002 in.)
2. Rear wheel drums ....inside diameter of new drum	180.00 mm (7.086 in.)	—
.............maximum permissible inside diameter	—	181.00 mm (7.125 in.)
.............maximum inside diameter after machining	—	180.50 mm (7.105 in.)
.............maximum radial runout or out-of-round	—	0.05 mm (.002 in.)
3. Rear wheel brake shoe linings ....remaining thickness (riveted linings)	—	2.50 mm (.100 in.)
.............remaining thickness (bonded linings)	—	1.50 mm (.060 in.)

SUSPENSION AND STEERING

Contents

2 ▉

Suspension and Steering

Both the VW Rabbit and the VW Scirocco have strut-type independent front wheel suspension. The struts, with their built-in hydraulic shock absorbers, are similar in many respects to the landing wheel struts being used on commercial airliners. In addition to providing excellent steering and handling, the system has the combined advantages of compact size and comparatively light weight.

The front struts have been designed to provide a negative roll radius. That is, each wheel's steering axis intersects the road at a point outboard of the wheel's vertical centerline. The resulting suspension geometry tends to steer the car automatically in the direction of incipient skids caused by unequal front wheel traction. Conventional front suspension geometry, which places the steering axes inboard of the tire centerlines, tends to steer the car away from the direction of this kind of skid—thereby increasing its severity.

The rack and pinion steering gearbox is notable for its light weight and compact size. The steering column is connected to the rack and pinion steering gearbox by a universal joint shaft. The universal joint shaft is angled in order to prevent collision impacts from forcing the steering wheel toward the driver.

The rear suspension has been designed for low unsprung weight, easy replacement of springs and shock absorbers, good riding qualities, and good handling. The axle beam is flexible and free to twist. Thus, it acts as an anti-roll bar whenever one rear wheel is deflected upward more than the other. This design offers many advantages over more complicated kinds of independent rear suspension.

Though the front suspension struts and track control arms can be disassembled for repair, this work requires special tools, experience, and clean shop conditions. If you lack the skills, tools, or a suitable workshop for suspension and steering work, we suggest you leave such repairs to an Authorized Dealer or other qualified shop. We especially urge you to consult your Authorized Dealer before attempting any repairs on a car still covered by the new-car warranty.

1. GENERAL DESCRIPTION

Fig. 1-1 shows the front suspension system. The control arms, sometimes called the wishbones or A-arms, are bolted to mounting points that are welded to the car's body structure. The struts have flexible rubber mountings at the top, encased in pressed steel housings. The housings are bolted to the car body.

Front Suspension Struts

Each front suspension strut consists of a hydraulic shock absorber inside a tubular strut housing and a concentrically-mounted coil spring. The front wheel bearing housing and its integral steering arm is a separate component that is bolted to a mounting welded to the lower end of the strut. The front suspension's upward travel is limited by a hollow rubber buffer, its lower limit of travel by a rubber stop inside the shock absorber.

Front Control Arms

The two Y-shaped control arms locate the suspension struts both longitudinally and laterally. Though the suspension ball joints are riveted to the control arm during manufacture, replacement ball joints can be installed with bolts. There are no adjustments for front wheel alignment on the control arms. Camber is adjusted by relocating the front wheel bearing housing on the suspension strut, and toe is adjusted by altering the length of the steering tie rods.

Rear Suspension

The entire rear suspension is shown removed from the car in Fig. 1-2. The rear axle beam is a welded assembly with a T-shaped cross section. Trailing arms, of tubular cross section, are welded to the outer ends of the axle beam. For easy replacement, the rear wheel stub axles are bolted to the trailing arms.

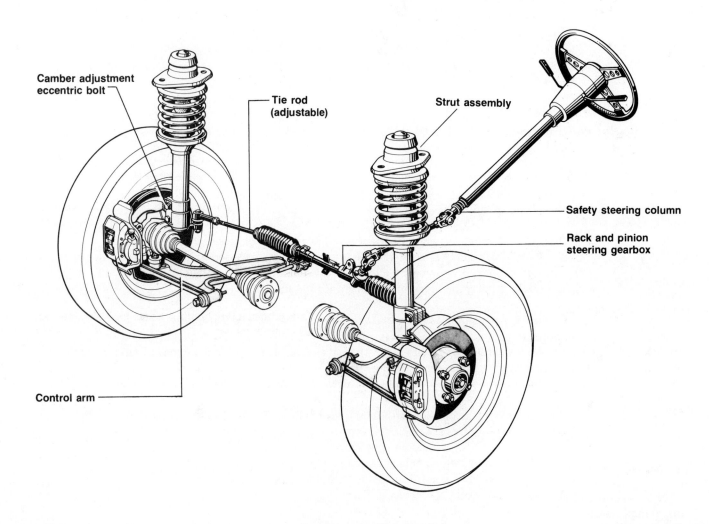

Camber adjustment eccentric bolt

Tie rod (adjustable)

Strut assembly

Safety steering column

Rack and pinion steering gearbox

Control arm

Fig. 1-1. Front suspension and steering layout used on cars covered by this Manual.

2

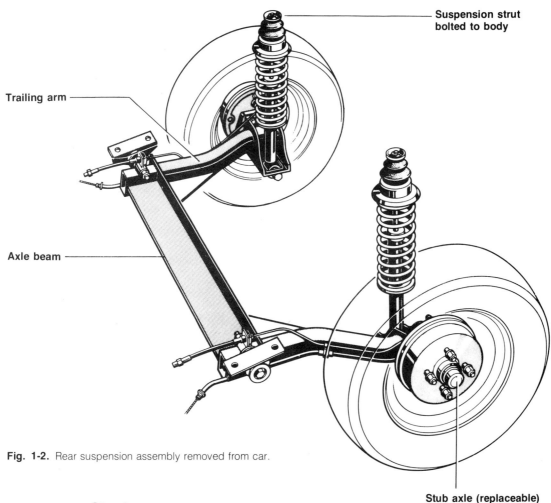

Suspension strut bolted to body

Trailing arm

Axle beam

Stub axle (replaceable)

Fig. 1-2. Rear suspension assembly removed from car.

Steering

The rack and pinion steering gearbox is located behind the engine and the transaxle. This location not only protects the steering gearbox from weather, but also shields the steering from damage in all but the most severe collisions. Because of its self-damping characteristics, the rack and pinion steering system does not have the hydraulic steering damper that is used on some other Volkswagen cars.

Neither the steering gearbox nor the tie rod ends require lubrication during their normal service lives. And, though there is an adjusting screw on the steering gearbox, it is not necessary to make any adjustment unless the steering either rattles or is stiff and does not self-center.

2. MAINTENANCE

The suspension and steering are virtually maintenance-free. The following items should be checked at the intervals prescribed in **LUBRICATION AND MAINTENANCE.** Instructions for making these

checks can be found either in **LUBRICATION AND MAINTENANCE** or under the listed heading in this section for the Manual.

1. Checking ball joint dust seals and tie rod end dust seals

2. Checking steering play

3. Checking steering gearbox boots for leaks, tearing, or other damage

4. Checking front wheel camber and toe. See **3.**

3. WHEEL ALIGNMENT

Only camber and toe are adjustable. Caster angle and king pin inclination are determined by the manufactured dimensions of the suspension parts, so damaged parts must be replaced in order to correct these alignment factors.

The following preparatory steps are essential to accurate alignment measurements:

1. Have the car on a level surface.

2. Inflate the tires to specifications and unload the car except for the spare wheel and a full fuel tank. Then jounce the car several times and let it settle into its normal position.

3. Check for excessive steering gearbox play. If play is excessive, adjust or replace the gearbox.

4. Make sure that there is no play in the tie rod ends or other parts of the steering linkage.

Measuring wheel camber and toe require suitable gauges. Although professional-grade instruments may cost several hundred dollars, modestly priced gauges that are adequate for home use are available from mail order houses. Instructions are supplied by the manufacturer.

3.1 Checking and Adjusting Front Wheel Camber

Camber is the angle at which wheels depart from the true vertical when viewed from directly in front of the car. If the tops of the wheels lean slightly outward, they are said to have positive camber. If they lean inward, they are said to have negative camber.

To check:

1. After placing the car on a level surface with the steering centered, apply a bubble protractor as shown in Fig. 3-1.

© 1974 VWoA—2196

Fig. 3-1. Bubble protractor against front wheel.

2. Using chalk, mark the wheel at the points where it contacts the protractor.

3. Turn the spirit level carrier on the protractor until the bubble is centered, then read the camber angle on the scale.

NOTE ——
If you are using a different kind of gauge, follow the manufacturer's instructions.

4. Roll the car forward a half-turn of the wheels and repeat the measurement at the chalk-marked points.

5. Take the new reading and average it with the one you obtained earlier. The result is the camber angle for the wheel.

6. Repeat the entire procedure on the other front wheel.

The front wheel camber should be +20' ±30'. Also, the difference in camber between the wheels should not vary more than 1°. If the camber of a wheel is not within specifications, it should be adjusted to as near 20' positive camber as possible.

To adjust camber:

1. Loosen the nuts and bolts that hold the front wheel bearing housing to the suspension strut.

NOTE ——
The car must be standing on its wheels while adjustments are being made.

2. Set the spirit level carrier on the protractor to the specified angle of 20' positive camber.

3. Turn the eccentric bolt indicated in Fig. 3-2 until the bubble in the protractor is centered when the protractor is applied to the chalk-marked points on the wheel.

44-020

Fig. 3-2. Eccentric bolt (arrow) that is used to adjust camber. This is the uppermost of the two bolts that hold the front wheel bearing housing to the suspension strut.

4. Torque the nuts of the bolts that hold the front wheel bearing housing to the suspension strut to 8.0 mkg (58 ft. lb.). Again check the camber and repeat the adjustments, if necessary, in order to bring the camber within specifications.

3.2 Checking and Adjusting Front Wheel Toe

The cars covered by this Manual are designed to operate with very little toe-in or toe-out. Shops with optical aligning devices should follow the equipment manufacturer's instructions to obtain a toe angle of $-15'$ $+10'$ or $-15'$, or $+10' \pm 15'$ after adding 8 to 12 kg (18 to 26 lb.) of extra weight above the wheel. The maximum toe change produced by the added weight should not exceed $20'$.

Most small shops and individual car owners check toe with a track gauge. This device is used to measure the distance between two points at the front edges of the rims, then the distance between the same two points after the car has been rolled ahead so that these points are at the rear. The measurement made at the rear should be nearly the same as the measurement at the front. In other words, adjust the front wheels to as near $0°$ toe as possible—with an infinitesimal amount of toe-out.

> **NOTE** ——
>
> All of the specifications given here apply only with the front wheels in their straight-ahead position. Specifications for toe angle difference at $20°$ of steering lock can be found in **7. Suspension and Steering Technical Data.** Specifications are also given there for caster angle and other front and rear alignment factors.

To check and adjust toe:

1. Turn the steering to its centered position (steering wheel spokes horizontal and front wheels pointed straight ahead).

2. Measure the toe. If a track gauge is used, mark the measuring points with chalk. Doing this will allow you to make measurements between the same two points after you have rolled the car forward a half-turn of the wheels.

3. If toe is not within specifications, loosen the locknut on the right-hand tie rod. (The nut is on the tie rod, adjacent to the right-hand tie rod end.)

4. Rotate the top of the right-hand tie rod toward the front of the car to increase toe-in or rotate the top of the right-hand tie rod toward the rear of the car to increase toe-out.

5. When the toe is correct, place an open end wrench on the flats of the right-hand tie rod end. Then, using a crow's foot wrench, torque the locknut to 4.0 mkg (29 ft. lb.).

6. Recheck the toe in order to make certain that it is correct. Repeat the adjustment, if necessary. Then position the tie rod end so that it is not angled; position the steering gearbox rubber boot on the tie rod so that the boot is not twisted.

If, after adjusting the toe to specifications, the steering wheel is not centered while you are driving straight ahead on a level surface, either the steering rack is not correctly adjusted, an incorrectly-adjusted replacement tie rod has been installed on the left side, the tie rods are not correctly installed on the steering rack, or the steering wheel is incorrectly installed. However, you should never assume that the steering wheel has been installed incorrectly until after you have checked the rack and the tie rods as described in **6.1 Removing and Installing Tie Rods, Tie Rod Ends, and Rubber Bushings** and **6.2 Adjusting Steering.** Also, check that the steering is not pulling to one side owing to unequally worn front tires or front tires with different tread patterns or inflation pressures. Lastly, there may be a bent tie rod or other damaged steering or suspension part, which should be replaced.

> **WARNING** ——
>
> *If there are worn, damaged, or misadjusted steering or suspension parts, never center the steering wheel either by altering its position on the column or by moving the column on the universal joint shaft. Doing these things leaves the real fault uncorrected. Always replace deformed parts. Bending them back to their original shapes could seriously weaken them structurally.*

3.3 Checking Rear Wheel Alignment

The rear wheel alignment cannot be adjusted. Incorrect alignment can only be corrected by replacing damaged parts. If you wish to check the rear wheel alignment, please refer to **5.2 Checking Axle Beam for Distortion.** Rear alignment specifications appear in **7. Suspension and Steering Technical Data.**

4. FRONT SUSPENSION

Though the cars covered by this Manual have front wheel drive, the front suspension is no more complex than that of a rear-drive automobile. All the front suspension parts that are subject to wear are quickly and easily replaceable. Some repairs, however, require equipment other than common hand tools. To avoid starting a job that you may not be able to complete, please read the entire procedure for the task before you begin work.

4.1 Checking Suspension Ball Joints

A special lever and a vernier caliper should be used to check ball joint play.

To check:

1. Lift the car so that the front wheels and suspension are unsupported.

2. Install the special lever as shown in Fig. 4-1.

Fig. 4-1. Lever installed on ball joint and control arm. Notice the spacer placed between lever and wheel rim for use as a fulcrum point. Moving lever as indicated by arrow will compress ball joint.

3. Fully compress the ball joint by prying the control arm upward with a lever. Then place a vernier caliper on the suspension as shown in Fig. 4-2.

4. Note the reading on the vernier caliper. Then, while slowly releasing the lever, note the caliper's travel. The increase in the reading is the ball joint play. Replace the ball joint if play is 2.50 mm (.100 in.) or more. The play in new ball joints is 1.00 mm (.040 in.).

Fig. 4-2. Ball joint play being measured. Place stationary inside-diameter caliper jaw against brake caliper; place sliding outside-diameter caliper jaw beneath control arm. Move lever as indicated by double arrow to compress and release ball joint.

4.2 Removing and Installing Suspension Ball Joints

1. Lift the car so that the front wheels and suspension are unsupported.

2. Remove the nut and clamp bolt that hold the ball joint stud in the bottom of the wheel bearing housing. Then pull the stud out of the bearing housing so that the control arm hangs down.

3. Drill out the rivets indicated in Fig. 4-3. On early cars with two rivets, use a 6-mm (or ¼-in.) drill; on later cars with three rivets, use a 7-mm ($^9/_{32}$-in.) drill. If necessary, cut the rivet heads off with a cold chisel after you have drilled them.

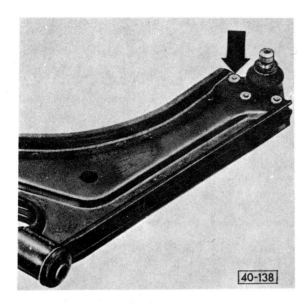

Fig. 4-3. Rivets (arrow) that hold suspension ball joint to control arm.

4. Remove the old ball joint.

5. On early control arms with two rivets, enlarge the holes to 8.3 mm ($^{21}/_{64}$ in.). Then install the new ball joint as shown in Fig. 4-4—using M 8 bolts and nuts torqued to 2.5 mkg (18 ft. lb.).

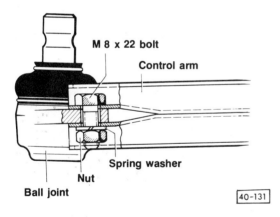

Fig. 4-4. Replacement ball joint installed in early control arm.

6. On late control arms with three rivets, install the new ball joint as shown in Fig. 4-5—using M 7 bolts and nuts torqued to 2.5 mkg (18 ft. lb.).

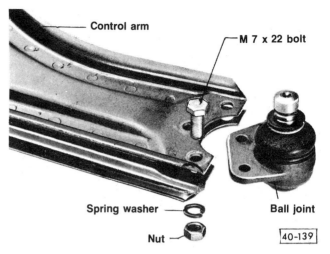

Fig. 4-5. Replacement ball joint being installed in late control arm.

7. Install the stud of the new ball joint in the bearing housing. Install the clamp bolt and torque its nut to 3.0 mkg (22 ft. lb.).

NOTE ——

It is not necessary to adjust the camber and toe if you have replaced a ball joint only.

4.3 Checking Front Suspension Control Arm for Distortion

If the front wheel alignment cannot be brought within specifications—or if there has been a collision—check the front suspension control arms for distortion. There should be no kinks or creases in the circled area of the control arm shown in Fig. 4-6. A straightedge should lie flat against the control arm when placed along the control arm's front edge.

Fig. 4-6. Control arm being checked with straightedge for rearward bending.

To check the control arm for bending in a horizontal plane, place the straightedge along the bottom, as shown in Fig. 4-7. If any fault is found in the control arm, replace it.

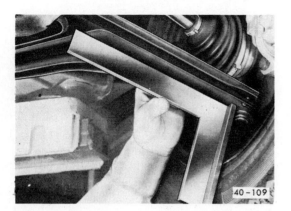

Fig. 4-7. Control arm being checked for horizontal bends.

WARNING ——

Never attempt to straighten a bent control arm. Bending it back to its original shape — while either heated or cold — will seriously weaken the control arm structurally.

4.4 Removing and Installing Front Suspension as a Unit

Unless you need to replace an individual component—such as the suspension strut or a wheel bearing—you can easily remove an entire front suspension assembly from the car. This is the best procedure when a complete front suspension rebuild is anticipated, or when the car is undergoing body work.

To remove:

1. Lift the car so that the front wheels and suspension are unsupported.

2. Disconnect the brake hose at the point indicated in Fig. 4-8. Quickly cap the brake line with a clean brake bleeder dust cap.

   CAUTION ——

   Do not hammer out the tie rod end. Doing this will ruin the threads and make reinstallation impossible.

3. Remove first the cotter pin and then the castellated nut that hold the tie rod end in the steering arm. Using a tool such as the one shown in Fig. 4-9, remove the tie rod end from the steering arm.

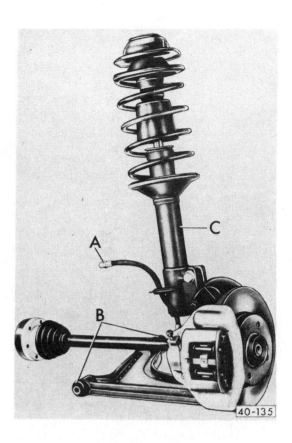

Fig. 4-8. Front suspension assembly removed from car. Brake hose is at **A**, pivots for control arm are at **B**, strut is at **C**.

Fig. 4-9. Puller in position for tie rod end removal. Car shown is not one of those covered by this Manual.

4. Remove the socket-head bolts that hold the inner constant velocity joint of the driveshaft to the transaxle's drive flange.

5. Remove the front pivot bolt of the control arm; remove the two retaining bolts for the U-shaped retainer for the control arm's rear pivot.

> **NOTE** ——
>
> In order to remove the front pivot bolts from cars with automatic transmissions, you must remove the front left engine mounting, the nut for the rear mounting, and the engine mounting support. Then, using the engine support bar shown in Fig. 4-10, or a jack, raise the engine/transaxle assembly until the front pivot bolts can be removed.

Fig. 4-10. Engine of car with automatic transmission being raised. Left engine mounting is at arrow. Threaded rod of engine support bar (Tool 10-222) can be tightened to raise engine and transaxle.

6. Support the front suspension assembly so that it will not fall, or have someone hold it. Then, working inside the engine compartment, remove the nuts that hold the toe mounting of the suspension strut to the body.

7. Carefully lower the entire suspension assembly from the car.

To install:

1. Position the front suspension assembly beneath the front fender. Bolt the top mounting of the suspension strut to the body. Torque the nuts to 2.0 mkg (14 ft. lb.).

2. Position the driveshaft on the transaxle and the control arm on the body. Install the front pivot bolt of the control arm to a torque of 6.0 mkg (43 ft. lb.); torque the bolts for the rear pivot's U-shaped retainer to 3.0 mkg (22 ft. lb.).

> **NOTE** ——
>
> In installing the front pivot bolt, place the convex surface of the lockwasher toward the bolt head. Always use a new bolt and lockwasher and coat the threads of the bolt with Loctite®. See Fig. 4-11. If the nut for the pivot bolt (which is welded to the body) is damaged, replace it as described in **BODY AND INTERIOR.**

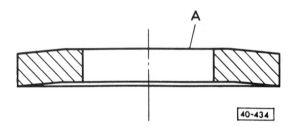

Fig. 4-11. Cross section of lock washer for front pivot bolt. Convex surface (**A**) must be toward bolt head.

3. On cars with automatic transmissions, lower the engine and reinstall the engine mountings. Torque the bolts that hold the engine to the mounting support to 5.5 mkg (40 ft. lb.).

4. Install the socket head bolts that hold the driveshaft's constant velocity joint to the transaxle's drive flange. Torque the bolts to 4.5 mkg (32 ft. lb.).

5. Reconnect the tie rod end to the steering arm. Torque the castellated nut to 3.0 mkg (22 ft. lb.). Advance it, if necessary, to uncover the cotter pin hole, then install a new cotter pin.

6. Reconnect the brake hose. Lubricate the threads with brake fluid, then torque the union to 1.5 to 2.0 mkg (11 to 14 ft. lb.).

7. Bleed the front brakes as described in **BRAKES AND WHEELS.**

8. Check and, if necessary, adjust the camber and toe as described in **3. Wheel Alignment.**

4.5 Removing and Installing Suspension Strut

Fig. 4-12 is an exploded view of the front suspension. If you wish to remove the driveshafts only, please use the procedure given in **MANUAL TRANSMISSION.** Detailed instructions for removing, repairing, and installing brake components can be found in **BRAKES AND WHEELS.**

> *WARNING* ――
>
> *Always loosen or tighten the axle nuts while the car is on the ground. The leverage needed for this job could topple the car from a hoist.*

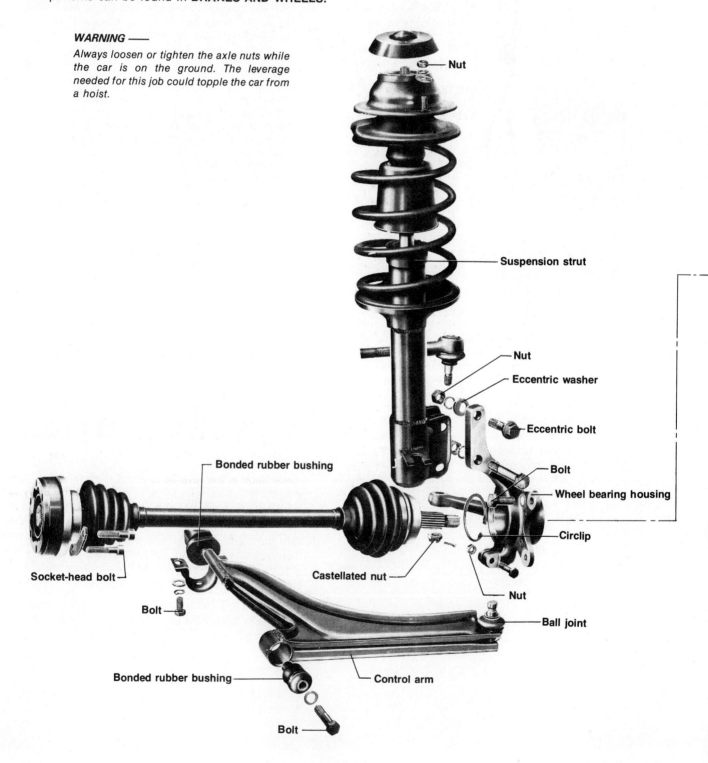

Nut

Suspension strut

Nut

Eccentric washer

Eccentric bolt

Bolt

Wheel bearing housing

Bonded rubber bushing

Circlip

Socket-head bolt

Castellated nut

Nut

Bolt

Ball joint

Control arm

Bonded rubber bushing

Bolt

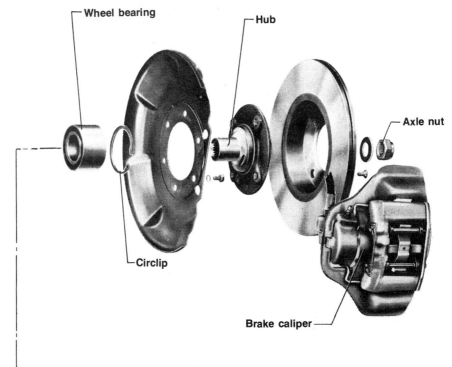

Wheel bearing

Hub

Axle nut

Circlip

Brake caliper

40-132

Fig. 4-12. Exploded view of front suspension. Since August 1975 washers have not been installed under the brake caliper mounting bolts.

To remove:

1. Lift the car so that the front wheels and suspension are unsupported.

2. Make a stiff wire hook that will be suitable for supporting the control arm, the wheel bearing housing, the driveshaft, and the brake assembly while the strut is off the car.

3. Remove the nuts from the bolts that hold the front wheel bearing housing to the suspension strut. (The uppermost bolt is the eccentric bolt used to adjust front wheel camber.) Then remove the bolts.

4. Using the stiff wire hook, suspend the brake assembly from the car body. Disengage the suspension strut from the wheel bearing housing.

5. Support the front suspension strut so that it will not fall, or have someone hold it. Then, working inside the engine compartment, remove the nuts that hold the top mounting of the suspension strut to the body.

6. Carefully remove the suspension strut assembly from the car.

Installation is the reverse of removal. Torque the nuts that hold the top of the suspension strut to the body to 2.0 mkg (14 ft. lb.). Install the bolts that hold the strut to the wheel bearing housing—being careful to install the eccentric washer and eccentric bolt as previously shown in Fig. 4-11. Adjust the front wheel camber and toe as described in **3. Wheel Alignment.** Then torque the bolts that hold the suspension strut to the front wheel bearing housing to 8.0 mkg (58 ft. lb.).

4.6 Disassembling, Checking, and Assembling Front Suspension Strut

Fig. 4-13 is an exploded view of the front suspension strut. The springs are selected from different tolerance groups and both springs on the car should be of the same group. Springs of different tolerance groups are identified by color. So, if you cannot obtain a replacement spring that is the same color as the original spring, replace both front springs with springs of the same color.

NOTE ——

To replace the end collar, shown in Fig. 4-13, it is necessary neither to remove the strut from the car nor to disassemble the strut. As long as the car is resting on its wheels, you can safely remove the suspension strut nut, the retainer, and the end collar. During assembly, torque the suspension strut nut to 8.0 mkg (58 ft. lb.).

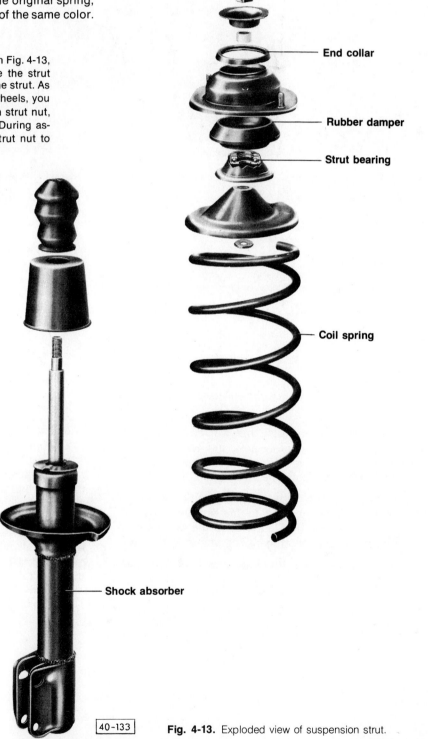

Suspension strut nut

End collar

Rubber damper

Strut bearing

Coil spring

Shock absorber

40-133

Fig. 4-13. Exploded view of suspension strut.

To disassemble strut:

1. Install the spring compressing appliance in a bench vise, then install the strut in the spring compressing appliance.

2. To compress the spring, tighten the long bolts a few turns at a time, working alternately (Fig. 4-14).

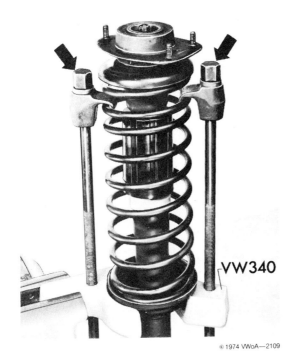

© 1974 VWoA—2109

Fig. 4-14. Strut mounted in spring compressing appliance. Arrows indicate the two long bolts. Strut shown is not for a car covered by this Manual.

3. Using an offset box wrench and an Allen wrench as shown in Fig. 4-15, remove the suspension strut nut from the shock absorber piston rod.

4. Working alternately, gradually loosen the two long bolts on the compressing appliance until spring tension is relieved. Then take the strut apart.

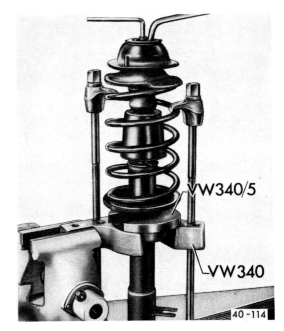

Fig. 4-15. Removing suspension strut nut from shock absorber piston rod.

Checking Shock Absorber

Worn-out shock absorbers often make knocking noises when the car is driven. You can hand-check a shock absorber by extending and compressing it while holding it in its installed position. It must operate smoothly and with uniform resistance throughout its entire stroke. If possible, compare the used unit with a new shock absorber. New shock absorbers that have been in storage may have to be pumped several times before they reach full efficiency.

Shock absorbers do not require maintenance. An adequate supply of fluid is placed in them during manufacture to compensate for small leaks. Minor traces of fluid leakage are acceptable if the shock absorber still functions efficiently. Faulty shock absorbers cannot be serviced and must be replaced.

Correcting Rattling Coil Springs

Sometimes rattles from the front suspension struts are caused by spring coils knocking together—not by worn-out shock absorbers. Usually, you will be able to see the places where the spring coils have been making contact, as all road dirt will be knocked off. To cure the problem, install a damping hose, part No. 321 511 123 A.

To install hose:

1. Remove the coil spring from the suspension strut as described previously in the disassembly procedure.

2. Coat the upper and the lower parts of the coil spring with vaseline. Cut the damping hose into two equal-length pieces and coat the insides of the hose pieces with vaseline.

3. Start one piece of hose onto the upper part of the coil spring. Then, while expanding the hose with compressed air as shown in Fig. 4-16, slide the piece of damping hose fully onto the spring.

4. Using the same procedure, install the second piece of hose on the lower part of the spring. Then reinstall the spring on the vehicle.

Fig. 4-16. Damping hose being installed on coil spring.

To assemble strut:

1. Install the protective sleeve and then the rubber buffer on the piston rod.

2. Install the shock absorber, the spring upper retainer, and the coil spring in the spring compressing appliance and gradually compress the spring. Continue compressing the spring until the threaded portion of the piston rod is fully visible.

3. Install the strut bearing, the rubber damper, and the other parts of the upper mounting. Then, while holding the piston rod stationary with the Allen wrench, torque the suspension strut nut to 8.0 mkg (58 ft. lb.).

4. Install the suspension strut on the car.

4.7 Removing and Installing Control Arm

You do not need to remove the control arm in order to replace the suspension ball joint. See **4.2 Removing and Installing Suspension Ball Joints.**

To remove control arm:

1. Lift the car so that the front wheels and suspension are unsupported.

2. Remove the nut and clamp bolt that hold the ball joint stud in the bottom of the wheel bearing housing. Then pull the stud out of the bearing housing so that the control arm hangs down.

3. Remove the front pivot bolt of the control arm; remove the two retaining bolts that hold the U-shaped retainer for the control arm's rear pivot.

NOTE ——

In order to remove the front pivot bolts from cars with automatic transmissions, you must remove the front left engine mounting, the nut for the rear mounting, and the engine mounting support. Then, using the engine support bar shown in Fig. 4-17, or a jack, raise the engine/transaxle assembly until the front pivot bolts can be removed.

Fig. 4-17. Engine being raised on car with automatic transmission. Left engine mounting is at arrow. Threaded rod of engine support bar (Tool 10-222) can be tightened to raise engine and transaxle.

4. Remove the control arm from the car. If the bushings need to be replaced, follow the instructions given under the next unnumbered heading.

To install:

1. Position the control arm on its pivots. Install the front pivot bolt of the control arm to a torque of 6.0 mkg (43 ft. lb.); torque the bolts for the rear pivot's U-shaped retainer to 3.0 mkg (22 ft. lb.).

NOTE ——

In installing the front pivot bolt, place the convex surface of the lockwasher toward the bolt head. Always use a new bolt and lockwasher and coat the threads of the bolt with Loctite®. See Fig. 4-18. If the nut for the pivot bolt (which is welded to the body) is damaged, replace it as described in **BODY AND INTERIOR.**

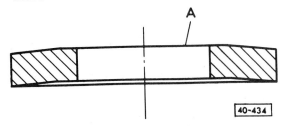

Fig. 4-18. Cross section of lock washer for front pivot bolt. Convex surface **(A)** must be toward bolt head.

2. Install the suspension ball joint stud in the bearing housing on the suspension strut. Install the clamp bolt and torque its nut to 3.0 mkg (22 ft. lb.).

3. Check and, if necessary, adjust the front wheel camber and toe as described in **3. Wheel Alignment.**

Replacing Control Arm Bushings

If the front pivot bushing of the control arm must be replaced, press it out as shown in Fig. 4-19. The bolt installed in the bushing has a depression in its head. This depression keeps the puller screw centered.

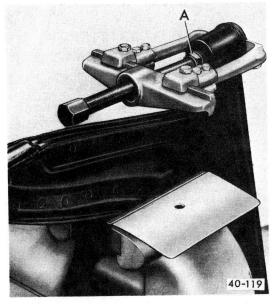

Fig. 4-19. Front pivot bushing being pressed out of control arm. Bolt with depression in head is at **A.**

To press the control arm out of its rear pivot bushing, support the bushing as shown in Fig. 4-20. Then place a drift punch of about 5 mm (7/32 in.) diameter between the press ram and the edge of the track control arm. Press the arm out of the rubber bushing a little at a time, working all around the edge of the control arm with the punch.

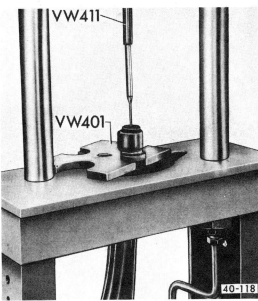

Fig. 4-20. Punch being used in repair press to force the rear pivot of the control arm out of the rubber bushing.

Install the front pivot bushing as shown in Fig. 4-21. In installing the rubber bushing for the rear pivot, simply slide it onto the control arm after lubricating the bushing and the pivot with silicone spray.

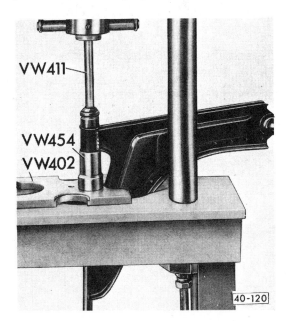

Fig. 4-21. Front pivot bushing being pressed into control arm.

NOTE ——

If you wish to replace the suspension ball joint, follow the instructions given in **4.2 Removing and Installing Suspension Ball Joints.**

4.8 Removing and Installing Front Wheel Bearing Housing

You must remove the front wheel bearing housing from the car before you can service or replace the front wheel bearings. Neither the hub, the drum brake backing plate, or the disc brake splash shield can be removed without making it necessary to replace the bearings.

To remove bearing housing:

1. With the car on the ground, loosen the axle nut. If necessary, refer to Fig. 4-12 given earlier. Also loosen the wheel lug bolts.

    WARNING ——

    Always loosen or tighten the axle nuts while the car is on the ground. The leverage needed for this job could topple the car from a hoist.

2. Lift the car so that the front wheels and suspension are not supported.

3. Remove the road wheel. Fully remove the axle nut and its washer.

4. On cars with drum front brakes, remove the countersunk screw that holds the brake drum to the wheel hub. Then remove the brake drum. Remove the brake shoes as described in **BRAKES AND WHEELS.** Disconnect the brake hose from the rear of the wheel cylinder and quickly cap the disconnected hose with a clean brake bleeder dust cap.

5. On cars with disc front brakes, unbolt the brake caliper from the bearing housing, then suspend it from the coil spring with a stiff wire hook. Remove the countersunk screw that holds the brake disc to the wheel hub and pull off the disc.

    CAUTION ——

    Never allow the caliper to hang by its hose. Doing this could damage the hose and cause brake failure. By leaving the hose attached to the caliper, you will avoid the job of bleeding the brakes.

6. Remove first the cotter pin and then the castellated nut that hold the tie rod end in the steering arm. Using a tool such as the one shown in Fig. 4-22, remove the tie rod end from the steering arm.

CAUTION ——

Do not hammer out the tie rod end. Doing this will ruin the threads and make reinstallation impossible.

© 1974 VWoA—2088

Fig. 4-22. Puller in position for tie rod end removal. Car shown is not one of those covered by this Manual.

7. Remove the nut and clamp bolt that hold the ball joint stud in the bottom of the wheel bearing housing. Then pull the stud out of the bearing housing so that the control arm hangs down.

8. Make a stiff wire hook that will be suitable for supporting the driveshaft.

9. Jerk outward on the bearing housing and the suspension strut in order to free the axle shaft portion of the driveshaft from the hub of the wheel bearing housing.

    NOTE ——

    Free the axle shaft only. Do not attempt to pull the bearing housing completely off the axle shaft at this time. If necessary, you can strike the end of the shaft sharply with a plastic hammer or a hardwood block. Do not use a metal hammer or you will deform the axle shaft threads.

10. Remove the nuts from the bolts that hold the front wheel bearing housing to the suspension strut. (The uppermost bolt is the eccentric bolt used to adjust front wheel camber.) Then remove the bolts while you support the bearing housing and the driveshaft.

11. Using the stiff wire hook, suspend the driveshaft from the coil spring. Then remove the bearing housing assembly from the car.

To install:

1. Position the bearing housing on the driveshaft's axle shaft splines and on the suspension strut. Loosely install the two bolts and nuts that hold the bearing housing to the strut, making sure that the eccentric bolt and washer are uppermost.

2. Install the stud of the suspension ball joint in the bearing housing. Install the clamp bolt and torque its nut to 3.0 mkg (22 ft. lb.).

3. Reconnect the tie rod end to the steering arm. Torque the castellated nut to 3.0 mkg (22 ft. lb.). Advance it, if necessary, to uncover the cotter pin hole, then install a new cotter pin.

4. Loosely install a new self-locking axle nut.

> **WARNING ——**
>
> *Always loosen or tighten the axle nuts while the car is on the ground. The leverage needed for this job could topple the car from a hoist.*

5. Install the brake system components. If you have disconnected the brake hose you will need to bleed the brakes before you drive the car. If necessary, consult **BRAKES AND WHEELS.**

6. Install the road wheel but do not fully tighten the lug bolts.

7. Lower the car to the ground. Torque the wheel lug bolts to 9.0 mkg (65 ft. lb.). Torque the axle nut to 24 mkg (173 ft. lb.).

> **CAUTION ——**
>
> *Failure to torque the axle nut adequately can cause noise and produce rapid wear on the axle splines.*

8. Check and, if necessary, adjust the front wheel camber and toe as described in **3. Wheel Alignment.**

4.9 Removing and Installing Front Wheel Bearings

Cleanliness and order are important in making the following repairs. Clean all metal parts thoroughly in solvent. Do not attempt to make repairs with makeshift tools. Once either the hub or the wheel bearing has been removed from the bearing housing, the bearing is no longer serviceable and must be replaced with a new bearing.

To remove the hub from the bearing housing of a car with disc brakes, use the tools shown in Fig. 4-23. To remove the hub from the bearing housing of a car with drum brakes, use the tools shown in Fig. 4-24. It is not possible to remove either the drum brake backing plate or the disc brake splash shield until the hub is removed.

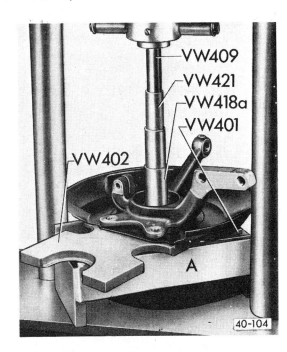

Fig. 4-23. Hub being pressed out of bearing housing of car with disc brakes. Support **A** consists of two parallel rails.

Fig. 4-24. Hub being pressed out of bearing housing of car with drum brakes.

Once you have removed the hub, you should remove the brake backing plate or the splash shield from the wheel bearing housing. Then, using circlip pliers, remove the two 64-mm × 2-mm circlips that are inside the housing—one at each end of the ball bearing race. With the circlips removed, press out the wheel bearing outer race and ball race as shown in Fig. 4-25. The wheel bearing inner race usually comes out along with the hub; remove the inner race from the hub as shown in Fig. 4-26.

CAUTION ——

The wheel bearing is destroyed in pressing out the hub. Once either the wheel hub or the bearing has been removed from the bearing housing, a new bearing must be installed.

To install a new wheel bearing, first install one circlip in the outermost groove in the bearing housing. Replace circlips that have lost tension, are burred, bent, or otherwise damaged. Using the setup shown in Fig. 4-27, press in the new bearing until it contacts the installed circlip. Then install the second circlip.

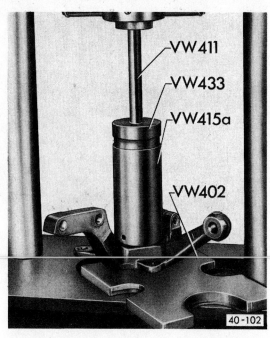

Fig. 4-25. Wheel bearing being pressed out of bearing housing.

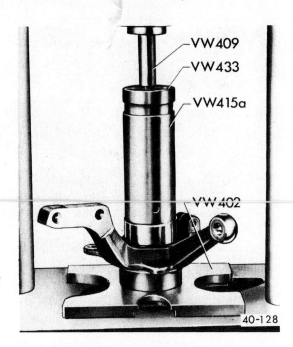

Fig. 4-27. Wheel bearing being pressed into bearing housing. Press tool must contact outer bearing race only.

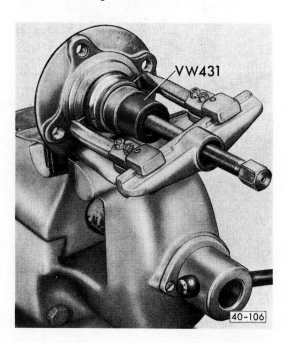

Fig. 4-26. Wheel bearing inner race being removed from hub.

Install the brake backing plate or the splash shield on the bearing housing. Hand start the hub into the wheel bearing's inner race. Then, on cars with disc brakes, press the bearing inner race down onto the hub as shown in Fig. 4-28. On cars with drum brakes, do the job using the tools shown in Fig. 4-29.

Fig. 4-28. Bearing and bearing housing being pressed onto hub of car with disc brakes. Press tool must contact bearing inner race only.

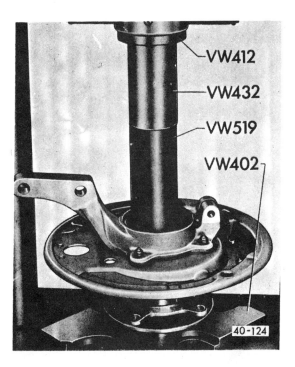

Fig. 4-29. Bearing and bearing housing being pressed onto hub of car with drum brakes. Press tool must contact bearing inner race only.

5. REAR SUSPENSION

The rear shock absorbers and the rear springs are assembled concentrically, in a strut arrangement. However, unlike the front suspension struts, you can separate the rear springs from the rear shock absorbers without a spring compressing appliance.

Though the rear wheel bearings do not routinely require lubrication and adjustment, this work is a necessary part of brake service. Therefore, many of the jobs described here will be carried out in conjunction with those described in **BRAKES AND WHEELS.**

5.1 Removing, Installing, and Adjusting Rear Wheel Bearings

The rear wheel bearings, the brake assembly, and the stub axle are shown in relation to the axle beam in Fig. 5-1. Repairs related to the brake assembly are described in **BRAKES AND WHEELS.**

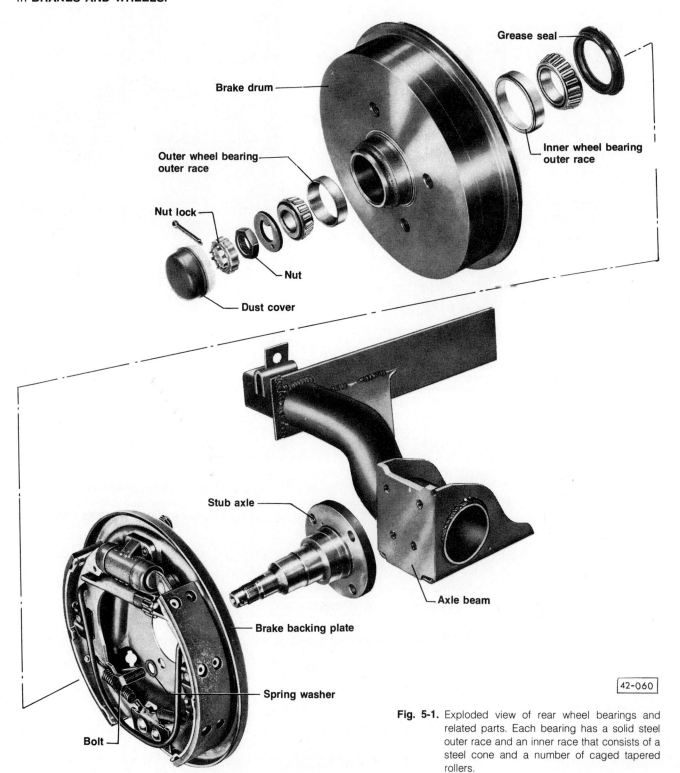

Fig. 5-1. Exploded view of rear wheel bearings and related parts. Each bearing has a solid steel outer race and an inner race that consists of a steel cone and a number of caged tapered rollers.

42-060

You can remove and install the wheel bearing inner races with common hand tools. The outer races, however, are pressed into the brake drum and should be installed with a hydraulic press and appropriate mandrels.

To remove bearing races:

1. Fully back off the brake adjuster. See **BRAKES AND WHEELS.** Remove the road wheel. Pry off the dust cover.

2. Remove the cotter pin and the nut lock. Remove the nut from the stub axle.

3. Pull off the brake drum, being careful not to let the thrust washer and the outer tapered-roller bearing inner race fall out and onto the floor.

4. Place the brake drum on the workbench, then carefully remove the thrust washer and the outer bearing's inner race. Store them in a clean, dust-free place.

5. Pry the grease seal out of its recess in the rear of the drum. Then lift out the inner tapered-roller bearing's inner race. Store it with the outer bearing's inner race.

To install inner races:

1. Carefully clean the bearing races with solvent, then dry them with compressed air.

> **CAUTION ——**
>
> *Do not use solvents such as gasoline because they remove all lubrication. Also, do not let blasts of compressed air spin the races. Unlubricated bearings can be damaged by rapid movement.*

2. Inspect the inner bearing races. Replace them if the race or the rollers are worn, burred, rough, or heat-blued.

3. Clean the brake drum hub and inspect the bearing outer races. Replace them if they are worn, rough, or heat-blued.

4. To replace the outer races, first use a brass drift to drive out the inner bearing's outer race. Then, using the same procedure, drive out the outer bearing's outer race.

5. To install the outer races, use a repair press and appropriate mandrels. Press in the outer bearing's outer race as shown in Fig. 5-2; press in the inner bearing's outer race as shown in Fig. 5-3.

Fig. 5-2. Outer bearing's outer race being pressed in.

Fig. 5-3. Inner bearing's outer race being pressed in.

6. Pack the inner bearing's inner race with multipurpose grease. If a pressure bearing lubricator is not available, get a palmful of multipurpose grease and thrust the edges of the roller bearing race into it, continuing around the bearing until it is completely filled. Coat the races inside the hub with the same lubricant. Do not pack large quantities of grease inside the hub; just coat the interior lightly to prevent corrosion.

> **CAUTION ——**
>
> *Use only multipurpose (lithium) grease to lubricate the rear wheel bearings. Other greases will not maintain adeqaute lubrication and may lead to bearing failure.*

7. Carefully place the inner bearing's inner race in the brake drum hub. Then, using clean tools, either press in a new grease seal or drive it in using a rubber hammer—tapping the seal at alternate sides.

8. Inspect the stub axle for burrs or blued areas. If satisfactory, lightly coat the stub axle with multipurpose grease.

9. Carefully slide the brake drum onto the stub axle so that the grease seal or the bearing races are not accidentally damaged by the sharp threads.

10. Using the same procedure you used in packing the inner bearing's inner race, pack the outer bearing's inner race with multipurpose grease. Then carefully slide it onto the stub axle and into the hub.

11. Install the thrust washer and the nut. Tighten the nut until the bearings just contact their outer races.

12. Before you install the nut lock and a new cotter pin, adjust the rear wheel bearings as described under the next heading. Then fill the dust cap with approximately 10 g ($5/16$ oz.) of multipurpose grease. Install the dust cap and the road wheel. Finally, adjust the brakes as described in **BRAKES AND WHEELS.**

Adjusting Rear Wheel Bearings

The rear wheel bearings must turn smoothly and not have excessive axial play. If the bearings feel gritty, have tight spots, or make noises as the brake drum turns, they probably need to be replaced. Excess axial play, though, can be corrected by adjusting.

To adjust bearings:

1. Raise the wheel. If not previously removed, pry off the dust cap. See Fig. 5-4.

2. If the bearings have just been installed, torque the nut on the stub axle to about 1.0 mkg (7 ft. lb.) while you hand-turn the brake drum.

> **CAUTION** ——
> *Never torque the nut to more than 1.3 mkg (9.5 ft. lb.). Doing this may damage the bearing races.*

3. Determine the wheel bearing axial play by testing the friction that is exerted on the thrust washer. To do this, turn the nut one way or the other until you can just move the thrust washer sideways with the tip of a screwdriver as shown in Fig. 5-5.

Fig. 5-4. Dust cap being removed with special tool. You can also use a large screwdriver.

Fig. 5-5. Friction on thrust washer being checked by moving thrust washer as indicated by arrow.

4. After the bearings have been adjusted, install the nut lock so that its projections do not cover the cotter pin hole. Then install a new cotter pin.

5. Install the dust cover and then lower the wheel to the ground.

Removing, Checking, and Installing Stub Axle

To remove the stub axle, first remove the brake drum and the wheel bearings. Then unbolt the rear brake assembly. The same mounting bolts that hold the brake assembly to the stub axle hold the stub axle to the axle beam. By pulling the brake assembly outward and toward the front of the car, you can remove the stub axle without disconnecting the brake line or the parking brake cable.

You can check the stub axle for distortion using a vernier caliper and a machinist's square as shown in Fig. 5-6. Make your measurements at a minimum of three points around the stub axle. The difference between any two measurements must not exceed 0.25 mm (.010 in.). Replace distorted stub axles.

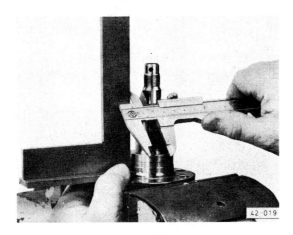

Fig. 5-6. Vernier caliper and machinist's square being used to check stub axle for distortion.

In installing the stub axle and the brake assembly on the axle beam, use new spring washers and torque the mounting bolts to 6.0 mkg (43 ft. lb.). Make certain that there is no dirt between the stub axle flange and the axle beam (which could upset wheel alignment), or between the brake backing plate and the stub axle (which could produce uneven braking or uneven brake lining wear).

5.2 Checking Axle Beam for Distortion

To check the rear axle beam for distortion, first raise the car. Visually check the axle beam reinforcing gusset (Fig. 5-7) for kinking. If there is any kink or other damage at this point, replace the axle beam. If you are in doubt, check the rear wheel toe and camber, which should be as follows:

Rabbit, through Chassis No. 176 3241 690
Scirocco, through Chassis No. 536 2031 722

  Toe: +10′ ±30′
  Camber: −1° ±35′

Rabbit, from Chassis No. 176 3241 691
Scirocco, from Chassis No. 536 2031 722

  Toe: +20′ ±30′
  Camber: −1° 15′ ±35′

Incorrect rear wheel alignment can be corrected only by replacing the axle beam or, if you find a distorted stub axle when you make the checks described under the preceding heading, by replacing the stub axle.

WARNING ——

Never attempt to straighten a bent or deformed axle beam. Doing this can seriously weaken the axle beam structurally.

Fig. 5-7. Reinforcing gusset (arrow) of rear axle beam.

5.3 Removing, Repairing, and Installing Rear Suspension Struts

The rear coil springs and rear shock absorbers are assembled concentrically into a strut arrangement. Fig. 5-8 is an exploded view that shows the components of one of the struts.

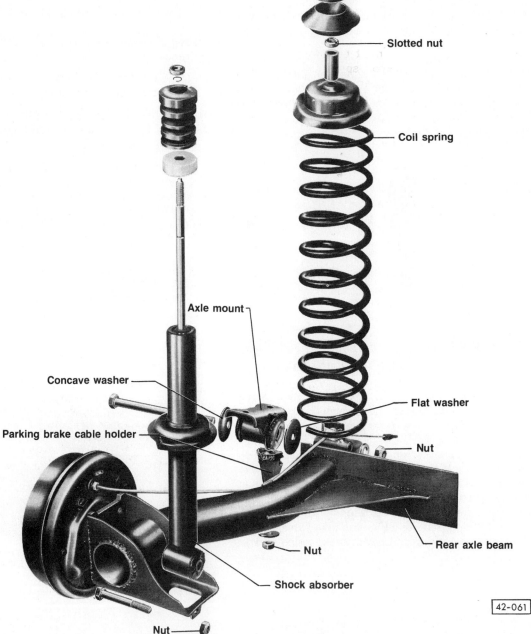

Nut

Slotted nut

Coil spring

Axle mount

Concave washer

Parking brake cable holder

Flat washer

Nut

Rear axle beam

Nut

Shock absorber

Nut

42-061

Fig. 5-8. Exploded view of rear suspension strut.

To remove:

1. Working inside the body with the car on the ground, remove the plastic cap that covers the rear suspension strut upper mounting. Remove the nut and the special washer that is beneath the nut.

2. Raise the car body slowly until the spring is unloaded and the top of the strut begins to pull away from the body.

3. Working beneath the car at the rear wheel, remove the nut and the bolt that hold the lower end of the suspension strut's shock absorber to the strut mounting on the axle beam.

4. Raise the car until it is possible to remove the strut from the car.

Installation is the reverse of removal. Torque the nut for the bolt that holds the lower end of the strut to the axle to 4.5 mkg (32 ft. lb.). Torque the nut that holds the upper end of the strut to the car body to 3.5 mkg (25 ft. lb.).

5.4 Disassembling, Checking, and Assembling Rear Suspension Strut

The rear suspension strut must be disassembled in order to replace either the coil spring or the shock absorber. Unlike the front suspension struts, it is not necessary to use a coil spring compressing appliance when you disassemble or assemble a rear suspension strut.

To disassemble:

1. Remove the rear suspension strut from the car and mount it in a vise as shown in Fig. 5-9.

2. While gripping the flats on the shock absorber piston rod with a suitable wrench, loosen the slotted nut.

3. Fully remove the slotted nut. Then separate the suspension strut into its individual components as shown previously in Fig. 5-8.

Fig. 5-9. Slotted nut being removed with special tool (Tool 50-200). Arrow indicates flats on piston rod.

Checking Shock Absorber

Worn-out shock absorbers often make knocking noises when the car is driven. You can hand-check a shock absorber by extending and compressing it while holding it in its installed position. It must operate smoothly and with uniform resistance throughout its entire stroke. If possible, compare the used unit with a new shock absorber. New shock absorbers that have been in storage may have to be pumped several times before they reach full efficiency.

Shock absorbers do not require maintenance. An adequate supply of fluid is placed in them during manufacture to compensate for small leaks. Minor traces of fluid leakage are acceptable if the shock absorber still functions efficiently. Faulty shock absorbers cannot be serviced and must be replaced.

Correcting Rattling Coil Springs

Sometimes rattles from the rear suspension struts are caused by spring coils knocking together—not by worn-out shock absorbers. Usually, you will be able to see the places where the spring coils have been making contact, as all road dirt will be knocked off. To cure the problem, install a damping hose, part No. 321 511 123 A.

To install hose:

1. Remove the coil spring from the suspension strut as previously described in the disassembly procedure.

2. Coat the upper part of the coil spring with vaseline. Cut the damping hose into two equal-length pieces and coat the inside of one piece with vaseline.

3. Start the piece of lubricated hose onto the upper part of the coil spring. Then, while expanding the hose with compressed air as shown in Fig. 5-10, slide the piece of damping hose fully onto the spring.

NOTE ——

On rear springs, it is usually adequate to install damping hose on the top part of the spring only. However, if there are marks on the lower part of the spring, indicating that the coils have been knocking together, use the procedure just described to install the second piece of hose on the lower part of the spring.

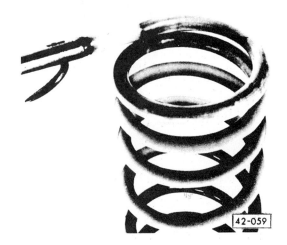

Fig. 5-10. Damping hose being installed on coil spring.

To assemble strut:

1. Install the protective cap and then the rubber buffer—large-diameter end uppermost—on the shock absorber piston rod. Install the snap ring and the washer.

   NOTE ——

   From car Chassis No. 175 3238 116, Rabbit models only have had different springs and different rubber buffers. The new replacement springs are identified by two green paint marks, whereas earlier springs had two white marks. The matching rubber buffers are shown in Fig. 5-11 and Fig. 5-12. Use only small buffers with white-marked springs and large buffers with green-marked springs.

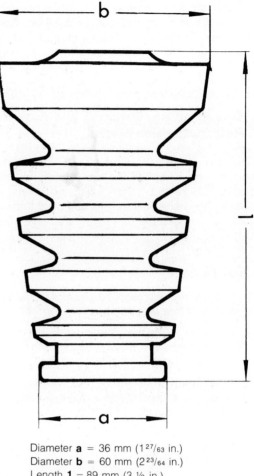

Diameter **a** = 36 mm (1 $^{27}/_{63}$ in.)
Diameter **b** = 60 mm (2 $^{23}/_{64}$ in.)
Length **1** = 89 mm (3 ½ in.)

Fig. 5-12. Large buffer used on Rabbit models from Chassis No. 175 3239 116.

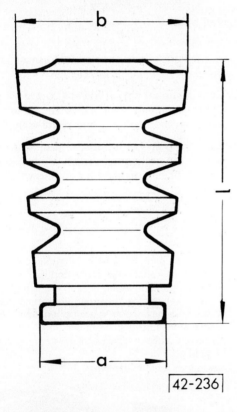

42-236

Diameter **a** = 36 mm (1 $^{27}/_{64}$ in.)
Diameter **b** = 48 mm (1 $^{57}/_{64}$ in.)
Length **1** = 71 mm (2 $^{51}/_{64}$ in.)

Fig. 5-11. Small buffer used on Scirocco models and on Rabbit models through Chassis No. 175 3238 115.

2. Install the spring, the spring upper retainer, and the spacer sleeve. Start the slotted nut onto the threads of the piston rod.

NOTE ——

If you must replace a spring on a Rabbit model, it must be the same kind of spring as that on the other side of the car. Alternatively, you can replace both springs with the same kind of spring. As stated previously, the buffers must match the springs. The differences in the springs are shown in Fig. 5-13 and Fig. 5-14. In production, springs with 1, 2, or 3 paint marks are installed, but spare parts are available only with 2 paint marks. If one spring is faulty, it is not necessary to replace both springs—even if the original spring that is retained has either 1 or 3 marks.

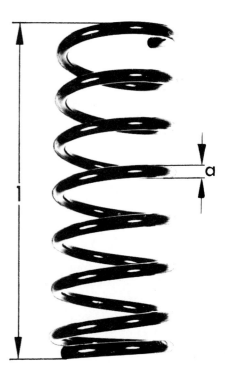

Diameter **a** = 9.40 mm (.370 in.)
Length **1** = 357 mm (14¹/₁₆ in.)
Replacement part identification:
    2 green paint marks

Fig. 5-14. Linear rate spring used on Rabbit models from Chassis No. 175 3238 116.

3. While you hold the piston rod stationary, use the special tool (Tool 50-200) to torque the slotted nut to 2.0 mkg (14 ft. lb.).

4. Install the other parts of the strut's upper mounting. Then install the strut on the car.

5.5 Removing and Installing Rear Suspension as a Unit

If the axle beam needs to be replaced, or if the rear suspension requires thorough reconditioning, use the procedure given here to remove the rear suspension as a unit from the car. Further disassembly can be carried out after the rear suspension has been removed.

To remove:

1. Working inside the body with the car on the ground, remove the plastic caps that cover the rear suspension strut upper mountings. Remove the nuts and the special washers that are beneath the nuts.

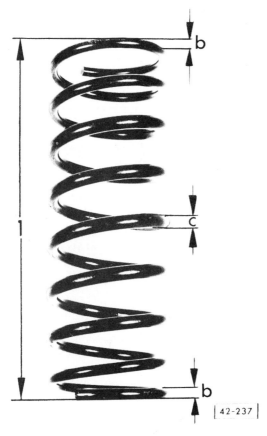

Diameters at **b** = 7.60 mm (.299 in.)
Diameter at **c** = 10.20 mm (.401 in.)
Length **1** = 389 mm (15⁵/₁₆ in.)
Replacement part identification:
    2 white paint marks

Fig. 5-13. Progressive rate spring used on Scirocco models and on Rabbit models through Chassis No. 175 3238 115.

2. Raise the car on a hoist or support the rear on jack stands with the front wheels firmly chocked.

NOTE ——

If you raise the car high off the floor with a hoist, you will need a floor jack with an axle adaptor in order to lower the dismounted rear suspension assembly from the car. It may be more convenient to work with the car near floor level so that, after you have un-bolted the rear suspension, you can raise the car and pull the suspension out toward the rear.

3. Detach the parking brake cables from the parking brake lever at the points indicated in Fig. 5-15.

4. One at a time, disconnect the brake hoses and quickly cap the brake lines with clean brake bleeder dust caps.

5. Detach the brake pressure regulator spring from the axle beam of cars with regulators. Then, with the axle beam supported, remove the two nuts that hold each axle beam mounting to the body. See Fig. 5-15.

6. Lower the rear suspension assembly and remove it from beneath the car toward the rear.

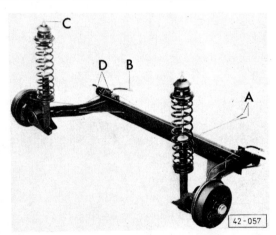

A. Parking brake cable ends
B. Brake hoses
C. Suspension strut upper mountings
D. Nuts that hold axle mountings to car body

Fig. 5-15. Points at which rear suspension assembly must be dismounted or disconnected from body. Brake pressure regulator spring must also be detached from axle beam of some models.

To install:

1. If you have removed the axle beam mountings from the axle beam, or loosened the pivot bolts and nuts, adjust the mounting(s) as indicated in Fig. 5-16. Otherwise, the torsional preload of the bonded rubber bushing will be incorrect.

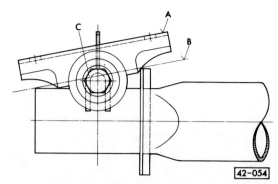

Fig. 5-16. Mounting being adjusted. Loosen pivot bolt and nut (**C**). Align mounting surface (**A**) with imaginary line (**B**). Then torque nut of pivot bolt (**C**) to 6.0 mkg (43 ft. lb.)

2. Position the rear suspension assembly on the body. Install the nuts and the washers that hold the axle beam mountings to the body. Torque the nuts to 4.5 mkg (32 ft. lb.).

3. Either raise the wheels or lower the car onto the wheels while guiding the tops of the suspension struts into their positions on the body.

4. Reconnect the parking brake cables.

5. Reconnect the brake hoses. Lubricate the threads with brake fluid, then torque the unions to 1.5 to 2.0 mkg (11 to 14 ft. lb.).

6. Bleed the brakes. Adjust both the foot brakes and the parking brakes. These jobs are covered in **BRAKES AND WHEELS.**

7. Lower the car to the ground. Install the nuts and the special washers that hold the tops of the rear suspension struts to the body. Torque the nuts to 3.5 mkg (25 ft. lb.). Install the plastic caps.

Replacing Axle Mounting Pivot Bushings

To replace an axle mounting pivot bushing without removing the axle beam, support the axle beam and the car body equally so that the axle beam pivot bolt is not under load. Remove the two nuts that hold the axle beam mounting to the car body. Then remove the pivot bolt so that you can remove the mounting from the axle beam. If necessary, refer to Fig. 5-8 given earlier.

Press out the old bonded rubber bushing. Then press a new bonded rubber bushing into the axle beam mounting. Loosely install the mounting on the axle beam. The concave washer and the bolt head should be toward the outside of the car with the bolt head recessed into the concave washer, as shown earlier in Fig. 5-8.

Align the mounting as shown earlier in Fig. 5-16, then torque the pivot bolt and nut to 6.0 mkg (43 ft. lb.). Install the mounting on the body, torquing the two nuts to 4.5 mkg (32 ft. lb.). Finally, remove the support from beneath the axle beam and lower the car to the ground.

6. STEERING

Fig. 6-1 is an exploded view of the rack and pinion steering gearbox and the components of the steering system that are connected to it. Though the non-adjustable left tie rod shown here is the kind of tie rod that is installed during production, replacement left tie rods have adjustable tie rod ends. The gearbox normally requires no lubrication during its service lifetime. If, however, the steering makes groaning noises as the steering wheel is turned, you should lubricate it as described in **6.2 Adjusting Steering.**

2

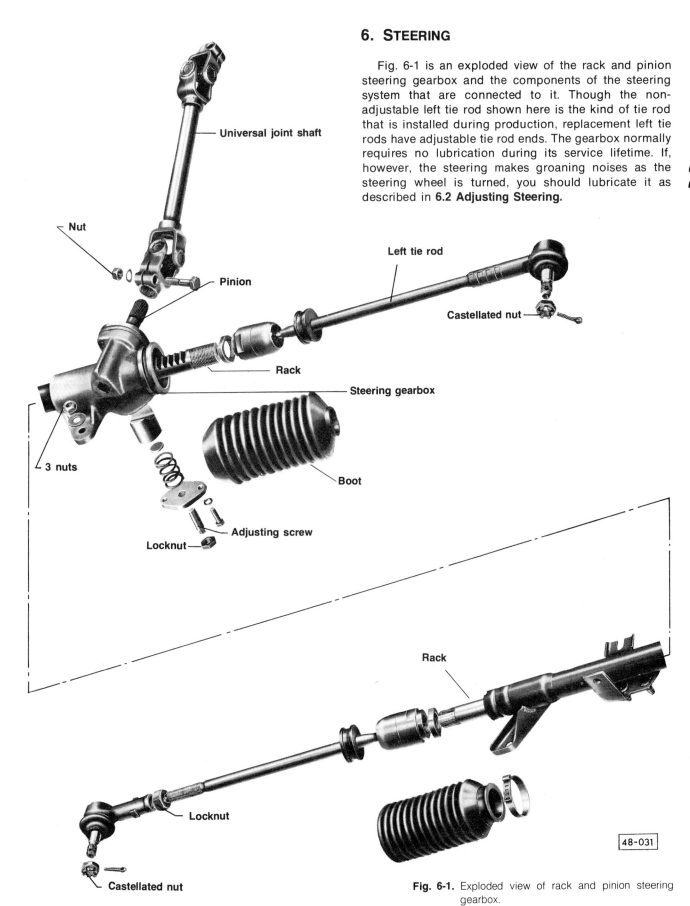

Fig. 6-1. Exploded view of rack and pinion steering gearbox.

6.1 Removing and Installing Tie Rods, Tie Rod Ends, and Rubber Bushings

You can replace the tie rod end on the right tie rod only, unless an adjustable left tie rod has been installed as a replacement part. To replace the tie rod end of a non-adjustable left tie rod, the entire rod must be replaced.

To remove tie rod:

1. Remove the cotter pin. Then remove the castellated nut that holds the tie rod end stud in the steering arm.

2. Using a puller as shown in Fig. 6-2, press the tie rod end stud out of the steering arm.

CAUTION ——

Do not hammer out the tie rod ends. Doing this will ruin the threads and make reinstallation impossible.

© 1974 VWoA—2088

Fig. 6-2. Puller being used to press tie rod end stud out of steering arm. Car shown is not one of those covered by this Manual.

NOTE ——

Though you may be removing only one tie rod, the inner ends of both tie rods must be exposed so that, by comparing the positions of the tie rod inner ball joint housings on the rack, you can install the removed tie rod to the correct dimension.

3. Remove the clamps that hold the boots to the rack tube of the steering gearbox. Pull both boots down off the tube and onto the tie rods in order to expose both tie rods' inner ball joint housings—if necessary, you can turn the boots inside out on the tie rods.

4. Loosen the locknut for the inner ball joint housing of the tie rod that is being removed. Then, gripping the flats of the inner ball joint housing with a wrench, unscrew the housing, together with its permanently-attached tie rod, from the steering rack.

To install:

1. If you are installing a new tie rod or a tie rod end, adjust the position of the tie rod end on the tie rod in order to obtain dimension **c,** as given in Fig. 6-3.

2. Center the steering (steering wheel spokes horizontal). Screw the tie rod's inner ball joint housing onto the steering rack until you obtain dimension **b,** as given in Fig. 6-4. Then tighten the locknut in order to hold the housing in this position on the steering rack.

NOTE ——

Dimension **b,** given in Fig. 6-4, will only be correct if the steering is accurately centered. If you are not sure that the steering rack is centered exactly when the steering wheel spokes are horizontal, carry out the adjustments described in **6.2 Adjusting Steering** before you install the new tie rod.

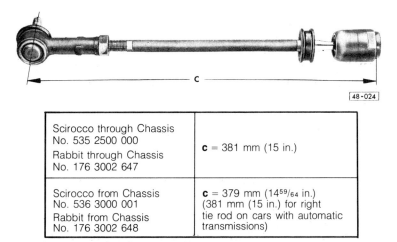

Scirocco through Chassis No. 535 2500 000 Rabbit through Chassis No. 176 3002 647	**c** = 381 mm (15 in.)
Scirocco from Chassis No. 536 3000 001 Rabbit from Chassis No. 176 3002 648	**c** = 379 mm (14⁵⁹/₆₄ in.) (381 mm (15 in.) for right tie rod on cars with automatic transmissions)

Fig. 6-3. Tie rod being adjusted prior to installation. Dimension **c** must be correct for the car.

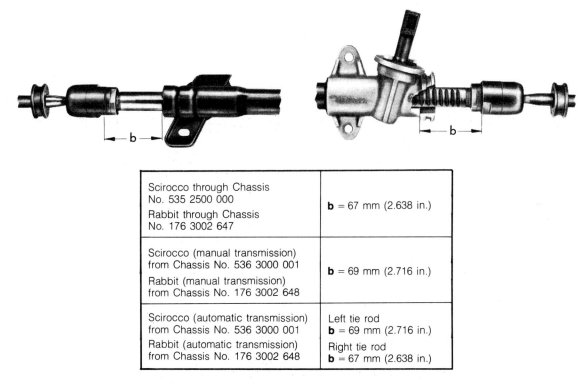

Scirocco through Chassis No. 535 2500 000 Rabbit through Chassis No. 176 3002 647	**b** = 67 mm (2.638 in.)
Scirocco (manual transmission) from Chassis No. 536 3000 001 Rabbit (manual transmission) from Chassis No. 176 3002 648	**b** = 69 mm (2.716 in.)
Scirocco (automatic transmission) from Chassis No. 536 3000 001 Rabbit (automatic transmission) from Chassis No. 176 3002 648	Left tie rod **b** = 69 mm (2.716 in.) Right tie rod **b** = 67 mm (2.638 in.)

Fig. 6-4. Dimension **b,** which should be adjusted during tie rod installation with the steering centered.

3. Reposition the boots on the tie rods and the steering rack tube. Install the clamps.

4. Reconnect the tie rod end to the steering arm. Torque the castellated nut to 3.0 mkg (22 ft. lb.). Advance it, if necessary, to uncover the cotter pin hole, then install a new cotter pin.

5. Adjust the toe as described in **3. Wheel Alignment.**

6.2 Adjusting Steering

The screw-and-locknut adjustment on the rack and pinion steering gearbox makes it possible to correct excessive steering wheel play and eliminate rattles from the steering rack. If, when you drive the car, the steering seems stiff or fails to self-center, the steering adjustment is probably too tight. If the steering rattles while you drive or if there is any visible play in the steering wheel with the road wheels pointed straight ahead, the adjustment is probably too loose. If the steering groans as you turn the wheel, lubricate the rack as described later under **Curing Groaning.** Fig. 6-5 is an exploded view of the adjustment components.

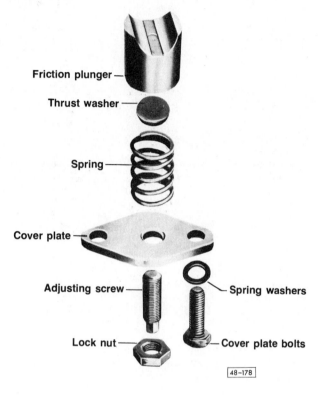

Fig. 6-5. Exploded view of adjustment components.

Labels: Friction plunger, Thrust washer, Spring, Cover plate, Adjusting screw, Lock nut, Spring washers, Cover plate bolts, 48–178

NOTE ——

If, after correctly adjusting the steering, there is still excessive play or rattling, check for loose tie rod ends, loose steering gearbox mounting bolts, or loose parts in the front suspension.

To adjust the steering gearbox, loosen the locknut. Hand-turn the adjusting screw until it just contacts the thrust washer. While holding the adjusting screw in this position, tighten the locknut as shown in Fig. 6-6. Then recheck the steering in order to determine whether or not your adjustment has corrected the steering fault that you observed earlier.

Centering Steering Rack

For correct steering, the steering rack must be precisely centered when the steering wheel spokes are horizontal and the car is moving straight ahead on a level surface. You should adjust the rack in order to center it whenever (1) you have removed and installed the steering gearbox, (2) the steering wheel spokes are not horizontal after you have adjusted the toe and (3) there is unequal steering lock to left and right—which may possibly cause the tires to strike the body.

First, check that the steering gearbox is firmly bolted to the body and that the steering column is correctly installed on the pinion shaft. If necessary, slightly reposition the steering gearbox on the body so that, with the steering wheel spokes horizontal, dimension **a**, given in Fig. 6-7, is identical on both sides.

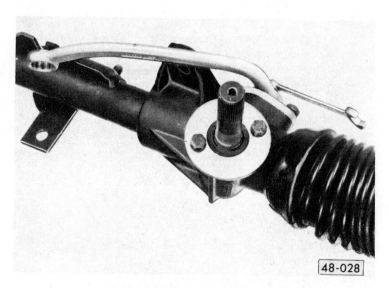

Fig. 6-6. Locknut being tightened while adjusting screw is held stationary. Though the steering gearbox is shown removed, it can be adjusted while it is installed on the car.

Fig. 6-7. Steering rack centered. Dimension **a** is identical on both sides.

It is possible that, though the steering rack is correctly centered, the tie rod ends' inner ball joint housings have been installed incorrectly on the steering rack. With the steering rack centered, dimension **b,** given in Fig. 6-8, must be correct for both tie rods.

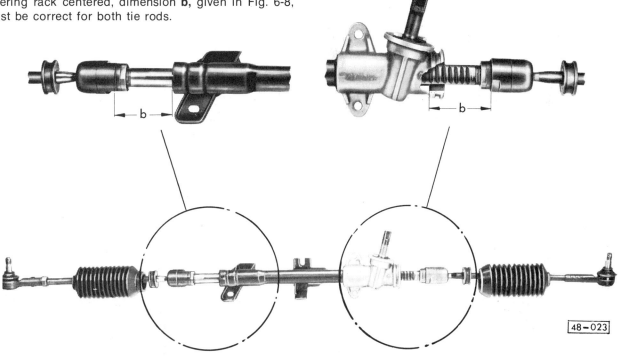

Scirocco through Chassis No. 535 2500 000 Rabbit through Chassis No. 176 3002 647	**b** = 67 mm (2.638 in.)
Scirocco (manual transmission) from Chassis No. 536 3000 001 Rabbit (manual transmission) from Chassis No. 176 3002 648	**b** = 69 mm (2.716 in.)
Scirocco (automatic transmission) from Chassis No. 536 3000 001 Rabbit (automatic transmission) from Chassis No. 176 3002 648	Left tie rod **b** = 69 mm (2.716 in.) Right tie rod **b** = 67 mm (2.638 in.)

Fig. 6-8. Correct tie rod installation dimensions with steering rack centered.

Curing Groaning

If the rack and pinion steering gearbox makes groaning noises as you turn the steering wheel, you can eliminate the noise by applying a special lubricant to the rack.

To cure groaning:

1. Turn the steering wheel completely to the left.

2. Loosen the clamp. Then detach the right-hand rubber boot from the steering gearbox's rack tube and pull the boot down onto the tie rod.

3. Wipe the grease from the exposed part of the steering rack.

4. Spray a thin film of Dow Corning Molykote® #321 lubricant, or its equivalent, onto the surface of the rack.

5. Allow the lubricant to dry for 10 minutes before you move the steering. Then reinstall the boot and the clamp.

6.3 Removing and Installing Rack and Pinion Steering Gearbox

You do not need to remove the rack and pinion steering gearbox fully in order to remove the steering universal joint shaft. Just detach the steering gearbox from the body, leaving the tie rod ends connected to the steering arms.

To remove gearbox:

1. Remove the cotter pin. Then remove the castellated nut that holds the tie rod end stud in the steering arm.

2. Using a puller, as shown in Fig. 6-9, press the tie rod end stud out of the steering arm.

> *CAUTION ——*
>
> *Do not hammer out the tie rod ends. Doing this will ruin the threads and make reinstallation impossible.*

© 1974 VWoA—2088

Fig. 6-9. Puller being used to press tie rod end stud out of steering arm. Car shown is not one of those covered by this Manual.

3. On cars with manual transmissions, dismount the gearshift linkage from the rack and pinion steering gearbox.

4. Loosen the clamp bolt and nut that hold the lower end of the universal joint shaft to the pinion shaft of the steering gearbox.

5. Remove the nuts and the washers that hold the rack and pinion steering gearbox to the body. Then remove the gearbox from the car.

To install:

1. If you are going to install a new rack and pinion steering gearbox on a car with an automatic transmission, modify the bracket as indicated in Fig. 6-10.

> **NOTE ——**
>
> If you have removed the tie rods from the steering rack, or if you are installing a replacement gearbox, do not install the tie rods until step 5 of this procedure.

2. Loosely install the steering gearbox on the car, guiding the pinion shaft into the lower universal joint of the universal joint shaft.

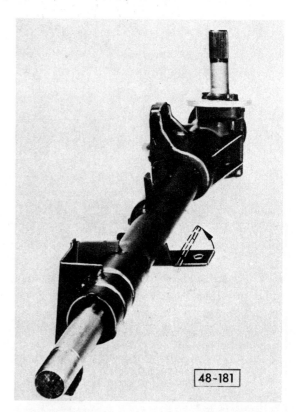

48-181

Fig. 6-10. Bracket on replacement gearbox being modified for use on car with automatic transmission. Bend bracket upward to approximately a 45° angle.

3. Loosely install the nuts and the washers that hold the gearbox to the car body. Center the steering rack with the steering wheel spokes horizontal, as described in **6.2 Adjusting Steering.** With the steering centered, install the clamp bolt for the universal joint shaft and torque the nut to 3.0 mkg (22 ft. lb.).

4. Keeping the steering wheel spokes horizontal and the steering rack centered, torque the nuts that hold the gearbox to the body to 2.0 mkg (14 ft. lb.).

5. If you are installing a replacement gearbox, or if you have removed the original tie rods from the original gearbox, install the tie rods with careful attention to the dimensions given in **6.1 Removing and Installing Tie Rods, Tie Rod Ends, and Rubber Bushings.**

6. On cars with manual transmissions, remount the gearshift linkage on the steering gearbox. Check the operation of the gearshift in order to make certain that all gears engage fully and easily. If necessary, consult **MANUAL TRANSMISSION.**

7. Reconnect the tie rod ends to the steering arms. Torque the castellated nuts to 3.0 mkg (22 ft. lb.). Advance each nut, if necessary, to uncover the cotter pin hole, then install a new cotter pin.

8. Adjust the toe as described in **3. Wheel Alignment.**

6.4 Removing and Installing Steering Wheel and Steering Column Switch Assembly

If the steering wheel spokes are not horizontal when the car is being driven straight ahead on a level surface, check the steering rack and the tie rods as described in **6.2 Adjusting Steering.** After you are sure that the steering rack is centered, that the tie rods are adjusted to the correct length, and that the tie rods are correctly installed on the steering rack, check the front wheel toe as described in **3. Wheel Alignment.** Only after you have checked these things, and corrected any faults, should you reposition the steering wheel, if necessary, in order to have the spokes horizontal with the steering centered.

To remove:

1. Disconnect the battery ground strap. Using your fingertips only, carefully pry off the padded cover of the horn control.

2. Remove the nut and the washer that hold the steering wheel to the steering column.

3. Pull the steering wheel off the steering column. Normally, it is not necessary to use any tool for this job.

4. If you must remove the steering column switch assembly, remove the socket-head bolt and the Phillips head screw from the recesses in the bottom of the switch housing.

5. Push the switch assembly as far as possible toward the dashboard. Then pry off the spacer sleeve that is on the steering column. See Fig. 6-11.

6. Pull the switch assembly upward. Then disconnect the wires at the multiple connector plugs. Pull the switch assembly up and off the steering column tube.

To install:

1. If you removed the switch assembly, slide it onto the column tube and reconnect the wires.

2. Drive on the spacer sleeve to the dimension given in Fig. 6-11. If the spacer sleeve is damaged or loose-fitting, replace it.

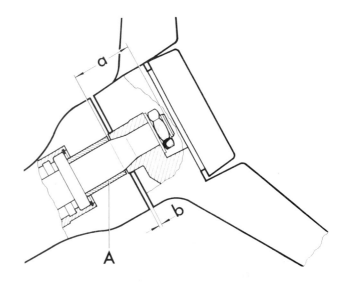

Fig. 6-11. Spacer sleeve **(A)** being installed. Drive on sleeve until dimension **a** is 41.5 mm (1.633 in.). When correctly installed, dimension **b** will be 2 to 4 mm (approximately $^1/_{16}$ to $^1/_8$ in.).

3. If necessary, pull the column switch upward until it contacts the spacer sleeve. Then install the Phillips head screw and the socket-head bolt. Torque the bolt to 1.0 mkg (7 ft. lb.).

4. Make certain that the steering is centered (front wheels pointed straight ahead). Then install the steering wheel. The spokes should be horizontal and the lug for the turn signal cancelling mechanism should point toward the left-hand side of the car.

5. Install the washer and the nut that hold the steering wheel to the column. Torque the nut to 5.0 mkg (36 ft. lb.).

6. Reinstall the pad on the horn control. Reconnect the battery ground strap.

6.5 Removing and Installing Universal Joint Shaft

Rabbit models do not have the same universal joint shaft as Scirocco models. So, if you must replace the shaft, make certain that you obtain the correct replacement part.

To remove:

1. On cars with manual transmissions, dismount the gearshift linkage from the rack and pinion steering gearbox.

2. Remove the nut and the clamp bolt that hold the lower end of the universal joint shaft to the pinion shaft of the steering gearbox.

3. Remove the nuts and the washers that hold the steering gearbox to the car body. Then pull the gearbox downward, disengaging its pinion shaft from the lower end of the universal joint shaft.

4. Carefully pry up the tab that holds the rubber boot to the lower universal joint. Then disengage the upper end of the boot and pull the boot off the universal joint shaft.

5. Remove the nut and the bolt that hold the upper end of the universal joint shaft to the steering column. Then remove the universal joint shaft by pulling it downward off the column.

To install:

1. Inspect the universal joint shaft. If the joints are loose or squeak when you move them, replace the universal joint shaft as a unit.

2. Install the universal joint shaft on the steering column as shown in Fig. 6-12. Torque the nut for the clamp bolt to 3.0 mkg (22 ft. lb.).

3. Install the boot and, where applicable, the damping grommet. If necessary, consult the exploded views given later in **6.6 Removing, Repairing and Installing Steering Column and Tube.**

4. Loosely install the steering gearbox on the car, guiding the pinion shaft into the lower universal joint of the universal joint shaft.

5. Loosely install the nuts and the washers that hold the gearbox to the car body. Center the steering (front wheels pointed straight ahead) with the steering wheel spokes horizontal. With the pinion and the universal joint shaft thus aligned, install the clamp bolt and torque the nut to 3.0 mkg (22 ft. lb.).

6. Keeping the steering wheel spokes horizontal and the steering rack centered, torque the nuts that hold the gearbox to the body to 2.0 mkg (14 ft. lb.).

7. On cars with manual transmissions, remount the gearshift linkage on the steering gearbox. Check the operation of the gearshift in order to make certain that all gears engage fully and easily. If necessary, consult **MANUAL TRANSMISSION.**

6.6 Removing, Repairing, and Installing Steering Column and Tube

Fig. 6-13, Fig. 6-14, and Fig. 6-15 are exploded views of the different steering columns that have been installed on the cars covered by this Manual. The pedal assembly shown with the late-type columns is similar to that used with the early-type column. The steering wheel and the steering column switch assembly shown on the early-type column are similar to those used on the late-type columns.

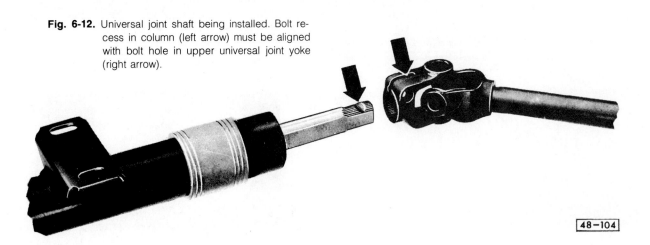

Fig. 6-12. Universal joint shaft being installed. Bolt recess in column (left arrow) must be aligned with bolt hole in upper universal joint yoke (right arrow).

48—104

Fig. 6-13. Exploded view of steering column used on 1975 cars.

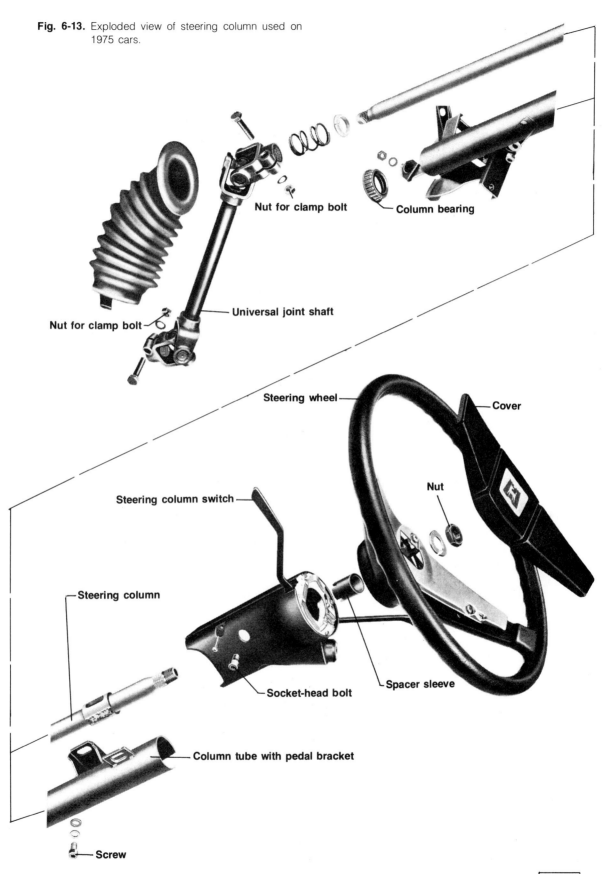

Nut for clamp bolt

Column bearing

Nut for clamp bolt

Universal joint shaft

Steering wheel

Cover

Nut

Steering column switch

Steering column

Socket-head bolt

Spacer sleeve

Column tube with pedal bracket

Screw

2

48-030

Fig. 6-14. Exploded view of steering column introduced on 1976 U.S. models. Column tube is detachable, held by a leaf spring.

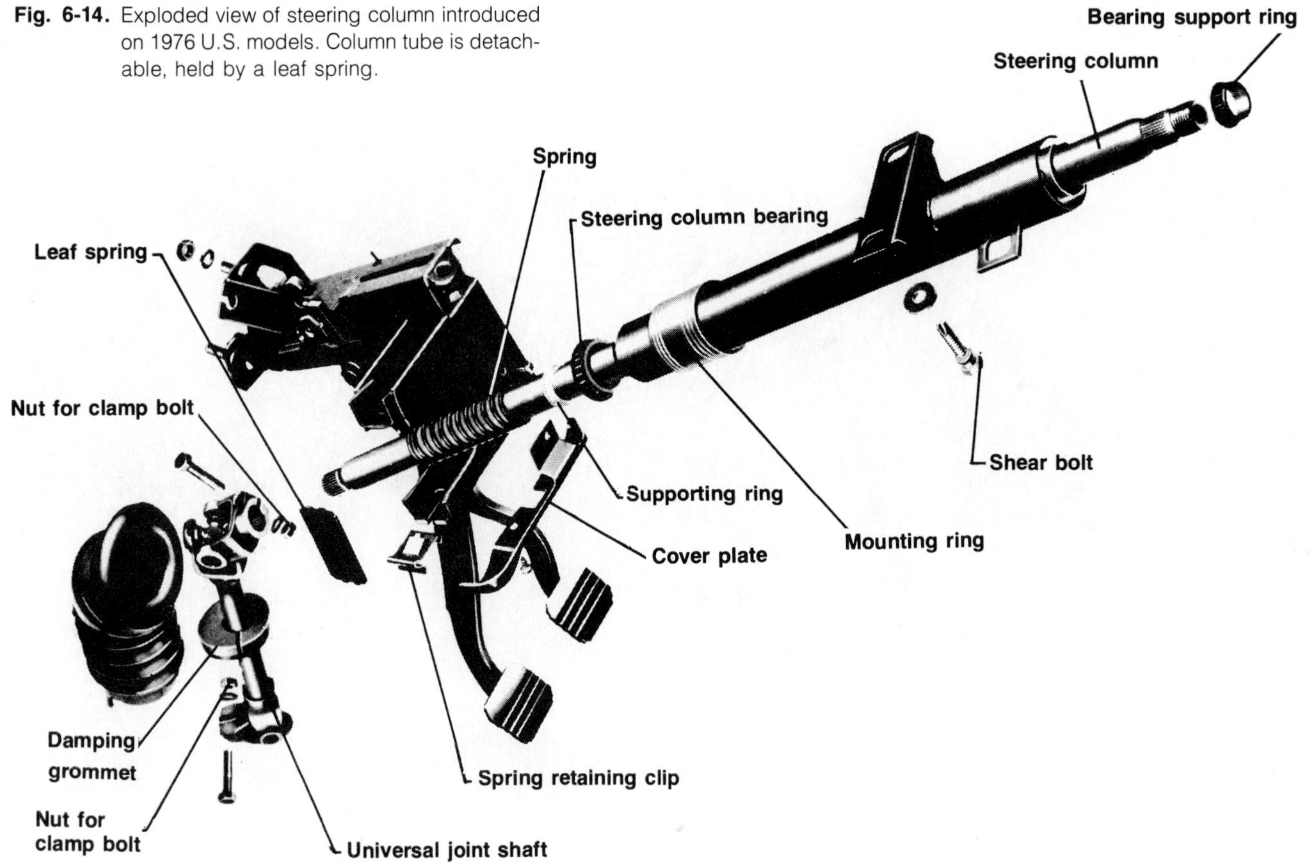

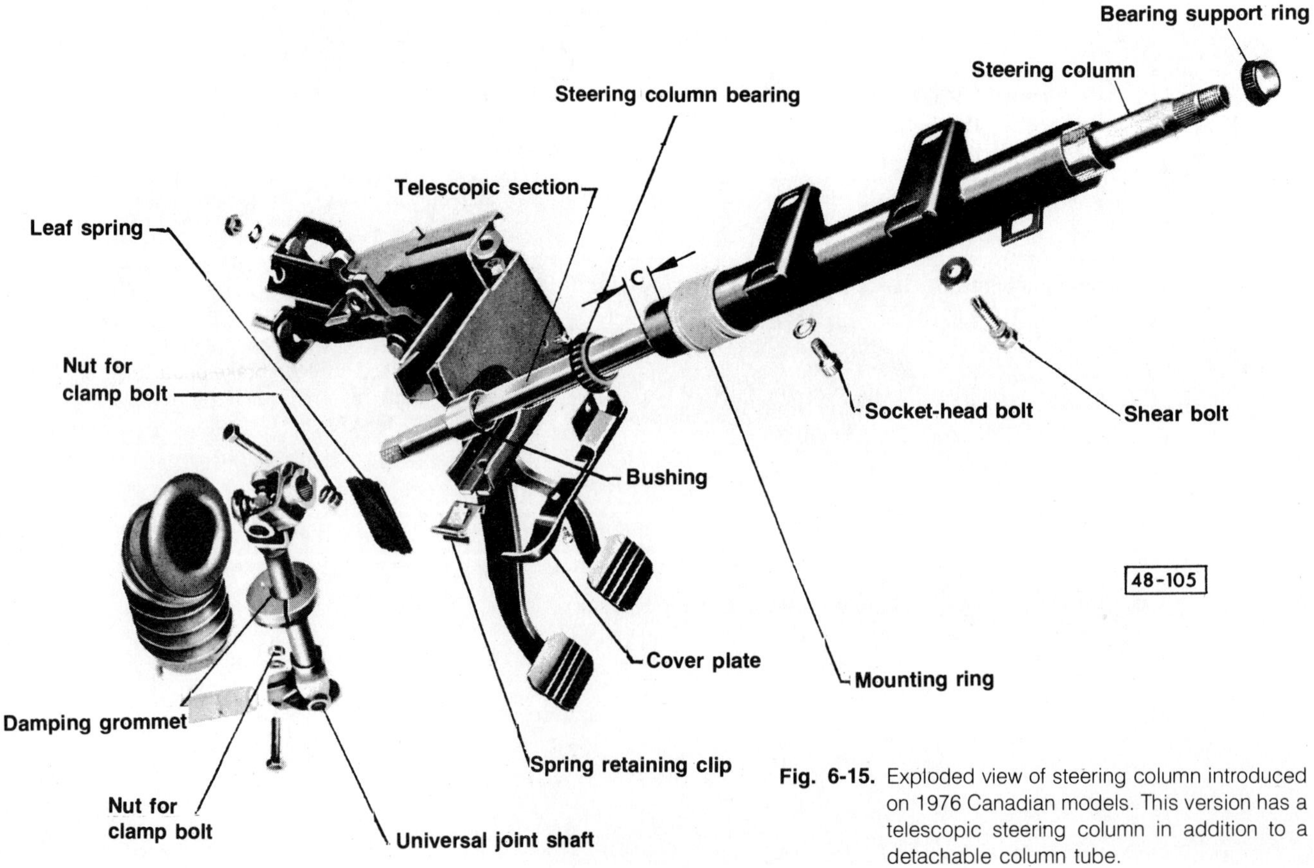

Bearing support ring

Steering column

Spring

Steering column bearing

Leaf spring

Nut for clamp bolt

Shear bolt

Supporting ring

Cover plate

Mounting ring

Damping grommet

Nut for clamp bolt

Spring retaining clip

Universal joint shaft

Bearing support ring

Steering column

Steering column bearing

Telescopic section

Leaf spring

C

Nut for clamp bolt

Socket-head bolt

Shear bolt

Bushing

Mounting ring

Damping grommet

Cover plate

Nut for clamp bolt

Spring retaining clip

Universal joint shaft

48-105

Fig. 6-15. Exploded view of steering column introduced on 1976 Canadian models. This version has a telescopic steering column in addition to a detachable column tube.

To remove the steering column use either Fig. 6-13, Fig. 6-14, or Fig. 6-15 as your guide. First disconnect the battery ground strap and then remove the steering wheel and the steering column switch as described in **6.4 Removing and Installing Steering Wheel and Steering Column Switch Assembly.** Remove the universal joint shaft as described in **6.5 Removing and Installing Universal Joint Shaft;** alternatively, you can disconnect the universal joint shaft from the steering column.

Detach the brake pedal push rod and the clutch cable from the pedals. Remove and install the leaf spring as indicated in Fig. 6-16 and Fig. 6-17. Remove the bolts that hold the column tube to the dashboard assembly. Shear bolts must be centerpunched and then drilled out. Once unbolted, you can remove the steering column and column tube from the car as a unit.

CAUTION ——

Do not attempt to remove the column from the tube without removing the entire assembly from the car. Always assemble the column and tube before you reinstall them as a unit. Otherwise, components will be damaged.

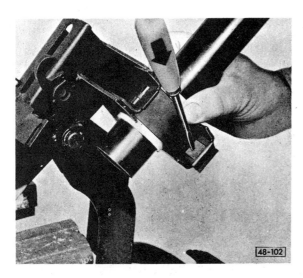

Fig. 6-16. Leaf spring being removed. Using a screwdriver, push spring retaining clip down as indicated by arrow. Remove retaining clip and then leaf spring.

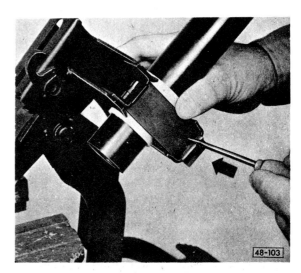

Fig. 6-17. Leaf spring being installed. Install leaf spring by pressing it over spring retaining clip as indicated by arrow.

Installation is the reverse of removal. Torque the regular bolts that hold the column tube to the dashboard assembly to 2.0 mkg (14 ft. lb.); use new shear bolts where necessary and tighten them until their heads shear off. The front wheels must be pointed straight ahead, and the steering wheel spokes horizontal, before you install the clamp bolt for the universal joint shaft. Please consult **6.5 Removing and Installing Universal Joint Shaft** for details. Torque the nut for the clamp bolt to 3.0 mkg (22 ft. lb.). Install the column switch and the steering wheel with careful attention to the instructions given in **6.4 Removing and Installing Steering Wheel and Steering Column Switch Assembly.**

NOTE ——

On cars with manual transmissions, you should adjust the clutch pedal freeplay as described in **ENGINE AND CLUTCH** after you have reconnected the clutch cable to the clutch pedal. The brake pedal pushrod yoke should be adjusted until the brake pedal is at the same height as the clutch pedal. See **BRAKES AND WHEELS.**

Steering Column and Column Tube Repairs

On 1976 and all later cars, the steering column tube is 10 mm (⅜ in.) longer than on the 1975 models. The longer tube has a mounting ring (bushing) with a slot and a lug. Some 1975 Rabbit models also have this tube and mounting ring. The new mounting ring (bushing) goes inside the tube and its lug projects through the slot indicated by the arrow in Fig. 6-18. The old mounting ring (bushing) fits over the outside of the column tube. To install it, you must first warm it in hot water and then slide it onto the tube until dimension **c**, given earlier in Fig. 6-15, is 31 mm (1¹/₁₆ in.).

New bearings can be pressed into the steering column tube as shown in Fig. 6-19. Drive the steering column out of the bearing and the column tube beforehand. Pressing the steering column into the column tube and the bearings should not require more than 45 to 90 kg (100 to 200 lb.) of force. If this much force is not adequate, something is wrong with the bearings or other components.

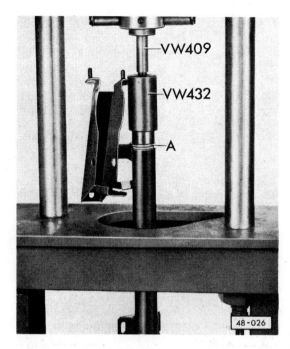

Fig. 6-19. Steering column bearing (**A**) being pressed into column tube.

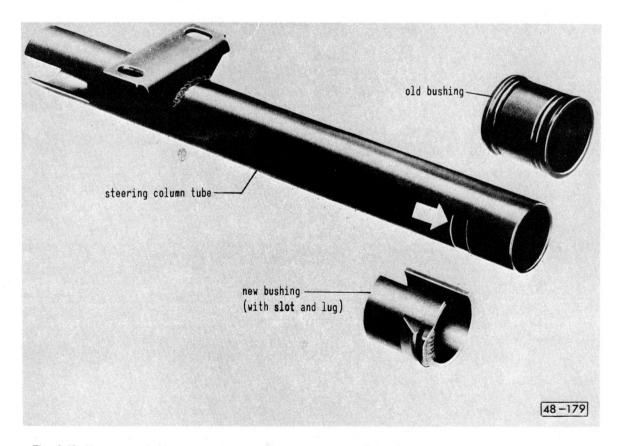

Fig. 6-18. New-type and old-type mounting rings (bushings). Arrow indicates slot for lug in new-type column tube.

7. Suspension and Steering
Technical Data

I. Tightening Torques

Location	Designation	mkg	ft. lb.
Tie rod end stud to steering arm	castellated nut	3.0	22
Tie rod end to tie rod	locknut	4.0	29
Replacement suspension ball joint to control arm	nut and bolt	2.5	18
Suspension ball joint stud to wheel bearing housing	clamp bolt & nut	3.0	22
Front suspension strut top mounting to car body	nut	2.0	14
Control arm front pivot to body	bolt (use Loctite®)	6.0	43
Control arm rear pivot U-retainer to body	bolt	3.0	22
Engine to engine mounting support	bolt	5.5	40
Driveshaft constant velocity joint to drive flange of transaxle	socket-head bolt	4.5	32
Brake hoses to brake lines	union nuts	1.5–2.0	11–14
Wheel bearing housing to front suspension strut	eccentric bolt & nut bolt & nut	8.0	58
Coil spring retainer to front strut piston rod	nut	8.0	58
Road wheel to hub or brake drum	lug bolt	9.0	65
Front hub to axle shaft (loosen and tighten only with car on ground)	self-locking nut	24.0	173
Nut on rear stub axle prior to rear wheel bearing adjustment	nut	1.0-max. 1.3 (while turning wheel)	7-max. 9.5 (while turning wheel)
Rear stub axle/brake backing plate to axle beam	bolt	6.0	43
Rear suspension strut shock absorber to axle beam	nut and bolt	4.5	32
Rear suspension strut shock absorber piston rod to car body	nut	3.5	25
Coil spring retainer to rear strut piston rod	slotted nut	2.0	14
Rear axle beam to rear axle mounting (Adjust mounting angle before torquing)	bolt and nut	6.0	43
Rear axle mounting to car body	nut	4.5	32
Steering universal joint shaft to steering column or steering gearbox pinion shaft	clamp bolt and nut	3.0	22
Rack and pinion steering gearbox to car body	nut	2.0	14
Steering column switch assembly to column tube	socket-head bolt	1.0	7
Steering wheel to steering column	nut	5.0	36
Steering column tube to dashboard assembly	regular bolt	2.0	14
	shear bolt	Tighten until heads shear off	

II. Wheel Alignment Specifications

Designation	Value
Front wheel alignment	
1. Total toe angle of front wheels, not pressed	−15′ +10′ or −15′
2. Total toe angle of front wheels, pressed	+10′ ±15′
3. Pressure applied above front wheels	10 ±2 kg (22 ±4 lb.)
4. Maximum permissible difference between total toe angle with wheels pressed and not pressed .	20′
5. Front wheel camber in straight ahead position	+20′ ±30′
6. Maximum permissible difference between sides	1°
7. Toe angle difference at 20° lock to left and right (not pressed)	−1°30′ ±30′
8. Offset between stub axles in direction of motion	5 mm maximum
9. Caster angle of a wheel	1°50′ ±30′
10. Corresponds to camber difference of a wheel on a lock from 20° left and 20° right	1°15′ ±20′
11. Maximum permissible difference between left and right	1° maximum
Rear wheel alignment	
1. Camber of rear wheels: Rabbit through Chassis No. 176 3241 690 and Scirocco through Chassis No. 536 2031 722	−1° ±35′
Rabbit from Chassis No. 176 3241 691 and Scirocco from Chassis No. 536 2031 723	−1°15′ ±35′
2. Maximum permissible camber deviation between sides	40′
3. Total toe of rear wheels: Rabbit through Chassis No. 176 3241 690 and Scirocco through Chassis No. 536 2031 722	+10′ ±30′
Rabbit from Chassis No. 176 3241 691 and Scirocco from Chassis No. 536 2031 722	+20′ ±30′
4. Deviation from driving direction (maximum difference in toe)	30′ maximum

III. Tolerances, Wear Limits, and Settings

Designation	New installation mm (in.)	Wear limit mm (in.)
1. Front suspension ball joints .... play	1.00 (.040)	2.50 (.100) using pry bar
2. Rear stub axle .... distortion	—	0.25 (.010) difference between any two measurements
3. Rear wheel bearing .... axial play	0.05–0.07 (.002–.0027)	—
4. Front track .... width	1390 (54.7)	—
5. Rear track .... width (Rabbit)	1350 (53.1)	—
.... width (Scirocco)	1358 (53.5)	—
6. Wheelbase .... length	2400 (94.5)	—

FUEL AND EXHAUST SYSTEMS

Contents

Fuel and Exhaust Systems

3

The fuel system handles five main tasks necessary for proper engine operation: (1) it provides storage space for the gasoline; (2) it includes the components necessary for delivering gasoline to the engine; (3) it is responsible for admitting the proper amount of filtered air to the engine; (4) it incorporates a system for mixing fuel and air in precisely controlled proportions and delivering this mixture to the cylinders; and (5) it modifies the density of the incoming air so that the combustion process does not produce an excess of undesirable exhaust emissions. The fourth function—mixing the fuel with air—is handled on early models by a carburetor and on later models by a fuel injection system.

On the carburetor-engined cars covered by this Manual, the carburetor is a dual-venturi, progressive opening one. That is, the primary venturi's throttle valve is directly controlled by the accelerator pedal and is the only throttle valve in operation during normal driving. During acceleration to high speeds and when cruising at high speeds, the secondary venturi's throttle valve also opens. By limiting the operation of the second venturi to periods of high-power demand, greater fuel economy is obtained during normal driving, when the power needed is either light or moderate.

The fuel injection system, used on the later cars covered by this Manual, has the same kind of progressive throttle valves as the carburetor already described. The throttle valves, however, are mounted in a separate throttle valve housing and control only the quantity of air that enters the engine's cylinders. The quantity of air going to the throttle valves is accurately measured by a separate unit, known as the air flow sensor.

The air flow sensor is built into a single unit with the fuel distributor. The amount of fuel injected into the engine's intake ports is metered precisely in proportion to the air entering the engine. Unlike a carburetor, fuel injection does not depend on the velocity of the incoming air to draw fuel into the engine. Instead, fuel is injected into the airstream under pressure. The system used on cars covered by this manual is a continuous-flow system—that is, the gasoline is injected in a continuous spray of varying quantity. By contrast, the fuel injection system used on Type 1 and Type 2 VWs injects the fuel in a uniform quantity but in pulses of varying duration.

The continuous injection system (CIS) is not an electronic system and requires few electrical tests for troubleshooting. A pressure gauge and one or two special tools are required, however. If you lack the skills, instruments, or other equipment necessary for testing either the carburetion system or the fuel injection system, we suggest you leave these tests or repairs to an Authorized Dealer or other qualified and properly equipped shop. We especially urge you to consult your Authorized Dealer before attempting repairs on a car still covered by the new-car warranty.

1. GENERAL DESCRIPTION

As noted earlier, the fuel system can be divided conveniently into five subsystems, each with a separate function. For brevity, these will be called fuel storage, pump and lines, air cleaner, carburetor or fuel injection, and emission controls.

Fuel Storage

The fuel tank is located beneath the car, ahead of the rear axle. Here it is protected by both the spare tire and the rear wheels, in the event of a rear-end collision. The tank has a capacity of 11.9 U.S. gallons (9.9 Imperial gallons or 45.0 liters).

The tank is equipped with a sending unit for the electrical fuel gauge, a pickup tube for the transfer of fuel to the engine, and three vent tubes routed into the evaporative emission control system. On cars with fuel injection, there is a second tube for the return of surplus fuel pump output to the tank. This return tube is built into the cover of the fuel gauge sending unit, as is the pickup tube on all models.

Pump and Lines

Engines with carburetors have a mechanical fuel pump located on the front side of the engine block. This pump is operated by an eccentric on the engine's intermediate shaft.

Engines with fuel injection have an electrical fuel pump located beneath the car, near the right-hand side of the fuel tank. The electrical fuel pump draws fuel from the tank and pumps the fuel into the pressure line to the fuel distributor.

The fuel lines that pass beneath the floor of the car are steel tubes housed in the floor pan tunnel. Hoses connect the steel lines to the fuel pump and to the carburetor or the fuel injection system. On fuel injection cars, the hoses are connected to banjo unions so that the unions can be disconnected easily without removing and installing the hoses on their connections.

Air Cleaner

All cars covered by this Manual have dry-type pleated paper filter elements. These filter elements are flat and rectangular in shape and located inside the air cleaner housing. On fuel injection cars, the air cleaner housing is attached to the bottom of the fuel metering unit.

1.1 Carburetor

A Zenith 32/32-2B2 carburetor is used on the models that have carburetors. The designation "32/32" indicates that each of the carburetor's two throttle valves is 32 mm in diameter. One throttle valve is used for mid-range operation. This gives good economy and throttle response with a minimum of exhaust emissions. At full load, a second throttle valve opens in addition to the first one.

The operating stages are shown in Fig. 1-1. Once the primary throttle valve has opened beyond a predetermined point, the secondary throttle valve is able to open to a degree that is proportional to engine vacuum, thus avoiding the hesitation that might occur if both throttle valves were fully opened at low speed on an engine tuned for maximum fuel economy and minimum exhaust emissions.

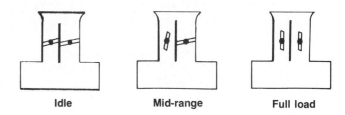

Idle   **Mid-range**   **Full load**

Fig. 1-1. Stages of dual-venturi carburetor operation. Secondary throttle valve is opened by vacuum chamber attached to carburetor.

Despite the two-stage design of the carburetor, hesitation, surging, and stalling were problems on some of the 1975 cars covered by this Manual. These cars were recalled for subsequent modification. The service and repair instructions given in this section for 1975 models apply to the modified carburetor and fuel system. In most instances, the modifications are described so that you can make them yourself if they have not already been made by an Authorized Dealer.

The carburetor has a built-in automatic choke operated by a thermostatic spring. The thermostatic spring closes the choke valve when the engine is cold. As the engine warms up, heated coolant is conducted to the carburetor by hoses, thus warming the thermostatic spring and causing the choke to open at a predetermined rate. In addition, there is an electric heating element that prevents the choke from opening too slowly in very cold weather. Whenever the throttle valve is closed—as at idle or during deceleration—a vacuum diaphragm overrides the thermostatic spring and causes the choke to open slightly.

1.2 Fuel Injection

Fig. 1-2 is a schematic view of the CIS (continuous injection system) that is used on the latest cars covered by this Manual. To help you understand this diagram, a brief explanation is given here of the function of each of

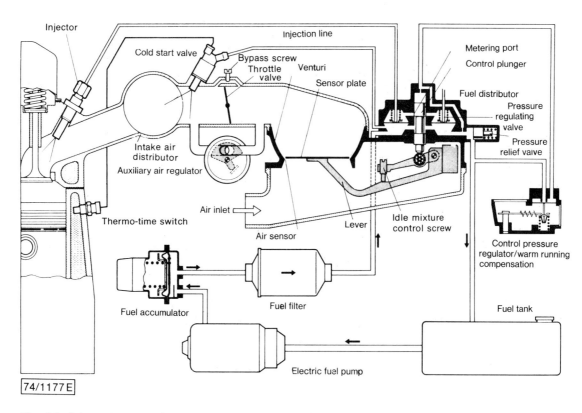

Fig. 1-2. Schematic view of CIS fuel injection.

the system's components. A detailed description of each component can be found under the heading for the particular component (for example, **7.8 Testing and Replacing Cold-start Valve**).

It is convenient to divide the fuel injection system into two subsystems: the fuel circuit and the air system.

Fuel Circuit

The electric fuel pump draws fuel from the tank and pumps it through the fuel accumulator and the fuel filter to the fuel distributor. The function of the fuel accumulator is to absorb the initial pressure surge when the pump starts, thereby preventing the control plunger of the fuel distributor's metering unit from being forced up before an adequate stable pressure has been reached. The fuel accumulator also serves as a reservoir to keep the system under pressure (1.5 bar to 2.5 bar) for a short time after the engine has been turned off. This residual fuel pressure is necessary to prevent vapor lock.

A pressure relief valve, built into the fuel distributor, keeps the pressure in the system at a predetermined level by allowing surplus fuel from the pump to flow back to the tank. The pressure is modulated according to engine temperature by the control pressure regulator. It too regulates pressure in the system by allowing a varying amount of fuel to flow back to the tank. In addition to being warmed by contact with the engine and engine oil, the control pressure regulator is warmed by an electrically heated thermostatic spring. The electric heating element ensures that the pressure will not be excessive when the outside air temperature is very cold.

In addition to the richer mixture produced for cold running by the control pressure regulator, there is a cold-start valve that injects additional fuel during starter operation when the engine is cold. Its function is analogous to the function of a choke on a carburetor. The cold-start valve, sometimes called the fifth injector, is operated electrically by current from the starter solenoid. However, the thermo-time switch interrupts the current if the engine is hot or after the starter has been in constant operation for more than a few seconds. The purpose of the thermo-time switch is to prevent flooding.

The main function of the four injectors is to atomize the continuous flow of fuel that is injected under pressure into the intake ports of the engine. Valves in the nozzles stop the flow of fuel when the fuel pressure drops below a certain point. The quantity of fuel injected is regulated by the fuel distributor's metering unit and, secondarily, by the control pressure regulator. The metering function of the fuel distributor is controlled by the quantity of air entering the engine, which is measured by the sensor plate.

Air System

The sensor plate of the mixture control unit is the heart of the fuel injection system. (The mixture control unit consists of the air volume sensor and the fuel distributor.) The greater the amount of air admitted to the engine past the throttle valve or the auxiliary air regulator, the higher the sensor plate is raised above the narrowest part of the venturi. A lever connected to the sensor plate raises or lowers the control plunger in the fuel distributor's metering unit—increasing the quantity of fuel to the injection nozzle when air flow increases or reducing the quantity of fuel when air flow diminishes.

In addition to the throttle valves, which are connected to the accelerator pedal, the quantity of air entering the engine can be changed by two other devices. The first of these is the auxiliary air regulator. When the engine is cold, the auxiliary air regulator admits additional air to the intake air distributor at closed throttle in order to provide a faster idle until the engine has warmed up. The auxiliary air regulator consists of a rotary valve operated by an electrically heated thermostatic spring. The spring begins to heat up as soon as the engine is started, gradually closing the valve and returning the engine to its normal idle rpm at a predetermined warm-up rate.

A second throttle valve bypass is adjustable by means of the bypass screw. This bypass screw, which is located in the throttle valve housing, is used to adjust the engine's idle speed.

As installed on the car, the intake air distributor is a large, cylindrical cast-aluminum chamber with four integral manifold tubes that conduct air to the intake ports of the engine. The intake air distributor provides mounting points for the throttle valve housing, the cold-start valve, and various air and vacuum hoses.

1.3 Emission Controls

The EEC (evaporative emission control) consists of the fuel tank ventilation hoses, an expansion tank, an activated charcoal filter canister, and the hoses from the canister to the engine. Its purpose is to keep fuel tank fumes from polluting the air. All of the engines covered by this Manual have a closed PCV (positive crankcase ventilation) system. The system contains no PCV valve that requires periodic cleaning or replacement but does include an oil separator.

An EGR (exhaust gas recirculation) system is installed on all cars covered by this Manual. Some cars are equipped with an AI (air injection) system and others have a CAT (catalytic converter). Which of these systems is on a given vehicle can be determined by inspecting the emission decal located in the engine compartment. Cars that are equipped with CATs are also identifiable by a fuel filler that will accept only the small pump nozzles used by filling stations for dispensing lead-free gasoline.

2. MAINTENANCE

There are only a few maintenance operations that must be carried out at a specified mileage or after a certain period of service. These are listed below and covered in **LUBRICATION AND MAINTENANCE** or under the listed headings in this section of the Manual.

1. Servicing the air cleaner
2. Replacing the fuel filter (see **3.2**)
3. Checking emission controls (see **5.** and **9.**)
4. Replacing catalytic converter (see **9.1** and **10.**)
5. Replacing activated charcoal filter canister
6. Checking PCV system.

3. FUEL TANK

If the fuel tank must be removed for cleaning or repairs, it is important that the connections leading to the tank be reinstalled correctly, without kinks, and in their original locations. Errors can lead to fuel starvation, a collapsed fuel tank, or the improper venting of fumes.

3.1 Removing and Installing Fuel Tank

To avoid the hazard of spilled fuel, the tank should be as nearly empty as possible during removal. Surplus fuel should be drained off. Removal and testing of the fuel gauge sending unit is described in conjunction with instruments in **ELECTRICAL SYSTEM.**

WARNING ——

Disconnect the battery ground strap. Do not smoke or work near heaters or other fire hazards. Have a fire extinguisher handy.

To remove:

1. On late 1976 cars and on all cars with fuel injection, raise up and remove the rear seat. Remove the sending unit access plate from the floor. (On most cars with carburetors manufactured up to the middle of 1976, the sending unit is accessible from under the car.)
2. Disconnect the wires from the fuel gauge sending unit. Use a pinch clamp or clamps to squeeze the fuel hose(s) shut at a point near the tank connection(s). Then pry off the clamp(s) and disconnect the fuel hose(s) from the sending unit.
3. Working beneath the car, loosen the hose clamps that hold the connecting hose to the fuel filler neck and to the filler pipe insert of the fuel tank.

Then remove the connecting hose so that the tank is no longer connected to the filler neck.

4. Remove the clamps for the ventilation hoses. Then detach the ventilation hoses from the fuel tank.

5. Unhook the rubber muffler support rings indicated at **1** in Fig. 3-1.

6. Disconnect the left rear brake hose from the brake line and the bracket on the car body. Seal the line with a clean brake bleeder dust cap.

7. Remove the two nuts that hold the left-hand rear axle mounting to the car body (**2** in Fig. 3-1). Then lower the axle on the left-hand side.

NOTE——
Though not absolutely necessary, tank removal is easier if the rear axle is dismounted and lowered at both sides.

8. Remove the two gasoline tank retaining straps, one of which is indicated at **3** in Fig. 3-1.

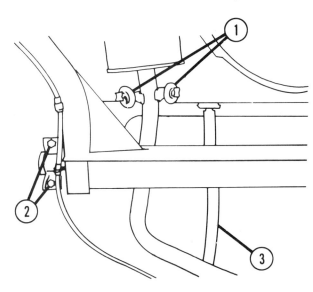

Fig. 3-1. Left-side disconnecting points. Muffler support rings are at **1**, bolts for left axle mount are at **2**, and retaining strap for fuel tank is at **3**.

9. If the car has a heatshield beneath the tank, remove it. All 1975 and 1976 cars should be equipped with a heatshield.

10. Remove the tank, sliding it out toward the left and to the rear.

On 1975 cars, check the distance from the fuel tank seam to the ventilation tube's outer end (Fig. 3-2). If it is less than 49 mm (1⅞ in.), bend the ventilation tube slightly in order to obtain the correct dimension, being careful not to damage the tube weld.

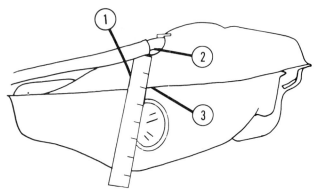

Fig. 3-2. Distance from tank seam to end of ventilation tube being measured. Ruler is at **1**, ventilation tube at **2**, and fuel tank seam at **3**.

If you have bent up the ventilation tube as just described, you may need to make a dimple in the body metal so that the ventilation hose does not contact the body with the tank installed. If the car is a 1975 or 1976 model and does not have the heatshield installed, install one as indicated in Fig. 3-3.

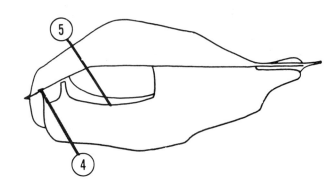

Fig. 3-3. Heatshield correctly installed on fuel tank. Front of heatshield clips over tank seam at front (**4**). Edge of heatshield (**5**) should scoop airflow over bottom of tank.

Installation is the reverse of removal. Connect the hoses and the wires to the sending unit as indicated in Fig. 3-4 or Fig. 3-5. Torque the axle mount nuts to 4.5 mkg (32 ft. lb.). Torque the brake line union to 1.5 to 2.0 mkg (11 to 14 ft. lb.). Then bleed the rear brakes as described in **BRAKES AND WHEELS.**

Fig. 3-4. Sending unit connections for cars with side-mounted sending units. Ground (brown) wire is at **1**, wire to fuel gauge at **2**, and fuel hose connection at **3**.

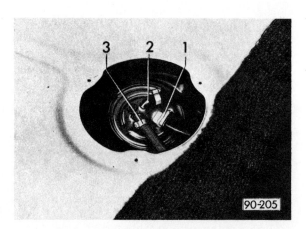

Fig. 3-5. Sending unit connections for cars with top-mounted sending units. Two-prong electrical connector is at **1**, suction line at **2**, and return line at **3**.

Fuel Tank Ventilation Hoses

In performing repairs on the evaporative emission control system and the fuel tank, it is important to reconnect the ventilation hoses correctly. Incorrect connections will impair proper fuel tank ventilation and could cause the tank to collapse. Connect the hoses as shown in Fig. 3-6 or Fig. 3-7. The expansion tank is located beneath the right-hand rear fender.

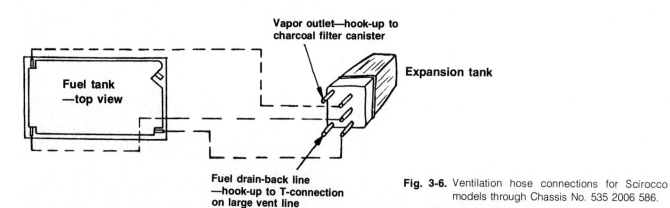

Fig. 3-6. Ventilation hose connections for Scirocco models through Chassis No. 535 2006 586.

Fig. 3-7. Ventilation hose connections for all Rabbit models and for Scirocco models from Chassis No. 535 2006 587.

3.2 Replacing Fuel Filter

Up to Rabbit Chassis No. 175 3394 504 and Scirocco Chassis No. 535 2052 617, the fuel filter is a strainer inside the fuel tank on the end of the fuel pickup tube of the fuel gauge sending unit. Normally, this strainer need not be checked or replaced. The strainer is accessible after you have removed the sending unit as described in **ELECTRICAL SYSTEM.**

Later cars have an in-line fuel filter as shown in Fig. 3-8 or Fig. 3-9, the strainer in the tank having been discontinued. This filter should be replaced every 30,000 miles. Install the new filter so that the arrow on the side indicates the direction of flow.

NOTE ——

The in-line filter has been dealer-installed on many early 1975 cars that did not originally have it.

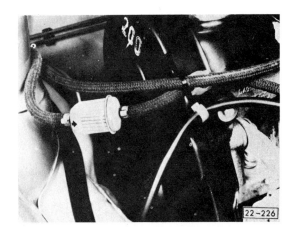

Fig. 3-8. In-line fuel filter for engines with carburetors. If you install this kind of filter on a car that originally had only the strainer in the tank, be sure to use hose clamps.

Fig. 3-9. In-line fuel filter for fuel injection engines. Arrow indicates direction of flow.

4. MECHANICAL FUEL PUMP
(CARBURETOR ENGINES ONLY)

On cars with carburetors, the fuel pump is mounted on the engine. It is a mechanical pump, operated by an eccentric on the engine's intermediate shaft. The stroke of the pump is nonadjustable.

4.1 Removing and Installing Mechanical Fuel Pump
(carburetor engines only)

1. Pry off or loosen the clamps. Then disconnect the fuel hoses from the fuel pump.

WARNING ——

Fuel will be expelled as you disconnect the hoses. Disconnect the battery ground strap. Do not smoke or work near heaters or other fire hazards. Have a fire extinguisher handy.

2. Remove the bolts that hold the fuel pump to the engine. Then take off the pump. See Fig. 4-1.

3. Remove the intermediate flange and the gasket.

Fig. 4-1. Socket-head bolts (arrows) that hold pump to engine. Fuel outlet is indicated by arrow superimposed on fuel hose. Hose clamp is circled.

Installation is the reverse of removal. Use a new seal beneath the intermediate flange. Torque the bolts to 2.0 mkg (14 ft. lb.). If the hose clamps are the clip kind without screws, replace them.

NOTE ——

If the original hoses are to be reinstalled, carefully inspect their ends to see that they have not been weakened or deformed by the previous installation of hose clamps. A new clamp may not seal hoses that have lost resiliency. In this case, a new hose should always be installed.

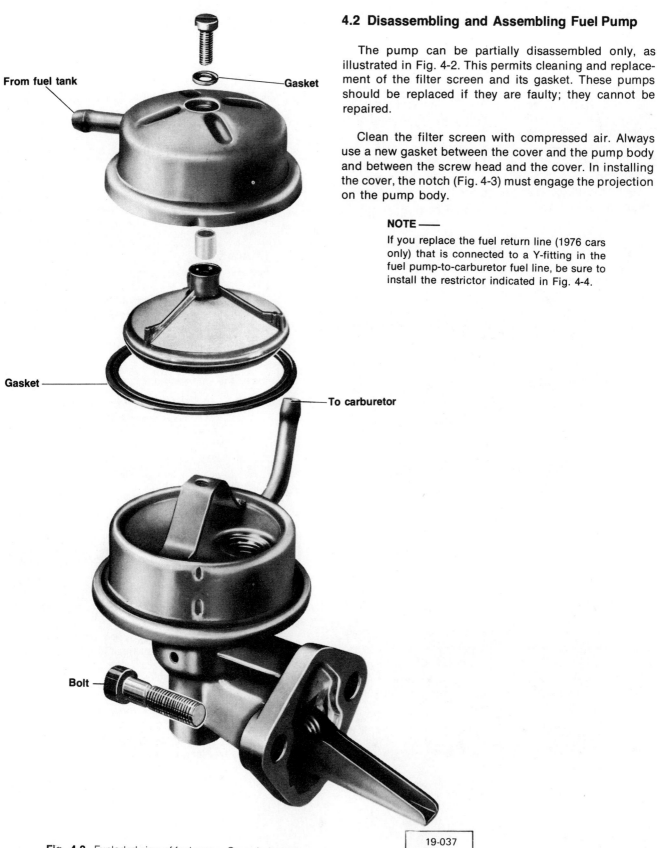

From fuel tank

Gasket

Gasket

To carburetor

Bolt

19-037

Fig. 4-2. Exploded view of fuel pump. Cover bolt, cover, filter screen, and gaskets are available as replacement parts.

4.2 Disassembling and Assembling Fuel Pump

The pump can be partially disassembled only, as illustrated in Fig. 4-2. This permits cleaning and replacement of the filter screen and its gasket. These pumps should be replaced if they are faulty; they cannot be repaired.

Clean the filter screen with compressed air. Always use a new gasket between the cover and the pump body and between the screw head and the cover. In installing the cover, the notch (Fig. 4-3) must engage the projection on the pump body.

NOTE ——

If you replace the fuel return line (1976 cars only) that is connected to a Y-fitting in the fuel pump-to-carburetor fuel line, be sure to install the restrictor indicated in Fig. 4-4.

Fig. 4-3. Notch (arrow) on pump cover.

Fig. 4-4. Restrictor (arrow) installed in 1976 model fuel return line.

5. ADJUSTING IDLE

Because haphazard idle adjustments will affect exhaust emissions adversely, please follow the instructions carefully and use the specified equipment. Professional mechanics should find out whether state authorization is required before a repair shop can make adjustments that influence exhaust emissions.

During routine maintenance, you should adjust the idle speed only. This is done by turning the bypass screw in the carburetor or on the throttle valve housing of the fuel injection system. Do not adjust the idle speed by turning the throttle valve adjustment, which is the procedure used on some other makes of cars. You need not adjust the idle mixture (CO content) unless (1) you have installed a different carburetor or, on fuel injection cars, a new mixture control unit, (2) you have removed,

repaired, or rebuilt the carburetor or the mixture control unit, (3) the engine has been extensively rebuilt, or (4) exhaust emissions are excessive.

In troubleshooting the engine, eliminate all other possible trouble sources before you touch the carburetor or fuel injection system adjustments. Also, adjusting the idle rpm should be the last step in a tune-up. Otherwise, valve and ignition adjustments will upset the previous idle adjustment. A preliminary idle speed adjustment should be made earlier only if the engine is idling too fast to check the ignition timing.

CAUTION ——

If you lack the skills, tools, or test equipment for adjusting the carburetor or the fuel injection, we suggest you leave this work to an Authorized Dealer or other qualified shop. We especially urge you to consult your Authorized Dealer before attempting repairs on a car still covered by the new-car warranty.

5.1 Adjusting Idle on Cars with Carburetors

The idle speed is adjusted by turning a bypass screw. Turning this screw will not alter exhaust emissions so long as the idle rpm is adjusted to the prescribed range. This idle mixture screw will alter emissions if it is turned and should not be adjusted without the aid of an exhaust gas analyzer.

Adjusting Idle Speed

If you suspect that someone has altered the factory throttle valve adjustment or has otherwise used incorrect procedures in adjusting the carburetor, you should check the various adjustments as described in **6.1 Removing, Rebuilding, and Installing Carburetor** before you attempt to adjust the idle speed. Always use the procedure given here to adjust the idle speed. Do not adjust the idle speed by turning the throttle valve adjustment.

To adjust idle speed:

1. Drive the car until the engine has reached an oil temperature of approximately 60°C (140°F).

2. Stop the car and set the parking brake firmly. Raise the hood and connect a dwell meter/tachometer according to the instructions furnished by the instrument's manufacturer. Set the instrument to measure rpm for a four-cylinder engine.

3. With the engine running, read the idle rpm. If the idle speed is not between 900 and 1000 rpm, adjust

it to specifications by turning the bypass screw (Fig. 5-1). Turning the bypass screw counterclockwise will increase the idle speed; turning it clockwise will decrease the idle speed.

NOTE ——

If turning the bypass screw makes little difference in the idle speed, it is likely that someone has tampered with the throttle valve adjustment.

Fig. 5-1. Location of bypass screw used to adjust idle speed.

Adjusting Idle Mixture
(CO content)

Do not attempt to adjust the idle mixture without a good quality infrared exhaust gas analyzer such as the Sun® EPA 75 Performance Analyzer. The instrument that you use for making idle mixture adjustments should measure parts per million of hydrocarbons and CO percentages.

To adjust idle mixture:

1. Adjust the idle speed as described under the preceding heading.

2. Disconnect the EEC (evaporative emission control) purge hose that goes between the activated charcoal filter canister and the carburetor's air intake elbow (Fig. 5-2). Disconnect the PCV (positive crankcase ventilation) hose from the elbow at the point indicated in Fig. 5-3. Plug both openings in the elbow.

3. Disconnect the air injection hose from the check valve. Plug the connection as indicated in Fig. 5-4.

Fig. 5-2. Point at which EEC purge hose should be disconnected (arrow).

Fig. 5-3. Point at which PCV hose should be disconnected (arrow).

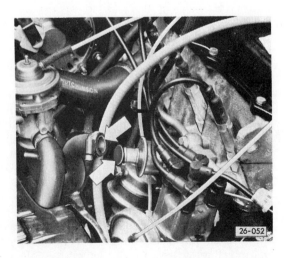

Fig. 5-4. Rubber plug (right arrow) installed on connection of diverter valve. Disconnected hose is at left arrow.

4. Connect the exhaust gas analyzer to its power source and turn it on. On cars without catalytic converters, insert the probe into the tailpipe; on cars with catalytic converters, insert the probe into the port provided in the EGR (exhaust gas recirculation) filter (Fig. 5-5).

NOTE ——

The 1976 models do not have an EGR filter. The CO test port is located in the EGR feedpipe.

Fig. 5-5. Exhaust analyzer probe connected to EGR filter (arrow).

5. With the engine fully warmed up and idling, compare the exhaust analyzer readings with the prescribed ranges for CO emissions and, where applicable, for hydrocarbon emissions. The applicable specifications are listed on the engine's emissions decal or are prescribed by the state government. If the decal is missing, check that the CO volume percentage at idle is within the range given for the car in **Table a.**

NOTE ——

The cooling fan should not be running. The engine oil temperature must be between 50° and 70°C (122° and 158°F).

6. If the CO level is outside the prescribed range, use a screwdriver to turn the idle mixture control screw (Fig. 5-6).

NOTE ——

Turning the idle mixture control screw clockwise (screwing it in) makes the mixture leaner.

7. If necessary, connect a dwell meter/tachometer and readjust the idle speed to 900 to 1000 rpm by turning the bypass screw.

Table a. CO Volume Percentages for Cars with Carburetors

Car model	Transmission	CO volume percent
1975 USA	Manual or Automatic	2.0 ± 0.5 at EGR filter (use 1976 specifications if catalytic converter has been eliminated)
1975 Canada	Manual	2.0 ± 0.5 at tailpipe
	Automatic	1.0 ± 0.5 at tailpipe
1976 USA	Manual	1.5 ± 0.7 at EGR feed pipe (or at tailpipe if catalytic converter has been eliminated)
	Automatic	1.0 ± 0.7 at EGR feed pipe (or at tailpipe if catalytic converter has been eliminated)
1976 Canada	Manual	0.8 to 2.2 at tailpipe
	Automatic	0.3 to 1.7 at tailpipe

3 ■

Fig. 5-6. Idle mixture control screw (arrow).

8. Reconnect the hose to the diverter valve. The CO percentage should drop noticeably. Measured at the tailpipe, the CO reading should be less than 0.4%. If not, test the air injection system as described in **9. Emission Controls.**

9. If both the idle speed and the idle mixture (CO content) are correct on cars with catalytic converters, check the CO percentage with the exhaust gas analyzer probe inserted into the car's tailpipe. The CO reading should be less than 0.4%. If it is not, the catalytic converter is probably faulty and should be replaced.

NOTE ——

When you reinstall the threaded plug in the probe opening in the EGR filter, coat the threads with graphite or Moly-Kote®.

10. If the tailpipe reading is satisfactory, disconnect the dwell meter/tachometer and the exhaust gas analyzer. Then reconnect the EEC and PCV hoses.

Troubleshooting Cold Idle Valve
(1976 cars only)

The cold idle valve (Fig. 5-7) is a temperature-controlled, vacuum-operated valve that admits additional fuel into the carburetor's secondary side for improved cold idling. The separate temperature valve that controls the supply of vacuum to the cold idle valve is located on a temperature valve manifold that is installed in one of the cooling system's heater hoses. This temperature valve should supply vacuum to the cold idle valve at coolant temperatures below approximately 13°C (55°F) and should close off the supply of vacuum at coolant temperatures above approximately 20°C (68°F). If it does not, replace the temperature valve.

Fig. 5-7. Cold idle valve (arrow).

Typically, the engine will idle roughly during the warm-up phase of operation if the cold idle valve is failing to admit fuel. First check the hoses and the temperature valve by blowing through them while the coolant is cold and again after the coolant temperature has risen to above 20°C (68°F). If the hoses are not clogged and if the temperature valve is opening and closing as previously described, check the cold idle valve.

To troubleshoot cold idle valve:

1. Run the engine at idle for about five minutes. Then connect an exhaust gas analyzer as previously described. The PCV and EEC hoses should be disconnected from the air intake elbow, and the air injection hose should be disconnected from the diverter valve.

2. Disconnect the vacuum hose from the large (first stage) choke pull-down vacuum unit. Then connect

the hose to the cold idle valve in place of the hose from the temperature valve. The idle speed should increase slightly, and the CO value should increase by about 5% to 8%.

3. If the idle speed and CO value did not increase during the check described in step 2, the cold idle valve is faulty and should be replaced.

5.2 Adjusting Idle on Cars with Fuel Injection

The idle speed is adjusted by turning a bypass screw in the throttle valve housing. Turning this screw will not alter exhaust emissions so long as the idle rpm is adjusted to the prescribed range. The idle mixture screw, located in the mixture control unit, will alter emissions if it is turned. It should not be adjusted without the aid of an exhaust gas analyzer.

> *CAUTION ——*
>
> *Do not try to cure engine operating problems by making idle adjustments. Incorrect adjustments are seldom the cause of such problems as hard starting, rough running, or lack of power. If the engine does not seem to be running right, refer to **7.1 Troubleshooting Fuel Injection.** Carry out the checks and tests suggested there before you attempt to adjust the idle.*

Adjusting Idle Speed

Always use the procedure given here to adjust the idle speed. Do not adjust the idle speed by altering the throttle valve position.

To adjust idle speed:

1. Drive the car until the engine has reached an oil temperature between 50° and 70°C (122° and 158°F).

2. Stop the car and set the parking brake firmly. Raise the hood and make sure that the auxiliary air regulator has fully closed. To check this, temporarily disconnect the hose from the end of the auxiliary air regulator that is opposite the electrical connection. You should feel no vacuum when you place your thumb against the connection on the valve. If you do, check the valve as described in **7.9 Testing and Replacing Auxiliary Air Regulator.**

3. If the auxiliary air regulator is closed, reconnect the hose. Then connect a dwell meter/tachometer according to the instructions furnished by the instrument's manufacturer. Set the instrument to measure rpm for a four-cylinder engine.

4. Turn the headlights on to high beam. With the engine running, read the idle rpm. If the idle speed

is not between 900 and 1000 rpm, adjust it to specifications by turning the bypass screw (Fig. 5-8). Turning the bypass screw counterclockwise will increase the idle speed; turning it clockwise will decrease the idle speed.

NOTE ——

If turning the bypass screw makes little difference in the idle speed, either someone has tampered with the throttle valve adjustment, there is a leak in the air system somewhere on the intake air distributor (which will also cause a rough idle), or the auxiliary air regulator is not fully closed.

Fig. 5-8. Location of bypass screw (arrow) on throttle valve housing. This screw is used to adjust the idle speed.

Adjusting Idle Mixture (CO content)

Do not attempt to adjust the idle mixture without a good-quality infrared exhaust gas analyzer such as the Sun® EPA 75 Performance Analyzer. The instrument that you use for making idle mixture adjustments should measure parts per million of hydrocarbons and CO percentages.

To adjust idle mixture:

1. Adjust the idle speed as described under the preceding heading. The headlight high beams should be turned on during idle speed adjustment and left on while you adjust the mixture.

2. Disconnect the EEC (evaporative emission control) purge hose that goes between the activated charcoal filter canister and the air cleaner, disconnecting it at the air cleaner end.

3. Connect the exhaust gas analyzer to its power source and turn it on. Insert the probe into the tailpipe, including the tailpipes of cars with catalytic converters.

4. With the engine idling, compare the exhaust analyzer readings with the prescribed ranges for CO emissions and, where applicable, for hydrocarbon emissions. The applicable specifications are listed on the engine's emissions decal or are prescribed by the state government. If the decal is missing, check that the CO volume percentage at idle conforms to the specifications given in **Table b.**

NOTE ——

The cooling fan should not be running. The engine oil temperature must be between 50° and 70°C (122° and 158°F).

Table b. CO Volume Percentages for Cars with Fuel Injection

Place where car was first sold	Transmission	CO volume percent
Canada and USA except California	Manual	1.5 maximum
	Automatic	1.0 maximum
California	Manual	0.3 maximum
	Automatic	0.3 maximum

5. If the CO level is outside the prescribed range, remove the rubber plug from the top of the mixture control unit's housing. There is a looped wire handle attached to this plug so that the plug can easily be pulled out of its hole.

6. Use the adjusting tool shown in Fig. 5-9 to turn the idle mixture control screw. Remove the tool after each adjustment, install the plug, and accelerate the engine briefly before you read the CO percentage with the engine at idle.

CAUTION ——

Do not push the adjusting tool down or accelerate the engine while the tool is in place. Doing these things can damage the air flow sensor.

Fig. 5-9. Idle mixture (CO content) being adjusted with Tool P377. Notice removed plug atop battery.

You can readily see what mechanical change your adjustment will accomplish by studying the schematic diagram given in **1.2 Fuel Injection.** Turning the screw clockwise makes the mixture richer; turning it counterclockwise makes it leaner.

7. If necessary, connect a dwell meter/tachometer and readjust the idle speed to 900 to 1000 rpm by turning the bypass screw on the throttle valve housing.

8. If both the idle speed and the idle mixture (CO content) are correct, turn off the headlights and stop the engine. Firmly reinstall the rubber plug in the mixture control unit. Reconnect the EEC hose.

9. Disconnect the dwell meter/tachometer and the exhaust gas analyzer.

6. REPAIRING CARBURETOR

Carburetor repairs consist of cleaning the carburetor, replacing the soft parts (gaskets, O-rings, and seals), replacing the jets and similar hard components, and making various pre-installation adjustments. If you install a new carburetor or a factory-rebuilt carburetor, you should still check the various adjustments before you install it on the car.

6.1 Removing, Rebuilding, and Installing Carburetor

If a carburetor must be replaced, it is important that the new carburetor have the same part number as the original or that the new carburetor be the correct replacement for the car model being serviced. Always obtain replacement carburetors and carburetor parts with reference to the carburetor part number and the engine number.

To remove carburetor:

1. Take off the nut. Then remove the air intake elbow from the top of the carburetor. Detach all hoses from the elbow, and remove the elbow from the car.

2. Obtain two corks of appropriate diameter. Disconnect the coolant hoses from the automatic choke, and quickly plug them with the corks to prevent the loss of coolant.

3. Disconnect the accelerator cable from the pin on the throttle arm. Then remove the three screws that hold the accelerator cable conduit bracket to the carburetor. Remove the bracket, leaving it attached to the cable conduit. By removing the bracket, you will avoid having to adjust the accelerator cable.

4. Disconnect all electrical wires from the carburetor, marking them for correct reinstallation if necessary.

WARNING ——

Fuel will be spilled during removal of the carburetor. Disconnect the battery ground strap to prevent accidental electrical sparks. Do not work near heaters or other fire hazards. Have a fire extinguisher handy.

5. Disconnect the fuel hose and the vacuum hoses from the carburetor. Plug the disconnected fuel hose with a screw, a pencil, or a golf tee.

6. Remove the bolts that hold the carburetor to the intake manifold. Then remove the carburetor and its gasket from the manifold.

Disassembling and Assembling Carburetor

In disassembling the carburetor, follow the exploded view of the carburetor that is supplied with the rebuilding kit. The jet sizes and other specifications for the carburetor can be determined from the table that appears in **11. Fuel and Exhaust Systems Technical Data.** If you are working on an early 1975 car that has not already been modified at factory expense by an Authorized Dealer, either have the modifications made or make the modifications yourself as described in the procedures that follow. Fig. 6-1 and Fig. 6-2 show the locations of the various jets.

1. Secondary full load enrichment
2. Primary air correction jet
3. Secondary air correction jet
4. Primary idle air and idle fuel jets
5. Secondary idle air and idle fuel jets
6. Primary auxiliary air jet and auxiliary fuel jet (fuel jet is below air jet)

Fig. 6-1. Locations of jets that are accessible after the air cleaner is removed.

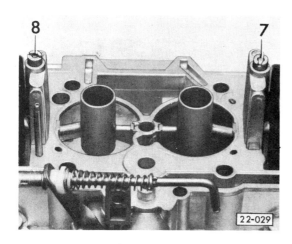

7. Primary main jet
8. Secondary main jet

Fig. 6-2. Locations of jets that are accessible after removing carburetor upper part.

The following basic sequence should be followed in disassembling the carburetor:

1. Remove the carburetor upper part from the carburetor body.

2. Remove the various jets and adjustment screws. Remove the float valve and the choke components from the carburetor upper part.

3. Disassemble the accelerator pump and linkage.

4. Take out the screws, and remove the throttle body and the spacer from the bottom of the carburetor body.

5. Remove the electromagnetic cutoff valve from the throttle body.

CAUTION ——

It is not recommended that you try to disassemble the throttle valves and shafts. The screws that hold the throttle valves to the shafts are peened and are likely to strip or break if you try to remove them.

With the exception of the choke heating element (on carburetors that have a supplemental electrical heating element), the pump diaphragm, the floats, the vacuum diaphragm, and similar nonmetallic parts, wash all old parts that are to be reused in lacquer thinner, acetone, or commercial carburetor cleaner.

WARNING ——

Do not smoke or work near heaters or other fire hazards. The cleaning agents are highly combustible.

Blow out all jets, valves, and drillings with compressed air. Do not clean them with pins or pieces of wire, which could upset the precise calibration of these parts. Assembly of the carburetor is the reverse of disassembly. As you assemble the carburetor, install the new components from the rebuilding kit, and carry out the adjustments described under the following unnumbered headings.

In obtaining new gaskets or a rebuilding kit, make certain that you have the correct gaskets. The large gasket that goes between the carburetor upper part and the carburetor body is different on 1976 models from the gasket used on 1975 models (Fig. 6-3).

3

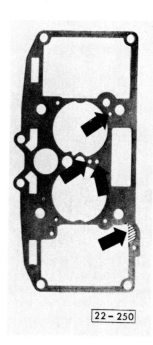

Fig. 6-3. Carburetor gasket changes. 1975 gasket on left (Part No. 055 129 281 A) has different arrangement of holes from 1976 gasket on right (Part No. 049 129 281).

If you are working on an early 1975 car and find that there is a hole in the carburetor flange gasket that does not align with a hole in the carburetor, you should drill a hole in the carburetor as shown in Fig. 6-4. This hole, which is factory-drilled in carburetors built since late 1975, allows moisture to drain from the choke linkage channel. Trapped moisture could freeze, causing the choke linkage to stick.

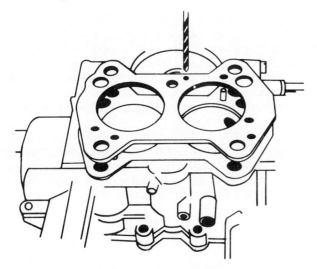

Fig. 6-4. Linkage channel drainage hole being drilled. Use gasket Part No. 055 129 341 A as a template. Use a 2-mm (or ¹/₁₆-in.) drill, and thoroughly clean out all metal shavings before assembling carburetor.

Installing, Checking, and Adjusting Automatic Choke

Check that the thermostatic spring is centered as indicated in Fig. 6-5. If the car is a 1975 model and does not already have the new-type choke cover with a thermo switch (Fig. 6-6), replace the choke cover with kit 055 198 580.

In installing the automatic choke, the end of the choke valve operating lever must be inserted between the two tabs on the spring end (Fig. 6-7). Install the choke cover and housing so that the index mark is aligned with the index mark on the choke housing of the carburetor.

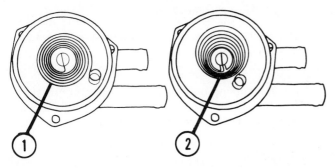

Fig. 6-5. Correctly centered thermostatic spring (**1**) and distorted spring (**2**). Replace choke cover if spring is not centered.

NOTE ——
If the catalytic converter has been eliminated as described in **9.1 Emission Controls for Engines with Carburetors**, adjust the index mark on the cover to a position that is about 5 mm (.20 in. or about ³/₁₆ in.) clockwise from the index mark on the choke housing of the carburetor.

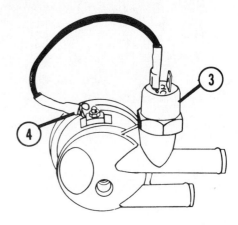

Fig. 6-6. Choke cover with thermo switch factory installed on 1976 cars. To service install on a 1975 car, connect short wire from kit between choke heating terminal (**4**) and thermo switch (**3**). Connect wire formerly attached to switch to other thermo switch terminal.

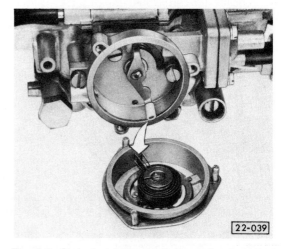

Fig. 6-7. Choke installation. End of operating lever must go between tabs on spring end, as indicated by arrow.

To test the thermo switch, use a battery-powered test light or an ohmmeter, as indicated in Fig. 6-8. At a coolant temperature below approximately 42° to 48°C (108° to 118°F), the test lamp should light or the ohmmeter should indicate 0 ohms. At coolant temperatures above approximately 52° to 58°C (126° to 136°F), the test lamp should not light or the ohmmeter should indicate infinite ohms.

Fig. 6-8. Ohmmeter being used to check automatic choke thermo switch.

Adjusting Throttle Valve Gaps

The throttle valve gaps need to be adjusted only if the factory settings have been unintentionally altered. Never move the throttle valve adjustments from their factory settings unless this is necessary during carburetor repairs. After you have adjusted either throttle valve, it is necessary to readjust the idle mixture (CO content) as described in **5.1 Adjusting Idle on Cars with Carburetors.**

To adjust primary throttle valve gap:

1. Remove the plastic cap from the slotted end of the throttle valve adjusting screw (Fig. 6-9).

Fig. 6-9. Plastic cap (arrow) on end of throttle valve adjusting screw.

2. Turn the adjusting screw out until there is a gap between the throttle valve lever and the screw.

3. Turn in the adjusting screw until it just contacts the throttle valve lever with the choke valve fully open and the throttle valve fully closed. Then turn the adjusting screw in one-quarter turn further so that there will be a slight amount of clearance between the throttle valve and the carburetor bore, thus preventing bore wear.

4. Reinstall the plastic cap on the slotted end of the adjusting screw.

To adjust secondary throttle valve gap:

1. Hold the choke valve fully open; hold both throttle valves fully closed.

2. Turn in the secondary throttle valve adjusting screw until there is no clearance noticeable between the activating cam and the roller. See Fig. 6-10.

3. From this no-clearance position, turn the adjusting screw out one-quarter turn—or as much as one-half turn in order to provide noticeable clearance at the lever.

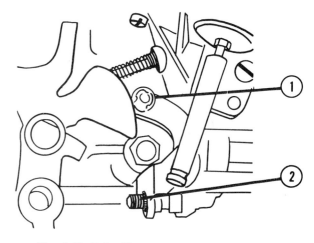

Fig. 6-10. Roller (**1**) and adjusting screw (**2**).

Adjusting Fast Idle

The fast idle setting must be adjusted any time the carburetor has been disassembled. A final check, with the engine running, should be made with the carburetor installed on the car.

To adjust fast idle (carburetor removed):

1. Hold the choke valve fully closed.

2. You should be able to insert a 0.45-mm (.018-in.) drill between the primary throttle valve and its bore

(Fig. 6-11), but you should not be able to insert a 0.50-mm (.020-in.) drill.

3. If the gap is not between 0.45 and 0.50 mm (.018 and .020 in.) as measured in step 2, adjust the gap by turning the screw indicated in Fig. 6-11.

Fig. 6-11. Drill being used to measure fast idle opening.

To adjust fast idle (carburetor installed):

1. Check that the ignition timing is correct. See **ENGINE AND CLUTCH.** Allow the engine to warm up fully.

2. Stop the engine. Remove the plastic cap (Fig. 6-12) from the fast idle adjusting screw.

3. On 1976 cars, detach the vacuum hose from the small choke pull-down vacuum unit (second stage). Then plug the hose.

4. Slightly open the throttle valve. Hold the choke valve fully closed; then release the throttle valve. When you release the choke valve, it should open fully, but the adjusting screw should rest on the full choke step as shown in Fig. 6-12.

Fig. 6-12. Fast idle adjusting screw resting on full choke step of fast idle cam. Arrow indicates plastic cap on adjusting screw.

5. Start the engine without touching the accelerator. Cars with manual transmissions should idle at 3150 to 3250 rpm; cars with automatic transmissions should idle at 3350 to 3450 rpm.

6. If the fast idle speed is outside the prescribed range, adjust it by turning the fast idle adjusting screw. Then install the plastic cap on the screw.

Adjusting 1975 Choke Vacuum Pull-down

Using the tip of a screwdriver, push the pull-down rod fully into the choke vacuum unit. With the pull-down rod in this position, hold the choke valve as nearly closed as possible. Then use a drill bit or gauge rod as shown in Fig. 6-13 to measure the gap between the choke valve and the air horn. The gap should be between 3.80 and 4.20 mm (.150 and .165 in.) on cars with no air injection diverter valve or 4.30 and 4.70 mm (.170 and .185 in.) on cars with a diverter valve. If the gap is not correct, adjust the vacuum pull-down by turning the screw indicated in Fig. 6-14.

Fig. 6-13. Vacuum pull-down being measured. Push pull-down rod in direction of arrow. Insert drill or gauge rod as shown.

Fig. 6-14. Choke vacuum pull-down adjusting screw (arrow).

Adjusting 1976 Choke Vacuum Pull-down

The 1976 models have a two-stage vacuum pull-down activated by two separate vacuum units. The large vacuum unit (Fig. 6-15) operates the first stage. To adjust, use the tip of a screwdriver to push the pull-down rod fully into the large vacuum unit. With the pull-down rod in this position, hold the choke valve lightly in its closed direction. Measured with a drill bit or gauge rod, the gap between the choke valve and the air horn should be 3.50 mm (.138 in.). If it is not, adjust the first stage pull-down by turning the screw in the center of the large vacuum unit. See Fig. 6-13 and Fig. 6-14 given earlier.

Fig. 6-16. Thermo-time vacuum valve (left arrow) and second stage choke pull-down vacuum unit (right arrow).

Fig. 6-15. Large vacuum unit (arrow) that operates first stage of choke vacuum pull-down.

The operation of the second stage choke pull-down vacuum unit is controlled by an electrically heated vacuum valve (thermo-time valve). This valve (Fig. 6-16) permits the second stage choke pull-down vacuum unit to operate only at temperatures above 9° to 19°C (48° to 66°F). With both the first stage and the second stage pull-down rods pressed fully into their respective vacuum units, the gap between the choke valve and the air horn should be 5.00 mm (.197 in.). If it is not, slightly bend the choke valve lever to obtain the correct gap.

You can check the thermo-time vacuum valve by cooling it to just below 9°C (48°F) and then trying to blow through it. No air should pass through. If the valve is closing correctly, repeat the test with the valve warmed to just above 19°C (66°F). Air should then pass through freely. (Between 9° and 19°C (48° and 66°F), the valve may be either open or closed.) There should be electrical continuity between the electrical connections when you test the valve's heating element with an ohmmeter or a battery-powered test light. Replace faulty valves.

Adjusting Accelerator Pump

The accelerator pump's injection quality is adjustable. The adjustment is made by turning a threaded adjusting sleeve that is on the end of the accelerator pump connecting link.

To measure the injection quantity, first be sure that the float bowl is filled with fuel. Then place a funnel in the top of a glass graduate and hold the carburetor over the funnel so that fuel expelled by the accelerator pump will run out of the carburetor's primary throttle bore and into the funnel. Slowly and steadily open the throttle valve exactly ten times—while holding the choke valve open. Divide the amount of fuel caught by ten to get the average quantity of a single injection pulse.

3 ■

The average quantity should be 0.75 to 1.05 cm^3 on 1975 USA cars with manual transmissions. On 1975 USA cars with automatic transmissions and on all 1976 USA and Canada cars with carburetors, the average quantity should be 0.60 to 0.90 cm^3 with no vacuum applied to the check valve (Fig. 6-17) or 1.30 to 1.70 cm^3 if you simulate engine vacuum by placing a hose on the check valve and sucking. On 1975 Canadian models, the average quantity should be 0.90 to 1.20 cm^3.

Fig. 6-17. Accelerator pump check valve (**2**). Vacuum to check valve is controlled by temperature valve on temperature valve manifold installed in heater hose. Temperature valve supplies vacuum below approximately 45°C (113°F) and cuts off vacuum above approximately 61°C (142°F).

If the injection quantity is not correct, turn the adjusting sleeve indicated in Fig. 6-18 either to increase or to decrease the injection quantity as required.

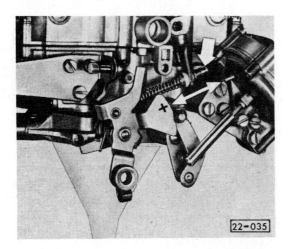

Fig. 6-18. Accelerator pump adjustment. Threaded adjusting sleeve is indicated by the broad arrow. Screw the sleeve further onto the connecting link to increase the quantity (+) or further off the link to decrease the quantity (−).

Recheck the injection quantity again after making the adjustment to see that it is within specifications. Best economy is obtained with the adjustment near the minimum specified quantity. Exhaust emissions will be adversely affected if the quantity is increased above the maximum.

The temperature-controlled check valve was not originally installed on 1975 cars with automatic transmissions. To install the valve in an unmodified carburetor, remove the plug, drill the jet orifice to 0.60 mm, and then blow out all shavings. Install the check valve as indicated in Fig. 6-19, and connect it to a new thermostatic valve, which is part of the modification kit. See **9.1 Emission Controls for Engines with Carburetors.** You should also check that the new-type discharge nozzle and the new-type acceleration pump rod spring are installed on all 1975 cars. Replace old-type parts with new-type parts. See Fig. 6-20.

CAUTION ——

For emission control reasons, you should retain the old-type discharge nozzle if the catalytic converter has been eliminated, as described in 9.1 Emission Controls for Engines with Carburetors.

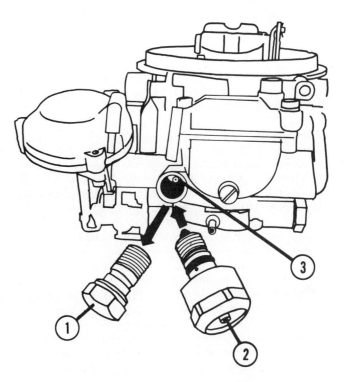

Fig. 6-19. Modification of 1975 carburetor for car with automatic transmission. Plug is at **1**, check valve at **2**, jet orifice at **3**.

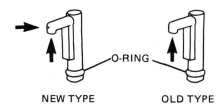

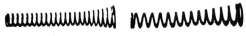

Fig. 6-20. Old-type and new-type acceleration pump system components. New-type discharge nozzle has two orifices, old-type has one (arrows).

Fig. 6-21. Float position being measured (dimension **a**) with needle valve fully seated.

3 ■

Checking Electromagnetic Cutoff Valve

The electromagnetic cutoff valve can be checked while it is installed. Turn on the ignition without starting the engine. Then remove the wire from the terminal on the electromagnetic cutoff valve. Touch the wire to the terminal several times. The valve should make a clicking sound each time contact is made.

The same test can be carried out with the electromagnetic cutoff valve removed from the car. Connect negative battery current to the valve's outer casing and apply positive battery current to the terminal. You may have to apply slight finger pressure to the electromagnetic cutoff valve before the plunger will retract.

Checking Fuel Level in Float Bowl

The carburetor upper part must be removed before you can check the float level. Invert the carburetor upper part. Then measure from the uppermost part of the float to the surface of the carburetor upper part to determine dimension **a,** as given in Fig. 6-21. Dimension **a** for the float on the carburetor's primary side should be 28 mm ±0.50 mm (1.102 in. ±.020 in.). Dimension **a** for the float on the carburetor's secondary side should be 30 mm ±0.50 mm (1.181 in. ±.020 in.). If necessary, correct the level by bending the tongue of the float hinge that contacts the needle valve.

Adjusting Dashpot

(when fitted)

Make sure that the choke valve is fully open and that the primary throttle valve is closed. Push the plunger fully into the dashpot. The gap between the plunger and the throttle valve arm should be 3 mm (or ⅛ in.). If it is not, loosen the dashpot mounting nuts and reposition the dashpot in its bracket until the gap is correct. Then tighten the nuts. See Fig. 6-22.

NOTE ——

If the dashpot is not already removed as part of the 1975 Quality Improvements program, you can remove it from 1975 cars with automatic transmissions. If the catalytic converter has been eliminated as described in **9.1 Emission Controls for Cars with Carburetors,** the dashpot should be retained. However, upon removal of the catalytic converter, the gap should be adjusted to 1 mm (.040 in.).

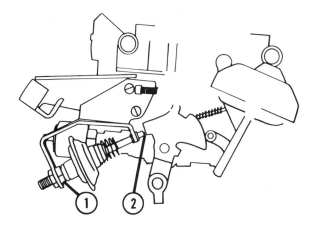

Fig. 6-22. Dashpot adjustment. Measure gap at **2** with dashpot plunger pressed in. Mounting nuts are at **1.**

Replacing and Adjusting
Secondary Throttle Valve Vacuum Unit

Replacement vacuum units for the secondary throttle valve must be adjusted during installation. Do this before you connect the vacuum unit operating rod to the throttle valve arm. Hold the choke valve fully open and both throttle valves fully closed. Then, by loosening the locknut and turning the operating rod, adjust the length of the vacuum unit operating rod until the ball socket in the rod extends 1 to 2 mm (or $1/32$ to $1/16$ in.) beyond the ball on the throttle valve arm. Then tighten the locknut and connect the operating rod to the ball. See Fig. 6-23.

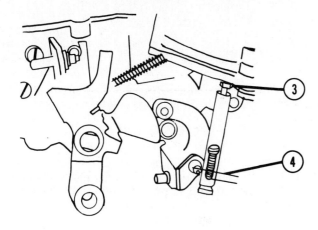

Fig. 6-23. Secondary throttle valve vacuum unit being adjusted. Locknut is at **3**. Dimension indicated at **4** should be 1 to 2 mm (or $1/32$ to $1/16$ in.).

Check that there is a vacuum delay jet for the secondary throttle valve vacuum unit. If this jet is not on the connection (Fig. 6-24), check whether there is a vacuum delay jet in the vacuum hose by blowing through it. If there is a delay jet in the hose, very little air will pass. If no vacuum delay jet is installed, install one in the hose, pressing it far enough into the hose to permit proper installation of the hose on the connection.

On all 1976 cars and on 1975 Canadian models with manual transmissions, the secondary throttle valve vacuum unit is supplied with vacuum only when the engine coolant temperature is 43° to 49°C (110° to 120°F) or above. The temperature valve that controls this vacuum supply must be closed at coolant temperatures below this point. You can check the temperature valve by blowing through it (Fig. 6-25).

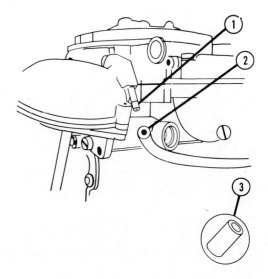

Fig. 6-24. Vacuum delay jet installation being checked. One kind of vacuum delay jet is shown at **1**. Another kind of jet (**3**) can be installed in hose (**2**).

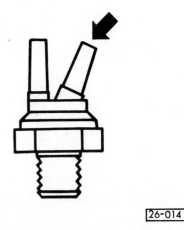

26-014

Fig. 6-25. Temperature valve being checked. Blow through as indicated by arrow.

Installing Carburetor

Lightly lubricate the choke valve shaft and the throttle valve shafts with engine oil and the external linkage with molybdenum grease. Using a new gasket, install the carburetor on the intake manifold. Then torque the bolts to 2.0 mkg (14 ft. lb.). Secure the fuel hose with a new hose clamp. Make sure that all wires and vacuum hoses have been installed in their correct locations. If necessary, consult **9. Emission Controls.**

After you have reconnected the accelerator cable, make certain that full throttle can be obtained before you install the air intake elbow. See **8. Accelerator Cable.** Torque the air intake elbow mounting nut to 1.0 mkg (7 ft. lb.). Replace the air intake duct if it is torn or otherwise damaged.

7. FUEL INJECTION TROUBLESHOOTING AND REPAIR

Before you begin troubleshooting or repairing the CIS (continuous injection system), you should be thoroughly familiar with the diagram and the general description of the system that appears in **1.2 Fuel Injection.** The system has very few electrical components, and a minimum knowledge of electrical circuits should suffice for troubleshooting purposes.

7.1 Troubleshooting Fuel Injection

Before you begin troubleshooting the fuel injection system, make sure that the engine trouble is not caused by something other than a fuel system problem. As with carburetors, no fuel injection test or adjustment should be made until you are confident that the engine has adequate compression and that the ignition system is not faulty.

Misfiring is not a typical symptom of a faulty fuel injection system. If you encounter misfiring—or if the car starts hard, fails to start, or has inadequate power—check for carbon tracking at the distributor rotor and distributor cap (Fig. 7-1) and the coil (Fig. 7-2). Replace faulty components. Also check the resistance of the spark plug connectors and the distributor rotor as described in **ENGINE AND CLUTCH.** Neither rotor nor connector resistance should exceed 10,000 ohms.

© 1975 VWoA—3835   © 1975 VWoA—3836

Fig. 7-1. Typical carbon tracks in distributor cap.

© 1975 VWoA—3837

Fig. 7-2. Typical carbon track on coil tower.

Finally, do not overlook incorrect valve clearances, faulty spark plugs, a dirty air cleaner, or a restricted exhaust system as possible causes of engine trouble. Because the fuel metering is highly dependent on the measurement of intake air volume, any air entering the engine that does not pass through the mixture control unit will cause the engine to operate incorrectly. Typically, it will start hard, idle slowly, or stall at idle, and give symptoms of lean operation at driving speeds. Look for a loose-fitting oil filler cap, leaking or disconnected ventilation hoses, or a leaking cylinder head cover gasket.

Troubleshooting Procedures

The Bosch CIS (continuous injection system) has been designed so that you can make all the necessary electrical tests using only a test lamp and an ohmmeter. In addition to these two electrical instruments, you will need a fuel pressure gauge to test the fuel pump and the control pressure regulator.

Do not try to correct engine trouble by adjusting the idle speed or the idle mixture (CO content). Changing these adjustments will hinder you in locating trouble in other parts of the fuel injection system. Before you adjust the idle on an engine that is not running right because of a fuel system problem, make a thorough inspection of the system in the following sequence:

1. Inspect the system visually for loose hoses, disconnected wires, and damaged components. See **7.2 Visual Inspection.**

2. Make electrical tests in order to determine whether current is reaching the right places at the right times. See **7.3 Electrical Tests.**

3. Make pressure tests and a pump delivery rate test so that you will know whether adequate fuel pressure is available under all conditions. See **7.4 Testing and Replacing Fuel Pump and Fuel Pressure Accumulator.**

4. Inspect the individual injection system components and test those that seem most likely to be trouble sources in light of the engine running conditions, the fuel pressure tests, and the electrical tests previously made. See headings **7.5** through **7.12.** Correct the trouble.

5. Adjust the idle. See **5.3 Adjusting Idle on Cars with Fuel Injection.**

Troubleshooting Table

As previously stated, you should always check the engine for ignition and mechanical problems before doing any fuel injection system troubleshooting. Make sure that there is fuel in the tank and that the battery is not run down.

Table c lists engine operating problems, their possible causes, and where the applicable fuel injection system troubleshooting or repair procedures can be found. The numbers listed after each possible cause indicate the

Table c. Fuel Injection System Troubleshooting

I. Engine hard to start or fails to start when cold (battery not discharged, starter current draw not excessive)
1. Cold-start valve not opening. See **7.8.**
2. Thermo-time switch defective. See **7.7.**
3. Wiring or pump relay faulty. See **7.3.**

II. Engine hard to start or fails to start when hot (battery not discharged, engine not overheated, oil supply and viscosity adequate)
1. Cold-start valve leaking or operating continuously. See **7.8.**
2. Control pressure regulator faulty. See **7.6.**
3. Wiring or pump relay faulty. See **7.3.**
4. Fuel leaks in the system. See **7.4.**

III. Engine fails to start under any condition (battery not discharged, fuel in tank)
1. Large air leaks. See **7.2.**
2. Insufficient fuel. See **7.4.**
3. Cold-start valve faulty. See **7.8.**
4. Thermo-time switch faulty. See **7.7.**
5. Decel valve faulty. See **9.2.**
6. Mixture control unit faulty. See **7.5.**
7. Auxiliary air regulator faulty. See **7.9.**
8. Control pressure regulator faulty. See **7.6.**

IV. Idle speed varies
1. Check idle speed and mixture (CO content). See **5.2.**
2. Small air leaks. See **7.2.**
3. Control pressure regulator faulty. See **7.6.**
4. Injection nozzles or nozzle seals faulty. See **7.10.**
5. EGR valve faulty or not being switched off at idle. See **9.2.**
6. Leaking fuel lines. See **7.11.**
7. Cold-start valve leaking. See **7.8.**
8. Mixture control unit faulty. See **7.5.**

V. Engine starts but stalls at idle
1. Control pressure regulator faulty. See **7.6.**
2. Cold-start valve leaking or operating continuously. See **7.8.**
3. Thermo-time switch faulty. See **7.7.**
4. Auxiliary air regulator faulty. See **7.9.**
5. "Engine warm" control pressure incorrect. See **7.4.**
6. Idle incorrectly adjusted. See **5.2.**

VI. Engine rpm fails to drop to idle speed when accelerator is released
1. Binding accelerator linkage or cable; lubricate linkage. See **8.**
2. Auxiliary air regulator not closing. See **7.9.**
3. Decel valve leaking. See **9.2.**

VII. Engine hesitates on acceleration (if engine backfires into intake air distributor, check engine for valve and other mechanical faults)
1. Air leaks. See **7.2.**
2. Injection nozzles not delivering uniform quantities. See **7.10.**
3. Fuel distributor faulty. See **7.5.**
4. Cold-start valve leaking. See **7.8.**
5. "Engine warm" control pressure incorrect. See **7.4.**
6. Idle mixture incorrectly adjusted. See **5.2.**

VIII. High fuel consumption
1. Leaking fuel lines. See **7.11.**
2. Control pressures incorrect. See **7.4.**
3. Control pressure regulator faulty. See **7.6.**
4. Cold-start valve leaking. See **7.8.**
5. Idle mixture incorrectly adjusted. See **5.2.**

IX. Engine continues to run after ignition is turned off
1. Sensor plate stuck above "off" position. See **7.5.**
2. Injection nozzles leaking. See **7.10.**
3. Fuel pressures excessive. See **7.4.**

headings in this section of the Manual where appropriate testing and repair instructions are described. Troubleshoot the possible causes in the order in which they appear. To troubleshoot fuel injection problems not covered by this table use the sequence given under the preceding heading.

7.2 Visual Inspection

You should inspect the entire system visually for fuel and air leaks before undertaking any adjustments or tests on the CIS (continuous injection system). Before you make any electrical tests, please read **7.3 Electrical Tests.** Unless you observe the precautions described there, you could accidentally damage solid-state components in the car. Loose wires that you may find during your visual examination can be reconnected so long as the ignition is turned off and you are sure that you are reconnecting the wires to their correct terminals. Fig. 7-3 and Fig. 7-4 show the locations of the various fuel injection components on the engine.

3

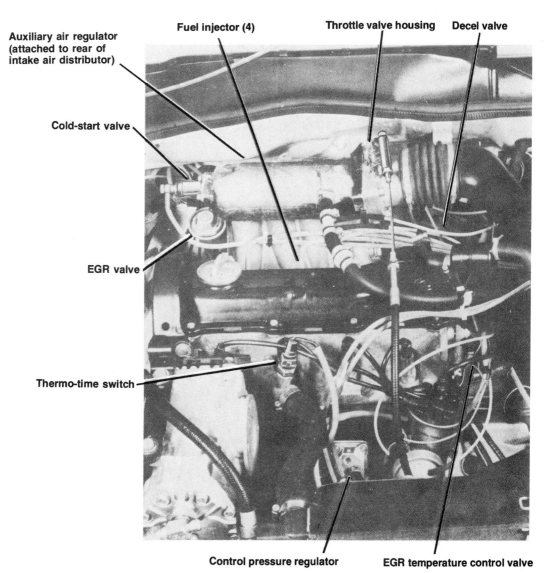

Auxiliary air regulator (attached to rear of intake air distributor)

Fuel injector (4)

Throttle valve housing   Decel valve

Cold-start valve

EGR valve

Thermo-time switch

Control pressure regulator

EGR temperature control valve

Fig. 7-3. Fuel injection components on engine. EGR valve, decel valve, and EGR temperature control valve are covered in **9.2 Emission Controls for Engines with Fuel Injection**.

Vacuum amplifier

**Mixture control unit
(air flow sensor and
fuel distributor)**

Fuel distributor

25·018

Fuel filter

Air flow sensor

Fig. 7-4. Fuel injection components located in left-hand side of engine compartment.

Checking Fuel Line Connections

Place the car on a hoist or support it on jack stands. Then check the fuel line connections at the fuel tank, the fuel pump, and the fuel pressure accumulator. With the car on the ground, check the connections at the fuel filter, shown previously in Fig. 7-4.

The other fuel line connections in the engine compartment can also be examined while the car is sitting on its wheels. Replace damaged fuel lines as described in **7.11 Replacing Plastic Fuel Lines.** If there are leaks around the banjo unions, torque them to no more than 1.0 mkg (7 ft. lb.) in an attempt to stop the leak. If torquing is not adequate to seal the leaking gasket, replace the gasket. Do not overtighten the union.

Checking Air System

Leaks in the air system that will affect engine operation are those that allow air to enter at some point between the mixture control unit's sensor plate and the engine's intake valves. Only a large air leak will prevent the engine from starting. Look for a torn or loose connecting duct between the mixture control unit and the throttle valve housing. The engine will start if there are only small leaks, such as from disconnected vacuum hoses, a loose-fitting oil filler cap, or a loose duct clamp. Typically, small air leaks will cause the engine to run or idle irregularly.

Any air leak in the critical area between the sensor plate and the intake valves will cause uncontrolled lean mixtures and result in poor engine output. Check especially the connecting duct, the hoses connected to the auxiliary air regulator, the intake air distributor flange gaskets, the air hose connections on the intake air distributor, the cold-start valve flange gasket, the injection nozzle seals, the vacuum lines at the vacuum-powered brake servo, the vacuum lines at the throttle valve housing and the vacuum amplifier, and the vacuum connection at the EGR valve. Make sure that the wires are connected to the auxiliary air regulator. Otherwise the auxiliary air regulator may not be closing completely.

7.3 Electrical Tests

The electrical testing of individual components is described under the heading for that component—for example, **7.8 Testing and Replacing Cold-start Valve.** In making electrical tests, refer to the current flow diagrams given in the Wiring Diagrams topic of **ELECTRICAL SYSTEM.**

Except for the cold-start valve, which receives current from terminal 50, all other electrical components of the fuel injection system receive positive current via the pump relay. This relay is located in the car's fuse/relay box. In making electrical tests, keep in mind that terminals numbered 30 are permanently connected to positive battery current. Terminals numbered 50 provide positive battery current only while the starter is being operated; they are connected to the control circuit of the starter solenoid. Terminals numbered 15 provide positive battery current whenever the ignition is turned on.

> *CAUTION* —
>
> *Before you make any electrical tests on an engine that is not running but has the ignition turned on, disconnect the positive wire from the alternator. Otherwise, testing may damage the alternator diodes. Disconnect the high tension cable from terminal 4 of the ignition coil so that the engine will not start when you run the starter.*

7.4 Testing and Replacing Fuel Pump and Fuel Pressure Accumulator

Absolute cleanliness is essential when you work with fuel circuit components of the CIS. Even a minute particle of dirt can cause trouble if it reaches an injector. Before you disconnect any of the fuel line connections, thoroughly clean the unions. Use clean tools.

Pressure Tests

Special care is required when you check the control pressure because the control pressure influences all engine operating characteristics, such as idle, partial throttle, and full throttle response, starting and warm-up, engine power, and emission levels.

To test "Engine cold" control pressure:

1. Disconnect the control pressure line from the center of the top of the fuel distributor. Connect the outlet hose of the pressure gauge's three-way valve to the fuel distributor in place of the control pressure line. See Fig. 7-5 and Fig. 7-6.

> **NOTE** —
>
> The engine must be completely cold for an "Engine cold" control pressure test. For this test, the vehicle should not be operated for several hours—preferably left unused overnight.

3 ∎

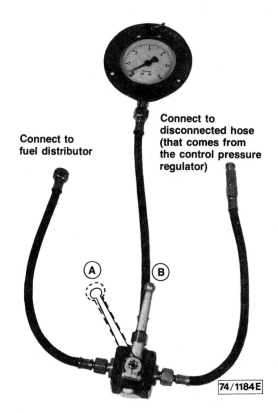

Connect to fuel distributor

Connect to disconnected hose (that comes from the control pressure regulator)

Ⓐ   Ⓑ

74/1184E

Fig. 7-5. Pressure gauge used for testing control pressures and system pressure and for detecting leakage.

Fig. 7-6. Pressure gauge correctly installed. Operating lever of three-way valve is at position **A**.

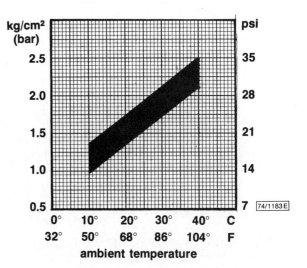

Fig. 7-7. Graph of acceptable "Engine cold" control pressures. For example, at 30°C (86°F), the "Engine cold" control pressure should be between 1.70 and 2.10 bar.

2. Connect the hose you disconnected from the fuel distributor to the inlet hose of the pressure gauge's three-way valve.

3. Disconnect the electrical plug from the control pressure regulator; disconnect the positive wire from the alternator.

4. Allow the pressure gauge to hang down so that the three-way valve is uppermost. This is necessary in order to bleed air from the pressure gauge.

5. Turn on the ignition so that the fuel pump runs. While the pump is running, move the operating lever on the three-way valve at 10-second intervals about five times between position **B** (flow blocked) and position **A** (flow to control pressure regulator).

6. With the gauge bled, hang the gauge from the hood so that it can be read easily. Start the engine and allow it to idle. Move the three-way valve to position **A** (flow to control pressure regulator). The pressure gauge reading should be in the nominal range for the corresponding ambient temperature, as shown in Fig. 7-7. If it is not, replace the control pressure regulator.

CAUTION ——

Run the engine for no more than one minute. If it is run for a longer time, this and subsequent tests may be inaccurate.

To test "Engine warm" control pressure:

1. Conduct the "Engine cold" test just described. If no fault is found, again turn on the ignition. Leave the three-way lever at position **A** (flow to control pressure regulator).

2. Observe the pressure gauge. As the warm running compensation heating element in the control pressure regulator warms up, the control pressure should rise and stabilize between 3.40 and 3.80 bar (48 and 54 psi).

3. If an "Engine warm" control pressure between 3.40 and 3.80 bar (48 to 54 psi) cannot be obtained, replace the control pressure regulator.

To check system pressure:

1. Move the three-way lever on the pressure gauge to position **B** (flow blocked) as shown in Fig. 7-8. By blocking the flow, the escape of fuel past the fuel distributor's pressure relief valve will be eliminated.

2. With the engine idling, the pressure should build up to 4.50 to 5.20 bar (64 to 74 psi).

3. If the system pressure is not within the prescribed range, check for leaks between the pump and the control pressure regulator. Clean, inspect, and adjust the pressure relief valve as described in **7.5 Testing and Repairing Mixture Control Unit.** Repeat the test.

Fig. 7-8. Pressure gauge three-way lever at position **B** (flow blocked).

NOTE——

If system pressure in the prescribed range still cannot be obtained, adjust or replace the fuel distributor as described in **7.5 Testing and Repairing Mixture Control Unit.** If the pressure is still out of tolerance, the fuel pump is probably faulty and should be replaced.

4. If the system pressure is within the prescribed range but the engine is operating with an excessively lean mixture, the pump's check valve may be faulty. To test the check valve, run the engine until the pressure is between 4.50 and 5.20 bar (64 and 74 psi). Then turn off the ignition. If the pressure drops below 1.8 bar (25 psi) within 10 minutes, replace the check valve as described later in the procedure for replacing the fuel pump and the fuel pressure accumulator.

5. If the system maintains pressure in the preceding test but the engine still operates with an excessively lean mixture, carry out the tests described in the next two procedures.

To pressure-test system for leaks:

1. Warm up the engine until the oil temperature is 50° to 70°C (122° to 158°F). Place the three-way lever at position **A** (Fig. 7-9).

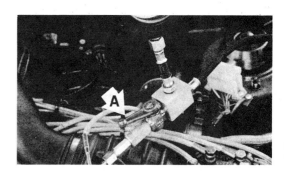

Fig. 7-9. Pressure gauge three-way lever at position **A** (flow to control pressure regulator).

2. Operate the starter or run the engine at idle until the pressure reading is 3.40 to 3.80 bar (48 to 54 psi). Then turn off the ignition.

3. Wait 10 minutes. At this time the gauge reading should be at least 1.80 bar (25 psi).

4. If the pressure does not drop below 1.80 bar (25 psi) in 10 minutes, increase the test time to 20 minutes.

5. If the pressure has not fallen below 1.60 bar (23 psi) after 20 minutes, repeat the entire test sequence with the pressure gauge three-way lever at position **B** (flow blocked).

6. If the pressure does not drop below 1.80 bar (25 psi) in 10 minutes or below 1.60 bar (23 psi) in 20 minutes with the three-way lever at position **B,** the control pressure regulator is faulty and should be replaced as described in **7.6 Testing and Replacing Control Pressure Regulator.**

7. If the pressure does drop excessively, even with the three-way lever at position **B,** check for leaks in the lines, the fuel distributor, the injectors, the cold-start valve, and the fuel pump—especially the fuel pump check valve. Replace faulty components.

3

To test fuel pump delivery rate:

1. Disconnect the high tension cable from terminal 4 of the ignition coil.

2. Disconnect the fuel return line from the fuel distributor.

> **WARNING ——**
>
> *Fuel will be expelled as you disconnect the union. Do not disconnect any wires that could cause electrical sparks. Do not smoke or work near heaters or other fire hazards. Have a fire extinguisher handy. Hold the end of the return line hose in an 800-cm³ or 1000-cm³ glass graduate (or a one-quart graduate). See Fig. 7-10.*

Fig. 7-10. Glass graduate being used to measure fuel delivery rate.

3. Run the starter for exactly 30 seconds so that the fuel pump operates for precisely that period of time.

4. If the fuel filter is not clogged—and if the pump is actually running—you should have collected at least 750 cm³ (about 24 oz.) of fuel during the 30 seconds of pump operation.

> **NOTE ——**
>
> If the pump did not run, make the test described later under **Fuel Pump Electrical Tests.** If the output was inadequate, replace the fuel filter as described in **3.2 Replacing Fuel Filter.** If the output is still inadequate, replace the pump.

Fuel Pump Electrical Tests

The following electrical tests should be made if the pump does not run or if it fails to deliver adequate volume or fuel pressure because of erratic pump operation. Before you make any other test, check the fuel pump

relay. Checking the relay will determine whether the fault is in the relay or in the pump and wiring.

To check pump relay:

1. Check the fuse for the electric fuel pump. This fuse is located atop the pump relay (Fig. 7-11).

Fig. 7-11. Fuel pump fuse atop relay (arrow).

2. Remove the cover from the fuse relay box. Remove the fuel pump relay. If necessary, consult **ELECTRICAL SYSTEM** in order to determine accurately the relay's location.

3. Make a test jumper such as the one shown in Fig. 7-12. Use 1.5 mm² (14-gauge) wire and an 8-amp fuse in the in-line fuse hold.

4. Turn on the ignition.

> **CAUTION ——**
>
> *Before you make any electrical tests on a car that is not running but has the ignition turned on, disconnect the positive wire from the alternator. Otherwise, testing may damage an alternator diode.*

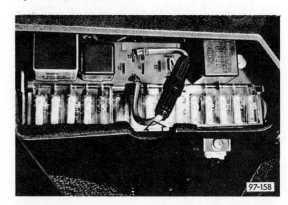

Fig. 7-12. Fuel pump relay being checked. Arrow indicates test jumper.

5. Using the test jumper, bridge terminals L13 and L14. If the pump did not run previously (or ran erratically) with the relay installed but runs

smoothly when the terminals are bridged, the relay is faulty and should be replaced. If the fuse blows or the fuel pump fails to run correctly, there is trouble in the pump or the wiring to the pump.

To determine whether current from the pump relay is reaching the fuel pump, install a pump relay that you know is in good condition. Alternatively, keep the test jumper installed between terminal L13 and terminal L14. Working under the car, disconnect the electrical plug from the fuel pump. Then, with the ignition turned on, measure the voltage at the disconnected wires with a voltmeter. If there is no voltage, there is a faulty wire or connection between the pump relay and the fuel pump. If the voltage is less than full battery voltage, there is a corroded connector or other high-resistance connection somewhere between the relay and the pump.

To test the fuel pump's current draw, disconnect the electrical plug from the pump and connect an ammeter in series between the disconnected positive wire and the pump terminal. Use a jumper wire to connect the negative wire to the other pump terminal. Then turn on the ignition so that the pump operates. The current draw indicated by the ammeter must not exceed 8.5 amperes. If the current draw is higher, replace the pump. Though the current draw is not excessive, you should still replace the pump if it fails to attain the minimum delivery rate prescribed earlier under **Pressure Tests.**

Replacing Fuel Pump and Fuel Pressure Accumulator

The fuel pressure accumulator and the fuel pump are located beneath the car, just ahead of the fuel tank. Each of these components can be removed separately. Both are held to the car body by bolts, as shown in Fig. 7-13.

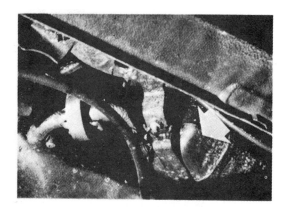

Fig. 7-13. Fuel pump (arrow) installed beneath car. Notice the bolt that holds the pump to the mounting bracket and the drum-shaped damper installed in the fuel intake hose.

To replace pump:

1. Make certain that the ignition is turned off. Disconnect the electrical connections from the fuel pump.

2. Thoroughly clean the fuel line unions before you disconnect them. Then disconnect both fuel lines from the pump. Quickly insert a rubber plug into the hose that comes from the tank.

   ***WARNING* ——**

   Fuel will be discharged as you disconnect the unions. Do not smoke or work near heaters or other fire hazards. Have a fire extinguisher handy.

3. Remove the bolts that hold the pump's sound-absorbing box to the mounting brackets. Then remove the box and pump.

4. Remove the fuel pump check valve. Remove the fuel pump from its sound-absorbing box.

Installation is the reverse of removal. See Fig. 7-14. If the electrical plug is broken, corroded, or otherwise damaged, replace it. Turn on the ignition after you have installed the pump so that you can check for leaks around the unions with the system under pressure.

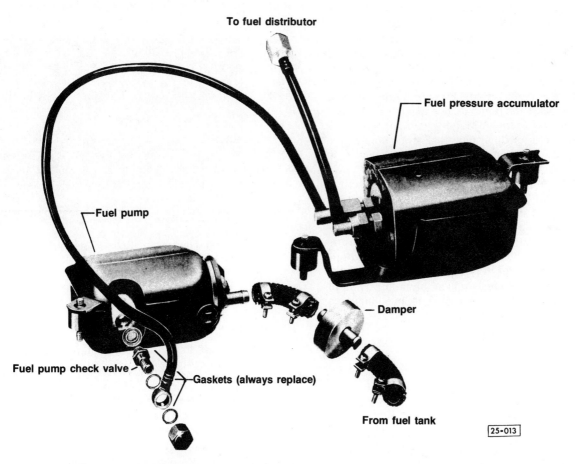

Fig. 7-14. Fuel pump and fuel pressure accumulator (shown in their sound-absorbing boxes). Damper isolates pump from fuel surges caused by movement of fuel in tank.

The fuel pressure accumulator should be replaced if it is leaking or if it fails to maintain residual pressure in the system for a few minutes after the engine has been turned off. The failure to maintain residual pressure can cause vapor lock. The fault is usually a ruptured diaphragm in the fuel pressure accumulator. See Fig. 7-15.

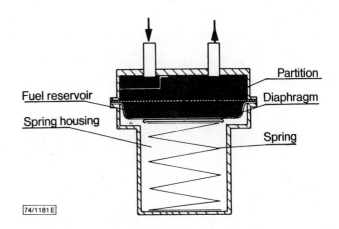

Fig. 7-15. Schematic cross-section of fuel pressure accumulator. The unit cannot be disassembled for repair.

To replace pressure accumulator:

1. Thoroughly clean the fuel line unions before you disconnect them from the fuel pressure accumulator.

2. Disconnect both fuel lines from the fuel pressure accumulator. To minimize the loss of fuel, quickly insert rubber plugs into the disconnected lines.

> **WARNING ——**
>
> *Fuel will be discharged as you disconnect the unions. Do not smoke or work near heaters or other fire hazards. Have a fire extinguisher handy.*

3. Remove the bolts that hold the fuel pressure accumulator's sound-absorbing box to the car body. Then remove the box and fuel pressure accumulator from the car.

4. Remove the fuel pressure accumulator from its sound-absorbing box.

Installation is the reverse of removal. Following installation, turn on the ignition so that the fuel pump operates. Check for leaks around the unions on the fuel pressure accumulator.

7.5 Testing and Repairing Mixture Control Unit

The mixture control unit governs the fuel/air ratio. It consists of an air flow sensor and the fuel distributor. The sensor plate of the air flow sensor is connected to the control plunger of the fuel distributor's metering unit. A simplified diagram of the mixture control unit is given in Fig. 7-16.

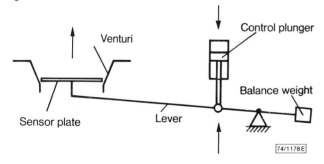

Fig. 7-16. Simplified diagram of mixture control unit.

As air enters from the air cleaner, it must pass between the sensor plate and its venturi before it can enter the connecting duct and flow toward the throttle valves. The balance weight partially offsets the weight of the lever and the sensor plate. The intake air lifts the air sensor plate until an equilibrium is reached between the air flow rate and the hydraulic counterpressure that acts on the lever through the control plunger.

The control plunger, in moving up or down in its cylinder, uncovers or covers the square-shaped metering ports of the fuel distributor's metering unit. Each injection outlet of the fuel distributor has its own metering port. Thus, the flow of fuel to the injectors is always metered in direct proportion to the quantity of air entering the engine.

A detailed layout of the fuel distributor's metering unit appears in Fig. 7-17. There are four of the steel-diaphragm, pressure-regulating valves—one for each injector hose outlet. These valves maintain a constant pressure drop in the metering ports regardless of fuel flow, fuel pump pressure, or injector opening pressure.

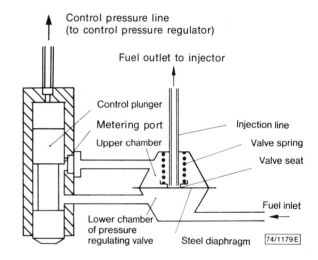

Fig. 7-17. Schematic layout of fuel distributor's metering unit.

To test mixture control unit:

1. Disconnect the connecting duct from the outlet of the mixture control unit's air flow sensor. This is the large rubber duct that connects the mixture control unit with the plastic duct that leads to the throttle valve housing.

2. Turn on the ignition for about five seconds so that the fuel pump will operate and pressurize the system. This pressure will press the fuel distributor metering unit's control plunger against the sensor plate lever.

3. Using a magnetic tool, lift the sensor plate by hand, as indicated in Fig. 7-18. There should be uniform resistance throughout the plate's entire range of travel. (With rapid downward movement, the lever will encounter more resistance because of the residual hydraulic pressure being exerted on the control plunger.)

Fig. 7-18. Magnetic tool being used to raise and lower sensor plate.

4. If the sensor plate is hard to move or moves with uneven resistance, remove the top of the air flow sensor in order to determine why the sensor plate is hard to move. If the pivot is dirty or lacks lubrication, you should clean and relubricate it so that it moves smoothly.

5. If the resistance encountered in moving the sensor plate is caused by a binding control plunger, replace the fuel distributor as described in the next two steps. Faulty control plungers cannot be replaced separately because each plunger is a precision fit with its own fuel distributor.

6. To replace the fuel distributor, first disconnect the fuel line banjo unions from the old fuel distributor.

WARNING ——

Fuel will be expelled as you remove the unions. Do not smoke or work near heaters or other fire hazards. Have a fire extinguisher handy.

7. Remove the screws that hold the fuel distributor to the cover of the air flow sensor housing (Fig. 7-19).

8. Remove the old fuel distributor. Then, using a new gasket (Fig. 7-20), install the new fuel distributor.

Adjust the idle speed and CO volume percentage as described in **5.2 Adjusting Idle on Cars with Fuel Injection.**

Fig. 7-19. Screws (arrows) that hold fuel distributor to air flow sensor.

Fig. 7-20. Gasket for fuel distributor. In installing the fuel distributor on the air flow sensor housing, torque the screws to 35 to 40 cmkg (30 to 35 in. lb.).

CAUTION ——

The control plunger can fall out of the fuel distributor easily (Fig. 7-21). It is best to hold the cover of the air flow sensor housing in an inverted position during removal or installation of the fuel distributor. If the plunger of the new fuel distributor falls, it may be damaged —thereby rendering the entire fuel distributor unserviceable. Always wash the plunger with gasoline before you install it in the fuel distributor.

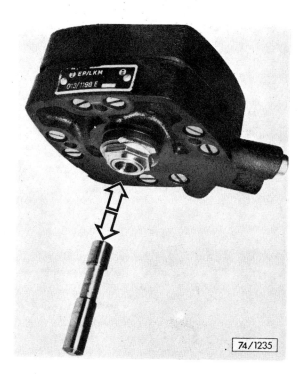

Fig. 7-21. Control plunger and fuel distributor. The plunger can be removed easily or inserted, as indicated by the arrows. Notice that the longest land on the plunger goes toward the air flow sensor.

9. If the sensor plate moved with uniform resistance in step 3, check the rest position of the sensor plate. Before you can do this, you must depressurize the system by loosening the control pressure line union at the control pressure regulator.

   NOTE ——

   The control pressure regulator is located on the front side of the engine block. The control pressure line is the fuel line that connects the control pressure regulator with the center of the top of the fuel distributor.

   WARNING ——

   Fuel will be expelled as you loosen the union. Do not smoke or work near heaters or other fire hazards. Have a fire extinguisher handy.

10. With the system depressurized, the edge of the sensor plate nearest the fuel distributor should be aligned with the narrowest point of the venturi, as indicated in Fig. 7-22. If the sensor plate is higher, or more than 0.50 mm (.020 in.) lower, correct the position as described in the next three steps.

11. Take out the screws. Then remove the cover from the air flow sensor.

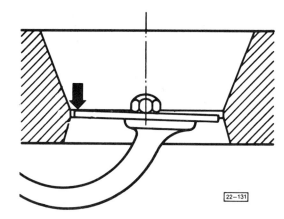

Fig. 7-22. Sensor plate correctly aligned (arrow) with narrowest part of venturi.

3

12. By bending the wire clip indicated in Fig. 7-23, adjust the spring stop so that the sensor plate is correctly aligned with the narrowest point of the venturi when the sensor plate is in its rest position.

13. Use a new gasket when you install the cover on the air flow sensor.

Fig. 7-23. Wire clip (arrow).

Adjusting System Pressure

During manufacture of the fuel distributor, the system pressure is preset by the installation of the correct shims behind the pressure relief valve spring (Fig. 7-24). If the system pressure is not between 4.50 and 5.20 bar (64 and 74 psi) when tested as described in **7.4 Testing and Replacing Fuel Pump and Fuel Pressure Accumulator,** you may be able to correct the system pressure by installing different shims. The addition or removal of a 0.10-mm shim will change the system pressure by approximately 0.06 bar (about 1 psi). The addition or removal of a 0.50-mm (.020-in.) shim will change the system pressure by approximately 0.30 bar (about 4 psi). If you cannot adjust the fuel distributor, replace it.

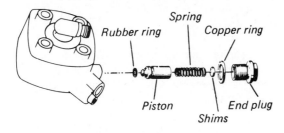

Fig. 7-24. Exploded view of pressure relief valve, showing location of adjusting shims.

Removing and Installing Mixture Control Unit

Fig. 7-25 is an exploded view of the entire fuel injection system. Before the mixture control unit can be disassembled as shown, you must remove it from the car using the procedure given here. If you must remove the fuel distributor, use the procedure given earlier.

To remove:

1. Thoroughly clean the fuel unions on the fuel distributor. Then disconnect all fuel lines from the fuel distributor. Attach tags to the removed banjo unions so that later you will be able to install them in their original positions.

WARNING ——

Fuel will be discharged as you remove the unions. Disconnect the battery ground strap. Do not smoke or work near heaters or other fire hazards. Have a fire extinguisher handy.

2. Loosen the hose clamp. Then disconnect the connecting duct from the air flow sensor outlet. Disconnect the crankcase ventilation hose from the air cleaner top part.

3. Using the tip of a screwdriver, snap loose the retainers that hold the bottom part of the air cleaner to the bracket on the car body. Steady the mixture control unit as you loosen the retainers so that the unit does not fall.

4. Being careful not to damage the intake air preheating duct as you disengage it from its connection on the air cleaner, remove the mixture control unit and the air cleaner from the car.

Installation is the reverse of removal. After you have reinstalled the mixture control unit, connect the battery ground strap. Then turn on the ignition so that the fuel pump operates. Check for leaks at the fuel line unions on the fuel distributor. Following installation of a new or a repaired mixture control unit, you must adjust the idle as described in **5.3 Adjusting Idle on Cars with Fuel Injection.**

3

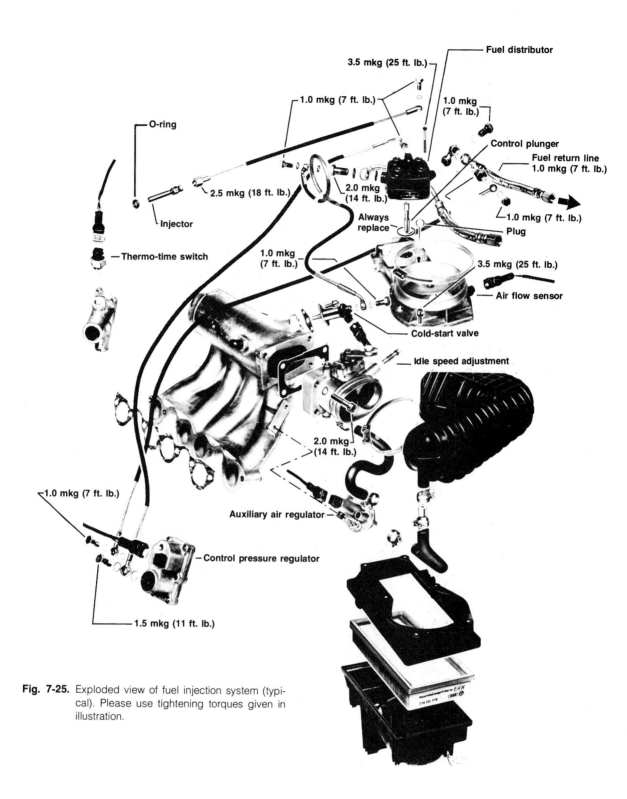

Fig. 7-25. Exploded view of fuel injection system (typical). Please use tightening torques given in illustration.

7.6 Testing and Replacing Control Pressure Regulator

To test the control pressure regulator, use the "Engine cold" and "Engine warm" control pressure tests described in **7.4 Testing and Replacing Fuel Pump and Fuel Pressure Accumulator.** Replace the control pressure regulator if it fails to maintain fuel pressures that are within the prescribed ranges.

Fig. 7-26 is a schematic diagram that shows the relationship of the control pressure regulator to the fuel distributor's metering unit. If the pressure on the top of the control pressure regulator's diaphragm increases because of the wider metering port openings in the fuel distributor, the control pressure regulator's diaphragm is pressed down—thus allowing more fuel to flow to the injectors. As the diaphragm's movement increases the flow to the injectors, the increased pressure from the fuel distributor is relieved, and the pressure in the system is balanced to maintain its regulated level. The control pressure regulator therefore serves to permit increases or reductions in the quantity of fuel delivered to the injectors without any change in the pressure at the nozzles.

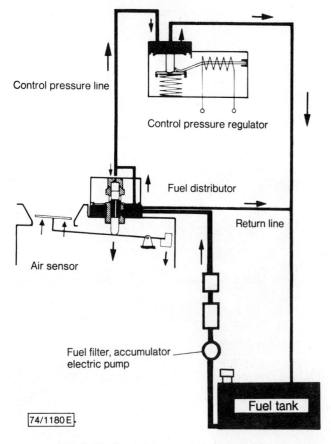

Fig. 7-26. Schematic diagram of control pressure regulator and related components. Notice the electrical heating element wound around the thermostatic spring of the control pressure regulator.

A coil spring exerts pressure on the diaphragm of the control pressure regulator. The coil spring pressure works counter to the fuel pressure. When the engine is cold, a flat thermostatic spring works in conjunction with the fuel pressure to compress the coil spring. This increases the quantity of fuel flowing to the injectors—thereby preventing the excessively lean mixture that would otherwise result from the cold air that is entering the engine.

As the engine and engine oil warm up, the thermostatic spring is deflected, placing less compressing force on the coil spring. The coil spring then exerts greater pressure on the diaphragm, reducing the quantity of fuel reaching the injectors.

In addition to responding to heat from the engine and engine oil, the control pressure regulator's thermostatic spring responds to an electrical heating element. This heating element prevents the fuel pressure from remaining high for an excessively long period of time in cold weather. The following electrical tests should be made to detect trouble in the warm running compensation heating element.

To test heating element:

1. Disconnect the positive wire from the alternator. Turn on the ignition without starting the engine.

2. Disconnect the electrical plug from the control pressure regulator. Then measure the voltage available at the plug.

3. If there was no voltage at the electrical plug when you made the test described in step 2, test the pump relay as described in **7.3 Electrical Tests.** If voltage is available at the pump relay, then there is trouble in the wire that connects the control pressure regulator plug with the relay.

4. If voltage is reaching the electrical plug correctly, test the heating element with an ohmmeter as indicated in Fig. 7-27. If the heating element is open

Fig. 7-27. Terminals on control pressure regulator (arrow) where ohmmeter test should be made.

(infinite ohms) or if the resistance is greatly more or less than the normal 20 ohms, replace the control pressure regulator.

To replace control pressure regulator:

1. Disconnect the fuel unions from the control pressure regulator.

> ***WARNING***
>
> *Fuel will be expelled as you disconnect the unions. Disconnect the battery ground strap. Do not smoke or work near heaters or other fire hazards. Have a fire extinguisher handy.*

2. Disconnect the electrical plug from the control pressure regulator.

3. Remove the bolts that hold the control pressure regulator to the engine block. Remove the regulator and its gasket.

Installation is the reverse of removal. Use a new gasket. Torque the mounting bolts to 1.5 mkg (11 ft. lb.).

7.7 Testing and Replacing Thermo-time Switch

The thermo-time switch (Fig. 7-28) controls the operation of the cold-start valve. When the engine temperature is above the cutoff temperature stamped on the hexagon of the thermo-time switch, the cold-start valve does not inject fuel during starter operation. If the starter is operated for longer than normal, the thermo-time switch cuts off the cold-start valve in order to prevent engine flooding. The time limit is also stamped on the hexagon of the thermo-time switch. It is not possible to check the timing and cutoff temperature exactly with normal workshop equipment.

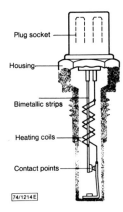

Fig. 7-28. Cross-section of thermo-time switch. The contact points are opened either by engine heat or, if the starter is operated for a longer-than-normal period of time, by the electrical heating coils.

To test thermo-time switch:

1. Make sure that the temperature of the engine coolant is below 35°C (or 95°F). If necessary, allow the engine to sit overnight, or cool the thermo-time switch with ice. The location of the thermo-time switch is shown in Fig. 7-29.

Fig. 7-29. Location of thermo-time switch (arrow).

2. Carefully disconnect the electrical plug from the cold-start valve. Disconnect the ignition high-tension cable from terminal 4 of the ignition coil in order to prevent the engine from starting.

3. Attach the leads of a test lamp or a voltmeter to the terminals of the disconnected plug (Fig. 7-30). Operate the starter without interruption for 10 to 15 seconds. The test lamp should first light brightly and then become noticeably dimmer—or go out—after one to eight seconds of starter operation. Alternatively, the voltmeter should at first indicate battery voltage and then fall off toward zero.

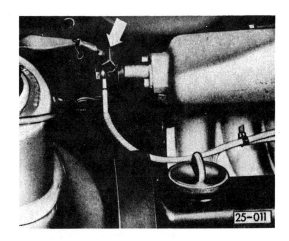

Fig. 7-30. Electrical plug (arrow) on cold-start valve.

4. If the test lamp does not light at all, attach one of the test lamp leads to ground on some clean, unpainted metal part of the engine. The other lead should remain connected to one of the plug terminals.

5. Operate the starter. If the test lamp does not light, repeat the test with the test lamp connected to the other terminal of the disconnected plug. If the lamp does not light in either test, the wiring to the starter solenoid is faulty.

> **NOTE** ——
>
> If the test lamp lights whether the starter is operating or not, someone has misconnected the wires at the starter solenoid, installing the wire that belongs on terminal 50 on terminal 30 instead.

6. If battery current is reaching the plug, but the test lamp did not light when the starter was operated in step 3, the thermo-time switch is faulty and should be replaced.

To replace thermo-time switch:

1. Drain the cooling system as described in conjunction with replacing hoses in **ENGINE AND CLUTCH.**

> *CAUTION* ——
>
> *Do not drain the coolant while the engine is hot. Doing this could warp the cylinder head or the engine block.*

2. Disconnect the electrical plug from the thermo-time switch.

3. Using a socket wrench, unscrew the thermo-time switch from the radiator hose connection.

4. Install a new thermo-time switch in the hose connection. Reconnect the electrical plug to the thermo-time switch. Then refill the cooling system as described in **ENGINE AND CLUTCH.**

7.8 Testing and Replacing Cold-start Valve

The cold-start valve (Fig. 7-31), sometimes called the fifth injector, sprays fuel into the intake air distributor only during the first few seconds of starter operation and only when the engine and the surrounding air are cold. The valve's operation is controlled by the thermo-time switch and by current from terminal 50 of the starter solenoid. The cold-start valve is located at the extreme right-hand end of the intake air distributor.

If the cold-start valve fails to inject fuel during the cranking of a cold engine, it will be difficult or impossible to start the engine. If the cold-start valve is leaky, the engine may flood during starting, especially if the engine is hot.

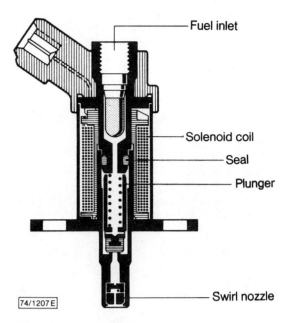

Fig. 7-31. Cross-section of cold-start valve.

To test cold-start valve:

1. Carefully disconnect the electrical plug from the cold-start valve. Put tape over the plug terminals to prevent accidental electrical sparks. Disconnect the positive wire from the alternator.

2. Remove the two screws that hold the cold-start valve to the intake air distributor. Remove the valve from the intake air distributor but leave the fuel hose connected to the valve.

3. Disconnect the ignition high-tension cable from terminal 4 of the ignition coil so that the engine will not start.

4. Wipe dry the nozzle of the cold-start valve. Turn on the ignition so that the fuel pump operates. No drops of fuel should form on the nozzle within one minute from the time that the pump begins to operate.

> *WARNING* ——
>
> *Do not smoke or work near heaters or other fire hazards. Have a fire extinguisher handy.*

5. If the cold-start valve leaks fuel when the ignition is on, owing to normal pressure from the fuel pump, replace the cold-start valve.

6. If the valve did not leak, reconnect the electrical plug to the cold-start valve. Then disconnect the electrical plug from the thermo-time switch and, using a jumper wire, bridge the two terminals of the disconnected plug.

7. To test the cold-start valve's operation, place the

cold-start valve above a glass receptacle as shown in Fig. 7-32. This will permit you to examine the spray pattern without spilling the fuel that is expelled.

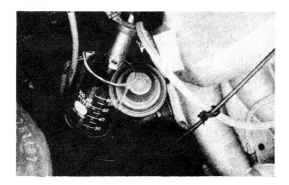

Fig. 7-32. Cold-start valve operation being checked.

WARNING —

Fuel will be expelled. Do not smoke or work near heaters or other fire hazards. Have a fire extinguisher handy.

8. Have someone operate the starter while you observe the spray from the cold-start valve. The valve should spray fuel in an even conical pattern. An irregular pattern indicates a dirty or damaged valve, which should be replaced.

9. If the cold-start valve is working correctly, it can be reinstalled on the intake air distributor. Test the termo-time switch if you suspect that the cold-start valve is failing to operate when the engine is cold.

10. If no fuel is expelled from the cold-start valve during starter operation, disconnect the electrical plug from the cold-start valve. Then connect one lead of a test lamp or a voltmeter to the positive plug terminal (Fig. 7-33). Connect the other test lead to ground on some clean, unpainted metal part of the engine.

11. Operate the starter. If the test lamp does not light or the voltmeter indicates no battery voltage, the wiring to the starter solenoid terminal 50 is faulty or the pump relay is faulty.

12. To check the fuel pump relay, remove it from the relay plate of the fuse box. Then make a test jumper using 1.5 mm² (14-gauge) wire and an 8-amp fuse in an in-line fuse holder. Use the jumper to bridge terminals L13 and L14. See Fig. 7-34.

13. Operate the starter. If the test lamp failed to light or if there was no voltage in step 11 but now there is voltage or the light operates, the pump relay is faulty and should be replaced.

Fig. 7-33. Plug for cold-start valve. Negative terminal is grounded by thermo-time switch. The test described here is made independently of the thermo-time switch.

Fig. 7-34. Test jumper with fuse (arrow) being used in place of fuel pump relay.

14. If battery current is reaching the cold-start valve but the valve does not operate, the valve is faulty and should be replaced. You can also use an ohmmeter to test for continuity between the two terminals on the cold-start valve. If there is no continuity, the valve is definitely faulty.

To replace cold-start valve:

1. Disconnect the electrical plug from the cold-start valve. Disconnect the fuel union.

WARNING —

Fuel will be expelled as you remove the union. Disconnect the battery ground strap. Do not smoke or work near heaters or other fire hazards. Have a fire extinguisher handy.

2. Remove the two screws that hold the cold-start valve to the intake air distributor. Then remove the cold-start valve and its gasket.

3. Install the new cold-start valve and a new gasket. Then reconnect the fuel union, the electrical plug, and the battery ground strap. Reconnect any other wires that you removed earlier during testing.

7.9 Testing and Replacing Auxiliary Air Regulator

Fig. 7-35 is a schematic view of the auxiliary air regulator. When open, a rotary valve in the auxiliary air regulator provides additional air—and consequently additional fuel—during engine warm-up. The auxiliary air regulator's function in the air system is shown in Fig. 1-2 in **1.2 Fuel Injection.**

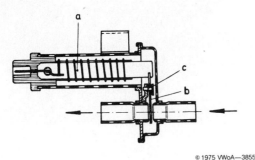

a. Bimetallic strip	b. Rotary valve	c. Pivot

Fig. 7-35. Schematic view of auxiliary air regulator. Arrows indicate air flow through valve.

On the car, the auxiliary air regulator is located on the right-hand rear side of the intake air distributor (Fig. 7-36). When the engine is started, current from the pump relay begins to warm the heating element that is wound around the auxiliary air regulator's bimetallic strip. Heat—whether from the heating element or from hot air surrounding the engine—causes the bimetallic strip to deflect gradually, closing the rotary valve and cutting off the additional air.

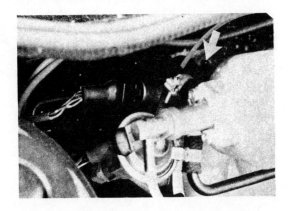

Fig. 7-36. Auxiliary air regulator on engine's intake air distributor (arrow).

To test the auxiliary air regulator, disconnect both hoses from it. Also disconnect the positive wire from the alternator. Turn on the ignition. After about five minutes, the rotary valve of the auxiliary air regulator should be closed completely—if you are working in a workshop that is heated to room temperature. You can check this by looking through the auxiliary air regulator with the aid of a mirror. See Fig. 7-37.

Fig. 7-37. Inspection point for auxiliary air regulator (arrow). You should be able to see the rotary valve close by looking into the hose connections (regulator removed for clarity).

If the auxiliary air regulator does not close after five minutes (outside, in cold weather, considerably more time may be required), stop the engine. Disconnect the electrical plug from the auxiliary air regulator. Using an ohmmeter, measure the resistance between the terminals on the auxiliary air regulator. The reading should be 30 ohms. If the ohmmeter reads infinity or if the resistance is considerably less than 30 ohms, replace the auxiliary air regulator.

If the auxiliary air regulator resistance is in the correct range, use a test light as shown in Fig. 7-38 to determine whether battery voltage is reaching the heating element while the engine is running. If it is not, you should make further tests at the pump relay.

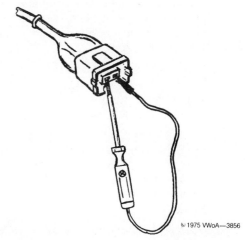

Fig. 7-38. Test light being used to check for current at the auxiliary air regulator plug while engine is running.

To replace auxiliary air regulator:

1. Disconnect both air hoses from the auxiliary air regulator.

2. Disconnect the electrical plug from the auxiliary air regulator. Then remove the two screws that hold the auxiliary air regulator to the intake air distributor.

3. Remove the old auxiliary air regulator. Then install the new auxiliary air regulator using a reverse of the removal procedure.

7.10 Checking and Replacing Injectors

The injectors are held in the manifold tubes of the intake air distributor by their rubber seals. You can remove individual injectors by pulling them out as indicated in Fig. 7-39. By removing an injector, you can check its operation with the ignition turned on.

Fig. 7-39. Injector being removed. Pull straight out as indicated by arrow.

To check injector:

1. Remove one injector from the manifold tube, leaving the fuel hose attached to the injector. Pull the injector straight out, as indicated previously in Fig. 7-39.

2. Remove the fuel pump relay and bridge relay plate terminals L13 and L14 with the fused jumper wire, shown previously in Fig. 7-34.

3. Remove the rubber duct from the top of the mixture control unit. Turn on the ignition without starting the engine.

4. Point the injector into a glass jar. Then, using the magnetic tool as indicated in Fig. 7-40, lift the sensor plate and observe the injector's spray pattern, which should be even and cone-shaped.

WARNING ——

Fuel will be discharged during this check. Do not smoke or work near heaters or other fire hazards. Have a fire extinguisher handy.

Fig. 7-40. Magnetic tool being used to lift sensor plate.

5. Turn off the ignition. Hold the injector in a horizontal position. It must not drip fuel.

6. If any injector has an irregular spray pattern or if it dribbles fuel after the ignition is turned off, replace the injector.

7. In installing an injector in the manifold tube, first moisten the rubber seal with gasoline. Soak new seals in gasoline for several minutes before installing them. Then press the injector fully into its seat.

If the idle speed varies, there may be air leaks around the injectors where they are pressed into the engine. Replace the rubber seals. If you suspect that the four injectors are not delivering equal amounts of fuel because of foreign matter in the injectors or defective injector valves, replace all four injectors and hoses with new ones. This is the only sure test for faulty injectors. Run the engine in order to determine whether the new injectors have cured the operating problem.

To replace injector:

1. Pull the injector straight out of its seat in the manifold tube. See Fig. 7-39 given earlier.

2. Detach the union that holds the fuel line to the injector and remove the injector from the fuel line.

WARNING ——

Fuel will be discharged as you disconnect the fuel line union. Do not smoke or work near heaters or other fire hazards. Have a fire extinguisher handy.

3. If you intend to install a new injector—or if the old rubber seal is hard, cracked, deformed, or other-

wise damaged—remove the rubber seal from the injector.

4. Thoroughly clean the holes in the engine, removing all loose dirt and hardened foreign matter.

Installation is the reverse of removal. Before you install the rubber seal, soak it in gasoline for a few minutes. Always lubricate the seals with fuel before you press the injectors into the engine. Torque the fuel line union to 2.5 mkg (18 ft. lb.).

7.11 Replacing Plastic Fuel Lines

The special tool shown in Fig. 7-41 is used for installing new plastic fuel lines on the banjo unions or at other points. Damaged fuel injection lines should always be replaced. Do not attempt to repair them.

Fig. 7-41. Special tool used for installing new plastic fuel lines. This tool will install lines of two different diameters.

To remove a plastic fuel line, heat it with a soldering iron as shown in Fig. 7-42. If the line has a braided sheath, push back the sheath before you apply the soldering iron.

WARNING ——

Do not heat the fuel line with a torch or other open flame. This could cause a fire or explosion. Never cut the old lines open, because this would damage the cone-shaped connections on the unions or adaptors, causing incurable leakage.

Use the special tool to install the new plastic fuel line, as shown in Fig. 7-43. The new fuel line should protrude from the tool for a distance that is equal to the length of

the cone-shaped connection on the union or adaptor. Grip the plastic line in the tool by tightening the wing nut.

CAUTION ——

Never heat the new plastic fuel line preparatory to installation. Doing this may prevent a tight fit. The fuel line should be shoved onto the connection cold. Once removed, it should not be reinstalled. Replace removed plastic lines.

Fig. 7-42. Plastic fuel line being heated with soldering iron (**a**). Car is not one of those covered by this Manual.

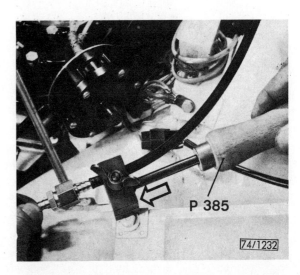

Fig. 7-43. New plastic fuel line being shoved onto connection.

7.12 Removing and Installing Throttle Valve Housing and Intake Air Distributor

The intake air distributor of cars with fuel injection is the part that corresponds to the intake manifold of cars with carburetors. Normally, you will need to remove the intake air distributor only when you are preparing to remove the cylinder head. If you must remove the intake air distributor with the engine installed, follow the procedure given here.

To remove:

1. Disconnect the battery ground strap.

2. Loosen the clamps. Then completely remove the rubber and plastic ducts that connect the throttle valve housing with the mixture control unit.

3. Disconnect all hoses from the intake air distributor and the throttle valve housing. Mark each hose as you remove it so that you will be able to install it in its original location.

4. Remove the cable-end clamp. Then disconnect the accelerator cable from the throttle valve lever. If necessary, consult **8. Accelerator Cable.**

5. Disconnect the EGR pipe and the vacuum hose from the EGR valve. Then remove the bolts, and take the EGR valve off the intake air distributor.

6. Remove all four injectors as described in **7.10 Checking and Replacing Injectors.**

7. Remove the cold-start valve as described in **7.8 Testing and Replacing Cold-start Valve.**

8. For working clearance, remove the decel valve. See **9.2 Emission Controls for Engines with Fuel Injection.**

   NOTE ——

   If you intend to remove the throttle valve housing from the intake air distributor, you can do this without removing the intake air distributor. In fact, prior removal of the throttle valve housing will make removal of the intake air distributor easier.

9. Working in the engine compartment, remove the two outermost socket-head bolts that hold the intake air distributor to the cylinder head.

10. Working beneath the car, remove the four remaining socket-head bolts that hold the intake air distributor to the cylinder head. Then remove the intake air distributor and its gasket from the engine.

Installation is the reverse of removal. Thoroughly clean all old gasket material from the port face of the cylinder head and from the manifold tube flange of the intake air distributor. Use a new gasket when you install the intake air distributor on the engine. Torque the socket-head bolts to 2.5 mkg (18 ft. lb.). Use a new gasket on the cold-start valve and new rubber seals, soaked in gasoline, on the injectors.

Adjust the accelerator cable as you install it, using the procedure described in **8. Accelerator Cable.** When installation of all components is complete, adjust the idle as described in **5.2 Adjusting Idle on Cars with Fuel Injection.**

8. ACCELERATOR CABLE

A number of different accelerator cables have been used on the cars covered by this Manual. In replacing an accelerator cable or, on cars with automatic transmissions, an accelerator cable or a throttle cable, it is wise to take along the old cable for comparison with the replacement cable. In addition, be sure that you have written down your car's chassis number, which will help the parts department to determine the correct replacement cable for the vehicle.

The removal and installation of the cable on its brackets and levers will be obvious from an examination of the car. During installation, adjust the cable(s) as described in **8.1 Adjusting Accelerator Cable.**

> *CAUTION ——*
>
> *Be very careful not to kink the cable during installation. A kinked cable will cause erratic throttle operation. New cables bend easily in one direction only and should be installed in that position. The installed cable must be perfectly straight from the bracket on the carburetor or cylinder head cover to the throttle valve lever. If necessary, bend the bracket to align the cable. The cable must also be perfectly straight between the grommet in the floorboard and the accelerator pedal. If necessary, bend the cable end of the pedal to align the cable.*

8.1 Adjusting Accelerator Cable

Cars that have automatic transmissions have two accelerator cables. One cable extends from the accelerator pedal to a lever on the automatic transmission. A second cable extends from the lever on the automatic transmission to the throttle valve lever of the fuel injection system or the carburetor.

To adjust cable on cars with manual transmissions:

1. Push the accelerator pedal down to its full throttle position.

2. Loosen the locknuts that hold the cable conduit to the bracket on the carburetor or, on fuel injection engines, to the bracket on top of the cylinder head cover.

3. Using the locknuts, adjust the position of the cable conduit in the bracket until the primary throttle valve is fully open—but with 1 mm (.040 in.) of clearance between the throttle valve lever and its fully open stop on the carburetor or the throttle valve housing.

> **CAUTION**
>
> *If the throttle valve lever contacts its fully open stop before the accelerator pedal reaches the floor, excessive strain will be placed on the cable during full-throttle operation. Always check the adjustment carefully in order to prevent broken cables.*

4. When the adjustment is correct, tighten both locknuts—without overtightening.

5. Operate the accelerator several times, and check that there is no more than 1 mm (.040 in.) of clearance at the throttle valve lever stop with the accelerator fully depressed.

To adjust cable on cars with automatic transmissions:

1. Loosen the locknuts that hold the cable conduit in its bracket on the carburetor or, on fuel injection cars, on the engine's cylinder head cover.

2. Make certain that the carburetor or fuel injection system primary throttle valve is fully closed. On cars with carburetors, you will need to open the choke valve by hand in order to get the throttle off its fast idle position on the fast idle cam.

3. Press the operating lever on the transmission to its end position as indicated in Fig. 8-1.

4. Being sure that the transmission operating lever remains in position, turn the locknuts (**1** in Fig. 8-1) until no play remains in the cable with the primary throttle valve closed. Then tighten the locknuts.

> **NOTE**
>
> If you can remove and install the cable ball socket on the upper end of the operating lever (at **9** in Fig. 8-1) without either tensioning the cable or moving the operating lever, you have adjusted the cable correctly.

5. To adjust the pedal cable (**2** in Fig. 8-1), push the pedal (**8** in Fig. 8-1) to the stop (**7** in Fig. 8-1). Hold it there with a weight.

6. Loosen the locknut (**5** in Fig. 8-1). Then, by turning the knurled adjusting nut, eliminate all play in the

operating lever in the direction indicated by the arrow at **6** in Fig. 8-1. Tighten the locknut.

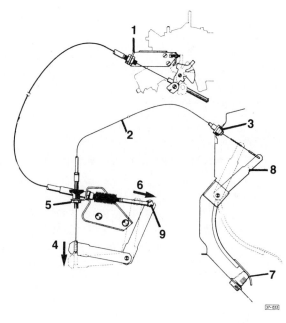

Fig. 8-1. Cable layout on cars with automatic transmissions. Move operating lever in direction indicated by arrow at **4**.

7. Recheck the adjustment by releasing and depressing the accelerator pedal several times. With the pedal fully depressed to its stop, there should still be no play at the operating lever. If necessary, repeat the adjustment procedure to eliminate play.

9. Emission Controls

Several kinds of emission controls have been used on the cars covered by this Manual. The procedures given here are designed to keep these controls in good working order. Individual emission control system components cannot be repaired and must be replaced if testing shows them to be faulty.

9.1 Emission Controls for Engines with Carburetors

Fig. 9-1, Fig. 9-2, Fig. 9-3, and Fig. 9-4 show the vacuum hose connections on the emission control components used on 1975 cars. The anti-backfire valve and the diverter valve are parts of the air injection system. The two-way valve and the EGR valve are parts of the EGR (exhaust gas recirculation) system.

NOTE——

As part of the procedure given for eliminating the catalytic converter in this section, the EGR system will have been modified on all USA cars other than California cars and 1976 cars with automatic transmissions. If this modification has been made, the vacuum hoses that connect the EGR valve to the carburetor and to the two-way valve will have been removed. There will be a plastic cap on the carburetor and brake servo hose vacuum connection and on the EGR valve's vacuum connection(s); the latter caps are pricked with a needle so that they are not completely airtight.

CAUTION——

Be careful not to interchange the vacuum hose connections when removing or installing emission control system components. Doing this will cause poor running and possible engine damage. The connections for each vacuum circuit should be the same color; for example, both connections for the hose from the carburetor to the anti-backfire valve are dark blue.

3 ■

Fig. 9-1. Emission control components of 1975 cars sold in the USA, showing vacuum line connections as originally installed by factory. Also refer to Fig. 9-4.

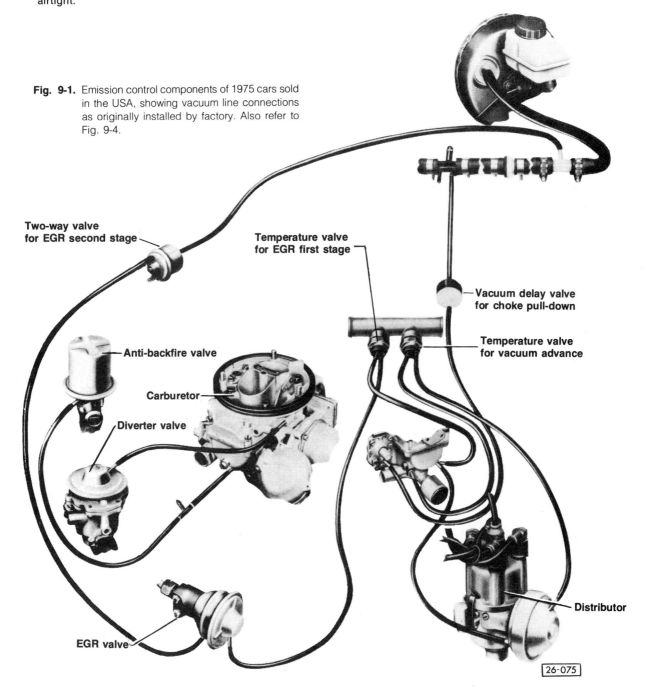

Two-way valve for EGR second stage

Temperature valve for EGR first stage

Vacuum delay valve for choke pull-down

Temperature valve for vacuum advance

Anti-backfire valve

Carburetor

Diverter valve

Distributor

EGR valve

26-075

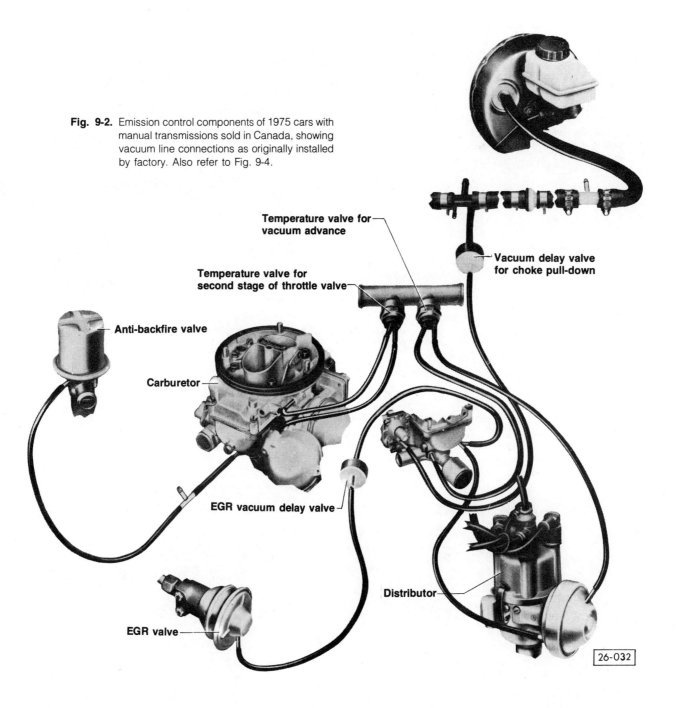

Fig. 9-2. Emission control components of 1975 cars with manual transmissions sold in Canada, showing vacuum line connections as originally installed by factory. Also refer to Fig. 9-4.

Temperature valve for vacuum advance

Temperature valve for second stage of throttle valve

Vacuum delay valve for choke pull-down

Anti-backfire valve

Carburetor

EGR vacuum delay valve

Distributor

EGR valve

26-032

3 ■

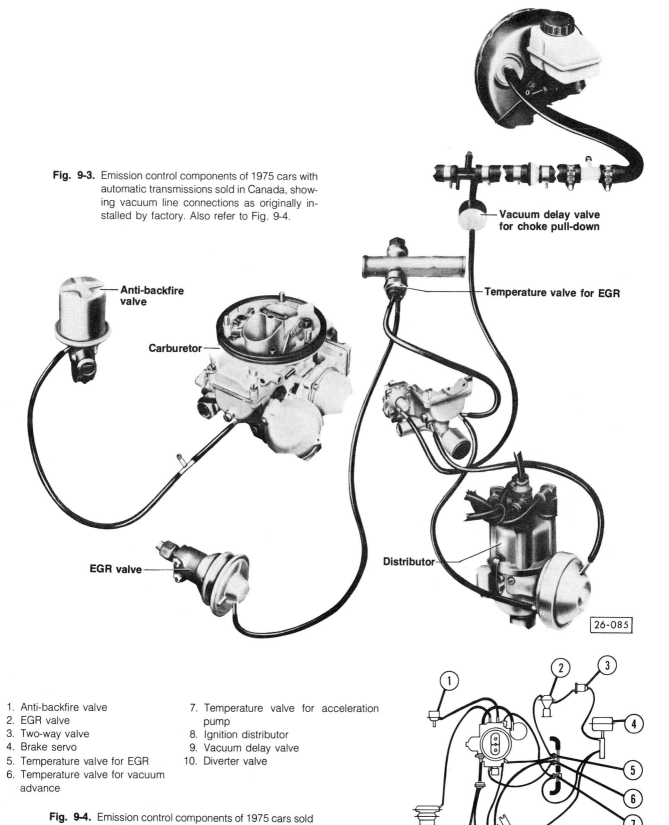

Vacuum delay valve for choke pull-down

Temperature valve for EGR

Anti-backfire valve

Carburetor

EGR valve

Distributor

26-085

Fig. 9-3. Emission control components of 1975 cars with automatic transmissions sold in Canada, showing vacuum line connections as originally installed by factory. Also refer to Fig. 9-4.

1. Anti-backfire valve
2. EGR valve
3. Two-way valve
4. Brake servo
5. Temperature valve for EGR
6. Temperature valve for vacuum advance
7. Temperature valve for acceleration pump
8. Ignition distributor
9. Vacuum delay valve
10. Diverter valve

Fig. 9-4. Emission control components of 1975 cars sold in USA after being dealer-modified in accordance with the 1975 Quality Improvements program. Canadian models do not have all of the emission control components shown here.

Fig. 9-5 and Fig. 9-6 show the vacuum hose connections on the emission control components used on 1976 cars. The individual components are identical to, or very little different from, corresponding components of 1975 cars. Any differences are pointed out in the testing and replacement procedures that appear later.

Fig. 9-5. Schematic layout of emission control components of 1976 cars with carburetors sold in USA, showing vacuum hose connections.

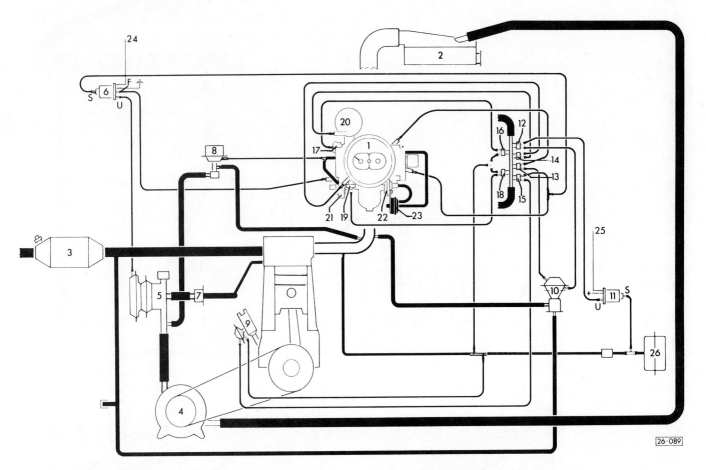

1. Carburetor
2. Air cleaner
3. Catalytic converter
4. Air pump for air injection system
5. Diverter valve
6. Two-way valve for air injection system
7. Check valve for air injection system
8. Anti-backfire valve for air injection system
9. Ignition distributor
10. EGR valve
11. Two-way valve for EGR second stage (California only)
12. Temperature valve for EGR second stage (California only)
13. Temperature valve for EGR first stage
14. Temperature valve for carburetor secondary throttle valve vacuum unit
15. Temperature valve for vacuum advance cutoff
16. Temperature valve for acceleration pump
17. Check valve for temperature-controlled acceleration pump system
18. Temperature valve for cold idle valve
19. Cold idle valve
20. Vacuum unit for carburetor secondary throttle valve
21. Vacuum unit for choke pull-down first stage
22. Vacuum unit for choke pull-down second stage
23. Thermo-time vacuum valve for choke pull-down second stage
24. Electrical wire to relay in two-way valve
25. Electrical wire to microswitch
26. Vacuum powered brake servo

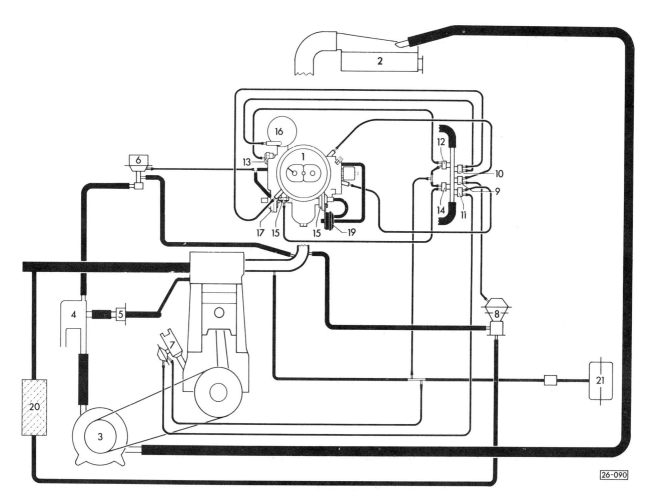

3

1. Carburetor
2. Air cleaner
3. Air pump for air injection system
4. Diverter valve for air injection system
5. Check valve for air injection system
6. Anti-backfire valve for air injection system
7. Ignition distributor
8. EGR valve
9. Temperature valve for EGR first stage
10. Temperature valve for carburetor secondary throttle valve vacuum unit
11. Temperature valve for vacuum advance cutoff
12. Temperature valve for acceleration pump
13. Check valve for temperature-controlled acceleration pump system
14. Temperature valve for cold idle valve
15. Cold idle valve
16. Vacuum unit for carburetor secondary throttle valve
17. Vacuum unit for choke pull-down first stage
18. Vacuum unit for choke pull-down second stage
19. Thermo-time vacuum valve for choke pull-down second stage
20. EGR filter
21. Vacuum powered brake servo

Fig. 9-6. Schematic layout of emission control components of 1976 cars with carburetors sold in Canada, showing vacuum hose connections.

Exhaust Gas Recirculation (EGR)

Three systems of exhaust gas recirculation have been used on the cars covered by this Manual. A single-stage system is used on 1975 and 1976 cars sold in Canada. The 1975 models sold in the USA, including California, have a two-stage EGR system. The 1976 models sold in California also have a two-stage system, but it is slightly different from that used in 1975. The 1976 models sold in the other states have the two-stage EGR valve, but only the first stage is connected and in operation.

NOTE ——

As part of the procedure given in this section for eliminating the catalytic converter, the EGR system will have been modified on all USA cars other than California cars and 1976 cars with automatic transmissions. The vacuum hoses will have been removed and the connections capped. The microswitch will have been removed from the carburetor and the wires cut and insulated. On cars with automatic transmissions, other than those sold in California, a gasket with a 3-mm orifice will have been installed between the EGR valve and the flange.

Troubles in the EGR system can cause engine starting difficulty, rough idling, stalling, hesitation with the engine cold, and poor performance. Each of the three systems is covered separately in the procedures that follow.

To test 1975 and 1976 Canada EGR system:

1. Check that the vacuum hoses are correctly attached to the EGR valve, the temperature valve, and the carburetor. See Fig. 9-7.

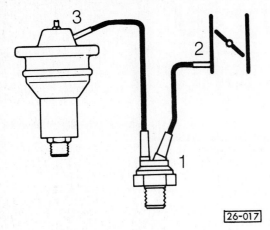

26-017

Fig. 9-7. Single-stage EGR system used on 1975 and 1976 Canadian models. Temperature valve is at **1**, carburetor at **2**, and EGR valve at **3**.

2. Start the engine and allow it to idle.

3. Disconnect the vacuum hose from the EGR valve. Then disconnect the vacuum hose from the anti-backfire valve for the air injection system, and temporarily connect it to the EGR valve. The idle speed should drop, indicating that exhaust gases are being recirculated.

4. If the idle speed does not drop during the test described in step 3, check for the following conditions: (1) EGR filter clogged (1975 cars only), (2) EGR line or fitting in exhaust manifold clogged, (3) EGR valve faulty or clogged.

   NOTE ——
   Clogged EGR valves can be cleaned as described in a later procedure under this heading. Replace clogged filters and lines.

5. If the idle speed drops during the test described in step 3, but the engine still gives trouble during starting and warm-up, you can test the temperature valve by removing it and placing it in a pan of water. Gradually heat the water. Below a water temperature of 43° to 49°C (110° to 120°F), the valve should be closed. Above these temperatures, you should be able to blow through the valve as indicated in Fig. 9-8. Replace faulty valves.

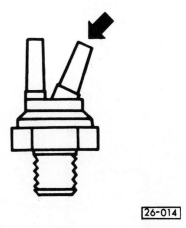

26-014

Fig. 9-8. Temperature valve being checked. Blow through valve as indicated by arrow.

To test 1975 USA EGR system:

1. Check that the vacuum hoses are correctly attached to the EGR valve, the temperature valve, the two-way valve, and the carburetor. See Fig. 9-9.

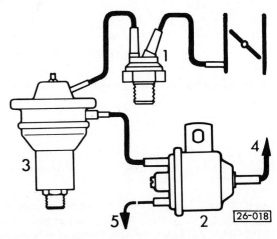

26-018

Fig. 9-9. Two-stage EGR system used on 1975 USA models. Temperature valve is at **1**, two-way valve at **2**, and EGR valve at **3**. Vacuum line at **4** goes to brake servo vacuum hose; electrical connection is at **5**.

2. Start the engine and allow it to idle.

3. To check the EGR valve first stage, disconnect the vacuum hose from the EGR valve at the connection indicated in Fig. 9-10. Then disconnect the vacuum hose from the anti-backfire valve for the air injection system, and temporarily connect it to the EGR valve. The idle speed should drop, indicating that exhaust gases are being recirculated.

4. If the idle speed does not drop during the test described in step 3, check for the following conditions: (1) EGR filter clogged, (2) EGR line or fitting

in exhaust manifold clogged, (3) EGR valve faulty or clogged.

NOTE ——

Clogged EGR valves can be cleaned as described in a later procedure under this heading. Replace clogged filters and lines.

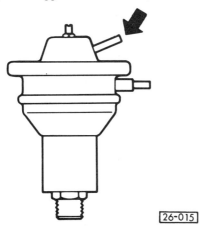

Fig. 9-10. EGR valve first-stage vacuum connection (arrow).

5. If the idle speed drops during the test described in step 3 but the engine still gives trouble during starting and warm-up, you can test the temperature valve by removing it and placing it in a pan of water. Gradually heat the water. Below a temperature of 43° to 49°C (110° to 120°F), the valve should be closed. Above these temperatures, you should be able to blow through the valve as indicated in Fig. 9-11. Replace faulty valves.

Fig. 9-11. Temperature valve being checked. Blow through valve as indicated by arrow.

6. To test the EGR valve second stage, operate the microswitch by raising the roller (Fig. 9-12) while the engine is idling. The idle speed should decrease drastically or the engine should stall.

NOTE ——

Though all 1975 cars originally had the microswitch, this switch was removed from cars other than those sold in California as part of the 1975 Quality Improvements program. If the microswitch has not been removed, you can remove it. Then cut off the microswitch wire where it comes out of the wiring harness and insulate the cut end of the wire with tape.

Fig. 9-12. Roller (arrow) on operating arm of microswitch.

7. If the engine does not slow down or stall when you make the test described in step 6 and if the EGR first-stage is working correctly, test the microswitch and the two-way valve with a voltmeter to determine whether there is an electrical fault. The two-way valve should make an audible click when battery current is applied to it. Replace faulty components.

NOTE ——

In installing a new microswitch, you must adjust it as described in a later procedure under this heading.

3

To test 1976 USA EGR system:

1. Check that the vacuum hoses are correctly attached to the various EGR system components, as shown in Fig. 9-13 or Fig. 9-14.

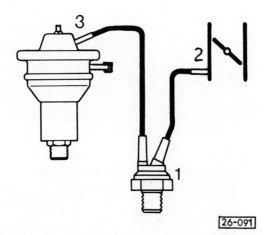

Fig. 9-13. EGR system used in USA except in California. Temperature valve is at **1**, carburetor at **2**, and EGR valve at **3**. Two-stage EGR valve is used, with connection for second-stage vacuum line capped.

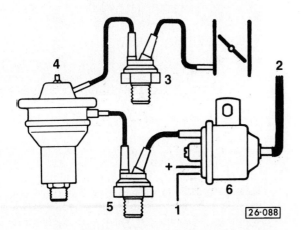

Fig. 9-14. Two-stage EGR system used in California. Electrical connection (**1**) goes to microswitch on carburetor. Vacuum line (**2**) goes to vacuum hose for brake servo. First-stage temperature valve is at **3**, EGR valve at **4**, second-stage temperature valve at **5**, and two-way valve at **6**.

2. Start the engine and allow it to idle.

3. To check the EGR valve first stage, disconnect the vacuum hose from the EGR valve at the connection indicated in Fig. 9-15. Then disconnect the vacuum hose from the anti-backfire valve for the air injection system and temporarily connect it to the EGR valve. The idle speed should drop, indicating that exhaust gases are being recirculated.

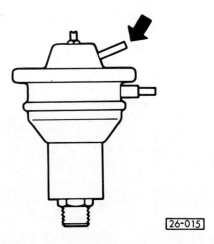

Fig. 9-15. EGR valve first-stage vacuum connection (arrow).

4. If the idle speed does not drop during the test described in step 3, check for the following conditions: (1) EGR line or fitting in exhaust manifold clogged, (2) EGR valve faulty or clogged.

NOTE ——
Clogged EGR valves can be cleaned as described in a later procedure. Replace clogged lines.

5. If the idle speed drops during the test described in step 3 but the engine still gives trouble during starting and warm-up, you can test the temperature valve by removing it and placing it in a pan of water. Gradually heat the water. Below a water temperature of about 27°C (81°F), the valve should be closed. At temperatures above about 49°C (120°F), you should be able to blow through the valve as indicated in Fig. 9-16. Replace faulty valves.

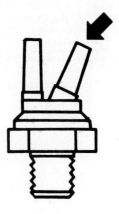

Fig. 9-16. First-stage or second-stage EGR system temperature valve being checked. Blow through valve as indicated by arrow.

6. To test the EGR valve second stage (California cars only), warm up the engine until the coolant temperature is above 49°C (120°F). Then operate the microswitch by raising the roller (Fig. 9-17) while the engine is idling. The idle speed should decrease drastically or the engine should stall.

Fig. 9-17. Roller (arrow) on operating arm of microswitch.

7. If the engine does not slow down or stall when you make the test described in step 6 and if the EGR first-stage is working correctly, test the temperature valve as shown earlier in Fig. 9-16. If the temperature valve is not faulty, test the microswitch and the two-way valve with a voltmeter to determine whether there is an electrical fault. The two-way valve should make an audible click when battery current is applied to it. Replace faulty components.

NOTE ——

In installing a new microswitch, you must adjust it as described in one of the later procedures under this heading.

To clean EGR valve:

1. Remove the EGR valve from the engine.

2. Clean the passage indicated in Fig. 9-18.

3. Check that the EGR valve plunger moves when engine vacuum is applied to the EGR valve connection(s). Replace faulty EGR valves.

4. Reinstall the EGR valve on the engine, using new gaskets and seals where applicable.

Fig. 9-18. EGR valve passage (arrow).

To adjust microswitch:

1. Remove the automatic choke's water housing as a unit, leaving the coolant hoses attached.

2. Remove the nut from the throttle valve shaft, and then install a protractor as shown in Fig. 9-19.

Fig. 9-19. Protractor installed on carburetor's primary throttle valve shaft.

3. Check that the throttle valve is closed. (It may be necessary to open the choke by hand in order to release the fast-idle mechanism.) Then zero the protractor.

4. Slowly open the throttle valve. The microswitch should click at the following switching points: at 30° and 67° for cars with manual transmissions and at 23° and 63° for cars with automatic transmissions.

5. If the adjustment is incorrect, correct it by moving the microswitch on its mounting bracket.

To reset EGR indicator light:

1. Service the EGR system by testing and cleaning the components as described in the preceding procedures.

2. Reset the elapsed mileage odometer by depressing the button indicated in Fig. 9-20.

3. Check that the EGR indicator light is out.

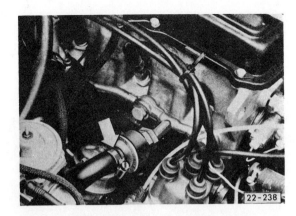

Fig. 9-21. Hose connection (arrow) on check valve.

Fig. 9-20. Reset button (arrow) for EGR indicator light.

Air Injection System

During routine maintenance, you should check the air injection system as follows. First, disconnect the hose from the check valve (Fig. 9-21) and plug the check valve opening. Then start the engine and allow it to idle while you check whether air is flowing out of the disconnected hose. If it is not, test the components as described in the next procedures.

If the system seems to be working well but emissions do not drop when the air injection hose is connected following idle mixture adjustment, the distributor tube may be clogged. Take out the union bolts and remove the distributor tube. Then clean out the bores in the union bolts and in the engine. You can clean the banjo unions and the tube with solvent and compressed air.

If air is not being injected because of a stuck check valve, you can clean the check valve by blowing it out with compressed air. The valve should be removed from the distributor tube and air blown through the valve in the direction of normal air flow.

Backfiring when the car is coasting could indicate a faulty anti-backfire valve in the air injection system. Check that a restrictor with a 4-mm diameter hole is installed on the suction side of the anti-backfire valve.

To check anti-backfire valve:

1. Disconnect the air hose from the anti-backfire valve as indicated in Fig. 9-22.

2. Start the engine and allow it to idle until full oil pressure has been established.

3. Place your hand over the connection on the anti-backfire valve. Run the engine at high rpm for a moment; then allow the throttle to snap closed suddenly. You should feel a vacuum at the anti-backfire valve for a period of from one to three seconds.

4. If no vacuum can be felt—and the hoses connected to the anti-backfire valve are neither clogged nor kinked—the anti-backfire valve is faulty and should be replaced.

Fig. 9-22. Hose removed from anti-backfire valve. Place your hand over the hose's connection on the valve (arrow).

Before you check the diverter valve on a 1975 car that has a catalytic converter (1975 USA models), look for a two-way valve installed on the diverter valve's mounting bracket (on top the radiator). If this two-way valve has been dealer-installed as part of the 1975 Quality Improvements program, check the diverter valve and the two-way valve as described later for 1976 USA cars. If the two-way valve has not been installed, either install it as described in the next procedure or check the diverter valve as described later for 1975 USA and 1976 Canada models.

NOTE ——

If the catalytic converter has been eliminated as described in a later procedure under this heading, the modification described below—including installation of relay Part No. 055 906 086 A—should still be carried out on USA models.

To install two-way valve for secondary air shutoff:

1. Install the two-way valve on the diverter valve bracket as indicated in Fig. 9-23. Make the vacuum connections shown, using the components supplied with the secondary air shutoff installation kit.

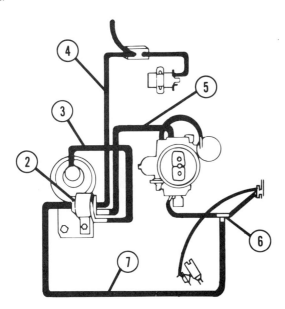

1. Temperature valve for vacuum advance
2. Two-way valve
3. Vacuum hose from diverter valve to connection **U** on two-way valve
4. Wiring harness for two-way valve, connected to ignition coil ballast resistance
5. Vacuum hose from connection **F** on two-way valve to carburetor
6. T-connector
7. Vacuum hose from connection **S** on two-way valve to T-connection

Fig. 9-23. Secondary air shutoff modification for 1975 USA cars, which have diverter valve and catalytic converter.

2. Disconnect the battery ground strap. Connect the wiring harness from the installation kit, as shown at **4** in Fig. 9-23. Push the brown (ground) wire of the harness through the firewall at the heater control cable grommet so that the wire can be connected to the relay plate of the fuse box.

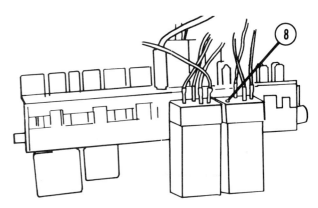

Fig. 9-24. Point at which brown (ground) wire should be connected (**8**).

3. Remove the fuse box from its bracket beneath the dashboard. Then plug the brown wire into the left top opening (Fig. 9-24) at the back of the socket for relay Part No. 055 906 086. (The number is on the relay.)

4. Remove relay Part No. 055 906 086. Install relay Part No. 055 906 086A (from the parts kit).

5. Reinstall the fuse box. Reconnect the battery ground strap.

To check 1975 USA and 1976 Canada diverter valve:

1. Pull the vacuum hose off the diverter valve. See Fig. 9-25.

2. Disconnect the vacuum hose from the anti-backfire valve. Then connect this hose to the diverter valve.

3. Start the engine and allow it to idle. You should be able to feel air flow from the diverter valve muffler (at the arrow in Fig. 9-25).

4. If the air pump, the air pump filter, and the hoses have already been checked and found to be in good condition, the diverter valve is faulty if there is no air flow. Replace faulty diverter valves.

> **NOTE** ──
>
> If the pump is found to be faulty, it must be replaced; no repairs are possible.

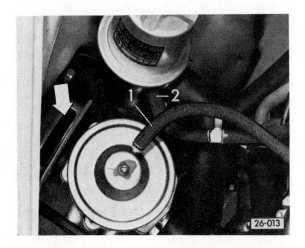

Fig. 9-25. Diverter valve test for 1975 USA cars and 1976 Canada cars. Diverter valve vacuum hose is at **1**, anti-backfire valve vacuum hose at **2**. Arrow indicates diverter valve muffler.

To check 1976 USA diverter valve and two-way valve:

1. Disconnect the vacuum hose marked **F** in Fig. 9-26.

2. Disconnect the vacuum hose marked **S** in Fig. 9-26. Then reconnect it to the two-way valve at the point where hose **F** is normally connected.

3. Start the engine and allow it to idle. You should be able to feel air flow from the diverter valve muffler.

4. If you feel no air flow and if the air pump, the air pump filter, and the hoses have already been checked and found to be in good condition, check that vacuum is present when you disconnect hose **U** (Fig. 9-26) from the diverter valve. If there is vacuum, the diverter valve is faulty and should be replaced.

> **NOTE** ──
>
> If the pump is faulty, it must be replaced; no repairs are possible.

Fig. 9-26. Vacuum hose connections to diverter valve. Hose **S** comes from T-connection near temperature valve, hose **F** comes from carburetor, and hose **U** goes to diverter valve.

5. To test the two-way valve, reconnect the vacuum hoses in their original locations. Then pull the electrical wire off the two-way valve.

6. With the engine idling, connect a jumper wire from the battery's positive (+) post to the electrical terminal on the two-way valve.

7. Increase the engine rpm and check for air flow from the muffler of the diverter valve. If there is no air flow, and if the diverter valve and the air and vacuum hoses have already been found to be in good condition, the two-way valve is faulty and should be replaced.

Temperature-controlled Vacuum Advance

Fig. 9-27 is a schematic view of the temperature-controlled vacuum advance system. This system is used on all cars with carburetors other than the 1975 Canadian models with automatic transmissions. Vacuum from the carburetor is shut off by the temperature valve whenever engine coolant temperatures are below 45°C (113°F). At temperatures above 61°C (142°F), the valve is fully open, allowing vacuum to reach the vacuum unit of the ignition distributor.

If the idle speed is too high during the warm-up phase of engine operation, the temperature valve may not be closing correctly at cold temperatures. If the temperature valve fails to open at higher temperatures, there will be hesitation or poor transition from lower to higher vehicle speeds, and fuel consumption will be too high. Test the temperature valve if any of these faults is observed.

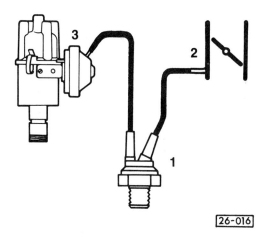

26-016

Fig. 9-27. Schematic view of temperature-controlled vacuum advance. Temperature valve is at **1**, carburetor at **2**, and ignition distributor at **3**.

To test temperature valve:

1. Remove the temperature valve and place its threaded end in a pan of water that contains a thermometer.

2. Heat the water. Attach a piece of hose to the angled connection of the temperature valve. (See Fig. 9-25 given earlier.) By placing the hose in your mouth, you should not be able to blow air through the valve until the water temperature reaches 58° ± 3°C (136° ± 5°F).

3. If the valve fails to open at the prescribed temperature or if the valve is open at low temperatures, replace the temperature valve.

Intake Air Preheating

Fig. 9-28 is a phantom view of the air cleaner, showing the thermostatically controlled flap for the intake air preheating system. To check the thermostat, remove the top part of the air cleaner housing; then take out the pleated paper filter element. Check that the intake air regulating flap is not loose. The thermostat should cause the flap to seal the cold air opening when the air temperature inside the air cleaner housing is below 30°C (86°F). When the air temperature inside the air cleaner housing is above 36°C (97°F), the flap should seal the warm air opening. Replace faulty thermostats.

Positive Crankcase Ventilation (PCV)

Beginning with the 1976 models, the check valve for the PCV (positive crankcase ventilation) system was replaced by the deflector indicated in Fig. 9-29. Also, an additional restrictor with an approximate 7-mm inside diameter was installed in the connecting hose (Fig. 9-30). If the PCV system is clogged by sludge when you inspect the hoses during routine maintenance, clean the hoses with solvent and a long brush. Replace kinked or leaking hoses.

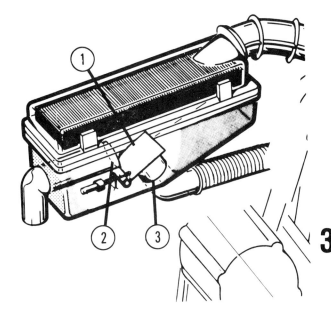

Fig. 9-28. Phantom view of air cleaner. Flap is at **1**, cold air opening at **2**, and warm air opening at **3**.

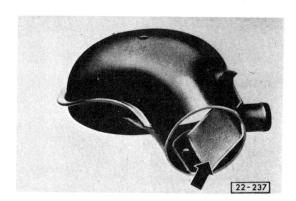

22-237

Fig. 9-29. Deflector (arrow) over PCV connection on air intake elbow.

22-236

Fig. 9-30. Restrictor (arrow) installed in PCV connecting hose.

Catalytic Converter

The catalytic converter is shown in Fig. 9-31. Catalytic converter overheating and incipient damage, which are indicated by a flickering of the CAT light in the speedometer, can be caused by the following:

1. Misfiring because of bad spark plugs, spark plug cables, or other ignition system components

2. Incorrect ignition timing that causes the engine to get too hot

3. CO value too high ahead of the converter (mixture too rich)

4. A faulty diverter valve in the air injection system that does not shut off at high rpm

5. A faulty temperature sensor on the catalytic converter.

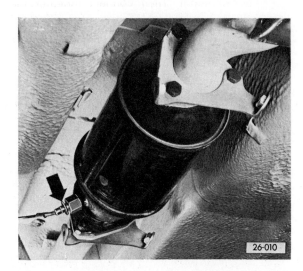

Fig. 9-31. Catalytic converter. Arrow indicates temperature sensor that controls CAT light in speedometer.

The CAT light may flicker when the engine is under extreme load resulting from trailer towing, prolonged high-speed driving in hot weather, and other similar conditions. Normally, the CAT light will go out if the driver reduces speed. The converter should be checked as described below if there has been prolonged driving with a flickering CAT light or if there is (1) poor engine output, (2) stalling at idle, (3) a rattle in the exhaust system, or (4) CO value (at tailpipe) of more than 0.4 volume percent at idle.

To check catalytic converter:

1. Hold the catalytic converter up to strong light and look through both ends. You should not see any evidence of damage to the ceramic insert.

WARNING ——
Wear safety glasses to protect your eyes from loose material that may spill out of the catalytic converter.

CAUTION ——
Do not drop or hit the catalytic converter. Any sharp blow will destroy the ceramic insert and ruin the catalytic converter.

2. Check the ceramic insert for blockage. Air should pass through easily.

3. If the catalytic converter is blocked or if the ceramic insert is damaged, replace the catalytic converter. Then reset the CAT indicator light as described in the following procedure.

To reset CAT indicator light:

1. Service the catalytic converter, replacing it as described in **10. Exhaust System.**

2. Reset the elapsed mileage odometer by depressing the button indicated in Fig. 9-32.

3. Check that the CAT indicator light is out.

Fig. 9-32. CAT indicator light reset button (arrow). Press to reset elapsed mileage odometer.

Eliminating Catalytic Converter

Late in 1976, the United States Environmental Protection Agency approved the elimination of the catalytic converter from the 1975 and 1976 Rabbits and Sciroccos in operation outside the state of California. Authorized Volkswagen Dealers can make this change, under the condition that the car will still meet legal emissions requirements. It is therefore no longer necessary to replace the catalytic converter in case of failure but rather to modify the emission control system according to the procedures given here.

NOTE——

If the catalytic converter has been removed by an Authorized Dealer, the emissions decal in the engine compartment should read "Engine Family 32 NC" on 1975 cars or "Engine Family 32 F/NC" on 1976 cars. There should no longer be a "catalytic converter cautions" label on the back of the sun visor on 1975 cars. On 1976 cars, the "Catalyst" label on the left front pillar will have been replaced by a "Non-catalyst" label.

To eliminate catalytic converter:

1. Remove the heatshield that is beneath the catalytic converter.

2. Disconnect the wires from the temperature sensor that is on the catalytic converter. Then, by unscrewing it, remove the sensor.

3. Remove the catalytic converter from the car by taking out the bolts and nuts.

4. Smash the ceramic insert out of the catalytic converter using a hammer and a rod. Shake out the dust and the broken pieces.

WARNING——

In order to protect your hands and eyes from sharp fragments, wear gloves and safety glasses when hammering out the ceramic insert.

5. Install the emptied catalytic converter. Reinstall the temperature sensor.

NOTE——

After you reinstall the temperature sensor, reconnect the wires. Then cut and insulate the wire at terminal 4 of the elapsed mileage odometer, and cut and insulate the wire at terminal 8 behind fuse box relay Part No. 055 906 086A.

6. Modify the car as described in one or the other of the next two procedures in order to ensure that the vehicle fulfills the EPA Exhaust Emissions Standards for the 1975 or the 1976 model year.

To modify 1975 car:

1. Install a 112.5 primary main jet and a 120 scondary main jet in the carburetor. Also install a 52.5 idle jet (the existing jet is probably the correct size) and a 140 idle air jet—both in the carburetor's primary side.

2. If necessary, replace the new-type (two orifice) acceleration pump discharge nozzle with the old-type (single orifice) nozzle. On cars with automatic transmissions, the temperature-controlled check valve must be installed. See the instructions given for adjusting the acceleration pump in **6.1 Removing, Rebuilding, and Installing Carburetor.**

3. If not already removed, remove the vacuum delay valve for the choke's vacuum pull-down (removal is not necessary if the car has an automatic transmission). Then connect together the two vacuum hoses with a short piece of tubing. If necessary, consult Fig. 9-1 and Fig. 9-4, given earlier.

4. Check that there is a vacuum delay jet for the secondary throttle valve vacuum unit. If not, install one. See **6.1 Removing, Rebuilding, and Installing Carburetor.**

5. Check that the new-type choke cover with a thermo switch has been installed. If not, install one as described in **6.1 Removing, Rebuilding, and Installing Carburetor,** using kit 055 198 580. Then adjust the choke by turning the cover clockwise so that the index mark on the cover is about 5 mm (.20 in. or about 3/16 in.) from the index mark on the choke housing of the carburetor.

6. Check the choke vacuum pull-down to be sure it is set to the specifications given in **6.1 Removing, Rebuilding, and Installing Carburetor.**

7. Reset the throttle valve dashpot so that the gap between the plunger and the throttle valve arm is 1 mm (.040 in.). See **6.1 Removing, Rebuilding, and Installing Carburetor.** (Install a dashpot if the car does not already have one.)

NOTE——

According to the Factory instructions, Authorized Dealers have been instructed to install fuel filters and to modify the PCV system at the same time as the catalytic converter is eliminated. The modification to the PCV system consists of removing the baffle shown earlier in Fig. 9-29 and installing a tube. Also, the restrictor shown in Fig. 9-30 must be removed and a PCV valve, Part No. 211 129 101, installed in the hose between the cylinder head cover and the air intake elbow.

8. As a first step in modifying the EGR system, remove and discard the vacuum hoses that are

connected to the EGR valve, the carburetor, and the two-way valve. Then plug the EGR vacuum connections on the carburetor and the brake servo hose with caps. Plug the vacuum connections on the EGR valve itself with caps that have had small holes pricked in them, as by a needle.

9. As a final step in modifying the EGR system, remove the microswitch from the carburetor. Cut and insulate the wire that is connected to terminal 2 at the elapsed mileage odometer in the engine compartment. On cars with automatic transmissions, install a gasket with a 3-mm orifice between the EGR valve and the flange.

10. Check and, if necessary, adjust the ignition dwell and timing as described in **ENGINE AND CLUTCH.** Check and, if necessary, adjust the idle speed and the idle mixture (CO percentage) as described in **5.1 Adjusting Idle on Cars with Carburetors.**

NOTE ——

Measured at the tailpipe, the CO volume percentage should be 1.5% ± 0.7% (manual transmission) or 1.0% ± 0.7% (automatic transmission) after carrying out the modifications just described and after the elimination of the catalytic converter.

CAUTION ——

In order to prevent fuel-fouled (sooty) spark plugs following the modifications given above, it may be necessary to use hotter spark plugs, such as the Champion N-9Y, Bosch W 175 T30, and Beru 175/14/3A. Examine the spark plugs after an extended period of normal driving. Change to the hotter spark plugs specified here if there is evidence of fuel fouling.

To modify 1976 car:

1. Install a 112.5 primary main jet and a 120 secondary main jet in the carburetor. Also install a 52.5 idle jet (the existing jet is probably the correct size) and a 140 idle air jet—both in the carburetor's primary side.

2. Readjust the choke by turning the cover clockwise so that the index mark on the cover is about 5 mm (.20 in. or about $^3/_{16}$ in.) from the index mark on the choke housing of the carburetor.

3. Reset the throttle valve dashpot so that the gap between the plunger and the throttle valve arm is 1 mm (.040 in.). See **6.1 Removing, Rebuilding, and Installing Carburetor.** (Install a dashpot if the car does not already have one).

NOTE ——

According to the Factory instructions, Authorized Dealers have been instructed to modify the PCV system at the same time as the catalytic converter is eliminated. The modifications consist of removing the baffle shown earlier in Fig. 9-29 and installing a tube. Also, the restrictor shown previously in Fig. 9-30 must be removed and a PCV valve, Part No. 211 129 101, installed in the hose between the cylinder head cover and the air intake elbow.

4. To modify the EGR system of cars with manual transmissions only, remove and discard the vacuum hoses that are connected to the EGR valve, the carburetor, and the EGR temperature valve. Then plug the EGR vacuum connection on the carburetor with a cap. Plug the vacuum connections on the EGR valve itself with caps that have had small holes pricked in them, as by a needle.

5. On cars with automatic transmissions, install a gasket with a 3-mm orifice between the EGR valve and the flange.

6. On cars with manual transmissions, cut and insulate the wire that is connected to terminal 2 at the elapsed mileage odometer in the engine compartment.

7. Check and, if necessary, adjust the ignition dwell and timing as described in **ENGINE AND CLUTCH.** Check and, if necessary, adjust the idle speed and the idle mixture (CO percentage) as described in **5.1 Adjusting Idle on Cars with Carburetors.**

NOTE ——

Measured at the tailpipe, the CO volume percentage should be 1.5% ± 0.7% (manual transmission) or 1.0% ± 0.7% (automatic transmission) after carrying out the modifications just described and after the elimination of the catalytic converter.

9.2 Emission Controls for Engines with Fuel Injection

Fig. 9-33 shows the vacuum hose connections on the emission control components used on cars with fuel injection. The vacuum booster (vacuum amplifier) and the vacuum accumulator are made necessary by the low vacuum level that is characteristic of engines equipped with fuel injection. The vacuum amplifier and the vacuum accumulator are part of the EGR (exhaust gas recirculation) system.

Troubles in the EGR system can cause engine starting difficulty, rough idling, stalling, hesitation with the engine cold, and poor performance. Check the EGR system if any of these troubles is observed. Otherwise, check the EGR system at the mileage interval prescribed in **LUBRICATION AND MAINTENANCE** and indicated by the EGR indicator light in the instrument cluster.

3

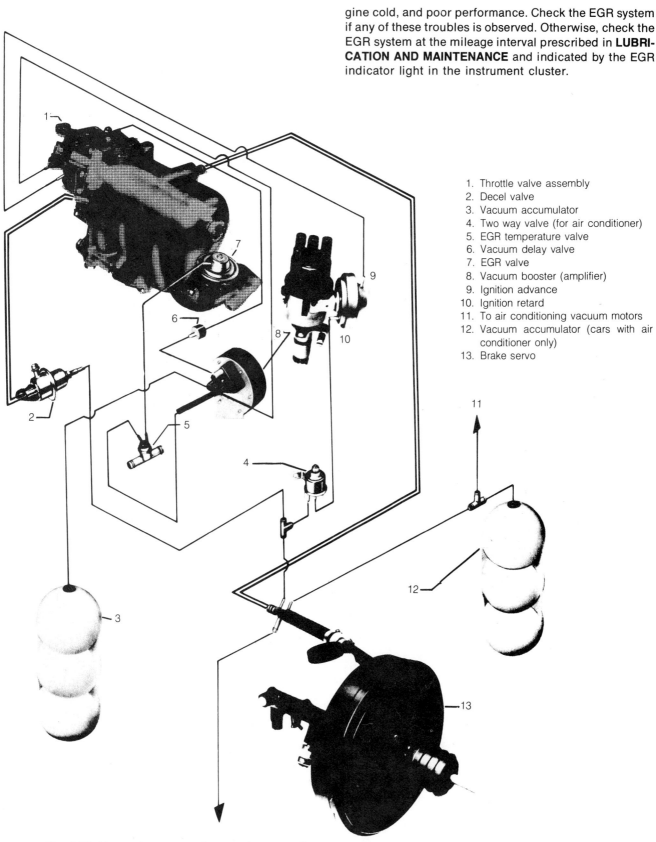

1. Throttle valve assembly
2. Decel valve
3. Vacuum accumulator
4. Two way valve (for air conditioner)
5. EGR temperature valve
6. Vacuum delay valve
7. EGR valve
8. Vacuum booster (amplifier)
9. Ignition advance
10. Ignition retard
11. To air conditioning vacuum motors
12. Vacuum accumulator (cars with air conditioner only)
13. Brake servo

Fig. 9-33. Vacuum hose connections used on cars with fuel injection. Intake air distributor is not for a car covered by this Manual.

25-019

To test EGR system:

1. Make sure that the vacuum connections and hoses are not leaking and are connected as shown previously in Fig. 9-33.

2. Start the engine and warm it up until the oil temperature is between 50° and 70°C (122° and 158°F).

3. With the engine idling, check that there are no leaks in the exhaust gas feed line that connects the EGR valve with the exhaust manifold. Replace leaking feed lines.

4. Disconnect the vacuum hose from the EGR valve (Fig. 9-34). Then temporarily connect a vacuum hose from the vacuum powered brake servo hose to the EGR valve.

   NOTE———

   The easiest way to make this connection is to install a T-fitting in the vacuum line to the retard side of the ignition distributor. Then run a separate vacuum hose from the T-fitting to the EGR valve.

Fig. 9-34. Location of EGR valve (arrow) on engine's intake air distributor.

5. When you connect the temporary vacuum hose to the EGR valve, the engine's idle speed should drop or the engine should stall. If the engine idle speed does not drop during the test described in step 4, check for the following conditions: (1) EGR valve clogged, (2) EGR feed line clogged, (3) EGR valve faulty.

   NOTE———

   Clogged EGR valves can be cleaned as described in a later procedure. Replace faulty EGR valves and clogged lines.

6. If the idle speed drops during the test described in step 3 but the engine still gives trouble during starting and warm-up, you can test the temperature valve by connecting a vacuum gauge to the tem-

perature valve (Fig. 9-35) in place of the vacuum hose that goes to the EGR valve. With the engine thoroughly warmed up, there should be 50 to 90 mm/Hg (2 to 4 in./Hg) available. If not, replace the temperature valve.

Fig. 9-35. Temperature valve (arrow) for EGR system, located on heater hose connection at left-hand end of engine's cylinder head.

To test vacuum booster (vacuum amplifier):

1. Using a T-fitting, connect a vacuum gauge to the vacuum hose that extends from the vacuum amplifier to the throttle valve port of the carburetor.

2. Start the engine and allow it to idle. The vacuum gauge should indicate 5 to 8 mm/Hg (0.2 to 0.3 in./Hg). If it does not, clean the throttle valve port in the throttle valve housing, which is probably clogged.

3. When you have determined that vacuum is reaching the vacuum amplifier from the throttle valve port, connect the vacuum gauge between the vacuum amplifier and the temperature valve, using the T-fitting. At idle, the gauge should read 50 to 90 mm/Hg (2 to 4 in./Hg).

4. If the specified vacuum is not obtained in the test described in step 3, the vacuum amplifier is faulty and should be replaced.

   NOTE———

   Install the new vacuum amplifier with careful reference to the hose connections shown previously in Fig. 9-33.

To clean EGR valve:

1. Remove the EGR valve from the engine.

2. Clean the passage indicated in Fig. 9-36.

3. Check that the EGR valve plunger moves when engine vacuum is applied to the EGR valve connection. Replace faulty EGR valves.

4. Reinstall the EGR valve on the engine, using new gaskets and seals where applicable.

Fig. 9-36. EGR valve passage (arrow).

To reset EGR indicator light:

1. Service the EGR system by testing and cleaning the components as described in the preceding procedures.

2. Reset the elapsed mileage odometer by depressing the button indicated in Fig. 9-37.

3. Check that the EGR indicator light is out.

Fig. 9-37. Reset button (arrow) for EGR indicator light.

Decel Valve

The decel (deceleration) valve prevents a high vacuum forming in the engine's intake air distributor during deceleration on a closed throttle. By limiting the vacuum, lower exhaust emissions are achieved.

To check decel valve:

1. Disconnect the hose from the decel valve, as indicated in Fig. 9-38.

Fig. 9-38. Hose (at fingertip) disconnected from decel valve.

2. Start the engine and allow it to idle until full oil pressure is achieved.

3. Increase the engine speed to about 3000 rpm for a few seconds; then allow the throttle valve to snap closed. At the same moment, you should be able to feel suction at the hose connection with your finger.

4. If you feel no suction during the check described in step 3, disconnect the vacuum hose from the decel valve. Repeat the test. If there is vacuum present, the decel valve is faulty and should be replaced.

5. If you feel suction during the check described in step 3, disconnect the vacuum hose from the T-fitting and then cap the T-fitting. With the engine running at about 3000 rpm, you should feel no suction at the air hose disconnected from the decel valve. If there is suction, the decel valve is faulty and should be replaced.

Catalytic Converter

A catalytic converter is installed only on fuel injection cars sold in California. Because the catalytic converter is unchanged from that used on earlier cars with carburetors, you can check the catalytic converter as described earlier in **9.1 Emission Controls for Engines with Carburetors.** If necessary, replace the catalytic converter as described in **10. Exhaust System.**

Temperature-controlled Intake Air Preheating

Cars sold in Canada with fuel injection have temperature-controlled intake air preheating. Replace the thermostat if the cold air inlet is not closed at low air temperatures and if the warm air inlet is not closed when the air temperature inside the air cleaner is above approximately 36°C (97°F).

10. EXHAUST SYSTEM

The checking of the catalytic converter used on some of the cars covered by this Manual is described in **9.2 Emission Controls for Engines with Fuel Injection.** To replace a catalytic converter, first remove the heatshield indicated in Fig. 10-1. Then disconnect the wire, and remove the temperature sensor indicated in Fig. 10-2. Remove the bolts and nuts that hold the catalytic converter to the exhaust pipe flanges, being careful not to drop or strike the catalytic converter. Remove the catalytic converter from the car.

Installation is the reverse of removal. Use new gaskets at both ends of the catalytic converter. Torque the nuts and bolts to 2.0 mkg (14 ft. lb.). Be sure to use the lock washers when you install the heatshield.

Fig. 10-1. Heatshield (**1**) and catalytic converter temperature sensor (**2**).

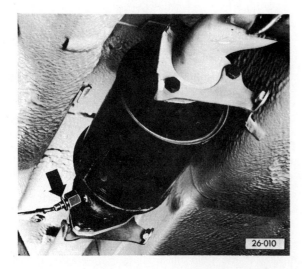

Fig. 10-2. Temperature sensor (arrow). Notice the nuts and bolts that hold the catalytic converter to the exhaust pipe flanges.

In replacing the exhaust system components, you may find that the replacement parts are not identical to those originally installed on the car. The new parts, however, can be used on earlier vehicles.

Fig. 10-3 shows the intermediate pipe and muffler used on USA models through Rabbit Chassis No. 175 3255 399 and Scirocco Chassis No. 525 2032 546, and the new intermediate pipe and muffler used on cars with later Chassis Numbers.

NOTE——

The Part Numbers given in Fig. 10-3 are for general reference only. Always check with your Parts Department for the latest information.

	Intermediate pipes	Mufflers
Old	055 253 201 A	055 253 609 C
New	055 253 201 G	055 253 609 A

Fig. 10-3. Early-type and late-type intermediate pipes and mufflers for USA models.

You can install the new-type muffler on an early-type USA intermediate pipe by cutting off the intermediate pipe as indicated in Fig. 10-4, discarding the other end of the intermediate pipe. Do not cut the front pipe off the new-type muffler.

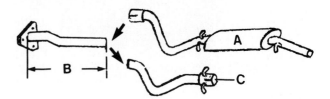

Fig. 10-4. Modification of early-type USA intermediate pipe. Cut so that dimension **B** is 798 mm (31⅜ in.). Discard part **C** and install new-type muffler **A**.

Fig. 10-5 shows the intermediate pipe and muffler used on Canadian models through Rabbit Chassis No. 175 3255 399 and Scirocco Chassis No. 535 2032 546, and the new intermediate pipe and muffler used on cars with later Chassis Numbers.

NOTE——

The Part Numbers given in Fig. 10-5 are for general reference only. Always check with your Parts Department for the latest information.

	Intermediate pipes	Mufflers
Old	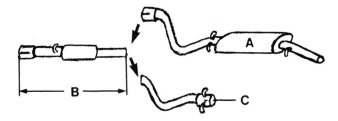 055 253 209 C	055 253 609 C
New	055 253 201 C	055 253 609 A

Fig. 10-5. Early-type and late-type intermediate pipes and mufflers for Canada models.

You can install the new-type muffler on an early-type Canadian intermediate pipe by cutting off the intermediate pipe as indicated in Fig. 10-6, discarding the other end of the intermediate pipe. Do not cut the front pipe off the new-type muffler.

Fig. 10-6. Modification of early-type Canadian intermediate pipe. Cut so that dimension **B** is 1107 mm (43 9/16 in.). Discard part **C** and install new-type muffler **A**.

In installing the exhaust system, it is important that the various components be carefully aligned before you tighten any of the clamps. Align the front exhaust pipe shown in Fig. 10-7 so that the bracket on the transaxle is free of tension. Then tighten the nuts. Align the rear exhaust pipe shown in Fig. 10-8 so that the rubber retaining ring is free of tension. Then tighten the clamp bolts.

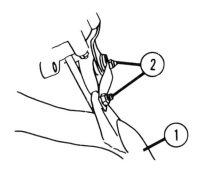

Fig. 10-7. Front exhaust pipe (**1**) being aligned. Nuts for bracket are at **2**.

3 ∎

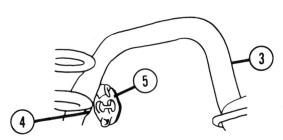

Fig. 10-8. Rear exhaust pipe (**3**) being aligned so that rubber retaining ring (**5**) is free of tension. Clamp bolts are at **4**.

Adjust the depth to which the pipes go together so that the rubber retaining rings hang down straight (Fig. 10-9). Then tighten the clamps that hold the pipes together.

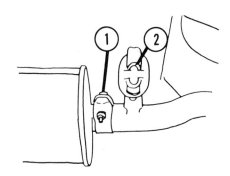

Fig. 10-9. Exhaust pipe being adjusted for length. Rubber retaining ring is at **2**, clamp is at **1**.

11. FUEL AND EXHAUST SYSTEMS TECHNICAL DATA

I. CIS Fuel Injection Specifications

Item	Specification
Fuel pump delivery rate	750 cm³ (24 oz.)/30 sec. minimum
Control pressure (engine cold) **NOTE —** Control pressure varies with ambient temperature. See graph.	 Ambient temperature
Control pressure (engine warm—oil temp. 50–70°C or 122–158°F)	3.40–3.80 bar (48–54 psi)
System pressure	4.50–5.20 bar (64–74 psi)
Pressure test for leaks: after 10 min., minimum pressure after 20 min., minimum pressure	1.8 bar (25 psi) 1.6 bar (23 psi)
Fuel injectors: opening pressure pressure difference between injectors	2.5–3.5 bar (35–50 psi) 0.6 bar (8.5 psi) max.

II. 1975 Carburetor Jets and Settings

Country where sold	USA		Canada	
Transmission	Manual	Automatic	Manual	Automatic
Engine Code letter Engine No.	FC FC 000 001	FG FG 000 001	FC FC 000 001	FG FG 000 001
Carburetor Type Spare Part No.	2B2 055 129 017B	2B2 055 129 017C	2B2 055 129 017H	2B2 055 129 017J
Venturi diameters	24/27 mm	24/27 mm	24/27 mm	24/27 mm
Main jet (factory-installed)	115/115	115/115	115/115	115/115
Main jet (dealer-installed after eliminating catalytic converter)	112.5/120 (except Calif.)	112.5/120 (except Calif.)	—	—
Air correction jet	140/92.5	140/92.5	140/92.5	140/92.5
Idle jet	52.5/70	52.5/70	52.5/70	52.5/70
Idle air jet (factory-installed)	135/100	135/100	135/100	135/100
Idle air jet (dealer-installed after eliminating catalytic converter)	140/100 (except Calif.)	140/100 (except Calif.)	—	—
Auxiliary fuel jet	42.5	42.5	42.5	42.5
Auxiliary air jet	127.5	127.5	127.5	127.5
Power fuel system (with ball)	—/1.0	—/1.0	—/1.0	—/1.0
Injection quantity	0.90 ±0.15 cm³/stroke	0.90 ±0.15 cm³/stroke	0.90 to 1.20 cm³/stroke	0.90 to 1.20 cm³/stroke
Float valve needle diameter	2.0 mm	2.0 mm	2.0 mm	2.0 mm

3

III. 1976 Carburetor Jets and Settings

Country or state where sold	USA except California		California		Canada	
Transmission	Manual	Automatic	Manual	Automatic	Manual	Automatic
Engine Code letter Engine No.	FN FN 000 001	FN FN 000 001	FN FN 000 001	FN FN 000 001	FN FN 000 001	FN FN 000 001
Carburetor Type Spare Part No.	2B2 055 129 021	2B2 055 129 021A	2B2 055 129 021B	2B2 055 129 021C	2B2 055 129 021D	2B2 055 129 021E
Venturi diameters	24/27 mm	24/27 mm	24/27 mm	24/27 mm	24/27 mm	24/27 mm
Main jet (factory-installed)	117.5/110	117.5/110	117.5/110	117.5/110	115/110	115/110
Main jet (dealer-installed after eliminating catalytic converter)	112.5/120	112.5/120	—	—	—	—
Air correction jet	130/92.5	130/92.5	130/92.5	130/92.5	140/92.5	140/92.5
Idle jet	52.5/65	52.5/65	52.5/65	52.5/65	52.5/65	52.5/65
Idle air jet (factory-installed)	135/140	135/140	135/140	135/140	140/140	140/140
Idle air jet (dealer-installed after eliminating catalytic converter)	140/140	140/140	—	—	—	—
Auxiliary fuel jet	42.5	42.5	42.5	42.5	42.5	42.5
Auxiliary air jet	127.5	127.5	127.5	127.5	127.5	127.5
Power fuel system (without ball)	—/1.1	—/1.1	—/1.1	—/1.1	—/1.1	—/1.1
Injection quantity cold (per stroke) warm	1.3–1.7 cm³ 0.6–0.9 cm³	1.3–1.7 cm³ 0.6–0.9 cm³	1.3–1.7 cm³ 0.6–0.9 cm³	1.3–1.7 cm³ 0.6–0.9 cm³	1.3–1.7 cm³ 0.6–0.9 cm³	1.3–1.7 cm³ 0.6–0.9 cm³
Float needle valve diameter	2.0 mm	2.0 mm	2.0 mm	2.0 mm	2.0 mm	2.0 mm

ENGINE AND CLUTCH

Contents

Engine and Clutch

4

The four cylinder inline engine is front mounted and water cooled. It has inline valves that are operated by a belt-driven single overhead camshaft. The piston displacement of 1975 engines is 1471 cm^3 (89.7 in.^{3}); the piston displacement of 1976 and later engines is 1588 cm^3 (96.9 in.^{3}). Basic simplicity, proven mechanical concepts, and a highly accessible arrangement of external components make the engine exceptionally easy to service and maintain.

The engine is bolted to a bellhousing on the transaxle and is inclined toward the rear of the car—thereby permitting a lower hood line and improving weight distribution. (A low, flat front body profile improves forward visibility and makes the car less sensitive to strong or gusty crosswinds.) The radiator cooling fan is mounted left of center. Its position, together with the canted engine, improves access to the drive belts, the water pump, and the alternator.

The engine's crosswise placement makes possible a roomier passenger compartment and concentrates weight over the (front) driving wheels, where it will improve traction in mud or snow. Despite a slight forward weight bias when the car is empty, total vehicle weight is distributed about equally on the front and rear wheels when the car is loaded. Equal weight distribution increases vehicle stability and assures precise handling.

The car is equipped with a network of test wiring for the Computer Analysis system. On the engine, there is a sensor in the high tension cable leading to No. 1 cylinder (for obtaining spark timing data) and a battery-testing wire attached to the starter solenoid. Another timing sensor is installed in the flywheel bellhousing. All sensor wires must remain properly attached if the Computer Analysis system is to work as designed. Never connect any device other than the test plug of the Computer Analysis system to the test network central socket in the engine compartment. Incorrect equipment could damage the plug connectors, the test sensors, or the components that contain sensors.

The information in this section of the Manual is intended to serve as a guide to both car owners and professional mechanics. Some of the operations may require special equipment and experience that only a trained mechanic will normally have. If you lack the skills, tools, or a suitable workshop for servicing the engine, we suggest you leave these repairs to an Authorized Dealer or other qualified shop. We especially urge you to consult your Authorized Dealer before attempting any repairs on a car still covered by the new-car warranty.

1. GENERAL DESCRIPTION

A cutaway view of the water-cooled, overhead camshaft engine appears in Fig. 1-1. Notice the drive belt, the camshaft, and the intermediate shaft. The intermediate shaft drives the oil pump, the distributor, and the fuel pump.

Engine Mounting

The engine and the transaxle are supported as a single unit by bonded rubber mountings. Bolts join the engine to the bellhousing of the transaxle. The engine cannot be removed without also removing the transaxle, though the transaxle can be removed without removing the engine.

Engine Block

The engine block is made of cast iron. For extra strength, the sides of the crankcase extend well below the main bearing centerline. The cylinders are integral with the block and completely exposed on all sides to the coolant that circulates through the water jacket.

Crankshaft and Bearings

The fully-counterweighted crankshaft revolves in five split-shell main bearings. The center bearing shells are flanged to take crankshaft end thrust. Seals, pressed into lightweight alloy seal carriers, are used at both ends of the crankshaft to prevent oil leakage.

Valve Train

The single overhead camshaft is driven by the crankshaft via a toothed, steel-reinforced belt. The cam lobes operate on hardened steel valve adjusting disks that are placed in recesses atop the bucket-type cam followers. Dual valve springs are used on both the intake valves and the exhaust valves.

Cylinder Head

The cylinder head is an aluminum alloy casting with integral bearing surfaces for the overhead camshaft. Pressed-in valve guides are used but the bores for the cam followers are machined directly into the cylinder head material.

Fig. 1-1. Cutaway view of the engine.

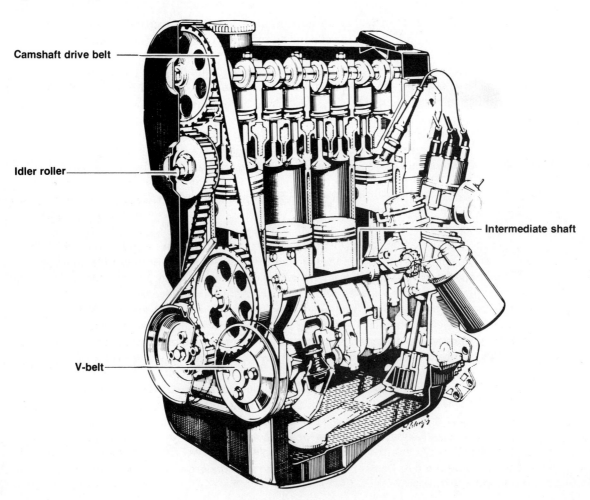

Camshaft drive belt

Idler roller

V-belt

Intermediate shaft

Connecting Rods and Pistons

The connecting rods are steel forgings. Split-shell bearings are used at the crankshaft end, and lead-bronze coated steel bushings at the piston pin end. The pistons are of the three-ring type with full-floating pins secured by circlips.

Flywheel and Drive Plate

The drive plate, used on cars with automatic transmissions, is mounted on the crankshaft with six steel bolts. On engines used with manual transmissions, the clutch pressure plate assembly is mounted on the crankshaft with six steel bolts and the flywheel is held to the pressure plate assembly at its periphery by six other steel bolts. This is a reverse of the design found on most cars, which have the flywheel bolted to the crankshaft and the pressure plate assembly bolted to the flywheel. Both the flywheel and the drive plate are equipped with ring gears for the starter drive.

Cooling System

Coolant is circulated through the radiator and the engine by a centrifugal-type water pump. The pump is crankshaft-driven by the same V-belt that drives the alternator. The radiator cooling fan is powered by an electric motor and begins to operate only at coolant temperatures of 90°C (194°F) or above. The coolant, warmed by the engine, is used to heat the car interior, the intake manifold, and, on 1974 and 1975 models, the carburetor's automatic choke.

Emission Controls

Exhaust emissions are controlled by engine modifications, exhaust gas recirculation (EGR), and—on cars sold in California—air injection (AI). The closed positive crankcase ventilation (PCV) system, which eliminates crankcase emissions, contains no PCV valve that would require periodic servicing or replacement. Some models have a catalytic converter built into the exhaust system.

Ignition System

The ignition is a conventional coil and battery system. The distributor, which has both vacuum and centrifugal advance mechanicsms, is driven by the intermediate shaft.

Lubrication System

A gear-type oil pump, driven by the distributor shaft, draws oil through a strainer in the bottom of the oil pan and forces it through a cartridge-type filter and into the engine's oil passages. A pressure relief valve limits the pressure in the system and a filter bypass valve assures lubrication even if the filter is plugged.

Clutch

The engines used with manual transmissions have a dry, single-plate clutch. The pressure plate assembly, which has a diaphragm spring, is bolted to the crankshaft. The flywheel is bolted to the periphery of the pressure plate assembly and must be removed for access to the driven plate. The operating lever on the transaxle's clutch release shaft is operated by a cable that is attached to the clutch pedal.

2. MAINTENANCE

The following routine maintenance steps are covered briefly in **LUBRICATION AND MAINTENANCE** or in this section under the headings listed after some of the items.

1. Changing engine oil and checking the oil level
2. Servicing and replacing spark plugs. **3.5**
3. Checking distributor and the ignition timing. **3.2**
4. Checking valve clearance. **5.2**
5. Checking compression
6. Servicing the air cleaner
7. Checking the exhaust system
8. Checking clutch pedal freeplay. **9.2**
9. Checking V-belt adjustment
10. Checking and adjusting idle (described in detail in **FUEL AND EXHAUST SYSTEMS**)
11. Checking the cooling system. **4.**

3. IGNITION SYSTEM

The ignition is a conventional coil and battery system. Because they have a vital influence on performance, fuel economy, and exhaust emissions, all components of the ignition system must be kept in good condition and, where applicable, correctly adjusted to the specifications given in this Manual, the Owner's Manual, or on the engine's emissions decal.

3.1 Coil

By the process of electrical induction, the coil steps up the primary circuit's 12-volt battery current to as much as 20,000 volts. This high voltage is required to ionize the air in the spark plug gaps so that a spark can jump across them. Despite the painful electrical shock that spark current can produce, its low amperage (current flow) renders it harmless. When you test the spark, you can avoid getting shocks either by wearing rubber gloves or by holding the high tension cable with a spring-type clothespin. A cable with sound insulation, however, is safe to handle.

When installing the coil, please be sure you connect the wire from the ignition switch to terminal 15 and the wire from the distributor to terminal 1. Reversing the coil wires will change the polarity of the spark current from positive to negative. Reversed polarity limits the ability of the spark voltage to ionize the air in the spark plug gaps, causing misfiring at high speeds or during hard acceleration.

Keep the coil tower clean and dry and make sure that the rubber boot surrounding the high tension cable is tight-fitting and waterproof. Otherwise, spark current may begin arcing from terminal 4 to ground. A short such as this can prevent the engine from running well or even from running at all. The arcing may also burn irreparable carbon tracks into the coil tower.

Ignition coils seldom produce trouble. However, if all the other ignition components are sound and the car still misses or is hard to start, check the coil. First test the battery as described in **ELECTRICAL SYSTEM** to make sure it is not run down. Then disconnect the high tension cable from the center terminal of the distributor cap and hold it about 10 mm (⅜ in.) from the engine block. Have someone run the starter while you observe the spark produced. If the spark is weak and yellowish, fires only when the cable is moved close to the engine block, or fails to fire at all, the coil is probably weak and should be replaced.

Since faulty wiring between the ignition switch and the coil, distributor faults, or a weak condenser can produce similar symptoms, it is best to have the coil tested before investing in a new one. If the coil proves satisfactory, use a voltmeter to check the voltage between coil terminals 15 and 1. The distributor points must be closed and the ignition turned on. If the voltage at the coil is below 9.6 volts, check for poor distributor point contact, a shorted condenser, or high resistance in the ignition switch or the wires that connect the switch to the coil.

NOTE——
The early cars covered by this manual have a ballast resistor installed in the wire that connects the ignition switch with terminal 15 of the coil. Instead of a ballast resistor, the latest cars have a resistance wire in this circuit that connects fuse box terminal A12 with terminal 15 of the coil. Use an ohmmeter to test either a ballast resistor or a resistance wire. The resistance should be between 0.85 and 0.95 ohms. Resistance wires can be identified by their insulation, which is clear with violet stripes. Replacement wires, Part No. N 900 120 01, are 1280 mm (50⅜ in.) long and have a conductor diameter of 0.75 mm (.030 in.).

3.2 Distributor

Servicing the distributor includes checking, replacing, and adjusting the breaker points, checking and possibly replacing the rotor and cap, checking the spark advance

mechanism, and adjusting the ignition timing. The condenser should not be replaced routinely but only when electrical testing proves it defective.

Removing and Installing Distributor

You should remove the distributor in order to protect it during engine disassembly. Many experienced mechanics also prefer to remove the distributor from the engine before servicing the breaker points or other distributor parts.

To remove distributor:

1. Remove the distributor cap. Using a wrench on the bolt that is in the center of the crankshaft pulley, handturn the crankshaft clockwise until the distributor rotor tip points to the No. 1 cylinder mark on the distributor body (Fig. 3-1).

Fig. 3-1. Distributor rotor aligned with the No. 1 cylinder mark on the distributor body.

2. If not previously removed, disconnect all hoses and wiring from the distributor.

3. Remove the distributor hold-down bolt and the hold-down clamp. Then lift out the distributor.

4. Lift off the washer that surrounds the distributor shaft opening in the engine block. Cover the opening to keep out dirt.

To install:

1. Check to see that the lug on the oil pump drive gearshaft is in the position shown in Fig. 3-2. If it is not, use a screwdriver to reposition it.

2. If the crankshaft was turned while the distributor was out of the engine, hand-turn the crankshaft until the No. 1 cylinder is in position to fire and the top dead center (TDC) mark is next to the pointer. The pointer is inside the hole for the Computer Analysis TDC sensor, as shown in Fig. 3-3. Remove the plastic plug (or remove the TDC sensor with special tool US 4463).

NOTE ——

To check the position of the No. 1 cylinder, look through the oil filler and see whether both cam lobes for the No. 1 cylinder are pointing upward. If the lobes are not up, hand-turn the crankshaft one full revolution to realign the TDC mark. The cylinders are numbered consecutively from the right (curb side) to the left (driver's side) of the engine. For example, the No. 4 cylinder is at the end of the engine that is bolted to the flywheel bellhousing of the transaxle.

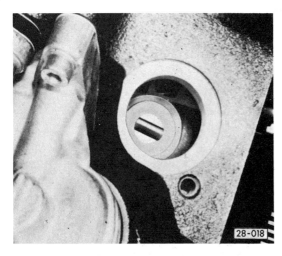

Fig. 3-2. Lug on oil pump drive gearshaft. The lug must be parallel to the engine's crankshaft.

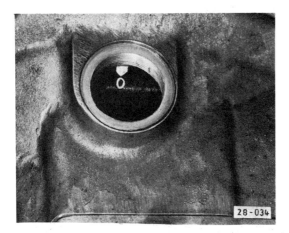

Fig. 3-3. TDC mark aligned with pointer in TDC sensor hole in bellhousing. TDC is designated by the numeral zero (0).

3. Place the large washer in the recess that surrounds the distributor shaft opening in the engine block.

4. Before you install the distributor, hand-turn the distributor shaft until the rotor tip points to a position approximately 18° clockwise from the No. 1 cylinder mark on the distributor housing.

5. Insert the distributor into the engine. As the helical gears mesh, the rotor should turn counterclockwise 18° and the lug on the oil pump drive gearshaft should engage the slot in the lower end of the distributor shaft.

6. Make sure that the distributor housing's mounting flange and washer are firmly seated against the engine block and that the rotor tip is aligned with the No. 1 cylinder mark on the distributor housing.

7. Loosely install the hold-down clamp and the hold-down bolt.

8. Install the distributor cap. Then adjust the ignition timing as described in **3.3 Adjusting Timing** before torquing the hold-down bolt to 2.0 mkg (14 ft. lb.).

4 ◼

Disassembling and Assembling Distributor

A screwdriver is the only tool required for disassembling the distributor. Though it is possible to disassemble the breaker plate, the centrifugal advance mechanism, and the distributor shaft for cleaning and inspection, only the components shown in Fig. 3-4 are available as replacement parts.

The distributor cap, the rotor, and the shield plate must be removed for access to the breaker points. A single fillister head screw holds the one-piece breaker point assembly to the breaker plate. The same screw locks the breaker points in adjustment. A slip-on terminal connects the point wire with the primary wire from the coil. In removing the vacuum advance unit, you must pry off the E-clip that holds the vacuum advance unit's pull rod to the pin on the breaker plate.

The distributor's breaker points should be replaced and adjusted at the intervals prescribed in **LUBRICATION AND MAINTENANCE.** Remove the old point assembly, then wipe clean the inside of the distributor. Make sure that the contacts of the new point assembly meet squarely. If the contacts do not meet squarely, carefully bend the stationary contact to align the points. Never bend the movable contact arm since doing this will impair its strength.

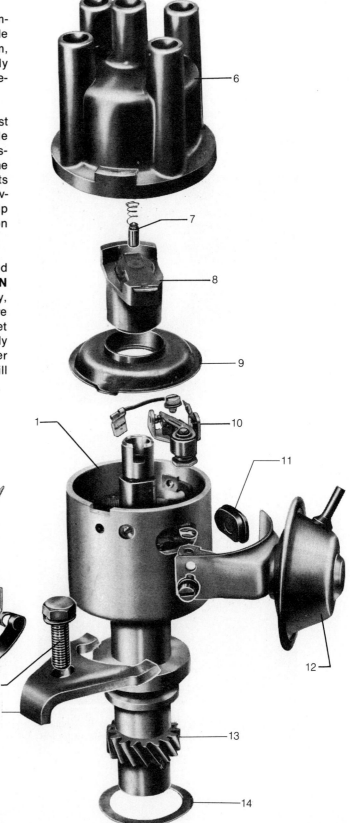

1. Distributor housing assembly
2. Condenser
3. Spring clip and bracket
4. Hold-down bolt
5. Hold-down clamp
6. Distributor cap
7. Carbon brush and spring
8. Rotor
9. Shield plate
10. Breaker point assembly
11. Rubber seal
12. Vacuum advance unit
13. Drive gear
14. Washer

Fig. 3-4. Exploded view of the distributor. The condenser is integral with the primary wire and the point wire terminal.

28-040

Lubricate the distributor as indicated in Fig. 3-5. Wipe off any excess lubricants so that they will not be thrown onto the point contacts, then adjust the breaker points.

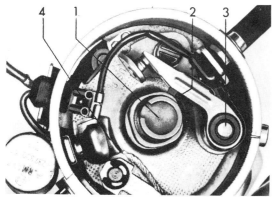

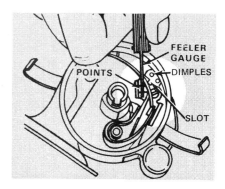

Fig. 3-6. Feeler gauge inserted between points. To adjust the point gap, engage a screwdriver in the slot in the breaker point assembly and between the dimples on the breaker plate.

© 1973 VWoA—1167

Fig. 3-5. Distributor lubrication. Saturate felt wick (**1**) with engine oil. Apply a small amount of multipurpose grease to the distributor cam and point rubbing block (**2**), one drop of engine oil to the breaker point pivot (**3**), and a small amount of multipurpose grease to the breaker plate ball (**4**).

Adjusting Points

The breaker points must be adjusted after you have installed them. The adjustment can be checked either with a feeler gauge or with a dwell meter.

To adjust with feeler gauge:

1. Remove the distributor cap and rotor.

2. Using a wrench on the bolt that is in the center of the crankshaft pulley, hand-turn the crankshaft clockwise until the breaker point rubbing block is on a high point on the distributor cam (points wide open).

   > **NOTE**
   >
   > If you are doing a complete tune-up, adjust the points while the spark plugs are out. This will make it easier to turn the crankshaft to the correct position.

3. To determine whether the points are gapped correctly, insert a 0.40-mm (.016-in.) feeler gauge in the point gap. The points are gapped correctly if the feeler gauge just slips into the gap without forcing the contacts apart (Fig. 3-6).

4. If necessary, loosen the breaker point assembly mounting screw. Then, using the tip of a screwdriver as shown in Fig. 3-7, move the fixed contact one way or the other until you get the specified breaker point gap.

Fig. 3-7. Breaker point gap being adjusted.

5. Tighten the breaker point assembly mounting screw, then recheck the gap. If the gap is incorrect, repeat the adjustment. If the gap is correct, install the shield plate, the distributor rotor, and the cap. Then adjust the ignition timing as described in **3.3 Adjusting Timing.**

To adjust with dwell meter:

1. If the points have not already been gapped with a feeler gauge, do so to make sure that the engine will start. The adjustment can be approximate.

2. Connect the dwell meter. The black clip should be attached to ground on any bare metal part and the colored clip attached to terminal 1 at the coil.

3. Switch the dwell meter to the tachometer position. Start the engine and run it at 1000 rpm.

4. Switch the meter to measure dwell. Read the dwell.

NOTE ——

The dwell should be between 44° and 50°. Points that have been in service for less than 15,000 mi. (24,000 km) can be retained in service without adjustment so long as dwell is between 42° and 58°.

5. If necessary, remove the distributor cap, the rotor, and the shield plate. Then adjust the dwell. To adjust dwell, loosen the breaker point assembly mounting screw. Using the tip of a screwdriver, as shown previously in Fig. 3-7, move the stationary contact either to widen the gap and decrease dwell, or to narrow the gap and increase dwell.

NOTE ——

You can run the engine with the starter to check the dwell during adjustment but always make the final check with the engine running.

6. Fully tighten the breaker point assembly mounting screw. Then install the distributor rotor and cap. Check the dwell at 1000 rpm to make sure that it is within the specified range.

7. Run the engine at about 2000 rpm. The dwell should not vary more than ±1° from the reading obtained at 1000 rpm. Larger deviations indicate a worn distributor, which should be replaced.

8. After you have adjusted the dwell to specifications, adjust the ignition timing as described in **3.3 Adjusting Timing**.

Abnormal Point Wear

Moderate contact pitting and build-up with bright contact surfaces can be considered normal breaker point wear. When properly installed, aligned, and lubricated, the breaker point assembly should provide reliable service without further attention until the mileage specified for point replacement is reached.

Vehicle operating symptoms that suggest abnormal point wear include engine missing at high speeds or during acceleration, rough idling, hard starting, or the failure to start. You will often be able to find the cause of such trouble by using **Table a** to diagnose the abnormal point condition that accompanies the operating symptom.

If the abnormal condition is severe, it may be necessary to replace or adjust the breaker point assembly before the normal replacement mileage. Filing or honing the point contacts to correct abnormal pitting or build-up, or to remove hard deposits, is not recommended.

Table a. Abnormal Point Condition Diagnosis

Abnormal Condition	Probable Cause	Remedy
1. Blued point contacts	Weak spark owing to defective coil or condenser	Test coil and condenser. Replace either if it is faulty. See **3.1, 3.2**.
2. Gray point surfaces	a. Point gap adjusted too narrow b. Point gap narrowed by rapid rubbing block wear c. Point spring weak	a. Readjust points. See **3.2**. b. Replace points. Lubricate distributor cam and rubbing block with multipurpose grease. See **3.2**. c. Use a spring scale to measure spring tension. Replace points if tension is below 400 to 600 g (14⅞ to 21⅛ oz.). See **3.2**.
3. Point contacts have yellow or black markings. A smudgy line may appear directly under the contacts	a. Oil or grease on point contacts owing to excessive distributor lubrication b. Oil on points owing to dirty feeler gauge c. Points fouled by engine oil that has been forced up around the distributor shaft by excessive crankcase pressure	a. Replace points. Lubricate to specifications, then wipe away excess lubricants. See **3.2**. b. Replace points. Clean feeler gauge with solvent before adjusting points. See **3.2**. c. Replace points. Clean distributor. Locate and remove restrictions in the crankcase ventilation system. See **3.2** and **FUEL AND EXHAUST SYSTEMS**.
4. One point contact pitted, metal transferred to other point	a. Misaligned points b. Electrical system voltage excessive owing to a faulty regulator c. Condenser faulty d. Extended engine operation outside normal speed range	a. Replace points. Make sure that new point contacts meet squarely. See **3.2**. b. Test charging system. Replace regulator, if faulty. Replace points if build-up exceeds 0.05 mm (.002 in.); if it is less, adjust points with dwell meter. See **3.2** and **ELECTRICAL SYSTEM**. c. Test condenser and replace if faulty. Replace points if build-up exceeds 0.05 mm (.002 in.); if it is less, adjust points with dwell meter. See **3.2**. d. Replace points if build-up exceeds 0.05 mm (.002 in.); if it is less, adjust points with dwell meter. See **3.2**.

3.3 Adjusting Timing

Adjust the timing after you install or adjust the breaker points, or whenever you reinstall the distributor. A change of only 0.10 mm (.004 in.) in the point gap will alter ignition timing about 3°.

To adjust timing:

1. On early cars with manual transmissions, disconnect the wire from the Computer Analysis TDC sensor, which is on the bellhousing. Using a special wrench (VW Tool US 4463), remove the TDC sensor. On late cars with manual transmissions, which do not have permanently installed TDC sensors, remove the plastic plug from the TDC sensor hole.

2. Following the instrument manufacturer's instructions, install a tachometer and a stroboscopic timing light.

3. Start the engine and allow it to warm up until the idle stabilizes at 850 to 1000 rpm. Do not disconnect the vacuum hoses from the distributor.

4. On cars with manual transmissions, aim the timing light at the TDC sensor hole in the flywheel bellhousing. The 3° ATDC (after top dead center) timing mark should appear in line with the pointer in the hole, as shown in Fig. 3-8.

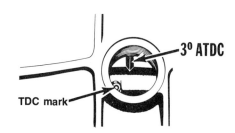

Fig. 3-8. The 3° ATDC mark in line with pointer in TDC sensor hole in flywheel bellhousing (manual transmission).

5. On cars with automatic transmissions, aim the timing light at the timing pointer hole, which is in the bellhousing—slightly toward the driver's side of the car from the engine's ignition distributor. The 3° ATDC (after top dead center) timing mark should appear in line with the pointer in the hole, as shown in Fig. 3-9.

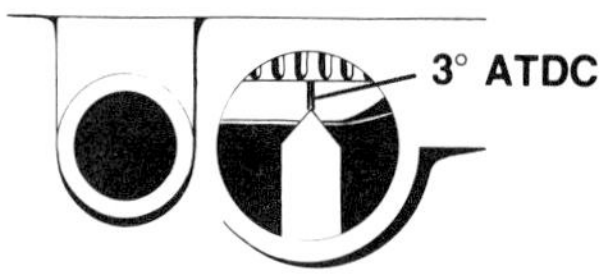

Fig. 3-9. The 3° ATDC mark on drive plate aligned with pointer in large hole in bellhousing (automatic transmission).

6. If the 3° ATDC timing mark is not aligned with the pointer, loosen the distributor hold-down bolt. Then, with the engine idling at 850 to 1000 rpm, hand-turn the distributor housing clockwise or counterclockwise until the 3° ATDC mark, illuminated by the timing light, is aligned with the pointer.

7. While you hold the distributor in the correct position, tighten the hold-down bolt.

8. Torque the hold-down bolt to 2.0 mkg (14 ft. lb.). Then recheck the timing. Repeat the adjustment procedure given in step 6 if the timing is incorrect.

9. Using the special wrench, install the TDC sensor on early cars with manual transmissions, then reconnect the Computer Analysis wire. On later cars with manual transmissions, install the plastic plug.

The throttle valve must close adequately for accurate timing adjustments. To check, disconnect the green (retard) hose from the distributor with the engine idling. The timing mark should shift considerably in the advance direction. If the timing does not shift, the throttle valve is not closing adequately and the throttle valve gap must be adjusted as described in **FUEL AND EXHAUST SYSTEMS.** Readjust the timing after adjusting the throttle valve gap.

Checking Spark Advance Mechanism

The distributor has both vacuum and centrifugal spark advance mechanisms. Special timing lights are available that incorporate a built-in meter you can use to measure spark advance. The instructions supplied with these timing lights tell you how to use the device to check the centrifugal advance mechanism. By using the special timing light in conjunction with a vacuum gauge (attached to T-fittings inserted in the two hoses that are connected to the distributor), you can also check the vacuum advance mechanism.

4

Table b lists the rpm and vacuum levels where critical changes in the spark advance curve take place. Comparing actual distributor operation to the data in the table will help you locate dirty, binding advance mechanisms or mechanical faults in the distributor. The distributor number is stamped on the distributor itself.

If testing reveals irregularities in the spark advance curve, first clean and lubricate the moving parts of the distributor. If the vacuum advance still fails to conform to specifications, install a new vacuum unit. If retesting reveals discrepancies in the centrifugal advance curve, it indicates worn internal parts. In that case you should replace the distributor body and internal parts as a unit.

Though you may not have a special timing light for checking the spark advance curve, you can still quick-check the spark advance mechanisms without running the engine. To check the vacuum advance, hand-turn the breaker plate counterclockwise. It should move without grittiness and spring back solidly to its original position when released. To check the vacuum unit for leaks, disconnect the vacuum hoses. Turn the breaker plate as far as it will go counterclockwise, cover the hose connections on the vacuum unit with your fingers, then release the breaker plate. Vacuum should keep the breaker plate from returning fully to its original position until you uncover the hose connections. If the breaker plate returns fully, there is a leak in the diaphragm or the vacuum unit housing.

To quick-check the centrifugal advance, hand-turn the distributor rotor clockwise. When you release it, the rotor should return automatically to its original position. If it does not, either the mechanism is dirty or the distributor body and internal parts are faulty and should be replaced as a unit.

Cleaning Spark Advance Mechanism

Clean the distributor if dirt or hardened grease is causing the spark advance mechanism to jam, or if the interior of the distributor has become oil soaked. First remove and disassemble the distributor as described in **3.2 Distributor.** Then wash the distributor body assembly thoroughly in clean solvent. Blow the distributor body assembly dry with compressed air.

CAUTION ——
Be careful not to direct a strong blast of air into the housing at close range. Doing this could damage the calibrated springs in the centrifugal advance mechanism.

Thoroughly lubricate the distributor shaft and bearings with engine oil by applying the oil to the space between the drive gear and the distributor body. With the distributor body inverted, hand-turn the shaft until the oil has

Table b. Spark Advance Curves

| Distributor | Centrifugal Advance Range | | | | | | |
| | Begin ──────────────────────────────────────▶ End | | | | | | |
	rpm	rpm	degrees	rpm	degrees	rpm	degrees
055 905 205 B (1975 cars)	1050–1350	2200	14–20	4000	22–26	5000	26–30
055 905 205 F (1976 cars with carburetors)	1100–1400	2100–2200	15–19	3000	18–23	5000	26–30
049 905 205 A (fuel injection cars)	1120–1400	2000–2400	11–21	4800	25–29	5200	26–30

| | Vacuum Advance Range | | |
| | Begin ─────────────────▶ End | | Timing direction |
	mbar (mm/Hg, in./Hg)	mbar (mm/Hg, in./Hg)	degrees	
055 905 205 B (1975 cars)	373–442 (280–333, 11.0–13.1)	452 (340, 13.3)	10°–12° maximum	advance
	213–293 (160–220, 6.4–8.8)	327–393 (245–295, 9.8–11.6)	8°–10° maximum	retard
055 905 205 F (1976 cars with carburetors)	267–327 (200–245, 8.0–9.8)	467 (350, 14.0)	11°–15° maximum	advance
	200–293 (150–220, 5.9–8.8)	333–400 (250–300, 10.0–11.8)	8°–9° maximum	retard
049 905 205 A (fuel injection cars)	267–333 (200–250, 8.0–10.0)	360–386 (270–290, 10.5–11.5)	4°–8° maximum	advance
	133–267 (100–200, 4.0–8.0)	280–373 (210–280, 8.25–11.0)	8°–10° maximum	retard

worked its way all along the shaft. The shaft should turn smoothly without binding. Apply one drop of engine oil to each pivot point in the centrifugal advance mechanism and to the breaker plate bearing. If necessary, you can remove the breaker plate to gain access to the centrifugal advance.

3.4 Secondary Circuit

The secondary circuit of the ignition system consists of the distributor rotor, the distributor cap, the spark plug cables, and the high tension cable that links the coil with the distributor cap. Secondary circuit resistance, for radio suppression and to reduce spark plug gap erosion, is built into the distributor rotor and the spark plug connectors. This resistance allows the use of metallic conductor ignition cables.

You can check the rotor resistor with an ohmmeter as shown in Fig. 3-10. You can test individual plug connectors the same way. Rotor resistance should not exceed 10,000 ohms; plug connector resistance should range from 5000 to 10,000 ohms.

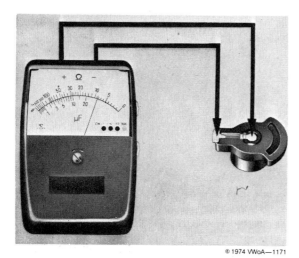

Fig. 3-10. Rotor resistance being measured.

To prevent spark flashover, which could cause irreparable carbon tracks on the distributor cap and rotor, keep the cap and the rotor clean and dry. Also keep the ignition cables clean and replace them when the insulation shows signs of cracking or deterioration. The rubber boots at the coil tower, the distributor cap towers, and the plug connectors must be sound and tight fitting if the secondary circuit is to remain waterproof.

3.5 Spark Plugs

Replace the spark plugs each 15,000 mi. (24,000 km). After this distance, the electrodes will have worn to the

point that ionization of the spark plug gap is discouraged. The color of the deposits on the firing tip of the used plugs may vary, indicating the following combustion chamber conditions:

1. Gray or light tan deposits indicate good combustion, proper fuel mixtures, and consistently good spark plug performance.

2. Light gray or chalky-white deposits indicate too lean a fuel/air mixture or an overheated spark plug.

3. Soft, fluffy, black deposits indicate a plug that is misfiring or too rich a fuel/air mixture.

4. A spark plug fouled by oil indicates severe oil leakage past the piston rings or valve guides, or a spark plug that is no longer firing.

Replacement spark plugs must be of the correct heat range and physical dimensions. The plug reach (the length of the threaded portion of the shell) should be ¾ in.; the thread diameter should be 14 mm. Suitable spark plugs are listed in **12. Engine and Clutch Technical Data.** Before you install the spark plugs, measure their gaps as illustrated in Fig. 3-11.

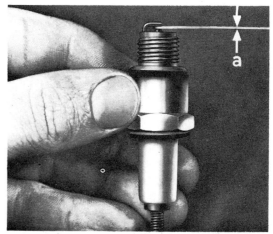

Fig. 3-11. Spark plug gap being measured. Dimension **a** should be 0.60 to 0.70 mm (.024 to .028 in.).

If the spark plug gap is too wide or too narrow, adjust the gap by bending the side electrode only. Never attempt to bend the center electrode. If you attempt to do this you will break the insulator and render the spark plug unserviceable. If the old spark plugs were difficult to remove, the spark plug holes in the cylinder head should be cleaned with a thread chaser made especially for the job.

During installation, lightly coat the spark plug threads with anti-seize compound or multipurpose grease. If nothing else is available, lubricate the spark plug threads with engine oil. Lubrication will prevent corrosion damage and stuck spark plugs.

CAUTION ――

Most anti-seize compounds contain graphite, which must not contact the plug electrodes or insulator. If it does, the graphite could short out the spark plug.

Start the plug in the cylinder head with your fingertips or by hand-holding the spark plug socket. This will give improved feel and help prevent accidental cross-threading. Turn the spark plug in until you feel the gasket contact the cylinder head. Then install a torque wrench on the spark plug socket and torque the plug to 2.5 to 3.0 mkg (18 to 22 ft. lb.).

4. COOLING SYSTEM

To maintain the anti-corrosion properties of the coolant, you should use a permanent-type anti-freeze year-round. If coolant must be added, use the same proportion of water to anti-freeze that is already in the cooling system. Typical proportions are given in **Table c.**

CAUTION ――

Never add cold water or coolant while the engine is hot or overheated. Doing this could crack the engine block or the cylinder head.

The cooling system is unusual in that the thermostat is mounted in the external-type water pump and the cooling fan is powered by an electric motor. The cooling fan does not operate constantly, but only after the coolant has reached a temperature of 90° to 95°C (194° to 203°F) or above. The advantages of this system are fast warm-up, stable operating temperature, low noise level while driving, fast heater reaction, and more available power from the engine. The thermo switch turns off the fan when the coolant temperature falls to between 85° and 90°C (185° and 194°F) or below.

4.1 Replacing Hoses

To prevent hose failure and overheating, you should periodically inspect both the heater hoses and the radiator hoses. Replace hoses that are hard and cracked, spongy, rotted, or that have a tendency to collapse.

To replace:

1. Remove the radiator cap or the expansion tank cap. Place a receptacle beneath the water pump for catching the draining coolant. Then disconnect the lower radiator hose from the thermostat housing and allow the coolant to drain. (If you must completely drain the coolant, also remove the plug that is in the engine block, at the rear.)

CAUTION ――

Never drain the coolant while the engine is hot. Doing this could warp the engine block or the cylinder head.

2. Using a screwdriver, loosen the hose clamps at each end of the hose you must remove. Then slide the clamps toward the center of the hose.

3. Pull the hose off of its connections.

CAUTION ――

If a radiator hose is stuck to the radiator connection by sealer, it is best to cut the old hose off the connection. Prying the hose loose can damage the brass connection or the radiator.

4. Clean bits of old hose and sealer off the connections. Lightly coat the connections with water resistant sealer.

5. Slip the hose clamps onto the hose. Then slide the hose onto its connections.

Table c. Anti-freeze-to-Water Proportions

For outside temperatures down to	Anti-freeze			Water		
	Quarts	Imp. Quarts	Liters	Quarts	Imp. Quarts	Liters
−20°C (−4°F)	2.5	2.1	2.4	4.4	3.65	4.2
−25°C (−13°F)	2.8	2.3	2.6	4.1	3.4	3.9
−30°C (−22°F)	3.1	2.6	2.9	3.8	3.1	3.6
−35°C (−31°F)	3.5	2.8	3.3	3.4	2.8	3.2
−40°C (−40°F)	3.6	3.0	3.4	3.3	2.7	3.1

6. Position the hose clamps so that they are past the bead on the connection, but no nearer than 2.5 mm (⅛ in.) to the end of the hose. Then tighten the hose clamps just enough to compress the hose firmly around the connections.

CAUTION ——

Overtightening the clamps will cause them to cut into the hose material. This damage may eventually lead to hose failure.

7. Using water resistant sealer, install the lower radiator thermostat housing. If previously removed, install the drain plug in the rearward side of the engine block. Then refill the radiator with the original coolant or with the mixture of water and permanent-type anti-freeze that was given earlier in **Table c.** Do not fill above the **Max.** marks indicated in Fig. 4-1 or Fig. 4-2.

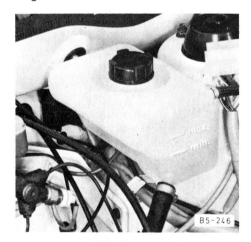

Fig. 4-1. Separate expansion tank used on early models. Fill to between **Max.** and **Min.** marks.

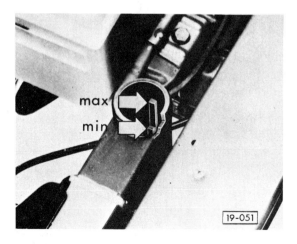

Fig. 4-2. Late-type radiator with built-in expansion tank. Fill to a point between the marks indicated by the arrows.

4.2 Cooling System Troubleshooting

Most cooling system malfunctions not caused by leaks can be traced to a faulty thermostat, a restricted hose, a faulty radiator cap, or a clogged radiator. Clogged radiators and heater cores should be repaired only by an Authorized Dealer or a qualified radiator repair shop.

Virtually all clogged cooling systems are caused by neglect or the addition of substances to the coolant that are not recommended by the car manufacturer. Because radiator repairs are expensive, it is not wise economically to neglect the cooling system in an attempt to save the few dollars that proper maintenance will cost. You will never have to worry about a clogged radiator or heater core if you observe the following precautions:

1. To prevent the formation of rust and scale, keep the cooling system filled with at least a 40% solution of an approved-quality, permanent-type anti-freeze. Change the anti-freeze solution as recommended by the manufacturer, or when a chemical test shows the old solution lacking in anti-corrosion protection.

2. Never add more than one can of leak sealer to the cooling system as a precaution against leaks. Doing this is especially likely to clog rust-filled, neglected cooling systems.

3. Never fill the radiator from a roadside ditch, a stream, or other water sources that may contain silt and organic material.

4. Do not add engine oil to the coolant as a rust preventative. Doing this will encourage the formation of oil sludge in the cooling system and will damage the heater hoses and radiator hoses.

4 ■

Table d lists possible overheating and underheating symptoms, their probable causes, and suggested repairs. The boldface numbers in the suggested repair column refer to the numbered headings in this section where the suggested repairs are described.

Testing Thermostat

To test the thermostat, first remove it from the water pump as described in **4.4 Disassembling and Assembling Water Pump.** You should also test new thermostats before you install them in the car.

Measure the thermostat to determine dimension **a** given in Fig. 4-3. If it exceeds 31 mm (1.220 in. or $1\,^7/_{32}$ in.), the thermostat is not closing fully and should be replaced. If dimension **a** is correct, place the thermostat in a pan of cool water together with a thermometer for measuring the water temperature. Heat the water. The thermostat should begin to open at approximately 80°C (176°F). At 94°C (200°F), dimension **b**, given in Fig. 4-3, should be at least 38 mm (1.496 in. or 1½ in.). If not, replace the thermostat.

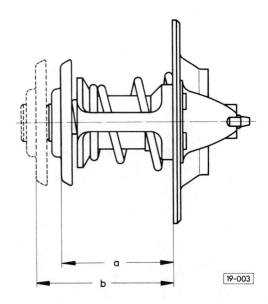

Fig. 4-3. Thermostat test dimensions. Dimension **a** is the closed (cold) length; dimension **b** is the open (hot) length.

Table d. Cooling System Troubleshooting

Symptom	Probable cause	Suggested repair
Inadequate heater output, temperature gauge reads normal	a. Installed position of heater hoses reversed b. Heater hose restricted c. Heater core clogged d. Heater control out of adjustment	a. Install heater hoses. See **4, 4.1.** b. Replace hose. See **4.1.** c. Replace heater core or have core cleaned. See **4.5.** d. Adjust control cables. See **BODY AND INTERIOR.**
Inadequate heater output, temperature gauge reads low	a. Faulty thermostat b. Electric fan not switching off	a. Remove and test thermostat. See **4.2, 4.3.** b. Replace thermo switch for fan. See **4.5.**
Temperature gauge reads low, heater output normal	Faulty temperature gauge or sending unit	Test temperature gauge and sending unit. Replace faulty part. See **4.2.**
Engine overheats	a. Low coolant level b. Burst hose c. Radiator hose restricted (lower hose may collapse only at highway speeds) d. V-belt loose or broken e. Faulty thermostat f. Electric fan not switching on g. Faulty radiator cap h. Clogged radiator i. Incorrect ignition timing or valve timing	a. Fill the radiator to **Max.** mark. Check cooling system for leaks with pressure tester. See **4.2.** b. Replace hose. Refill radiator to **Max.** mark. See **4.1.** c. Replace hose. See **4.1.** d. Adjust or replace V-belt. See **4.3.** e. Remove and test thermostat. Replace if necessary. See **4.2, 4.3.** f. Test thermo switch and fan. Replace faulty part. See **4.2, 4.5.** g. Test pressure relief valve in cap. Replace faulty caps. See **4.2.** h. Replace radiator or have core cleaned. See **4.2, 4.5.** i. Check camshaft drive belt installation. Adjust ignition timing and check spark advance. See **3.3, 5.1.**

Pressure Testing Radiator Cap and Cooling System

Various kinds of cooling system pressure testers are available. In carrying out pressure tests, follow the instructions supplied by the tester's manufacturer and use a procedure that is suitable to the tester's design.

To pressure test the cooling system, pump the pressure up to approximately .95 atu (14 psi). Observe the gauge on the pressure tester pump (Fig. 4-4). The gauge should not indicate a pressure loss during a two-minute waiting period. If it does, there are leaks in the system that should be shown by the seepage of coolant.

—VW1274

19-011

Fig. 4-4. Pressure tester pump installed on expansion tank. On late cars, install pump on radiator.

CAUTION ——

Never pump the pressure above 1.02 atu (15 psi)—the maximum pressure permitted by the radiator cap or expansion tank cap's relief valve. Exceeding this pressure could burst the radiator.

To test the expansion tank cap or radiator cap, install the cap on the pressure tester pump. Pump the pressure up to 0.88 to 1.02 atu (13 to 15 psi). If the cap's pressure relief valve opens within this range—but not at a lesser pressure—the cap is working correctly. Replace faulty caps.

Testing Thermo Switch and Cooling Fan

If the electric cooling fan fails to operate, check the coolant temperature. If a defective thermostat is not allowing the coolant to warm up to the switch's cut-in temperature of 90° to 95°C (194° to 203°F), the fan will not be switched on by the thermo switch.

If the coolant is reaching the thermo switch's cut-in temperature, bridge the terminals on the thermo switch. If the fan operates, the thermo switch is defective and should be replaced. If the fan still does not operate, use a voltmeter to test the fan circuit. The wiring is shown in the current flow diagrams given in **ELECTRICAL SYSTEM.**

Testing Temperature Gauge and Sending Unit

If the temperature gauge needle remains at its rest position even though the engine has been operating for some time, turn on the heater so that you can judge the temperature of the coolant. If the heater delivers little or no heat, the thermostat is probably defective. If the heater delivers adequate heat, the trouble is in the gauge or the sending unit.

Should the preceding check indicate that the coolant is reaching normal operating temperatures but the gauge does not indicate heat, turn on the ignition. Then pull the gauge wire off of the sending unit that is screwed into the heater hose connection on the left end of the cylinder head. Ground the wire on some clean, unpainted metal part of the car. If the gauge needle moves upward, the sending unit is faulty and should be replaced. If the needle does not move, the wire or the gauge is faulty.

You can make another similar test if the temperature gauge needle advances to the high end of the dial whenever the ignition is switched on. Should the needle fall when you disconnect the wire from the sending unit, the sending unit is faulty. If the needle does not fall to a lower reading, the wire leading to the gauge is probably grounded. If the gauge itself is stuck or has an internal short circuit to ground, replace the gauge.

4.3 Removing and Installing Water Pump

The right-hand part of the water pump, which contains the shaft, the seals, the bearing and the impeller, can be replaced separately. However, you can avoid removing the camshaft drive belt and sprockets by removing the water pump as a unit before you disassemble it.

To remove:

1. Drain the coolant (see **4.1 Replacing Hoses**). Loosen the upper and lower alternator mounting bolts. Loosen the bolt that holds the alternator belt adjusting bracket to the cylinder head.

2. Push the alternator as far as possible toward the engine. Then take the V-belt off the alternator and water pump pulleys.

4 ■

NOTE ——

Unless you are going to remove the water pump by working under the car, you may wish to remove the alternator completely for better access to the water pump mounting bolts. If you want to remove the alternator/water pump V-belt completely from certain cars sold in California, you must first remove the belt for the air injection pump. To do this, loosen the air pump mounting bolts. Push the air pump as far as possible toward the engine, then remove the air pump V-belt.

3. Remove the nut from the T-head bolt that holds the camshaft drive belt cover to the water pump. Then remove the T-head bolt from the water pump. The two spacer washers and the rubber grommet can remain in the drive belt cover.

4. Disconnect both hoses from the left end of the water pump. See **4.1 Replacing Hoses.**

5. Take out the four bolts that hold the water pump to the engine block. Two short bolts are at the top of the pump, one long bolt is at about the center of the pump, and one long bolt is between the two hose connections. Remove the pump as you take out the last bolt.

To install:

1. Install a new O-ring in the recess that surrounds the water outlet in the pump's mounting flange. Clean the surface of the engine block where it will be contacted by the pump and the O-ring.

NOTE ——

Do not use sealer between the water pump mounting flange and the engine block.

2. Using all four mounting bolts, loosely install the water pump on the engine. Then, tightening each bolt a little at a time, torque the mounting bolts to 2.0 mkg (14 ft. lb.).

3. Install the V-belt on the crankshaft pulley, the water pump pulley, and the alternator pulley.

4. By pulling the alternator away from the engine block, adjust the V-belt tension so that you can depress the V-belt 10 to 15 mm (3/8 to 9/16 in.) at the point indicated in Fig. 4-5.

5. When the V-belt tension is correct, torque the lower alternator mounting bolts to 2.5 mkg (18 ft. lb.) and the bolts that hold the adjusting bracket on the alternator and the cylinder head to 2.0 mkg (14 ft. lb.). On California cars that are so equipped, install the air pump V-belt and adjust it using the same procedure used to adjust the alternator/water pump belt.

CAUTION ——

Do not tension the V-belts too tightly. Doing this may cause the alternator bearings, the water pump bearings, or the air pump bearings to fail after only a short period of service.

Fig. 4-5. Point at which V-belt should be depressed. Dimension **a** should be 10 to 15 mm (3/8 to 9/16 in.).

6. Install the hoses as described in **4.1 Replacing Hoses.** Install the T-head drive belt cover bolt and tighten the nut just enough to compress slightly the rubber grommet that is in the drive belt cover. Fill the cooling system as previously described.

4.4 Disassembling and Assembling Water Pump

By working under the car, you can easily remove the thermostat housing and the thermostat with the water pump installed on the engine. Once you have removed the thermostat, you can test it as described in **4.2 Cooling System Troubleshooting.** The mechanical (right-hand) part of the water pump can also be removed from the water pump housing with the pump installed, but it is usually more convenient to remove the water pump first.

To disassemble:

1. Remove the three bolts and washers that hold the pulley on the water pump shaft.

NOTE ——

Though it is not absolutely necessary to remove the pulley, removing it will improve access to the bolts that hold the water pump together.

2. Remove the seven bolts and washers that hold the right-hand part of the pump to the housing. Then remove the right-hand part of the pump and the gasket.

3. Remove the two bolts and washers that hold the thermostat housing to the water pump housing. Then remove the thermostat housing, the O-ring, and the thermostat as shown in Fig. 4-6.

Assembly is the reverse of disassembly. Use a new O-ring between the thermostat housing and the water pump housing and a new gasket between the water pump housing and the right-hand part of the pump. Tighten each of the seven bolts a little at a time until all are torqued to 1.0 mkg (7 ft. lb.). Torque the bolts that hold the pulley to the water pump hub to 2.0 mkg (14 ft. lb.).

4.5 Removing and Installing Radiator, Cooling Fan, and Air Ducts

The cooling fan is mounted on the radiator. It can be removed from the radiator while the radiatior is installed in the car, or the radiator and the cooling fan can be removed together as a unit.

To remove:

1. Remove the radiator cap. Place a receptacle beneath the water pump for catching the draining coolant. Then disconnect the bottom radiator hose from the thermostat housing and allow the coolant to drain.

> **CAUTION** ——
>
> *Never drain the coolant while the engine is hot. Doing this could warp the engine block or the cylinder head.*

2. Disconnect the upper and the lower radiator hoses from the radiator. See **4.1 Replacing Hoses.**

> **CAUTION** ——
>
> *If the radiator hoses are stuck to the radiator connections by sealer, it is best to cut the old hoses off the connections, then replace the hoses. Prying the hoses loose can damage the brass connections or the radiator.*

3. Disconnect the battery ground strap. Then disconnect the wires from the thermo switch that is on the radiator and from the connector that is on the fan motor.

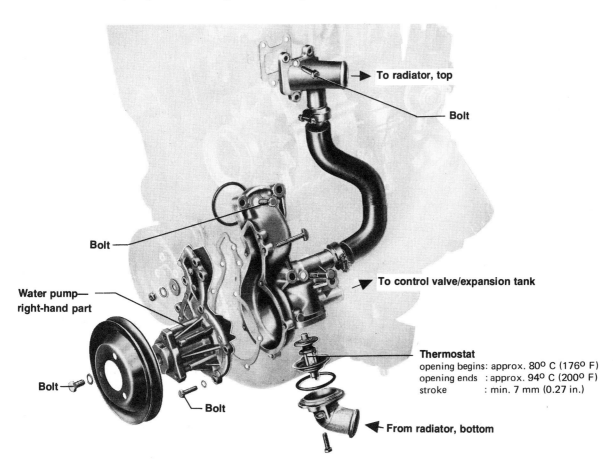

Fig. 4-6. Exploded view of the water pump and related parts.

- To radiator, top
- Bolt
- Bolt
- To control valve/expansion tank
- Water pump—right-hand part
- Bolt
- Bolt
- **Thermostat**
  opening begins: approx. 80° C (176° F)
  opening ends : approx. 94° C (200° F)
  stroke   : min. 7 mm (0.27 in.)
- From radiator, bottom

19-016

4. Remove the clips, the nuts, and the bolts. Then remove the fiberboard air ducts.

5. Remove the lower radiator mounting nuts, but leave the bonded rubber mountings attached to the radiator.

6. Move the radiator slightly to the left and tilt it toward the engine. Then lift the radiator out upward, complete with the fan and the fan duct.

7. If necessary, unbolt the fan and the fan duct from the radiator.

> **NOTE ——**
>
> To remove the cooling fan with the radiator installed, disconnect the battery ground strap and the wire to the fan. Unbolt the fan duct from the radiator and remove the duct and motor. Then unbolt the fan motor from the fan duct.

Installation is the reverse of removal. Align the radiator by sliding the mountings in their elongated bolt holes. Install the hoses as described in **4.1 Replacing Hoses.** Then refill the cooling system.

5. VALVES, CAMSHAFT, AND CYLINDER HEAD

The camshaft drive belt, the camshaft, and the cylinder head can be removed from the engine without first removing the engine from the car. You do not need to replace the camshaft drive belt unless inspection shows it to be faulty.

5.1 Removing, Installing, and Adjusting Camshaft Drive Belt

The removal of the camshaft drive belt and related parts is illustrated in Fig. 5-1. In replacing the drive belt, you need not remove the drive belt sprockets.

To remove camshaft drive belt:

1. On cars with carburetors, remove the air cleaner and all of the related air ducts. This step is unnecessary on cars with fuel injection.

2. Only on certain cars sold in California, remove the V-belt for the air injection pump. To do this, loosen the air pump mounting bolts, push the pump toward the engine, then remove the air pump V-belt.

3. Loosen the upper and the lower alternator mounting bolts. Loosen the bolt that holds the alternator belt adjusting bracket to the cylinder head. Push the alternator toward the engine, then remove the alternator V-belt.

4. Take out the three bolts that hold the water pump pulley to the water pump and remove the pulley. Remove the nuts and the bolts that hold the camshaft drive belt cover to the water pump and to the front of the engine. Then remove the cover.

5. Loosen the camshaft drive belt tension adjuster locknut. Using a wrench on the tension adjuster, turn the adjuster counterclockwise so that tension is removed from the drive belt. Then remove the drive belt. (Work it off the sprockets toward the front of the car.)

Fig. 5-1. Camshaft drive belt removal.

1. Camshaft sprocket
2. Drive belt tensioner
3. Tension adjuster locknut
4. Camshaft drive belt
5. V-belt
6. Crankshaft sprocket retaining bolt
7. Socket head screw for crankshaft pulley
8. Bolt for water pump pulley
9. Intermediate shaft sprocket retaining bolt
10. Crankshaft sprocket
11. Intermediate shaft sprocket
12. Oil seal

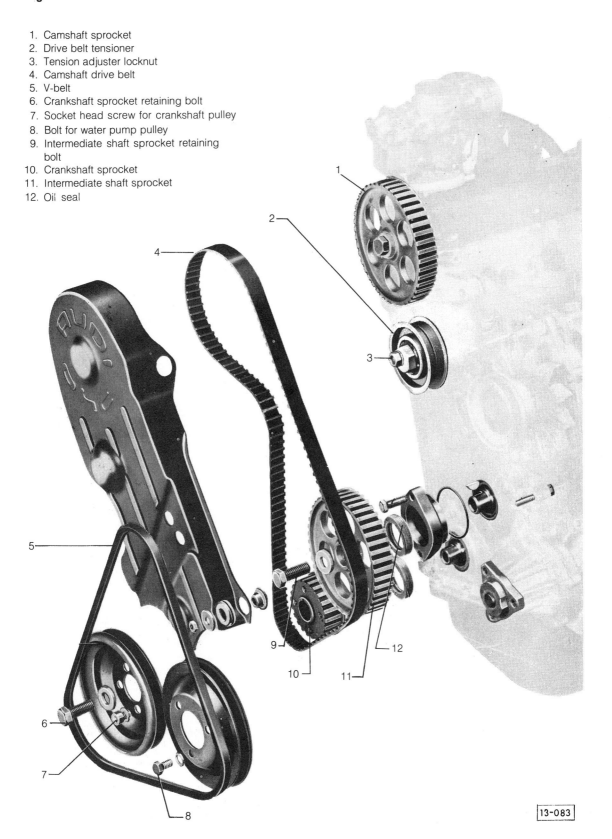

13-083

To install and adjust drive belt:

1. Hand-turn the camshaft sprocket until the centerpunch mark indicated in Fig. 5-2 is exactly in line with the upper surface of the cylinder head cover's mounting flange.

Fig. 5-2. Centerpunch mark (arrow) on camshaft sprocket aligned with the upper surface of the cylinder head cover mounting flange. Align the mark with the flange on the front (spark plug) side of the engine and never with the flange on the opposite (manifold) side of the engine.

2. Hand-turn the crankshaft and the intermediate shaft until the centerpunch mark on the intermediate shaft sprocket is positioned in the V-notch on the crankshaft pulley (Fig. 5-3).

Fig. 5-3. Centerpunch mark (arrow) on intermediate shaft sprocket positioned within the V-notch on the crankshaft pulley.

3. Being careful not to move any of the sprockets, install the camshaft drive belt first at the bottom and then at the top so that there is no slack between the crankshaft and intermediate shaft sprockets or between the intermediate shaft and camshaft sprockets.

4. Using a wrench on the tension adjuster, tighten the belt until it can just be finger-twisted 90° at a point halfway between the camshaft and intermediate shaft sprockets (Fig. 5-4). Then torque the tension adjuster locknut to 4.5 mkg (32 ft. lb.). If the timing marks have moved from their setting positions, repeat the installation and adjustment procedure.

Fig. 5-4. Drive belt being adjusted.

The remainder of installation is the reverse of removal. Adjust the V-belt tension as shown in Fig. 5-5. You should just be able to depress the V-belt 10 to 15 mm (3/8 to 9/16 in.). Make the adjustment by pulling the alternator away from the engine. When the V-belt tension is correct, torque the lower alternator mounting bolts to 2.5 mkg (18 ft. lb.) and the bolts that hold the adjusting bracket to the alternator and the cylinder head to 2.0 mkg (14 ft. lb.). Use the same procedure to adjust the air pump V-belt tension on California cars that are so equipped.

CAUTION ——

Do not tension the V-belts too tightly. Doing this may cause the alternator bearings, the water pump bearings, or the air pump bearings to fail after only a short period of service.

Fig. 5-5. Point at which V-belt should be depressed. Dimension **a** should be 10 to 15 mm (³/₈ to ⁹/₁₆ in.).

5.2 Adjusting Valves

The clearance between the heel of the cam lobe and the bucket-type cam follower is adjustable by means of replaceable adjusting disks (shims), as shown in Fig. 5-6.

The adjusting disks are available in twenty-six different thicknesses from 3.00 to 4.25 mm (.1181 to .1673 in.). The disks most frequently required in making adjustments fall in the thickness range of 3.55 to 3.80 mm (.1397 to .1496 in.). **Table e** lists the available disks by thickness and part number. The thickness of each disk is etched on its underside.

Table e. Adjusting Disk Thicknesses and Part Numbers

Thickness mm	Part No.	Thickness mm	Part No.
3.00	056 109 555	3.65	056 109 568
3.05	056 109 556	3.70	056 109 569
3.10	056 109 557	3.75	056 109 570
3.15	056 109 558	3.80	056 109 571
3.20	056 109 559	3.85	056 109 572
3.25	056 109 560	3.90	056 109 573
3.30	056 109 561	3.95	056 109 574
3.35	056 109 562	4.00	056 109 575
3.40	056 109 563	4.05	056 109 576
3.45	056 109 564	4.10	056 109 577
3.50	056 109 565	4.15	056 109 578
3.55	056 109 566	4.20	056 109 579
3.60	056 109 567	4.25	056 109 580

You can adjust the valves with the engine hot—coolant temperature approximately 35°C (95°F)—or with the engine cold. However, the clearance will be different depending on whether the engine is hot or cold.

Cam follower

Valve adjusting disk

Valve stem seal

Intake port

Fig. 5-6. Cross section of cylinder head showing the relationship of the cam lobe and cam follower. Adjusting disk fits in a recess in the follower.

To adjust valve clearance:

1. Remove the eight bolts and cylinder head cover retaining plates. Then carefully lift off the cylinder head cover and its gasket. If the gasket is stuck to the cylinder head, use a dull knife to separate the gasket from the head.

2. Using a wrench on the bolt that is in the center of the crankshaft pulley, hand-turn the crankshaft clockwise until both cam lobes for the No. 1 (right) cylinder are pointing upward. Then, to determine the valve clearance, insert feeler gauges of various thicknesses between the cam lobes and the adjusting disks (Fig. 5-7).

> **NOTE** ——
>
> The cylinders are numbered consecutively from the right (curb side) to the left (driver's side) of the engine. For example, the No. 4 cylinder is at the end of the engine that is bolted to the flywheel bellhousing of the transaxle.

> **NOTE** ——
>
> With the engine hot, the intake valve clearance should be between 0.20 and 0.30 mm (.008 and .012 in.); exhaust valve clearance should be between 0.40 and 0.50 mm (.016 and .020 in.). With the engine cold, the intake valve clearance should be between 0.15 and 0.25 mm (.006 and .010 in.); exhaust valve clearance should be between 0.35 and 0.45 mm (.014 and .018 in.).

Fig. 5-7. Valve clearance being measured. Notice that both cam lobes for No. 1 cylinder are pointing up, away from the cam followers. The feeler gauge is inserted between the cam lobe and the adjusting disk that is on top of the cam follower.

3. If either the intake or the exhaust valve clearance is incorrect, write down the actual clearance that you have measured. Then depress the cam followers with special tool VW 546 and lift out the adjusting disk(s) with special pliers (Fig. 5-8).

Fig. 5-8. Adjusting disk being removed. Special tool depresses both cam followers simultaneously. Special pliers (Tool 10-208) are used to remove disk from cam follower.

4. Read the thickness that is etched on the underside of the removed disk. (If the number has worn off, check the disk thickness with a micrometer.) Then determine the thickness of the required replacement disk as described in one of the next two steps.

5. If the measured clearance was less than the specified clearance range for the valve, subtract the measured clearance from the specified maximum clearance. Then subtract the difference from the thickness of the original disk in order to determine the thickness of the required replacement disk. If the computed thickness comes out equal to a standard disk thickness, or if the computed thickness is less than a standard disk thickness, use the next thicker disk.

6. If the measured clearance was greater than the specified clearance range for the valve, subtract the specified maximum clearance from the measured clearance. Then add the difference to the thickness of the original disk in order to determine the thickness of the required replacement disk. If the computed thickness comes out equal to a standard disk thickness, or if the computed thickness is less than a standard disk thickness, use the next thicker disk.

7. Install the required replacement disk(s) with the etched numbers toward the cam follower. Remove the special cam follower depressing tool. Then recheck the clearance to make sure that it is within the specified range.

8. Using a wrench on the bolt that is in the center of the crankshaft, hand-turn the crankshaft 180° clockwise and repeat steps 1 through 7 on the No. 3

cylinder. Hand-turn the crankshaft another 180°
and adjust the valves of the No. 4 cylinder, and,
finally, 180° farther to adjust the valves of the No. 2
cylinder.

9. Install the cylinder head cover. Torque the bolts to
1.0 mkg (7 ft. lb.).

5.3 Removing and Installing
Cylinder Head and Manifolds

The cylinder head can be removed without removing
the engine from the car and without removing the camshaft or other valve gear prior to cylinder head removal.

To remove cylinder head and manifolds:

1. On cars with carburetors, remove the air cleaner
and all of the related air ducts. On cars with fuel
injection, disconnect the rubber duct that links the
throttle valve housing with the mixture control unit.
If necessary, consult **FUEL AND EXHAUST SYS-
TEMS.**

2. Remove the radiator cap or the expansion tank
cap. Place a receptacle beneath the water pump for
catching the draining coolant. Then remove the
bottom radiator hose from the thermostat housing
and allow the coolant to drain.

> *CAUTION —*
>
> *Never drain the coolant while the engine is
> hot. Doing this could warp the engine block
> or the cylinder head.*

3. Remove the camshaft drive belt as described in
**5.1 Removing, Installing, and Adjusting Camshaft
Drive Belt.**

4. On cars with carburetors, disconnect all of the
hoses, cables, and wires that are connected to the
carburetor and the intake manifold. On certain cars
sold in California, disconnect the air lines from the
air injection connections on the exhaust manifold.

5. On cars with fuel injection, pull the injectors out of
the manifold tubes of the intake air distributor.
Disconnect all of the hoses, cables, and wires that
are connected to the throttle valve housing and the
intake air distributor. If necessary, consult **FUEL
AND EXHAUST SYSTEMS.**

6. Remove the six nuts that hold the exhaust pipe to
the exhaust manifold. Unbolt the exhaust pipe
support from the engine/transaxle assembly. See
Fig. 5-9.

7. Remove the nuts and the bolts that hold the
exhaust manifold and the intake manifold (or intake air distributor) to the cylinder head. Then remove the manifolds (or manifold and intake air
distributor) from the cylinder head as a unit.

Fig. 5-9. Exhaust pipe support (left arrow) and exhaust
pipe flange (center arrow). Disregard arrow at
right.

8. Remove the upper alternator mounting bolt. Then
unbolt the alternator V-belt adjusting bracket from
the cylinder head and remove the bracket.

9. Disconnect all coolant hoses from the cylinder
head. Disconnect the wire for the temperature
gauge.

10. Disconnect the spark plug cables from the spark
plugs. Disconnect the high tension cable from the
coil at terminal 4. Then remove the distributor cap
complete with the spark plug cables and the high
tension cable.

11. Remove the spark plugs.

12. Remove the eight bolts and cylinder head cover
retaining plates. Then carefully lift off the cylinder
head cover and its gasket. If the gasket is stuck to
the cylinder head, use a dull knife to separate the
gasket from the head.

13. Beginning at the outer ends of the cylinder head
and working toward the center from both directions, use a hex-shaped driver to remove the
eight socket head cylinder head bolts.

14. Lift the cylinder head off the engine block. If the
head is stuck, insert two wooden hammer handles
in the outermost exhaust ports. Then, using a tilting motion, pull the head free.

4

To install:

1. Thoroughly clean the cylinder head.

> **CAUTION ——**
>
> *Do not use a metal scraper or a power-driven wire brush to clean the combustion chambers or gasket sealing surface. Doing this can gouge the aluminum, which could cause the head gasket to leak, or leave scratches in the combustion chambers that could become "hot spots." Instead, use solvent to soften combustion chamber deposits, dried sealer, and material torn from the old head gasket. Then remove this foreign matter with a wooden or plastic scraper.*

2. Thoroughly clean the gasket sealing surface of the cylinder block. Then clean the threads in the head bolt holes.

> **NOTE ——**
>
> To keep out dirt, stuff clean rags into the cylinder bores and seal all water and oil passages with tape. After you have cleaned the sealing surface of the block, use a thread-cutting tap or thread chaser to clean the bolt holes. It is extremely important that all debris be removed from the bottoms of the holes after you have cleaned the threads.

3. Check the cylinder head for warping. To do this, lay a straightedge lengthwise across the sealing surface of the head as shown in Fig. 5-10. You should not be able to insert a 0.13-mm (.005-in.) feeler gauge between the sealing surface and the straightedge at any point. Repeat the check with the straightedge placed diagonally across the surface in both directions.

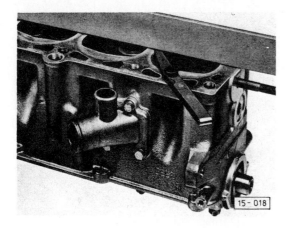

Fig. 5-10. A 0.10-mm (.004-in.) feeler gauge inserted between the straightedge and cylinder head sealing surface. 0.10 mm (.004 in.) is the maximum allowable distortion.

> **NOTE ——**
>
> If a 0.13-mm (.005-in.) feeler gauge can be inserted at any point, either replace the cylinder head or take it to an automotive machine shop where the head can be milled to obtain a true surface.

4. Using the procedure you used for the head, check the engine block for warping. Warped blocks can also be milled but the engine must be removed and completely disassembled beforehand.

5. Using a thread-cutting die, clean the cylinder head bolt threads. Do not use a power-driven wire brush, which could distort the threads. Replace damaged or distorted bolts. Then coat the bolt threads and the head bolt washers with anti-seize compound.

6. Install a new cylinder head gasket as shown in Fig. 5-11. Place two 200-mm long, 9-mm diameter (8-in. long, ⅜-in. diameter) wooden dowels in two of the outermost head bolt holes in order to hold the gasket on the engine block and to serve as guides when you install the cylinder head.

Fig. 5-11. Cylinder head gasket installed on block. The word OBEN (top) identifies the top surface of the gasket, which must be upward.

> **CAUTION ——**
>
> *Never reinstall a cylinder head gasket that has previously been compressed by tightening the cylinder head bolts. Once compressed, these gaskets lose their resilience and will not produce a reliable seal if reused.*

7. Using the two dowels as a guide, carefully lower the cylinder head onto the new cylinder head gasket and the engine block. Then immediately install, but do not tighten, several head bolts and washers. With the cylinder head thus supported, remove the dowels and loosely install the remaining head bolts and washers.

8. Following the sequence given in Fig. 5-12, torque the head bolts to 3.0 mkg (22 ft. lb.). Go over the sequence a second time, torquing the bolts to 6.0 mkg (43 ft. lb.), then a third time, torquing the bolts to 7.5 mkg (54 ft. lb.).

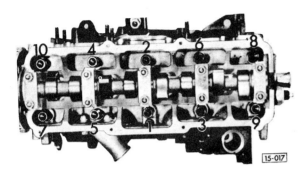

Fig. 5-12. Head bolt tightening sequence.

9. Install the remaining engine parts. See **5.1 Removing, Installing, and Adjusting Camshaft Drive Belt** and **4.1 Replacing Hoses.** Use a new gasket when you install the cylinder head cover and torque the bolts to 1.0 mkg (7 ft. lb.). Install new gaskets for the manifolds, then install the manifolds and torque the nuts and the bolts to 2.5 mkg (18 ft. lb.). Reconnect the hoses, cables, and wires to the induction system as described in **FUEL AND EXHAUST SYSTEMS.** Fill the cooling system as described in **4. Cooling System.**

10. Start the engine. When it has warmed up to the specified temperature, adjust the idle speed to 850 to 1000 rpm as described in **FUEL AND EXHAUST SYSTEMS.**

11. After the car has been driven for approximately 1000 miles (1500 km), remove the cylinder head cover with the engine stopped.

12. Following the reverse of the sequence given earlier in Fig. 5-12, loosen all of the cylinder head bolts by turning each one approximately 30° counterclockwise.

13. Following the sequence given earlier in Fig. 5-12, torque each cylinder head bolt to 7.5 mkg (54 ft. lb.) if the engine is cold or to 8.5 mkg (61 ft. lb.) if the engine is warm (coolant temperature 35°C (95°F) or above).

14. Check the valve clearances and, if necessary, adjust the clearances as described in **5.2 Adjusting Valves.**

15. Install the cylinder head cover. Use a new gasket if the old gasket is hardened or damaged.

5.4 Disassembling and Assembling Cylinder Head

You should not completely disassemble the cylinder head in one continuous operation. Instead, disassemble the head in stages, following the sequence given here, so that you can make various checks and measurements at each stage of disassembly. By doing this, you will be able to determine which parts can be reused and which parts require reconditioning or replacement.

4 ■

Camshaft and Cam Followers

To check the condition of the camshaft and its bearings, you must first relieve the pressure that is exerted on the cam lobes by the valve springs. Relieving the pressure requires only that the camshaft be removed, the cam followers lifted out, and the camshaft reinstalled. The valves and valve springs need not be removed.

The camshaft is held to the cylinder head by five bearing caps. Each cap is held by two nuts that thread onto studs. The bearing caps and the nuts are shown in Fig. 5-13. Notice that each camshaft bearing cap is numbered, beginning at the camshaft drive end of the cylinder head, to simplify correct installation. The numbered sides of the caps should always be installed toward the manifold side of the head.

To remove the camshaft, remove the nuts and washers from bearing caps 5, 1, and 3 in that order. Then, loosening each of the four nuts a little at a time so that the valve spring tension is relieved evenly, simultaneously remove bearing caps 2 and 4. If this procedure is not followed, the camshaft may tilt in its bearings, which could damage the bearings or bend the camshaft.

To check camshaft axial play, remove the camshaft and lift out the cam followers. Number each cam follower as you remove it so that the followers can be reinstalled in their original bores. Install the camshaft using only bearing caps 1 and 5. Install a dial indicator as shown in Fig. 5-14. Move the camshaft forward and backward while you observe the dial indicator. Axial play should not exceed 0.15 mm (.006 in.). If the play is greater, the head or the camshaft is worn and must be replaced.

Fig. 5-14. Dial indicator being used to measure camshaft axial play.

To check the camshaft for bending and runout, install the camshaft between centers as shown in Fig. 5-15. Mount a dial indicator so that its gauge pin is against the center bearing journal on the camshaft. Then rotate the camshaft and observe the runout range shown by the dial indicator. If runout exceeds 0.01 mm (.0004 in.), replace the camshaft.

To measure camshaft bearing clearance, either install one bearing cap at a time and measure the camshaft's radial play with a dial indicator, or use Plastigage®. Plastigage is available from automotive supply stores. Further information on its use can be found in **10.1 Removing, Checking, and Installing Pistons, Piston Rings, Connecting Rods, and Connecting Rod Bearings.** Camshaft bearing clearance should be between 0.02 and 0.05 mm (.0008 and .002 in.).

Fig. 5-13. Camshaft bearing caps and bearing cap nuts. There is a flat washer under each nut. It is important that the bearing caps be removed in the correct sequence.

Fig. 5-15. Dial indicator being used to measure camshaft runout.

Inspect the cam followers for galling and signs of seizure—conditions that indicate a lack of lubrication. If aluminum from the cylinder head is found adhering to a cam follower, replace the cam follower. The cylinder head should be replaced if any of the cam follower bores is rough, gouged, worn, or otherwise damaged.

To install the cam followers and the camshaft, first clean all the parts in order to remove sludge and abrasive dirt. Lightly lubricate the cam follower bores with assembly lubricant (available from automotive supply stores), or with a thin coating of multipurpose grease. Then, with reference to the numbers marked on the cam followers during removal, install each cam follower in its original bore. If undamaged, install the original adjusting disks so that the valve clearance can be measured after you have installed the camshaft.

4

Inspect the camshaft lobes for wear (Fig. 5-16). Worn cam lobes are caused by a lack of lubrication. So always lubricate the cam lobes and the adjusting disks on the cam followers during assembly and make certain that the engine's oil passages are clear. Replace worn camshafts and worn adjusting disks.

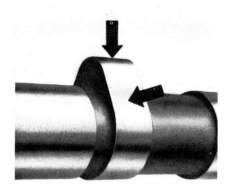

© 1974 VWoA—1242

Fig. 5-16. Cam lobe. Toe of cam (top arrow) should not be scored or worn unevenly. There should be no sign of wear at the second arrow. If there is wear at the second arrow, check for incorrect valve clearances, abrasive substances in the oil, or inadequate lubrication.

Coat the tops of the adjusting disks, the camshaft bearing surfaces, and the cam lobes with assembly lubricant or with a thin coating of multipurpose grease, then position the camshaft on the cylinder head. Loosely install bearing caps 2 and 4. Gradually tighten all four bearing cap nuts until the camshaft is drawn down fully and evenly into the bearing saddles. Then install bearing caps 5 and 3. Finally, install a new oil seal on the front of the camshaft and install bearing cap 1. See Fig. 5-17. Torque the bearing cap nuts to 2.0 mkg (14 ft. lb.). Install the end plug at the left-hand (driver's side) end of the cylinder head. Obtain a new plug if the original is damaged or does not fit tightly.

If previously removed, install the drive belt sprocket on the camshaft. Then, gripping the sprocket, hand-turn the camshaft to the required positions so that you can adjust the valve clearances as described in **5.2 Adjusting Valves.**

NOTE

If the cylinder head is not installed on the engine block, you can delay the valve adjustment until after the cylinder head has been installed. By doing so, your adjustments will take into account minor clearance changes that may result from the torquing of the cylinder head bolts.

Valves and Valve Guides

You must remove the camshaft and the cam followers before you can remove the valves. Do not remove the valve guides unless they are worn badly enough to require replacement. The components of a valve assembly are shown disassembled in Fig. 5-18.

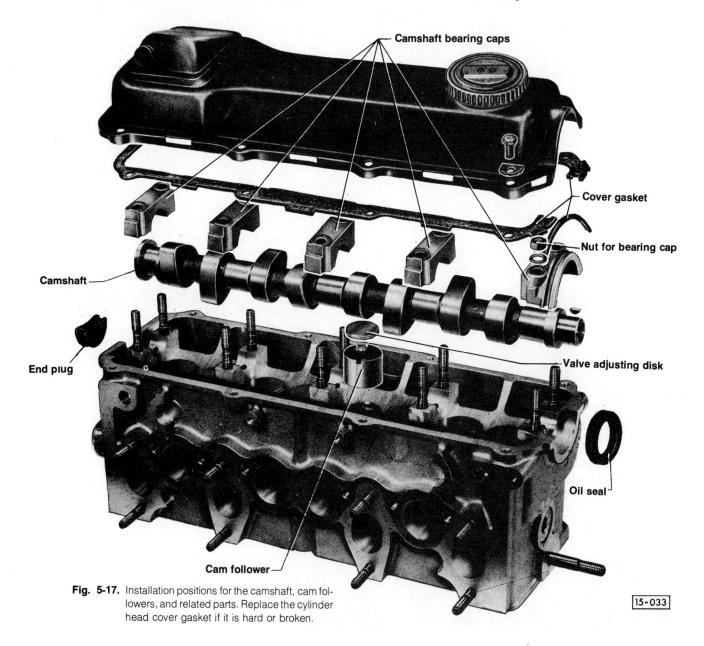

Fig. 5-17. Installation positions for the camshaft, cam followers, and related parts. Replace the cylinder head cover gasket if it is hard or broken.

15-033

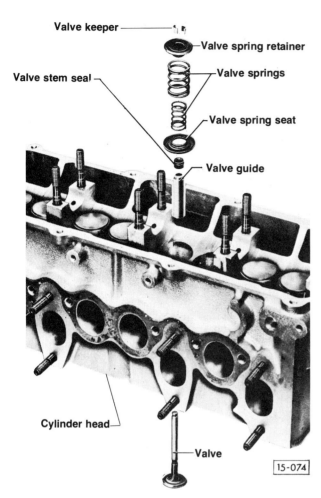

Fig. 5-18. Components of a valve assembly. The valve guides are a press fit in the cylinder head.

Fig. 5-19. Lever tool that is used to press down the valve spring retainer and compress the valve springs. The plate, placed beneath the cylinder head, has projections on it that support the valve heads.

4 ■

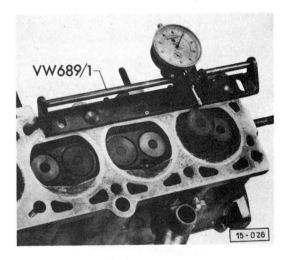

Fig. 5-20. Dial indicator being used to measure the rock of the valves in their guides.

To remove valves:

1. With the camshaft and cam followers removed and the cylinder head removed from the engine, compress the valve springs as shown in Fig. 5-19. Doing this should press the valve spring retainer down the valve stem so that the split valve keeper is uncovered.

2. Remove the split keeper halves from the valve stem. Release the compressing tool. Then take off the spring retainer and the valve springs.

3. Using long-nose pliers, remove the valve spring seat and the valve stem seal.

4. When all eight valve assemblies have been disassembled, install a dial indicator as shown in Fig. 5-20 so that you can check the valve guides for wear.

> **CAUTION** ——
>
> *If the keeper grooves in the valve stems are burred, file them smooth before proceeding. If the burred stems are forced into the valve guides, the guides will be ruined.*

5. One at a time, lift each valve off its seat until the tip of the valve stem is flush with the top of the valve guide. Position the dial indicator's gauge pin against the valve head. Then rock the valve from side to side in its guide while you observe the play range shown by the dial indicator.

> **NOTE** ——
>
> If the rocking play of an intake valve exceeds 1.00 mm (.039 in.), or the rocking play of an exhaust valve exceeds 1.30 mm (.051 in.)—even when a new valve is used—the guides are excessively worn. The inside diameter of valve guides should be between 8.013 and 8.035 mm (.315 and .316 in.).

CAUTION

Before you decide to replace the valve guides, determine whether new guides and the proper installation equipment are available. If guides and tools are unavailable, replace the entire cylinder head. Do not replace the valve guides routinely; replace them only if they are worn. To replace valve guides, follow the procedure given below.

NOTE

Surging at steady throttle, despite good carburetion, may indicate excessive guide wear. If you have observed this operating condition, it is especially important that you check the guides as just described.

6. Remove the dial indicator. Remove the valves, numbering each one so that you can reinstall the valves in their original locations.

7. To determine whether the original valve springs can be reused, check them with a valve spring tester as shown in Fig. 5-21. The outer valve spring should indicate a load of 43.5 to 48.0 kg (96 to 106 lb.) when compressed to a length of 22.3 mm (⁷⁄₈ in.). The inner valve spring should indicate a load of 21.0 to 23.0 kg (46 to 51 lb.) when compressed to a length of 18.3 mm (²³⁄₃₂ in.). Replace weak springs.

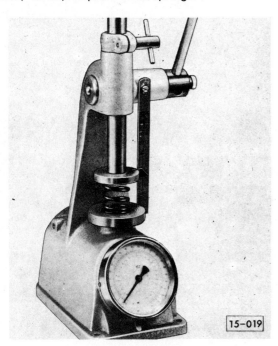

Fig. 5-21. Valve spring tester with spring in place.

NOTE

If you do not have a spring tester, have the springs tested by your Authorized Dealer or by a qualified automotive machine shop.

8. To check the keepers, oil them and then install them on a removed valve. Hold the keeper halves together while you turn the valve. The valve stem should rotate freely in the assembled keeper. If the keeper is a loose fit, you can grind the mating surfaces to make it fit tighter.

9. Inspect the valve seats and the valve facings as described in **5.5 Reconditioning Valves and Valve Seats**. If necessary, recondition (grind) the seats and the facings.

CAUTION

The exhaust valves must not be machine-ground. If their facing is too deeply worn or pitted to be restored by lapping, replace the valve.

To replace valve guides:

1. Clean and carefully inspect the cylinder head. Do not replace the valve guides in a cylinder head that is cracked or warped. Do not replace the valve guides if the valve seats are too badly worn to be refaced.

2. Using a repair press, press out the worn guides from the combustion chamber side, as shown in Fig. 5-22.

Fig. 5-22. Valve guide being pressed out.

3. Coat the new valve guides with engine oil. Then press the new guides into the cold cylinder head from the camshaft side until the shoulder on the guide firmly contacts the top of the cylinder head. The correct replacement guide, with the shoulder, is Part No. 056 103 419A.

CAUTION

Once the shoulder on the guide is seated against the head, do not use more than 1 ton pressure or the shoulder may break.

4. Ream the guides in order to obtain a uniform inside diameter of from 8.013 to 8.035 mm (.315 to .316 in.). See Fig. 5-23. Lubricate the reamer with cutting oil during the reaming operation.

NOTE ——

The correct tool for checking the guide bore is a "go/no-go" bore gauge that has a "go" diameter of 8.013 mm (or .315 in.) and a "no-go" diameter of 8.035 mm (or .316 in.). The 8.013-mm (.315-in.) end of the gauge should enter the guide easily but it should be impossible for the 8.035-mm (.316-in.) part of the gauge to enter the guide bore.

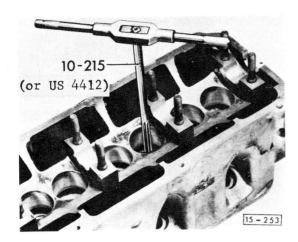

Fig. 5-23. New valve guide being reamed.

5. To ensure that the valve seats are concentric with the new valve guides, reface the seats as described in **5.5 Reconditioning Valves and Valve Seats.**

To install valves:

1. Lubricate the valve stems with engine oil. Then, with reference to the numbers marked on the valves during removal, install the valves in their original locations.

2. Place the cylinder head upright atop the plate for the valve removal tool. Then install plastic caps over the valve stem ends (Fig. 5-24).

3. Using the installing tool shown in Fig. 5-24, or a plastic tube of suitable diameter, press the new valve stem seals down over the valve stems and onto the tops of the valve guides.

CAUTION ——

If you do not have the plastic protective cap, wrap the valve stem ends with smooth plastic tape. If you force the new valve stem seals over the bare valve stems, the keeper grooves will damage the seals and the engine will use excessive oil.

Fig. 5-24. Plastic protective cap (**A**), new valve stem seal (**B**), and installing tool—part 10-204.

4. Install the valve spring seats. Then install the valve springs so that the closely-spaced coils of the outer springs are against the spring seats.

5. Install the spring retainers. Then compress the springs with the valve spring compressing tool and install the keepers.

Removing and Installing Valve Springs and Seals
(cylinder head installed)

A worn valve stem seal, a broken valve spring, a damaged keeper, or a damaged spring retainer can be replaced without removing the cylinder head. To replace these parts, use the procedure that follows.

To remove spring:

1. Remove the spark plug, the cylinder head cover, the camshaft drive belt, the camshaft, and the cam follower. Install air hose adapter VW 653/2 in the spark plug hole. Install the valve spring compressing tool as shown in Fig. 5-25.

Fig. 5-25. Spring compressing tool and air hose adapter installed.

2. Hand-turn the crankshaft until the piston of the cylinder you are working on is at bottom dead center (BDC). Then apply a constant air pressure of at least 85 psi (6 kg/cm²) to the cylinder.

3. Compress the valve spring retainer and the valve springs. Then remove the keeper.

4. Replace the worn or damaged parts. Then reassemble the valve assembly using a reverse of the disassembly procedure.

5.5 Reconditioning Valves and Valve Seats

Carefully inspect used valves in order to determine whether they are suitable for reuse. You can reface intake valves, but not exhaust valves, by machine-grinding. In doing this work, follow a procedure suitable to the valve refacing machine that you have. Alternatively, have worn intake valves refaced by an Authorized Dealer or a qualified automotive machine shop.

To inspect and recondition used valves:

1. Discard any valve with damaged keeper grooves or with a stem that has been warped or galled by seizure.

2. Using a motor-driven wire brush, remove the combustion chamber deposits from the valves.

3. Examine the part of the valve facing that contacts the valve seat for pits, burns, and other signs of wear. If the damage to an intake valve is too extensive to be corrected by machine-grinding, replace the valve. Replace any exhaust valve that has pitting or wear that is too extensive to be corrected by lightly hand-lapping the valve into its seat.

   NOTE ——

   Because of the extreme conditions under which exhaust valves operate, many experienced mechanics routinely replace any exhaust valve that has been in service for 25,000 mi. (40,000 km) or more.

4. After you have refaced the intake valves by machine-grinding, the remaining margin must not be less than the minimum specified in Fig. 5-26. Discard any intake valve that has an irregular margin after machine-grinding—a condition that indicates a warped valve.

   CAUTION ——

   Do not machine-grind exhaust valves. Doing this will shorten their service life. Exhaust valves should be hand-lapped only.

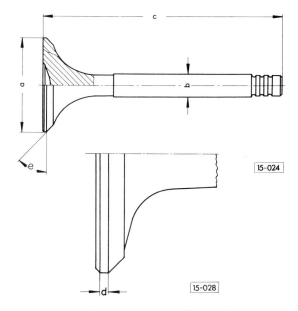

15-024

15-028

Dimension **a**, valve head diameter	Intake: 34.00 mm (1.338 in.) Exhaust: 31.00 mm (1.220 in.)
Dimension **b**, valve stem diameter	Intake: 7.97 mm (.314 in.) Exhaust: 7.95 mm (.313 in.)
Dimension **c**, valve length	Intake: 98.70 mm (3.886 in.) Exhaust: 98.50 mm (3.878 in.)
Dimension **d**, valve head margin	Intake: 0.50 mm (.020 in.) minimum Exhaust: Do not machine-grind
Dimension **e**, facing angle	Intake: 45° Exhaust: 45°

Fig. 5-26. Dimensions for reusable valves.

To inspect and reface valve seats:

1. If any valve seat is cracked or so badly gas-cut that it cannot be refaced to the specified dimensions, replace the cylinder head.

2. If inspection has shown that the valve guides are no longer serviceable (see **5.4 Disassembling and Assembling Cylinder Head**), either replace the guides or replace the cylinder head. If the correct replacement guides and replacement tools are available, replace the guides before you reface the valve seats.

3. Whether you use a hand-operated seat cutter or a power-driven seat grinder, make sure that the tool pilot fits the valve guides with little or no play.

4. Select a 45° seat cutter or a 45° seat grinding stone. Cutter blades should be straight and not chipped; grinding stones should be freshly dressed to the prescribed 45° angle.

5. Cut or grind to 45° the contact areas of the intake and the exhaust valve seats. See Fig. 5-27 for the finished dimensions of the intake valve seats; see

Fig. 5-28 for the finished dimensions of the exhaust valve seats. Remove no more metal than is necessary to erase wear and pitting—the less metal removed the better.

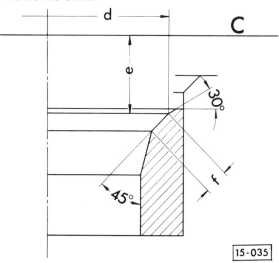

15-035

C. Gasket sealing surface of cylinder head
d. Diameter: 33.20 mm (1.307 in.)
e. Depth: 9.00 mm (.354 in.)
f. Seat contact area width: 2.00 mm (.079 in.)
30°. Angle of correction chamfer
45°. Angle of valve seat contact area

Fig. 5-27. Dimensions for finished intake valve seat.

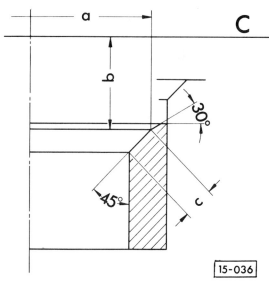

15-036

C. Gasket sealing surface of cylinder head
a. Diameter: 30.80 mm (1.212 in.)
b. Depth: 9.60 mm (.378 in.)
c. Seat contact area width: 2.40 mm (.094 in.)
30°. Angle of correction chamfer
45°. Angle of valve seat contact area

Fig. 5-28. Dimensions for finished exhaust valve seat.

6. Using a 30° hand seat cutter or a 30° grinding stone, chamfer the seats so that the contact areas are narrowed to the widths specified in Fig. 5-27 or Fig. 5-28.

CAUTION ——

Do not neglect narrowing the valve seats to specifications. Overly wide seats produced by using only a 45° cutter or stone tend to trap carbon particles and other deposits.

To hand-lap valves and seats:

1. Lubricate the valve stem with engine oil. Coat the valve seat contact area with a small amount of valve grinding compound (available from automotive supply stores).

2. Using a suction cup tool as shown in Fig. 5-29, turn the valve clockwise and counterclockwise against the seat. Lift the valve off the seat every few turns in order to avoid cutting concentric grooves into the seat.

Fig. 5-29. Suction cup tool used to turn valve against seat, as indicated by the curved double arrow.

3. Clean away every trace of grinding compound. Inspect the valve and the seat. There should be a uniform dull-gray band completely around the valve facing and the seat contact area.

4. To check the valve seating, lightly coat the valve facing with Prussian blue. Then install the valve. While applying light pressure to the valve, rotate the valve about a quarter turn against its seat.

5. Remove the valve and examine the contact pattern. If the seating is correct, the valve will leave an even coating of Prussian blue on the seat. If it does not, either the valve is warped and must be replaced or the seat must be reconditioned with greater care.

6. LUBRICATION SYSTEM

Oil pressure for the lubrication system is supplied by a gear-type oil pump that is located inside the engine's crankcase. The oil from the pump passes through a full-flow oil filter before it reaches the moving parts of the engine. Instructions for replacing the oil filter are given in **LUBRICATION AND MAINTENANCE.**

Fig. 6-1 is a schematic view of the lubrication system. In the event that the filter becomes plugged, the filter bypass valve permits oil to bypass the filter and reach the engine's bearings until a new filter can be installed. Whenever the pressure in the system exceeds a predetermined level, the pressure relief valve opens in order to return oil to the crankcase. By doing this, the pressure relief valve prevents over-pressurization of the system, which could increase oil consumption or burst the filter. To ensure that pressure indications accurately reflect the pressure of the entire system, the oil pressure switch is installed in that part of the system that is most remote from the pump. The switch closes when oil pressure falls below a predetermined level, thereby causing the oil warning light in the instrument panel to light up.

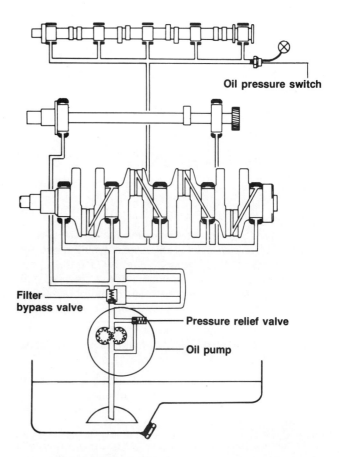

Fig. 6-1. Schematic view of the lubrication system. Pressure relief valve is integral with pump.

6.1 Testing and Replacing
Oil Pressure Switch

The oil pressure switch is located at the left end of the cylinder head, opposite the camshaft drive end. If the oil pressure warning light in the instrument panel fails to light when the ignition is turned on (engine not running), check the bulb for the warning light and replace it if necessary. If the bulb is not burned out, turn on the ignition. Then remove the wire from the oil pressure switch and ground the wire against a clean, unpainted metal part of the engine. If the warning light comes on, the pressure switch is defective and must be replaced. If the light fails to come on, the wiring is faulty. Troubleshoot faulty wiring using the wiring diagrams given in **ELECTRICAL SYSTEM.**

If the oil pressure warning light comes on while the engine is operating, and if the oil level in the crankcase is correct, test the accuracy of the oil pressure switch before you assume that there is trouble in the lubrication system.

To test the oil pressure switch, remove the switch from the cylinder head. Then install a pressure gauge (Fig. 6-2) that has a T-fitting or other provision for the installation of the switch. Ground the switch housing and connect the warning light wire to the terminal on the switch. The warning light should come on when the ignition is turned on (engine not running).

Fig. 6-2. Pressure gauge installed in place of oil pressure switch. The switch has been installed in the base of the gauge. Wire on switch goes to warning light; wire on base goes to ground.

Start the engine; if there is no pressure, immediately stop the engine. On Rabbit models through Chassis No. 176 3119 462 and Scirocco models through Chassis No. 536 2018 901, the warning light should go out when the gauge indicates a pressure of 0.3 to 0.6 kg/cm² (4.3 to 8.5 psi)—or more. On cars with later Chassis Nos., the warning light should go out when the gauge indicates a pressure of 0.15 to 0.45 kg/cm² (2.1 to 6.4 psi)—or more.

If the light stays on despite adequate oil pressure, replace the switch. Torque the switch to 1.0 mkg (7 ft. lb.). With SAE 10W oil at an oil temperature of 60°C (140°F), the minimum permissible pressure at 2000 rpm is 2.0 atu (28 psi). If the pressure is less, remove and inspect the oil pump.

6.2 Removing, Checking, and Installing Oil Pump

Because the oil pump is housed inside the crankcase, you must remove the oil pan before you can remove the pump. This is a relatively easy job owing to the transverse position of the engine ahead of the front suspension mounting points.

To remove and check oil pump:

4 ■

1. Place a receptacle of at least one gallon (or four liters or one Imperial gallon) capacity beneath the engine. Then remove the oil drain plug and allow the engine oil to drain into the receptacle. If necessary, consult **LUBRICATION AND MAINTENANCE.**

2. On 1975 cars, use a 5-mm hex driver on a 175 or 200-mm (7 or 8-in.) extension to remove the socket head pan bolts and their square washers. On 1976 and later cars, use a 10-mm socket wrench on a 175 or 200-mm (7 or 8-in.) extension to remove the pan bolts. See Fig. 6-3.

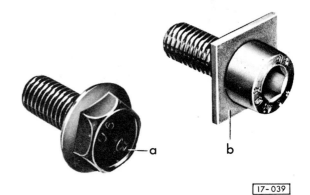

Fig. 6-3. New-type (**a**) and old-type (**b**) pan bolts.

3. Remove the oil pan from the engine. If the pan is stuck in place with sealer, tap the sides of the pan with a rubber mallet to break the pan free with a tilting motion.

4. Remove the two M 8 pump-mounting bolts. Then remove the oil pump from the engine, leaving the oil pump's pickup tube attached.

5. With the oil pump on the workbench, remove the pickup tube from the pump body.

NOTE ——
If necessary, you can pry off the oil baffle plate with a screwdriver.

6. Using feeler gauges of various thicknesses, determine the backlash clearance between the pump gears as shown in Fig. 6-4. The clearance should be between 0.05 and 0.20 mm (.002 and .008 in.) If the clearance is greater, replace the gears or replace the pump.

Fig. 6-4. Feeler gauges being used to determine backlash.

7. Using a machinist's square and feeler gauges of various thicknesses, determine the axial play of the oil pump gears as shown in Fig. 6-5. If the play exceeds 0.15 mm (.006 in.), replace the pump.

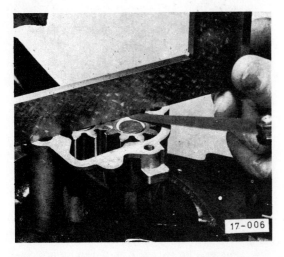

Fig. 6-5. Gear axial play being measured.

To install oil pump:

1. Thoroughly clean the strainer and the pickup tube.

2. Assemble the pump (Fig. 6-6). Torque the M 6 bolts that hold the pickup tube to the housing to 1.0 mkg (7 ft. lb.).

3. Thoroughly clean the mating surfaces of the oil pump and the engine block. Turn the drive gearshaft until it is positioned to engage the distributor drive gear. Then install the pump and torque the M 8 mounting bolts to 2.0 mkg (14 ft. lb.).

4. Clean the mating surfaces of the engine block and the oil pan. Then, using a new gasket, install the oil pan on the engine block. Torque old-type socket-head bolts to 1.0 mkg (7 ft. lb.); torque the new-type hexagon-head bolts to 2.0 mkg (14 ft. lb.). Wait several minutes for the gasket to compress, then retorque to the same specifications.

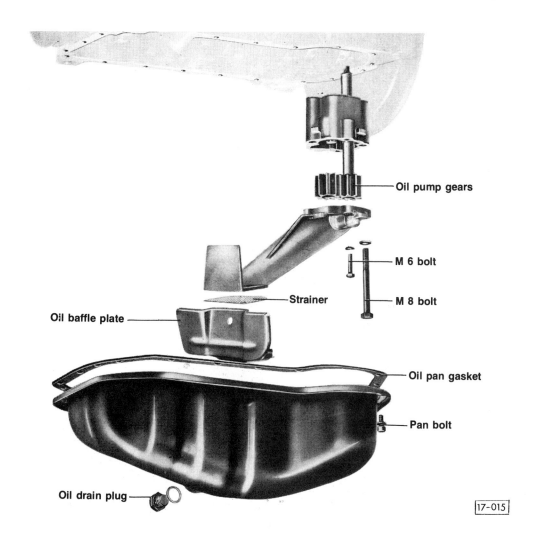

Oil pump gears

M 6 bolt

Strainer

M 8 bolt

Oil baffle plate

Oil pan gasket

Pan bolt

Oil drain plug

17-015

Fig. 6-6. Relative positions of parts in oil pump.

7. REMOVING AND INSTALLING ENGINE

Though it is possible to remove the oil pan and the cylinder head so that the pistons and connecting rods can be removed and installed with the engine in the car, more extensive engine reconditioning should be performed only with the engine removed. The engine and the transaxle must be removed as a unit. Once removed, the engine can be separated from the transaxle.

The procedure for removing the engine/transaxle assembly of a car with an automatic transmission is different from the procedure used for removing the engine/transaxle assembly from a car with a manual transmission. These two procedures are given separately.

Removing and Installing Engine with Manual Transmission

1. Disconnect the battery ground strap.

   NOTE ——

   It is not necessary to remove the car's hood unless it will interfere with the kind of hoisting equipment you will use in lifting out the engine/transaxle assembly.

2. Remove the radiator cap or the expansion tank cap. Place a receptacle beneath the water pump for catching the draining coolant. Then disconnect the lower radiator hose from the thermostat housing and allow the coolant to drain.

   CAUTION ——

   Never drain the coolant while the engine is hot. Doing this could warp the engine block or the cylinder head.

3. Disconnect the heater hoses and the radiator hoses from the engine. See Fig. 7-1.

Fig. 7-1. Hose connections at water pump. Disconnect hoses **A** first in order to drain coolant. Thermostat housing is at **B**.

4. Following the directions given in **4.5 Removing and Installing Radiator, Cooling Fan, and Air Ducts,** remove the fan, the fan duct, and the radiator as a unit.

5. On cars with air conditioners, loosen the bolts on the compressor support so that you can lift up the compressor. Dismount the condenser from the body. See Fig. 7-2.

CAUTION ——

Do not loosen or disconnect any of the refrigerant hose connections. If you do, it will make necessary costly and time-consuming air conditioning repairs.

Fig. 7-2. Condenser (**C**) and compressor (**K**) for air conditioning system.

6. Place the compressor and the condenser on a table next to the car, as shown in Fig. 7-3.

Fig. 7-3. Condenser (**C**) and compressor (**K**) removed from engine compartment without disconnecting refrigerant hoses.

7. On cars with fuel injection, pull the injectors out of the manifold tubes of the intake air distributor. Disconnect all fuel lines other than the injector lines from the fuel distributor. Then remove the mixture control unit, the air cleaner, and the intake air duct from the engine. Disconnect the fuel return line and the electrical plug from the control pressure regulator. If necessary, consult **FUEL AND EXHAUST SYSTEMS.**

WARNING ——

Fuel will be expelled as you disconnect the lines. Do not smoke or work near heaters or other fire hazards. Have a fire extinguisher handy.

8. On cars with carburetors, disconnect the fuel hose, the accelerator cable, and the coolant hoses indicated in Fig. 7-4.

WARNING ——

Fuel will be expelled as you disconnect the fuel hose. Do not smoke or work near heaters or other fire hazards. Have a fire extinguisher handy.

9. Disconnect the electrical wiring at the points indicated in Fig. 7-5. On cars with fuel injection, also disconnect the wiring plug from the auxiliary air regulator. On cars with carburetors, remove the air cleaner and all associated air ducts.

Fig. 7-4. Fuel hose (bottom arrow), accelerator cable (top arrow), and coolant hoses (three central arrows).

Fig. 7-5. Wiring connections on engine. Late engines usually have a plastic plug and no wire at arrow **A**.

10. Disconnect the speedometer cable and move it aside. Plug the hole in the transaxle in order to prevent the loss of hypoid oil. Detach the clutch cable and its conduit from the transaxle. Remove the engine/transaxle front mounting indicated in Fig. 7-6.

11. In order to provide clearance for lifting the engine/transaxle assembly out of Scirocco models, remove the headlight cap that is indicated in Fig. 7-7.

12. Disconnect the gearshift linkage from the relay lever. Disconnect the short gearshift linkage rod from the transaxle. See Fig. 7-8.

Fig. 7-6. Engine transaxle front mounting (bottom arrow), clutch cable (center arrow), and speedometer cable (top arrow). Unbolt mounting from both the engine and the body.

Fig. 7-7. Right, inboard headlight cap (Scirocco only).

Fig. 7-8. Relay lever (**a**) and short gearshift linkage rod (**b**).

13. Install an engine hoisting chain as shown in Fig. 7-9. The lifting eyes are provided on the engine's cylinder head.

14. Remove all slack from the hoist chain—raising the engine and the front of the car only slightly.

Fig. 7-9. Engine hoisting chain installed on engine.

15. Working beneath the car, remove the six nuts that hold the exhaust pipe to the exhaust manifold flange. Detach the exhaust pipe support from the engine/transaxle assembly. See Fig. 7-10.

16. Detach the transaxle-to-body electrical ground strap from the transaxle. Remove the transmission rear mounting that is indicated in Fig. 7-10.

Fig. 7-10. Exhaust pipe flange (center arrow) and exhaust pipe support (left arrow). Completely remove the transaxle rear mount indicated by the right arrow.

17. Remove the socket head bolts that hold the inboard constant velocity joints of the front wheel driveshafts to the drive flanges on the transaxle. Suspend the disconnected driveshafts from the car body on stiff wire hooks.

18. Remove the engine carrier that is on the right.

19. Completely remove the transaxle left mounting. The engine/transaxle assembly should now be supported solely by the hoist.

20. Using the special wrench (US 4463), remove the TDC sensor of the Computer Analysis system from the bellhousing. If the engine has the plastic plug, remove the plug.

21. Lift out the engine/transaxle assembly, guiding it carefully to avoid damage to the body and checking that no wires, hoses, or cables have become tangled with the engine.

22. With the engine/transaxle assembly fully removed, use a wrench on the bolt that is in the center of the crankshaft pulley to turn the crankshaft and align the mark indicated in Fig. 7-11. Only in this position can the engine and the transaxle be separated.

Fig. 7-11. Disassembly mark on flywheel aligned with timing pointer in hole for Computer Analysis TDC sensor.

23. With both the engine and the transaxle supported, take out the bolts that hold the engine to the transaxle. You must remove the cover plate indicated in Fig. 7-12 for access to one of the bolts. Separate the engine from the transaxle without placing any strain on the transmission mainshaft.

CAUTION ———

At no time should the weight of either the engine or the transaxle be supported by the transmission mainshaft. If it is, you may damage the clutch, bend the clutch pushrod, or bend the mainshaft.

Fig. 7-12. Cover plate (arrow) that must be removed for access to one of the engine-to-transaxle bolts.

Installation is basically the reverse of removal. Before you can install the engine on the transaxle, you must position the flywheel so that the recess indicated in Fig. 7-13 is aligned as shown (at the same level as the clutch driven plate hub with the engine in its installed position). Torque the bolts that hold the engine to the transaxle to 5.5 mkg (40 ft. lb.). Torque the bolts that hold the cover plates to the bellhousing to 1.5 mkg (11 ft. lb.).

Fig. 7-13. Flywheel positioned for transaxle installation. Recess (arrow) must be at same level as clutch driven plate hub with engine in its installed position.

With the engine/transaxle assembly positioned in the car, install the transaxle left mounting on the transaxle and torque the bolts to 2.5 mkg (18 ft. lb.). Align the engine/transaxle assembly in an approximate way, then loosely install the remaining engine/transaxle mountings. Install the driveshaft constant velocity joints on the drive flanges of the transaxle, torquing the socket-head bolts to 4.5 mkg (32 ft. lb.).

NOTE ——

The engine/transaxle assembly should be aligned and the mounts tightened only after all other components have been installed. Otherwise, the added weight of the oil, the coolant, the air conditioning compressor, and similar accessories might alter the alignment of the mountings. Please see the instructions given under the next unnumbered heading.

Adjust the accelerator cable as described in **FUEL AND EXHAUST SYSTEMS**. Adjust the clutch cable as described in **9.2 Adjusting Clutch Pedal Freeplay**. If the car has air conditioning, install the components as described in the following procedure.

To install air conditioning components:

1. Install the condenser, then install the radiator, the air ducts, and the radiator cooling fan and fan duct.

2. Loosely install the compressor on the engine.

3. Align the V-belt pulley of the compressor with those of the crankshaft and the alternator.

4. Install a pry bar on the bracket as shown in Fig. 7-14 so that you will be able to lift the compressor upward on its support.

Fig. 7-14. Setup used to lift compressor. Pry bar is at **A**, support is at **B**, and bracket is at **C**.

5. Using the pry bar, lift the compressor up on its support. Then tighten bolt **1**, as given in Fig. 7-15. Check that the pulleys are still aligned, then tighten bolts **2**, **3**, and **4**, as given in Fig. 7-15.

Fig. 7-15. Bolts that hold compressor.

6. Adjust the V-belt tension for the compressor. To do this, place a screwdriver in the mounting bolt bracket as shown in Fig. 7-16. With a second screwdriver, lift the alternator on the bracket until it is just possible to deflect the V-belt 10 to 15 mm (⅜ to ⁹/₁₆ in.) by pressing the belt at a point halfway between the compressor and crankshaft pulleys. Then tighten the adjusting nut on the bracket.

Fig. 7-16. Belt tension being adjusted at compressor. Support is at **B**, screwdriver in mounting bracket is at **F**. Screwdriver at **G** is being used to lift alternator on bracket, as indicated by arrow.

After you have completed the engine installation, refilled the cooling system and, if necessary, refilled the engine and the transaxle with oil, you must align the engine/transaxle assembly with the body as described under the following unnumbered heading.

NOTE ——

You must align the engine/transaxle assembly with the body before you tighten the bolts and the nuts that hold the engine/transaxle mountings to the car. If the assembly is not correctly aligned, there will be excessive engine vibration (buzzing inside the car).

Aligning Engine/Transaxle Assembly Mountings

Normally, it is necessary to align the engine/transaxle assembly mountings only after the engine/transaxle assembly has been installed in the car. If, however, there is excessive engine vibration, indicated by buzzing noises inside the car, you should check and, if necessary, adjust the alignment of the engine/transaxle assembly. Following this work, you should check and, if necessary, correct the alignment of the exhaust pipes and the muffler. This work is covered in **FUEL AND EXHAUST SYSTEMS.** Misaligned exhaust system components can also be responsible for buzzing noises inside the car.

To align engine/transaxle:

1. If not previously loosened during removal and installation of the engine/transaxle assembly, loosen the bolts and the nuts that are indicated in Fig. 7-17.

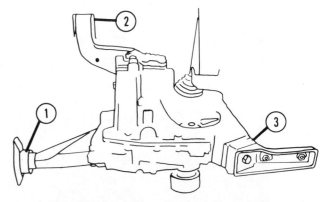

Fig. 7-17. Mountings that must be loosened prior to aligning the engine/transaxle assembly with the body. Engine/transaxle front mounting is at **1**, transaxle left mounting is at **2**, and transaxle rear mounting is at **3**. All nuts and bolts should be loosened.

2. Move the engine/transaxle assembly from side to side until the transaxle rear mounting is straight, with no twisting or strain in the bonded rubber part. See Fig. 7-18. Then torque the nuts to 4.0 mkg (29 ft. lb.) and recheck the rubber part for twisting or strain.

3. Move the engine/transaxle assembly from front to rear until the transaxle left mounting is centered in its bracket as indicated in Fig. 7-19. Then torque the bolt to 4.0 mkg (29 ft. lb.).

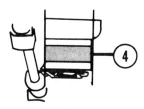

Fig. 7-18. Transaxle rear mounting (**4**) aligned without strain or twisting of rubber part.

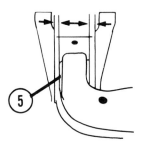

Fig. 7-19. Transaxle left mounting (**5**) centered in bracket on body. Spaces indicated by arrows will be equal on both sides when the engine/transaxle assembly is correctly aligned.

4. Move the engine/transaxle front mounting on the body (usually, you must push it upward) until the rubber core is centered in the mounting's housing (Fig. 7-20). Then torque the bolts to 4.0 mkg (29 ft. lb.).

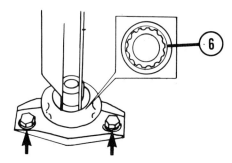

Fig. 7-20. Engine/transaxle front mounting being aligned. Move mounting on bolts (arrows) until rubber core (**6**) is centered.

CAUTION ——

After you have aligned the engine/transaxle assembly of a car with a manual transmission, check that the gearshift works smoothly and that the gears engage fully. If necessary, adjust the gearshift linkage as described in MANUAL TRANSMISSION.

Removing and Installing Engine with Automatic Transmission

1. Disconnect the battery ground strap.

    NOTE ——

    It is not necessary to remove the car's hood unless it will interfere with the kind of hoisting equipment you will use in lifting out the engine/transaxle assembly.

2. Remove the radiator cap or the expansion tank cap. Place a receptacle beneath the water pump for catching the draining coolant. Then disconnect the lower radiator hose from the thermostat housing and allow the coolant to drain.

    CAUTION ——

    Never drain the coolant while the engine is hot. Doing this could warp the engine block or the cylinder head.

3. Disconnect the heater hoses and the radiator hoses from the engine. See Fig. 7-21.

Fig. 7-21. Hose connections at water pump. Disconnect hoses **A** first in order to drain coolant. Thermostat housing is at **B**.

4. Following the directions given in **4.5 Removing and Installing Radiator, Cooling Fan, and Air Ducts,** remove the fan, the fan duct, and the radiator as a unit.

5. On cars with air conditioners, loosen the bolts on the compressor support so that you can lift up the compressor. Dismount the condenser from the body. See Fig. 7-22.

CAUTION ――

Do not loosen or disconnect any of the refrigerant hose connections. If you do, it will make necessary costly and time-consuming air conditioning repairs.

Fig. 7-22. Condenser (**C**) and compressor (**K**) for air conditioning system.

6. Place the compressor and the condenser on a table next to the car, as shown in Fig. 7-23.

Fig. 7-23. Condenser (**C**) and compressor (**K**) removed from engine compartment without disconnecting refrigerant hoses.

7. On cars with fuel injection, pull the injectors out of the manifold tubes of the intake air distributor. Disconnect all fuel lines other than the injector

lines from the fuel distributor. Then remove the mixture control unit, the air cleaner, and the intake air duct from the engine. Disconnect the fuel return line and the electrical plug from the control pressure regulator. If necessary, consult **FUEL AND EXHAUST SYSTEMS.**

WARNING ――

Fuel will be expelled as you disconnect the lines. Do not smoke or work near heaters or other fire hazards. Have a fire extinguisher handy.

8. On cars with carburetors, remove the air cleaner and its associated ducts. Disconnect the fuel tank-to-engine fuel hose from the fuel pump, disconnect all wiring and coolant hoses from the carburetor and the intake manifold.

WARNING ――

Fuel will be expelled as you disconnect the fuel hose. Do not smoke or work near heaters or other fire hazards. Have a fire extinguisher handy.

9. Detach the accelerator cable from the throttle lever of the carburetor or from the fuel injection system's throttle housing assembly. Dismount the cable conduit mounting bracket as indicated in Fig. 7-24.

CAUTION ――

Always dismount the cable conduit support bracket from the carburetor or from the bracket on the engines of cars with fuel injection. If you disconnect the cable conduit from the bracket, you will alter an adjustment that is difficult to restore.

Fig. 7-24. Screws that hold cable conduit bracket to carburetor. On fuel injection cars, bracket should be removed from engine.

10. Disconnect all electrical wiring from the engine. On cars with fuel injection, disconnect the wiring plug from the auxiliary air regulator.

11. Disconnect the speedometer cable and move it aside. Plug the hole in the transaxle in order to prevent the loss of oil.

12. Install an engine hoisting chain as shown in Fig. 7-25. The lifting eyes are provided on the engine's cylinder head.

13. Remove all slack from the hoist chain—raising the engine and the front of the car very slightly.

Fig. 7-25. Engine hoisting chain installed on engine.

14. Remove the alternator. If necessary, consult **ELECTRICAL SYSTEM.**

15. Remove the engine/transaxle front mounting, unbolting it from both the engine and the body.

16. In order to provide clearance for lifting the engine/transaxle assembly out of Scirocco models, remove the headlight cap that is indicated in Fig. 7-26.

Fig. 7-26. Right, inboard headlight cap (Scirocco only).

17. Working beneath the car, disconnect the transaxle-to-body ground strap. Disconnect the automatic transmission selector lever cable from the lever on the transaxle. Disconnect the throttle cable ball socket from the lever and unhook the accelerator pedal cable from the lever. Take out the bolts that hold the cable conduit bracket to the transaxle. See Fig. 7-27.

Fig. 7-27. Cables being disconnected from transaxle. Selector lever cable is at **1**, throttle cable to carburetor or fuel injection is at **2**, accelerator pedal cable is at **3**. Bolts at **4** hold cable conduit bracket to transaxle.

18. Fully remove the engine/transaxle assembly rear mounting from both the body and the transaxle by removing the nuts indicated in Fig. 7-28. Also remove the six nuts that hold the exhaust pipe to the exhaust manifold flange. Detach the exhaust pipe support from the engine/transaxle assembly.

Fig. 7-28. Nuts (arrows) that hold rear mounting to body and to transaxle.

19. By taking out the bolts, remove the cover from the engine end of the bellhousing. Then detach the torque converter from the drive plate by taking out the bolts, one of which is indicated in Fig. 7-29.

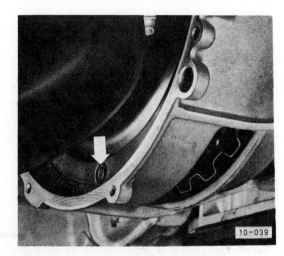

Fig. 7-29. One of three bolts (arrow) that hold torque converter to drive plate. Use a wrench on bolt in center of crankshaft pulley to turn bolts into position for removal.

20. Remove the socket-head bolts that hold the in-board constant velocity joints of the front wheel driveshaft to the drive flanges of the transaxle. Detach the constant velocity joints from the drive flanges and suspend the disconnected driveshafts from the body on stiff wire hooks.

21. Fully remove the engine/transaxle assembly left mounting. Remove the engine carrier that is on the right. The engine/transaxle assembly should now be supported solely by the hoist.

22. Lift out the engine/transaxle assembly, guiding it carefully to avoid damage to the body and check-ing that no wires, hoses, or cables have become tangled with the engine.

23. With both the engine and the transaxle supported, take out the bolts that hold the engine to the transaxle. Separate the engine from the transaxle—being careful to see that the drive plate pulls cleanly away from the torque converter without pulling the torque converter off its support.

CAUTION —

As soon as you have the engine off the transaxle, install a bar across the mouth of the bellhousing in order to keep the torque converter from falling out.'

Installation is basically the reverse of removal. Before you install the engine on the transaxle, make certain that the torque converter has not slipped off its support inside the bellhousing. Torque the bolts that hold the engine to the transaxle to 5.5 mkg (40 ft. lb.). Torque the bolts that hold the engine's drive plate to the torque converter to 3.0 mkg (22 ft. lb.).

With the engine/transaxle assembly positioned in the car, install the transaxle left mounting on the transaxle and torque the bolts to 2.5 mkg (18 ft. lb.). Align the engine/transaxle assembly in an approximate way, then loosely install the remaining engine/transaxle mountings. Install the driveshaft constant velocity joints on the drive flanges of the transaxle, torquing the socket head bolts to 4.5 mkg (32 ft. lb.).

NOTE —

The engine/transaxle assembly should be aligned and the mounts tightened only after all other components have been installed. Otherwise, the added weight of the oil, the coolant, the air conditioning compressor, and similar accessories might alter the alignment of the mountings. Please see the instructions given under the preceding un-numbered heading.

Adjust the accelerator pedal and throttle cable relative to the carburetor by following the instructions given in **FUEL AND EXHAUST SYSTEMS.** If you have not altered the positions of the cable conduits on their brackets, it should be unnecessary to carry out the complete cable adjustment procedure.

After reconnecting the automatic transmission's selector lever cable, check that all gears engage correctly when the selector lever is adjacent to the correct drive range letter or letter/number. If necessary, consult **AUTOMATIC TRANSMISSION.** If the car has air condi-tioning, install the components as described in the following procedure.

To install air conditioning components:

1. Install the condenser, then install the radiator, the air ducts, and the radiator cooling fan and fan duct.

2. Loosely install the compressor on the engine.

3. Align the V-belt pulley of the compressor with those of the crankshaft and the alternator.

4. Install a pry bar on the bracket as shown in Fig. 7-30 so that you will be able to lift the compressor upward on its support.

5. Using the pry bar, lift the compressor up on its support. Then tighten bolt **1**, as given in Fig. 7-31. Check that the pulleys are still aligned, then tighten bolts **2**, **3**, and **4**, as given in Fig. 7-31.

Fig. 7-30. Setup used to lift compressor. Pry bar is at **A**, support is at **B**, and bracket is at **C**.

Fig. 7-31. Bolts that hold compressor.

6. Adjust the V-belt tension for the compressor. To do this, place a screwdriver in the mounting bolt bracket as shown in Fig. 7-32. With a second screwdriver, lift the alternator on the bracket until it is just possible to deflect the V-belt 10 to 15 mm (⅜ to ⁹/₁₆ in.) by pressing the belt at a point halfway between the compressor and crankshaft pulleys. Then tighten the adjusting nut on the bracket.

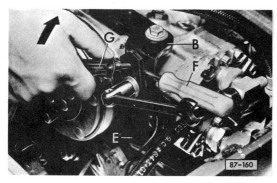

Fig. 7-32. Belt tension being adjusted at compressor. Support is at **B**, screwdriver in mounting bracket is at **F**. Screwdriver at **G** is being used to lift alternator on bracket, as indicated by arrow.

After you have completed the engine installation, refilled the cooling system and, if necessary, refilled the engine and the transaxle with oil, you must align the engine/transaxle assembly with the body as described under the preceding unnumbered heading.

8. TORQUE CONVERTER AND DRIVE PLATE

Cars equipped with automatic transmissions have a drive plate rather than a conventional flywheel. The torque converter is held to the drive plate by three bolts that are taken out when the engine is removed. Torque converter repair and replacement are covered in **AUTOMATIC TRANSMISSION.**

8.1 Removing and Installing Drive Plate

If you must disassemble the engine, remove the drive plate before you remove the crankshaft. The starter ring gear is an integral part of the drive plate assembly. If the gear is faulty, replace the drive plate.

To remove:

1. Mark the drive plate so that you can install it in the exact original position on the crankshaft.

2. Install a drive plate holding fixture—a dog that engages the starter ring gear teeth—on the engine. Alternatively, use coathanger wire to bind a bolt hole in the drive plate to a bolt hole in the engine block's transaxle mounting flange.

3. Remove the six bolts and the washer that hold the drive plate to the crankshaft. Then remove the drive plate and, where applicable, the shim.

To install:

1. If the crankshaft oil seal is leaking, replace the seal as described in **11.1 Replacing Crankshaft and Intermediate Shaft Oil Seals.**

2. With reference to the marks made prior to removal, install the drive plate on the crankshaft. Install the washer and two of the six bolts, then check dimension **a** as shown in Fig. 8-1.

Fig. 8-1. Dimension **a** being measured with a depth gauge. **a** = 31.30 mm ± 0.80 mm (1.232 in. ± .031 in.).

3. If dimension **a**, measured in step 2, is less than 31.30 mm ± 0.80 mm (1.232 in. ± .031 in.), install a shim or shims between the drive plate and the crankshaft in order to bring dimension **a** within tolerance. See Fig. 8-2.

> **NOTE** ——
>
> If dimension **a** exceeds the specified range, and there are no shims that can be removed from between the drive plate and the crankshaft, check the drive plate and replace it if there is excessive runout or other distortion.

4. Clean and dry all six drive plate mounting bolts and mounting bolt holes.

Fig. 8-2. Drive plate installation. Washer is at **1**, shim is at **2**. Drive plate shown is not for a car covered by this Manual.

5. With the drive plate holding fixture in place, apply an even coating of Loctite® 270 or 271 to the bolt threads. Then install all six drive plate mounting bolts and torque them to 7.5 mkg (54 ft. lb.).

6. Remove the drive plate holding fixture.

9. FLYWHEEL AND CLUTCH

The flywheel and clutch assembly remain on the crankshaft when you separate the engine from the transaxle. The clutch release bearing and related parts stay in the transaxle bellhousing. Unlike most other cars, the clutch's pressure plate assembly is bolted to the crankshaft and the flywheel is then bolted to the periphery of the pressure plate assembly. See Fig. 9-1.

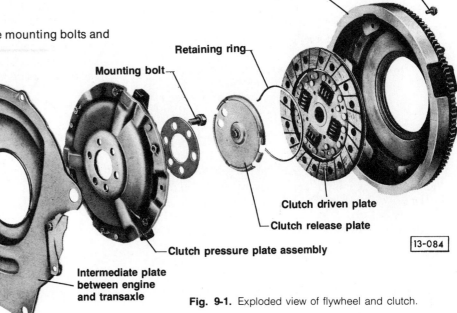

Fig. 9-1. Exploded view of flywheel and clutch.

9.1 Removing, Checking, and Installing Flywheel and Clutch

If you must disassemble the engine, remove the flywheel and the clutch before you remove the crankshaft. The starter ring gear is an integral part of the flywheel and cannot be replaced separately.

To remove:

1. To ensure proper reinstallation, mark the flywheel and the clutch pressure plate assembly and a matching point on their periphery.

2. If available, install the flywheel holding fixture shown in Fig. 9-2. Loosen the six flywheel-to-pressure plate mounting bolts a quarter turn at a time. Work around the flywheel until the pressure is relieved, then remove the bolts completely.

Fig. 9-2. Flywheel holding fixture installed so that it engages the teeth of the starter ring gear.

3. Remove the flywheel and the clutch driven plate by pulling the flywheel off its dowel pins. Then, using a screwdriver, carefully pry out the retaining ring and remove the clutch release plate.

4. Install the flywheel holding fixture on the pressure plate assembly, as shown in Fig. 9-3. Alternatively, you can use coathanger wire to bind a bolt hole in the pressure plate assembly to a bolt hole in the engine block's transaxle mounting flange.

5. Using a correctly-fitting 17-mm socket wrench, remove the six bolts and the washer that hold the clutch pressure plate assembly to the crankshaft. Then remove the pressure plate assembly.

Fig. 9-3. Holding fixture reversed and bolted to pressure plate assembly.

To check and install:

1. Inspect the levers on the diaphragm spring (Fig. 9-4). If they are out of line with one another, replace the pressure plate assembly.

2. Thoroughly clean the pressure plate assembly. Then inspect the rivets and the straps that connect the pressure plate with the pressure plate assembly mounting cover. If any rivet is loose, or if any strap is cracked or broken, replace the pressure plate assembly.

Fig. 9-4. Pressure plate assembly, showing release levers on the diaphragm spring. Also check the pressure plate friction surface for cracks, scoring, and other damage. Replace worn pressure plate assemblies.

4

3. Using a straightedge and feeler gauges, as shown in Fig. 9-5, check the pressure plate for wear and distortion. If the inward taper of the pressure plate exceeds 0.30 mm (.012 in.), replace the pressure plate assembly.

Fig. 9-5. Pressure plate being checked for inward taper and distortion. You should not be able to insert a feeler gauge thicker than 0.30 mm (.012 in.) between the pressure plate and the straightedge at any point.

4. Clean the friction surface inside the flywheel and inspect it for wear, cracks, and grooves. Replace unserviceable flywheels.

5. Check the driven plate for wear. There should be at least 2.00 mm (about $1/16$ in.) of friction material remaining above the rivet heads. When checked at a diameter of 175 mm (6⅞ in.), as shown in Fig. 9-6, runout should not exceed 0.40 mm (.016 in.).

Fig. 9-6. Dial indicator being used to measure driven plate runout. Rotate plate, note gauge movement.

6. Inspect the splines in the driven plate and on the transmission mainshaft. The splines must not be broken or distorted. Lubricate the splines with molybdenum disulfide powder, or with a thin coating of multipurpose grease. Then see that the driven plate slides freely on the mainshaft without undue radial play. If the driven plate is in any way unserviceable, replace it.

7. Clean and dry all six pressure plate assembly mounting bolts and all six holes in the crankshaft flange.

8. With the holding fixture in place and the pressure plate assembly positioned on the crankshaft, apply an even coating of Loctite® 270 or 271 to the bolt threads. Then install all six mounting bolts and torque them to 7.5 mkg (54 ft. lb.).

9. Remove the holding fixture. Lightly lubricate the contact surface of the clutch release plate with molybdenum grease or multipurpose grease. Similarly lubricate the socket for the pushrod, which is in the center of the release plate.

10. Install the clutch release plate. Then install the retaining ring, making sure that the ends rest between the two slots as indicated in Fig. 9-7.

Fig. 9-7. Retaining ring correctly installed. Ring ends (arrows) are in place between the two slots.

11. Place the clutch driven plate inside the flywheel, so that is projecting hub is visible through the small-diameter opening of the flywheel. Then, with reference to the marks you made earlier, loosely position the flywheel on the dowels and start one or two flywheel mounting bolts in their holes.

12. Center the driven disk, using the special tool shown in Fig. 9-8. Then, with the driven plate centered in the flywheel, install all six flywheel

mounting bolts—tightening them a little at a time to tension the clutch and finally torquing them to 2.0 mkg (14 ft. lb.).

Fig. 9-8. Driven plate being centered in flywheel with special centering tool.

13. If you have installed a new replacement flywheel, you must cut a timing mark into it as indicated in Fig. 9-9. Try to duplicate the shape of the timing mark that was in the original flywheel.

Fig. 9-9. Location for timing mark on flywheel. Cut the timing mark 6 mm (.236 in. or about ¼ in.) to the right of the TDC mark—as shown by dimension **a**. This will produce a timing mark at 3° ATDC.

14. After you have installed the engine on the transaxle and installed the engine/transaxle assembly in the car, adjust the clutch pedal freeplay as described under the next heading.

9.2 Adjusting Clutch Pedal Freeplay

As the clutch linings wear, the clearance between the release lever and the pushrod inside the transaxle is reduced. If this condition progresses until there is no clearance at all, clutch pressure will decrease and permit slippage that can lead to burned linings. When checking for the proper clearance, you should be able to depress the clutch pedal about 15 mm (⅝ in.) before you encounter working resistance. If not, adjust the clutch cable in order to obtain the prescribed amount of freeplay.

To adjust the cable, raise the hood and locate the adjusting nut, which is on the cable conduit (Fig. 9-10). To increase clutch pedal freeplay, loosen the locknut. Then turn the adjuster until you can pull the cable conduit upward out of the bracket about 3 or 4 mm (or about ⅛ in.). Then check the freeplay at the pedal. If it is about 15 mm (⅝ in.), tighten the cable adjuster locknut. If necessary, make additional adjustments in order to obtain the correct freeplay before you tighten the locknut.

Fig. 9-10. Clutch freeplay adjustment. Locknut is at top arrow, adjuster is at middle arrow. To keep the battery cable from being damaged by the clutch cable, make sure that it is held as indicated by the bottom arrow.

Replacing Clutch Cable

To replace the clutch cable, loosen the freeplay adjustment so that you can disengage the clutch cable conduit from the bracket that is on the transaxle. With the conduit disengaged from the bracket, unhook the cable end from the clutch operating lever that is on the side of the transaxle. Working beneath the dashboard, unhook the cable end from the clutch pedal. Then pull the cable and its conduit out of the firewall and into the engine compartment. After you have installed a replacement cable, following the reverse of the removal procedure, adjust the clutch pedal freeplay to 15 mm (⅝ in.) as previously described. If you have installed a new cable, again check the clutch pedal freeplay after 300 mi. (500 km) of driving and, if necessary, correct the freeplay.

Clutch Troubleshooting

Road testing is an important part of troubleshooting the clutch because it lets you base your diagnosis on first-hand information. For example, trouble described as "lack of power" might be caused by a slipping clutch and not inadequate engine output. Similarly, a complaint that "It's hard to shift gears" may mean a dragging clutch, not transmission trouble. **Table f** lists the most common clutch complaints, their probable causes, and suggested repairs. The numbers in bold type in the Suggested Repair column refer to the headings in this section where the repairs are described.

Table f. Clutch Troubleshooting

Problem	Probable cause	Suggested repair
1. Clutch noise	a. Loose clutch release plate retaining ring b. Driven plate fouling pressure plate c. Diaphragm spring weak or tension uneven d. Broken clutch part(s) trapped inside flywheel, causing rattling	a. Correctly install a new retaining ring. See **9.1** b. Replace driven plate. See **9.1** c. Replace pressure plate assembly. See **9.1** d. Disassemble and inspect clutch; replace faulty part(s). See **9.1**
2. Clutch grabbing	a. Engine/transaxle mountings loose b. Clutch cable binding c. Pressure plate contacting unevenly d. Release plate not running true e. Driven plate spring segments deformed	a. Tighten mounting bolts and nuts. See **7** b. Replace clutch cable. See **9.2** c. Replace pressure plate assembly. See **9.1** d. Replace release plate. See **9.1** e. Replace driven plate. See **9.1**
3. Clutch dragging	a. Excessive pedal freeplay b. Cable conduit faulty c. Driven plate not running true d. Driven plate linings broken e. Driven plate spring segments deformed f. Splines on mainshaft or in clutch driven plate dirty, burred, or deformed g. Sticky clutch linings (lining dust and grease on linings) h. Stiffness in clutch pedal bearing or operating mechanism inside transaxle	a. Adjust pedal freeplay to 15 mm (⅝ in.). See **9.2** b. Replace clutch cable. See **9.2** c. Replace driven plate. See **9.1** d. Replace driven plate. See **9.1** d. Replace driven plate. See **9.1** f. Clean splines and lubricate with molybdenum disulfide powder or multipurpose grease. Replace damaged parts. See **9.1** g. Replace driven plate. See **9.1** h. Lubricate pedal bearing with multipurpose grease. See **BRAKES AND WHEELS.** Or repair operating mechanism as described in **MANUAL TRANSMISSION**
4. Clutch slipping	a. Insufficient pedal freeplay b. Oily linings c. Clutch linings worn out d. Pressure plate has lost tension	a. Adjust pedal freeplay to 15 mm (⅝ in.). See **9.2** b. Replace driven plate; replace engine or transaxle oil seal, if necessary. See **9.1** c. Replace driven plate. See **9.1** d. Replace pressure plate assembly. See **9.1**

10. PISTONS, PISTON RINGS, AND CONNECTING RODS

Though it is possible to remove the cylinder head and the oil pan so that the connecting rods and pistons can be removed and installed with the engine in the car, that procedure is advisable mainly for the purpose of inspecting the piston rings and the connecting rod bearings. Any work that requires grinding or machining—such as removing the top-cylinder ridge or honing the cylinder bores—should be done with the engine removed and disassembled. Otherwise, abrasive dirt and metal particles will remain in the engine, causing bearing damage and rapid wear.

The components of the piston/connecting rod assembly for one cylinder of the engine are shown in Fig. 10-1.

10.1 Removing, Checking, and Installing Pistons, Piston Rings, Connecting Rods, and Connecting Rod Bearings

Because the pistons, the connecting rods, and many of their related parts must be reinstalled in their original locations and positions, you should mark the parts as you remove them. Replacement parts must be selected with careful reference to the cylinder bore, the original part, and to the other parts in the piston/connecting rod assembly.

To remove, check, and install:

1. Unless you are replacing connecting rod bearings only, or are removing the piston and connecting rod for inspection purposes only, remove the engine as described in **7. Removing and Installing Engine.**

2. Remove the cylinder head as described in **5.3 Removing and Installing Cylinder Head and Manifolds.** Remove the oil pan and the oil pump as described in **6.2 Removing, Checking, and Installing Oil Pump.**

4

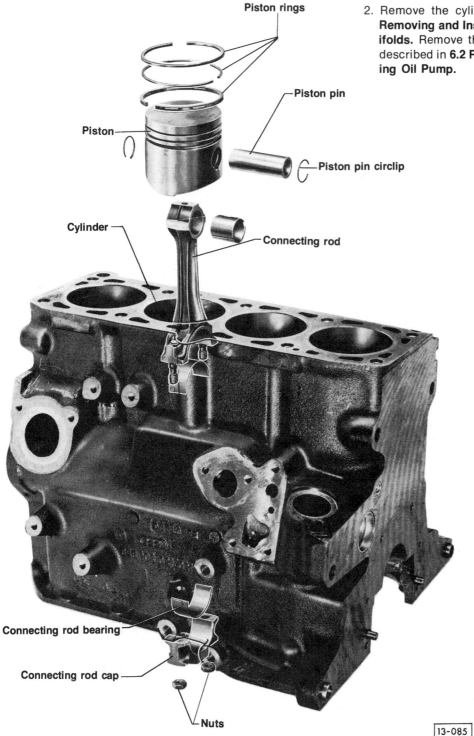

Fig. 10-1. Components of piston/connecting rod assembly.

3. Mark the cylinder number on the crown of each piston. If necessary, mark arrows on the piston crowns to indicate which side of each piston is toward the camshaft drive end of the engine block. See Fig. 10-2.

Fig. 10-2. Cylinder numbers and arrows marked on piston crowns.

4. Remove the connecting rod nuts. Remove the connecting rod cap from the connecting rod bolts. Then, using a wooden hammer handle, push the piston/connecting rod assembly away from the crankshaft and out through the top of the cylinder.

CAUTION ——

If the engine block has pronounced top-cylinder ridges, remove them with a cylinder ridge reamer before you remove the pistons. Otherwise, the piston rings and pistons may be damaged during removal. A top-cylinder ridge is a band of unworn cylinder wall that remains above the part of the cylinder that has been worn to a larger diameter by contact with the piston rings.

5. As soon as you remove each piston/connecting rod assembly, mark the cylinder number on both the rod cap and connecting rod as shown in Fig. 10-3.

Fig. 10-3. Numerals **1** (arrows) marked on the connecting rod and the rod cap for No. 1 cylinder.

6. Using needle-nosed pliers or a punch, as shown in Fig. 10-4, remove the piston pin circlips from both ends of each piston pin. Then press out the piston pin and remove the piston from the rod.

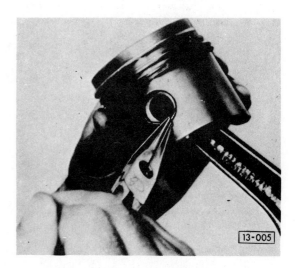

Fig. 10-4. Circlip being removed. Notice the notch in the piston where the pliers have been inserted.

7. Check each piston for wear as shown in Fig. 10-5. Measure the piston at right angles to the piston pin at a point approximately 15 mm (⅝ in.) from the lower edge of the piston skirt.

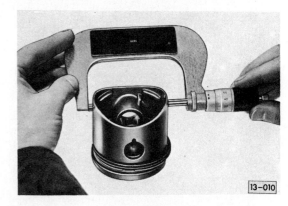

Fig. 10-5. Piston diameter being measured.

8. Compare the measurement obtained in step 7 with the nominal piston diameter that is marked on the piston crown (Fig. 10-6). This comparison will give an indication of the extent to which the piston is worn. However, you can determine whether the piston is suitable for reuse only after measuring the cylinder bore as described in step 9 of this procedure.

9. Using a dial indicator device, as shown in Fig. 10-7, determine the cylinder diameter and the degree of wear.

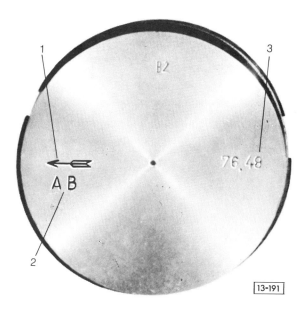

1. Arrow that must point to front of engine
2. Weight class
3. Nominal diameter in mm

Fig. 10-6. Markings on piston crown.

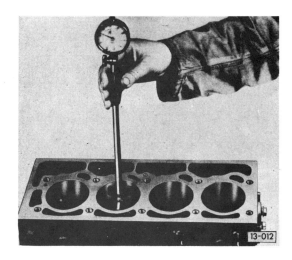

Fig. 10-7. Cylinder bore being measured with a special dial indicator.

NOTE ——

When checking the cylinder bores, make your measurements at three points throughout each cylinder and at right angles to one another (Fig. 10-8). Minor variations in cylinder diameter can be corrected by honing, as described in later steps of this procedure. If, however, there are variations of 0.05 mm (.002 in.) or more among the measurements made in any one cylinder, the cylinder must be rebored to accept an oversize piston.

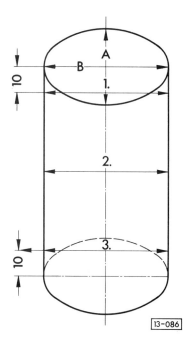

Fig. 10-8. Cylinder bore measuring points. Measurement **1** should be made 10 mm (⅜ in.) from the top of the cylinder, measurement **2** should be made in the middle of the cylinder, and measurement **3** should be made 10 mm (⅜ in.) from the bottom of the cylinder. Make each measurement first in direction **A** and then in direction **B**.

10. Write down the largest bore diameter measurement you obtain for each of the cylinders.

11. Compare the measurements written down in step 10 with the honing group that is marked on the engine block (Fig. 10-9). This comparison will give an indication of the extent to which the cylinder is worn.

Fig. 10-9. Honing group code stamped on the engine block. This number is derived from the diameter of the original cylinder bore. For example, code 653 indicates that, when manufactured, the cylinders were honed to a diameter of 76.53 mm.

NOTE ——

If the measured bore diameter of any cylinder exceeds the largest cylinder diameter listed for the basic dimension or repair stage (as given in **Table g**) by 0.04 mm (.0015 in.) or more, all the cylinders must be rebored and honed to accept new pistons from the next larger repair stage. If the original bore diameter was at the lower limit of the basic dimension or repair group tolerance range, you can hone the cylinders to accept a larger piston from the same basic dimension or repair stage. However, your goal should always be to obtain a clearance of 0.03 mm (.001 in.) between the pistons and the cylinders of a repaired or rebuilt engine.

12. Compute the clearance between the original pistons and their cylinders. To do this, subtract the measurements obtained in step 7 from the measurements that you obtained in step 9. With new parts, the clearance should be 0.03 mm (.0011 to .0012 in.). The wear limit is 0.07 mm (.0025 in.).

13. If the piston clearance exceeds the wear limit, but the cylinders are not worn to a diameter more than 0.04 mm (.0015 in.) greater than their original

honing group, you can correct the clearance by installing new pistons of the original diameter for the cylinder honing group, or by honing the cylinders to the next larger diameter in the same basic dimension or repair stage and then installing new pistons to match the new honing group.

14. If the piston clearance exceeds the wear limit because of cylinder wear, then the cylinders must be rebored and honed to accept new pistons from the next larger repair stage. This work can be done by your Authorized Dealer or by a qualified automotive machine shop.

15. Using feeler gauges of various sizes, determine the side clearance of all the piston rings as shown in Fig. 10-10.

NOTE ——

The piston ring side clearance should be from 0.02 to 0.05 mm (.0008 to .002 in.) with new parts. If you install new piston rings, make certain that side clearance is not less than 0.02 mm (.0008 in.). If there is too little clearance, either replace the piston or have the grooves reconditioned by your Authorized Dealer or a qualified automotive machine shop.

Table g. Piston and Cylinder Diameters

Engine	Repair stage	Piston diameter mm (in.)	Cylinder bore mm (in.)	Honing group
1471 cm³ (89.7 in.³)	Basic dimension	76.48 (3.0110) 76.49 (3.0114) 76.50 (3.0118)	76.51 (3.0122) 76.52 (3.0126) 76.53 (3.0130)	651 652 653
	Repair stage 1	76.73 (3.0209) 76.74 (3.0213) 76.75 (3.0217)	76.76 (3.0221) 76.77 (3.0224) 76.78 (3.0228)	676 677 678
	Repair stage 2	76.98 (3.0307) 76.99 (3.0311) 77.00 (3.0315)	77.01 (3.0319) 77.02 (3.0323) 77.03 (3.0327)	701 702 703
	Repair stage 3	77.48 (3.0504) 77.49 (3.0508) 77.50 (3.0512)	77.51 (3.0516) 77.52 (3.0520) 77.53 (3.0524)	751 752 753
1588 cm³ (96.9 in.³)	Basic dimension	79.48 (3.1291) 79.49 (3.1295) 79.50 (3.1299)	79.51 (3.1303) 79.52 (3.1307) 79.53 (3.1311)	951 952 953
	Repair stage 1	79.73 (3.1390) 79.74 (3.1394) 79.75 (3.1398)	79.76 (3.1402) 79.77 (3.1406) 79.78 (3.1409)	976 977 978
	Repair stage 2	79.98 (3.1488) 79.99 (3.1492) 80.00 (3.1496)	80.01 (3.1500) 80.02 (3.1504) 80.03 (3.1508)	001 002 003
	Repair stage 3	80.48 (3.1685) 80.49 (3.1689) 80.50 (3.1693)	80.51 (3.1697) 80.52 (3.1701) 80.53 (3.1705)	051 052 053

Fig. 10-10. Piston ring side clearance being measured. Insert the feeler gauge between the piston ring and one of the piston lands. Then move the gauge completely around the piston. The clearance must not be outside the specified range at any point.

16. Using a tool such as the one shown in Fig. 10-11, remove the piston rings from the pistons.

CAUTION ——

If you intend to install new rings, it is of no consequence if you break the rings during removal. However, if you intend to reuse the rings, you must work carefully to prevent accidental breakage. It is imperative that used rings be reinstalled in their original grooves and on their original pistons. Otherwise, poor sealing will result—which may cause excessive oil consumption or lost power.

Fig. 10-11. Piston ring being removed from piston.

17. Push each ring about 15 mm (⅝ in.) into the bottom of its cylinder. Then measure the ring gap as shown in Fig. 10-12.

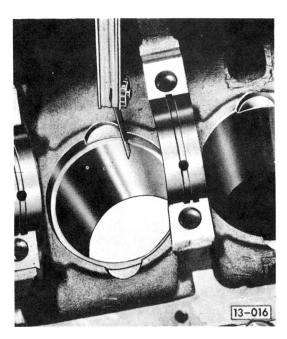

Fig. 10-12. Ring gap being measured with feeler gauge.

NOTE ——

Replacement rings for engines with oversize pistons must be the correct size for the oversize cylinder honing group. If you are checking the end gaps of new rings, which you should always do, the gap should be 0.30 to 0.45 mm (.012 to .018 in.) for the upper and lower compression rings or 0.25 to 0.40 mm (.010 to .016 in.) for the oil scraper ring. If the gap is too narrow, enlarge it with a file or an oil stone. If you are checking used piston rings, the measurement obtained in step 17 must not exceed 1.00 mm (.039 in.)—which is the wear limit. Replace worn out rings.

18. Check the piston pin fit in each piston. The pin must be a light push fit with the piston heated to approximately 60°C (140°F) in an oil bath. If not, replace both the piston and the pin.

19. Check the piston pin fit in each connecting rod. If the clearance exceeds 0.04 mm (.0015 in.), the wear limit, either replace the rod and pin or fit a new pin and a new rod bushing. Hone the new bushing to obtain a clearance of 0.01 to 0.02 mm (.0004 to .0008 in.), then check the rod's alignment. This work can be done by your Authorized Dealer or by a qualified automotive machine shop.

NOTE ——

If for any reason you replace pistons or connecting rods, all four must be of the same weight class. Connecting rod weight classes are designated by a number on the rod cap. Unmarked replacement pistons must be within 10 grams of the weight of the other pistons in the engine. Beginning early in 1975, the factory stopped supplying individual connecting rods that were marked according to weight groups. Present factory replacement rods are available only as sets of four rods of the same weight group.

20. Using the tool shown previously in Fig. 10-11, install the piston rings as indicated in Fig. 10-13.

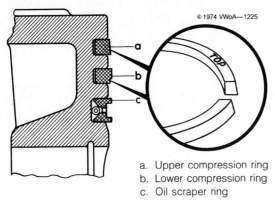

© 1974 VWoA—1225

a. Upper compression ring
b. Lower compression ring
c. Oil scraper ring

Fig. 10-13. Proper ring installation. Word TOP must be toward piston crown.

21. Install one circlip only in one end of the piston pin bore of each piston. Then heat all of the pistons to approximately 60°C (140°F) in an oil bath.

22. With reference to the cylinder numbers you marked on the pistons and the connecting rods during removal, install the pistons on their original connecting rods so that, when the arrow marked on the piston crown is pointing toward the camshaft drive end of the engine, the marks indicated in Fig. 10-14 will be toward the engine's intermediate shaft.

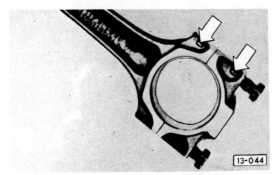

Fig. 10-14. Forged marks (arrows) that must be toward the engine's intermediate shaft with the connecting rod and piston installed in the engine.

23. Working quickly, so that the pistons do not have an opportunity to cool, hand-press the piston pins into position as shown in Fig. 10-15. Seat the pin against the circlip that you have already installed in the piston, then install the other circlip. Make sure that all circlips are firmly engaged in the grooves in the pistons.

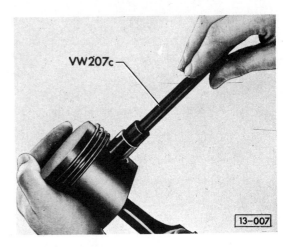

Fig. 10-15. Special drift being used to press piston pin into piston and connecting rod.

24. If the cylinders have not been rebored, but you have installed new piston rings, inspect the cylinders to see whether there are top-cylinder ridges. Remove top-cylinder ridges with a cylinder ridge reamer. Then—whether there were ridges or not—lightly hone the cylinder bores with a hone that has fine (220-grit) stones. Move the spinning hone smoothly in and out of the bore to produce a fine cross-hatch pattern on the cylinder walls.

NOTE ——

A top-cylinder ridge is a band of unworn cylinder wall that remains above the part of the cylinder that has been worn to a larger diameter by contact with the piston rings. If the ridge is not removed, the new upper compression ring will strike the ridge, breaking the ring and damaging the piston. The object of honing the cylinder is to remove "glaze" that could keep the new rings from seating. In breaking the glaze, remove as little metal as possible.

25. Thoroughly clean the engine block to remove metal particles and abrasive dust. Then install the crankshaft, the intermediate shaft, and their bearings and oil seals. (See **11. Crankshaft and Intermediate Shaft.**) Hand-turn the crankshaft to place the connecting rod journal for No. 1 cylinder at bottom dead center (BDC).

26. Thoroughly lubricate the cylinder bores and the piston rings with engine oil only. Stagger the ring

gaps so that the oil scraper ring's gap will be toward the left or the right end of the engine and the other two ring's gaps will be offset 120° to each side of the scraper ring's gap. Then install a piston ring compressor on the piston for No. 1 cylinder and fully compress the rings (Fig. 10-16).

Fig. 10-16. Piston ring compressor installed on piston. Rings must be pressed into their grooves so that piston can be pushed into the cylinder.

27. If previously removed, install the connecting rod bearing shells in the connecting rod and the connecting rod cap. Make sure that the anti-rotation tabs on the bearing shells engage the notches in the rod and the cap. Do not install the cap on the rod.

28. Install the piston/connecting rod assembly in the No. 1 cylinder until the piston ring compressor band contacts the engine block.

29. Being careful to guide the connecting rod bolts over opposite sides of the crankshaft journal, use a wooden hammer handle to tap the piston out of the ring compressor and into the cylinder. Then use the hammer handle to press the piston down in the cylinder until the connecting rod bearing is seated squarely on the crankshaft journal.

CAUTION ——

Check the progress of the connecting rod as you press the piston toward the crankshaft. The rod bearing or the crankshaft will be damaged if you drive them together at an angle.

30. Loosely install the connecting rod cap. Using the same procedure you used on the No. 1 cylinder,

install the piston/connecting rod assembly of the No. 4 cylinder. Then hand-turn the crankshaft 180° and install the piston/connecting rod assemblies of the No. 2 and No. 3 cylinders.

31. One at a time, remove the connecting rod caps. Then place a piece of Plastigage® (available at automotive supply stores) on the crankshaft journal. Do not lay the Plastigage across the oil hole in the crankshaft journal.

NOTE ——

In checking the clearance of new bearings, you can use green Plastigage, which measures clearances from 0.025 to 0.076 mm (.001 to .003 in.). In checking used bearings or new bearings installed in high-mileage engines, use red Plastigage, which measures clearances from 0.050 to 0.150 mm (.002 to .006 in.).

32. Install the connecting rod cap. Torque the nuts to 3.5 mkg (25 ft. lb.), then remove the nuts and the connecting rod cap.

NOTE ——

Torquing the nuts will compress and flatten the Plastigage, which you will measure to determine the connecting rod bearing clearance. Do not turn the crankshaft as you compress the Plastigage. Doing this will spread the Plastigage and cause inaccurate measurement.

33. To determine the bearing clearance, compare the flattened Plastigage to the scale that is printed on the edge of the Plastigage package. Read the clearance printed adjacent to the scale band that has the same width as the flattened Plastigage strip (Fig. 10-17).

Fig. 10-17. Flattened Plastigage being measured to determine connecting rod bearing clearance.

NOTE ——

Used bearings must be installed in their original positions in their original connecting rod. New bearings must be installed so that their anti-rotation tabs engage the notches in the connecting rod and rod cap. With new parts, the connecting rod bearing clearance should be from 0.028 to 0.088 mm (.0011 to .0035 in.). If clearance is at or near the 0.12-mm (.0047-in.) wear limit, check the crankshaft as described in **11.2 Removing, Checking, and Installing Crankshaft and Main Bearings.** Then replace the bearings.

CAUTION ——

Use solvent to remove the flattened Plastigage. Scraping off the Plastigage could damage the connecting rod bearings.

34. If bearing clearance is correct, lightly coat the connecting rod bearing shells and the crankshaft journals with assembly lubricant.

NOTE ——

If assembly lubricant is not available from your automotive supply store, use a light coating of multipurpose grease instead.

35. Install the connecting rod caps. Torque the connecting rod nuts to 4.5 mkg (32 ft. lb.).

36. Using feeler gauges of various thicknesses, determine the connecting rod bearing axial play. To do this, push each connecting rod as far as possible toward one side of the crankshaft journal. If you can insert an 0.25-mm (.010-in.) feeler gauge between the opposite side of the journal and the connecting rod (Fig. 10-18), the clearance is excessive. Excessive clearance can be corrected by installing new bearings, a new

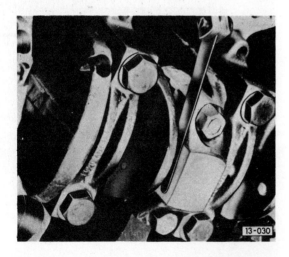

Fig. 10-18. Connecting rod axial play (side clearance) being measured with a feeler gauge.

crankshaft, a new connecting rod, or all three—depending on the extent to which any of these parts is worn.

37. Install the oil pump and the oil pan as described in **6.2 Removing, Checking, and Installing Oil Pump.** Install the cylinder head as described in **5.3 Removing and Installing Cylinder Head and Manifolds.** Then install the engine, if previously removed, as described in **7. Removing and Installing Engine.**

11. CRANKSHAFT AND INTERMEDIATE SHAFT

You must remove the engine if you intend to remove the crankshaft or the intermediate shaft from the engine block. The front oil seals for both shafts can be replaced with the engine installed. However, you can replace the crankshaft's rear oil seal only after you have removed the transaxle or the engine/transaxle assembly. See **MANUAL TRANSMISSION** or **AUTOMATIC TRANSMISSION.**

The crankshaft revolves in five split-shell main bearings. The center (No. 3) main bearing shells are flanged. The flanges control crankshaft axial play. The intermediate shaft runs in two ring-type bearings that are driven into bores in the front and the rear of the engine block.

11.1 Replacing Crankshaft and Intermediate Shaft Oil Seals

The oil seals used at the front ends of the crankshaft, the intermediate shaft, and the camshaft are identical. See **5.4 Disassembling and Assembling Cylinder Head** for information on the replacement of the camshaft oil seal.

To replace crankshaft front oil seal:

1. Remove the camshaft drive belt as described in **5.1 Removing, Installing, and Adjusting Camshaft Drive Belt.** Then remove the crankshaft sprocket.

2. Being careful not to damage the light alloy seal carrier, pry out the old oil seal (Fig. 11-1).

3. Using the tool shown in Fig. 11-2, press in the new seal until it is flush with the front of the seal carrier.

4. Remove the seal-installing tool. Then, so that it does not get stuck in the seal recess, remove the steel driving sleeve from the tool. Using the aluminum part of the tool only, press in the seal until it is recessed 2 mm (.080 in.) from the front of the seal carrier. Then remove the tool and install the sprocket and the camshaft drive belt.

NOTE ——

You can mark the outer surface of the seal-installing tool at a point 2 mm (.080 in.) from the end of the tool that contacts the seal. Press in the seal until the mark on the tool is flush with the seal carrier.

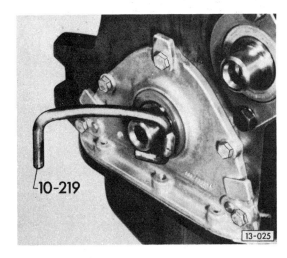

Fig. 11-1. Crankshaft front oil seal being removed. Special tool hooks under inner edge of seal.

Fig. 11-2. Seal being pressed in. Turn bolt (threaded into crankshaft) as indicated by arrow.

To replace crankshaft rear oil seal:

1. Remove the transmission. Remove the flywheel as described in **9.1 Removing, Checking, and Installing Flywheel and Clutch** or remove the drive plate as described in **8.1 Removing and Installing Drive Plate.**

2. Carefully insert a large screwdriver between the crankshaft's flywheel flange and the inner edge of the old oil seal. Then, bracing the screwdriver against the flange, pry out the oil seal.

3. Install the seal guide sleeve tool over the crankshaft flange as shown in Fig. 11-3 or Fig. 11-4. Then hand-start the new oil seal into the seal recess in the oil seal carrier.

NOTE ——

The crankshafts with 82-mm (3 15/64-in.) flywheel mounting flanges, mentioned in Fig. 11-3, were installed only on early 1975 cars, through engine Nos. FC 008 936 and FG 000 301. Later cars have crankshafts with 85-mm (3 11/32-in.) flywheel mounting flanges.

Fig. 11-3. Crankshaft rear oil seal being started in recess (cars with 82-mm (3 15/64-in.) flywheel mounting flanges). Press in as indicated by arrows.

Fig. 11-4. Crankshaft rear oil seal being started in recess (cars with 85-mm (3 11/32-in.) flywheel mounting flanges).

4. Remove the guide sleeve. Then, using the driving plate shown in Fig. 11-5 or Fig. 11-6, press in the seal by alternately tightening the two flywheel or drive plate mounting bolts so that the plate advances evenly toward the seal carrier. When the seal is flush with the carrier, remove the plate and the bolts, install the flywheel or drive plate, then install the transaxle.

Fig. 11-5. Seal driving plate and two flywheel mounting bolts being used to press in rear oil seal (cars with 82-mm (3^{15}/$_{64}$-in.) flywheel mounting flanges).

Fig. 11-6. Seal driving plate and two flywheel mounting bolts being used to press in rear oil seal (cars with 85-mm (3^{11}/$_{32}$-in.) flywheel mounting flanges).

To replace intermediate shaft oil seal:

1. Remove the camshaft drive belt as described in **5.1 Removing, Installing, and Adjusting Camshaft Drive Belt.** Remove the intermediate shaft sprocket.

Use the tools and procedure given for replacing the crankshaft front oil seal, press the seal in only until it is flush with the seal carrier. (Alternatively, you can remove the two bolts and take off the intermediate shaft oil seal carrier, then remove and install the seal as described in the next two steps.)

2. Press the old oil seal out of the carrier. Then press in the new seal as shown in Fig. 11-7.

3. Using a new O-ring, install the seal carrier and seal. Torque the two bolts to 2.0 mkg (14 ft. lb.). Then install the sprocket and the camshaft drive belt.

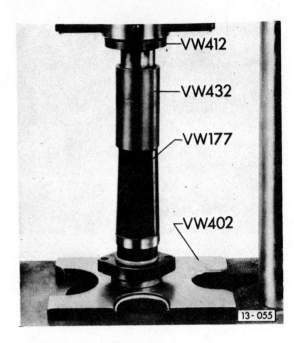

Fig. 11-7. Oil seal being pressed in until it is flush with front of seal carrier.

11.2 Removing, Checking, and Installing Crankshaft and Main Bearings

Fig. 11-8 illustrates the removal of the crankshaft, the crankshaft bearings, and the intermediate shaft. In removing the crankshaft, both crankshaft oil seal carriers must be removed from the engine block.

Though the bearing shells for main bearings 1, 2, 4, and 5 are identical, you must always reinstall used bearing shells in their original locations. Similarly, the main bearing caps must always be reinstalled on their original bearing saddles.

To remove, check, and install:

1. Remove the engine. Remove the pistons and connecting rods as described in **10.1 Removing, Checking, and Installing Pistons, Piston Rings, Connecting Rods, and Connecting Rod Bearings.** Remove the flywheel and clutch or the drive plate.

Fig. 11-8. Exploded view of the crankshaft, crankshaft bearings, intermediate shaft, and related parts.

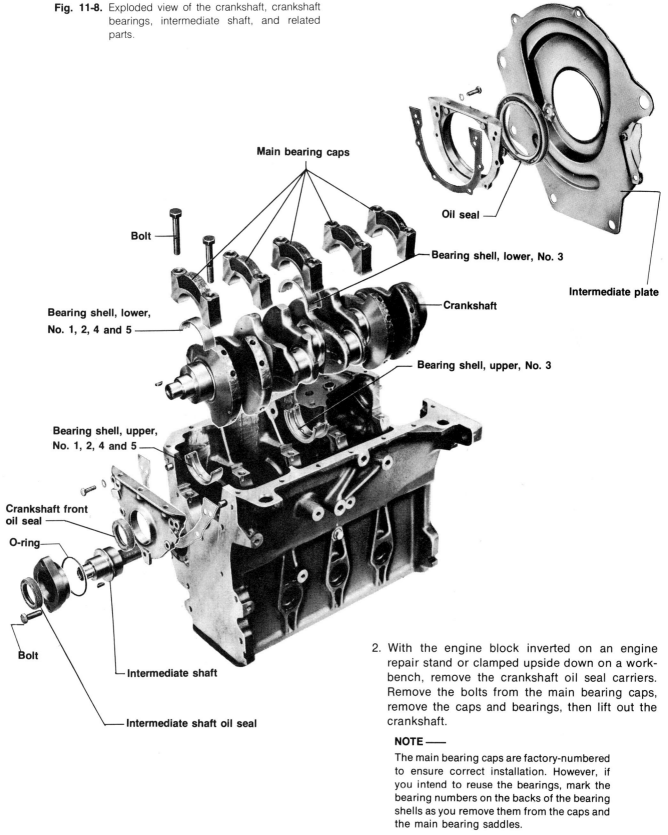

Main bearing caps

Bolt

Bearing shell, lower, No. 1, 2, 4 and 5

Bearing shell, upper, No. 1, 2, 4 and 5

Crankshaft front oil seal

O-ring

Bolt

Intermediate shaft

Intermediate shaft oil seal

Oil seal

Bearing shell, lower, No. 3

Crankshaft

Bearing shell, upper, No. 3

Intermediate plate

2. With the engine block inverted on an engine repair stand or clamped upside down on a workbench, remove the crankshaft oil seal carriers. Remove the bolts from the main bearing caps, remove the caps and bearings, then lift out the crankshaft.

NOTE

The main bearing caps are factory-numbered to ensure correct installation. However, if you intend to reuse the bearings, mark the bearing numbers on the backs of the bearing shells as you remove them from the caps and the main bearing saddles.

3. Using a micrometer, measure the crankshaft's main bearing and connecting rod journals. Then

compare the measurements with the dimensions given in **Table h.** So that you can be certain the journals are not worn to a taper, duplicate each measurement at opposite sides of each journal. To determine eccentricity, make a second pair of measurements at a point 90° from the initial measurements. Alternatively, check the eccentricity (out-of-round) of the main bearing journals by placing main bearing journals 1 and 5 on V-blocks, and then rotating the crankshaft against a dial indicator positioned, one journal at a time, against main bearing journals 2, 3, and 4.

NOTE ——

If the journals are rough or scored, tapered, exceed the limit for maximum out-of-round, or have worn to such a degree that the connecting rod or the main bearing clearances exceed the wear limit even with new bearings, the crankshaft must be either replaced or reconditioned. You can exchange your worn crankshaft for a new crankshaft or for an undersize reconditioned crankshaft at your Authorized Dealer's parts department. Alternatively, a specialty shop can recondition your worn crankshaft to one of the undersizes listed in **Table h.**

4. Using the original bearings, original-size replacement bearings, or undersize main bearings—depending on the condition of the crankshaft as determined in step 3—install the upper main bearing shells (with oil holes and lubrication grooves) in the bearing saddles of the engine block (Fig. 11-9). Make certain that the bearing saddles are clean and that the anti-rotation tabs engage the notches in the saddles.

Fig. 11-9. Upper main bearing shells, identified by oil groove (lower arrow). Oil holes (upper arrow) must align with oil holes in engine block.

5. Place the crankshaft in the engine block. Install the lower main bearing shells in the bearing caps. Then, making sure you install the caps as shown in Fig. 11-10, use Plastigage® to check the bearing clearance with the bolts torqued to 3.5 mkg (25 ft. lb.). Plastigage measurement is described in **10.1 Removing, Checking, and Installing Pistons, Piston Rings, Connecting Rods, and Connecting Rod Bearings.**

6. With new bearings, the bearing clearance (measured with Plastigage) should be between 0.03 and 0.08 mm (.0012 and .003 in.). If the clearance with used bearings exceeds the wear limit—0.17 mm (.007 in.)—replace the bearings. If the clear-

Table h. Crankshaft Journal Sizes

Sizes	Crankshaft main bearing journal		Crankshaft connecting rod journal	
	diameter in mm (in.)	maximum out-of-round mm (in.)	diameter in mm (in.)	maximum out-of-round mm (in.)
Original grade 1 grade 2	54.00 −0.04 (2.126 −.0015) 54.00 −0.06 (2.126 −.002)	0.03 (.0012) 0.03 (.0012)	46.00 −0.04 (1.811 −.0015) 46.00 −0.06 (1.811 −.002)	0.03 (.0012) 0.03 (.0012)
Undersize I grade 1 grade 2	53.75 −0.04 (2.1161 −.0015) 53.75 −0.06 (2.1161 −.002)	0.03 (.0012) 0.03 (.0012)	45.75 −0.04 (1.8012 −.0015) 45.75 −0.06 (1.8012 −.002)	0.03 (.0012) 0.03 (.0012)
Undersize II grade1 grade 2	53.50 −0.04 (2.1063 −.0015) 53.50 −0.06 (2.1063 −.002)	0.03 (.0012) 0.03 (.0012)	45.50 −0.04 (1.7913 −.0015) 45.50 −0.06 (1.7913 −.002)	0.03 (.0012) 0.03 (.0012)
Undersize III grade 1 grade 2	53.25 −0.04 (2.0965 −.0015) 53.25 −0.06 (2.0965 −.002)	0.03 (.0012) 0.03 (.0012)	45.25 −0.04 (1.7815 −.0015) 45.25 −0.06 (1.7815 −.002)	0.03 (.0012) 0.03 (.0012)

ance exceeds the wear limit even with new bearings, the crankshaft must be replaced or reconditioned to accept bearings for one of the three undersize ranges.

Fig. 11-10. Main bearing cap numbers. Number **1** is at front of engine. All numbers must be toward the right (manifold) side of the engine.

7. Remove the flattened Plastigage strips. Then lift out the crankshaft.

CAUTION —

Use solvent to remove the flattened Plastigage. Scraping off the Plastigage could damage the main bearings.

8. Lightly coat the main bearing shells and the main bearing journals with assembly lubricant.

NOTE —

If assembly lubricant is not available from your automotive supply store, use a light coating of multipurpose grease instead.

9. Place the crankshaft in the engine block, install the bearing caps as shown earlier in Fig. 11-10, then torque the bolts to 6.5 mkg (47 ft. lb.).

10. Using feeler gauges of various thicknesses, determine the crankshaft's axial play. To do this, push the crankshaft as far as it will go toward the rear of the engine. Then insert the feeler gauge between the crank throw for No. 2 cylinder and the front flange of the No. 3 main bearing, as shown in Fig. 11-11.

NOTE —

With new parts, axial play should be between 0.07 and 0.17 mm (.0025 and .0065 in.). If you can insert a 0.37-mm (.015-in.) feeler gauge between the bearing and the crank throw, the clearance is excessive. Excessive clearance can usually be corrected by replacing the No. 3 main bearing.

Fig. 11-11. Crankshaft axial play being measured.

4 ■

11. Using new gaskets, install the crankshaft oil seal carriers. Install the clutch and flywheel or the drive plate. Install the pistons and connecting rods as described in **10.1 Removing, Checking, and Installing Pistons, Piston Rings, Connecting Rods, and Connecting Rod Bearings.** Then install the engine.

11.3 Removing and Installing Intermediate Shaft

The intermediate shaft and its bearings are subject to very little wear. Nevertheless, remove the shaft during engine rebuilding so that abrasive particles and other foreign matter can be thoroughly cleaned off the bearings and out of the oil passages.

To remove the intermediate shaft, first remove the engine as described in **7. Removing and Installing Engine.** Then remove the distributor as described in **3.2 Distributor** and, on engines with carburetors, remove the fuel pump as described in **FUEL AND EXHAUST SYSTEMS.** Remove the camshaft drive belt as described in **5.1 Removing, Installing, and Adjusting Camshaft Drive Belt.**

Remove the two bolts, then remove the intermediate shaft oil seal carrier. Being careful not to damage the bearings, the gear that drives the distributor, or the eccentric for the fuel pump, withdraw the intermediate shaft from the engine block.

Installation is the reverse of removal. If the oil seal is cracked or worn, replace it as described in **11.1 Replacing Crankshaft and Intermediate Shaft Oil Seals.** If the bearings are worn so that their copper backing shows through the silvery bearing surfaces, drive out the old bearings. Then, being careful to align the oil holes in the new bearings with the oil holes in the engine block, drive in first the rear bearing and then the front bearing. You must use a bearing driver that accurately fits the inside of the bearings and the oil holes must align with the bearings installed.

Coat the bearings with assembly lubricant or multipurpose grease before you install the shaft. Also apply assembly lubricant or multipurpose grease to the eccentric for the fuel pump and the gear that drives the distributor. Torque the two bolts for the intermediate shaft oil seal carrier to 2.0 mkg (14 ft. lb.).

12. ENGINE AND CLUTCH TECHNICAL DATA

I. Tolerances, Wear Limits, and Settings

Designation	New parts on installation mm (in.)	Wear limit mm (in.)
A. Crankshaft		
1. Journal dimensions		
a. Main journals .... grade 1, diameter	54.00 −0.04 (2.126 −.0015)	—
.... grade 2, diameter	54.00 −0.06 (2.126 −.002)	—
b. Connecting rod journals .... grade 1, diameter	46.00 −0.04 (1.811 −.0015)	—
.... grade 2, diameter	46.00 −0.06 (1.811 −.002)	—
c. Three undersizes of 0.25 mm (.010 in.) each	—	—
2. Main journals .... out-of-round	—	0.03 (.0012)
3. Connecting rod journal .... out-of-round	—	0.03 (.0012)
4. Main bearing/main journal .... clearance	0.03–0.08 (.0012–.003)	0.17 (.007)
5. Connecting rod bearing/rod journal .... clearance	0.028–0.088 (.0011–.0035)	0.12 (.0047)
6. Crankshaft/main bearing No. 3 .... axial play	0.07–0.17 (.0025–.0065)	0.25 (.010)
B. Connecting rods		
a. Piston pin/connecting rod bushing .... clearance	0.01–0.02 (.0004–.0008)	0.25 (.010)
b. Connecting rod/crankshaft .... side clearance	—	0.25 (.010)
C. Pistons and Cylinders		
1. Piston and cylinder sizes		
a. Pistons, 1471-cm³ (89.7-in.³) engine .... grade 1, diameter	76.48 (3.0110)	—
.... grade 2, diameter	76.49 (3.0114)	—
.... grade 3, diameter	76.50 (3.0118)	—
Three oversizes of 0.25 mm (.010 in.) each	—	—
b. Cylinders, 1471-cm³ (89.7-in.³) engine ...... grade 1, diameter	76.51 (3.0122)	76.55 (3.0138)
...... grade 2, diameter	76.52 (3.0126)	76.56 (3.0141)
...... grade 3, diameter	76.53 (3.0130)	76.57 (3.0146)
Three oversizes of 0.25 mm (.010 in.) each	—	—
c. Pistons, 1588-cm³ (96.9-in.³) engine .... grade 1, diameter	79.48 (3.1291)	—
.... grade 2, diameter	79.49 (3.1295)	—
.... grade 3, diameter	79.50 (3.1299)	—
Three oversizes of 0.25 mm (.010 in.) each	—	—
d. Cylinders, 1588-cm³ (96.9-in.³) engine ...... grade 1, diameter	79.51 (3.1303)	79.55 (3.1319)
...... grade 2, diameter	79.52 (3.1307)	79.56 (3.1323)
...... grade 3, diameter	79.53 (3.1311)	79.57 (3.1327)
Three oversizes of 0.25 mm (.010 in.) each	—	—
2. Cylinders .... maximum taper or out-of-round	—	0.05 (.002)
3. Piston/cylinder .... clearance	0.03 (.001)	0.07 (.0025)
4. Piston ring/piston .... side clearance	0.02–0.05 (.0008–.002)	—
5. Ring gap (with ring installed in cylinder)		
a. Compression rings .... end gap	0.30–0.45 (.012–.017)	1.00 (.039)
b. Oil scraper rings .... end gap	0.25–0.40 (.010–.016)	1.00 (.039)
D. Camshaft, Valves, and Cylinder Head		
1. Camshaft .... axial play	—	0.15 (.006)
2. Camshaft (measured at center bearing, bearings 1 and 5 on V-blocks) .... runout	—	0.01 (.0004)
3. Camshaft/camshaft bearings .... clearance	0.02–0.05 (.0008–.002)	—
4. Valve spring tensions		
a. Outer spring at loaded length of 22.3 mm (⅞ in.) .... load	43.5–48.0 kg (96–106 lb.)	—
b. Inner spring at loaded length of 18.3 mm (²³/₃₂ in.) .... load	21.0–23.0 kg (46–51 lb.)	—

I. Tolerances, Wear Limits, and Settings (continued)

Designation	New parts on installation mm (in.)	Wear limit mm (in.)
5. Valve seats		
a. Contact area facing .... angle	45°	—
b. Intake .... width of 45° facing	2.00 (.079)	—
c. Intake .... outside diameter of 45° facing	33.20 (1.307)	—
d. Intake .... distance from head gasket surface on head to outer edge of 45° facing	9.00 (.354)	—
e. Exhaust .... width of 45° facing	2.40 (.094)	—
f. Exhaust .... outside diameter of 45° facing	30.80 (1.212)	—
g. Exhaust .... distance from head gasket surface on head to outer edge of 45° facing	9.60 (.378)	—
h. Seat width correction chamfer .... angle	30°	—
6. Valve guides		
a. Valve guide intake valve stem .... rock	—	1.00 (.039)
b. Valve guide/exhaust valve stem .... rock	—	1.30 (.051)
c. Valve guide .... inside diameter	8.013–8.035 (.315–.316)	—
d. Tops of valve guides below cover gasket surface on cylinder head .... distance	56.00 ±0.50 (2.204 ±.020)	—
7. Valve stem		
a. Intake .... diameter	7.97 (.314)	—
b. Exhaust .... diameter	7.95 (.313)	—
c. Intake .... overall valve length	98.70 (3.886)	—
d. Exhaust .... overall valve length	98.50 (3.878)	—
8. Valve head		
a. Intake .... diameter	34.00 (1.338)	—
b. Exhaust .... diameter	31.00 (1.220)	—
c. Intake .... margin	—	0.50 (.020) min.
d. Exhaust .... margin	—	Do not machine-grind
9. Valve clearance		
a. Intake (cold) .... setting	0.15–0.25 (.006–.010)	—
b. Intake (hot—coolant temp. approx. 35°C (95°F)) .... setting	0.20–0.30 (.008–.012)	—
c. Exhaust (cold) .... setting	0.35–0.45 (.014–.018)	—
d. Exhaust (hot—coolant temp. approx. 35°C (95°F)) ...... setting	0.40–0.50 (.016–.020)	—
10. Cylinder head		
a. Cylinder head warp .... twist or arch	—	0.10 (.004)
b. Engine block deck warp .... twist or arch	—	0.10 (.004)
E. Cooling System		
1. Radiator cap .... relief pressure	0.88–1.02 atu (13–15 psi)	—
2. Thermostat		
a. Begins opening .... temperature	80°C (176°F)	—
b. Fully open .... temperature	94°C (200°F)	—
3. Radiator fan thermo switch		
a. Fan goes on .... temperature	90°–95°C (194°–203°F) and above	—
b. Fan goes off .... temperature	85°–90°C (185°–194°F) and below	—
4. V-belt tension—deflection under thumb pressure at a point midway between the alternator and the crankshaft pulleys	10–15 (³⁄₈–⁹⁄₁₆)	—
F. Lubrication System		
1. Oil pressure		
a. Warning light goes out Rabbit through Chassis No. 176 3119 462; Scirocco through Chassis No. 536 2018 901 .... pressure	0.30–0.60 kg/cm² (4.3–8.5 psi) or more	—
Later cars .... pressure	0.15–0.45 kg/cm² (2.1–6.4 psi)	—
b. Normal oil pressure (@ 2000 rpm with SAE 10 W oil at 60°C (140°F)) .... minimum	—	2.0 kg/cm² (28 psi)
2. Oil pump		
a. Oil pump gears .... backlash clearance	0.05–0.20 (.002–.008)	—
b. Oil pump gears .... axial play	—	0.15 (.006)
G. Drive Plate or Flywheel and Clutch		
1. Rear surface of drive plate—distance from rear surface of engine block	31.30 ±0.80 (1.232 ± .031)	—
2. Clutch pressure plate .... inward taper of friction surface	—	0.30 (.012)
3. Clutch driven plate ...... runout at a diameter of 175 mm (6⅞ in.)	—	0.40 (.016)
4. Clutch freeplay measured at pedal .... distance	15 (⅝)	—

4

II. Tightening Torques

Location	Designation	mkg	ft. lb.
Distributor hold-down to engine block	bolt	2.0	14
Spark plug in cylinder head	spark plug	2.5–3.0	10–22
Temperature gauge sensor in heater hose connection	sensor	0.7	5 (60 in. lb.)
Hose connections to engine block and cylinder head	bolt	1.0	7
Water pump to engine block	bolt	2.0	14
Alternator adjusting bracket to head and alternator	bolt/socket-head bolt	2.0	14
Alternator to mounting bracket	nut	2.5	18
Alternator mounting bracket to engine block	bolt	3.3	24
Water pump front part to water pump housing	bolt	1.0	7
Camshaft drive belt tensioner	locknut	4.5	32
Camshaft drive belt cover to engine	nut	1.0	7
Camshaft drive belt sprockets to camshaft, crankshaft, and intermediate shaft	bolt	8.0	58
Camshaft bearing caps to cylinder head	nut	2.0	14
Cylinder head to engine block (engine cold)	socket-head bolt	7.5	54
Cylinder head to engine block (engine hot)	socket-head bolt	8.5	61
Coolant drain plug in engine block	hex-head plug	3.5	25
Manifolds or intake air distributor to cylinder head	nut or bolt	2.5	18
Guard to exhaust manifold	nut	2.0	14
Exhaust pipe to exhaust manifold	nut	2.5	18
Intake manifold support to intake manifold	bolt	2.0	14
Intake manifold support to exhaust manifold	bolt	2.5	18
Core plug in front of cylinder head	socket-head plug	6.0	43
Cylinder head cover to cylinder head	bolt	1.0	7
V-belt pulleys to water pump hub, air pump hub, or crankshaft sprocket	bolt	2.0	14
Oil filter mounting flange to engine block	socket-head bolt	1.0	7
Fuel pump to engine block	socket-head bolt	2.0	14
Oil pressure warning light switch in cylinder head	sensor	1.0	7
Oil pickup tube to oil pump housing	bolt	1.0	7
Oil pump to engine block	M 8 bolt	2.0	14
Oil pan to engine block (retorque after waiting 5 minutes)	socket-head screw	1.0	7
	special M 6 bolt	2.0	14
Oil drain plug in oil pan	hex-head plug	3.0	22
Engine/transaxle mountings	M 10 bolt or nut	4.0	29
Transaxle left mounting to transaxle	nut and bolt	2.5	18
Torque converter to drive plate	bolt	3.0	22
Engine to transmission bellhousing	nut	5.5	40
Clutch pressure plate assembly or drive plate to crankshaft (use Loctite® 270 or 271)	bolt	7.5	54
Flywheel to clutch pressure plate assembly	bolt	2.0	14
Connecting rod cap to connecting rod	nut	4.5	32
Crankshaft and intermediate shaft oil seal carriers to engine block	bolt	2.0	14
Main bearing cap to engine block	bolt	6.5	47

III. General Engine Data

Engine code letter	Manual transmission— 1975: FC 1976: FN 1976–1977 fuel injection: EE Automatic transmission— 1975: FG 1976: FN 1976–1977 fuel injection: EF
Number of cylinders	4
Cylinder layout	Inline, transverse engine
Valve operation	Belt-driven single overhead camshaft
Cylinder bore	1975: 76.50 mm (3.012 in.) 1976–1977: 79.50 mm (3.130 in.)
Piston stroke	80.00 mm (3.150 in.)
Piston displacement	1975: 1471 cm³ (89.7 in.³) 1976–1977: 1588 cm³ (96.9 in.³)
Compression ratio	1975–early 1976: 8.2:1 Late 1976–1977: 8.0:1
Fuel requirement	91 octane RON—lead-free for cars with catalytic converters
Horsepower	Code letters FC, FG: 74 DIN (55 kw) @ 5800 rpm 70 SAE net @ 5800 rpm Code letter FN: 75 DIN (55 kw) @ 5600 rpm 71 SAE net @ 5600 rpm Code letters EE, EF: 82 DIN (60 kw) @ 5500 rpm 78 SAE net @ 5500 rpm (California models slightly less)
Torque	Code letters FC, FG: 11.7 mkg DIN @ 3500 rpm 80 ft. lb. SAE @ 3500 rpm Code letter FN: 11.9 mkg DIN @ 3000 rpm 86 ft. lb. SAE @ 3000 rpm Code letters EE, EF: 11.8 mkg DIN @ 3200 rpm 83 ft. lb. SAE @ 3200 rpm (California models slightly less)

IV. Basic Tune-up Specifications

Coolant capacity	6.8 U.S. quarts (5.7 Imperial quarts, 6.0 liters)
Oil capacity	With filter change: 3.7 U.S. quarts (3.2 Imperial quarts, 3.5 liters) Without filter change: 3.2 U.S. quarts (2.6 Imperial quarts, 3.0 liters)
Firing order	1–3–4–2
Cylinder location	No. 1 at camshaft drive end of engine, cylinders numbered consecutively from curb side of car to driver's side
Valve clearance	Intake (cold): 0.15–0.25 mm (.006–.010 in.) Intake (hot): 0.20–0.30 mm (.008–.012 in.) Exhaust (cold): 0.35–0.45 mm (.014–.018 in.) Exhaust (hot): 0.40–0.50 mm (.016–.020 in.)

IV. Basic Tune-up Specification (continued)

Compression pressure	142–184 psi (10–13 atu) Wear limit: 107 psi (7.5 atu)—or a cylinder-to-cylinder difference exceeding 42 psi (3.0 atu)
Electrical system	12-volt, negative ground
Spark plug type	Carburetor engine: Champion N-8Y Bosch W 200 T30 Beru 200/14/3A1 After elimination of catalytic converter (see **FUEL AND EXHAUST SYSTEMS**), it may be necessary to use the following spark plugs in order to avoid fuel (soot) fouling: Champion N-9Y Bosch W 175 T30 Beru 175/14/3A Fuel injection engine: Champion N-7Y Bosch W 215 T30 Beru 215/14/3A or 215/14/3A1
Spark plug gap	0.60 to 0.70 mm (.024 to .028 in.)
Plug connector resistance	5000 to 10,000 ohms
Distributor rotor resistance	10,000 ohms maximum
Point gap	0.40 mm (.016 in.)
Dwell angle	44° to 50° on installation of new points 42° to 58° wear limit
Ignition timing	3° after TDC at 850 to 1000 rpm with the vacuum hose(s) connected
Idle speed	850 to 1000 rpm
CO content (carburetor engines only)	USA including California (measured ahead of catalytic converter)— 1975 with manual transmission: 2.0% ± 0.5% 1975 with automatic transmission: 2.0% ± 0.5% (If the catalytic converter has been eliminated from a 1975 car (see **FUEL AND EXHAUST SYSTEMS**), use the 1976 CO content specifications) 1976 with manual transmission: 1.5% ± 0.7% 1976 with automatic transmission: 1.0% ± 0.7% Canada (measured at tailpipe)— 1975 with manual transmission: 2.0% ± 0.5% 1975 with automatic transmission: 1.0% ± 0.5% 1976 with manual transmission: 0.8% to 2.2% 1976 with automatic transmission: 0.3% to 1.7%
CO content (fuel injection engines only)	Canada and USA, except California (measured at tailpipe)— With manual transmission: 1.5% maximum With automatic trans.: 1.0% maximum California (measured at tailpipe)— With manual transmission: 0.3% maximum With automatic trans.: 0.3% maximum

4 ■

ELECTRICAL SYSTEM

Contents

Electrical System

The electrical system is basically an efficient means for transmitting power from the engine to remote parts of the car. It does this with the help of an alternator that converts some of the engine's mechanical energy into electrical energy. The electrical energy is carried over wires to motors that convert it back into mechanical energy or to bulbs that convert it into heat and light. The battery in the system supplies electrical power mainly when the engine is not running.

5

Every terminal in the electrical system is numbered. The terminal numbers for all major electrical connections are given in the wiring diagrams that appear at the end of this section. The terminal number is usually stamped on the component itself as an aid to correct installation.

Though most of the electrical terminal numbers are used only once to denote a particular terminal on a particular component, there are several numbers that do not designate specific terminals and which appear in numerous locations throughout the electrical system. These numbers identify main sources of electrical current. All terminals numbered 15 originate at the ignition switch and supply current only when the ignition switch is in its on position. Terminals numbered 30 supply positive polarity current directly from the battery with no intervening switch that can be used to turn it off. Terminals numbered 31 are ground connections and the ground wires connected to them are always brown. Terminals identified by the number 50 receive current only when the ignition switch is in its start position. A letter suffix is sometimes added to the terminal number to distinguish separate parts of the same circuit or to prevent confusion between two circuits that have similar functions.

All electrical circuits other than those required for starting and operating the engine are protected by fuses. To prevent accidental shorts that might blow a fuse or damage wires and electrical components that are not protected by fuses, you should always disconnect the ground strap from the negative post of the battery before working on the electrical system of your car. If you lack the skills or the equipment needed for testing and repairing the electrical system, we suggest that you leave this work to an Authorized Dealer or other qualified shop. We especially urge you to consult your Authorized Dealer before attempting repairs on a car still covered by the new-car warranty.

1. GENERAL DESCRIPTION

The components of the electrical system are discussed in detail in later parts of this section. However, a brief description of the principal components is presented here for purposes of familiarization.

System Voltage and Polarity

The cars covered by this Manual have a 12-volt, negative-ground electrical system. In other words, the voltage regulator keeps voltage in the system at approximately the 12-volt rating of the battery and the negative pole of the battery is connected directly to the car's chassis.

Battery

The six-cell, 12-volt lead-acid battery is located in the left-hand side of the engine compartment. All Scirocco models and those Rabbit models with air conditioning have a battery that is rated at 54 ampere-hours. The Rabbit model without air conditioning has a battery rated at 45 ampere-hours.

Starting System

The 0.7-horsepower starter is series-wound and has an overrunning clutch. The starter and its attached solenoid are located at the front of the engine/transaxle assembly on cars with manual transmissions or behind the engine on cars with automatic transmissions.

Charging System

The charging system consists of a belt-driven alternator and a regulator. The regulator is integral with the alternator brush holder on Bosch alternators. On Motorola alternators, the regulator is a separate component held to the alternator housing by screws. The Bosch alternators and the Motorola alternators used on most models are rated at 55 amperes with a maximum output of 770 watts. However, beginning with the 1977 models, a 65-ampere Bosch alternator is used on cars with factory air conditioning.

Ignition System

The ignition is a conventional coil and battery, distributor-controlled system. Ignition troubleshooting and repair is covered in **ENGINE AND CLUTCH**. Radio suppression is by resistance built into the spark plug connectors and distributor rotor.

Wiring

All components of the electrical system (except for the heavy battery cables) have push-on connectors. A system of fuses prevents short circuits or excessive current from damaging the electrical system and wiring.

Lights

The lighting system includes the parking lights, the side marker lights, the turn signals, the back-up lights, the interior lighting, and the sealed beam headlights. The dimmer control is on the steering column. Except on 1977 and later cars, the actual switching is carried out by a dimmer relay mounted on the fuse box.

Computer Analysis

The cars covered by this Manual are equipped with a network of wiring that serves the Computer Analysis system. A central socket in the engine compartment receives the individual wires that are connected to various measuring points on the car. These connections are identified by encircled numbers in the wiring diagrams that appear in this section.

Although they are not vital to car operation, all these connections must be kept intact if the Computer Analysis system is to work properly. Never connect any device other than the test plug of the Computer Analysis system to the test network central socket in the engine compartment. Incorrect equipment could damage the plug connectors, the test sensors, or the vehicle components that contain sensors.

Heating and Ventilation Fan

The heating and ventilation system includes a two- or three-speed fan. The fan, which is used primarily to assist heating and ventilation while the car is being driven slowly or standing still, is controlled by a dashboard-mounted switch. Removal and installation of the fan is covered in **BODY AND INTERIOR.**

Windshield Wipers

The blade(s) of the two-speed windshield wiper system park automatically when the wiper switch is turned off. The wiper switch includes a windshield washer control. The washers are supplied with fluid by a motor-driven pump.

Instruments

The instrument cluster of basic Rabbit models consists of a speedometer with a built-in fuel gauge. Other Rabbit models have a speedometer and a clock—with a water temperature gauge and a fuel gauge built into the clock face. As an option, a tachometer can be obtained in place of the clock. All Scirocco models have the tachometer with built-in water temperature and fuel gauges and a speedometer that has a resettable trip odometer. On all models, the speedometer is operated by a flexible cable that is driven by a gear in the transaxle. Warning lights are used to inform the driver of charging system and oil pressure irregularities. Instead of a gauge, basic Rabbit models have a warning light to signal excessive water temperature.

2. MAINTENANCE

No routine lubrication of the alternator, the starter, or the other motors is required. However, the following checks are covered in **LUBRICATION AND MAINTENANCE** or under the listed headings in this section of the Manual.

1. Checking the lights and switches

2. Checking the windshield wipers and washers

3. Checking the battery

4. Testing the charging and starting systems. See **3., 4., 5.2.**

3. BATTERY

Each of the six battery cells contains a set of brown lead oxide positive plates and gray sponge lead negative plates. The cells are connected in series by heavy lead bars and are enclosed in a plastic case having six compartments. The battery case also serves as a tank for the electrolyte—a solution of sulfuric acid diluted with water to a specific gravity of 1.285, which means that the electrolyte weighs 1.285 times as much as an equal volume of water. The battery plates that make up the cells are completely immersed in the electrolyte.

The terminal posts are labeled + and − and are further identified by having a positive post that is the thicker of the two. A ground strap connects the negative (−) post to the chassis of the car. Two cables are attached to the positive (+) post; one cable connects the battery to the starter solenoid and the other (thinner) cable connects the battery to the fuse box and the rest of the electrical system.

Discharging

The battery does not store electricity. Rather, it produces electrical current by means of a reversible electrochemical reaction. When a circuit is completed between the two battery posts, sulfuric acid from the electrolyte combines with the lead in the plates to produce lead sulfate, releasing a great many electrons in the process.

Charging

The electrochemical reaction by which the battery produces electrical current is reversed when direct current is sent back into the cells. The charging system of the car supplies this current. When the discharged battery plates are charged with direct current from an outside source, the lead sulfate in the plates is converted back to its original state, returning sulfuric acid to the solution in the electrolyte.

A battery can never be charged to a voltage level in excess of the voltage it is capable of producing electrochemically. As charging proceeds, the battery's voltage builds to a peak called terminal voltage. If charging is continued beyond the terminal voltage, the water in the electrolyte begins to decompose into hydrogen and oxygen. This condition is called gassing.

Temperature Effects

Temperature changes modify the efficiency of the battery as well as alter the specific gravity of its electrolyte. Low outside temperatures can create slow starting by thickening the engine and transmission oils and simultaneously reducing the battery power available for running the starter motor. For example, the current-producing capacity of a battery chilled to −15°C (5°F) is only half its capacity at 20°C (68°F).

In addition, there is danger of partly-discharged batteries freezing in cold weather owing to the higher proportion of water in the electrolyte. A frozen battery will produce no current, but can usually be restored to service if thawed out slowly. The following list shows the safe low temperature limits for batteries in various states of charge.

Specific gravity	Freezing point
1.285	−68°C (−90°F)
1.200	−27°C (−17°F)
1.120	−11°C (12°F)

3.1 Servicing and Testing Battery

The level of the electrolyte should never be allowed to fall below the tops of the plates in any cell. As water is lost through evaporation and electrolysis, fresh water must be added in order to maintain the electrolyte's level at the bottoms of the indicator tubes built into the battery filler openings. Use only distilled water to replenish the electrolyte. Water that is not chemically pure may have an adverse effect on battery life and efficiency.

The battery will lose more water in summer than in winter. In very hot weather it may be necessary to check the electrolyte level as often as once a week. Never overfill the cells. This could cause the electrolyte to boil over during a long daylight drive when the load on the electrical system is light and alternator output is high.

Battery terminals must be tight-fitting and free of corrosion and acid salts. If you notice even a trace of corrosion, disconnect the positive cable and the ground strap from the battery posts and clean the posts and the terminal clamps with a battery terminal cleaning tool. After the terminals have been cleaned and the positive cable and the ground strap tightly installed on the battery posts, the terminals and posts should be coated lightly

5

with petroleum jelly or sprayed with a commercial battery terminal corrosion inhibitor.

WARNING ——

Keep sparks and open flame away from the top of the battery. Hydrogen gas from the battery could explode violently.

The top of the battery should always be kept clean. Even a thin layer of dust containing conductive acid salts can cause the battery to discharge. Corrosion and acid salt accumulations should be washed away with a baking soda solution. Be extremely careful that none of this solution enters the cells through the vent holes. Even a drop or two will seriously impair the efficiency of the battery.

You should make periodic battery tests in order to keep track of battery condition. These tests can also be made to help pinpoint the source of suspected battery trouble.

WARNING ——

Wear goggles when you work with battery electrolyte and do not allow the liquid to contact your skin or clothing. Electrolyte is corrosive and can cause severe burns. If it should spill onto your skin, flush the area of contact immediately with large quantities of water. Spilled electrolyte can be neutralized with a strong baking soda solution.

Hydrometer Testing

The simplest tool for testing the battery is a hydrometer. It consists of a glass cylinder with a freely moving float inside. When electrolyte is drawn into the cylinder by squeezing and releasing a rubber bulb, the level to which the float sinks indicates the specific gravity of the electrolyte. A specific gravity scale on the float is read at the point where it intersects the surface of the electrolyte. The more dense the concentration of sulfuric acid in the electrolyte, the less the float will sink and the higher the reading. Specific gravity values for different states of charge are as follows:

State of charge	Specific gravity
Fully charged	1.280 to 1.285
75% charged	1.240
50% charged	1.200
25% charged	1.160
Fully discharged	1.120

Voltage Testing

Total battery voltage can be tested with a special voltmeter. The tester should consist of a voltmeter connected in parallel with a test load of approximately

110 amps. The minimum voltage indicated should not be less than 9.6 volts. If total voltage drops below this value during the 5- to 10-second test, the battery is either discharged or sulfated. A sulfated battery is one in which the plates are covered by a layer of lead sulfate that is difficult to reconvert. Sulfating is visible as a gray coating on the plates.

CAUTION ——

A discharged battery should be recharged immediately. Otherwise, sulfating will lead to the loss of active plate materials and to reduced battery capacity.

The voltage of an individual cell should not vary from the others by more than 0.2 volts. This can be determined by applying one prong of the tester to the negative battery post, then dipping the other prong into the electrolyte of successive cells, and finally applying it to the positive post (Fig. 3-1). The readings should be 2, 4, 6, 8, 10, and 12 volts. This test should last for no more than 10 seconds.

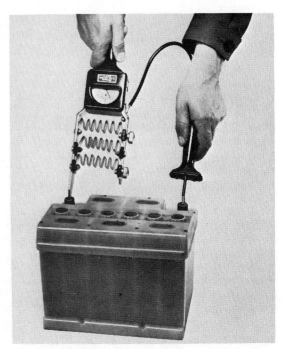

© 1974 VWoA—1329

Fig. 3-1. Using voltmeter to test total voltage of battery.

3.2 Removing and Installing Battery

The battery is fastened in position by a bolt and hold-down plate (Fig. 3-2). Before removing the bolt, disconnect first the ground strap and then the positive cable from the battery posts. Remove the hold-down plate bolt, then remove the battery.

When installing the battery, clean and install the terminals as described earlier in **3.1 Servicing and Testing Battery.** The battery must be mounted firmly to the body during installation in order to prevent road shocks and vibration from damaging the plates.

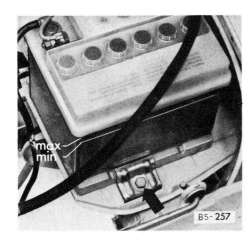

Fig. 3-2. Battery installed, showing hold-down plate and bolt (arrow). Minimum (**min**) and maximum (**max**) electrolyte levels are indicated.

3.3 Charging

Normally, a battery should be charged at no more than 10 percent of its rated capacity. For example, a charging current of 5.4 amperes would be used on a battery having 54 Ah (ampere-hours) capacity. However, a current as low as 5 percent of the rated capacity (2.7 amps for a 54 Ah battery) can be used in normal charging and should always be used the first time a new battery is charged.

In normal charging, the battery is considered fully charged when it is gassing freely and the voltage of the individual cells has risen to 2.5 to 2.7 volts each (about 15 volts for the battery). An hour or so after you have switched off the charging current, use the voltmeter/tester to determine the rest voltage of the battery. This should be 2.1 to 2.2 volts per cell, or approximately 12.5 to 13.0 volts for the battery.

Quick-charging

To save time in an emergency, a higher current can be used to charge batteries in good condition. Only sound batteries that are already in service are suitable for quick charging. Neither factory-new nor sulfated batteries should ever be quick-charged.

WARNING ——
Do not boost a sulfated battery at a high charging rate. Doing this could cause the battery to explode.

To quick-charge:

1. Remove the battery caps, then connect a battery charger and voltmeter to the battery. Quick-charge 45 Ah batteries at 36 to 40 amperes for three minutes. Quick-charge 54 Ah batteries at 44 to 48 amperes for three minutes.

2. Observe the voltmeter reading during charging. If total battery voltage exceeds 15.5 volts, the battery plates are sulfated or worn out and the battery should be replaced.

3. If the total voltage is less than 15.5 volts, test the individual cell voltages. If cell voltages vary by more than 0.1 volt, the battery plates are worn out and the battery should be replaced. If cell voltages are within 0.1 volt, measure the specific gravity and continue quick-charging at 44 to 48 amperes for 54 Ah batteries or 36 to 40 amperes for 45 Ah batteries (80 to 90 percent of total battery capacity). Use the following times:

Specific gravity	Period of charge
1.150	1 hour
1.150 to 1.175	45 minutes
1.175 to 1.225	15 minutes
Above 1.225	Slow charge only

WARNING ——
Smoking and open flames should not be permitted in a room where batteries are charged. Charging causes excess water in the electrolyte to decompose into hydrogen and oxygen, a dangerously explosive combination of gases.

CAUTION ——
Do not store precision tools in a room where batteries are charged. The corrosive fumes generated can severely damage the tools.

Storing Battery

A battery that is not in use will gradually discharge itself. At room temperature it will lose about one percent of its remaining capacity a day. The rate of discharge increases with higher temperatures. If the battery is allowed to remain in a partly or fully discharged condition for long periods, it will become badly sulfated and may never be serviceable again. The following procedure is recommended to prevent this happening in a battery that is to be stored either in or out of the car.

To store battery:

1. Charge the battery. Check the electrolyte level and the specific gravity, then make corrections as necessary.

2. Store the battery in a cool, dry place.

3. Every 6 to 8 weeks, discharge the battery and recharge it.

4. Before returning the battery to service, charge it with a very low current (not over 3 amps).

4. STARTING SYSTEM

Three slightly different starters, manufactured by Bosch, are used in the cars covered by this Manual. One starter, Part No. 055 911 023 A, is used only on cars with automatic transmissions. Cars with manual transmissions manufactured through June 1975 have the starter (Part No. 055 911 023) shown in Fig. 4-1. All later cars with manual transmissions have the starter (Part No. 055 911 023 B) shown in Fig. 4-2. The late-type starter cannot be used as a replacement part on cars manufactured prior to July 1975.

Fig. 4-1. Early-type starter used on cars with manual transmissions through June 1975.

Fig. 4-2. Late-type starter used on cars with manual transmissions from July 1975.

All three starters are of the multipolar series wound variety with four brushes and aluminum field coils. A solenoid is used to engage the starter's drive pinion with the starter ring gear on the engine's flywheel or drive plate.

To minimize wear and stress on the starter's drive pinion and the starter ring gear, the solenoid is designed so that it does not switch starting current to the starter motor until the drive pinion has fully engaged the ring gear. Also, the drive pinion is mounted on an overrunning clutch so that, in the event that the driver does not immediately release the ignition key as soon as the engine has started, the starter motor will not sustain overspeed damage in being driven by the engine.

4.1 Starting System Troubleshooting

Troubleshooting procedures that are applicable to the starting system appear in **Table a.** The bold numbers in the Remedy column refer to the headings in this section under which the prescribed service and repair procedures are described. If more than one test or probable cause is listed, check them one by one in the order in which they appear.

Table a. Starting System Troubleshooting

Problem	Test and Probable Cause	Remedy
1. Starter does not operate when ignition is turned to start position (1974 seat belt interlock bypassed or in good working order)	Turn lights on for test: a. Lights are out. Loose battery connections or battery run down b. Lights go out when key is moved to starting position. Insufficient current owing to loose battery connections or corroded terminals c. Lights become dim when key is moved to starting position. Battery run down d. Lights stay bright, solenoid operates (clicks). Connect jumper cable from starter terminal 30 to solenoid's starter connector strap terminal. Solenoid contacts are faulty if starter runs e. Lights stay bright, solenoid does not operate (car with automatic transmission). Connect jumper cable between terminals on neutral safety switch. If starter can be operated normally, neutral safety switch is defective f. Lights stay bright, solenoid does not operate, neutral safety switch not defective. Connect a jumper cable between starter terminals 30 and 50. If starter runs, wire from terminal 30 of main lighting switch to terminal 30 of ignition switch is faulty, the seatbelt interlock relay is faulty, or there is an open circuit in wire 50 between the ignition switch and the relay or between the relay and the solenoid	a. Check battery cable terminals. Test battery. Charge if necessary. See **3.1, 3.3**. b. Clean and tighten all battery cable connections. See **3.1, 3.2**. c. Charge battery. See **3.3**. d. Replace solenoid. See **4.3**. e. Replace neutral safety switch. See **AUTOMATIC TRANSMISSION.** f. Eliminate open circuits. Replace defective parts. At least 7 volts must be available at terminal 50 for the solenoid to operate. See **8.3, 12**.
2. Starter does not operate when battery cable is directly connected with terminal stud of connector strip	a. Brushes sticking b. Brushes worn c. Weak spring tension. Brushes do not make contact d. Commutator dirty e. Commutator rough, pitted, or burned f. Armature or field coils defective	a. Clean brushes and guides of brush holders. See **4.3**. b. Replace brushes. See **4.3**. c. Replace springs. See **4.3**. d. Clean commutator. See **4.3**. e. Recondition or replace starter motor. See **4.2, 4.3**. f. Recondition or replace starter motor. See **4.2, 4.3**.
3. Starter turns too slowly or fails to turn the engine over	a. Battery run down b. Insufficient current flowing to loose or corroded connections c. Brushes sticking d. Brushes worn e. Commutator dirty f. Commutator rough, pitted, or burned g. Armature or field coils defective	a. Charge battery. See **3.3** b. Clean battery terminals and cable clamps, tighten connections. See **3.1, 3.2**. c. Clean brushes and guides of brush holders. See **4.3**. d. Replace brushes. See **4.3**. e. Clean commutator. See **4.3**. f. Recondition or replace starter motor. See **4.2, 4.3**. g. Recondition or replace starter motor. See **4.2, 4.3**.
4. Starter makes unusual sounds, cranks engine erratically, or fails to crank	a. Drive pinion defective b. Flywheel or drive plate ring gear defective	a. Replace drive pinion. See **4.3**. b. Replace flywheel or drive plate. See **ENGINE AND CLUTCH.**
5. Drive pinion does not disengage	a. Drive pinion or armature shaft dirty or damaged b. Solenoid switch defective	a. Recondition or replace starter motor. See **4.2, 4.3**. b. Replace solenoid switch. See **4.3**.

5

4.2 Removing and Installing Starter

Because of the starter location, you can remove one or two of its mounting bolts and the electrical connections by working in the engine compartment. Remove the remaining mounting bolt(s) from under the car. On early cars with manual transmissions, the starter is held to the transaxle by a support bracket in addition to being bolted to the flywheel bellhousing.

To remove:

1. Disconnect the ground strap from the negative post of the battery. Then disconnect the wires from the starter solenoid.

2. On cars with manual transmissions built through June 1975, remove the bolt that holds the support bracket to the transaxle. Remove the nuts that hold the support bracket to the starter motor, then remove the support bracket.

3. Remove the nuts or the bolts that hold the starter to the bellhousing. Then withdraw the starter from the bellhousing and remove the starter from the car.

To install:

1. Except on cars with manual transmissions built through June 1975, inspect the starter bushing that is pressed into the transaxle's bellhousing. If the bushing is worn or damaged, replace it as described in **MANUAL TRANSMISSION.**

2. Lubricate the starter bushing with multipurpose grease. Then apply a good sealing compound around the starter's mounting flange.

3. Insert the starter in the bellhousing and loosely install the mounting bolts or nuts.

4. Working alternately, gradually torque the nuts or the bolts to 3.0 mkg (22 ft. lb.).

5. On early cars that have a support bracket (Fig. 4-3), make sure that the starter motor through bolts are torqued to 1.5 mkg (11 ft. lb.). Then loosely install the bracket on the starter and the transaxle. First torque the bolt to 1.5 mkg (11 ft. lb.) and then torque the nuts to 60 cmkg (52 in. lb.).

6. Clean the wires and the terminals. Tightly install the two wires and the cable on the solenoid (Fig. 4-4). On cars with manual transmissions and no starter support bracket, route the battery cable as shown in Fig. 4-5.

Fig. 4-3. Starter support bracket (**1**) used on early cars with manual transmissions. If bracket places a strain on starter when bolt is tightened, enlarge the bracket holes at **2**.

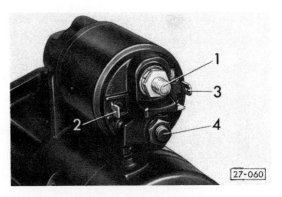

1. Terminal for battery cable (+)
2. Terminal 15a for wire from ignition coil terminal 15
3. Terminal 50 for start wire from ignition switch (routed through main wiring harness)
4. Terminal for field winding connecting strap

Fig. 4-4. Terminals on starter solenoid.

Fig. 4-5. Correct routing for battery cables on cars with starter 055 911 023 B. Positive (+) cables (arrow) should point toward rear of car.

4.3 Disassembling and Assembling Starter

If a faulty starter proves to have a number of defects, it is often best economically to replace it with a new or rebuilt starter rather than to attempt repairs. Some tasks, such as removing the pole shoes and the field windings, may require special tools.

CAUTION ——

If you lack the skills, tools, or test equipment needed to repair the starter, we suggest you leave these repairs to an Authorized Dealer or a qualified automotive electrical shop. We especially urge you to consult your Authorized Dealer before attempting repairs on a car still covered by the new-car warranty.

Removing and Installing Solenoid

If troubleshooting has shown the solenoid to be faulty, it can be replaced separately. New and rebuilt starters are delivered with solenoids installed. The removal of the solenoid, as well as complete disassembly of the starter motor and starter drive, is illustrated in Fig. 4-6. The starter connector strap is shown attached to the field coils.

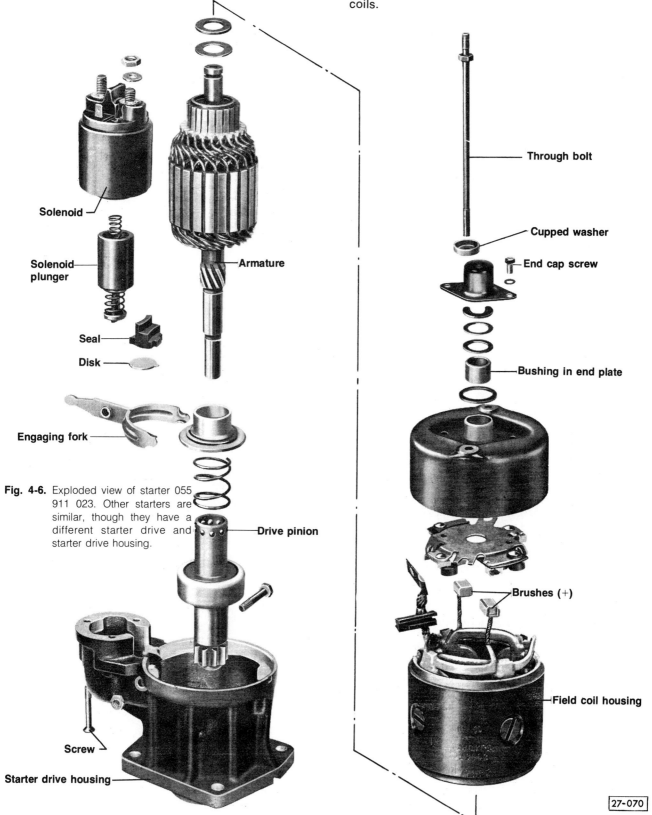

Fig. 4-6. Exploded view of starter 055 911 023. Other starters are similar, though they have a different starter drive and starter drive housing.

Solenoid

Solenoid plunger

Armature

Seal

Disk

Engaging fork

Drive pinion

Screw

Starter drive housing

Through bolt

Cupped washer

End cap screw

Bushing in end plate

Brushes (+)

Field coil housing

5

27-070

To remove solenoid:

1. Remove the starter from the car.

2. Remove the nut and the starter connector strap from the starter connector terminal on the solenoid. Then remove the two screws that hold the solenoid to the starter drive housing.

3. Lift the solenoid plunger's pull rod upward and off the engaging fork. (It will be easier to do this if you turn the drive pinion and pull it outward at the same time.)

4. Withdraw the solenoid.

To install:

1. Make sure that the seal and the disk are tight and correctly positioned in the starter drive housing. Also check the rubber seal for the starter connector strap.

2. Place a thin strip of plastic sealing compound around the outer edge of the solenoid end face.

3. Withdraw the drive pinion as far as possible. Then hook the solenoid plunger's pull rod over the engaging fork. The spring and spring cup on the pull rod should be compressed toward the plunger.

4. Position the solenoid against the starter drive housing. Then allow the drive pinion to return to its disengaged position.

5. Apply sealer to the screw heads. Then install the two screws that hold the solenoid to the starter drive housing.

6. Install the starter connector strap and the nut on the solenoid's connector strap terminal.

Disassembling and Assembling Starter Motor and Starter Drive

You must disassemble the starter motor in order to inspect, repair, or replace the starter drive or replace the brushes.

To disassemble:

1. Remove the starter. Then remove the solenoid.

2. Remove the nuts and washers from the through bolts.

3. Remove the end cap screws. Remove the end cap and its gasket. Then pry the C-clip off the end of the armature shaft and remove the two spacer washers. If there are burrs beside the C-clip groove in the armature shaft, remove them with a file in order to prevent damage to the bushing as the end plate is removed.

4. Remove the through bolts. Remove the end plate from the motor.

5. Lift aside the brush springs. Remove the positive (+) brushes from the brush holder. Then remove the brush holder.

6. Lift the field coil housing off the armature.

7. On starter 055 911 023 B, use a tool such as the one shown in Fig. 4-7 to press the stop ring off the snap ring. (The snap ring is concealed beneath the stop ring in a groove in the armature shaft.)

8. On starter 055 911 023 B, use circlip pliers to remove the snap ring from the armature shaft. Remove the stop ring. If there are burrs beside the snap ring groove in the armature shaft, remove them with a file.

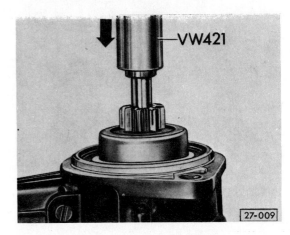

Fig. 4-7. Stop ring being pressed off snap ring toward drive pinion (starter 055 911 023 B).

9. Remove the bolt, the nut, and the washer that hold the engaging fork in the starter drive housing. Remove the seal, the disk, and then the engaging fork. Take out the armature.

10. Except on starter 055 911 023 B, remove the drive pinion as shown in Fig. 4-8. (On starter 055 911 023 B, simply slide the drive pinion off the armature shaft.)

Fig. 4-8. Drive pinion being removed from starter 055 911 023 or 055 911 023 A. Pull sleeve off balls, then pull pinion off shaft.

11. If the field coils must be replaced, loosen the pole shoe screws as shown in Fig. 4-9. If the screws cannot be loosened in this manner, take the field coil housing to your Authorized Dealer or to a qualified automotive machine shop where special tools are available for removing pole shoe screws.

12. Remove the pole shoes and the field coils from the field coil housing.

Fig. 4-9. Punch being used to loosen pole shoe screw. Strike punch with hammer in order to turn screw counterclockwise.

To inspect and assemble:

1. Wipe clean all of the parts for the starter motor and starter drive.

> **CAUTION** —
>
> *Do not wash the armature, the field coils, the self-oiling end plate bushing, or the drive pinion assembly in solvent. Doing this may damage the insulation of the armature or the field coils and will destroy the factory-installed lubricants in the bushing and in the drive pinion's overrunning clutch.*

2. If there has been trouble in the starter, make the electrical tests described under the next heading. If necessary, replace the armature, the field coils, or the entire starter.

> **NOTE** —
>
> If you replace the armature, make certain that you obtain the correct replacement part. The helical grooves are different on starters for cars with automatic transmissions, as shown in Fig. 4-10.

3. Inspect the bushing in the end plate. If the bushing is worn or damaged, press it out. Then press in a new bushing as shown in Fig. 4-11.

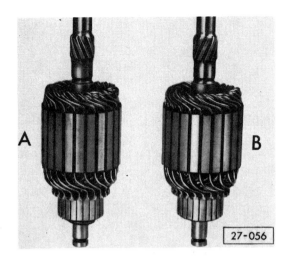

Fig. 4-10. Armature for car with manual transmission (**A**) and armature for car with automatic transmission (**B**).

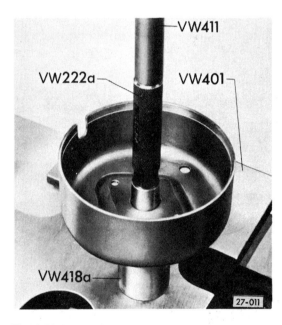

Fig. 4-11. New bushing being pressed into end plate.

4. Inspect the brushes. If the brushes have worn to a length of less than 13 mm (½ in.), replace the brushes.

5. To replace the negative (−) brushes, replace the entire brush holder. Alternatively, check whether new brushes are available. If so, unsolder the brush wires from the brush holder. Then install the new brushes, soldering on their wires in place of the original wires.

6. To replace the positive (+) brushes, replace the field coils with new field coils that have brushes attached. Alternatively, check whether new brushes are available. If so, crush the old brushes

in a vise, then solder the new brushes onto the original brush wires. Because the field coils are aluminum, the brush wires are welded to the field coils and cannot be detached.

7. Inspect the commutator for taper and uneven wear. (The commutator is a ring of brass bars permanently affixed to the armature.) To check the commutator for out-of-round, place the armature shaft on V-blocks and hand-turn the commutator against a machinist's square that has been positioned beside the commutator. If there is more than 0.03 mm (.001 in.) of taper, uneven wear, or out-of-round, the commutator must be machined.

NOTE ——

The commutator should be machined by an Authorized Dealer or by a qualified automotive machine shop. The commutator diameter must not be reduced to less than 33.50 mm (1.319 in.). After the commutator has been turned on a lathe, the insulation strips between the commutator bars must be undercut by about 0.50 mm (.020 in.) below the surfaces of the bars.

8. Inspect the drive pinion for chipped and burred teeth. Make sure that the overrunning clutch operates smoothly without noise or binding. If any of these faults is found, replace the drive pinion assembly.

9. To prevent damage to the bushing in the end plate or to the interior of the drive pinion, remove any burrs from the snap ring and C-clip grooves in the armature shaft.

10. On starter 055 911 023 and starter 055 911 023 A, install the drive pinion on the armature shaft. Use multipurpose grease to lubricate the helical grooves of the armature shaft and as an adhesive to hold the balls in place in the drive pinion.

CAUTION ——

Do not grease the smooth part of the shaft or the inside of the drive pinion. Do not use grease on the shaft of starter 055 911 023 B. Grease may cause the starter drive to jam in cold weather.

11. Install the armature in the starter drive housing.

12. On starter 055 911 023 B, install the drive pinion. Install the stop ring on the armature shaft, then install a new snap ring as shown in Fig. 4-12. With the stop ring supported on the press bed, press down the armature shaft as shown in Fig. 4-13 until the snap ring is seated beneath the stop ring.

Fig. 4-12. Stop ring and snap ring installed on armature shaft.

Fig. 4-13. Snap ring being seated beneath stop ring.

13. With the exception of the end cap, assemble the remaining parts of the starter and starter drive. During assembly, all points indicated in Fig. 4-14 should be made weatherproof with a good sealer.

14. After you have installed the spacer washers and the C-clip on the armature shaft, use feeler gauges of various thicknesses to determine the clearance between the C-clip and the washers. By doing this you will be measuring the armature's axial play. Axial play should be between 0.10 and 0.15 mm (.004 and .006 in.). If it is not, either add or remove spacer washers in order to obtain armature axial play that is within the prescribed range.

15. Using sealer on the screw heads, install the end cap. Then install the starter on the car.

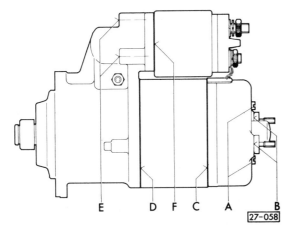

A. Holes for end cap screws
B. Holes for through bolts
C. Joint between field coil housing and end plate
D. Joint between field coil housing and starter drive housing
E. Holes for solenoid mounting screws
F. Surface between solenoid and starter drive housing

Fig. 4-14. Sealing locations on starter. Do not install end cap and screws until you have checked armature's axial play.

Testing Disassembled Starter

If the troubleshooting checks given in **4.1 Starting System Troubleshooting** indicate trouble in the armature or in the field coils, further tests can be made after you have removed and disassembled the starter. Several of these tests can be made with a simple battery-powered test light, although an ohmmeter is preferable.

Short circuits in the armature occur when the insulation between the windings breaks down. An armature tester called a growler is used to test for shorts. Growlers are available at most automotive supply stores that offer machine shop service. The shop will test an armature for you at low cost. If the armature is shorted, it must be replaced.

Armature grounds occur when the insulation breaks down and allows the windings to come into electrical contact with the armature laminations or the shaft. It is easy to detect this condition with a battery-powered test light or with an ohmmeter, as shown in Fig. 4-15.

Occasionally, carbon dust from the brushes will short an armature. If arcing current has not permanently damaged the insulation, cleaning with trichloroethylene or a similar solvent will usually cure the short.

To check the armature for open circuits, inspect the commutator bars. Burn marks between the bars indicate that there is an open circuit in the winding coil that is

Fig. 4-15. Armature ground test. If testing for continuity between commutator and armature body or shaft produces an ohmmeter reading or causes a battery-powered test lamp to light, the windings are grounded.

connected to one of the bars. You can also test for open circuits by applying the test probes of an ohmmeter or a battery-powered test light to adjacent bars all around the commutator. There should be electrical continuity among all of the bars. If not, there is an open circuit and the armature must be replaced.

A minimum of 7 volts must be available at terminal 50 in order to operate a removed solenoid. A minimum of 8 volts must be available at terminal 50 for the solenoid to hold the pinion in engagement under load. Sometimes, though the voltage at terminal 50 is adequate, an installed solenoid will fail to work properly. In these cases it is necessary to distinquish trouble caused by a binding starter drive from trouble caused by faulty solenoid windings.

To test the solenoid windings, connect a switch and a fully-charged 12-volt automobile battery as indicated in Fig. 4-16. Close the switch **(S)**. Normally, the solenoid plunger will pull in. However, on some removed solenoids it may be necessary to start the plunger into the solenoid housing by hand. Immediately after the plunger pulls in, open the switch **(S)**. The plunger must drop out of the housing at once. If it does not, the windings are unserviceable and the solenoid must be replaced.

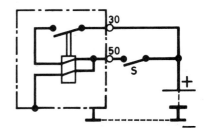

Fig. 4-16. Solenoid test hookup. Switch **(S)** goes between battery's positive pole and terminal 50 on solenoid. Solenoid housing is connected to battery's negative (−) post.

Because of the high conductivity of the aluminum field coils and the relatively few windings in each coil, it is not practical to test the coils for shorts by comparing the relative resistance or the relative current flow through the coils. However, you can test the field coils in order to determine whether they are short-circuited (grounded) to the starter's field coil housing. To locate this kind of trouble, test for continuity between the field coils and the housing. Make certain that neither positive (+) brush is touching the housing when this test is made. If there is continuity between the coil windings and the housing, replace the field coils.

To test the field coils for open circuits, apply one test probe of an ohmmeter or a battery-powered test light to the starter connector strap and the other test probe alternately to each of the positive (+) brushes. If there is no electrical continuity, there is an open circuit and the field coils must be replaced.

Testing Assembled Starter

A battery, or several batteries wired in parallel, with a rated capacity of 135 ampere-hours should be available for starter bench tests. This will ensure that decreasing battery power does not influence the test readings. Automotive electrical shops that have starter motor test stands will find the data given here useful in determining how closely starters conform to factory specifications. Testing should be carried out in the following sequence:

No-load test—starter motor running freely:

The starter should run at 6000 to 8000 rpm, the voltage should read 11.5, and the current draw should be between 35 and 55 amperes.

If the rpm is below 6000 rpm and the current is above 55 amps, either the mechanical parts are binding or there are shorts in the armature or in the field coils. If the rpm is below 6000 rpm and the current draw is below 35 amps, inadequate voltage is reaching all or part of the starter. Check for worn-out solenoid contacts, unsoldered connections between the armature windings and the commutator bars, or poor contact between the brushes and the commutator. Severe brush sparking indicates an out-of-round commutator, protruding commutator insulation strips, or armature windings that are open-circuited or unsoldered from the commutator bars.

Load test—starter braked to approximately 1000 rpm:

This is a simple functional test which must last no longer than 10 seconds. Look for severe brush sparking.

If the commutator is not out-of-round and the commutator insulation strips are properly undercut, severe brush sparking indicates that the armature windings or the field coil windings are shorted or that the armature windings are open-circuited or unsoldered from the commutator bars.

Stall test—starter braked to a standstill under load:

This test must last no longer than 1 or 2 seconds. At a voltage of 8.5, the current draw should be 340 to 430 amps. At a voltage of 7.5, the current draw should be 290 to 380 amps. Not less than 8 volts must be available at terminal 50 on the solenoid.

If the current draw is above 430 amps at 8.5 volts or above 380 amps at 7.5 volts, there are either internal short circuits or a short circuit to ground. If the current draw is below 340 amps at 8.5 volts or below 290 amps at 7.5 volts, check for poor contact between the brushes and the commutator, open-circuited armature windings, or armature windings that are unsoldered from the commutator bars. If none of these faults is found, there is an open circuit in the field coils.

5. CHARGING SYSTEM

Three kinds of alternators, two manufactured by Bosch and the one manufactured by Motorola, are used in the cars covered by this Manual. Most are rated at 55 amperes with a maximum output of 770 watts. However, beginning with the 1977 models, a 65-ampere Bosch alternator is used on cars with factory air conditioning.

The alternator is belt-driven by the same V-belt that drives the water pump. The regulator, which is transistorized, is mounted on the end of the alternator housing. To prevent damage to the alternator and the regulator when you are making tests and repairs, please observe the following precautions:

1. If you connect a battery charger or a booster battery to the battery in the car, make certain that you connect the negative cable to the battery's negative (−) post and the positive cable to the battery's positive (+) post. Otherwise, the diodes (transistors) will be damaged—even by momentary reversed polarity.

2. In installing a battery in the car, make certain that the ground strap is connected to the battery's negative (−) post and that the cable that goes to terminal 30 on the starter solenoid is connected to the battery's positive (+) post.

3. In installing the alternator or a replacement alternator on the car, never attempt to polarize the alternator. This is a practice required by the DC (direct current) generators used on some cars, but it is unnecessary on alternators and will damage the alternator used on the cars covered by this Manual.

4. Never operate the alternator while the battery cables are disconnected. Also, never operate the alternator with its output terminal (B+) disconnected and the other terminals connected.

5. Never short, bridge, or ground any terminals of the

charging system except as specifically described in **5.1 Charging System Troubleshooting.**

6. Do not test the alternator diodes with an outside power source of more than 1.5 volts.

5.1 Charging System Troubleshooting

Charging system trouble is indicated by an alternator warning light that does not function normally, an undercharged battery, or an overcharged battery. Before you proceed with any testing, however, make sure that the alternator V-belt is correctly adjusted as described in **5.3 Removing and Installing Alternator.** Visually inspect all electrical connections. The terminals and the connectors must be clean and tight-fitting; the alternator must be properly grounded (by a ground strap from terminal 31 on the alternator to a bolt on the engine). Replace wires that have cracked or broken insulation.

In addition to alerting the driver to charging system malfunctions, the warning light has another important function. In order to explain this other function, it is necessary to describe briefly the operation of the alternator.

The alternator generates electrical power by means of electrical induction. That is, a magnetic field is placed in motion so that its invisible magnetic lines of force sweep over many stationary coils of wire. When they do this, the magnetic lines of force produce electrical current in the coils. The alternator's rotor is the electromagnet that produces this magnetic field. When the field is set into motion by the turning of the rotor, electrical power is generated in the windings of the alternator's stator. (The stator consists of overlapping coils of wire mounted on a soft iron core inside the alternator housing.)

Once the alternator has started to convert mechanical energy from the engine into electrical current in the stator coils, some of that current is used to magnetize the rotor. However, battery current must be used to magnetize the rotor until the alternator is generating enough electricity to become self-sufficient (or, to use the correct technical terminology, self-exciting).

The necessary battery current is supplied to the rotor through the filament of the alternator warning light bulb. As soon as the alternator's output has risen to a level that is equal to the battery's voltage, the current through the warning light bulb reaches a state of equilibrium and the light goes out.

Normally, the warning light should be off when the ignition is off and the engine is stopped. The light should be on with the ignition turned on and the engine stopped. The light should be off with the ignition turned on and the engine running. If the light does not function as described, carry out the tests and checks given in **Table b.**

5 ■

Table b. Warning Light Troubleshooting

Symptom	Test and Probable Cause	Remedy
1. Ignition off, engine not running. Warning light glowing or on	**(TEST)** Disconnect connector plug from alternator: a. Light goes out. Shorted diode carrier or faulty positive (+) diode in diode carrier b. Light does not go out. Short in wiring harness or in connector plug	a. Replace diodes and diode carrier as a unit. See **5.4.** b. Repair or replace faulty wiring. See **12.**
2. Ignition on, engine not running. Warning light off	a. Battery discharged **(TEST)** Remove and test warning light bulb: b. Bulbs burned out **(TEST—bulb not burned out)** Disconnect connector plug from alternator. Using a voltmeter, test between the plug terminal for the red wires and ground: c. No voltage. Open circuit between connector plug and battery positive (+) pole **(TEST—bulb not burned out, battery voltage reaching connector plug)** Disconnect the connector plug from the alternator. With the ignition on, ground the plug terminal for the blue wire against a clean, unpainted metal part of the engine: d. Light does not come on. Faulty bulb socket, open circuit in blue wire, or open circuit in wire between socket and terminal 15 on the ignition switch e. Light comes on. Loose connection between regulator and alternator or loose connection between brushes and regulator f. Light comes on, regulator properly connected. Worn out brushes, dirty slip rings (on rotor), or both	a. Charge battery. See **3.3.** b. Replace bulb. See **11.3.** c. Repair wire or connections. See **12.2.** d. Replace faulty socket. Repair wires or connections. See **11.3, 12.2.** e. Correct loose connections. See **5.4.** f. Clean slip rings. Measure brushes. Replace brushes that have worn to a length of 5 mm ($^7/_{32}$ in.) or less See **5.4.**

(continued on next page)

Table b. Warning Light Troubleshooting (continued)

Symptom	Test and Probable Cause	Remedy
	g. Light comes on, regulator properly connected. Brushes not excessively worn and slip rings clean. Burned-out field winding in rotor	g. Using an ohmmeter or a battery-powered test light, test for continuity between slip rings. If there is no continuity, replace the rotor. See **5.4.**
	h. Light comes on, regulator properly connected; brushes, slip rings, and rotor not defective. Faulty regulator	h. Replace regulator. See **5.4.**
3. Ignition on, engine running. Engine can be accelerated to 2000 rpm or more but warning light stays on	a. Loose or broken alternator V-belt	a. Replace or adjust V-belt. See **5.3.**
	b. Exciter diodes burned out	b. Test diodes. If diodes are faulty, replace the diodes and the diode carrier as a unit. See **5.4.**
	c. Faulty regulator or faulty alternator windings	c. Test charging system with engine running. Replace faulty regulator, alternator, or both. See **5.2, 5.4.**

If the warning light operates in the normal way, but the battery is undercharged or overcharged, you should make the tests described in **5.2 In-car Testing of Alternator and Regulator.** Overcharging is usually indicated by a frequent need to add large quantities of distilled water to the battery electrolyte. Since a worn-out battery will also exhibit a greater-than-normal need for water, make sure that the battery is fully charged and in good condition before you assume that there is trouble in the charging system.

An undercharged battery is usually associated with starting trouble. Again, make sure that the battery is in good condition and capable of accepting a full charge before you blame the charging system. Other causes of a run-down (undercharged) battery are the simultaneous use of a great many electrical accessories for long periods of time, leaving accessories or lights in operation with the engine stopped, frequent long periods of starter usage, and frequent short-trip driving that does not provide adequate time for the battery to recharge after operation of the starter. Broken or frayed charging system wiring and worn, corroded, or loose battery cable connections will also prevent adequate charging or increase the time required for the battery to become fully recharged.

5.2 In-car Testing of Alternator and Regulator

Fig. 5-1 shows the hook-up for testing alternator output. The positive battery cable must be disconnected and a battery cutout switch installed as shown, with the cable reconnected to the cutout switch.

CAUTION ———

An alternator must never be run with the battery disconnected. Doing this will severely damage the alternator, the regulator, or both.

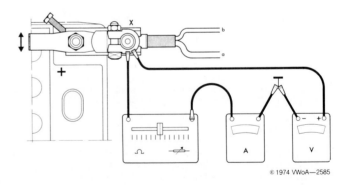

© 1974 VWoA—2585

a. To starter
b. To fuse box terminal 30

X. Battery cutout switch (SUN electric No. 7052-003 or similar equipment)

Fig. 5-1. Alternator charging system test. Variable resistance, ammeter, and voltmeter are connected in series as shown. Note that the ammeter lead and the negative voltmeter lead connected to it are both grounded to the chassis. The double arrow at the left indicates switch operation.

To test:

1. With the engine stopped (alternator stationary), remove the battery ground strap. Then make the test connections and connect the battery ground

strap. Close the cutout switch as shown in Fig. 5-2, then start the engine.

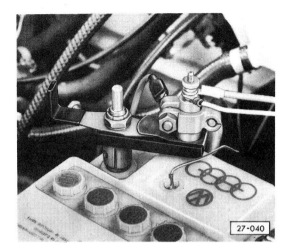

Fig. 5-2. Battery cutout switch in closed position. Notice the test connections.

2. In testing a 55-ampere alternator, run the engine at 2500 to 3000 rpm and adjust the variable resistance so that the ammeter gives a reading between 20 and 30 amps. In testing the 65-ampere alternator introduced on 1977 cars with factory air conditioning, run the engine at 3000 rpm and adjust the variable resistance to 44 amps.

> **NOTE ——**
>
> If there is no charging system output, and earlier troubleshooting has uncovered no open circuits, loose connections, or trouble in the brushes or the rotor, the trouble is in the alternator. Test the diodes as described in **5.4 Disassembling and Assembling Alternator.** If open diodes are found, replace the diodes and the diode carrier as a unit. If the diodes are not faulty, there are open circuits in the stator coil windings and the entire alternator should be replaced.

3. Move the cutout switch as shown in Fig. 5-3 in order to cut the battery out of the test circuit. The load current is now determined by the variable resistance.

4. Readjust the variable resistance, if necessary, so that the ammeter reading is 25 amps with the engine at 2500 to 3000 rpm—or 44 amps at 3000 rpm if you are testing a 65-ampere alternator.

5. Read the voltage indicated on the voltmeter. It should be between 12.5 and 14.5 volts.

If charging system output is above the prescribed range (overcharging), the trouble is probably a faulty regulator. However, test the diodes as described in **5.4 Disassembling and Assembling Alternator** before you replace the regulator. If any diodes are open-circuited, replace the diodes and the diode carrier as a unit. If there is still an overcharge, or if the diodes are not faulty, replace the regulator.

If the charging system output is below the prescribed range (undercharging), test the diodes as described in **5.4 Disassembling and Assembling Alternator.** If any diodes are shorted, replace the diodes and the diode carrier as a unit. If the diodes are not faulty, test the stator for grounded coil windings as described in **5.4 Disassembling and Assembling Alternator.** If there are grounded windings, replace the alternator. If neither the diodes nor the stator windings are faulty, the trouble is in the regulator, which should be replaced.

Fig. 5-3. Battery cutout switch in open position.

Noisy Alternator

Alternator noises are usually mechanical in origin but a high, soft whistling sound may be produced by an alternator that is overcharging because of a faulty regulator or open diode. The same sound may be heard if there is a shorted diode that is placing abnormal electrical strain on the alternator. Some alternators make this sound when operating normally at maximum output.

Alternator mechanical noises are usually the result of misalignment between the V-belt and the pulley, a loose or broken pulley, worn bearings, or a bent rotor shaft. If any of these faults are found, either replace the faulty parts as described in **5.4 Disassembling and Assembling Alternator** or replace the entire alternator.

5.3 Removing and Installing Alternator

Owing to differences in the shape and hole pattern of the mounting flange, the alternators used on 1977 and later cars cannot be installed on earlier models. To prevent shorts and electrical damage, always disconnect the battery ground strap before you begin to remove the alternator. Battery current reaches the alternator even when the ignition is turned off.

To remove:

1. Remove the connector plug from the alternator. Take off the nut, then disconnect the ground strap (which goes to the alternator mounting bracket on the engine block) from the alternator housing.

> **NOTE** ——
>
> On 65-ampere alternators, the wire to the B+ terminal is attached with a nut, as shown in Fig. 5-4.

Fig. 5-4. Terminal locations on 65-ampere alternator introduced on 1977 cars with factory air conditioning.

2. Loosen the upper and lower alternator mounting bolts. See Fig. 5-5. Loosen the bolt that holds the alternator belt adjusting bracket to the cylinder head.

3. Push the alternator as far as possible toward the engine. Then take the V-belt off the alternator and water pump pulleys.

> **NOTE** ——
>
> If you want to remove the alternator V-belt completely from a car with air injection emission control, you must first remove the belt for the air injection pump. To do this, loosen the air pump mounting bolts. Push the air pump as far as possible toward the engine, then remove the air pump V-belt.

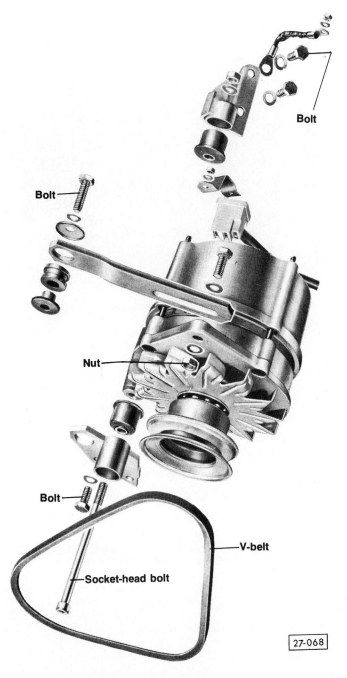

Fig. 5-5. Alternator and mountings.

4. Remove the lower alternator mounting bolt (Fig. 5-6). Then remove the upper alternator mounting bolt and remove the alternator from the engine.

Fig. 5-6. Socket-head bolt being removed from alternator's lower mounting. Pull bolt out only as far as is necessary to disengage it from alternator.

Fig. 5-7. Point at which V-belt should be depressed (arrows). Dimension **a** should be 10 to 15 mm (⅜ to ⁹/₁₆ in.).

To install:

1. Position the alternator on its lower mounting brackets, then loosely install the lower mounting bolt.

2. Loosely install the alternator's upper mounting bolt. Push the alternator as far as it will go toward the engine. Then install the V-belt on the crankshaft pulley, the water pump pulley, and the alternator pulley.

3. By pulling the alternator away from the engine block, adjust the V-belt tension so that you can depress the V-belt 10 to 15 mm (⅜ to ⁹/₁₆ in.) at the point indicated in Fig. 5-7.

4. When the V-belt tension is correct, torque the alternator lower mounting bolt to 2.0 mkg (14 ft. lb.) and the bolts that hold the adjusting bracket to the alternator and the cylinder head to 2.0 mkg (14 ft. lb.).

   NOTE ——

   The bolts that hold the alternator mounting bracket to the engine block—including the bolt for the ground strap—should be torqued to 3.0 mkg (22 ft. lb.).

5. On cars with air injection emission control, install the air pump V-belt and adjust it using the same procedure used to adjust the alternator belt.

   CAUTION ——

   Do not tension the V-belts too tightly. Doing this can cause the alternator bearings, the water pump bearings, or the air pump bearings to fail after only a short period of service.

5

Rotor bearing

Rotor

Pulley-end housing

Fan

Pulley

Pulley nut

5.4 Disassembling and Assembling Alternator

The Bosch alternator is shown separated into its replaceable components in Fig. 5-8. The ball bearing races are a press fit on the rotor shaft. Do not reuse bearings that have been pressed off the shaft. In installing new bearings, use a press tool that will apply pressure to the inner bearing race only.

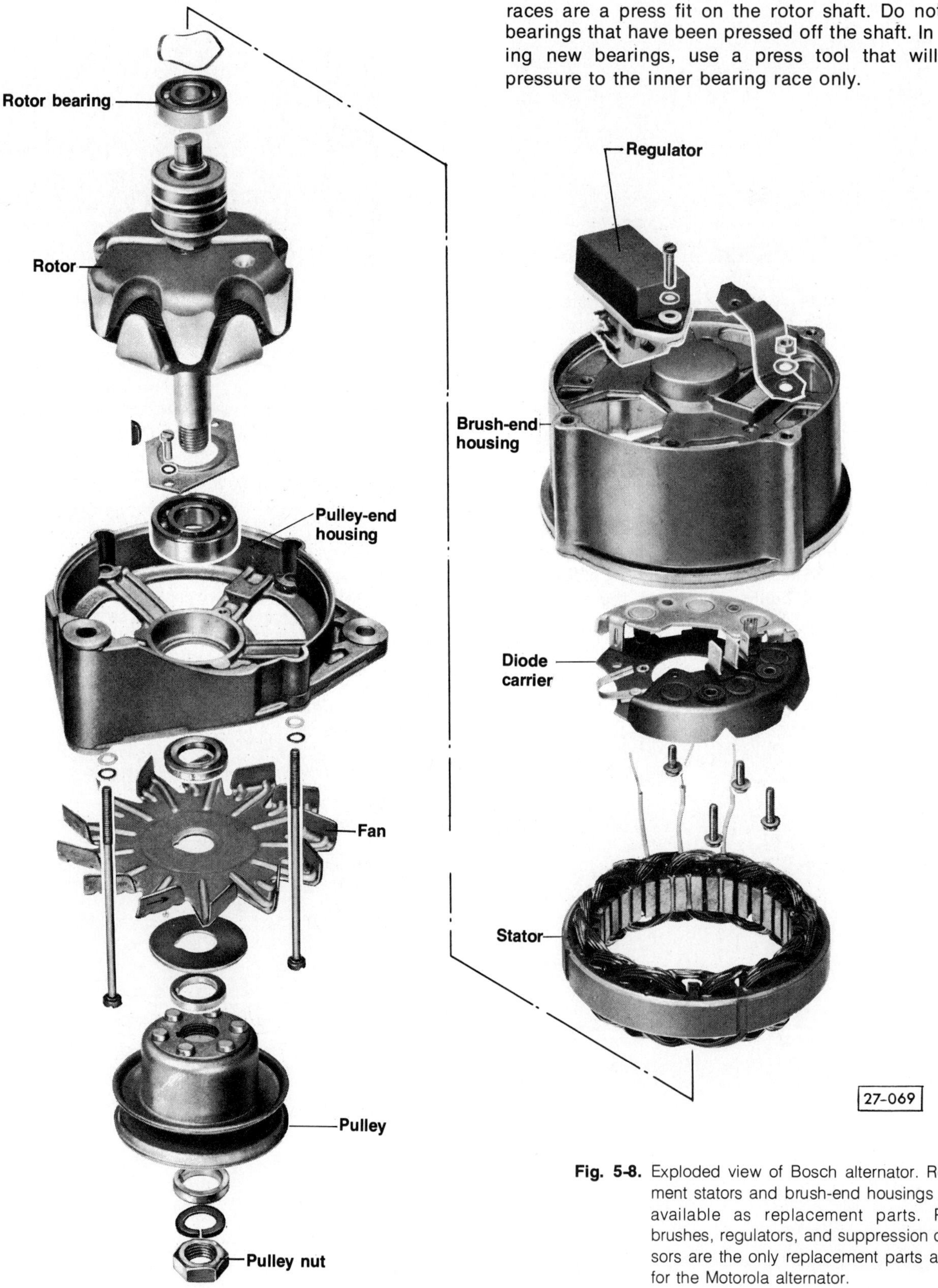

Regulator

Brush-end housing

Diode carrier

Stator

27-069

Fig. 5-8. Exploded view of Bosch alternator. Replacement stators and brush-end housings are not available as replacement parts. Pulleys, brushes, regulators, and suppression condensors are the only replacement parts available for the Motorola alternator.

NOTE —

Though the Motorola alternator can be taken apart for testing, the degree of repair is limited by the few replacement parts available. For identification purposes, the Bosch alternator and the Motorola alternator are shown in Fig. 5-9. Other than regulator replacement, the following repairs and tests are applicable mainly to the Bosch alternator.

The diodes and diode carrier must be replaced as a unit. If either the diode carrier or the stator is replaced, the stator wires must be unsoldered from the diode carrier and the connections resoldered after the faulty component has been replaced. In using the soldering iron, you must be careful not to overheat the diodes. Overheating will cause the diodes to open-circuit or short. Before applying the soldering iron to the connection, grip the diode wire near the diode with a pair of needle-nose pliers. Alternatively, install a special heat sink on the diode lead wire. By absorbing heat from the lead wire, the heat sink or pliers will prevent excessive heat from reaching the diode itself.

5 ∎

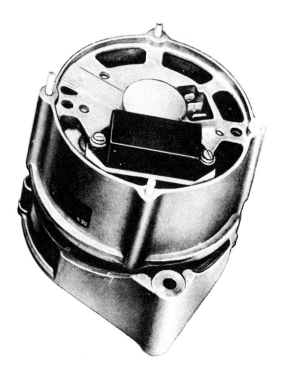
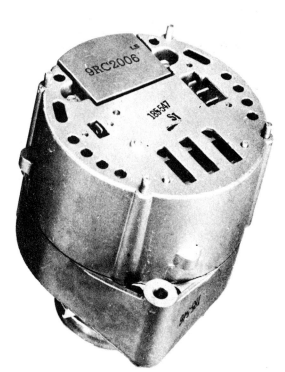

27-274

Bosch alternator
Part No. 055 903 023 A

Motorola alternator
Part No. 055 903 023 E

Fig. 5-9. Bosch alternator and Motorola alternator compared.

If you use a screwdriver to hold the fan while you remove the pulley nut (Fig. 5-10), be careful not to bend the fan vanes. During installation of the pulley and the fan, torque the nut to 3.5 to 4.5 mkg (25 to 32 ft. lb.).

NOTE——

A 61-mm (2⅜-in.) pulley is used on fuel injection engines in order to increase alternator output, as is necessary owing to the electric fuel pump. Do not install the 66-mm (2¹⁹⁄₃₂-in.) pulley used on engines with carburetors.

You can press the rotor out of the pulley-end housing as shown in Fig. 5-11. Once the rotor is removed, you can remove the bearing as shown in Fig. 5-12. If you must replace the rotor, always replace the bearings also.

Fig. 5-10. Fan being held with screwdriver so that pulley nut can be removed.

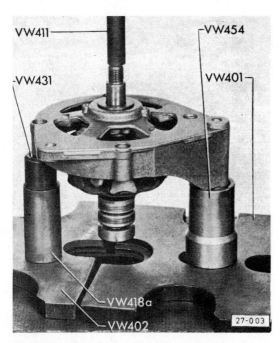

Fig. 5-11. Rotor being pressed out of alternator's pulley-end housing.

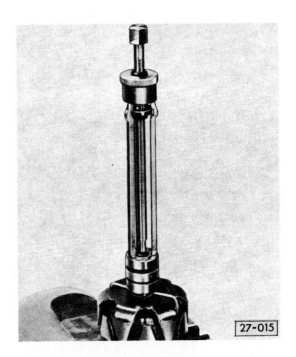

Fig. 5-12. Puller being used to remove ball bearing race from rotor shaft. Press on new bearings using a sleeve-type driver that will contact inner bearing race only.

Brushes and Regulator

You can remove the regulator and brush holder from the Bosch alternator by taking out the two screws indicated in Fig. 5-13. If the brushes are worn to less than 5 mm (⁷⁄₃₂ in.), replace the brushes. See Fig. 5-14.

To replace the regulator on a Motorola alternator, remove the two screws that hold the regulator to the alternator's brush-end housing. Then lift off the regulator and disconnect its wires from the terminals of the alternator.

Fig. 5-13. Screws (arrows) that hold regulator and brush holder to Bosch alternator.

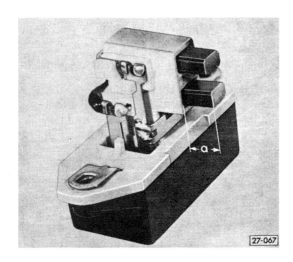

Fig. 5-14. Brush length being checked. Length (dimension **a**) of new brushes is 10 mm (⅜ in.). Replace brushes that have worn to 5 mm (⁷/₃₂ in.) or less.

Installation is the reverse of removal. Connect the wires of the regulator as indicated in Fig. 5-15.

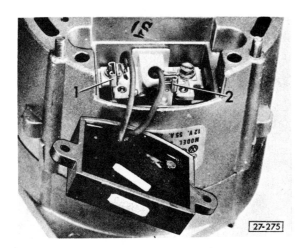

1. Green wire to terminal DF
2. Red wire to terminal D+

Fig. 5-15. Regulator connections on Motorola alternator.

Testing Alternator Components

A diode is a kind of transistor that has the unique property of permitting electrical current to flow through it in only one direction. To test the diodes in the alternator's diode carrier, first unsolder the connections for the stator wires. You will notice that there are three diode groups of three diodes each in the diode carrier. Unsolder the connections that join the three groups. This will isolate each group from the other two.

Using an ohmmeter or a 1.5-volt battery-powered test light, apply one test probe to the diode's lead wire and the other test probe to the diode's case. Then reverse the positions of the two test probes. The ammeter should show a reading (or the test light should light) with the test probes in one position but not in the other. If no reading (or light) is obtained in either position, the diode (or diode group) is open-circuited and the diodes and the diode carrier should be replaced as a unit.

You should also replace the diode carrier if the ammeter produces a reading (or the test light comes on) with the test probes in both positions. This is an indication that one or more of the diodes is shorted.

If all three diode groups show continuity in one test probe position but not in the other, it is still possible that an individual diode is faulty. Unsolder each diode lead from its connection with the other diodes, then test the diodes individually. If one or more diodes show no continuity in either position, replace the diodes and the diode carrier as a unit.

NOTE ——

Voltage surges in the car's electrical system may damage the alternator diodes. When you replace the diodes, install a suppression condenser (Part No. 059 035 271) if the alternator did not originally have this condenser. The condenser, shown installed on a Bosch alternator in Fig. 5-16, should prevent a recurrence of the trouble. The same condenser is also suitable for use with the Motorola alternator.

Fig. 5-16. Suppression condenser (Part No. 059 035 271) installed on alternator.

You can use an ohmmeter or a battery-powered test light to test the rotor's field coil. There should be no electrical continuity when the test probes are applied to

5 ■

the slip rings and to the rotor shaft or the poles (Fig. 5-17). If there is continuity, the field coil is grounded and the rotor must be replaced.

There should be no electrical continuity between any of the stator coil winding leads and the stator's laminated iron frame (Fig. 5-19). If there is continuity, the windings are grounded and the stator must be replaced.

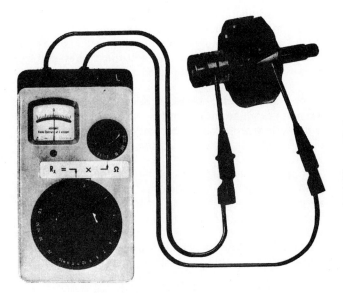

Fig. 5-17. Ohmmeter being used to test rotor for grounded field coil. The poles and the shaft should not be in electrical contact with the slip rings.

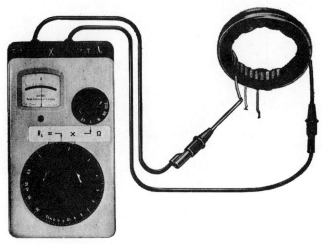

Fig. 5-19. Ohmmeter being used to test stator for grounded coil windings. You can also use a battery-powered test light for this test.

Using an ohmmeter, you can measure the resistance between the slip rings as shown in Fig. 5-18. If the resistance is significantly less than 3.40 to 3.74 ohms, the field coil is shorted (this specification is valid for 55-ampere Bosch alternators only). A battery-powered test light should be dim when the test probes are applied to the slip rings. If there is no continuity, the field coil is burned out.

If there is no electrical continuity between any two of the stator coil winding leads when checked as shown in Fig. 5-20, there is an open circuit in the windings. If the resistance between any two leads of a 55-amp alternator is significantly more or less than 0.14 to 0.15 ohms, the windings are shorted. Replace stators that have open or shorted windings.

Fig. 5-18. Ohmmeter being used to measure the resistance between the two slip rings. Resistance is created by the field coil, through which the test current must flow.

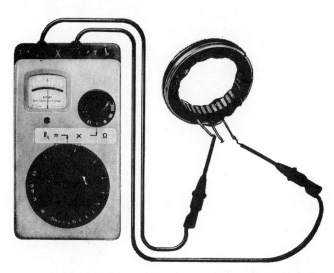

Fig. 5-20. Ohmmeter being used to check continuity and resistance through stator coil windings. A battery-powered test light can be used in testing continuity only.

6. TURN SIGNALS AND EMERGENCY FLASHERS

The turn signal switch and the flasher relay are often mistakenly blamed for troubles cause by dirty, corroded, or loose-fitting turn signal bulb contacts. Before you start to troubleshoot either the turn signal switch or the turn signal/emergency flasher relay, be sure that all bulb contacts are clean and tight.

6.1 Turn Signal and Emergency Flasher Troubleshooting

The turn signals and the emergency flashers share the same flasher relay. The flasher relay is labeled J² in the wiring diagrams that appear elsewhere in this section of the Manual.

The turn signals operate only with the ignition turned on. The emergency flashers operate whether the ignition is on or off. If the emergency flashers work but the turn signals do not, you can be certain that the flasher relay is not faulty. The same is true if the turn signals work but the emergency flashers do not. However, if neither system operates, you should not conclude that the flasher relay is faulty without further troubleshooting.

First, check that fuses 6 and 8 are not burned out, that the turn signal bulbs are not burned out, and that the bulb and bulb socket contacts are clean and tight. If one bulb is burned out or in poor electrical contact with its socket, the other bulbs may come on without flashing or may flash very slowly. If no other fault is found, and neither the turn signals nor the emergency flashers will work, replace the flasher relay.

If the turn signals work only on one side, or if the emergency flashers only work on one side of the car or fail to work at all, use **Table c, Table d,** or **Table e** to troubleshoot the problem. The bold numbers that appear

in the Test results and suggested repairs columns of the tables refer to headings in this section where the suggested repairs are described.

Before you replace a switch, it is wise to test the removed switch in order to make sure that you have made no error in troubleshooting. The tests can be simple continuity checks made with an ohmmeter or a battery-powered test light. Fig. 6-1 shows the turn signal terminal locations on the switch introduced on 1977 cars. The 1977 wiper/washer switch terminals are identified in **7.1 Windshield Wiper Motor Troubleshooting** and the 1977 headlight dimmer terminals are identified in **8. Lights and Switches.** For these and earlier cars, use the wiring diagrams given in **12. Wiring, Fuses, and Relays** as your test guides.

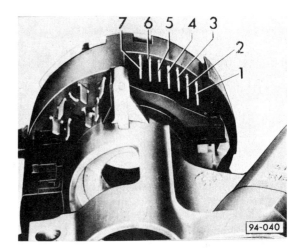

1. Terminal R	5. Terminal 71
2. Terminal 49a	6. Terminal P
3. Terminal L	7. Terminal PL
4. Terminal PR	

Fig. 6-1. Terminals of turn signal switch introduced on 1977 models.

Table c. Troubleshooting: Emergency Flashers Work, Turn Signals Work One Side Only

	Troubleshooting tests	Test results and suggested repairs
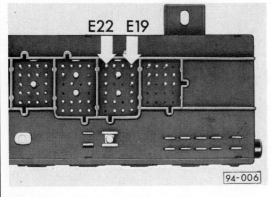 **Fig. 6-2.** Multiple connector for turn signal switch disconnected. Terminal R is at **1**, terminal 49a is at **2**, terminal L is at **3**. For 1977 and later cars, see Fig. 6-1 given earlier.	1. Disconnect multiple connector shown in Fig. 6-2. Bridge terminal 49a of female plug to terminal R and then to terminal L 2. Disconnect battery ground strap; remove emergency flasher switch from dashboard without disconnecting its wires. Make sure that no switch terminal is grounded, then reconnect battery ground strap. Use a jumper wire to connect emergency flasher terminal 49a to terminal R and then to terminal L of female plug indicated in Fig. 6-2	1. If turn signals work correctly on both sides, replace faulty turn signal switch. See **6.2**. If turn signals cannot be made to work correctly, make test 2. 2. If turn signals work correctly on both sides, trouble is in black/white/green wire from emergency flasher switch terminal 49a to turn signal switch terminal 49a. If turn signals cannot be made to work correctly, trouble is in wire from emergency flasher switch terminal L or R to turn signal switch terminal L or R. Replace faulty wiring. See **12**.

Table d. Troubleshooting: Turn Signals and Emergency Flashers Work One Side Only

	Troubleshooting tests	Test results and suggested repairs
Fig. 6-3. Terminals used in test 1. A6 is for left front, F19 for rear left, C18 for front right, and F16 for rear right.	1. Disconnect battery ground strap; detach relay plate from fuse box. Make sure that no relay plate terminal is grounded, then reconnect battery ground strap. Using a jumper wire connected to terminal 30 (+), make contact with the appropriate terminal(s), as given in Fig. 6-3	1. If turn signals work correctly, continue troubleshooting by making test 2. If turn signals cannot be made to work correctly, trouble is in black/white wire from relay plate to front or rear left turn signal or in black/green wire from relay plate to front or rear right turn signal. Replace faulty wiring. See **12**.
Fig. 6-4. Terminals used in test 2. E19 is for left turn signals, E22 is for right turn signals.	2. Connect the jumper wire from terminal 30 (+) to relay plate terminal E19 (left turn signals) or to terminal E22 (right turn signals). See Fig. 6-4	2. If turn signals work correctly, trouble is in black/white wire from emergency flasher switch to relay plate terminal E19 (left side of car) or in black/green wire from emergency flasher switch to relay plate terminal E2. If turn signals cannot be made to work correctly, relay plate is faulty and should be replaced. See **12**.

Table e. Troubleshooting: Emergency Flashers Do Not Work, Turn Signals Work Correctly

	Troubleshooting tests	Test results and suggested repairs
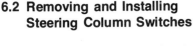 **Fig. 6-5.** Terminal D21 on relay plate.	1. Disconnect battery ground strap; remove emergency flasher switch from dashboard without disconnecting its wires. Make sure that no switch terminal is grounded, then reconnect battery ground strap. Disconnect white wire from emergency flasher switch terminal 49 and touch it to red/white wire on emergency flasher switch 30 2. Connect a jumper wire from terminal 30 (+) to relay plate terminal D21 (Fig. 6-5)	1. If emergency flashers work correctly, replace faulty emergency flasher switch. See **6.3.** If emergency flashers cannot be made to work correctly, make test 2. 2. If emergency flashers work correctly, trouble is in red/white wire from emergency flasher switch terminal 30 to relay plate terminal D21. If emergency flashers cannot be made to work correctly, replace the faulty relay plate. See **12.**

6.2 Removing and Installing Steering Column Switches

Three switches, the turn signal switch, the windshield wiper/washer switch, and the ignition switch, are mounted on the steering column, as shown in Fig. 6-6. Though the switches used on 1977 and later cars are shown, those of earlier models are similar—though not interchangeable.

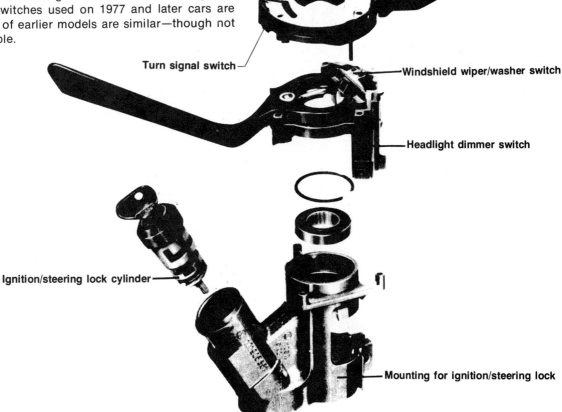

Fig. 6-6. Exploded view of steering column switches used on 1977 and later cars.

To remove the steering column switches, first disconnect the battery ground strap. Then carefully pry off the padded cover (Fig. 6-7) using your fingertips only. Remove the nut and the washer so that you can pull the steering wheel off the steering column. (Normally, it is not necessary to use any kind of tool for this.)

Remove the Phillips head screw and the socket-head bolt from the recesses in the bottom of the switch housing. Remove the bottom half of the housing. Push the switch assembly as far as possible toward the dashboard, then pry off the spacer sleeve. Pull the switch assembly upward so that you can disconnect the wires as shown in Fig. 6-8.

After you have pulled the switch assembly off the steering column and steering column tube, remove the screw that holds the turn signal switch to the wiper/washer switch. See Fig. 6-9. Separate the switches and remove the spacer sleeve that is between the two switches.

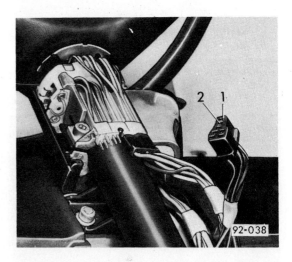

Fig. 6-8. Wires being disconnected from steering column switches. Two terminals for the windshield wiper motor are indicated by the numbers **1** and **2**. 1977 cars have third plug for headlight dimmer/flasher switch.

Fig. 6-7. Exploded view showing removal of steering wheel and steering column switches.

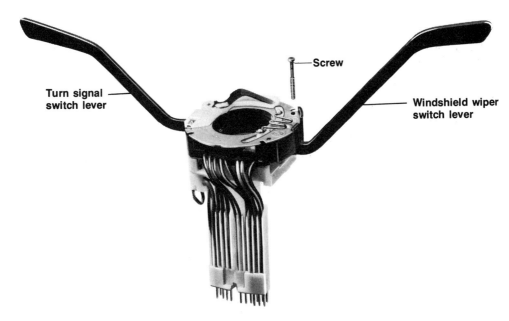

Fig. 6-9. Screw removed from switch assembly.

Installation is the reverse of removal. After you have reassembled the two switches using the screw and the spacer sleeve, slide the switch assembly onto the column tube and reconnect the wires. Drive on the spacer sleeve to the dimension given in Fig. 6-10. (If the spacer sleeve is damaged or loose-fitting, replace it.)

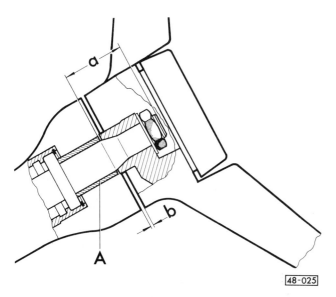

48-025

Fig. 6-10. Spacer sleeve (**A**) being installed. Drive on sleeve until dimension **a** is 41.5 mm (1.633 in.). When correctly installed, dimension **b** will be 2 to 4 mm (approximately 1/16 to 1/8 in.).

If necessary, pull the column switch assembly upward until it contacts the spacer sleeve. Then install the lower half of the housing and the Phillips head screw. Install the socket-head bolt to a torque of 1.0 mkg (7 ft. lb.).

Before you install the steering wheel, make certain that the steering is centered (front wheels pointed straight ahead). Then install the steering wheel so that its spokes are horizontal and the lug for the turn signal cancelling mechanism is pointed toward the left-hand side of the car. Install the washer, then install the nut and torque it to 5.0 mkg (36 ft.lb.). Reinstall the pad on the horn control. Reconnect the battery ground strap.

Removing and Installing Ignition Switch and Ignition/steering Lock Cylinder

The mounting for the ignition/steering lock need not be removed from the car in order to replace or repair the lock cylinder. If the mounting is faulty, you can remove it as described in conjunction with steering column removal in **SUSPENSION AND STEERING.**

5

To remove the ignition/steering lock cylinder from a 1975 or 1976 model, first remove the turn signal switch and wiper/washer switch as previously described. Using pliers, pull out the locking plate (Fig. 6-11). Insert the key and turn the lock cylinder approximately one key thickness clockwise. Then use the key to pull out the lock cylinder.

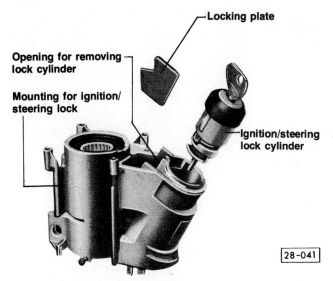

Fig. 6-11. Exploded view showing removal of 1975-1976 lock cylinder from mounting for ignition/steering lock.

Install the lock cylinder by pressing it in without the key installed. Install the locking plate, then lightly peen the mounting in order to hold the locking plate in place.

To remove the ignition/steering lock cylinder from a 1977 or later model, you must drill a 3-mm (⅛-in.) hole at the point indicated in Fig. 6-12. Then insert a pin through the hole in order to press down the spring that holds the lock cylinder in the mounting. If necessary, you can insert

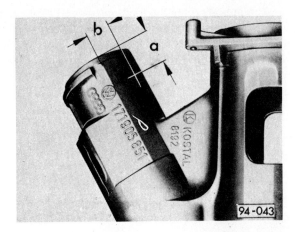

Fig. 6-12. Hole being located in mounting for ignition/steering lock. Dimension **a** is 12 mm ($^{15}/_{32}$ in.); dimension **b** is 10 mm (⅜ in.).

the key in order to pull out the cylinder. To install the cylinder, simply press it in without the key until it snaps into place.

To remove the ignition switch, remove the screw indicated in Fig. 6-13. The terminals are identified in the illustration in order to help in testing the switch electrically. Installation is the reverse of removal.

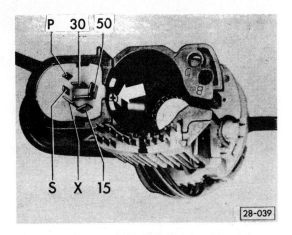

Fig. 6-13. Screw (arrow) that holds ignition switch in housing. Numbers and letters indicate terminal designations.

6.3 Removing and Installing Emergency Flasher Switch

The emergency flasher switch is located directly above the center of the dashboard bin or the optional radio. To remove the switch, first disconnect the battery ground strap. Remove the dashboard bin or the radio. Then reach behind the dashboard and squeeze together the retainers that are on either side of the emergency flasher switch. The switch can then be pressed out through the face of the dashboard and the wires disconnected. An exploded view, showing the removal of the emergency flasher switch, can be seen in **11. Instruments**.

Installation is the reverse of removal. After you have installed the emergency flasher switch, temporarily reinstall the battery ground strap so that you can test the operation of the emergency flashers. Replace the switch if it is faulty.

7. WINDSHIELD WIPERS AND WASHERS

The operation of the two-speed windshield wipers and the windshield washers is controlled by a lever on the steering column. The wiper blades park automatically when turned off. The windshield washers are supplied with water by a motor-driven pump. You can add the intermittent wiper operation feature, standard on Sciroccos, to any Rabbit model by following the instructions given in **12. Wiring, Fuses, and Relays.**

7.1 Windshield Wiper Motor Troubleshooting

Table f and **Table g** are designed to help you quickly determine the cause and the remedy for malfunctions in the windshield wiper motor. The bold numbers in the Test results and suggested repairs columns refer to

headings in this section where the suggested repairs are described.

NOTE ——

Before making any of the tests, check that no fuse is burned out and turn on the ignition.

Table f. Troubleshooting: Windshield Wiper Motor Does Not Run

	Troubleshooting tests	Test results and suggested repairs
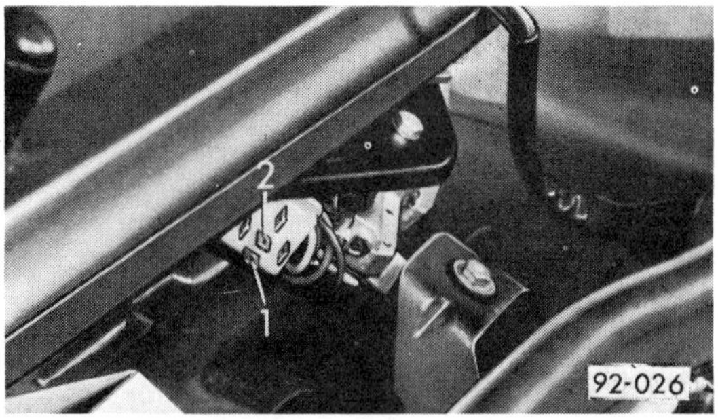 Fig. 7-1. Terminal 53 (**1**) and terminal 31 (**2**).	1. Disconnect multiple connector on wiper motor. Attach jumper wire from battery positive post to terminal 53 of motor. Use a second jumper wire to ground terminal 31. See Fig. 7-1	1. If wiper motor does not run, it is faulty and should be replaced. See **7.3.** If motor runs, make test 2.
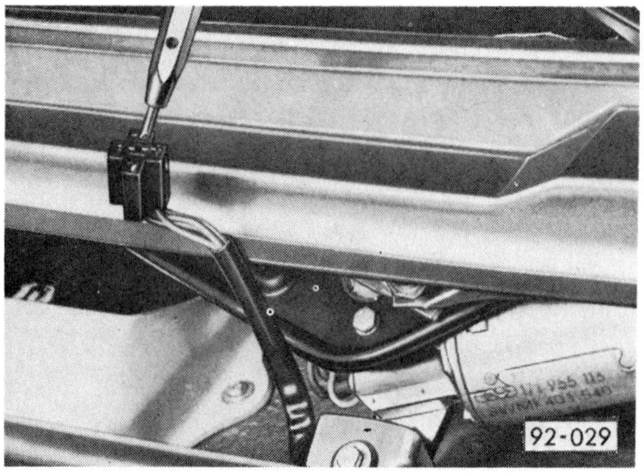 Fig. 7-2. Test probe of test light connected to terminal 53 of multiple connector plug.	2. Turn wiper switch on to low speed, then use a test light as shown in Fig. 7-2 to check for voltage at terminal 53 (green/black wire). Repeat test with second test probe grounded to terminal 31 of plug	2. If there is voltage at plug, terminals are dirty or loose-fitting and should be cleaned or repaired. See **12.** If there is no voltage at terminal 53, make test 3.
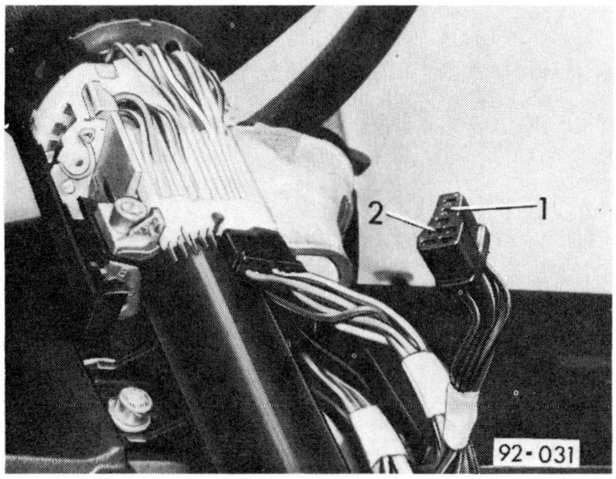 Fig. 7-3. Terminal 53a (**1**) and terminal 53 (**2**) on 1975 or 1976 car.	3. Reconnect multiple connector to motor. Remove Phillips head screw and take off bottom of steering column switch housing. Disconnect multiple connector from wiper/washer switch (Fig. 7-3 or Fig. 7-4). Use a jumper wire to connect terminal 53a of plug with terminal 53	3. If wiper motor runs, wiper/washer switch is faulty and should be replaced. See **6.2.** If motor does not run, make test 4.

5

(continued on next page)

Table f. Troubleshooting: Windshield Wiper Motor Does Not Run (continued)

	Troubleshooting tests	Test results and suggested repairs

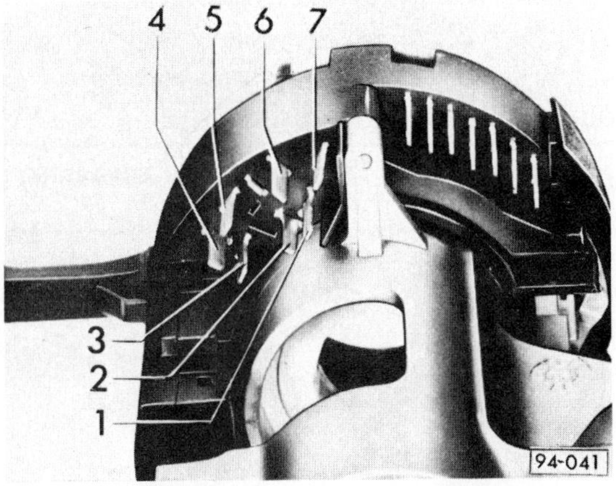

1. Terminal 51
2. Terminal S 1
3. Terminal 53e
4. Terminal 53
5. Terminal 53a
6. Terminal 53b
7. Terminal 53c

Fig. 7-4. Wiper switch terminals of 1977 and later cars. Make test at corresponding holes in plug.

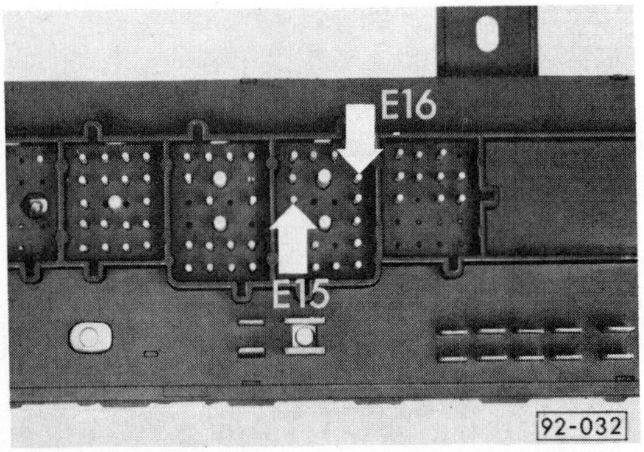

Fig. 7-5. Terminals E15 and E16 on relay plate.

4. Reconnect multiple connector to wiper/washer switch. Then disconnect battery ground strap. Detach relay plate from fuse box and disconnect multiple connector E from relay plate. Bridge terminals E15 and E16 (Fig. 7-5)

4. If wiper motor runs when wiper/washer switch is turned on, wire 53a or wire 53 from relay plate to switch or motor is faulty and should be replaced. See **12.** If motor does not run when switch is turned on, make test 5.

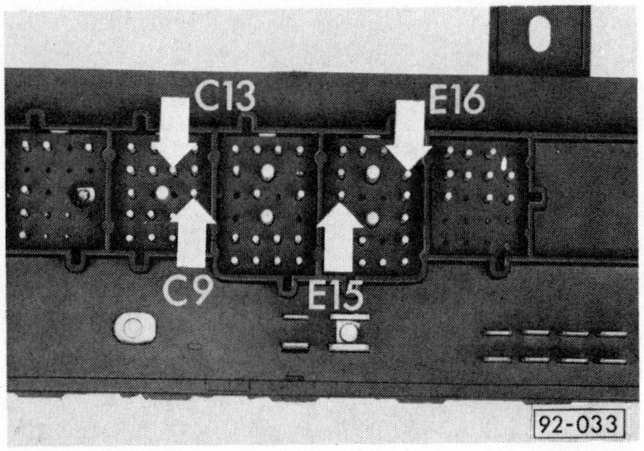

Fig. 7-6. Terminals used in making test 5.

5. Disconnect battery ground strap. Remove relay plate. Use an ohmmeter or a battery-powered test light to check continuity from terminal E16 to terminal C9 and from terminal E15 to terminal C13 (Fig. 7-6)

5. If there is no continuity in one of the tests, relay plate is faulty and should be replaced. If there is continuity in both tests, wiring harness from relay plate to wiper motor is faulty and should be replaced. See **12.**

Table g. Troubleshooting: Windshield Wipers Operate at Low Speed Only

	Troubleshooting tests	Test results and suggested repairs
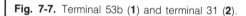	1. Turn wiper switch on to high speed. Disconnect multiple connector on wiper motor. Attach jumper wire from battery positive post to terminal 53b of motor. Use a second jumper wire to ground terminal 31. See Fig. 7-7	1. If wiper motor does not run, it is faulty and should be replaced. See **7.3.** If motor runs, make test 2.

Fig. 7-7. Terminal 53b (**1**) and terminal 31 (**2**).

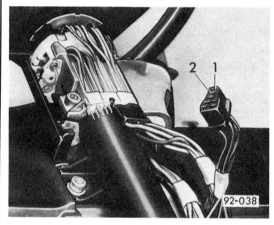

	2. Reconnect multiple connector to motor. Remove Phillips head screw and take off bottom of steering column switch housing. Disconnect multiple connector from wiper/washer switch. Use a jumper wire to connect terminal 53a (black/grey wire) with terminal 53b (green/yellow wire). On 1975 and 1976 cars, see Fig. 7-8; on 1977 cars, see Fig. 7-4 given earlier	2. If wiper motor runs, wiper/washer switch is faulty and should be replaced. See **6.2.** If motor does not run, make test 3.

Fig. 7-8. Terminal 53a (**1**) and terminal 53b (**2**).

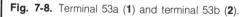
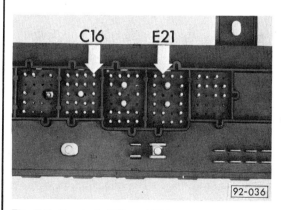

	3. Disconnect battery ground strap. Detach relay plate from fuse box and disconnect multiple connectors C and E from the relay plate. Using an ohmmeter or a battery-powered test light, test for continuity between terminal C16 and terminal E21. See Fig. 7-9	3. If there is no continuity, relay plate is faulty and should be replaced. If there is continuity, make test 4.
	4. Using an ohmmeter or a battery-powered test light, test wire 53b for continuity. (Wire 53b goes from relay plate to multiple connector on wiper/washer switch)	4. If there is continuity in wire 53b, trouble is in wiring harness from relay plate to wiper motor and the harness should be replaced. If there is no continuity in wire 53b, replace wire 53b with a new single wire running parallel to relay plate-to-steering column wiring harness.

Fig. 7-9. Terminals C16 and E21.

7.2 Removing, Servicing, and Installing Wiper Blades and Arms

To remove a wiper blade, first fold the wiper arm away from the windshield. Then turn the blade to an angle with the arm, as shown in Fig. 7-10.

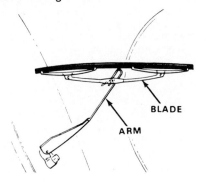

© 1974 VWoA—2671

Fig. 7-10. Wiper blade turned to an angle with wiper arm.

With the blade angled until it is against the stop, lift the retaining spring and slide the blade down the wiper arm until the hook of the arm is off the pivot pin. You may then lift the blade off upward. The sequence is illustrated in Fig. 7-11.

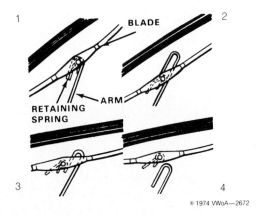

© 1974 VWoA—2672

Fig. 7-11. Blade removal sequence.

To install wiper blade:

1. Position the new blade on the arm. The arm must enter through the hole in the blade frame on the side opposite the retaining spring.

2. Slide the blade down the arm until you can slip the hook on the arm over the pivot pin.

3. Pull the blade upward until the retaining spring is fully enclosed in the hook, then place the wiper against the windshield. This installation procedure is the reverse of the sequence given previously in Fig. 7-11.

The rubber filler can be replaced without replacing the entire wiper blade. See Fig. 7-12.

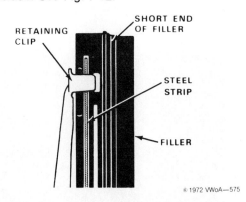

© 1972 VWoA—575

Fig. 7-12. Components of wiper blade filler assembly.

To replace filler:

1. Remove the wiper blade from the wiper arm.

2. Tightly compress the short end of the filler between your thumb and finger, then twist one side of the filler out of the retaining clip.

3. With the free side of the retaining clip resting in the groove with the steel strip, repeat the preceding step to free the other side of the filler from the retaining clip.

4. Slide the short end of the filler toward the center of the blade until the short end is completely free of the retaining clip.

5. Shift the filler sideways and unhook the steel strips from the retaining clip as indicated in Fig. 7-13. Then slide the filler out of the other retaining clips.

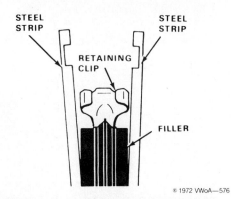

© 1972 VWoA—576

Fig. 7-13. Steel strips unhooked from retaining clip.

6. Place both steel strips in the grooves of the new filler. Make sure that the notches in the steel strips face the filler and engage the projections in the filler grooves.

7. Hold the filler so that the strips are kept in the grooves. Starting at the open end of the filler,

carefully slide the filler and the steel strips into the retaining clips.

8. When the closed end of the filler has reached the end retaining clip, compress the filler until the retaining clip rides over the raised edge next to the retaining clip recess in the end of the filler.

9. Make sure that the retaining clip completely engages the recess in the filler. Then install the wiper blade on the wiper arm.

Removing, Installing and Adjusting Wiper Arms

The wiper arm is held on the wiper shaft by a concealed M 6 hexagon nut. The nut is covered by a pressed-on cap. In removing the wiper arm, it is necessary to pry off the cap carefully in order to gain access to the mounting nut. See Fig. 7-14.

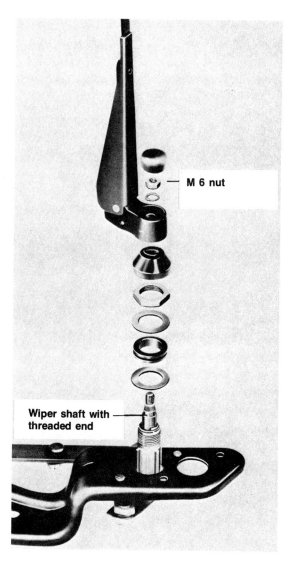

Fig. 7-14. Exploded view of wiper arm and wiper arm bearing mountings.

The wiper arm(s) must be adjusted to the correct angle(s) during installation. Correct wiper operation under all weather conditions is possible only when the arms are positioned accurately to the dimensions given in Fig. 7-15, Fig. 7-16, Fig. 7-17, or Fig. 7-18. Proper installation requires that the spring washer be seated under the nut. After you have adjusted the angle of the wiper arm(s), torque the nut(s) to 0.7 mkg (70 cmkg or 61 in. lb.) for windshield wipers or 40 to 60 cmkg (35 to 52 in. lb.) for rear window wipers.

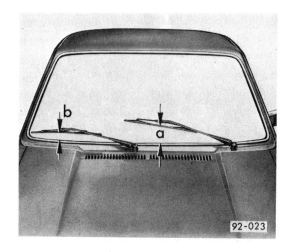

Fig. 7-15. Points where wiper arm adjustment is measured on Rabbit models. Dimension **a** is 35 mm (1 ⅜ in.); dimension **b** is 65 mm (2 ½ in.).

a = 25 mm (1 in.)
b = 30 mm (1 ³/₁₆ in.)
c = 325 to 375 mm (12 ¹³/₁₆ to 14 ¾ in.)
d = 150 to 250 mm (5 ²⁹/₃₂ to 9 ²⁷/₃₂ in.)
e = 235 to 285 mm (9 ¼ to 11 ⁷/₃₂ in.)
f = 400 to 500 mm (15 ¾ to 19 ¹¹/₁₆ in.)

Fig. 7-16. Points where wiper arm adjustment is measured on Scirocco models that have two wiper blades. Windshield washer adjustment dimensions are given also.

Fig. 7-17. Point where wiper arm adjustment is measured on Scirocco models that have one wiper blade. Dimension **a** is 55 mm (2 3/16 in.).

Fig. 7-18. Point where wiper arm adjustment is measured on rear window wiper. Dimension **a** is 30 mm (1 3/16 in.).

7.3 Removing and Installing Wiper Motor

The windshield wiper motor is mounted inside the ventilation compartment that is immediately to the rear of the engine compartment. The rear window wiper motor is housed inside the rear door. Because of differences in body design and wiper application, a different procedure must be followed in removing and installing the wiper motors of different models. Each procedure appears separately under the headings that follow.

Removing and Installing Windshield Wiper Motor

(1975 and later Rabbit, 1975 Scirocco only)

In removing the wiper motor, do not remove the wiper mounting frame from the car body. Also, you should not detach the drive crank from the wiper motor's drive gearshaft unless it is absolutely necessary. Once removed, the drive crank must be adjusted before you install the motor in the car.

To remove:

1. Fully raise the hood. Disconnect the battery ground strap.

2. Disconnect the multiple connector from the wiper motor.

3. Carefully pry the connecting rods off the ball pin on the motor's drive crank. It is unnecessary to detach the connecting rods at their other ends.

4. Remove the four bolts indicated in Fig. 7-19, then take out the wiper motor.

NOTE ——

On Scirocco models, first remove bolts 1, 2, and 4. Then apply battery current to the terminals indicated in Fig. 7-20, thus running the motor and moving the drive crank aside so that you can remove bolt 3. If the motor will not run, you must remove the drive crank before you can remove bolt 3.

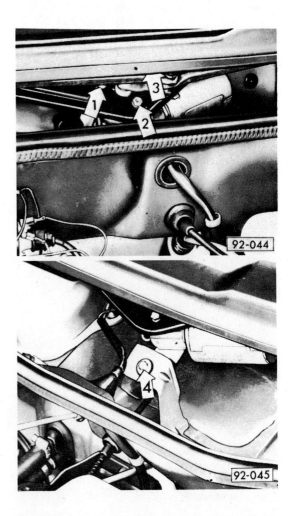

Fig. 7-19. Bolts that hold wiper motor to wiper mounting frame and car body.

Fig. 7-20. Terminals that operate motor. Use jumper wires to connect termiminal 53 (**1**) to battery positive (+) post and terminal 31 (**2**) to battery negative (−) post.

To install:

1. If you have removed the drive crank or if you are installing a new motor, adjust the drive crank before you install the motor in the car.

   NOTE

   To adjust the drive crank, you must temporarily reconnect the battery ground strap and the multiple connector for the motor. Otherwise, the motor will not park correctly. Run the motor for about 3 minutes. Then turn off the windshield wiper switch—without disconnecting the multiple connector. The motor will then stop in its parking position. Install the drive crank to the angle indicated in Fig. 7-21.

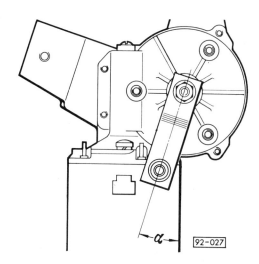

Fig. 7-21. Drive crank correctly installed with motor in parking position. Angle *a* should be 20°.

2. Install the wiper motor on the mounting frame and the car body, then install the four bolts.

3. Lubricate the plastic bushings in the connecting rods with universal grease. Then hand-press the connecting rods onto the ball pin of the motor's drive crank. The left (shortest) rod should be the first installed.

4. Reconnect the multiple connector for the electrical wires. Then reconnect the battery ground strap.

Removing and Installing Windshield Wiper Motor

(1976 and later Scirocco)

In removing the wiper motor, do not remove the wiper mounting frame from the car body.

To remove:

1. Fully raise the hood. Disconnect the battery ground strap.

2. Disconnect the multiple connector from the wiper motor.

3. Carefully pry the connecting rod off the ball pin on the motor's drive crank. It is unnecessary to detach the connecting rod at its other end.

4. Remove the nut that holds the drive crank to the motor's drive gearshaft. Then remove the serrated washer and the drive crank.

5. Remove the bolts that hold the motor to the mounting frame and the car body. Then slide the motor out from beneath the frame as indicated in Fig. 7-22.

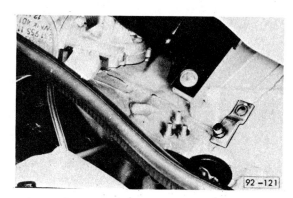

Fig. 7-22. Wiper motor being removed. Notice removed drive crank.

To install:

1. Install the wiper motor on the mounting frame and the car body, then install the bolts.

2. Install the multiple connector on the wiper motor. Then reconnect the battery ground strap.

3. Turn on the windshield wiper switch and allow the motor to run for about 3 minutes. Then turn off the motor using the switch—do not pull off the multiple connector. The motor will then stop in its parking position so that you can install the drive crank as indicated in Fig. 7-23.

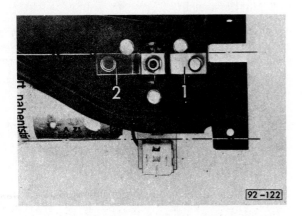

Fig. 7-23. Drive crank correctly installed (**1**) with motor in parking position. Do not install drive crank in position **2**. (Wiper mounting frame removed for clarity.)

4. Lubricate the plastic bushing in the connecting rod with universal grease. Then hand-press the connecting rod onto the ball pin of the motor's drive crank.

Removing and Installing Rear Window Wiper Motor

Fig. 7-24 is an exploded view of the rear window wiper and washer system. The washer system is covered separately in **7.4 Windshield and Rear Window Washers.**

To remove:

1. Disconnect the battery ground strap. Remove the trim panel from the inside of the rear lid.

2. Disconnect the multiple connector from the wiper motor.

3. Carefully pry the connecting rod off the ball pin on the motor's drive crank. It is unnecessary to detach the connecting rod at its other end.

4. Remove the nut that holds the drive crank to the motor's drive gearshaft. Then remove the serrated washer and the drive crank.

5. Remove the bolts that hold the motor to the mounting frame and the rear lid. Then remove the motor.

To install:

1. Install the wiper motor on the mounting frame and the rear lid, then install the bolts.

2. Install the multiple connector on the wiper motor. Then reconnect the battery ground strap.

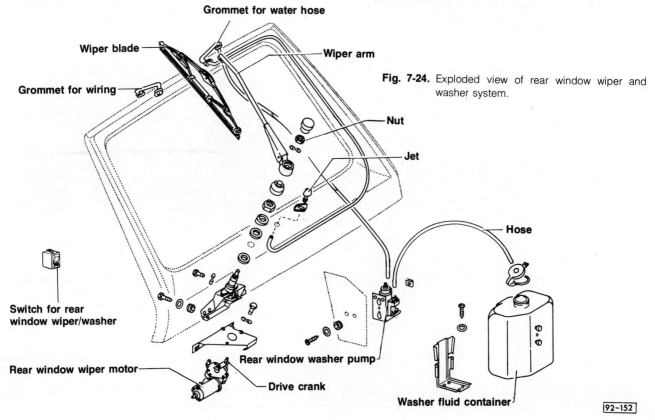

Grommet for water hose

Wiper blade

Wiper arm

Grommet for wiring

Fig. 7-24. Exploded view of rear window wiper and washer system.

Nut

Jet

Hose

Switch for rear window wiper/washer

Rear window washer pump

Rear window wiper motor

Drive crank

Washer fluid container

3. Turn on the rear window wiper switch that is on the dashboard and allow the motor to run for about 3 minutes. Then turn off the motor using the switch—do not pull off the multiple connector. The motor will then stop in its parking position so that you can install the drive crank as indicated in Fig. 7-25 or Fig. 7-26.

NOTE ——

A new linkage and a new motor, with a ribbed cast alloy cover instead of the smooth drivegear cover shown here, were introduced early in the 1977 model year. Parts for the new assembly cannot be interchanged with parts for the old.

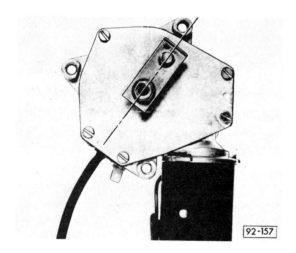

Fig. 7-25. Drive crank correctly installed on rear window wiper motor of Rabbit model (wiper motor removed for clarity).

Fig. 7-26. Drive crank correctly installed on rear window wiper motor of Scirocco model (wiper motor removed for clarity).

4. Lubricate the plastic bushing in the connecting rod with universal grease. Then hand-press the connecting rod onto the ball pin of the motor's drive crank.

Wiper Motor and Wiper Linkage Repairs

In addition to new wiper arm mounting components and wiper arm shaft/bearing assemblies, the connecting rods, the wiper frame, and the wiper motor are avilable as replacement parts. No individual components are available for repair of the wiper motor or its drive assembly. So, if either the drive or the motor is faulty, the motor must be replaced as a unit.

7.4 Windshield and Rear Window Washers

Fig. 7-27 shows a typical windshield washer installation. The electric motor-powered windshield washer pump is mounted on the side of the windshield washer fluid reservoir. The pump used on rear window washers is identical to the pump used on windshield washers. The rear fluid reservoir is also identical to the front reservoir used on 1976 and later cars. However, when used at the rear, the washer pump is not mounted on the reservoir. An exploded view of the rear window washer system was given earlier in Fig. 7-24. You can easily remove the pump from the plastic lugs of the windshield washer fluid reservoir in order to replace either the pump or the reservoir.

5 ■

Fig. 7-27. Typical windshield washer installation. Filler cap is at arrow. Notice the routing of the fluid hoses to and from the pump.

To clean a windshield washer jet, insert a fine steel wire into its orifice. If the spray does not strike the windshield or the rear window at a satisfactory angle, you can adjust the jets as shown in Fig. 7-28. On rear windows, the jet should be aimed to center the spray on the glass. Precise dimensions for adjusting the 1975 Scirocco washer jets are given in **7.2 Removing, Servicing, and Installing Wiper Blades and Arms.**

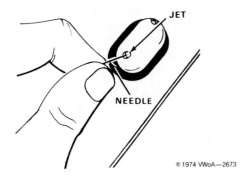

Fig. 7-28. Ball-shaped windshield washer jet being pivoted in its socket. A sewing needle inserted into the orifice is a satisfactory tool.

8. LIGHTS AND SWITCHES

For safety reasons, it is important that all lights on the vehicle be working properly at all times. Aside from the instrument panel light bulbs, the replacement of which is described in **11.4 Removing and Installing Instruments,** all light bulbs on the car are available as standard U.S. replacement numbers. Should it be necessary to troubleshoot the dimmer switch used on 1977 and later cars, you can make continuity tests at the switch terminals, which are identified in Fig. 8-1. On earlier models, use the wiring diagrams given in **12. Wiring, Fuses, and Relays.**

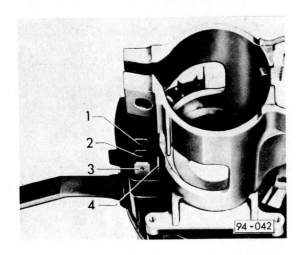

1. Terminal 56a   3. Terminal 56
2. Terminal 56b   4. Terminal 30

Fig. 8-1. Terminals of 1977 dimmer switch.

8.1 Removing and Installing Sealed Beam Units and Aiming Headlights

The radiator grille must be removed before you can replace a sealed beam unit. The grille is held by the Phillips head screws indicated in Fig. 8-2 or Fig. 8-3.

Fig. 8-2. Screws (arrows) that hold right-hand side of grille on Scirocco cars. Corresponding screws must be removed from left-hand side.

Fig. 8-3. Screws (arrows) that hold left-hand side of grille on Rabbit cars. Corresponding screws must be removed from right-hand side.

Once the grille has been removed, you can remove the sealed beam unit and its retaining ring by taking out the three short screws that hold the retaining ring to the support ring (Fig. 8-4 or Fig. 8-5). Then pull the sealed beam unit forward and disconnect the wiring harness from the terminals.

CAUTION ——

Do not alter the positions of the long headlight adjustment screws, located in the engine compartment. If you do, you will have to readjust the headlights.

When you install a sealed beam unit, be sure that its three glass lugs correctly engage the support ring. Install the retaining ring and then the grille. It should not be necessary to aim the headlights after changing a sealed beam unit. If you are in doubt, however, the aim should be checked.

Each headlight has two adjusting screws, accessible by raising the hood. Adjust vertical aim with the top screw; adjust lateral aim with the screw at the side of the support ring.

NOTE ——

Check your state laws to determine whether adjustments must be made by a licensed shop. your state may also have laws that specify different timing from that described here.

Fig. 8-4. Screws (arrows) that hold Scirocco sealed beam unit in place.

Fig. 8-5. Screws (arrows) that hold Rabbit sealed beam unit in place.

To check and adjust headlight aim:

1. Position the car on a level surface 7.65 m (25 ft.) from a vertical wall. Have the fuel tank about half-filled and make certain that the tire pressures are correct.

2. Roll the car back and forth a few yards to settle the suspension. Then load the driver's seat with one person or a weight of 70 kg (154 lb.).

3. Raise the hood for access to the adjustment screws.

4. Turn on the headlights and, if necessary, switch them to low beam. Cover one headlight at a time. The uncovered light's upper and left edges of high intensity should be in the positions shown in Fig. 8-6. If not, adjust the light's position using the adjustment screws that are located inside the engine compartment.

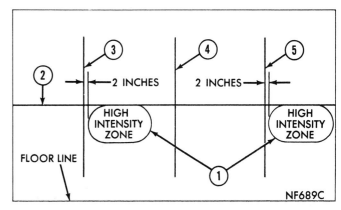

Fig. 8-6. Low beam aiming target on vertical wall. Light intensity areas are at **1**. Line **2** is at the height of the headlight centers. Vertical line **4** is the vehicle centerline. Vertical lines **3** and **5** are spaced equally on each side of line **4** and are exactly as far from one another as the centers of the (outermost) sealed beam units.

5. On Scirocco models only, switch the headlights to high beam. Check the aim of each headlight with the other three headlights covered. The high intensity zones of all four lights should fall on the target as shown in Fig. 8-7.

NOTE ——

It is unnecessary to adjust the Rabbit model's headlights on high beam. Nor do the outermost headlights of Scirocco models need to have their high beams adjusted if the low beam positions are correct. If there is any discrepancy, adjust the low beams correctly.

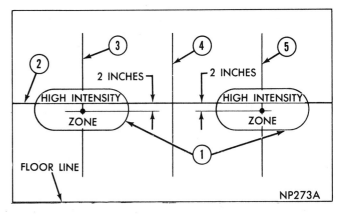

Fig. 8-7. High beam aiming target. Numbers represent the same factors given in Fig. 8-6.

8.2 Replacing Bulbs

Table h lists the bulbs and their applications. Except for the bulbs used in the dashboard for instrument illumination, all of the bulbs are available as standard U.S. parts.

Table h. Bulb Applications and Part Numbers

Bulb for	U.S. Trade No.	VW Part No.
Sealed beam (Scirocco high beam)	4001	ZAP 118 001
Sealed beam (Scirocco high/low beam)	4000	ZAP 118 000
Sealed beam (Rabbit high/low beam)	6014	ZVP 118 114
Front turn signals/parking lights	1034	ZVP 118 034
Side marker lights	57	ZPP 118 057
Rear turn signals	1073	ZVP 118 073
Stop lights	1073	ZVP 118 073
Taillights	67	ZVP 118 067
Back-up lights	1073	ZVP 118 073
License plate lights	57	ZPP 118 057
Illumination of the operating controls	—	N 17 751 2
Instrument illumination, indicator and warning lights ..	—	N 17 751 2
Glove compartment light (Scirocco)	—	N 17 726 2
Interior light	211	N 17 723 2
Luggage compartment light (Scirocco)	211	N 17 725 2

Replacing Side Marker Light Bulbs

To replace a side marker light bulb, first remove the two screws indicated in Fig. 8-8. Then pull the light assembly away from the fender so that you can pull the rubber cap off the back. Press the lugs on the housing outwards and remove the bulb holder. Take out the bulb.

Install the new bulb by pressing it into the bulb holder and turning the bulb clockwise. The remainder of installation is the reverse of removal. In installing the light assembly, tighten the screws evenly but do not overtighten them, since this may crack the lens.

Fig. 8-8. Screws (arrows) that hold side marker light to body.

Replacing Front Turn Signal/ Parking Light Bulb

On Scirocco models, open the hood. Pull the rubber cap off the back of the light housing, then squeeze together the lugs indicated in Fig. 8-9 and pull the bulb holder out of the housing. Press the bulb into the bulb holder, turn it counterclockwise, then take the bulb out.

Installation is the reverse of removal. Because of the asymmetrical pin arrangement on the double-filament bulb, there is no wrong way of inserting the bulb into the holder.

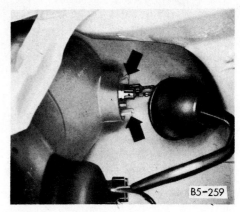

Fig. 8-9. Lugs (arrows) that hold Scirocco bulb holder in light housing.

On Rabbit models, take out the two screws indicated in Fig. 8-10. Then remove the lens. Press the bulb into its socket, turn it counterclockwise, then take out the bulb.

Installation is the reverse of removal. Make sure that the gasket is in good condition and correctly positioned when you install the lens. Tighten the screws evenly but do not overtighten them, since doing this may crack the lens.

Fig. 8-10. Screws (arrows) that hold turn signal/parking light lens in Rabbit bumper.

Replacing Rear Turn Signal, Stop/Taillight, or Back-up Light Bulb

The bulbs in the taillight assembly are accessible from inside the car's luggage compartment. Unscrew the knurled screw and take off the taillight assembly cover.

Depress the spring clip on the inboard side so that you can pull the bulb holder out of the taillight assembly.

Installation is the reverse of removal. Fig. 8-11 or Fig. 8-12 will show you the correct locations for the various bulbs.

1. Back-up light   3. Taillight
2. Stop light   4. Turn signal light

Fig. 8-11. Bulb locations on Scirocco taillight assembly.

1. Back-up light   3. Stop light
2. Taillight   4. Turn signal light

Fig. 8-12. Bulb locations on Rabbit taillight assembly.

Replacing License Plate Light Bulb

Remove the two screws indicated in Fig. 8-13, then take off the lens. Press the bulb into its holder, turn it counterclockwise, and remove the bulb.

Installation is the reverse of removal. The license plate will be correctly illuminated only if both bulbs are

functioning. In installing the lens, tighten the screws evenly but do not overtighten them, since doing this may crack the lens.

Fig. 8-13. Screws (arrows) that hold license plate light lens to car.

Replacing Interior Light Bulb

To replace the interior light bulb, press against the spring clip indicated in Fig. 8-14. Then withdraw the light assembly as shown. Take out the old bulb, snap the new bulb into place, then press the light assembly back into the body.

Fig. 8-14. Spring clip (arrow) that holds interior light assembly in body.

8.3 Back-up Light Switch

The back-up light switch for cars with automatic transmissions is built into the selector lever assembly. Instructions for removing and installing the contact assembly for this switch can be found in **AUTOMATIC TRANSMISSION.**

Three different kinds of back-up light switches have been used on cars with manual transmissions. The two earliest kind are operated by the gearshift linkage. The third kind is operated by a lug on the reverse shift fork inside the transmission. Fig. 8-15 shows the two earliest switches.

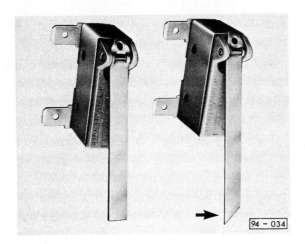

Fig. 8-15. Earliest kind (left) and later kind of linkage-operated back-up light switches. Later kind has longer, angled lever (arrow).

In replacing the earliest kind of back-up light switch, always use the later kind of linkage-operated switch. Both kinds of switch are adjusted by repositioning them after first loosening the mounting screws or bolts. However, the later kind is mounted on a bracket, as shown in Fig. 8-16, and should be adjusted by loosening the bolts and repositioning the switch and bracket as a unit.

Fig. 8-16. Later kind of linkage-operated back-up light switch installed on car. Bracket is at **1**, switch is operated by rod lever (**2**).

The latest kind of back-up light switch is installed beginning with Transmission No. 02 04 6. It is screwed

directly into the transaxle case, as indicated in Fig. 8-17. This switch requires no adjustment. The switch is easily replaceable by disconnecting the wires and unscrewing the switch from the transaxle. In installing the new switch, make certain that a sealing washer is installed in order to prevent transaxle leaks. A cross section of the transaxle, showing the internal parts that operate the switch, can be seen in **MANUAL TRANSMISSION.**

Fig. 8-17. Screw-in back-up light switch (arrow) used on latest cars with manual transmissions.

9. HORN AND BUZZER

The horn control in the steering wheel consists of simple contacts that you can inspect after removing the steering wheel. For good horn operation, the installation of the steering wheel spacer sleeve must be correct. See **6.2 Removing and Installing Steering Column Switches.** The horn circuit is controlled directly by the horn control on the steering wheel, there being no horn relay.

9.1 Horn Troubleshooting

Table i is designed to help you locate and repair horn malfunctions. Before you begin troubleshooting, check that fuse 9 is intact by turning on the ignition and engaging reverse gear. The fuse is burned out if the back-up lights do not come on. The ignition must also be turned on during the test described in the table. If it is necessary to replace a faulty wire or to replace the relay plate, do so with the help of the information given in **12. Wiring, Fuses, and Relays.**

All cars covered by this Manual are equipped with an ignition key warning buzzer that sounds if the ignition key is in the lock when the driver's door is opened. The same buzzer serves the seat belt warning system. The buzzer is an integral part of the seat belt warning system relay, which is located under the dashboard at the left side of the car. If the buzzer is faulty, the entire seat belt warning system relay must be replaced.

Table i. Troubleshooting: Horn Does Not Work

	Troubleshooting tests	Test results and suggested repairs
  Fig. 9-1. Positive (black/yellow wire) terminal (**1**), ground (brown) wire (**2**), jumper wire (**3**).	1. Disconnect both wires from horn. Use jumper wires to connect horn directly to battery posts 2. Reconnect positive wire to horn. Use jumper wire at negative terminal only, as shown in Fig. 9-1	1. If horn fails to sound, horn is faulty and should be replaced. If horn sounds, make test 2. 2. If horn does not sound, make test 3. If horn sounds, make test 4.
  Fig. 9-2. Relay plate terminal A11.	3. Reconnect ground wire to horn. Disconnect battery ground strap and disconnect positive wire from horn. Use a jumper wire to connect horn positive terminal with relay plate terminal A11 (Fig. 9-2), then reconnect battery ground strap	3. If horn sounds, replace black/yellow wire from relay plate to horn. If horn fails to sound, relay plate is faulty and should be replaced.
  Fig. 9-3. Jumper wire connected to multiple connector brown/blue wire.	4. Reconnect ground wire to horn. Disconnect multiple connector from steering column switch. Then use a jumper wire to ground brown/blue wire of multiple connector (Fig. 9-3)	4. If horn sounds, contacts in steering wheel require attention; check especially for correct routing of wiring from contact plate to horn button. If horn fails to sound, make test 5.

(continued on next page)

Table i. Troubleshooting: Horn Does Not Work (continued)

	Troubleshooting tests	Test results and suggested repairs
Fig. 9-4. Relay plate terminal E11.	5. Use jumper wire to ground relay plate terminal E11 (Fig. 9-4)	5. If horn sounds, brown/blue wire from multiple connector to relay plate is faulty and should be replaced. If horn fails to sound, make test 6.
Fig. 9-5. Relay plate terminal A7.	6. Use a jumper wire to connect relay plate terminal A7 to negative (ground) terminal of horn (Fig. 9-5)	6. If horn sounds, brown wire from relay plate terminal A7 to horn's negative terminal is faulty and should be replaced. If horn fails to sound, relay plate is faulty and should be replaced.

10. HEATING AND VENTILATION

The heater motor and the heater controls are covered in **BODY AND INTERIOR.** Faulty heater motors cannot be repaired and must be replaced as a unit.

Heated Rear Window

A relay located in the fuse box controls the temperature of the heated rear window. Disconnect the battery ground strap before you disconnect any of the wires related to the system. In removing the rear window, disconnect the two wires from the terminals that are at the edge of the glass. Removal and installation of the heated rear window are the same as for any other rear window. However, they should only be attempted by someone familiar with automotive glass work who has the special tools required.

If only the conductive grid is damaged, it is unnecessary to replace the window. Repair material is available at Authorized Dealers to patch broken circuits.

To repair:

1. Apply a strip of masking tape along each edge of the broken conductor.

2. Apply the repair material evenly over the break.

3. Allow the repair to dry for one hour at room temperature. Then remove the tape and test the heating effect.

11. INSTRUMENTS

Throughout this Manual you will find the instruction "remove the battery ground strap" given many times. Failure to remove the ground strap where instructed, or reinstalling the ground strap before all other electrical connections are made, can result in instrument damage or warning light malfunction—typically, a speedometer needle that will not return to zero or a brake warning light that will not go out.

If the brake warning light will not go out, and the trouble is not in the brake system, it is probably because of poor ground contact between the battery and the car body. If the ground strap for the engine/transaxle assembly is broken or disconnected, current may be forced to flow through the speedometer cable—especially during starting. The resultant heat inside the speedometer can soften the return spring for the speedometer needle so that the spring can no longer return the needle to zero.

To avoid damage, always disconnect the battery ground strap before you disconnect any other ground strap. Always reconnect the ground straps in the following sequence:

1. Connect the ground strap to the engine/transaxle assembly (**X** in Fig. 11-1).

2. Connect the ground straps to the body (**Y** in Fig. 11-1).

3. Connect the battery ground strap to the battery (**Z** in Fig. 11-1).

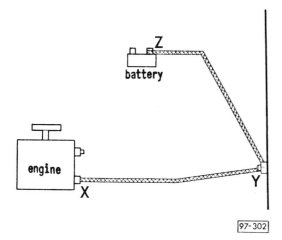

97-302

Fig. 11-1. Ground strap terminals. Battery ground strap (**Z**) should always be the first disconnected and the last reconnected. Terminal **Y** is on car body; terminal **X** is on engine/transaxle assembly.

NOTE——

Inaccurate instruments can be either replaced or returned to their manufacturer for repair or calibration (VDO Instruments, LTD., 116 Victor Avenue, Detroit, Michigan 48203).

11.1 Replacing Speedometer Cable

The speedometer is driven off the transaxle via two flexible cables. One cable extends from the speedometer drivegear assembly on the transaxle to the EGR/CAT elapsed mileage odometer and the second cable extends from the elapsed mileage odometer to the speedometer. The elapsed mileage odometer is covered in **FUEL AND EXHAUST SYSTEMS.**

To disconnect a speedometer cable from either the speedometer or the elapsed mileage odometer, unscrew the knurled ferrule nut that holds the cable to the odometer or the speedometer head. Use pliers or a special wrench to unscrew the cable union from the drivegear assembly on the transaxle.

NOTE——

Access to the rear of the speedometer can be obtained through the radio/dashboard bin opening, as shown in **11.3 Removing and Installing Instruments.**

In installing the cable, check it carefully to see that the cable has not been kinked or its conduit flattened. Check also that the ferrule nut is not dented or deformed. Do not lubricate the cable prior to installation. Make sure that the rubber grommets fully engage the holes in the panels and that the cable has no sharp bends. See Fig. 11-2.

5

CAUTION——

The radius of any bend must be at least 150 mm (6 in.). Otherwise the cable will soon break at the bend.

90·040

Fig. 11-2. Speedometer cable grommet correctly installed (Rabbit).

On Scirocco models, use the plastic retainer to attach the cable to the bracket at the point indicated in Fig. 11-3. Otherwise, the speedometer cable may make contact with the clutch cable, the movement of which will damage the speedometer cable conduit.

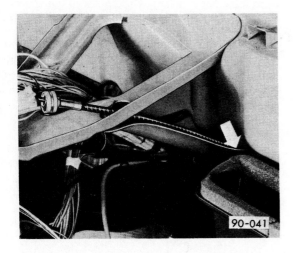

Fig. 11-3. Point (arrow) at which Scirocco speedometer cable should be held to bracket by plastic retainer.

Disassembling and Assembling Speedometer Drivegear Assembly

Fig. 11-4 is an exploded view of a typical speedometer drivegear assembly. A bolt and hold-down clamp keep the drivegear assembly attached to the transaxle. A special union, for holding the cable to the drivegear assembly, goes onto the threads on the exposed end of the assembly.

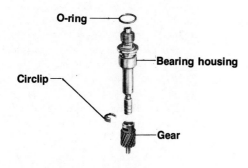

Fig. 11-4. Exploded view of typical speedometer drivegear assembly.

Early in 1976, a new kind of drivegear was introduced on transaxles with manual transmissions only (Fig. 11-5). The new kind of gear is installed with a different kind of circlip.

Fig. 11-5. Speedometer drivegears for cars with manual transmissions. Gear introduced early in 1976 has chamfer (arrow), earlier gear at right does not.

To remove the drivegear from the bearing housing, pry off the external type circlip and then pull off the gear (Fig. 11-6) or pull the gear off the internal type circlip (Fig. 11-7). Installation is the reverse of removal. However, in installing the gear over an internal type circlip, start the gear on the circlip at an angle, then push on the gear until you can see the circlip through the hole in the gear. The circlip's gap should be offset 180° from the hole in the gear.

NOTE ——

The old-type drivegear can be used with the internal type circlip if you chamfer the bore of the gear with a countersink.

1. Bearing housing
2. Drivegear
3. External type circlip

Fig. 11-6. Drivegear assembly with external type circlip.

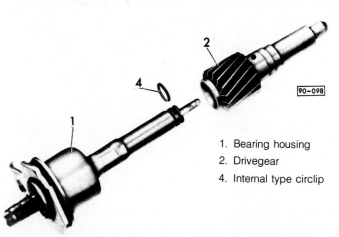

1. Bearing housing
2. Drivegear
4. Internal type circlip

Fig. 11-7. Drivegear assembly with internal type circlip. Install circlip in groove on bearing housing.

11.2 Fuel and Temperature Gauge Troubleshooting

Except for basic Rabbit models, which have a warning light for engine overheating, all cars covered by this Manual have both a fuel gauge and a coolant temperature gauge. These gauges are installed in the instrument cluster so that they are visible through the faces of the large dials of the speedometer, clock, or tachometer.

Fuel Gauge and Sending Unit Troubleshooting

The fuel gauge is controlled by an electromechanical sending unit in the fuel tank (Fig. 11-8 or Fig. 11-9). The late-type sending unit is accessible by removing a cover plate that is beneath the rear seat. This new location simplifies troubleshooting as well as simplifying replacement of the sending unit.

Fig. 11-8. Location under car of fuel gauge sending unit of cars with carburetors. Ground wire is at **1**, wire to fuel gauge at **2**, and fuel hose connection at **3**.

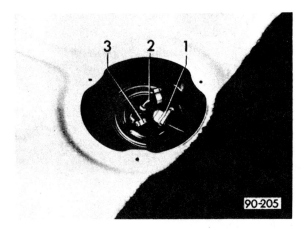

Fig. 11-9. Location beneath rear seat of fuel gauge sending unit of cars with fuel injection. Two-prong electrical connector is at **1**, suction line at **2**, and return line at **3**.

A fuel gauge that never moves from the 1/1 position has a grounded control circuit. Disconnect the violet/black control wire from the sending unit. If the gauge falls from the 1/1 mark, the trouble is in the sending unit. If it does not, the control wire is grounded somewhere between the sending unit and the gauge.

If the fuel gauge fails to register at all, remove the violet/black wire from the sending unit and ground it against a clean, unpainted metal part of the car. If the fuel gauge moves up to 1/1, the sending unit is faulty or not properly grounded via the brown wire. If the gauge still fails to move, the gauge or the violet/black wire is faulty.

Testing Fuel Gauge Accuracy

You can test the accuracy of the fuel gauge by installing resistances of a known capacity in the circuit in place of the sending unit (Fig. 11-10). The ignition must be turned on during the test. Use the following resistances:

Resistance R1 =   47 ohms ±5%
Resistance R2 = 100 ohms ±5%
Resistance R3 = 220 ohms ±5%

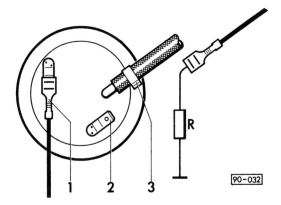

1. Ground (brown) wire
2. Terminal for violet/black wire
3. Fuel hose
R. Resistance used to ground violet/black wire

Fig. 11-10. Fuel gauge accuracy being tested. Resistance (**R**) should be used in place of sending unit with one side of resistance grounded and other side attached to violet/black wire.

NOTE

The sending unit used on cars with fuel injection has a two-prong electrical connection, as shown in Fig. 11-11. The test illustrated in Fig. 11-10, however, can still be carried out as it is not necessary for the ground wire to be connected.

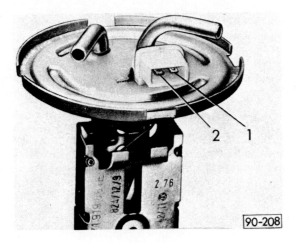

Fig. 11-11. Sending unit used on cars with fuel injection. Terminal **1** is for violet/black wire to gauge; terminal **2** is for brown ground wire.

Fig. 11-12 shows the correct positions for the fuel gauge needle with each of the three resistances installed. If the gauge is inaccurate in this test, you should check the voltage stabilizer on cars built since November 1975 as described under the next heading before you decide that the gauge is faulty.

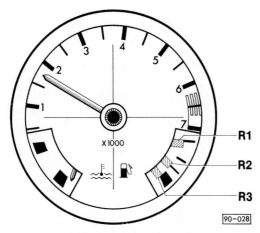

Fig. 11-12. Correct fuel gauge needle positions (shaded areas) with resistances **R1**, **R2**, and **R3** installed in place of sending unit.

Testing Voltage Stabilizer

On cars manufactured through November 1975, the fuel gauge and the water temperature gauge each has its own built-in voltage stabilizer. Beginning with cars manufactured in December 1975, the printed circuit of the instrument panel is changed and a single voltage stabilizer (Fig. 11-13) is used to serve both gauges.

Fig. 11-13. Location of voltage stabilizer (arrow) on speedometer housing.

To test the voltage stabilizer, turn on the ignition. Connect a voltmeter as indicated in Fig. 11-14. The voltage should be approximately 10 volts and, if it is above 10.5 volts or below 9.5 volts, the voltage stabilizer is faulty and should be replaced.

NOTE

For accurate testing, the voltmeter must have an internal resistance of at least 1000 ohms/volt and the battery must be charged and in good condition.

Fig. 11-14. Voltmeter connected to voltage stabilizer. Stabilizer terminal +E is for voltage input, terminal marked ⏚ is for ground, and terminal +A is for stabilized voltage output.

In installing a new voltage stabilizer, make sure that the metal plate indicated in Fig. 11-15 is against the speedometer housing in order to prevent reversed polarity through the stabilizer with consequent damage to its solid state components. Replacement voltage stabilizers manufactured by VDO and Motometer are interchangeable.

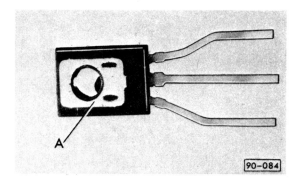

Fig. 11-15. Metal plate (**A**) on voltage stabilizer that should be installed against speedometer housing.

Testing Temperature Gauge Accuracy

You can test the accuracy of the temperature gauge by installing resistances of known capacity in the circuit in place of the sending unit (Fig. 11-16). The ignition must be turned on during the test. Use the following resistances:

Resistance R1 =   47 ohms ±5%
Resistance R2 = 150 ohms ±5%
Resistance R3 = 270 ohms ±5%

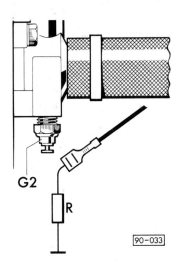

Fig. 11-16. Temperature gauge accuracy being tested. Resistance (**R**) should be used in place of sending unit (**G2**) with one side of resistance grounded and other side attached to wire disconnected from sending unit.

Fig. 11-17 shows the correct positions for the temperature gauge needle with each of the three resistances installed. If the gauge is inaccurate in this test, you should check the voltage stabilizer on cars built since November 1975 as described under the preceding heading before you decide that the gauge is faulty.

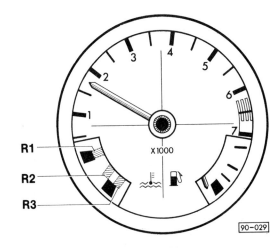

Fig. 11-17. Correct temperature gauge needle positions (shaded areas) with resistances **R1**, **R2**, and **R3** installed in place of sending unit.

11.3 Removing and Installing Fuel Gauge Sending Unit

Fuel gauge sending units cannot be repaired. If the sending unit is faulty, replace it.

To remove:

1. Disconnect the battery ground strap.

2. On cars with carburetors, have the tank as near empty as possible. On cars with fuel injection, the tank should be no more than ¾ full. If necessary, drain the tank with a siphon.

WARNING ——
Do not smoke or work near heaters or other fire hazards during any part of this procedure. Have a fire extinguisher handy.

3. On cars with fuel injection, remove the cover plate that is beneath the rear seat. On all cars, disconnect the wires from the terminals of the sending unit. If necessary, consult Fig. 11-8 or Fig. 11-9 given earlier.

4. Disconnect the fuel hose(s) and quickly plug each disconnected hose with a punch, a pencil, or a golf tee.

5. Mark the position of the sending unit on the tank. Then, using universal pliers, turn the sending unit's bayonet fitting counterclockwise to release the sending unit from the bayonet socket in the tank. Then remove the sending unit.

The sending unit can be tested by connecting a battery and a voltmeter in series between the ground terminal and the gauge wire terminal.

WARNING —

Do not make tests near the fuel tank. An electrical spark could cause an explosion.

Observe whether the voltmeter reading changes continuously as the sending unit's float is moved by hand through its full range. If the voltmeter needle does not move, or does not move smoothly, the sending unit is faulty and should be replaced.

Installation is the reverse of removal. Inspect the sealing ring and the fuel filter. Replace hard or cracked sealing rings; replace clogged or torn filters. Lubricate the sealing ring with glycerine or graphite so that it will not be twisted or deformed as the bayonet fitting is pressed in and turned clockwise. Refer to Fig. 11-8 given earlier if you are in doubt as to the correct installed positions for the wires.

11.4 Removing and Installing Instruments

The instrument cluster is shown removed and disassembled in Fig. 11-18. There are detail differences in the clusters used in different car models covered by this Manual. The components shown are available as replacement parts.

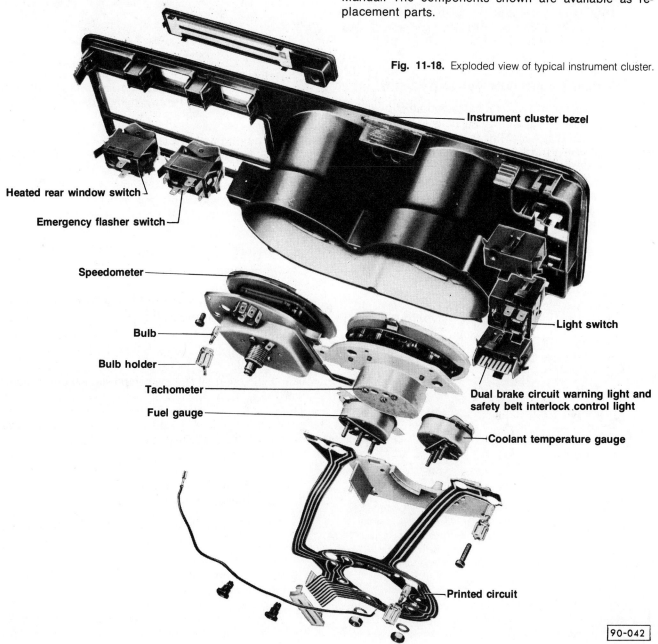

Fig. 11-18. Exploded view of typical instrument cluster.

Instrument cluster bezel

Heated rear window switch

Emergency flasher switch

Speedometer

Bulb

Bulb holder

Tachometer

Fuel gauge

Light switch

Dual brake circuit warning light and safety belt interlock control light

Coolant temperature gauge

Printed circuit

90-042

To remove instrument cluster:

1. Disconnect the battery ground strap.

2. Pull the knobs off the heating and ventilation controls. Then carefully pry off the trim plate for the controls.

3. Remove the radio or the dashboard bin, which is immediately above the heating and ventilation controls.

4. Disconnect the speedometer cable from the speedometer head by unscrewing the ferrule nut.

5. Remove the screw (Fig. 11-19) that holds the instrument cluster to the dashboard structure.

Fig. 11-19. Screw (arrow) that holds instrument cluster to dashboard structure.

6. Pull the instrument cluster out of the dashboard. Then disconnect the wiring harness plugs from the switches and from the multiple connector for the printed circuit.

7. Remove the instrument cluster from the car.

Installation is the reverse of removal. If you must disassemble the cluster in any way or replace any of the components, use as your guide Fig. 11-18, which was given earlier. Fig. 11-20 identifies the various terminals for the printed circuit's multiple connector plug. Using this illustration as your guide, you can test the printed circuits for continuity with an ohmmeter in order to separate printed circuit troubles from gauge troubles.

1. Turn signal indicator light (terminal 49a)
2. Alternator warning light (terminal 61)
3. High beam warning light positive wire (terminal 56a)
4. Tachometer (terminal 1) or clock positive wire (terminal 30)
5. Ground (terminal 31)
6. Instrument cluster light (terminal 58b)
7. Positive wire (terminal 15)
8. Fuel gauge (from sending unit)
9. Temperature gauge (from sending unit)
10. Catalytic converter control (where applicable)
11. Oil pressure warning light (from oil pressure switch)
12. EGR control (where applicable)

Fig. 11-20. Identification of terminals for printed circuit.

5 ■

Replacing Instrument Light Bulbs

It is unnecessary to remove the instrument cluster to replace instrument light bulbs. Remove the radio or the dashboard bin, then reach behind the instrument cluster and detach the appropriate bulb holder. To do this, turn the bulb holder until its lugs can be slipped out through the cutouts in the cluster. (If necessary, consult Fig. 11-18 which was given earlier.) Replace the faulty bulb, then insert the bulb holder and turn it so that its lugs engage the back of the instrument cluster.

11.5 Installing Radio Suppression Filter for Radiator Fan

The operation of the radiator fan motor may cause noise or static in radios that are not factory-installed. This radio interference problem can be fixed by installing a suppression filter, Part No. 171 035 257.

To install:

1. Disconnect the battery ground strap.

2. Disconnect the radiator fan wires from the wiring harness connector.

3. Cut off the radiator fan wires to a length of 30 mm (1³/₁₆ in.). Then install the new connector, which is provided with the filter kit, on the fan motor wires.

4. Attach the suppression filter to the fan motor and to the wiring harness as indicated in Fig. 11-21.

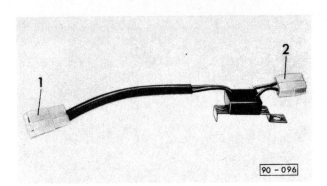

Fig. 11-21. Suppression filter installation. Plug **1** should be attached to wiring harness. Plug **2** should be attached to new connector on the radiator fan motor wires.

5. Using one of the fan mounting bolts, attach the filter to the fan shroud, as shown in Fig. 11-22.

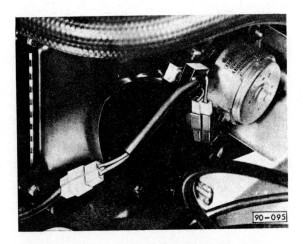

Fig. 11-22. Suppression filter bolted to fan shroud.

12. WIRING, FUSES, AND RELAYS

The intermittent windshield wiper feature, standard on Scirocco models, can be applied to the Rabbit by means of a minor change. Simply remove the bridge wire, shown later in Fig. 12-5, and install relay Part No. 111 955531 in its place. Then remove the wedge indicated in Fig. 12-1.

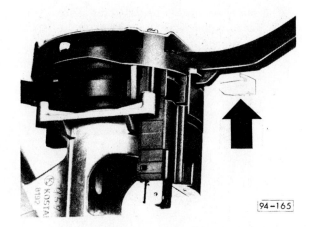

Fig. 12-1. Wedge (arrow) that prevents Rabbit wiper switch from being moved to intermittent position. See **6.2 Removing and Installing Steering Column Switches** for switch housing removal directions.

The fuses and the relays for the electrical system are arranged together in one centralized unit and are protected by a transparent cover. There are 15 fuses. You can determine which circuits are protected by each numbered fuse, either by consulting the Owner's Manual or by consulting the current flow diagrams given in **12.2 Wiring Diagrams.** In the diagrams, the fuse number is preceded by the letter S (*Schmelzeinsatz*). For example, S17 in the diagrams indicates fuse number 17 in the fuse box.

The terminals on the relay plate of the fuse box are all numbered, as indicated in Fig. 12-2. Eight wiring harnesses plug into the bottom of the relay plate. Their positions are identified by the letters A through H, as shown in Fig. 12-3. Terminal number 10 for wiring harness C is called terminal C10.

These kinds of terminal designations are given in the current flow diagrams as an aid to troubleshooting. For example, the wiring harness for the windshield wiper motor is connected to the bottom of the relay plate by plug C. Therefore, in the current flow diagrams, the wires to the wiper motor are marked C9, C16, C13, and C6 at the points where they are connected to the relay plate. These markings indicate the exact relay plate terminal to which each of these wiper motor wires is connected.

Description	Terminal	Terminal on relay	Connected to
Socket J (headlight dimmer relay)	1	56	terminal G10, D17, J12
	2	56	terminal J1
	3	56b	terminal J5, fuse S1 and S2
	4	56a	terminal G8, fuse S3 and S4
	5	56b	terminal J3
	6	30	terminals H1 to H7 (terminal 30)
	7	S	terminal E8
Socket K (rear window defogger relay)	8	86	terminal D10, L15, M18, N23 (terminal 31)
	9	30	terminals H1 to H7 (terminal 30)
	10	87	fuse S5
	11	85	terminal D7
Socket L	12	86	terminal A3
	13	30	terminals H1 to H7 (terminal 30)
	14	87	terminal A8
	15	31	terminal D10, K8, M18, N23 (terminal 31)
	16	15	fuse S8, S9
Socket M (windshield wiper intermittent relay on Scirocco only)	17	15	bridged for windshield wiper motor from M19 to M21 on Rabbit
	18	31	
	19	53s	
	20	S1	
	21	53m	
Socket N (turn signal/emergency flasher relay)	22	49a	terminal D1, D3
	23	31	terminal D10, L15, K8, M18 (terminal 31)
	24	+49	terminal D12
	25	C	terminal D6

Fig. 12-2. Top of relay plate. Capital letters A to N and numbers for connections are repeated in test instructions and current flow diagrams.

Fig. 12-3. Bottom of relay plate. Capital letters A to N and numbers for connections are repeated in test instructions and current flow diagrams.

Fig. 12-4 shows the fuse box relay plate with the fuses and the relays installed. Relay J31, for the intermittent operation of the windshield wipers (marked with a large X), is not installed on Rabbit models. Instead, terminals 19 and 21 are bridged as shown in Fig. 12-5.

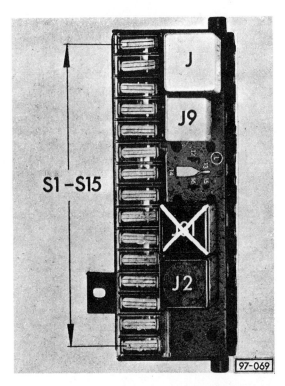

Fig. 12-4. Fuses and relays. Headlight dimmer relay (eliminated on 1977 cars) is at **J**, heated rear window relay is at **J9**, Scirocco-only wiper intermittent relay is at **J31**, and turn signal/emergency flasher relay is at **J2**.

A   – socket for front left harness
B   – socket for Analysis system wiring
C   – socket for front right harness
D   – socket for dashboard wiring
E   – socket for dashboard wiring
F   – socket for rear harness
G1 – connected to G6 via fuse S15
G2 – connected to terminal E7 and M20
G3 – connected to ignition/starter switch, terminal 15
G4 – connected to fuse S12
G5 – connected to alternator, terminal D+
G6 – connected to G1 via fuse S15
G7 – connected to ignition/starter switch, terminal X
G8 – connected to headlight dimmer switch, terminal 56a
G9 – connected to engine oil pressure switch
G10 – connected to light switch, terminal 56

H1
H2
H3
H4 } terminal 30
H5
H6
H7

Fig. 12-5. Bridge wire (**A**) used on Rabbit models in place of windshield wiper intermittent relay.

Replacing Fuses

Always replace white (8-amp) fuses with other white fuses, red (16-amp) fuses with other red fuses, and blue (25-amp) fuses with other blue fuses. If in doubt, consult the Owner's Manual supplied with the car or the current flow diagrams given in **12.2 Wiring Diagrams.**

CAUTION ——

Never patch a burned-out fuse with aluminum foil or replace the fuse with wire or a fuse of greater capacity. Doing this can damage the electrical system. Before you replace a fuse, disconnect the battery ground strap or, if this is not possible, turn off all electrical components, turn off the ignition, and remove the key. If you do not take these precautions, there is a chance that you may receive a minor electrical shock when you replace the fuse.

To replace a fuse, carefully disengage the fuse box clip, then lift up the lower side of the fuse box cover. (The fuse box is located under the car's dashboard, on the left-hand side.) Turn the fuses between the contact springs until the metal fuse strips are visible. In a burned-out (blown) fuse, the metal strip is separated.

Remove the burned-out fuse by pressing the upper contact spring away from the fuse—being careful not to deform either contact spring, as they must fit tightly against the new fuse. Carefully install the new fuse so that its metal strip is visible. Then install the fuse box cover.

Replacing Relays

The relays can easily be unplugged or plugged into the relay plate of the fuse box. Because each relay has a different plug pattern, there is no danger of accidentally installing a relay in the wrong location.

12.1 Removing and Installing Wiring Harnesses

The wiring harnesses attach to the bottom of the relay plate in the fuse box. Detach the relay plate and lift it out of the box if it is necessary to disconnect one of the wiring harnesses.

CAUTION ——

Before you begin to work on any part of the electrical system, always disconnect the battery ground strap. Otherwise, there is likely to be damage to the instruments and other electrical components of the car.

Fig. 12-6, Fig. 12-7, Fig. 12-8, and Fig. 12-9 identify the connections of the major wiring harnesses. On cars with fuel injection and on some cars with carburetors manufactured near the end of the 1976 model year, the front left and front right wiring harnesses were changed, as shown in Fig. 12-10.

1. Multiple connector F to relay plate
2. Ground wire for fuel gauge sending unit to body
3. Wire connector to fuel gauge sending unit
4. Ground wire to fuel gauge sending unit
5. Wire connector to left taillight
6. Wire connector to rear window defogger (positive)
7. Ground wire to left taillight
8. Ground wire to body
9. Wire connector to license plate light (positive)
10. Ground wire to license plate light
11. Wire connectors to right taillight

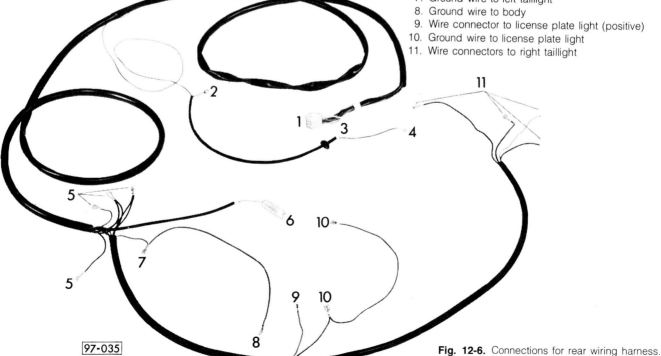

97-035

Fig. 12-6. Connections for rear wiring harness.

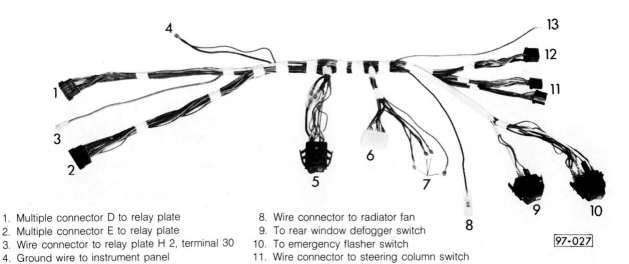

1. Multiple connector D to relay plate
2. Multiple connector E to relay plate
3. Wire connector to relay plate H 2, terminal 30
4. Ground wire to instrument panel
5. To headlight switch
6. Wire connector to instrument cluster
7. Ground wires to instrument panel
8. Wire connector to radiator fan
9. To rear window defogger switch
10. To emergency flasher switch
11. Wire connector to steering column switch
12. Wire connector to steering lock/ignition switch
13. Ground wire to instrument panel

Fig. 12-7. Dashboard wiring harness through 1976. For 1977 and later cars, see Fig. 12-16, given later.

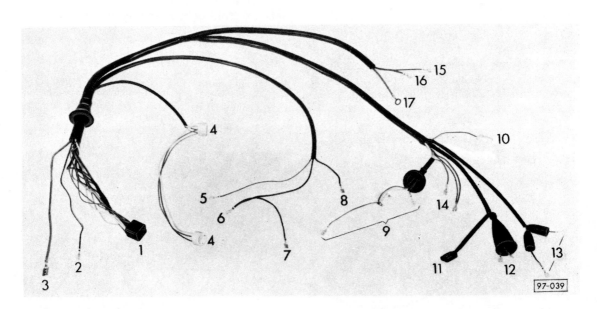

1. Multiple connector A to relay plate
2. Wire connector to relay plate G 1, terminal Z
3. Wire connector to relay plate H 1, terminal 30
4. Multiple connector to brake light switch
5. Wire connector to ignition coil, terminal 1
6. Wire connector to series resistance/ignition coil
7. Wire connector to ignition coil, terminal 15
8. Wire connector to series resistance/ignition coil
9. Wire connectors to left headlight
10. Wire connector to left turn signal
11. Wire connector (double) to radiator fan
12. Wire connector to thermo switch for radiator fan
13. Wire connector to horn
14. Ground wires to body
15. Wire connector to starter, terminal 16
16. Wire connector to starter, terminal 50
17. Eyelet terminal to starter, terminal 30

Fig. 12-8. Front left wiring harness (until late 1976).

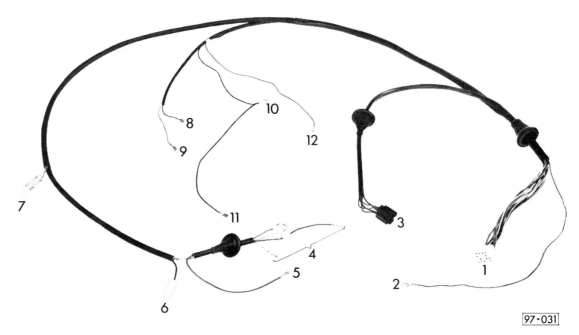

97-031

1. Multiple connector C to relay plate
2. Ground wire to instrument panel
3. Multiple connector to wiper motor
4. Wire connectors to right headlight
5. Ground wire to body
6. Wire connector to right turn signal
7. Wire connector (double) to alternator
8. Wire connector to oil pressure switch
9. Wire connector to temperature gauge sending unit
10. Wire connector (positive) to electromagnetic cutoff valve, terminal 15
11. Wire connector (positive) to automatic choke, terminal 15
12. Ground wire to carburetor housing

Fig. 12-9. Front right wiring harness (until late 1976).

5 ■

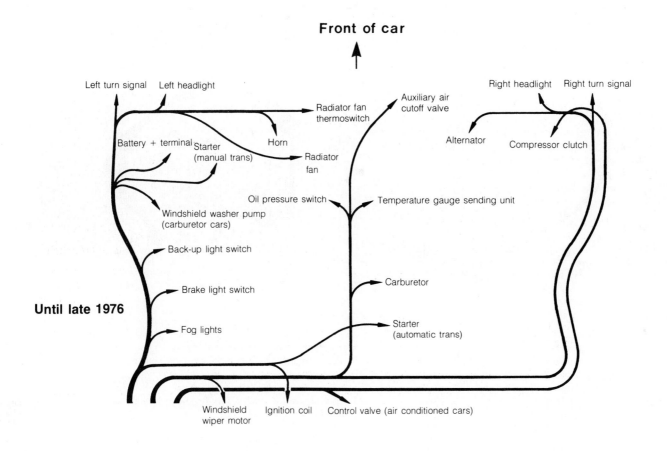

Until late 1976

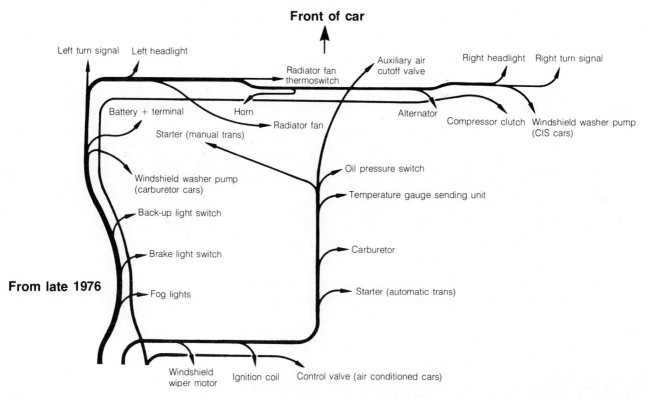

From late 1976

Fig. 12-10. Changes in front wiring harnesses made late in 1976 model year. CIS cars have fuel injection.

In addition to the changes in harness routing that were shown previously in Fig. 12-10, cars manufactured from late 1976 have changed wiring harness connections at the relay plate of the fuse box. These changes are the result of routing the right headlight, the right turn signal, the alternator and, on cars with fuel injection, the windshield washer pump wires through the front left wiring harness rather than through the front right wiring harness as on earlier cars. **Table j** shows the changes in connecting points at the relay plate.

In installing new wiring harnesses, it is important that they be routed correctly. Correct installation of the wiring harnesses will prevent damage to the wiring and will make troubleshooting easier in the event that there are electrical problems in the future. Fig. 12-11 through Fig. 12-15 show the correct installation of the various wiring harnesses at critical points on the car.

Fig. 12-11. Correct routing of left front wiring harness. Attach with clamps (arrows) to body above battery shelf.

Table j. Changed Connections at Fuse Box Relay Plate (introduced late in 1976)

Wire color and source	Relay plate terminal on early cars	Relay plate terminal from late 1976	Remarks
Blue/white wire to alternator B+ terminal	C19	A1	—
Blue wire to alternator D+ terminal	C2	A4	—
Red/black wire to starter terminal 50	A10	C10	—
Transparent/violet wire to coil terminal 15	A12	C15	—
Red/green wire to windshield washer pump (positive)	C17	C17	Three-point multiple connector inserted in harness (near relay plate)
Brown wire to windshield washer pump (negative)	Front left ground connection	Front right ground connection	—
Black/green wire to right front turn signal	C18	C18	—
Gray/red wire to right front parking light	C7	C7	Four-point multiple connector inserted in harness (near relay plate)
Yellow wire to right headlight low beam	C8	C8	
White wire to right headlight high beam	C11	C11	

5

1. Right front harness
2. Left front harness
3. Analysis system harness

Fig. 12-12. Correct routing of wiring harnesses through firewall.

Fig. 12-13. Correct routing for right front wiring harness. Attach body with clamp (arrow) near ignition coil.

Fig. 12-14. Correct routing for rear portion of right front wiring harness. Attach with clamps (arrows) to firewall.

Fig. 12-15. Correct routing for lower portion of right front wiring harness. Attach with clamps (arrows) as shown.

The routing of the dashboard wiring harness is changed beginning with the 1977 models. Fig. 12-16 should be used as a guide for correct installation.

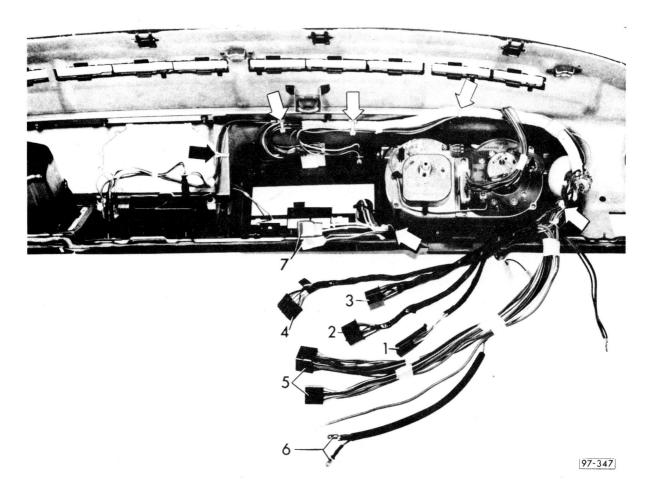

1. To steering column headlight dimmer/
   flasher switch
2. To steering column windshield wiper
   switch
3. To steering column ignition switch

4. To steering column turn signal switch
5. To relay plate, connectors D and E
6. To relay plate, socket J (in place of
   former headlight dimmer relay)
7. To heater fan motor

Fig. 12-16. Routing of dashboard wiring harness introduced on 1977 cars. Retain to dashboard
structure with clips (arrows).

12.2 Wiring Diagrams

The wiring diagrams given on the following pages are
of the current flow type and represent the individual
electrical components of the car schematically. The small
numbers in the wire lines indicate the wire's gauge in
mm². The test connections for the Computer Analysis
system are shown throughout these diagrams. Always
reconnect the test connection wires when servicing the
electrical system.

CAUTION ——

*Never connect any device other than the test
plug of the Computer Analysis system to the
test network socket in the engine compartment. Other test equipment will not guaran-
tee accurate readings and could damage the
socket, the test sensors, or the car components that contain sensors.*

The symbols used in the current flow diagrams are explained in Fig. 12-17. The thin black lines in the current flow diagrams are not actual wires but ground connections via the car's chassis. The thin black lines in the gray band at the top of the diagrams represent internal connection in the fuse box relay plate.

Along the bottom of each current flow diagram is a yellow band containing numbers that will help you find electrical components easily. Appearing after each component listed in the description are numbers in a yellow legend labeled "current track." These numbers indicate the current track in the diagram that contains the part you are looking for.

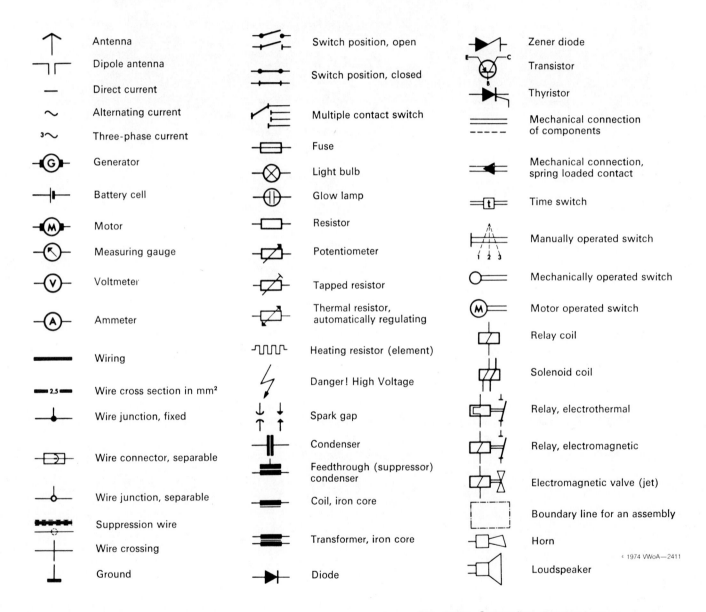

© 1974 VWoA—2411

Fig. 12-17. Current flow diagram symbols.

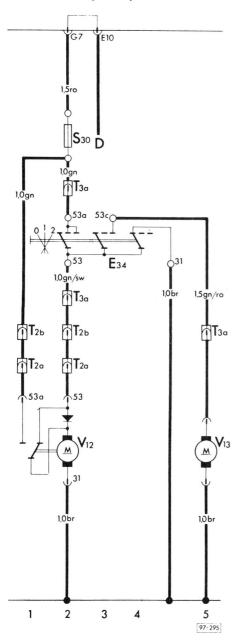

Relay/fuse plate

CAUTION ——

*Do not interchange wires of terminals 53 and
53a on the switch, as this will cause damage
to the diode on the rear window wiper motor.*

Description		Current track
D	– To ignition/starter switch	3
E34	– Rear window wiper switch	1–4
S30	– Single fuse	2
T2a	– Flat connector in rear door	1, 2
T2b	– Flat connector, near left taillight	1, 2
T3a	– Flat connector, near rear window wiper switch	2, 5
V12	– Rear window wiper motor	2
V13	– Rear window washer pump	5

Color code

gn – green
br – brown
ro – red
sw – black

5

1   2   3   4   5

97-295

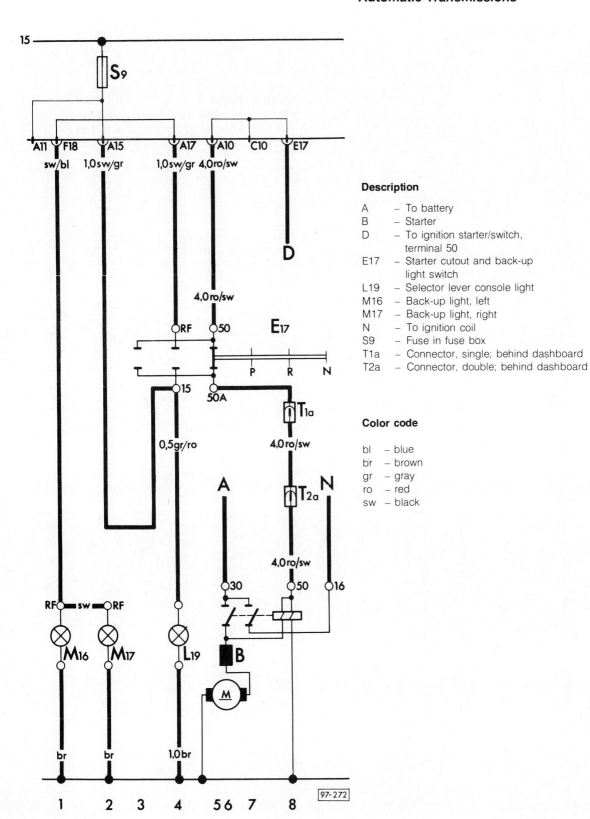

Description		Current track
A	– To battery	6
B	– Starter	6, 7, 8
D	– To ignition starter/switch, terminal 50	8
E17	– Starter cutout and back-up light switch	3, 4, 5
L19	– Selector lever console light	4
M16	– Back-up light, left	1
M17	– Back-up light, right	2
N	– To ignition coil	
S9	– Fuse in fuse box	
T1a	– Connector, single; behind dashboard	
T2a	– Connector, double; behind dashboard	

Color code

bl	– blue
br	– brown
gr	– gray
ro	– red
sw	– black

97-272

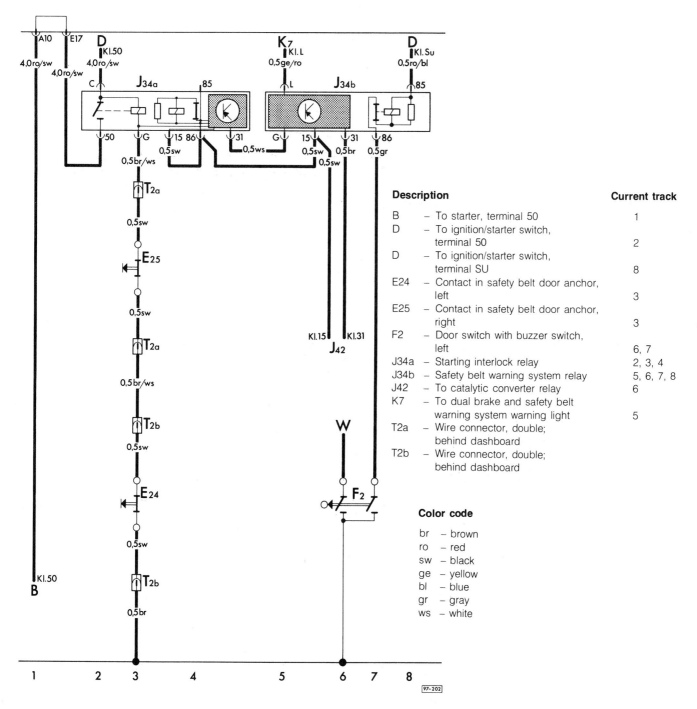

Description | **Current track**

B – To starter, terminal 50 | 1
D – To ignition/starter switch, terminal 50 | 2
D – To ignition/starter switch, terminal SU | 8
E24 – Contact in safety belt door anchor, left | 3
E25 – Contact in safety belt door anchor, right | 3
F2 – Door switch with buzzer switch, left | 6, 7
J34a – Starting interlock relay | 2, 3, 4
J34b – Safety belt warning system relay | 5, 6, 7, 8
J42 – To catalytic converter relay | 6
K7 – To dual brake and safety belt warning system warning light | 5
T2a – Wire connector, double; behind dashboard |
T2b – Wire connector, double; behind dashboard |

Color code

br – brown
ro – red
sw – black
ge – yellow
bl – blue
gr – gray
ws – white

5

97-202

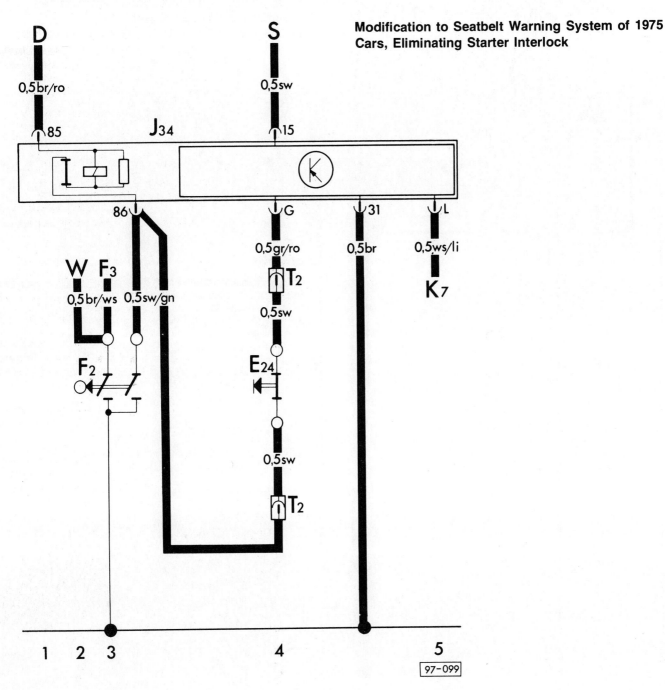

Modification to Seatbelt Warning System of 1975 Cars, Eliminating Starter Interlock

97-099

Description

D	– To ignition/starter switch, terminal SU
E24	– Contact in safety belt lock, right
F2	– Door contact switch for buzzer, left
F3	– Door contact switch, right
J34	– Safety belt warning system relay
K7	– To safety belt warning system and dual brake circuit warning light, terminal L
T2	– Wire connector, double; on frame
W	– Interior light
S	– To fuse box, terminal 15

Color code

br	–	brown
ro	–	red
sw	–	black
gr	–	gray
ws	–	white
gn	–	green
li	–	lilac

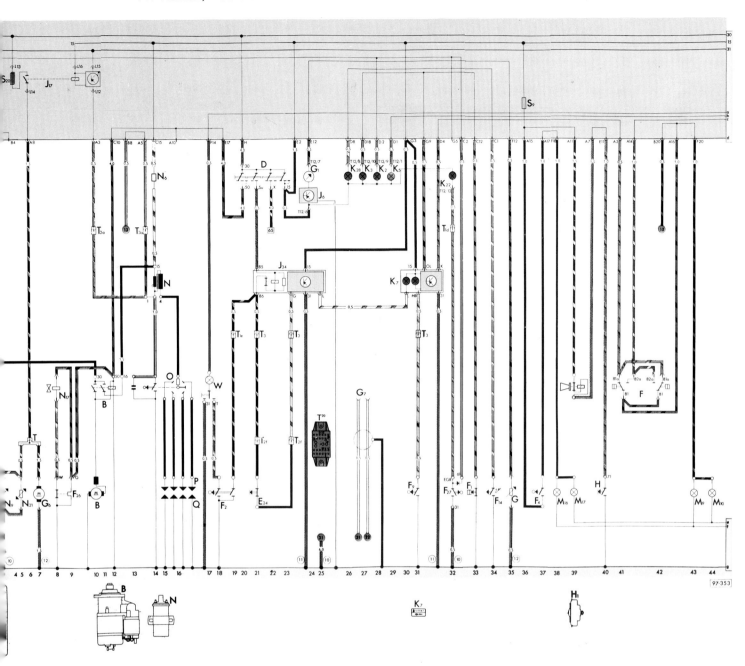

CAUTION ——

Disconnect the battery ground strap
before starting to work on any part of
the electrical system.

NOTE

The gray-colored area in the upper part of the currect flow diagram indicates the relay plate with fuse box.

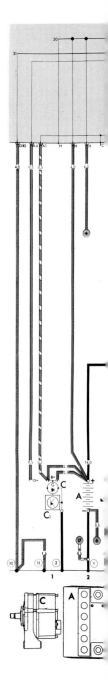

Description	Current track
A – Battery	2
B – Starter	10–12
C – Alternator	1
C 1 – Regulator	1
D – Ignition/starter switch	20–23
E 24 – Safety belt lock, left, with contact	21
F – Brake light switch	41,42
F 1 – Engine oil pressure switch	33
F 2 – Door contact switch, left	18
F 4 – Back-up light switch	37
F 9 – Parking brake warning light switch	31
F 14 – Coolant temperature warning light switch	34
F 26 – Thermo-time switch for cold-start device	8, 9
F 27 – Elapsed EGR mileage switch	32
G – Fuel gauge sending unit	35
G 1 – Fuel gauge	24
G 6 – Electrical fuel pump	7
H – Horn button	40
H 1 – Horn	39
J 6 – Voltage stabilizer	24
J 17 – Electrical fuel pump relay	6, 10
J 34 – Safety belt warning system relay	21–25
K 2 – Alternator charging warning light	28
K 3 – Engine oil pressure warning light	27
K 5 – Turn signal warning light	29
K 7 – Dual circuit brake, parking brake, and safety belt warning light	30, 31
K 22 – EGR warning light	32
K 28 – Coolant temperature warning light	26
M 9 – Brake light, left	43
M 10 – Brake light, right	44
M 16 – Back-up light, left	38
M 17 – Back-up light, right	39
N – Ignition coil	14
N 6 – Ballast resistor wire	14
N 9 – Control pressure regulator	3
N 17 – Cold start valve	8
N 21 – Auxiliary air regulator	5
O – Ignition distributor	15, 16
P – Spark plug connectors	15, 16
Q – Spark plugs	15, 16
S 9 – Fuse in fuse box	
S 20 – Fuse for electrical fuel pump (16-amp) on relay J 17	
T – Wire connector, single; in engine compartment	
T 1d – Wire connector, single; behind dashboard	
T 1e – Wire connector, single; next to relay board	
T 2f – Wire connector, double; on frame, left	
T 3 – Wire connector, 3-point; behind dashboard	
T 3a – Wire connector, 3-point; behind dashboard	
T 12 – Wire connector, 12-point (Canada 10-point) on dashboard cluster	
T 20 – Analysis system, analysis socket	25
W – Interior light	17,18

① – Ground strap, battery/body/engine

② – Ground strap, generator/engine

⑩ – Ground strap, steering column support

⑪ – Ground strap, next to instrument panel cluster

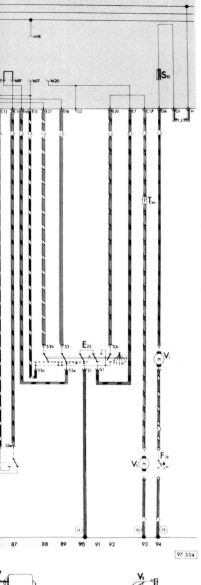

Description	Current track
E 1 – Light switch	66–69
E 2 – Turn signal switch	50
E 3 – Emergency flasher switch	46–53
E 4 – Headlight dimmer switch	63, 64
E 9 – Fresh air fan switch	81, 82
E 15 – Rear window defogger switch	84, 85
E 20 – Instrument panel lighting switch	69
E 22 – Windshield wash/wipe intermittent switch	88–92
F 18 – Radiator cooling fan thermo switch	94
J 2 – Emergency flasher relay	48–50
J 9 – Rear window defogger relay	83
K 1 – Headlight high beam warning light	62
K 6 – Emergency flasher warning light	52, 53
K 10 – Rear window defogger warning light	85
L 1 – Sealed beam unit, left	58, 60
L 2 – Sealed beam unit, right	59, 61
L 10 – Instrument panel light	52
L 16 – Fresh air operation lever light	68
L 25 – Ashtray light (custom model only)	67
L 28 – Cigarette lighter light (custom model only)	66
M 1 – Parking light, left	74
M 2 – Taillight, right	79
M 3 – Parking light, right	77
M 4 – Taillight, left	76
M 5 – Turn signal, front left	54
M 6 – Turn signal, rear left	55
M 7 – Turn signal, front right	56
M 8 – Turn signal, rear right	57
M 11 – Side marker lights, front	73, 78
M 12 – Side marker lights, rear	75, 80
N 23 – Ballast resistor for fresh air blower	81
S 1, S 2, S 3, S 4, S 5, S 6, S 7, S 8, S 10, S 11, S 12, S 13, S 14, S 15 } Fuses in fuse box	
T 1a – Wire connector, single; behind dashboard	
T 1c – Wire connector, single; behind dashboard	
T 1e – Wire connector, single; in luggage compartment, left	
T 1g – Wire connector, single; behind dashboard	
T 1i – Wire connector, single; in engine compartment, left	
T 1k – Wire connector, single; in engine compartment, right	
T 1m – Wire connector, single; in luggage compartment, right	
T 1n – Wire connector, single; in luggage compartment, left	
T 2c – Wire connector, double; in engine compartment, left	
T 2d – Wire connector, double; behind dashboard	
T 2e – Wire connector, double; behind dashboard	
T 3a – Wire connector, 3-point; behind dashboard	
T 4 – Wire connector, 4-point; behind dashboard	
T 12 – Wire connector, 12-point (Canada 10-point); on instrument panel cluster	
U 1 – Cigarette lighter	45
V – Windshield wiper motor	86
V 2 – Fresh air fan	82
V 5 – Windshield washer pump	93
V 7 – Radiator cooling fan	94
X – License plate light	71, 72
Z 1 – Rear window defogger element	83
⑩ – Ground strap, dashboard	
⑪ – Ground strap, next to instrument panel cluster	
⑮ – Ground strap, engine compartment; left	
⑯ – Ground strap, engine compartment; right	

NOTE ———

The gray-colored area in the upper part of the current flow diagram indicates the relay plate with fuse box.

Description

		Current track
A	– Battery	2
B	– Starter	10, 11
C	– Alternator	1
C 1	– Regulator	1
D	– Ignition/starter switch	16–19
E 24	– Safety belt lock switch, left	34
F	– Brake light switch	48, 49
F 1	– Engine oil pressure switch	27
F 2	– Door contact switch for buzzer alarm, left	32
F 3	– Door contact switch, right	31
F 4	– Back-up light switch	45
F 9	– Parking brake control light switch	39
F 26	– Thermo-time switch for cold-start device	8
F 27	– Elapsed EGR mileage switch (not for CANADA)	26
G	– Fuel gauge sending unit	29
G 1	– Fuel gauge	21
G 2	– Coolant temperature sending unit	28
G 3	– Coolant temperature gauge	22
G 5	– Tachometer	24
G 6	– Electric fuel pump	7
G 7	– to TDC sensor	19–21
G 10	– Oil pressure switch	36
G 11	– Oil pressure gauge	36
H	– Horn button	43
H 1	– Dual horn	40, 41
J 4	– Relay for dual horn	42, 43
J 6	– Voltage stabilizer	21
J 7	– Electric fuel pump relay	6, 11
J 34	– Safety belt warning relay	34, 35
K 2	– Alternator charging warning light	24
K 3	– Engine oil pressure warning light	23
K 5	– Turn signal warning light	25
K 7	– Dual circuit brake, parking brake, and safety belt warning light	37–39
K 22	– EGR warning light	26
M 9	– Brake light, left	50
M 10	– Brake light, right	51
M 16	– Back-up light, left	46
M 17	– Back-up light, right	47
N	– Ignition coil	13, 14
N 6	– Ballast resistor	13
N 9	– Warm-up regulator	3
N 17	– Cold-start regulator	8
N 21	– Auxiliary air regulator	5
O	– Ignition distributor	14, 15
P	– Spark plug connector	14, 15
Q	– Spark plugs	14, 15
S 9	– Fuse on fuse/relay panel	S
S 20	– Fuse for electric fuel pump (16-amp) from relay J 17	
T	– Wire connector; in engine compartment	
T 1c	– Wire connector, single; behind dashboard	
T 1h	– Wire connector, single; behind dashboard	
T 1i	– Wire connector, single; behind dashboard	
T 1j	– Wire connector, single; behind dashboard	
T 1l	– Wire connector, single; behind dashboard	
T 1r	– Wire connector, single; behind dashboard	
T 2a	– Wire connector, double; in engine compartment, front	
T 2b	– Wire connector, double; on frame, left	
T 3	– Wire connector, 3-point; behind dashboard	
T 3a	– Wire connector, 3-point; behind dashboard	
T 12	– Wire connector, 12-point; dashboard cluster	
T 20	– Analysis socket	
W	– Interior light	30

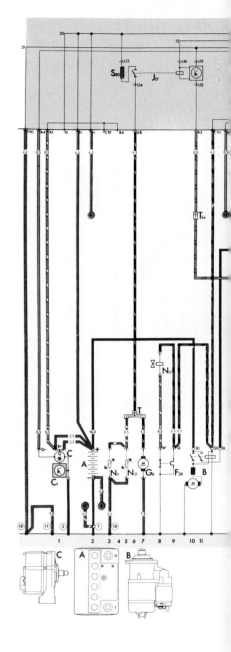

① – Ground strap, battery to body
② – Ground strap, alternator to engine
⑩ – Ground connector on steering colu[mn]
⑪ – Ground connector next to instrume[nt]

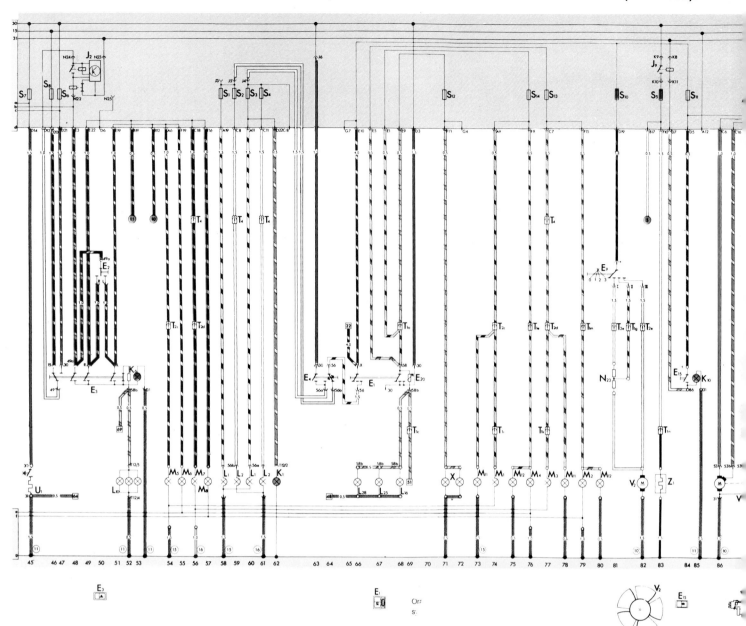

Computer Analysis System——

The orange-colored spots are connections in
the Computer Analysis System that are wired
to Socket T 20. The numbers in these spots
correspond to terminals in the Computer
Analysis socket.

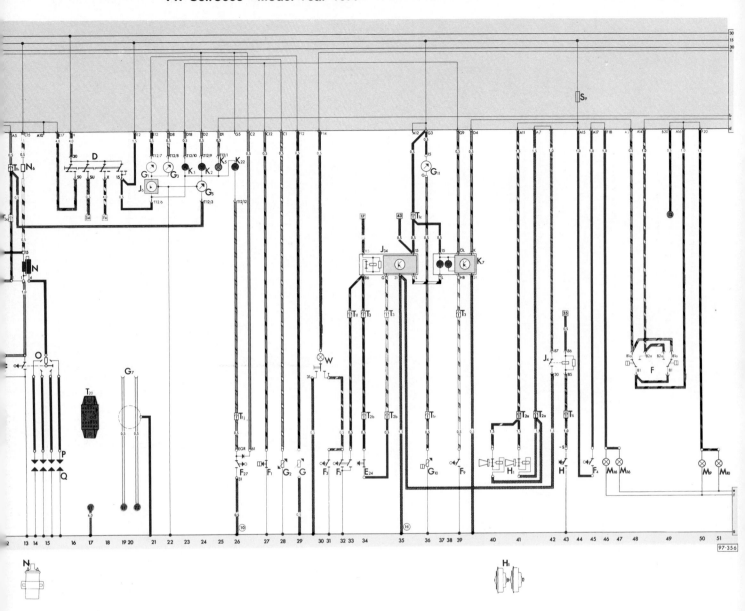

97-356

mn

nt cluster

CAUTION ——

Disconnect the battery ground strap
before starting to work on any part of
the electrical system.

MANUAL TRANSMISSION

Contents

6

TABLES

Manual Transmission

The four-speed manual transmission, standard equipment on the cars covered by this Manual, is fully synchronized in all forward gears. Both the transmission and the final drive are housed in a two-piece light alloy case. Taken as a unit, the transmission, final drive, and case are called the transaxle.

The transaxle with four-speed manual transmission operates on entirely different principles from those of the optional transaxle with automatic transmission. However, the constant velocity joint repairs described in this section of the Manual apply to both the standard and the optional transaxles. See **AUTOMATIC TRANSMISSION** for all other repairs related to the transaxle with automatic transmission.

Because of the transverse engine position, the transfer of power from the transmission gear train to the differential is by spur gears, rather than by bevel gears—the kind of gears used in other Volkswagen transaxles. The transaxle is also unique in that the mainshaft is hollow. Through its center passes the clutch pushrod. Information concerning the clutch release bearing and the pushrod is given in this section, whereas all other clutch troubleshooting, servicing, and repair procedures are given in **ENGINE AND CLUTCH.**

6 ■

The transaxle can be removed and installed without removing the engine. The engine, however, cannot be removed without also removing the transaxle. You can remove the engine and the transaxle as a unit, using the procedure given in **ENGINE AND CLUTCH,** or you can remove the transaxle first, using the procedure given in this section of the Manual. Removing the transaxle first will give you more room for hoisting the engine out of the car.

Though the home mechanic often lacks the tools and experience necessary to repair his car's transaxle, he may be perfectly capable of removing and installing it. If so, he should deliver the transaxle to an Authorized Dealer or other qualified repair shop after giving the case a thorough exterior cleaning but without doing any disassembly work. A partially disassembled transmission in a box or a basket is a mechanic's nightmare, so the car owner is not likely to be greeted with sympathy after trying a job that is over his head and then giving up.

Cleanliness and a careful approach are imperative when repairing either the transmission or the final drive. If necessary, mark the parts to show their proper assembly order. Also make sure that you have the necessary tools—particularly for procedures given only with metric specifications. Work that is designated by the lack of U.S. equivalents can be carried out correctly only with metric tools and instruments.

1. GENERAL DESCRIPTION

The gears on the mainshaft and on the drive pinion shaft are called the transmission gear train. The drive pinion, the ring gear, and the differential gears—all of which carry driving torque from the transmission gear train to the front wheel driveshafts—are called the final drive. Throughout this section of the manual, we will use the term *transmission gear train* when we are speaking of the gears that are used to select the four forward speeds and reverse. The term *final drive* will be used for the gears that drive the front axle driveshafts. The term *transaxle* will be used to designate the transmission gear train, the final drive gears, and the transaxle case when these three main components are handled as a unit.

Transaxle Case

The transaxle case, which contains the transmission gear train and the final drive gears, is die cast in magnesium alloy. There is no partition between the transmission gear train and the final drive, both of which are lubricated by the hypoid gear oil in the transaxle case. The flywheel bellhousing is integral with the transaxle case. All repairs related to the flywheel and the clutch are covered in **ENGINE AND CLUTCH.**

The drive flanges that carry driving torque to the front wheels extend from two openings at either side of the final drive part of the transaxle case. There is no removable cover for the differential, so the transaxle case must be taken apart for access to the final drive gears.

Transmission Gear Train

Fig. 1-1 is a cross section of the transaxle with manual transmission. The transmission gears are of the constant-mesh type with balk ring synchronizers. The 3rd and 4th gear synchronizers are on the mainshaft; the 1st and 2nd gear synchronizers are on the pinion shaft. The reverse sliding gear (idler gear) is at the bellhousing end of the transaxle case where it can be moved into engagement with the teeth on the outer surface of the 1st gear/2nd gear clutch gear assembly.

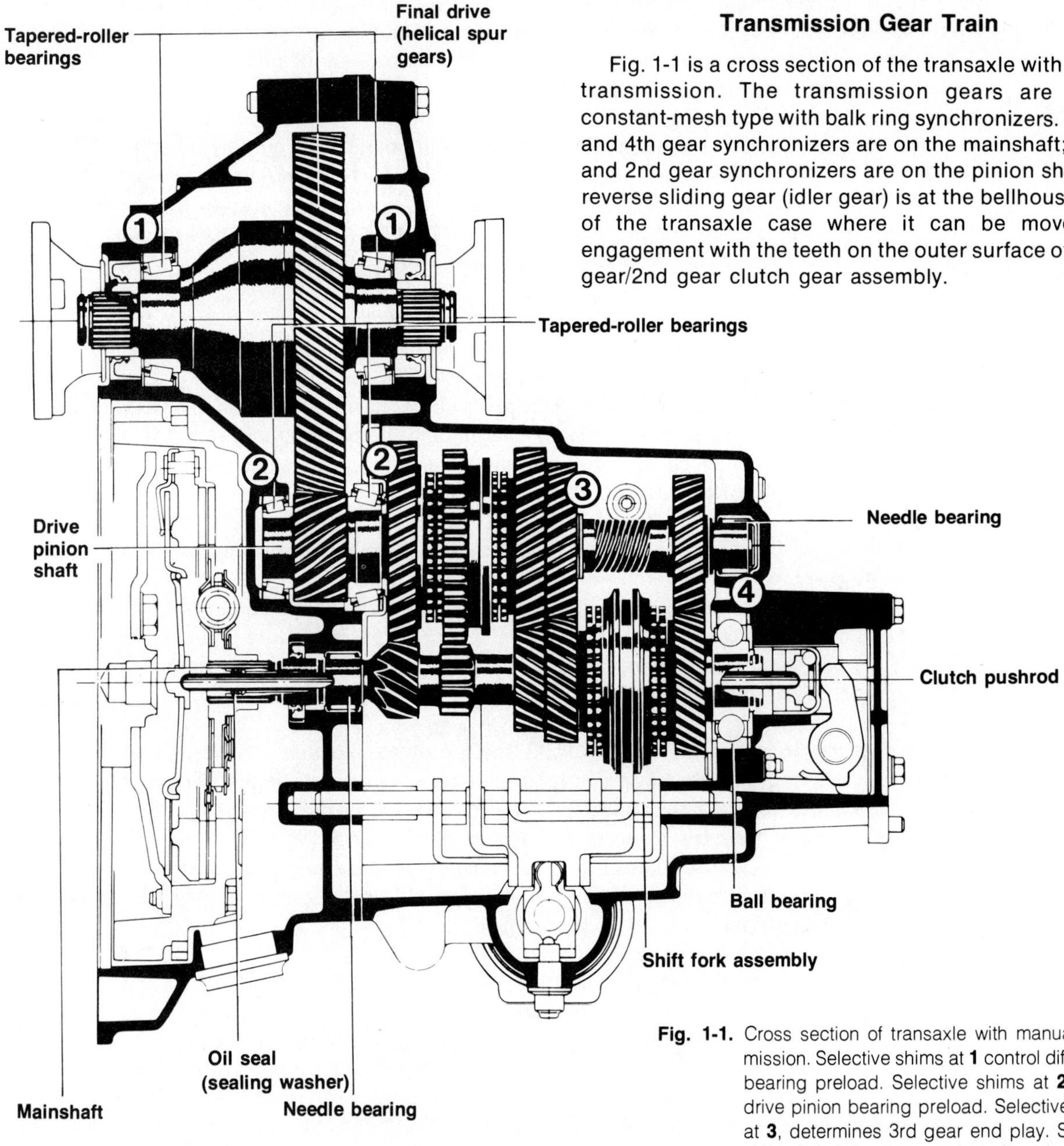

Fig. 1-1. Cross section of transaxle with manual transmission. Selective shims at **1** control differential bearing preload. Selective shims at **2** control drive pinion bearing preload. Selective circlip, at **3**, determines 3rd gear end play. Selective shim at **4** determines mainshaft end play.

Final Drive Gears

The ring and pinion gearset consists of two spur gears. One, the ring gear, is mounted on the differential housing; the other is an integral part of the drive pinion shaft. The teeth on the ring and pinion spur gears are helical-cut for silent running. The differential gearset, which consists of the two differential sidegears and the two differential pinions, allows the front wheels to turn at different speeds, as is necessary when making turns (the outside wheel must travel farther than the inside wheel in the same amount of time).

Driveshafts and Constant Velocity Joints

The front wheels are driven by the driveshafts, which have a constant velocity joint at each end. The repairs described in this section also apply to the driveshafts and constant velocity joints used with the optional transaxle with automatic transmission.

2. MAINTENANCE

Only two items, checking the constant velocity joint screws and boots, and checking and correcting the transaxle oil level, are required at a prescribed mileage. These jobs are described in **LUBRICATION AND MAINTENANCE.**

3. GEARSHIFT LEVER AND SHIFT LINKAGE

All 1975 cars have the same kind of gearshift lever. However, late 1975 cars have a completely different shift linkage from that used on early 1975 cars. On 1976 and later models, both the gearshift lever and the shift linkage are completely different from the lever and the linkages used on 1975 cars. Each kind of lever and linkage is covered separately under the following headings.

3.1 Removing, Adjusting, and Installing 1975 Gearshift Lever and Shift Linkage

Fig. 3-1 is an exploded view of the 1975 gearshift lever and related parts. For styling reasons, a different boot is used on some models.

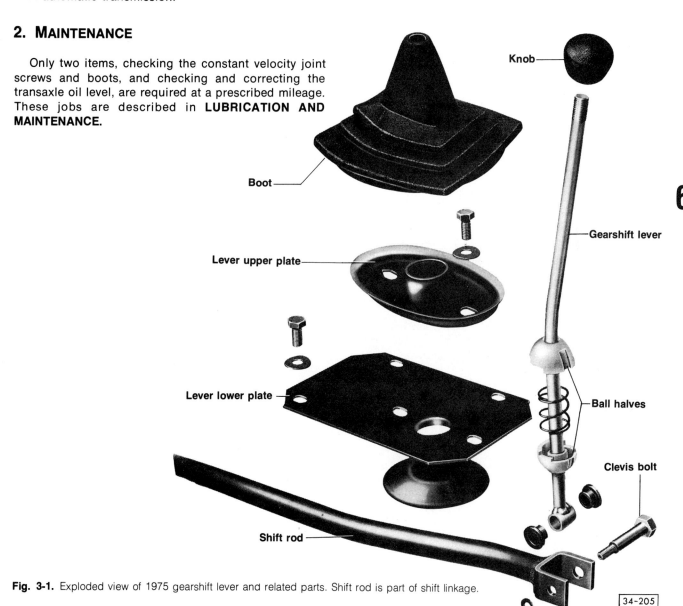

Fig. 3-1. Exploded view of 1975 gearshift lever and related parts. Shift rod is part of shift linkage.

34-205

To remove 1975 gearshift lever:

1. Unscrew the shift knob. Remove the boot by detaching it at the bottom and then pulling it upward off the gearshift lever.

2. Working beneath the car, remove the nut and the washer from the clevis bolt. Then withdraw the clevis bolt from the yoke on the shift rod and from the bushings in the eye of the gearshift lever.

3. Working in the passenger compartment, remove the two bolts and two washers that hold the lever upper plate to the lever lower plate and the car body. Remove the lever upper plate, then remove the gearshift lever.

   NOTE ——

   It is not necessary to remove the lever lower plate from the car body. The lever lower plate should not be removed unless absolutely necessary.

To install and adjust 1975 gearshift lever:

1. If you have removed the nylon ball halves and the coil spring from the gearshift lever, install them as shown earlier in Fig. 3-1. Make certain that the notches in the ball halves are toward the rear and that the lugs of the upper ball half engage the cutouts in the lower ball half.

2. Using molybdenum grease, lubricate the ball halves and the surfaces that the ball halves will contact. Then install the gearshift lever through the lever lower plate.

3. Install the lever upper plate so that the bolt hole with the arrow-like pointed slot is toward the front of the car. Press the plate down, making sure that the ball halves are correctly engaged. Then install the bolts and washers—finger-tight.

4. Check the fit of the clevis bolt in the bushings that are in the gearshift lever eye. Replace the bushings if there is play. Then coat the clevis bolt with

multipurpose grease and install the bolt and its nut to a torque of 2.0 mkg (14 ft. lb.).

5. Working inside the passenger compartment, slide the lever upper plate back and forth on its elongated bolt holes until the lower part of the lever is vertical, as indicated in Fig. 3-2. Then torque the bolts to 2.0 mkg (14 ft. lb.).

6. Install the boot. Install the shift knob. Check that all gears engage smoothly, easily, and fully. If they do not, adjust the shift linkage as described under the following heading.

Fig. 3-2. Gearshift lever being adjusted. Lower part of lever should be vertical, as indicated by white line.

Disassembling, Assembling, and Adjusting 1975 Shift Linkage

Fig. 3-3 is an exploded view of the shift linkage used on early 1975 cars. Beginning with Rabbit Chassis No. 175 3108 888 and Scirocco Chassis No. 535 2020 020, the 1975 models have a different shift linkage, which is shown in Fig. 3-4. If all of the late-type parts are used, the late 1975 shift linkage can be service-installed on early 1975 cars. Components of the earlier linkage, however, remain available as replacement parts.

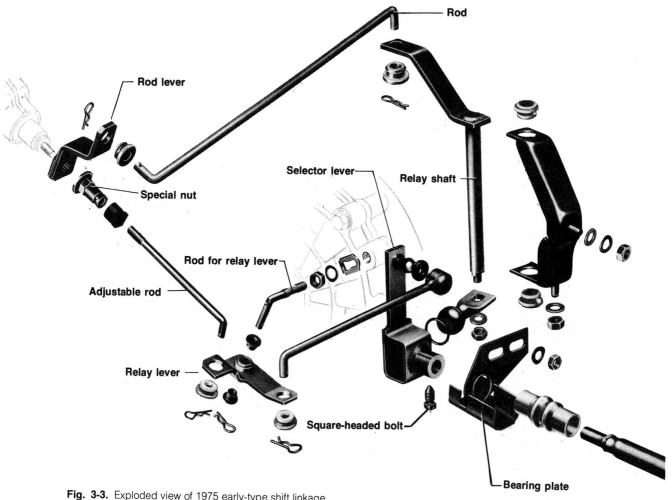

Fig. 3-3. Exploded view of 1975 early-type shift linkage. During assembly, torque the special nut to 1.5 mkg (11 ft. lb.).

34-210

6

Fig. 3-4. Exploded view of 1975 late-type shift linkage. Arrow indicates notch on end of rod that goes in rod lever.

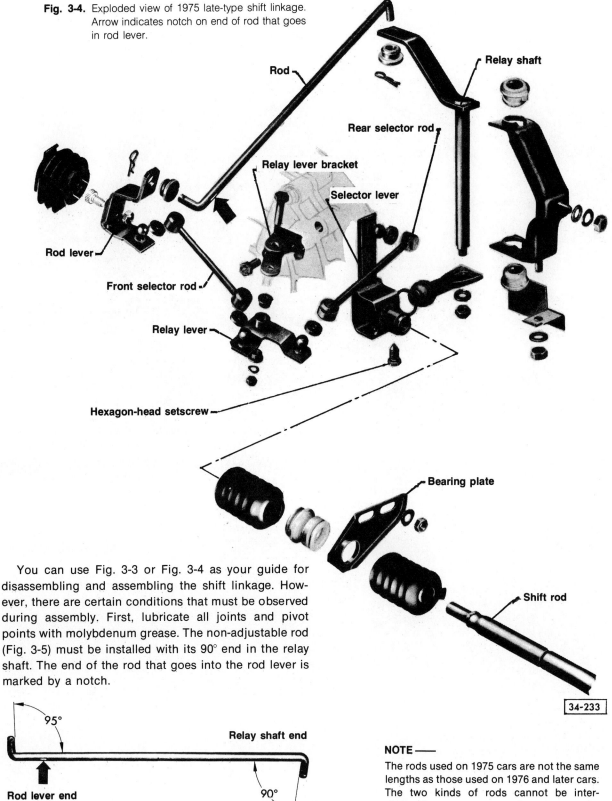

Rod

Relay shaft

Rear selector rod

Relay lever bracket

Selector lever

Rod lever

Front selector rod

Relay lever

Hexagon-head setscrew

Bearing plate

Shift rod

34-233

You can use Fig. 3-3 or Fig. 3-4 as your guide for disassembling and assembling the shift linkage. However, there are certain conditions that must be observed during assembly. First, lubricate all joints and pivot points with molybdenum grease. The non-adjustable rod (Fig. 3-5) must be installed with its 90° end in the relay shaft. The end of the rod that goes into the rod lever is marked by a notch.

95°

Relay shaft end

Rod lever end

90°

34-168

Fig. 3-5. Non-adjustable rod installation. Arrow indicates notch that identifies end of rod connected to rod lever on transaxle.

NOTE ——

The rods used on 1975 cars are not the same lengths as those used on 1976 and later cars. The two kinds of rods cannot be interchanged.

On early 1975 linkages, the shift rod (which connects the linkage to the gearshift lever) is secured in the selector lever by an M 8 square-head setscrew. These square-head setscrews can be reused but should always be locked in position with wire, as originally installed. The late 1975 linkage has a setscrew with a hexagon head, as indicated in Fig. 3-6. This kind of screw should be used only once and replaced by a new setscrew whenever it is removed. Alternatively, you can reinstall the original screw after thoroughly cleaning the threads and applying Loctite®. The new-type setscrew, which is removed and installed with a 10-mm wrench, can replace the early-type setscrew without other modification to the linkage. Torque either kind of setscrew to 1.5 mkg (11 ft. lb.) during installation.

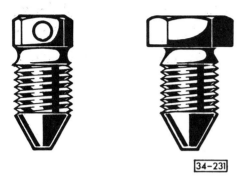

Fig. 3-6. Early-type square-head and late-type hexagon-head setscrews. Square-head setscrew is locked in place by wire; hexagon-head setscrew is locked by a factory-applied adhesive on its threads.

There are two adjustments on the 1975 early-type shift linkage that the 1975 late-type shift linkage does not have. On 1975 early-type linkages, the adjustable rod must be turned in the threaded part of the special nut until dimension **b**, given in Fig. 3-7, is correct. Torque the special nut to 1.5 mkg (11 ft. lb.) on the transaxle's selector shaft before you adjust the adjustable rod.

Fig. 3-7. Adjustable rod of 1975 early-type linkage being adjusted. Dimension **b** should be 163 to 165 mm (6 7/16 to 6½ in.).

The second linkage adjustment required on cars with the 1975 early-type linkage is adjusting the rod for the relay lever. Before installing the relay lever on the rod for the relay lever, loosen the locknut on the rod. Then adjust the rod for the relay lever to dimension **a**, as indicated in Fig. 3-8.

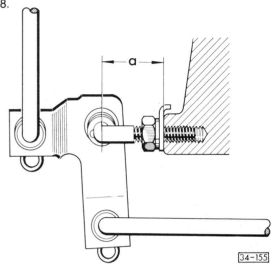

Fig. 3-8. Rod for relay lever of 1975 early-type linkage being adjusted. Dimension **a** should be 30 to 32 mm (1 3/16 to 1¼ in.).

The bearing plate requires adjustment both on cars with the 1975 early-type linkage and on cars with the 1975 late-type linkage. To adjust, engage first gear. Then move the bearing plate on its elongated bolt holes until the gearshift lever is vertical. Lock the plate in this position by torquing the nuts to 2.0 mkg (14 ft. lb.).

6

NOTE ——

The gearshift lever must have been adjusted as described earlier and, on cars with the 1975 early-type linkage, the adjustable rod and the rod for the relay lever must previously have been adjusted.

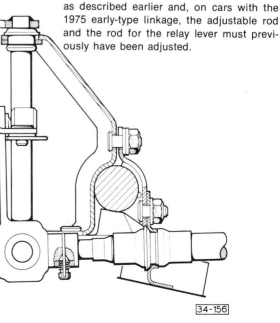

3.2 Removing, Adjusting, and Installing 1976 and Later Gearshift Lever and Shift Linkage

Fig. 3-9 is an exploded view of the gearshift lever and related parts that are used on 1976 and later cars. For styling reasons, a different boot is used on some models.

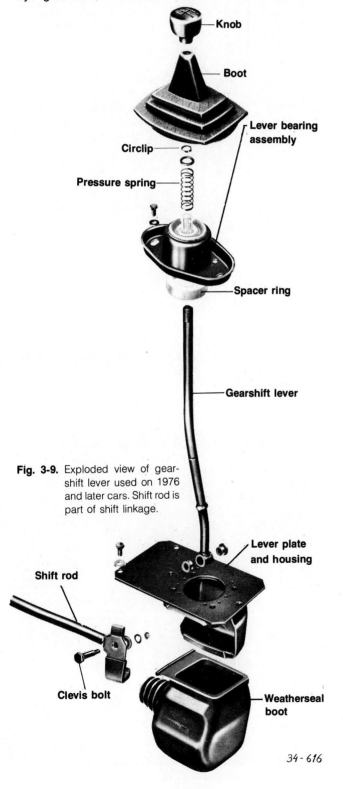

Fig. 3-9. Exploded view of gearshift lever used on 1976 and later cars. Shift rod is part of shift linkage.

34-616

To remove 1976 and later gearshift lever:

1. Unscrew the shift knob. Remove the boot by detaching it at the bottom and then pulling it upward off the gearshift lever.

2. Working beneath the car, detach the weatherseal boot from the bottom of the lever plate and housing. Then slide the weatherseal boot forward on the shift rod.

   NOTE ——
   It may be necessary to loosen screws in the lever plate and housing in order to free the weatherseal boot.

3. Remove the nut and the washer from the clevis bolt. Then withdraw the clevis bolt from the yoke on the shift rod and from the bushings in the eye of the gearshift lever.

4. Working in the passenger compartment, remove the two bolts and two washers that hold the lever bearing assembly to the lever plate and housing. Remove the gearshift lever and lever bearing assembly as a unit.

5. Though individual replacement parts are not available, the lever bearing can, if necessary, be disassembled for cleaning and lubrication. To disassemble the bearing, remove the circlip, the washer, and the pressure spring from the gearshift lever. Then pull the lever bearing assembly off the lever and separate the bearing into its individual components.

To install 1976 and later gearshift lever:

1. If you have not disassembled the lever bearing assembly, begin with step 5 of this procedure; if you have disassembled the lever bearing assembly, wash the parts in a low-volatility petroleum-based solvent and thoroughly dry them. Coat all surfaces of the bearing parts with molybdenum grease.

2. Place the bearing shells inside the rubber guide. Then press the lower ball half into the shells. The shoulder on the rubber guide should be uppermost (Fig. 3-10).

3. Insert the spring and the upper ball half by pushing the shells apart—slightly expanding the rubber guide. With the ball joint thus assembled, push the rubber guide and ball joint as a unit into the lever bearing plate.

4. Slide the lever bearing assembly onto the gearshift lever. Then install the pressure spring, the washer, and the circlip.

5. Using both bolts and washers, loosely install the gearshift lever on the lever plate housing.

6. To adjust the gearshift lever, move the lever bearing assembly on its elongated bolt holes until the

round holes indicated in Fig. 3-11 are perfectly aligned with the corresponding round holes in the lever plate and housing.

NOTE ——

If, after you have aligned the round holes, the bolts are not centered in the elongated holes, remove the bolts and turn the lever bearing assembly 180°. Then reinstall the bolts and adjust the lever.

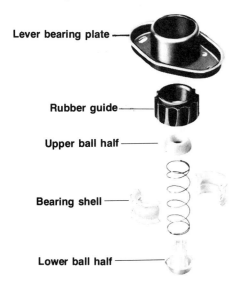

Lever bearing plate

Rubber guide

Upper ball half

Bearing shell

Lower ball half

Fig. 3-10. Exploded view of lever bearing assembly.

Fig. 3-11. Gearshift lever being adjusted. The round holes indicated by arrows **A** must be aligned with corresponding round holes in the lever plate and housing. Bolts should be centered in elongated holes (arrow **B**).

7. Check the fit of the clevis bolt in the bushings that are in the gearshift lever eye. Replace the bushings if there is play. Then coat the clevis bolt with multipurpose grease and install the bolt and its nut to a torque of 2.0 mkg (14 ft. lb.).

8. Unless you have removed and installed parts of the shift linkage and need to make adjustments, reinstall the weatherseal boot. Otherwise, leave off the weatherseal boot until you have adjusted the shift rod.

9. Working inside the passenger compartment, install the boot and the shift knob. Check that all gears engage smoothly, easily, and fully. If they do not, adjust the shift linkage as described under the following heading.

6

Disassembling, Assembling, and Adjusting 1976 and Later Shift Linkage

Fig. 3-12 is an exploded view of the shift linkage used on 1976 and later cars. This linkage cannot be installed on earlier cars. The procedure for engaging reverse is different and the new linkage must be used in conjunction with the changed transaxle components introduced on the 1976 models.

You can use Fig. 3-12 as your guide for disassembling and assembling the shift linkage. In removing the front selector rod or the rear selector rod, use a screwdriver to press back the clips on the plastic rod ends before you attempt to detach the rod ends from the ball pins of the levers.

Several things must be carefully observed during assembly of the shift linkage. First, lubricate all joints and pivot points with molybdenum grease. The rod, shown in Fig. 3-13, which connects the relay shaft with the rod

lever, must be installed with its 90° end in the relay shaft. The end of the rod that goes into the rod lever is marked by a notch.

NOTE—

The rods used on 1975 cars are not the same length as those used on 1976 and later cars. The two kinds of rods cannot be interchanged.

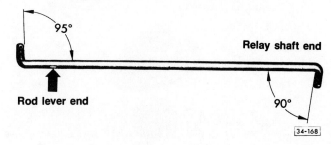

Fig. 3-13. Rod installation. Arrow indicates notch that identifies end of rod connected to rod lever on transaxle.

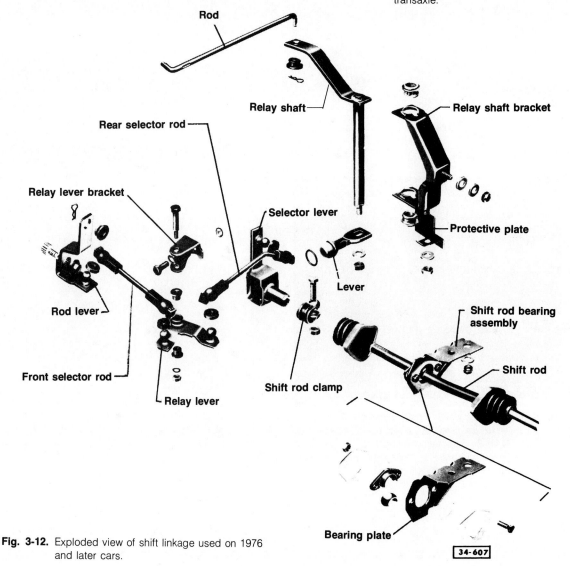

Fig. 3-12. Exploded view of shift linkage used on 1976 and later cars.

No adjustment to the linkage is necessary other than shift rod adjustments. Before you begin adjusting the shift rod, correctly adjust the gearshift lever's lever bearing assembly position—as described earlier in the procedure for installing the gearshift lever. If not previously loosened, loosen the shift rod clamp that is indicated in Fig. 3-14. Also, the weatherseal boot must be detached from the bottom of the gearshift lever's lever plate and housing, and then pushed forward on the shift rod. If necessary, consult Fig. 3-9 given earlier.

NOTE————

It may be necessary to loosen screws in the lever plate and housing in order to free the weatherseal boot.

Fig. 3-14. Shift rod clamp. To loosen clamp, loosen nut indicated by arrow.

Make sure that the transmission is in neutral. Then slide the shift rod backward and forward in its clamp until dimension **x,** indicated in Fig. 3-15, is equal at the front and rear edges of the stop on the shift rod. Lock the shift rod in this position by torquing the nut for the shift rod clamp to 2.0 mkg (14 ft. lb.).

Move the gearshift lever so that the stop finger is as far as possible away from the stop plate surface on the lever plate and housing. (The gearshift lever will be away from the driver's seat, aligned with the gate for 3rd and 4th gears.) In this position, dimension **a,** given in Fig. 3-16, should be 20 mm (just barely over ¾ in.). If dimension **a** is incorrect, loosen the shift rod clamp. Then slightly rotate the shift rod on the selector lever until dimension **a** is correct. Re-torque the nut on the clamp to 2.0 mkg (14 ft. lb.).

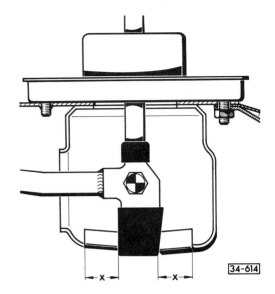

Fig. 3-15. Stop finger correctly positioned (transmission in neutral). Dimension **x** must be the same at both front and rear.

Fig. 3-16. Stop finger position being adjusted. With gearshift lever aligned with gate for 3rd and 4th gears, dimension **a** should be 20 mm (just barely over ¾ in.).

Following the shift rod adjustments, check that all gears engage smoothly, easily, and fully. If necessary, correct the adjustment of the shift rod. When gearshift operation is satisfactory, reinstall the weatherseal boot on the bottom of the lever plate and housing.

6 ■

4. Driveshafts

There are no differences between the driveshafts for cars with manual transmissions and the driveshafts for cars with automatic transmissions. The driveshaft used on the right-hand side is a solid steel shaft whereas the driveshaft for the left-hand side is tubular. In addition, the two kinds of driveshafts are of different lengths, as indicated in Fig. 4-1.

4.1 Removing and Installing Driveshaft

Because the inboard constant velocity joints are different from the outboard constant velocity joints, the procedure for disconnecting the driveshaft inner ends differs from the procedure for disconnecting the driveshaft outer ends. To avoid difficulty, follow the sequence given here.

To remove:

1. Pry off the dust cap that is pressed into the center of the front wheel hub. Then loosen, but do not remove, the axle shaft nut.

> **WARNING ——**
>
> *Loosen axle shaft nuts with the car on the ground. The leverage needed for this job is enough to topple a car off the lift.*

2. Raise the car on a hoist.

3. Remove the six socket-head bolts that hold the inboard constant velocity joint to the transaxle's drive flange.

4. Lower the inboard end of the driveshaft. Pull the axle shaft out of the wheel hub and remove the driveshaft from the car.

To install:

1. Inspect the boots. If they are torn or otherwise damaged, replace them. If the constant velocity joints are difficult to move by hand, or feel gritty, remove and disassemble the joints so that they can be inspected and, if necessary, replaced or cleaned and lubricated. See **4.2 Removing and Installing Constant Velocity Joints.**

2. Insert the shaft in the wheel hub. Raise the inboard end of the driveshaft and install the constant velocity joint on the flanged shaft. Torque the socket head bolts to 4.5 mkg (32 ft. lb.).

3. Loosely install the axle shaft nut. Then lower the car to the ground.

4. Torque the axle shaft nut to 24 mkg (173 ft. lb.).

> **WARNING ——**
>
> *Torque axle shaft nuts with the car on the ground. The leverage needed for this job is enough to topple a car off the lift.*

4.2 Removing and Installing Constant Velocity Joints

Fig. 4-2 is an exploded view of a driveshaft and its two constant velocity joints. Notice the ridges that are forged into the shaft for the purpose of holding the rubber boots in place.

To remove an outboard constant velocity joint, first cut off the clamp for the rubber boot. Then turn the boot inside out over the driveshaft. Clamp the driveshaft in a vise.

Working through the opening indicated at arrow **A** in Fig. 4-3, fully expand the circlip into the groove in the constant velocity joint's ball hub. With the circlip expanded, grasp the axle shaft (arrow **B** in Fig. 4-3) and pull the axle shaft and the constant velocity joint off the driveshaft. If necessary, use a rubber or plastic hammer to drive off the axle shaft and joint.

Fig. 4-1. Driveshaft lengths (dimension **a**). Solid right-hand driveshaft is 658.0 mm (25 $^{29}/_{32}$ in.) long; tubular left-hand driveshaft is 445.5 mm (17 $^{17}/_{32}$ in.) long.

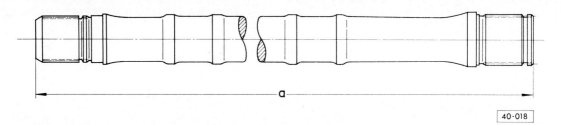

40-018

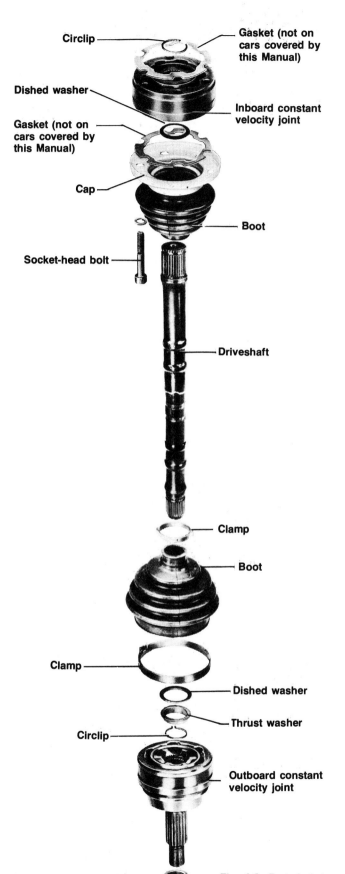

Fig. 4-3. Outboard constant velocity joint removal. Circlip is at arrow **A**; axle shaft is at arrow **B**.

If the rubber boot is torn or otherwise damaged, be sure to replace it before you install the constant velocity joint. When installing a rubber boot, either use a plastic guide sleeve or cover the driveshaft splines with tape in order to protect the boot's sealing surface as you slide the boot onto the driveshaft.

Install the dished washer and the thrust washer on the driveshaft in the positions shown in Fig. 4-4. Install a new circlip in the groove inside the constant velocity joint's ball hub. Using circlip pliers, fully expand the circlip while you start the constant velocity joint on the driveshaft splines. Then, using a rubber or plastic hammer, drive the axle shaft and the constant velocity joint onto the driveshaft until the circlip snaps firmly into the groove on the driveshaft.

6

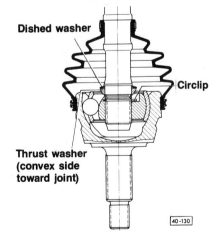

Fig. 4-4. Correct positions for washers and circlip. Convex side of thrust washer must be toward constant velocity joint; convex side of dished washer must be against shoulder on driveshaft.

Fig. 4-2. Exploded view of driveshaft and constant velocity joints.

If the constant velocity joint has not been disassembled, cleaned, and lubricated as described in **4.3 Servicing Constant Velocity Joints,** add just enough molybdenum grease to make up for any that was lost during removal and installation of the joint. Using a new clamp, secure the boot to the constant velocity joint as shown in Fig. 4-5. If the boot has been replaced, position its small end between the ridges on the driveshaft so that the boot is not twisted. Then secure it with a clamp.

NOTE ——

In installing a new large clamp, be sure to position it so that its locking projection will not interfere with the installation of any of the socket-head screws.

Fig. 4-5. Special pliers being used to tighten and lock the clamp for the rubber boot.

To remove an inboard constant velocity joint, remove the circlip as shown in Fig. 4-6. Then, using a drift and a hammer, drive the cap off the outer side of the joint and turn the boot inside out over the driveshaft.

CAUTION ——

After you have removed the cap and boot, do not tilt the ball hub more than 20° in the joint outer ring. If you do, the balls may fall out.

After removing the circlip and the cap and boot, slide the joint outer ring as far out as possible toward the end of the driveshaft. Then, with the ball hub supported, press the driveshaft out of the ball hub as shown in Fig. 4-7. Remove the dished washer from the driveshaft.

If the rubber boot is torn or otherwise damaged, be sure to replace it before you install the constant velocity joint. When installing a rubber boot, either use a plastic guide sleeve or cover the driveshaft splines with tape in order to protect the boot's sealing surface as you slide the boot onto the driveshaft.

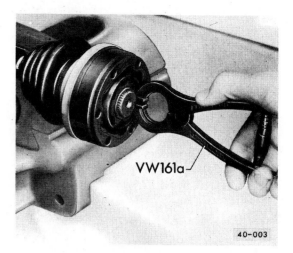

Fig. 4-6. Circlip being removed.

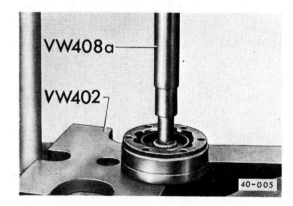

Fig. 4-7. Driveshaft being pressed out of constant velocity joint. Notice that only the ball hub is supported, so that no stress is placed on the balls or the outer ring.

Install the dished washer with its convex side against the shoulder on the driveshaft (Fig. 4-8). Then, with the driveshaft supported in a collet clamp, as shown in Fig. 4-9, press the constant velocity joint onto the driveshaft. While using the press to hold the ball hub down against the tension of the dished washer, install the circlip. After you have raised the press tool, use pliers to squeeze the circlip around its periphery until the circlip is completely seated in the groove.

If the constant velocity joint has not been disassembled, cleaned, and lubricated as described in **4.3 Servicing Constant Velocity Joints,** add just enough molybdenum grease to make up for any that was lost during removal and installation of the joint. Then install the cap and boot on the joint's outer surface. If the boot has been replaced, position its small end between the ridges on the driveshaft so that the boot is not twisted.

Fig. 4-8. Dished washer correctly installed with its convex side against the shoulder on the driveshaft.

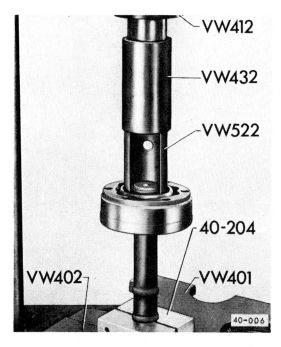

Fig. 4-9. Constant velocity joint being pressed onto driveshaft. Notice collet clamp that is positioned below ridge on driveshaft.

4.3 Servicing Constant Velocity Joints

It is not possible to repair the constant velocity joints. The components of each joint are factory-matched and cannot be replaced individually. The joints can, however, be disassembled for cleaning, inspection, and repacking with molybdenum grease. Because the outboard and the inboard constant velocity joints are constructed differently, separate procedures are given for servicing each kind.

To disassemble outboard joint:

1. Remove the constant velocity joint from the driveshaft as described in **4.2 Removing and Installing Constant Velocity Joints.**

2. Using a waterproof felt-tip marker, mark the relative positions of the ball hub, the ball cage, and the outer ring. Then tilt the ball cage and the hub as shown in Fig. 4-10 and remove the balls.

CAUTION ——

The ball cage, the outer ring, and the balls themselves are selected for matching tolerances. When disassembling more than one joint, be sure not to intermix the parts. If you do, the joints may seize, make noise, or wear rapidly.

Fig. 4-10. Balls being removed from outboard constant velocity joint. Notice the mark that has been made on the outer ring. Similar marks should be made on the ball hub and the ball cage.

3. Turn the ball cage and the ball hub so that the two large rectangular openings are positioned as shown in Fig. 4-11. Then remove the cage and the hub from the outer ring.

Fig. 4-11. Large rectangular opening (arrow) in position for cage and hub removal.

4. To remove the ball hub from the ball cage, turn the hub so that one ridge is in line with one of the large rectangular openings in the cage (Fig. 4-12). The ball hub now has sufficient clearance to be tipped out of the ball cage.

Fig. 4-12. Ball hub being removed or installed in the ball cage. Notice how the large rectangular opening in the cage just accommodates the ridge on the hub.

To assemble outboard joint:

1. Clean and inspect all parts. If any part is worn or damaged, replace the entire joint.

NOTE ———

In addition to galling, pitting, and other obvious wear, replace joints that have excessive radial clearance or excessive play when changes of load direction take place. Do not replace a joint merely because the parts appear polished or the ball track is clearly visible.

2. Thoroughly coat all parts with molybdenum grease. Then install the ball hub in the ball cage as illustrated earlier in Fig. 4-12.

3. Install the balls in the ball cage and ball hub. If necessary, use additional molybdenum grease as an adhesive to hold the balls in place.

4. Insert the ball hub together with the balls and ball cage into the outer ring, making sure that the marks made prior to disassembly are correctly aligned. Also make sure that the circlip-access groove in the ball hub is visible following assembly.

5. Repack the joint with 90 g (3.2 oz.) of molybdenum grease. Force about two-thirds of the grease into the joint and use the remaining third to pack the open side of the joint.

6. Install the constant velocity joint on the driveshaft.

To disassemble inboard joint:

1. Remove the inboard constant velocity joint from the driveshaft as described in **4.2 Removing and Installing Constant Velocity Joints.**

2. Using hand pressure, push the ball hub and ball cage out of the outer ring as shown in Fig. 4-13.

Fig. 4-13. Ball cage and ball hub being separated from outer ring. Position the ball hub and ball cage perpendicular to the outer ring, then push in the direction indicated by the arrow.

3. Lift the six steel balls out of the ball cage, taking care not to drop them.

> **CAUTION ——**
>
> *The ball cage, the outer ring, and the balls themselves are selected for matching tolerances. When disassembling more than one joint, be sure not to intermix the parts. If you do, the joints may seize, make noise, or wear rapidly.*

4. Rotate the ball hub into the position shown in Fig. 4-14. The groove in the ball hub must be in line with the outer edge of the ball cage. The ball hub now has sufficient clearance to be tipped out of the ball cage.

Fig. 4-14. Ball hub being removed from or installed in the ball cage. Arrows indicate the alignment of the ball hub groove with the ball cage edge.

To assemble inboard joint:

1. Clean and inspect all parts. If any part is worn or damaged, replace the entire joint.

2. Thoroughly coat all parts with molybdenum grease. Then install the ball hub in the ball cage as illustrated earlier in Fig. 4-14.

3. Install the balls in the ball cage and ball hub. If necessary, use additional molybdenum grease as an adhesive to hold the balls in place.

4. Insert the ball hub together with the balls and ball cage into the outer ring. The chamfer on the splines and the larger diameter portion of the outer ring must be on the same side of the joint.

> **NOTE ——**
>
> Insert the ball and hub assembly in the outer ring at a 90° angle, as shown in Fig. 4-15. The narrow ball hub grooves **b** and the wide outer ring grooves **a** must be positioned as illustrated.

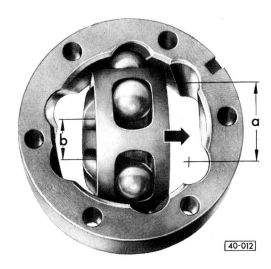

Fig. 4-15. Ball and hub assembly positioned in the outer ring. Arrow indicates the direction in which the ball and hub assembly must be turned to complete the installation.

5. Hold the ball and hub assembly steady and push it in the direction indicated in Fig. 4-16 (left arrow). This will align the balls with their respective grooves (right arrows) in the outer ring.

Fig. 4-16. Balls being aligned with the grooves of the outer ring. Apply finger pressure in the direction indicated by the left arrow.

6

6. When the balls are aligned with their grooves in the outer ring, firmly press the ball cage, as indicated in Fig. 4-17, until it swings fully into place. Heavy pressure should not be required.

Fig. 4-17. Balls being engaged in the grooves of the outer ring. Apply hand pressure at the point indicated by the arrow.

CAUTION ——

Excessive force will result in improper joint assembly. Double-check the previous steps if the joint does not go together readily. An improperly assembled joint will lock solidly and render the unit unserviceable.

7. Check the operation of the joint. The ball hub should be able to turn smoothly throughout the entire range of travel.

8. Repack the joint with 90 g (3.2 oz.) of molybdenum grease. Pack two-thirds of the grease between the joint and the cap. Use the remaining third to pack the open side of the joint.

9. Install the constant velocity joint on the driveshaft as described in **4.2 Removing and Installing Constant Velocity Joints.** Then hand-squeeze the boot tightly so that grease will be forced into the joint from the rear.

Replacing Drive Flange Oil Seal

With the driveshaft removed, you can replace a leaky drive flange oil seal without removing the transaxle from the car. Pry the dust cap out of the center of the drive flange. Remove the circlip and the dished washer, then use a puller such as the one shown in Fig. 4-18 to withdraw the drive flange from the transaxle.

Fig. 4-18. Drive flange being removed. Puller shown here mounts on drive flange with M 8 X 20 bolts. If you use another kind of puller, be careful not to damage threaded hole in differential sidegear shaft.

Use a hooked tool, or a large screwdriver, to pry the faulty seal out of its recess in the transaxle case (Fig. 4-19). Pack the open side of the new seal with multipurpose grease before you install the seal as shown in Fig. 4-20.

Fig. 4-19. Drive flange oil seal being removed.

Inspect the drive flange before you install it. Replace the flange if it has a groove worn into it at the point where it is contacted by the oil seal. Install the drive flange as shown in Fig. 4-21. The special tool screws into the threads that are in the center of the differential's sidegear shaft.

Fig. 4-20. Drive flange oil seal being installed. Drive in as indicated by arrow.

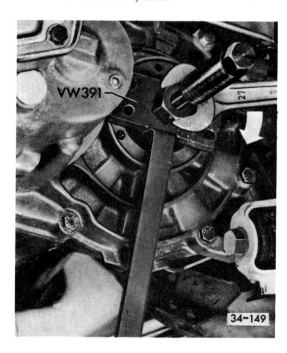

Fig. 4-21. Drive flange being installed.

With the drive flange fully seated in the transaxle, install the dished washer so that its convex side is away from the drive flange. Then, using circlip pliers, install a new circlip over the end of the differential's sidegear shaft—but do not attempt to seat the circlip in its groove. Drive the circlip inward against the tension of the dished washer, as shown in Fig. 4-22, until the circlip snaps into its groove. Install a new dust cap.

Fig. 4-22. Circlip being driven inward (arrow) against tension of dished washer until circlip snaps into its groove.

5. REMOVING AND INSTALLING TRANSAXLE

You can remove the transaxle and engine as a unit using the procedure described in **ENGINE AND CLUTCH.** If no engine repairs are required, you can, using the procedure described here, remove the transaxle without removing the engine.

To remove:

1. Disconnect the battery ground strap. Install an engine support such as the one shown in Fig. 5-1, then completely remove the transaxle left mounting.

Fig. 5-1. Support bar (**2**) installed. Disconnected battery ground strap is at **1**; transaxle left mounting is at **3**.

2. On cars that have a permanently installed TDC sensor, remove it using special tool US 4463; on late cars, remove the plastic plug from the sensor opening (item **4** in Fig. 5-2).

3. Using a wrench on the bolt that is in the center of the crankshaft pulley, turn the crankshaft in order to align the mark on the flywheel with the pointer in the TDC sensor hole. The mark and the pointer can be seen in Fig. 5-2. Only in this position can the transaxle be separated from the engine.

4. Detach the speedometer cable by taking out the bolt (item **5** in Fig. 5-2).

5. Remove the upper two transaxle-to-engine bolts, indicated by the number **6** in Fig. 5-2.

6. Disconnect the back-up light wire (item **7** in Fig. 5-2). Detach the clutch cable and its conduit from the transaxle (item **8** in Fig. 5-2).

Fig. 5-2. Preliminary detachment points on transaxle. TDC sensor hole is at **4** (notice alignment of mark and pointer). Speedometer cable retaining bolt is at **5**, transaxle-to-engine upper bolts are at **6**, back-up light connection is at **7**, clutch cable is at **8**.

7. Disconnect the shift linkage from the transaxle at the points indicated in Fig. 5-3.

NOTE————

Only the earliest-type shift linkage is shown. If necessary, consult the illustrations given in **3. Gearshift Lever and Shift Linkage.**

Fig. 5-3. Shift linkage being disconnected from transaxle. Remove rod and rod lever from transaxle's selector shaft (**9a**); dismount relay lever from rod or bracket on transaxle (**9b**).

8. Disconnect the transaxle-to-body ground strap (item **10** in Fig. 5-4). Remove the starter by first disconnecting the wires from the solenoid and then removing the bolts indicated by number **11** in Fig. 5-4.

9. Remove the transaxle-to-engine bolts indicated by number **12** in Fig. 5-4.

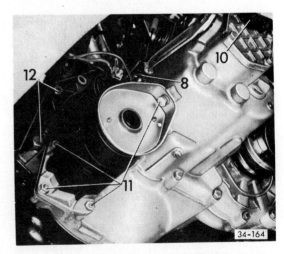

Fig. 5-4. Additional disconnecting points. Transaxle-to-body ground strap is at **10**, starter mounting bolts at **11**, transaxle-to-engine bolts at **12**.

10. Place a transmission jack or a floor jack with a transmission adaptor beneath the transaxle. Raise the jack so that the transaxle is supported. Then, by removing the nuts and the bolts indicated by number **13** in Fig. 5-5, completely remove the transaxle rear mount.

11. Detach the left-hand driveshaft from the trans-

axle's drive flange by taking out the socket-head bolts (one of which is indicated by number **14** in Fig. 5-5). Support the detached driveshaft by hanging it from the car body with a stiff wire hook.

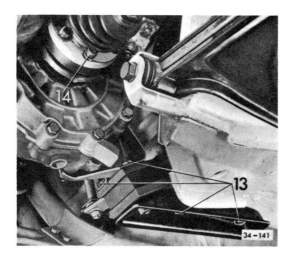

Fig. 5-5. Left side disconnecting points. Bolts for transaxle rear mount are indicated by number **13**. Socket-head screw for driveshaft is at **14**.

12. Detach the right-hand driveshaft from the transaxle's drive flange by taking out the socket-head bolts (one of which is indicated by number **15** in Fig. 5-6). Support the detached driveshaft by hanging it from the car body with a stiff wire hook.

13. Remove the cover plate bolts (item **16** in Fig. 5-6). (The cover plate will remain on the engine when the transaxle is removed.)

Fig. 5-6. Right side disconnecting points. Socket-head screw for driveshaft is at **15**, cover plate bolts at **16**, small cover plate bolt at **17**, and nut at **18**.

14. Remove the small cover plate by taking out the bolt indicated by number **17** in Fig. 5-6. Once removed, you can take out the transaxle-to-engine bolt that is concealed by the cover plate.

15. Remove the nut indicated by number **18** in Fig. 5-6. Then, by rolling the transaxle toward the left side of the car on the floor jack or transmission jack, separate the transaxle from the engine.

CAUTION ——

At no time should the weight of the transaxle be supported by the transmission mainshaft. Placing such a load on the clutch and transaxle components can damage them seriously.

16. Either lower the jack or raise the car for clearance. Then use the jack to pull the transaxle out from under the car.

NOTE ——

If you intend to disassemble the transaxle, remove the oil drain plug and drain the hypoid oil.

To install:

1. If you have turned the engine's crankshaft while the transaxle was removed, align the recess in the flywheel as indicated in Fig. 5-7.

6 ■

Fig. 5-7. Flywheel positioned for transaxle installation. Recess (arrow) must be at same level as clutch driven plate hub with engine in its installed position.

2. Position the transaxle on the engine, being careful not to damage the clutch driven plate, the clutch pushrod, or the mainshaft. If necessary, use a wrench on the bolt that is in the center of the

crankshaft pulley to hand-turn the crankshaft—so that the splines of the mainshaft will mesh with those in the hub of the clutch driven plate.

3. Install the bolts and the nut that hold the transaxle to the engine. Torque the bolts and the nut to 5.5 mkg (40 ft. lb.). Then install the small cover plate for the concealed bolt.

4. Install the starter. Torque the bolts to 3.0 mkg (22 ft. lb.). Then reconnect the starter wires and the transaxle-to-body ground strap.

5. Install the transaxle rear mount, but do not fully tighten the bolts and nuts.

6. Reconnect the driveshafts to the transaxle's drive flanges. Torque the socket-head bolts to 4.5 mkg (32 ft. lb.).

7. Install the bolts that hold the flywheel cover plate to the bellhousing to a torque of 1.5 mkg (11 ft. lb.).

8. Install the transaxle left mounting but do not fully tighten the bolts and nuts.

9. Reconnect the back-up light wires and the speedometer cable. Install the plastic plug, or the TDC sensor, in the TDC sensor hole of the bellhousing. Then, where applicable, reconnect the wire to the TDC sensor.

10. Reattach the shift linkage to the transaxle.

11. Reattach the clutch cable to the clutch operating lever and loosely install the cable conduit on the transaxle.

12. Remove the engine support bar. Reconnect the battery ground strap.

13. With careful reference to the instructions given in conjunction with engine installation in **ENGINE AND CLUTCH,** align the engine/transaxle mountings. With the mountings aligned and the nuts and bolts torqued, adjust the clutch pedal freeplay as described in **ENGINE AND CLUTCH.**

> **NOTE——**
> On early 1975 models with the early-type shift linkage, adjust the shift linkage as described in **3.1 Removing, Adjusting, and Installing 1975 Gearshift Lever and Shift Linkages.**

14. Check that all gears can be engaged smoothly, easily, and fully. If necessary, adjust the shift linkage.

> **NOTE——**
> If you have drained the hypoid oil, be sure to refill the transaxle as described in **LUBRICATION AND MAINTENANCE** before you start the engine or tow the car.

Repairing Engine/Transaxle Mountings
(cars with either manual or automatic transmissions)

After removing and installing any of the engine/transaxle mountings, you should always align the mountings as described in conjunction with engine installation in **ENGINE AND CLUTCH.** The mountings can be replaced, for the most part, using common hand tools. You will need a repair press, however, to replace the rubber bushing of the transaxle left mounting.

You need not remove the transaxle to repair the mountings. However, the engine's transaxle assembly must be supported while each mount is removed and no more than one mounting should be removed at any one time. Cut through the metal casing of the rubber bushing as shown in Fig. 5-8 before you press it out as shown in Fig. 5-9.

Fig. 5-8. Metal casing of rubber bushing being cut through with hacksaw. This will release tension and prevent damage to the mounting as the bushing is pressed out.

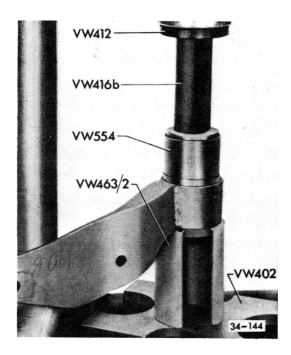

Fig. 5-9. Rubber bushing being pressed out of transaxle left mounting. Use this tool setup for the 60-mm (2⅜-in.) diameter bushings used through December 1975. For the 64-mm (2½-in.) diameter bushings used from January 1976, substitute tool 40-20 for VW 554.

Position the new rubber bushing in the transaxle left mounting so that the arrow on the bushing points straight up when the transaxle left mounting is in its installed position (Fig. 5-10). Then press in the new bushing as shown in Fig. 5-11 or Fig. 5-12.

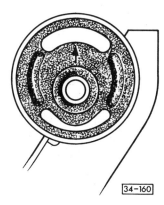

Fig. 5-10. Rubber bushing correctly positioned for installation in transaxle left mounting. Arrow points straight up with mounting in installed position.

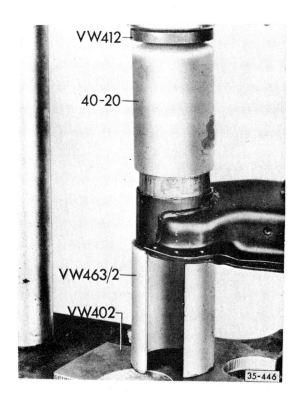

Fig. 5-11. Late-type rubber bushing being pressed into transaxle left mounting. Use this tool setup for the 64-mm (2½-in.) diameter bushings used from January 1976.

6

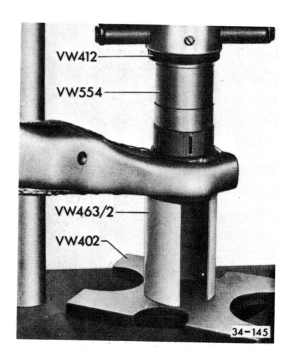

Fig. 5-12. Early-type rubber bushing being pressed into transaxle left mounting. Use this tool setup for the 60-mm (2⅜-in.) diameter bushings used through December 1975.

6. TRANSMISSION

Before you begin any transmission repair, thoroughly read the instructions. The transaxle should be removed from the car before attempting any repair that involves the transmission gear train.

Though the home mechanic often lacks the tools and experience necessary to repair the transmission, he may be able to remove and install the transaxle. If so, he should deliver the transaxle to an Authorized Dealer or other qualified repair shop after giving the transaxle a thorough exterior cleaning—but without doing any disassembly work.

> **CAUTION ——**
>
> *If you lack the skills, tools, or a clean workshop for transmission repairs, we suggest you leave these repairs to an Authorized Dealer or other qualified shop. We especially urge you to consult your Authorized Dealer before attempting repairs on a car still covered by the new-car warranty.*

6.1 Removing, Installing, and Adjusting Selector Shaft.

Fig. 6-1 is a cross section of the selector shaft and related parts. During the model years covered by this Manual, there have been a number of modifications to the selector shaft components. In obtaining replacement parts, always take the original parts with you for comparison. Whenever possible, we will point out the component differences during the procedures that follow.

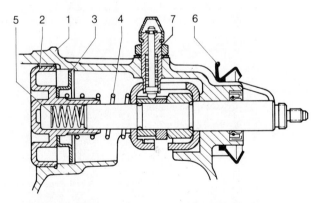

1. Gear carrier/shift housing portion of transaxle case
2. Selector shaft cover (tapered threads on early models)
3. Oil deflector plate
4. Selector control spring
5. Selector shaft control spring (installed on 1975 models only)
6. Selector shaft boot
7. Selector shaft adjuster

Fig. 6-1. Cross section of selector shaft and related parts.

The selector shaft should be removed before you attempt to separate the transaxle case into its two main parts. Though it is possible to remove, install, and adjust the selector shaft with the transaxle installed in the car, the procedure given here assumes that the transaxle has already been removed. The adjustments, described following the selector shaft installation procedure, can be carried out easily without removing any major components from the installed transaxle.

To remove selector shaft:

1. Remove the selector shaft boot. Carefully clean the exposed end of the selector shaft so that when the selector shaft is removed, dirt and corrosion on the shaft will not damage the oil seal or the transaxle case.

2. Make sure that the transmission gears are in neutral. If necessary, place the gears in neutral by moving the selector shaft.

3. Loosen the selector shaft adjuster's locknut. Then remove the selector shaft adjuster from the top of the gear carrier/shift housing portion of the transaxle case.

   > **NOTE ——**
   >
   > The earliest cars have an adjuster without a locknut. If necessary, refer to Fig. 6-6, which appears later.

4. Remove the selector shaft cover as shown in Fig. 6-2. As you take off the cover, be careful not to lose the oil deflector plate and the spring(s)—which you should remove along with the cover.

5. Remove the selector shaft by hand-pressing it out through the cover opening.

Fig. 6-2. Selector shaft cover being removed. Tool US 4463 is at **A**.

To install:

1. Inspect the selector shaft oil seal. If it is leaking, hard, cracked, or otherwise damaged, replace it. Pry out the old seal (Fig. 6-3) and then install the new seal using a suitable seal driving tool (Fig. 6-4).

Fig. 6-3. Selector shaft oil seal being removed.

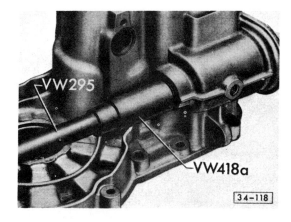

Fig. 6-4. Selector shaft oil seal being installed.

2. Make certain that the transmission gears are in neutral. Fully lubricate the oil seal and all surfaces of the selector shaft with multipurpose grease. Then, being careful not to damage the oil seal, install the selector shaft in the transaxle case.

3. Install the selector control spring and the oil deflector plate. Where applicable, install the selector shaft control spring inside the cover. Then install the cover to a torque of 4.5 mkg (32 ft. lb.). See Fig. 6-5.

    NOTE ——

    Some early 1976 cars have the 1976 transaxle, with the high-mounted starter, but have the 1975-type gearshift lever, shift linkage, and selector shaft/selector shaft adjuster. These cars have transmissions numbered 07 08 5 through 24 08 5.

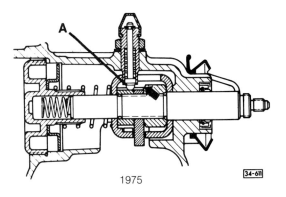

1975

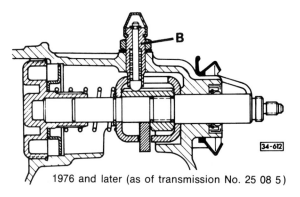

1976 and later (as of transmission No. 25 08 5)

Fig. 6-5. Differences in selector shaft used on 1976 and later cars. In 1975, reverse detent was provided by chamfer on selector (arrow) and beveled shoulder on adjuster ball end (**A**). 1976 and later cars have reverse detent in gearshift lever. Adjuster has round ball end (**B**); selector shaft control spring is no longer used.

6

4. Install the selector shaft adjuster and adjust it as described under the next heading. Then install the selector shaft boot.

Adjusting Selector Shaft

Three different selector shaft adjusters have been used. Each kind is covered separately in the following procedures.

To adjust the early-type selector shaft adjuster which has no locknut, as shown in Fig. 6-6, first place the transmission in neutral and remove the cap. Make sure that the locking bolt is torqued to 2.0 mkg (14 ft. lb.). Then turn the interlock plunger (the slotted screw) clockwise until the plunger bottoms—which is indicated by the nut starting to move out. From this position, turn the interlock plunger counter-clockwise ¼ turn, then reinstall the plastic cap.

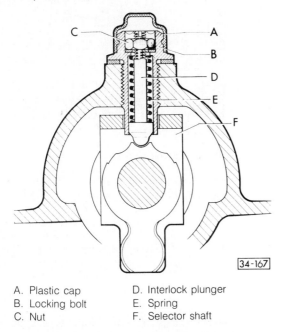

A. Plastic cap
B. Locking bolt
C. Nut
D. Interlock plunger
E. Spring
F. Selector shaft

Fig. 6-6. Cross section of early-type selector shaft adjuster.

Fig. 6-7 is a cross section of the selector shaft adjuster used on all but the earliest 1975 cars. To adjust, place the transmission in neutral. Remove the plastic cap (not shown) and loosen the locknut. Turn the adjusting bolt clockwise until the plunger bottoms—which is indicated by the lockring lifting away from the adjusting bolt. From this position, turn the adjusting bolt ¼ turn counter-clockwise. Then, while holding the adjusting bolt stationary, torque the locknut to 2.0 mkg (14 ft. lb.). Reinstall the plastic cap.

Fig. 6-8 is a cross section of the selector shaft adjuster that is used in conjunction with the new-type gearshift lever and shift linkage installed on 1976 and later models. To adjust, place the transmission in neutral. Remove the plastic cap (not shown) and loosen the locknut. Turn the adjusting bolt clockwise until the lockring lifts away from the adjusting bolt. Then turn the adjusting bolt counter-

clockwise until the lockring just contacts the adjusting bolt. While holding the adjusting bolt stationary, torque the locknut to 2.0 mkg (14 ft. lb.). To check the adjustment, hand-turn the selector shaft slightly. Repeat the adjustment if the lockring fails to lift as soon as the shaft is turned. When the adjustment is correct, reinstall the plastic cap.

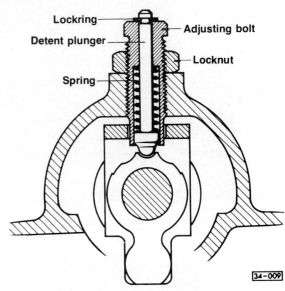

Fig. 6-7. Cross section of selector shaft adjuster used on most 1975 cars.

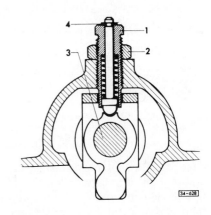

1. Adjusting bolt
2. Locknut
3. Selector shaft
4. Lockring

Fig. 6-8. Cross section of selector shaft adjuster used with new-type gearshift lever and shift linkage installed on 1976 and later models.

6.2 Removing and Installing Clutch Release Mechanism

To remove components of the clutch release mechanism, first take out the four bolts and washers that hold the clutch release cover to the extreme left-hand end of the transaxle case. The cover has waffle-pattern reinforcing ribs cast into it.

Remove the two circlips that are on each side of the clutch lever (Fig. 6-9). With the circlips removed, you can pull the clutch operating lever and release shaft assembly out of the case. Then lift the return spring and the clutch lever out of the transaxle case. If necessary, lift out the clutch release bearing, the release bearing guide sleeve, and the clutch pushrod. (The pushrod is concentric with the transmission's mainshaft.) An exploded view of the clutch release mechanism appears under the next heading in Fig. 6-12.

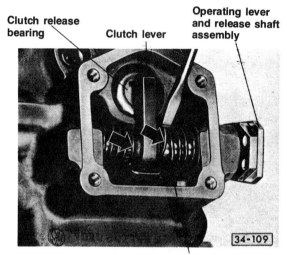

Fig. 6-9. Circlips being removed from or installed on clutch release shaft. Installed circlip is at left arrow. Screwdriver can be used to pry off circlips or to press them onto the shaft, as indicated by the right arrow.

If you have removed the clutch pushrod, thoroughly coat it with multipurpose grease before you insert it into the mainshaft. Similarly lubricate the sliding surfaces for the clutch release bearing and its guide.

NOTE ——

Check the release bearing by hand-turning it. If the bearing feels rough or makes noise, replace it. If the sealing washer for the clutch pushrod is leaky, or if the bushing for the clutch pushrod is worn or otherwise unserviceable, replace both parts using the procedure given in **6.4 Disassembling and Assembling Mainshaft.** Suspect a leaky sealing washer if the clutch is contaminated by oil.

Inspect the oil seal for the clutch operating lever and release shaft assembly. If the seal is worn, hard, cracked, or otherwise damaged, remove it as indicated in Fig. 6-10. Drive in a new oil seal as indicated in Fig. 6-11, then lubricate the seal lips with multipurpose grease. This job can also be done with the transaxle installed in the car.

Fig. 6-10. Oil seal for clutch operating lever and release shaft assembly being pried out.

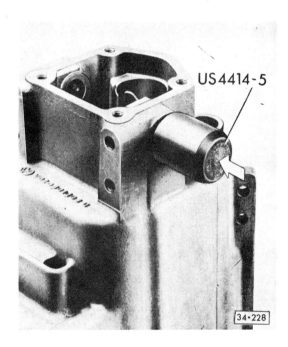

Fig. 6-11. Oil seal for clutch operating lever and release shaft assembly being driven in.

To assemble the clutch release mechanism, position the return spring and the clutch lever inside the transaxle case. The central hook of the return spring should lie atop the lug on the clutch lever and the spring's end hooks should point downward so that the clutch lever is held away from the release bearing.

NOTE ——

It is of no consequence if the spring is not under tension and the clutch lever is pointed away from the transaxle case—so long as the spring is correctly hooked to the lever and correctly positioned in the case.

Lightly coat the release shaft with multipurpose grease. Then insert the shaft, being careful that the splines do not damage the oil seal. Move the operating lever back and forth until the splines on the release shaft enter those in the clutch lever—the splines will mesh in only one position. Install the circlips as previously shown in Fig. 6-9. Then check that, when the operating lever is lifted up to its normal position, the return spring is correctly tensioned. After you are sure that the mechanism operates correctly, install the cover together with a new gasket. Torque the bolts to 1.5 mkg (11 ft. lb.).

6.3 Removing and Installing Mainshaft, Shift Forks, and Reverse Sliding Gear

Fig. 6-12 is an exploded view that shows the components you must remove in order to obtain access to the transmission gear train. The left half of the transaxle case, which is uppermost in the illustration, cannot be removed without first removing the transaxle from the car.

CAUTION ——

Clean the outside of the transaxle case before you begin any disassembly work. Otherwise, abrasive dirt is likely to enter the transaxle, causing rapid wear of the gears, bearings, and synchronizers.

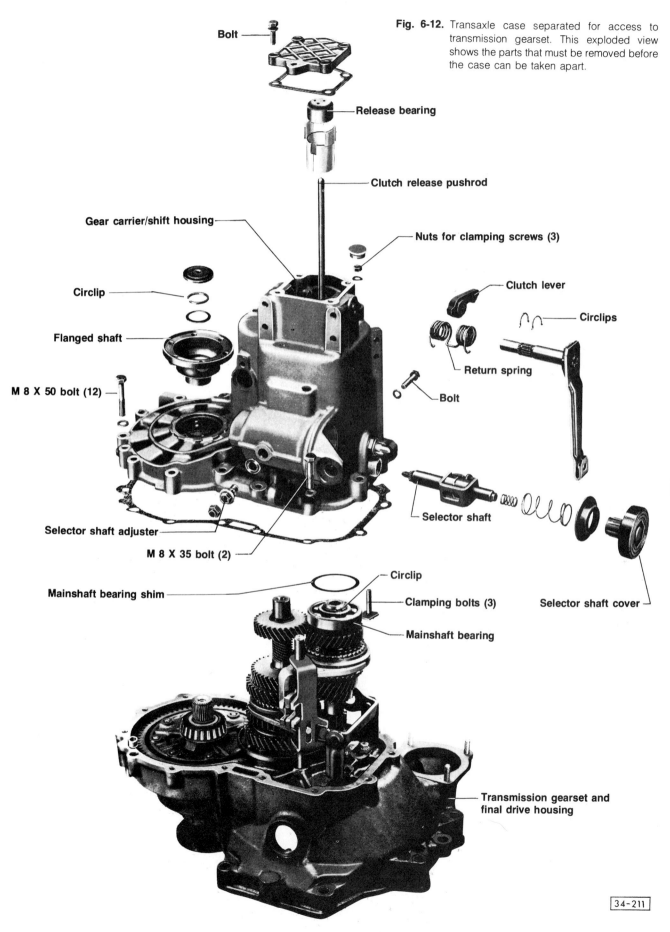

Fig. 6-12. Transaxle case separated for access to transmission gearset. This exploded view shows the parts that must be removed before the case can be taken apart.

Bolt

Release bearing

Clutch release pushrod

Gear carrier/shift housing

Nuts for clamping screws (3)

Clutch lever

Circlip

Circlips

Flanged shaft

Return spring

M 8 X 50 bolt (12)

Bolt

Selector shaft adjuster

Selector shaft

M 8 X 35 bolt (2)

Mainshaft bearing shim

Circlip

Clamping bolts (3)

Selector shaft cover

Mainshaft bearing

Transmission gearset and final drive housing

34-211

To remove:

1. Remove the transaxle as described in **5. Removing and Installing Transaxle.** From the bellhousing end, withdraw the clutch release pushrod from the center of the mainshaft.

2. Install the transaxle on a repair stand, as shown in Fig. 6-13.

Fig. 6-13. Transaxle installed on repair stand.

3. Install a bar across the mouth of the bellhousing in order to support the mainshaft solidly. The bar should have a central screw that can be used to take up the clearance between the bar and the mainshaft. See Fig. 6-14.

Fig. 6-14. Bar with mainshaft support screw (**A**).

4. Remove the entire speedometer drivegear assembly, withdrawing the gear through the top of the transaxle case. On transaxles built from Transmission No. 02 04 6, disconnect the wires and

remove the screw-in back-up light switch indicated in Fig. 6-15.

NOTE ——

Repair and replacement of the speedometer drivegear is covered in **ELECTRICAL SYSTEM** in conjunction with speedometer and speedometer cable repairs.

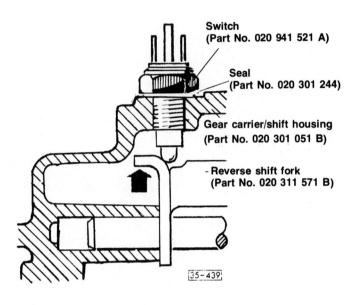

Fig. 6-15. Back-up light switch used on late-type transaxles. Remove switch so that lug (arrow) on shift fork will not damage switch as gear carrier/shift housing portion of transaxle case is removed.

5. Remove the selector shaft and related parts as described in **6.1 Removing, Installing, and Adjusting Selector Shaft.**

6. Remove the clutch release mechanism as described in **6.2 Removing and Installing Clutch Release Mechanism.**

7. Pry the plastic cap out of the center of the left driveshaft's drive flange. Remove the circlip and the dished washer. Then, using a puller such as the one shown in Fig. 6-16, remove the left drive flange.

8. Remove the circlip from the end of the mainshaft. This circlip is at the bottom of the clutch release bearing recess (Fig. 6-17).

9. For access to the nuts that hold the mainshaft bearing clamping bolts to the transaxle case, carefully pry off the two plastic caps indicated in Fig. 6-18. Remove the two nuts that are beneath the caps and the third nut which is inside the housing for the clutch release mechanism.

Fig. 6-16. Left drive flange being removed. Puller is held to drive flange by two M 8 X 30 bolts. Turn nut with wrench as indicated by arrow.

Fig. 6-17. Circlip being removed from end of mainshaft.

Fig. 6-18. Plastic caps (arrows) that cover two of nuts for mainshaft bearing clamping bolts.

NOTE ——

The mainshaft bearing should pull out of the case and remain on the mainshaft. The three clamping bolts will pull out of their holes in the case as the gear carrier/shift housing is pulled off the final drive housing.

CAUTION ——

Do not attempt to pry apart the case by inserting tools between the two halves. Doing this can damage or deform the castings. The input end of the mainshaft must be firmly supported by the bar shown earlier in Fig. 6-14. Otherwise, the mainshaft bearings may be damaged.

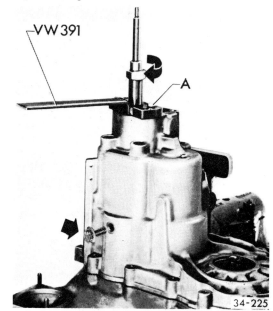

Fig. 6-19. Gear carrier/shift housing portion of transaxle case being removed. Reverse sliding gear's shaft support bolt is shown removed at lower arrow. Attach puller to housing with two M 8 X 30 bolts. Turn nut on puller as indicated by curved arrow to pull housing off gearset.

10. Remove the twelve M 8 X 50 bolts and the two M 8 X 35 bolts that hold the gear carrier/shift housing portion of the transaxle case to the final drive housing portion of the transaxle case.

11. Remove the reverse sliding gear's shaft support bolt, which is indicated in Fig. 6-19. Then, using a puller that will exert force against the end of the mainshaft, pull the gear carrier/shift housing portion of the transaxle case off the final drive portion of the transaxle case.

12. Take out the mainshaft bearing shim, which was between the mainshaft bearing outer race and the gear carrier/shift housing portion of the transaxle case. Store the three mainshaft bearing clamping bolts with their nuts and washers and the two plastic caps for the nuts.

13. Remove the two E-clips from the shift fork shaft. Then pull out the shaft and remove the shift fork assembly. If it must be replaced or repaired, unbolt the reverse sliding gear shift fork assembly from the case. See Fig. 6-20.

14. Pull out the reverse sliding gear and its shaft.

15. Remove the circlip from the end of the drive pinion shaft. Then lift off the drive pinion shaft 4th gear.

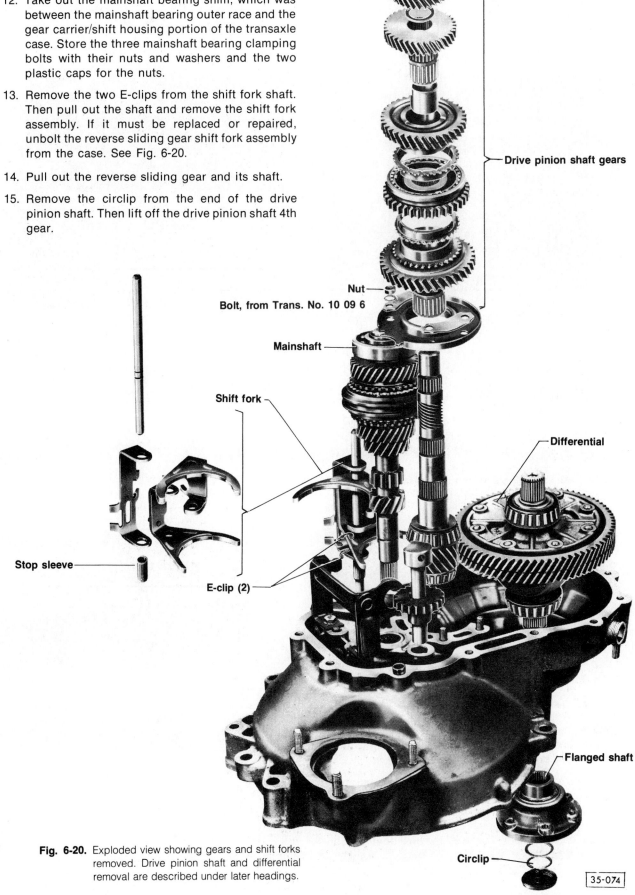

Drive pinion shaft gears

Nut

Bolt, from Trans. No. 10 09 6

Mainshaft

Shift fork

Differential

Stop sleeve

E-clip (2)

Flanged shaft

Circlip

35-074

Fig. 6-20. Exploded view showing gears and shift forks removed. Drive pinion shaft and differential removal are described under later headings.

16. Lift out the mainshaft, beaing careful not to damage the gear teeth, the mainshaft oil seal, or the mainshaft needle bearing.

17. Using a plate on the press bed that will support the mainshaft bearing's inner race only, press the mainshaft out of the mainshaft ball bearing as shown in Fig. 6-21.

CAUTION ——

If the bearing's outer race is supported, the bearing will be ruined. Be careful not to let the mainshaft drop, which could cause extensive damage.

Fig. 6-21. Mainshaft being pressed out of ball bearing.

NOTE ——

The transaxle cannot be reassembled without first removing the mainshaft ball bearing from the mainshaft as just described.

18. If you must replace the mainshaft needle bearing, remove it with a slide hammer and an expansion puller as shown in Fig. 6-22. Drive in the new needle bearing as shown in Fig. 6-23.

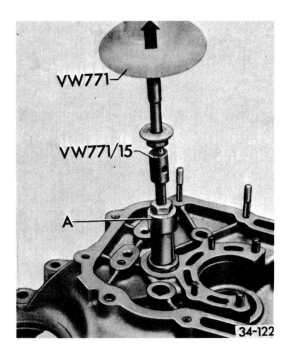

Fig. 6-22. Mainshaft needle bearing being removed from final drive portion of transaxle case (drive pinion shaft has been removed in this illustration). Expansion puller is at **A**. Move slide hammer as indicated by arrow.

6

Fig. 6-23. Mainshaft needle bearing being driven in. Thickest side of bearing cage should be toward the installing tool.

19. To remove the mainshaft oil seal, pry it out as indicated in Fig. 6-24.

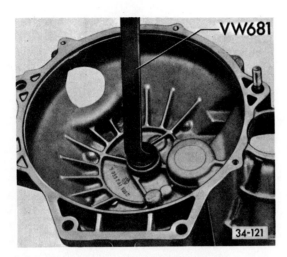

Fig. 6-24. Mainshaft oil seal being removed. This job can also be done with the mainshaft installed in the transaxle.

20. Inspect the recess for the oil seal. If there is a groove, as indicated by the arrow in Fig. 6-25, simply lubricate the new seal's periphery with multipurpose grease and drive in the seal as shown in Fig. 6-26. Early 1975 transaxles, without the groove, should have the seal recess coated with sealer. Also coat the periphery of the oil seal with sealer and allow it to dry for a short time before you drive in the seal.

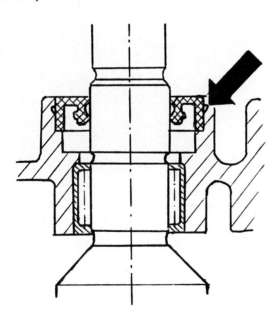

Fig. 6-25. Cross section of mainshaft needle bearing and oil seal. Except on early 1975 cars, the seal recess has a groove, as indicated by the arrow.

Fig. 6-26. Mainshaft oil seal being driven in (arrow).

To install:

1. Being careful not to damage the needle bearing, the mainshaft oil seal, or the gear teeth, install the mainshaft so that its teeth mesh with those of the drive pinion shaft.

   CAUTION ——

   Select a new mainshaft bearing shim as described in the next eight steps only if you have (1) replaced either half of the transaxle case, (2) replaced the mainshaft, or (3) replaced the 4th gear thrust washer (applicable only if the mainshaft has a 4th gear thrust washer). If no adjustment is required, use the original shim and proceed to step 10.

2. Using the bolt in the support bar (Fig. 6-27), adjust the position of the mainshaft until the side clearance between 2nd gear on the drive pinion shaft and 3rd gear on the mainshaft is 1.00 mm (.039 in.), when measured as shown in Fig. 6-28.

3. When the clearance is correct, tighten the locknut for the bolt in the support bar. Then recheck the side clearance (Fig. 6-29). If necessary, repeat the adjustment.

4. Install the dummy bearing and measuring sleeve shown in Fig. 6-30. Although the mainshaft you are adjusting may not have a 4th gear thrust washer, you must install a 4th gear thrust washer (Part No. 020 311 151) between the dummy bearing of the measuring sleeve and the shoulder on the mainshaft.

Fig. 6-27. Bolt (A) used to raise and lower mainshaft.

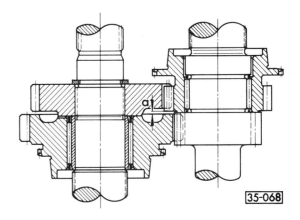

Fig. 6-29. Clearance (dimension **a**) between 2nd gear on drive pinion shaft and 3rd gear on mainshaft.

Fig. 6-28. 1.00-mm (.039-in.) feeler gauge being used to check side clearance between 2nd gear on drive pinion shaft and 3rd gear on mainshaft.

Fig. 6-30. Measuring sleeve with dummy bearing installed on mainshaft.

NOTE ——

The 4th gear thrust washer is a press fit on the mainshaft. If the washer is being used for adjustment purposes only, increase its inside diameter with a file so that the washer slides easily onto the mainshaft.

5. Install a new gasket on the mating surface of the final drive portion of the transaxle case. Then install the gear carrier/shift housing portion of the transaxle case—without the ball bearing or its clamping bolts. In order to hold the two halves of the transaxle case together, install five bolts torqued to 2.0 mkg (14 ft. lb.).

6. Install a dial indicator on a bridge so that its gauge pin is against the end of the measuring sleeve. Zero the dial indicator with a 3-mm preload. The tool setup is shown in Fig. 6-31.

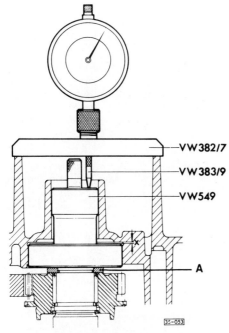

Fig. 6-31. Tool setup used to determine mainshaft bearing shim thickness (dimension **x**). A 4th gear thrust washer (**A**) must be installed adjacent to the dummy bearing of VW 549 even on mainshafts that do not have this thrust washer.

7. By grasping the knurled end of the measuring sleeve, move the measuring sleeve as far as possible up and down. Write down the range of play shown by the needle of the dial indicator. See Fig. 6-32.

Fig. 6-32. End play of measuring sleeve (dimension **x**) being measured. Move measuring sleeve up and down as indicated by double arrow.

8. Using the end play (dimension **x**) measured in step 7, select a new mainshaft bearing shim from **Table a.**

Table a. Mainshaft Bearing Shim Thicknesses

End play (dimension x)	Correct shim thickness	Part Number(s)
0.00 to 0.46 mm	use no shim	—
0.47 to 0.75 mm	0.30 mm	020 409 231 A
0.76 to 1.04 mm	0.60 mm	020 409 231 D
1.05 to 1.45 mm	0.90 mm (use two shims)	020 409 231 A plus 020 409 231 D

9. Remove the dial indicator. Remove the gear carrier/shift housing portion of the transaxle case and the gasket. Then remove the measuring sleeve.

10. Install the correct mainshaft bearing shim(s) in the bearing recess inside the gear carrier/shift housing portion of the transaxle case. Then press in the mainshaft bearing atop the shim(s) as shown in Fig. 6-33.

CAUTION ——

Position the bearing so that its plastic cage is toward the shims and the housing. If you install it backwards, the bearing will be ruined.

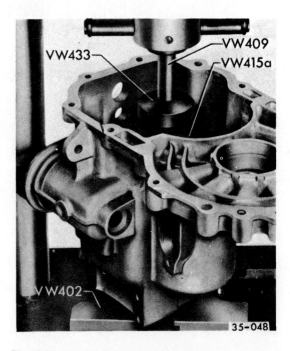

Fig. 6-33. Mainshaft ball bearing being pressed in atop shims. In order to prevent damage to bearing, press tool must contact bearing outer race only.

11. Install the clamping bolts (Fig. 6-34). Torque the nuts to 2.0 mkg (14 ft. lb.). Then install the plastic caps on the two nuts that are outside the housing for the clutch release mechanism.

Fig. 6-34. One of three clamping bolts (arrow) that hold mainshaft bearing to gear carrier/shift housing.

12. If you are working on a 1975 car that has a 4th gear thrust washer—but have installed the new-type bearing (Part No. 020 311 123 A) shown in Fig. 6-35—remove and discard the 4th gear thrust washer as described in **6.4 Disassembling and Assembling Mainshaft.**

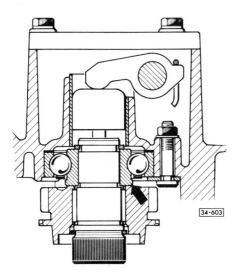

Fig. 6-35. Mainshaft bearing with wide inner race that eliminates need for 4th gear thrust washer. This improved bearing is factory-installed beginning with Transmission No. 18 06 5 (beginning with Chassis Nos. 175 3406 848 and 535 2058 206).

13. Inspect the reverse sliding gear and its shaft. Early transaxles have a stop sleeve that is pressed onto the shaft. If you must replace the gear, the shaft, or the bushing that is inside the gear, press off the stop sleeve. Heat the stop sleeve before you install it. Then press it onto the shaft so that dimension **a,** given in Fig. 6-36, is 41 mm (1.614 in.).

NOTE ——
Beginning with Chassis Nos. 175 3405 699 and 535 2058 516, end movement of the reverse sliding gear is limited by a stop on the drive pinion shaft bearing retainer (Fig. 6-37). There is no stop sleeve.

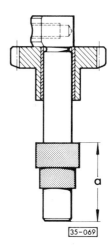

Fig. 6-36. Stop sleeve being installed (early transaxles only). Dimension **a** is 41 mm (1.614 in.).

Fig. 6-37. Reverse sliding gear shaft without stop sleeve. Gear end movement is limited by stop (arrow) on drive pinion shaft bearing retainer.

14. Loosely install the support bolt in the reverse sliding gear shaft. Align the shaft as indicated in

Fig. 6-38, then remove the bolt. If the shaft has a stop sleeve, the stop sleeve should be in contact with the transaxle case.

Fig. 6-38. Reverse sliding gear shaft being aligned. Support bolt should be equidistant from two bolt holes in flange of case, as indicated by arrows.

15. Assemble the shift forks. Insert the shift fork shaft, then use a screwdriver to press on the E-clips as indicated in Fig. 6-39.

    NOTE——

    If you are installing the reverse sliding gear shift fork, torque the bolts to 1.5 mkg (11 ft. lb.).

Fig. 6-39. E-clips (arrows) being installed on shift fork shaft. If necessary, refer to exploded view given earlier in Fig. 6-20.

16. Install 4th gear on the drive pinion shaft. Secure it in place with a new circlip.

17. Install a new gasket on the mating surface of the final drive portion of the transaxle case. Do not use sealer on this gasket.

18. Position the gear carrier/shift housing portion of the transaxle case on the gear train, making sure that the mainshaft is aligned with the ball bearing and that the drive pinion shaft is aligned with its needle bearing. The hollow dowels should align one half of the case with the other.

19. With the mainshaft firmly supported by the bar shown previously in Fig. 6-14 and Fig. 6-27, drive the mainshaft ball bearing onto the mainshaft. Doing this will, at the same time, move together the two halves of the transaxle case. Use a tool such as the one shown in Fig. 6-40, which will apply force only to the mainshaft bearing's inner race.

Fig. 6-40. Mainshaft bearing being driven onto supported mainshaft. Make sure that the hollow dowels of the case halves are aligned.

20. Install the support bolt for the reverse sliding gear shaft. Torque the bolt to 2.0 mkg (14 ft. lb.).

21. Install the 12 M 8 X 50 bolts and the two M 8 X 35 bolts that hold together the halves of the transaxle case. Working diagonally, gradually torque the bolts to 2.0 mkg (14 ft. lb.).

22. Install a new circlip on the end of the mainshaft where it projects through the ball bearing—making sure that the circlip is fully engaged in the groove.

23. Inspect the oil seal for the left drive flange. If it is worn, hard, cracked, or otherwise damaged, pry it out with a hooked tool or a large screwdriver. Pack the open side of the new seal with multipurpose grease before you install the seal as shown in Fig. 6-41.

Fig. 6-41. Drive flange oil seal being installed. Drive in as indicated by arrow.

24. Inspect the drive flange. Replace it if there is a groove worn into it at the point where it contacts the oil seal. Install the drive flange as shown in Fig. 6-42. The special tool screws into the threads that are in the center of the differential's sidegear shaft.

Fig. 6-42. Left drive flange being installed. Central screw threads into hole in differential's sidegear shaft. Turn nut with wrench as indicated by arrow.

25. With the drive flange fully seated, install the dished washer so that its convex side is away from the drive flange. Use circlip pliers to install a new circlip, but do not attempt to seat the circlip in its groove.

26. Drive the circlip inward against the tension of the dished washer, as shown in Fig. 6-43, until the circlip snaps into its groove. Install a new dust cap.

Fig. 6-43. Circlip being driven inward (arrow) against tension of dished washer until circlip snaps into its groove.

27. Install the speedometer drivegear assembly, being careful to mesh the drivegear with the helical teeth on the drive pinion shaft.

28. Install the clutch release mechanism as described in **6.2 Removing and Installing Clutch Release Mechanism.**

29. Install and adjust the selector shaft and related parts as described in **6.1 Removing, Installing, and Adjusting Selector Shaft.**

30. Remove the bar from the mouth of the bellhousing. Dismount the transaxle from the repair stand.

31. Insert the clutch pushrod through the center of the mainshaft. Install the transaxle in the car as described in **5. Removing and Installing Transaxle.**

6

6.4 Disassembling and Assembling Mainshaft

Fig. 6-44 is an exploded view of the mainshaft. The mainshaft bearing circlip, the mainshaft ball bearing, and the mainshaft bearing shim are removed when the mainshaft is removed from the transaxle. The transaxle cannot be reassembled unless the mainshaft bearing has been removed from the mainshaft. You can replace the bushing for the clutch pushrod without disassembling the transaxle, but the transaxle must be removed from the car.

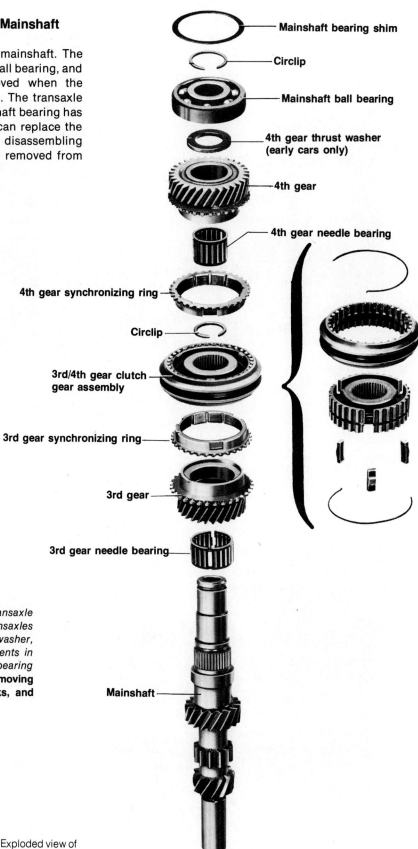

- Mainshaft bearing shim
- Circlip
- Mainshaft ball bearing
- 4th gear thrust washer (early cars only)
- 4th gear
- 4th gear needle bearing
- 4th gear synchronizing ring
- Circlip
- 3rd/4th gear clutch gear assembly
- 3rd gear synchronizing ring
- 3rd gear
- 3rd gear needle bearing
- Mainshaft
- Sealing washer for clutch pushrod
- Bushing for clutch pushrod

CAUTION —

If you replace either half of the transaxle case, the mainshaft itself or, on transaxles that have one, the 4th gear thrust washer, you must make precision measurements in order to select a new mainshaft bearing shim. This work is described in **6.3 Removing and Installing Mainshaft, Shift Forks, and Reverse Sliding Gear.**

Fig. 6-44. Exploded view of mainshaft. Exploded view of clutch gear assembly is at right. The 1st gear, 2nd gear, and reverse gear driving gears are integral with shaft itself.

35-072

To disassemble:

1. Remove the mainshaft as described in **6.3 Removing and Installing Mainshaft, Shift Forks, and Reverse Sliding Gear.** If you have not already done so, press the mainshaft out of its ball bearing, using a plate on the press bed that will support the mainshaft bearing's inner race only. See Fig. 6-45.

CAUTION ———

If the bearing's outer race is supported, the bearing will be ruined. Be careful not to let the mainshaft drop, which could cause extensive damage.

Fig. 6-45. Mainshaft being pressed out of ball bearing.

2. If the mainshaft that you are working on has no 4th gear thrust washer, lift off 4th gear, its needle bearing, and the 4th gear synchronizing ring. If the mainshaft has a 4th gear thrust washer, which is a press fit on the mainshaft, use a repair press as shown in Fig. 6-46 to remove 4th gear and the 4th gear thrust washer simultaneously. Then lift off the 4th gear synchronizing ring.

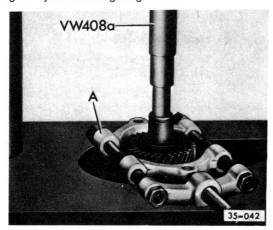

Fig. 6-46. Mainshaft being pressed out of 4th gear and 4th gear thrust washer. Separator tool US 4439 is at **A.**

3. Remove the circlip as shown in Fig. 6-47.

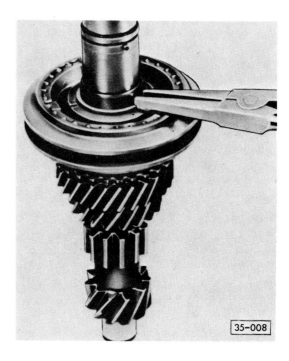

Fig. 6-47. Circlip for clutch gear assembly being removed. Notice the kind of pliers being used.

4. Using the setup shown in Fig. 6-48, simultaneously press off 3rd gear, the 3rd gear synchronizing ring, and the 3rd/4th gear clutch gear assembly. Then remove the 3rd gear needle bearing.

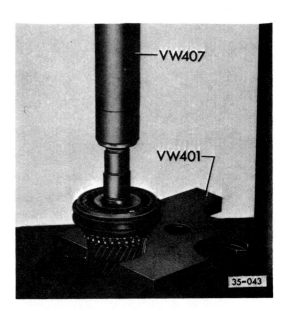

Fig. 6-48. 3rd gear, its synchronizing ring, and the clutch gear assembly being pressed off mainshaft.

5. Look for index lines that mark the position of the synchronizer hub in the operating sleeve; if there are none, mark the parts prior to any disassembly. Then, if necessary, remove the spring rings and separate the synchronizer hub from its operating sleeve as shown in Fig. 6-49.

1. Spring ring (2)
2. Operating sleeve
3. Synchronizer hub
4. Synchronizer key (3)

Fig. 6-49. Exploded view of clutch gear assembly.

To assemble:

1. Inspect all parts. Replace any part that is worn or damaged.

   NOTE ——

   There have been some changes in gear designs and tooth ratios. If you must replace a gear, first consult the Gear Application table in **10. Manual Transmission Technical Data.** Also, if you replace a gear on the mainshaft, you must also replace its meshing gear on the drive pinion shaft—the gears being available only as matched paris.

2. Hand-press the synchronizing rings into the gears as illustrated in Fig. 6-50. Measure clearance **a** with a feeler gauge. The wear limit is 0.50 mm (.020 in.). With new parts, clearance **a** should be between 1.12 and 1.75 mm (.044 and .069 in.) for 3rd gear and between 1.30 and 1.90 mm (.051 and .075 in.) for 4th gear.

Fig. 6-50. Clearance measurement **a**.

3. Assemble the clutch gear assembly with careful attention to the index lines you made or to the factory alignment marks indicated in Fig. 6-51.

   NOTE ——

   The spring rings on opposite sides of the clutch gear assembly must be installed 120° apart as shown in the illustration. If the car has been giving trouble by jumping out of 4th gear, install the new-type clutch gear assembly (Part No. 020 311 301), which can be identified by one or the other of the markings indicated in Fig. 6-52. Jumping out of gear can also be caused by incorrect mainshaft adjustment.

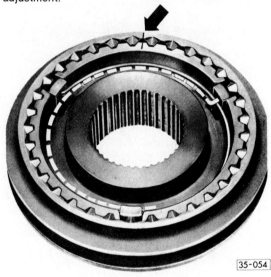

Fig. 6-51. Positions for spring rings. Make sure spring ring ends hook inside hollows of synchronizer keys. Arrow indicates alignment marks.

Fig. 6-52. New-type clutch gear assembly identification. Synchronizer hub has either circular groove on 4th gear side (white arrow) or lengthwise grooves on each spline (black arrow).

4. If the sealing washer for the clutch pushrod is leaky, or if the bushing for the clutch pushrod is worn, burred, or otherwise damaged, drive the bushing out with a 10-mm (or ⅜-in.) diameter rod, as indicated in Fig. 6-53. Always install a new sealing washer (Part No. 020 311 109). Then press in a new bushing as shown in Fig. 6-54.

NOTE ——

The sealing washer and the bushing can also be replaced with the transmission removed but not disassembled. Remove only the clutch release cover, the clutch operating lever and release shaft assembly, the release bearing, and the clutch pushrod. See **6.2 Removing and Installing Clutch Release Mechanism.**

Fig. 6-53. Bushing for clutch pushrod being driven out with rod (**A**). Drive rod in direction indicated by arrow.

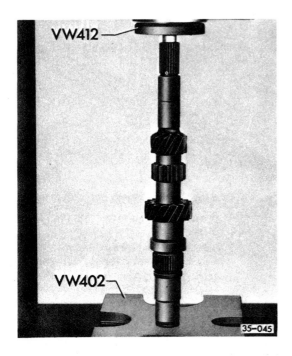

Fig. 6-54. New bushing for clutch pushrod being pressed in.

5. Install the 3rd gear needle bearing on the mainshaft.

6. Place the clutch gear assembly, the 3rd gear synchronizing ring, and 3rd gear in their correct relationship atop one another. The chamfered splines in the synchronizer hub of the clutch gear assembly must be toward 3rd gear. The notches in the 3rd gear synchronizing ring must engage the three synchronizer keys in the clutch gear assembly.

7. Press the mainshaft into the clutch gear, 3rd gear, and its synchronizing ring as shown in Fig. 6-55.

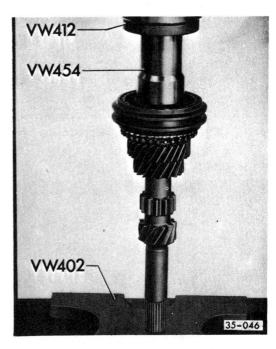

Fig. 6-55. Mainshaft being pressed into clutch gear splines. Align splines carefully.

8. Install a new circlip in the groove adjacent to the clutch gear assembly's synchronizer hub.

9. If necessary, use the repair press to move 3rd gear and the clutch gear assembly toward the snap ring until the synchronizer hub of the clutch gear assembly is in firm contact with the snap ring. Do not exceed a pressure of 2000 kg (4400 lb.).

10. Install the 4th gear synchronizing ring in the 4th-gear side of the clutch gear assembly. The notches in the ring must engage the three synchronizer keys in the clutch gear assembly.

11. Install the 4th gear needle bearing on the mainshaft.

12. Install 4th gear. If you are working on a 1975 car that has a 4th gear thrust washer—and have not replaced the original mainshaft ball bearing with the new-type ball bearing—press on a new 4th

gear thrust washer as shown in Fig. 6-56. See **6.3 Removing and Installing Mainshaft, Shift Forks, and Reverse Sliding Gear** for further information.

NOTE ——

In installing a 4th gear thrust washer, press on the washer until it contacts the shoulder on the mainshaft.

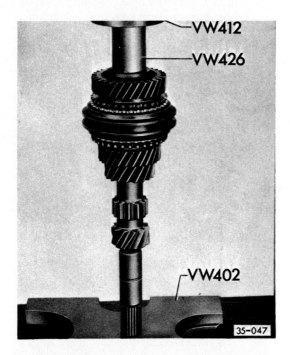

Fig. 6-56. 4th gear thrust washer, for use with early-type mainshaft bearings, being pressed on after installation of 4th gear.

13. With careful attention to the instructions given in **6.3 Removing and Installing Mainshaft, Shift Forks, and Reverse Sliding Gear,** install the mainshaft in the transaxle.

CAUTION ——

If you have replaced either half of the transaxle case, the mainshaft itself or, on mainshafts that have one, the 4th gear thrust washer, you must select a new mainshaft bearing shim (or shims) before you press the mainshaft ball bearing into its recess in the gear carrier/shift housing portion of the transaxle case. Failure to select the correct shim, for mainshaft adjustment, can result in abnormal gear wear and jumping out of gear.

6.5 Disassembling and Assembling Drive Pinion Shaft

You must disassemble the drive pinion shaft, as described under this heading, before you can remove the drive pinion or the differential assembly from the final drive portion of the transaxle case. Also, you must remove the mainshaft, the shift forks, and the reverse sliding gear, as described in **6.3 Removing and Installing Mainshaft, Shift Forks, and Reverse Sliding Gear,** before you can disassemble the drive pinion shaft. You will have already removed 4th gear and the circlip for 4th gear from the drive pinion shaft during removal of the mainshaft. See Fig. 6-57.

CAUTION ——

*If you replace the final drive portion of the transaxle case, the ring and pinion gearset, or the drive pinion shaft's tapered-roller bearings, you must select a new S_3 shim as described in **8.1 Adjusting Drive Pinion.** Failure to select the correct S_3 shim will result in gear noise and rapid transaxle wear.*

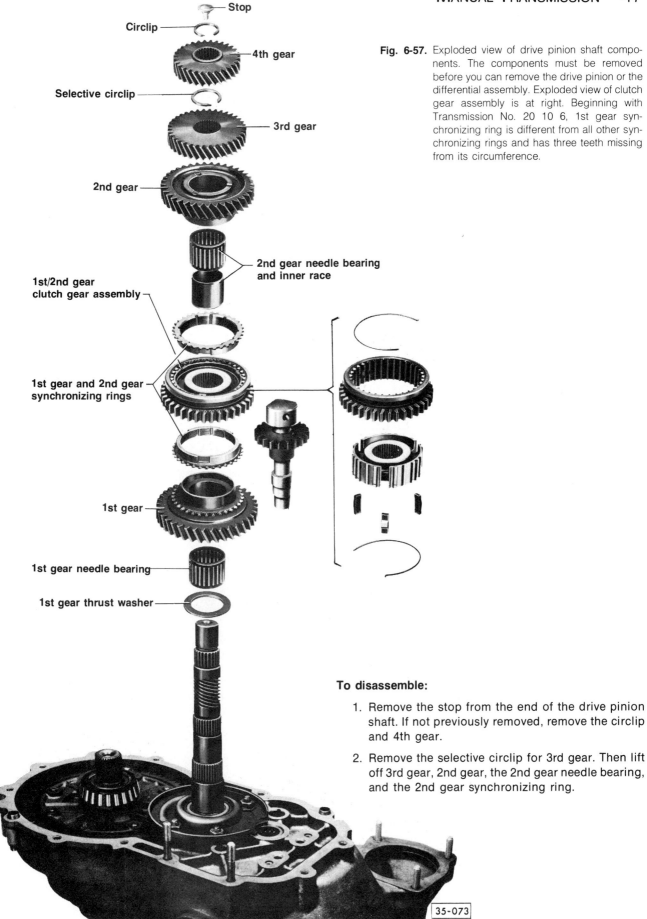

Stop

Circlip

4th gear

Selective circlip

3rd gear

2nd gear

2nd gear needle bearing and inner race

1st/2nd gear clutch gear assembly

1st gear and 2nd gear synchronizing rings

1st gear

1st gear needle bearing

1st gear thrust washer

35-073

Fig. 6-57. Exploded view of drive pinion shaft components. The components must be removed before you can remove the drive pinion or the differential assembly. Exploded view of clutch gear assembly is at right. Beginning with Transmission No. 20 10 6, 1st gear synchronizing ring is different from all other synchronizing rings and has three teeth missing from its circumference.

To disassemble:

1. Remove the stop from the end of the drive pinion shaft. If not previously removed, remove the circlip and 4th gear.

2. Remove the selective circlip for 3rd gear. Then lift off 3rd gear, 2nd gear, the 2nd gear needle bearing, and the 2nd gear synchronizing ring.

3. Using a puller, as shown in Fig. 6-58, simultaneously remove 1st gear, the 1st gear synchronizing ring, the 1st/2nd gear clutch gear assembly, and the 2nd gear needle bearing inner race.

4. Remove the 1st gear needle bearing. Remove the 1st gear thrust washer.

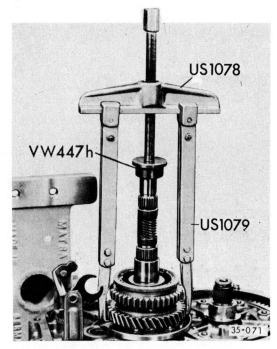

Fig. 6-58. 1st/2nd gear clutch gear assembly and 1st gear synchronizing ring being removed by applying a puller to 1st gear.

5. Look for index lines that mark the position of the synchronizer hub in the operating sleeve; if there are none, mark the parts prior to any disassembly. Then, if necessary, remove the spring rings and separate the synchronizer hub from its operating sleeve as shown in Fig. 6-59.

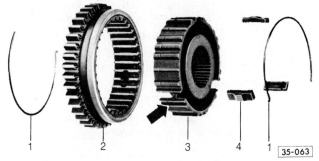

1. Spring ring (2)
2. Operating sleeve
3. Synchronizer hub
4. Synchronizer key (3)

Fig. 6-59. Exploded view of clutch gear assembly. Arrow indicates different spacing of splines that distinguishes the 1st/2nd gear synchronizer hub from the 3rd/4th gear synchronizer hub.

6. If you must replace the drive pinion shaft needle bearing, which is in the gear carrier/shift housing portion of the transaxle case, remove it with a slide hammer and expansion tool as shown in Fig. 6-60. Install the new needle bearing—with the thickest side of the cage against the installing tool—as shown in Fig. 6-61.

Fig. 6-60. Drive pinion shaft needle bearing being removed from transaxle case. Expansion tool is at **A**. Move slide hammer as indicated by arrow.

Fig. 6-61. Drive pinion shaft needle bearing being driven (arrow) into transaxle case.

7. If you need to remove the drive pinion, or replace the drive pinion's tapered-roller bearings, do so as described in **7.1 Removing and Installing Drive Pinion Shaft and Tapered-roller Bearings.**

NOTE ——

You should also read **8.1 Adjusting Drive Pinion** in order to determine whether precision measurements will be required for the selection of a new S₃ shim following the anticipated repairs.

To assemble:

1. Inspect all parts. Replace any part that is worn or damaged.

   NOTE ——

   There have been some changes in gear designs and tooth ratios. If you must replace a gear, first consult the Gear Application table in **10. Manual Transmission Technical Data.** Also, if you replace a gear on the drive pinion shaft, you must also replace its meshing gear on the mainshaft—the gears being available only as matched paris.

2. Hand-press the synchronizing rings into the gears as illustrated in Fig. 6-62. Measure clearance **a** with a feeler gauge. The wear limit is 0.50 mm (.020 in.). With new parts, clearance **a** should be between 1.10 and 1.70 mm (.043 and .067 in.).

Fig. 6-62. Clearance measurement **a**.

3. Assemble the clutch gear assembly with careful attention to the index lines you made or to the factory alignment marks indicated in Fig. 6-63.

   NOTE ——

   The spring rings on opposite sides of the clutch gear assembly must be installed 120° apart as shown in the illustration.

4. Install the 1st gear thrust washer, the 1st gear needle bearing, 1st gear, and the 1st gear synchronizing ring on the drive pinion.

5. Heat the 1st/2nd gear clutch gear assembly to 120°C (or 250°F) in an oven. Then press on the clutch gear assembly as shown in Fig. 6-64.

CAUTION ——

To prevent damage, you must align the 1st gear synchronizing ring with the synchronizer keys of the clutch gear assembly. (From Transmission No. 20 10 6, the 1st gear synchronizing ring is different from all other synchronizing rings and has three teeth missing from its circumference.) The shift fork groove in the assembly's operating sleeve must be toward the press tool—away from the previously-installed 1st gear.

Fig. 6-63. Positions for spring rings. Make sure spring ring ends hook inside hollows of synchronizer keys. Arrow indicates alignment marks.

Fig. 6-64. 1st/2nd gear clutch gear assembly being pressed (or driven) onto drive pinion shaft.

6. Drive on the 2nd gear needle bearing inner race as indicated in Fig. 6-65. The needle bearing inner race must be fully seated against the synchronizer hub of the clutch gear assembly.

Fig. 6-65. 2nd gear needle bearing inner race being driven (arrow) onto drive pinion shaft.

7. Install the 2nd gear needle bearing, 2nd gear, and 3rd gear. The side of the 3rd gear that has the collar should be toward 2nd gear.

8. Choose a selective circlip from **Table b** that, when installed, will limit the end play of 3rd gear to 0.00 to 0.20 mm (.000 to .008 in.)—the nearer 0.00 mm (.000 in.) the better. Measure the end play by inserting feeler gauges of various thicknesses between 3rd gear and the selective circlip, as shown in Fig. 6-66.

Table b. Selective Circlip Thicknesses

Part No.	Thickness	Color
020 311 381	2.50 mm	brown
020 311 381 A	2.60 mm	black
020 311 381 B	2.70 mm	shiny uncolored metal
020 311 381 C	2.80 mm	copper
020 311 381 D	2.90 mm	brass
020 311 381 E	3.00 mm	blue

NOTE ——
Always install a new circlip. Once removed, these circlips are no longer serviceable.

Fig. 6-66. End play of 3rd gear being determined by inserting feeler gauge between 3rd gear and selective circlip.

9. Install the stop in the end of the drive pinion shaft. Do not install 4th gear or its circlip until you have installed the mainshaft in the transaxle. Always use a new 4th gear circlip during assembly.

7. Final Drive

Neither the drive pinion shaft nor the differential can be removed from the final drive portion of the transaxle case until you have first removed the mainshaft, the shift forks, and the reverse sliding gear. The drive pinion shaft must then be disassembled, as described in **6.5 Disassembling and Assembling Drive Pinion Shaft.** Only then is it possible to remove first the drive pinion shaft and then the differential assembly.

Before you remove either the drive pinion shaft or the differential, please read **8. Adjusting Final Drive** in order to determine whether precision measurements must be made after you have repaired the transaxle. If the final drive is not correctly adjusted, it may make noise and wear rapidly.

CAUTION ——
If you lack the skills, tools, or a clean workshop for final drive repairs, we suggest you leave these repairs to an Authorized Dealer or other qualified shop. We especially urge you to consult your Authorized Dealer before attempting repairs on a car still covered by the new-car warranty.

7.1 Removing and Installing Drive Pinion Shaft and Tapered-roller Bearings

Fig. 7-1 is an exploded view of the drive pinion shaft and its tapered-roller bearings. Though each of the two tapered-roller bearing assemblies is available separately, you should always replace both bearings with new bearings at the same time. Otherwise, accurate adjustment will not be possible. Once a tapered-roller bearing

inner race has been removed from the drive pinion shaft, the bearing is no longer serviceable and must be replaced. If you replace the drive pinion shaft itself, you must replace the ring gear also. The two gears are factory-matched pairs and must not be combined with meshing gears from another gearset.

To remove the drive pinion shaft and its bearings from the final drive portion of the transaxle case, first disassemble the drive pinion shaft as described in **6.5 Disassembling and Assembling Drive Pinion Shaft.** On transmissions prior to Transmission No. 10 09 6, built during the early part of the 1977 model year, remove the four nuts, the washers, and the two reinforcement plates that hold the retainer to the transaxle case. (Beginning with Transmission No. 10 09 6, bolts without washers, but with special heads, are used instead of nuts and washers.) Lift off the retainer, then lift the drive pinion shaft and its bearings out of the case.

To remove the large tapered-roller bearing inner race from the drive pinion shaft, press the shaft out of the bearing as shown in Fig. 7-2. Press the shaft out of the small tapered-roller bearing inner race as shown in Fig. 7-3. Be careful that the drive pinion shaft does not fall or become damaged in some other way during these operations.

- Retainer with large tapered-roller bearing outer race
- Large tapered-roller bearing inner race
- Drive pinion shaft
- Small tapered-roller bearing inner race
- Small tapered-roller bearing outer race
- S₃ shim

39-176

Fig. 7-1. Exploded view of drive pinion shaft and tapered-roller bearing assemblies.

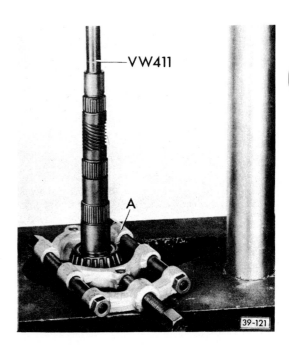

Fig. 7-2. Drive pinion shaft being pressed out of large tapered-roller bearing inner race. Separator tool US 4439 is at **A**.

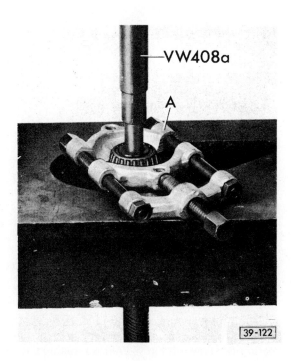

Fig. 7-3. Drive pinion shaft being pressed out of small tapered-roller bearing inner race. Separator tool US 4439 is at **A**.

To install the new tapered-roller bearing inner races on the drive pinion shaft, first heat the inner races to approximately 100°C (212°F) in a pan of oil placed in a larger pan of boiling water. Alternatively, you can heat the bearing races in an oven. Press on the small tapered-roller bearing inner race as shown in Fig. 7-4. Press on the large tapered-roller bearing inner race as shown in Fig. 7-5.

CAUTION ——

Never install a tapered-roller bearing inner race that has been removed from a drive pinion shaft. Once removed, the bearings are no longer serviceable.

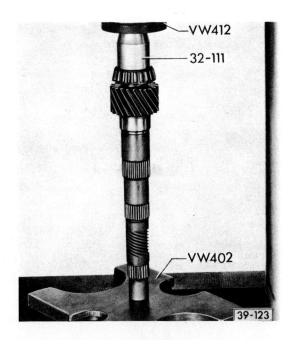

Fig. 7-4. Small tapered-roller bearing inner race being pressed onto drive pinion shaft.

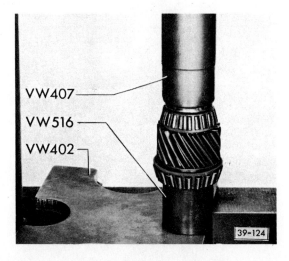

Fig. 7-5. Large tapered-roller bearing inner race being pressed onto drive pinion shaft.

Use an expansion puller to withdraw the small tapered-roller bearing outer race from the final drive portion of the transaxle case. See Fig. 7-6. Remove the S_3 shim, which is located beneath the outer race.

NOTE ——

It is neither necessary nor desirable to remove the large tapered-roller bearing outer race from the retainer. A new retainer, with a factory-installed outer race, is supplied with large tapered-roller bearing replacement assemblies.

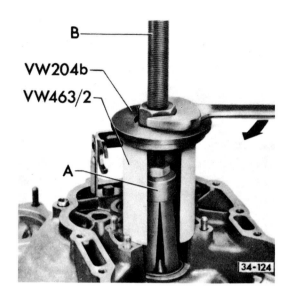

Fig. 7-6. Small tapered-roller bearing outer race being removed. Expansion puller US 1099 is at **A**, puller screw is at **B**. Turn nut with wrench as indicated by arrow.

If you have replaced the final drive portion of the transaxle case, the ring and pinion gearset, or the drive pinion shaft's tapered-roller bearings, select a new S_3 shim as described in **8.1 Adjusting Drive Pinion.** Otherwise, install the original S_3 shim. Then drive in the small tapered-roller bearing outer race as indicated in Fig. 7-7.

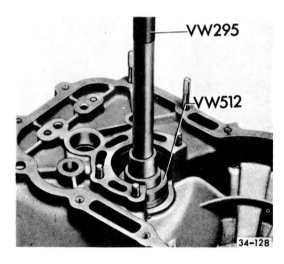

Fig. 7-7. Small tapered-roller bearing outer race being driven in atop correct S_3 shim.

To install the drive pinion shaft, first install the differential—if previously removed. Lubricate the pinion head and the tapered-roller bearings with hypoid oil only. Then install the drive pinion shaft in the case, meshing the teeth of the pinion head with the teeth of the ring gear. Install the retainer, the reinforcement plates, and

where applicable the washers. Install the nuts or the bolts. Then, working diagonally, gradually torque nuts to 2.5 mkg (18 ft. lb.) or bolts to 4.0 mkg (29 ft. lb.). Hand-turn the drive pinion in order to make sure that the bearings are evenly lubricated and are not binding.

7.2 Removing and Installing Differential

You cannot remove the differential from the final drive portion of the transaxle case until you have removed the drive pinion shaft as described under the preceding heading. It is important that the differential is solidly supported during removal and installation of the drive flange.

To remove differential:

1. Invert the final drive portion of the transaxle case. Position the case over the workbench so that the lower end of the differential is solidly supported.

2. Pry out the plastic dust cap that is in the center of the drive flange. Then, using circlip pliers, remove the circlip that is in the center of the drive flange, in a groove on the differential's sidegear shaft. Remove the dished washer.

3. Using a puller as shown in Fig. 7-8, remove the right drive flange.

Fig. 7-8. Right drive flange being removed. Puller is held to drive flange by two M 8 X 30 bolts. Turn nut with wrench as indicated by arrow.

4. Remove the differential assembly from the final drive portion of the transaxle case.

To install:

1. Inspect the oil seal for the right drive flange. If it is worn, hard, cracked, or otherwise damaged, pry it

6

out with a hooked tool or a large screwdriver. Pack the open side of the new seal with multipurpose grease before you install the seal as shown in Fig. 7-9.

Fig. 7-9. Drive flange oil seal being installed. Drive in as indicated by arrow.

2. Lubricate the differential tapered-roller bearings, the ring gear teeth, and the differential gears and shafts with hypoid oil only. Then install the differential assembly in the final drive portion of the transaxle case.

> **CAUTION ——**
>
> *If you are installing a new differential or a new differential case—or if you have replaced either half of the transaxle case or a differential tapered-roller bearing—you must adjust the final drive before you install the differential. See **8.2 Adjusting Differential.***

3. With the differential firmly supported, install the right drive flange as indicated in Fig. 7-10.

4. With the drive flange fully seated, install the dished washer so that its convex side is away from the drive flange. Use circlip pliers to install a new circlip—but do not attempt to seat the circlip in its groove.

5. Drive the circlip inward against the tension of the dished washer, as shown in Fig. 7-11, until the circlip snaps into its groove. Install a new dust cap.

6. Turn over the final drive portion of the transaxle case so that you can install the drive pinion shaft and other transaxle components.

Fig. 7-10. Right drive flange being installed. Central screw threads into hole in differential's sidegear shaft. Turn nut with wrench as indicated by arrow.

Fig. 7-11. Circlip being driven inward (arrow) against tension of dished washer until circlip snaps into its groove.

7.3 Disassembling and Assembling Differential

Fig. 7-12 is an exploded view of the differential. The tapered-roller bearing inner races need be removed only if they require replacement. See **7.4 Removing and Installing Differential Tapered-roller Bearings.** If you replace the bearings, the differential housing, or the ring and pinion gearset, you must adjust the final drive as described in **8. Adjusting Final Drive** before you install the repaired differential.

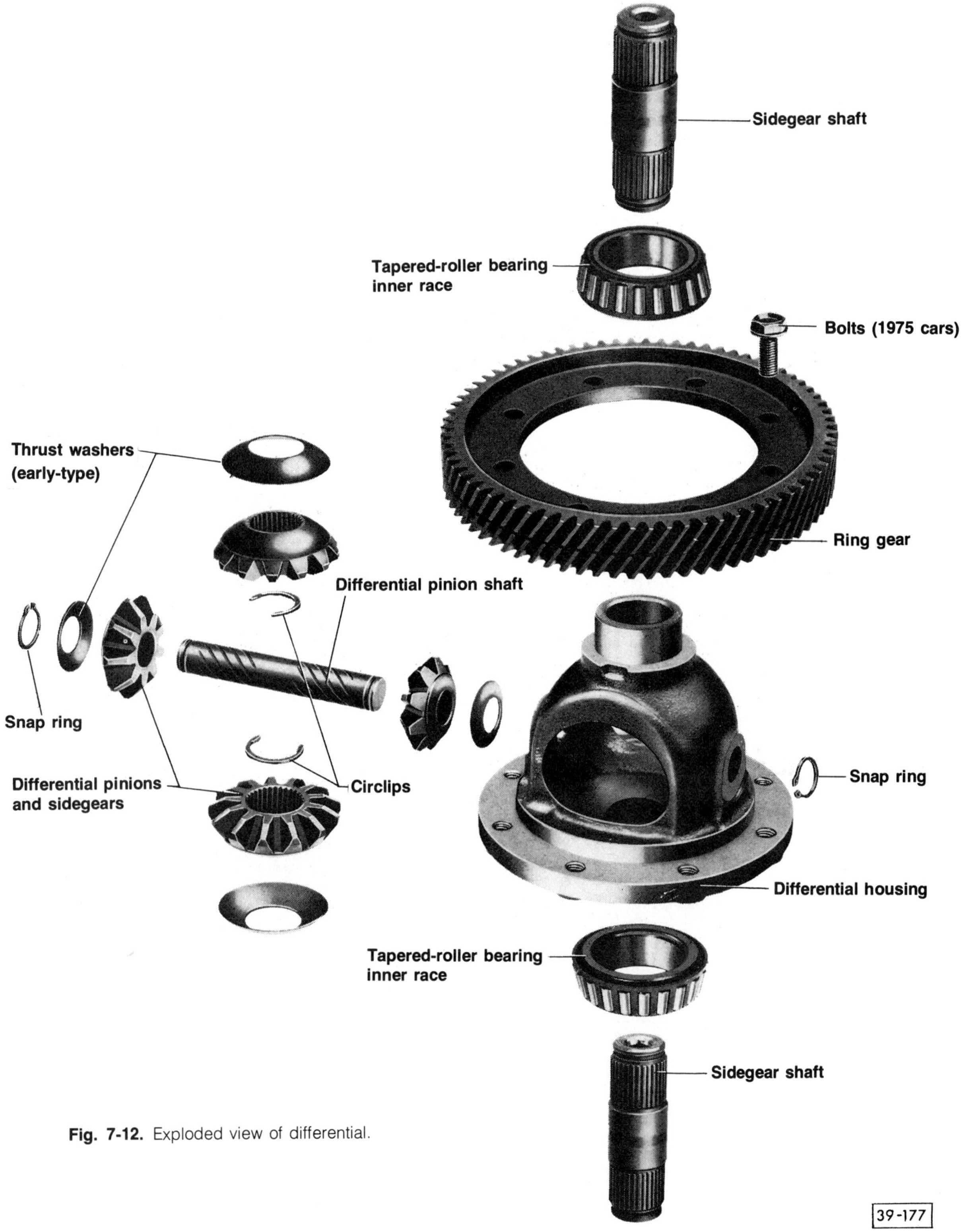

Sidegear shaft

Tapered-roller bearing
inner race

Bolts (1975 cars)

Ring gear

Thrust washers
(early-type)

Differential pinion shaft

Snap ring

Snap ring

Differential pinions
and sidegears

Circlips

Differential housing

Tapered-roller bearing
inner race

Sidegear shaft

Fig. 7-12. Exploded view of differential.

6

39-177

To disassemble:

1. If you are working on a 1976 or later car, the ring gear is held to the differential housing by rivets—unless the ring gear has previously been removed. If the gear is riveted, drill off the rivet heads with a 12-mm ($^{15}/_{32}$-in.) drill bit, as shown in Fig. 7-13. Then knock the rivets out with a drift.

> **CAUTION ——**
>
> *Protect the tapered-roller bearings from flying metal chips while you drill the rivets. Thoroughly clean the differential in order to remove all metal particles. Metal chips and shavings in the transaxle will quickly ruin the gears and bearings.*

Fig. 7-13. Ring gear rivets being drilled out of 1976 and later differential assembly.

2. If the ring gear is held to the differential housing by bolts, as shown earlier in Fig. 7-12—or if the rivets have been drilled out of a 1976 or later differential and replaced by special bolts with nuts—remove the bolts or the nuts that hold the ring gear to the differential housing.

3. Using the setup shown in Fig. 7-14, press the differential out of the ring gear—being careful not to let the differential fall.

4. Using snap ring pliers, remove the snap rings for the differential pinion shaft. Then drive the shaft out of the differential housing, the differential pinions, and the pinion thrust washers.

5. Remove the circlips that hold the differential sidegears to the differential sidegear shafts. Withdraw the shafts from the differential housing. Then remove the differential pinions, the sidegears, and the thrust washers.

Fig. 7-14. Differential being pressed out of ring gear.

> **NOTE ——**
>
> At approximately the beginning of the 1976 model year, the four separate thrust washers were eliminated and, in their place, a thrust spacer cage was introduced. This is a one-piece metal fabrication that has four round openings centered in the hemispherical parts of the cage that serve as thrust washers.

To assemble:

1. Insert the pinion thrust washers or the thrust cage. Insert the differential pinions. Drive in the differential pinion shaft—being especially careful not to damage the thrust washers or thrust cage.

2. Install the snap rings for the differential pinion shaft.

3. On differentials with thrust washers, insert the sidegears and their thrust washers as shown in Fig. 7-15. Position the sidegears so that they are meshed with the pinions and are 180° apart. Then rotate the sidegears and their thrust washers into position inside the housing.

4. On differentials with a thrust cage, rotate the thrust cage inside the housing until the sidegear shaft holes in the cage are aligned with the sidegear shaft holes in the housing. Then position the sidegears so that they are meshed with the pinions and are 180° apart. Rotate the sidegears into position inside the housing.

5. Install the sidegear shaft. Push each sidegear shaft as firmly as possible against the differential pinion shaft. Then install the thickest possible circlip. See Fig. 7-16.

There are two available circlips. One is 2.00 mm thick (Part No. 020 409 299) and the other is 2.30 mm thick (Part No. 020 409 299 A). If the thicker circlip jams sideways when you install it, use the thinner circlip.

39-136

Fig. 7-15. Sidegears being installed in differential housing. Insert sidegears through opening, then rotate into position as indicated by arrow.

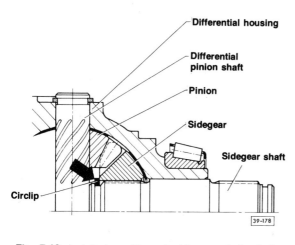

Differential housing

Differential pinion shaft

Pinion

Sidegear

Sidegear shaft

Circlip

39-178

Fig. 7-16. Installed position of sidegear shaft circlip (arrow).

6. If the ring gear was originally held by rivets, drive the special bolts into the differential housing. The special bolts and nuts are included in a kit, Part No. 171 498 088. See Fig. 7-17.

7. Heat the ring gear to approximately 100°C (212°F) in a pan of oil placed in a larger pan of boiling water. Alternatively, you can heat the ring gear in an oven. Install the heated ring gear on the differential housing as shown in Fig. 7-18.

The guide pins shown in Fig. 7-18 are helpful for installing the ring gear on a 1975 differential housing. The pins can be made by grinding the heads off two long bolts that fit the threads in the differential housing.

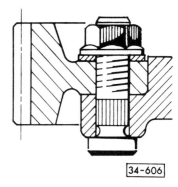

34-606

Fig. 7-17. Special bolt, washer, and nut used to replace factory-installed rivets on 1976 and later ring gears. Serrations on bolt shank lock bolt into position in housing when bolt is driven in.

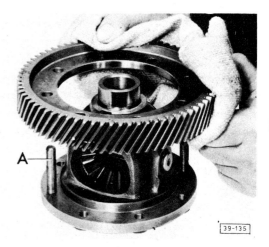

39-135

Fig. 7-18. Heated ring gear being installed on differential. One of two guide pins is at **A**. Protect your hands with gloves or hold the hot ring gear with rags, as shown.

8. On 1975 differentials, which have tapped holes in the housing, install the ring gear retaining bolts and torque them to 5.0 mkg (36 ft. lb.). On 1976 and later differentials, which must be equipped with special bolts after the rivets have been removed, install the washers and the ring gear retaining nuts to a torque of 7.0 mkg (50 ft. lb.).

If you have replaced the ring gear, you must replace the drive pinion also. The two gears are factory-matched pairs and must not be combined with meshing gears from another gearset.

6

7.4 Removing and Installing Differential Tapered-roller Bearings

Remove the tapered-roller bearing races only if the bearings must be replaced. Replace bearings that are noisy, obviously worn, rough, galled, flattened, or heat-blued. It is unnecessary to remove the tapered-roller bearing inner races in order to disassemble the differential.

You can remove the tapered-roller bearing inner races with a puller, as shown in Fig. 7-19. The tapered-roller bearing inner race that is opposite the ring gear can also be removed with a repair press, as shown in Fig. 7-20.

NOTE ———

You must remove the differential sidegear shafts, as described in **7.3 Disassembling and Assembling Differential**, before you can either remove or install the tapered-roller bearing inner races.

Fig. 7-19. Puller (**A**) being used to remove tapered-roller bearing inner race. Recesses are provided in differential housing to accommodate puller hooks.

Before you install a tapered-roller bearing inner race, heat it to approximately 100°C (212°F) in a pan of oil placed in a larger pan of boiling water. Alternatively, you can heat the inner race in an oven. Press on the tapered-roller bearing inner race as shown in Fig. 7-21 or Fig. 7-22.

CAUTION ———

If you replace a tapered-roller bearing inner race, you must replace the outer race also, using the matching race from the bearing set. If you remove more than one bearing at a time, be careful not to mix up the races with those of the other bearing. If you install new bearings, you must adjust the differential as described in **8.2 Adjusting Differential.**

Fig. 7-20. Tapered-roller bearing inner race opposite ring gear being removed with repair press.

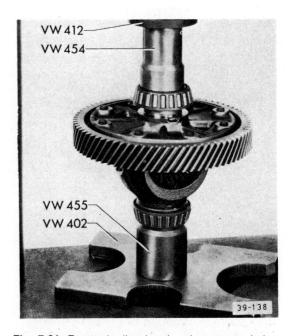

Fig. 7-21. Tapered-roller bearing inner race being pressed onto ring gear side of differential.

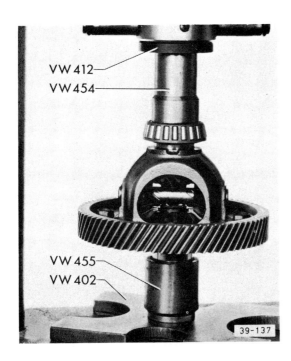

Fig. 7-22. Tapered-roller bearing inner race being pressed onto end of differential housing that is opposite ring gear.

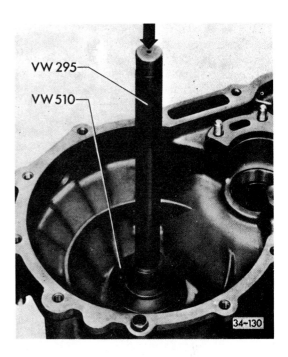

Fig. 7-24. Tapered-roller bearing outer race being driven into final drive housing atop S_2 shim (a 1-mm spacer).

To remove the tapered-roller bearing outer race from the final drive housing portion of the transaxle case, first pry out the drive flange oil seal. Then press out the tapered-roller bearing outer race as shown in Fig. 7-23. Remove the S_2 shim that is between the bearing race and the transaxle case. If the S_2 shim is in good condition, it can be reused. The S_2 shim is a 1-mm thick spacer and is never exchanged for a thicker or thinner shim for purposes of adjusting the final drive. Install the S_2 shim, then press in the tapered-roller bearing outer race as shown in Fig. 7-24.

To remove the tapered-roller bearing outer race from the gear carrier/shift housing portion of the transaxle case, first pry out the drive flange oil seal. Then press out the tapered-roller bearing outer race as shown in Fig. 7-25. Remove the S_1 shim(s) located between the bearing race and the transaxle case.

6 ∎

Fig. 7-23. Tapered-roller bearing outer race being pressed out of final drive housing portion of transaxle case.

Fig. 7-25. Tapered-roller bearing outer race being pressed out of gear carrier/shift housing portion of transaxle case.

If you have replaced either half of the transaxle case, the differential housing, or either of the differential tapered roller bearings, you must select a new S_1 shim as described in **8.2 Adjusting Differential**. If you must select a new S_1 shim, install the tapered-roller bearing outer race in the gear carrier/shift housing portion of the transaxle case without any S_1 shim. If you do not need to select a new S_1 shim, install the original shim(s) and then press in the tapered-roller bearing outer race. See Fig. 7-26.

Fig. 7-26. Tapered-roller bearing outer race being pressed into gear carrier/shift housing portion of transaxle case.

8. ADJUSTING FINAL DRIVE

Owing to the use of spur gears in the final drive, adjustment of the mesh between the ring gear and the drive pinion is not necessary during repair of the transaxle. Nevertheless, careful adjustment of the drive pinion shaft tapered-roller bearings and the differential tapered-roller bearings is essential to ensure long life and quiet operation.

The final drive requires adjustments only when parts directly affecting the adjustment have been replaced, or when careless disassembly has resulted in the loss of the original S_1 and S_3 shims. **Table c** lists what adjustments must be made when certain parts are replaced. Mainshaft adjustment, to determine the thickness of the mainshaft bearing shim, is described in **6.3 Removing and Installing Mainshaft, Shift Forks, and Reverse Sliding Gear.**

8.1 Adjusting Drive Pinion

If not previously removed, remove the drive pinion shaft's small tapered-roller bearing outer race from the final drive housing portion of the transaxle case, as shown in Fig. 8-1. Remove the original S_3 shim, which is beneath the outer race. Then install, as a temporary S_3 shim, the shim Part No. 020 311 391, which is 0.75 mm thick. Press in the tapered-roller bearing outer race as shown in Fig. 8-2.

To prepare the drive pinion for adjustment, install the drive pinion shaft in the final drive housing portion of the transaxle case. Torque the nuts for the retainer to 2.5 mkg (18 ft. lb.). Then install a dial indicator as shown in Fig. 8-3. Zero the dial indicator with a 1-mm preload.

CAUTION ——

Do not turn the drive pinion shaft while you are installing it, during installation of the dial indicator, or during subsequent measurements. If the shaft is turned, the bearings will settle, thus producing incorrect dial indicator readings. The bearings should not be lubricated during the following measurement.

Table c. Necessary Adjustments for Replaced Parts

Part replaced	Parts to be adjusted		
	Mainshaft	Differential	Drive pinion
Gear carrier/shift housing portion of transaxle case	X	X	
Final drive housing portion of transaxle case	X	X	X
One or both differential tapered-roller bearings		X	
Ring and pinion gearset			X
Differential housing		X	
Drive pinion tapered-roller bearings (always replace both bearings)			X
Mainshaft	X		
4th gear thrust washer (only on early transaxles that have this washer)	X		

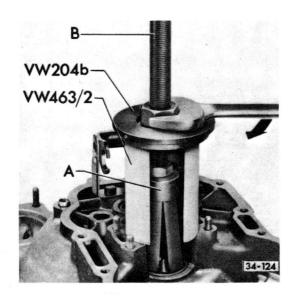

Fig. 8-1. Expansion tool (**A**) and puller (**B**) being used to remove drive pinion shaft's small tapered-roller bearing from transaxle case. Turn nut with wrench as indicated by arrow.

Fig. 8-2. Drive pinion shaft's small tapered-roller bearing outer race being pressed into transaxle case atop temporary 0.75-mm thick S_3 shim.

To obtain a bearing play reading, move the drive pinion shaft up and down once as indicated in Fig. 8-4. Write down the maximum dial indicator reading.

To compute the correct thickness for the permanent S_3 shim, add the dial indicator reading to the thickness of the temporary S_3 shim (0.75 mm). To this, add the constant 0.20 mm which is to compensate for normal bearing preload. The sum of these three numbers is the correct thickness for the permanent S_3 shim. (See the example on the next page.)

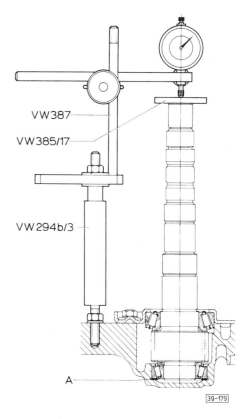

Fig. 8-3. Tool setup used to measure drive pinion shaft end-play with temporary 0.75-mm S_3 shim (**A**) installed. Tool VW 385/17 is a magnetic plate that provides a smooth surface for the dial indicator's gauge pin.

6

Fig. 8-4. Bearing play being measured. Move drive pinion shaft up and down once, as indicated by double arrow.

CAUTION ——

The dial indicator reading and the permanent S_3 shim thickness in the following example are imaginary. Using them for actual adjustments could cause serious damage.

Example:

Dial indicator reading	0.30 mm
Temporary shim thickness	+0.75 mm
Constant figure for preload	+0.20 mm
Permanent S_3 shim thickness	=1.25 mm

Select the new permanent S_3 shim from **Table d.** Then remove the small tapered-roller bearing inner race as previously shown in Fig. 8-1. Remove the temporary S_3 shim used during measuring and install the new permanent S_3 shim. Press in the bearing inner race as previously shown in Fig. 8-2.

Table d. Available S_3 Shims

Part Number	Shim thickness
020 311 391	0.75 mm
020 311 391 A	0.80 mm
020 311 391 B	0.85 mm
020 311 391 C	0.90 mm
020 311 391 D	0.95 mm
020 311 391 E	1.00 mm
020 311 391 F	1.05 mm
020 311 391 G	1.10 mm
020 311 391 H	1.15 mm
020 311 391 I	1.20 mm
020 311 391 K	1.25 mm
020 311 391 L	1.30 mm
020 311 391 M	1.35 mm
020 311 391 N	1.40 mm
020 311 391 P	0.65 mm (Newly available)
020 311 391 Q	0.70 mm (Newly available)

If you have installed new drive pinion shaft tapered-roller bearings, lubricate the bearings with hypoid oil. Then install the drive pinion shaft in the final drive housing portion of the transaxle case. Torque the nuts to 2.5 mkg (18 ft. lb.). Using the torque gauge shown in Fig. 8-5, spin the drive pinion 15 or 20 turns in each direction. While spinning the pinion rapidly, the turning torque should be 5 to 15 cmkg (4.5 to 13 in. lb.). Recheck the pinion adjustment if the turning torque is incorrect.

NOTE ——

Used bearings cannot be checked as described here. For this reason, special care should be given to the correct selection of an S_3 shim whenever a drive pinion shaft with used bearings is being installed in a new final drive housing.

Fig. 8-5. Drive pinion turning torque with new bearings being checked with torque gauge (**A**).

8.2 Adjusting Differential

The differential adjustment is by two shims installed between the differential tapered-roller bearing outer races and the transaxle case. The S_2 shim, which is installed in the final drive housing portion of the transaxle case, is a 1-mm thick spacer and is never exchanged for a thicker or thinner shim for purposes of adjusting the final drive. The S_1 shim is installed in the gear carrier/shift housing portion of the transaxle case. The precision measurements described under this heading are necessary in order to determine the thickness of the S_1 shim.

If you have not already done so, install the S_2 shim (the 1-mm thick spacer, Part No. 020 409 298) in the final drive housing portion of the transaxle case. Then drive in the tapered-roller bearing outer race as indicated in Fig. 8-6. Make sure that you install the outer race that is a matched pair with the tapered-roller bearing inner race that is installed on the side of the differential opposite the ring gear.

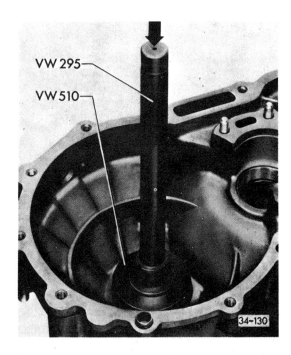

Fig. 8-6. Tapered-roller bearing outer race being driven into final drive housing atop S_2 shim (a 1-mm spacer).

If you have not already done so, drive out the tapered-roller bearing outer race that is in the gear carrier/shift housing portion of the transaxle case in order to remove the S_1 shim(s). See Fig. 8-7. Using the tools illustrated previously in Fig. 8-6, reinstall the outer race—without an S_1 shim.

Fig. 8-7. Tapered-roller bearing outer race being driven (arrow) out of gear carrier/shift housing portion of transaxle case.

To prepare the differential for adjustment, install the differential in the final drive housing portion of the transaxle case. Install a new gasket on the mating surface, then install the gear carrier/shift housing portion of the transaxle case. Torque the bolts to 2.0 mkg (14 ft. lb.). Then install a dial indicator as shown in Fig. 8-8. Zero the dial indicator with a 1-mm preload.

CAUTION ——

Do not turn the differential while you are installing it, during installation of the dial indicator, or during subsequent measurements. If the differential is turned, the bearings will settle, thus producing incorrect dial indicator readings. The bearings should not be lubricated during the following measurement.

Fig. 8-8. Tool setup used to measure differential end-play with no S_1 shim installed. Tool VW 385/17 is a magnetic plate that provides a smooth surface for the dial indicator's gauge pin.

To obtain a bearing play reading, move the differential up and down once by pushing upward on the left sidegear shaft. Write down the maximum dial indicator reading. To compute the correct thickness for the S_1 shim, add the dial indicator reading to the constant 0.40 mm which is to compensate for normal bearing preload. The sum of the measurement plus the constant equals the thickness of the S_1 shim.

CAUTION ——

The dial indicator reading and the S_1 shim thickness in the following example are imaginary. Using them for actual adjustments could cause serious damage.

Example:

Dial indicator reading	0.90 mm
Constant figure for preload	+0.40 mm
S_1 shim thickness	=1.30 mm

Select the new S_1 shim(s) from **Table e.** Use as few shims as possible in making up the required thickness. If necessary, you can use one or two shims in addition to the 1-mm thick spacer (Part No. 020 409 298).

Table e. Available S_1 shims

Part Number	Shim thickness
020 409 231	0.15 mm
020 409 231 A	0.30 mm
020 409 231 B	0.40 mm (replacement part unavailable)
020 409 231 C	0.50 mm (replacement part unavailable)
020 409 231 D	0.60 mm
020 409 231 E	0.70 mm
020 409 231 F	0.80 mm
020 409 298	1.00 mm (also used as S_2 shim)

Disassemble the transaxle case and remove the differential. Then remove the tapered-roller bearing outer race from the gear carrier/shift housing portion of the transaxle case, as previously illustrated in Fig. 8-7. Install the correct S_1 shim(s)—thickest shim first and thinnest shim against the bearing race. Press in the tapered-roller bearing outer race atop the shim(s).

Lubricate the differential bearings with hypoid oil. Then reinstall the differential in the transaxle case. Using the torque gauge shown in Fig. 8-9, spin the differential 15 or 20 turns in each direction. While spinning the differential, the turning torque with used bearings should not be less than 3 cmkg (2.6 in. lb.). If it is less, install new bearings and select a new S_1 shim. If new bearings do not provide a turning torque well above the used bearing minimum, something is wrong with the bearings or you have not selected the correct S_1 shim(s).

9. TRANSAXLE CASE

The transaxle case is assembled from two halves, or housings. The right-hand half is referred to in this Manual as the final drive housing portion of the transaxle case. The left-hand half is referred to as the gear carrier/shift housing portion of the transaxle case. The halves are not matched pairs. So, if one half is damaged or worn, you can replace it without also replacing the other half.

> **CAUTION ——**
>
> *Precision measurements and adjustments will be required if you replace one or both halves of the transaxle case. Before deciding to replace the case halves, please read* **8. Adjusting Final Drive**.

Fig. 9-1 is an exploded view of the final drive housing portion of the transaxle case. An exploded view of the gear carrier/shift housing portion of the transaxle case is given in Fig. 9-2. All of the components shown in these illustrations must be transferred from the original housing if you replace either half of the transaxle case.

The callout keys that accompany the illustrations tell how to remove and install the transaxle case components or, alternatively, list the headings in this section of the Manual where instructions can be found. In some cases, another section is listed, wherein you will find the applicable removal and installation procedures.

Fig. 8-9. Differential turning torque being checked with torque gauge (**A**).

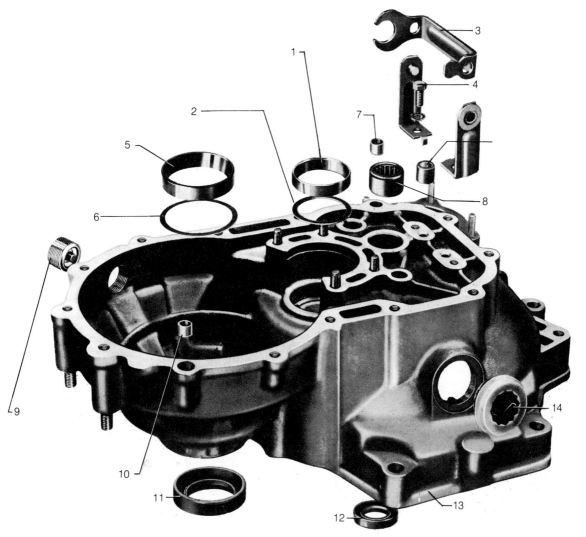

34-213

1. Drive pinion small tapered-roller bearing outer race—see **7.1**
2. S₁ shim—see **7.1**
3. Reverse sliding gear shift fork—see **6.3**
4. Bolt—torque to 1.5 mkg (11 ft. lb.)
5. Differential tapered-roller bearing outer race (side opposite ring gear)—see **7.4**
6. S₂ shim—see **7.4**
7. Starter drive bushing—see **9.1**
8. Mainshaft needle bearing—see **6.3**
9. Oil drain plug—torque to 2.0 mkg (14 ft. lb.)
10. Hollow dowel (2)—remove and install with pliers
11. Drive flange oil seal—see **7.2**
12. Mainshaft oil seal—see **6.3**
13. Final drive housing
14. TDC sensor (or plastic plug)—see **5.**

Fig. 9-1. Exploded view of final drive housing portion of transaxle case.

Fig. 9-2. Exploded view of gear carrier/shift housing portion of transaxle case.

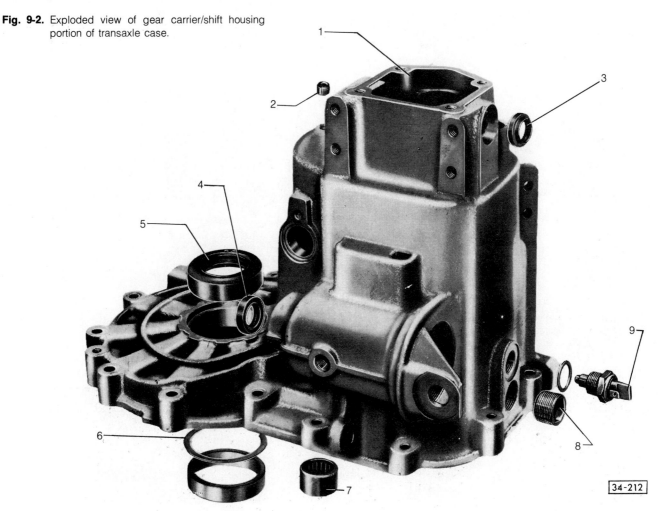

1. Gear carrier/shift housing
2. Oil level plug—torque to 1.0 mkg (7 ft. lb.)
3. Oil seal for clutch operating lever and release shaft assembly—see **6.2**
4. Oil seal for selector shaft—see **6.1**
5. Drive flange oil seal—see **6.3**
6. S₁ shim—see **7.4**
7. Drive pinion shaft needle bearing—see **6.5**
8. Oil filler plug (early cars only)—torque to 2.0 mkg (14 ft. lb.).
9. Back-up light switch—see **ELECTRICAL SYSTEM**

9.1 Removing and Installing Starter Drive Bushing

The starter drive bushing can be removed and installed either with the transaxle removed or with the transaxle installed in the car. For access to the bushing on an installed transaxle, you must first remove the starter as described in **ELECTRICAL SYSTEM.** An expansion tool, or a puller that can be screwed into threads that you have tapped into the old bushing, should be used to remove the bushing from the transaxle case. See Fig. 9-3. Drive in the new bushing as indicated in Fig. 9-4.

Fig. 9-3. Starter drive bushing being removed.

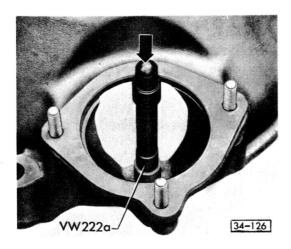

Fig. 9-4. Starter drive bushing being installed.

10. MANUAL TRANSMISSION TECHNICAL DATA

I. Tightening Torques

Location	Designation	mkg	ft. lb.
Shift rod to gearshift lever	fitted bolt and nut	2.0	14
Gearshift lever assembly to bearing plate/car body	bolt	2.0	14
Shift linkage rod lever to transaxle selector shaft	nut or special nut	1.5	11
1975 model shift rod to selector lever	square-head or hex-head setscrew	1.5	11
Shift linkage bearing plate to body	nut	2.0	14
1976 and later model shift rod clamp	bolt and nut	2.0	14
Inboard constant velocity joint to drive flange	socket-head bolt	4.5	32
Front wheel hub to axle shaft of outboard constant velocity joint	nut	24	173
Flywheel cover plate to bellhousing	bolt	1.5	11
Starter to bellhousing	bolt	3.0	22
Selector shaft adjuster in transaxle case (earliest cars only)	adjuster assembly	2.0	14
Selector shaft adjuster locknut (except earliest cars)	nut	2.0	14
Clutch release mechanism cover to transaxle case	bolt	1.5	11
Transaxle case halves to one another	bolt	2.0	14
Reverse sliding gear shaft to transaxle case	bolt	2.0	14
Mainshaft ball bearing to transaxle case	bolt	2.0	14
Reverse sliding gear shift fork assembly to transaxle case	clamping bolt and nut	1.5	11
Drive pinion shaft bearing retainer to transaxle case	self-locking nut	2.5	18
	special bolt	4.0	29
1975 ring gear to differential housing	bolt	5.0	36
1976 and later ring gear to differential housing (following removal of original rivets)	special bolt and nut	7.0	50

6

II. Tolerances, Wear Limits, and Settings

Description	New installation mm (in.)	Wear limit mm (in.)
1. Synchronizing rings (measured between coupling teeth on ring and coupling teeth on gear)		
1st gear/2nd gear . . . . clearance	1.10–1.70 (.043–.067)	0.50 (.020)
3rd gear . . . . clearance	1.12–1.75 (.044–.069)	0.50 (.020)
4th gear . . . . clearance	1.30–1.90 (.051–.075)	0.50 (.020)
2. Drive pinion shaft 3rd gear/3rd gear selective circlip (adjust as near lower limit as possible) . . . . clearance	0.00–0.20 (.000–.008)	—
3. Front wheel driveshafts		
Manual and automatic transmissions . . . . length of left driveshaft	445.5 (17 $^{17}/_{32}$)	—
. . . . length of right driveshaft	658.0 (25 $^{29}/_{32}$)	—
4. Preload on drive pinion shaft tapered-roller bearings (new bearings only) . . . . turning torque	5–15 cmkg (4.5–13 in. lb.)	—
5. Preload on differential tapered-roller bearings (used bearings only) . . . . minimum turning torque	3 cmkg (2.6 in. lb.)	—
6. Molybdenum grease for constant velocity joint . . . . quantity	90 g (3.2 oz)	—

III. Gear Applications

Gear	Model	Location	No. of teeth	Numerical ratio of gearset	Spare part number
1st	all	mainshaft	11	3.45	integral with mainshaft 020 311 101
1st	all	drive pinion shaft	38		014 211 257
2nd	1975 through Sept. '74	mainshaft	19	1.94	integral with mainshaft 020 311 101
2nd	1975 through Sept. '74	drive pinion shaft	37		020 311 261
2nd	all from Oct. '74	mainshaft	18	1.94	integral with mainshaft 020 311 101 A
2nd	all from Oct. '74	drive pinion shaft	35		020 311 261 A
3rd	all	mainshaft	27	1.37	020 311 273 (matched set)
3rd	all	drive pinion shaft	37		
4th	all	mainshaft	32	0.97	020 311 339 (matched set)
4th	all	drive pinion shaft	31		
Reverse	all	—	12:38 tooth ratio	3.17	020 311 501 (sliding gear)
Final drive	all	—	19:74 tooth ratio	3.9	020 409 143 (matched ring and pinion gearset)

IV. Basic Data for Transaxle with Manual Transmission

Designation	Specification
1. Transaxle identification code	GC
2. Oil required to fill transaxle to correct level	1.25 liters (1.3 U.S. quarts or 1.1 Imperial quarts)
3. Hypoid oil recommended	SAE 80W or SAE 80W/90 that meets specifications MIL-L 2105 and API/GL 4 (sulphur-phosphorous additive)

AUTOMATIC TRANSMISSION

Contents

TABLES

Automatic Transmission

A transmission Number is sometimes referred to in this section of the Manual. This number, located atop the bellhousing, consists of a code letter—EQ for example—followed by five numerals. The transmission Number 15 10 7 indicates that the transaxle was manufactured on 15 October, 1977. (The code letter is not used in the text references found in this Manual.)

The automatic transmission itself is housed in a cast aluminum alloy case that is held by studs to a separate final drive housing. Taken as a unit, the transmission and final drive are called the transaxle. Though the transaxle with automatic transmission operates on entirely different principles from those of the transaxle with manual transmission, the constant velocity joints and front wheel driveshafts of the two transaxles are identical. Please consult **MANUAL TRANSMISSION** for repairs related to the driveshafts and constant velocity joints.

Because of the transverse engine position, the transfer of power from the automatic transmission's planetary gear system to the differential is by spur gears, rather than by bevel gears—the kind of gears used in other Volkswagen transaxles. Though the transaxle with manual transmission also employs spur gears in the final drive, these gears are not interchangeable with those used in the transaxle with automatic transmission.

Cleanliness and a careful approach are imperative when repairing the transaxle. Familiarize yourself with the instructions before you begin a job and make sure that you have the necessary tools—particularly for procedures given with metric specifications only. Specifications that lack U.S. equivalents require that the related work be carried out only with metric tools and instruments.

Though you may not have the tools or the skills for carrying out actual repairs, you may be able to remove the transaxle, which can help to reduce service time. In this case, we recommend that the transaxle be thoroughly cleaned on the outside and then taken to the shop as is—partial disassembly will not make repairs easier and may indeed complicate them. We especially urge you to consult an Authorized Dealer before attempting repairs on a car still covered by the new-car warranty.

7 ■

1. GENERAL DESCRIPTION

The transaxle with automatic transmission is shown in Fig. 1-1. At the right end of the transaxle is the final drive housing, which has an integral bellhousing for the torque converter. Inside the final drive housing are the differential, the ring and pinion gearset, and the intermediate gear—which is interposed between the drive pinion and the ring gear. The governor for the automatic transmission is located beneath the round cover on top the final drive housing.

The final drive housing, which contains hypoid oil for lubricating the final drive gears, is completely sealed off from the transmission case. The transmission case contains the ATF pump, the hydraulic controls, and the planetary gear system. The planetary gear system is lubricated solely by the ATF that is circulated through the transmission by the ATF pump. Because the ATF does not circulate unless the engine is running, it is important to remember that the transmission parts are only partially lubricated when the engine is turned off and the car is being towed.

CAUTION

Never tow a car with an automatic transmission faster than 30 mph (48 kph) or farther than 30 mi. (48 km). Bearings can be damaged by lack of lubrication. If you must tow the car farther, lift the front wheels or remove the driveshafts that connect the front wheels to the transaxle.

Torque Converter

The torque converter is a large doughnut-shaped assembly located between the engine and the transaxle. The torque converter not only receives engine output and passes it on to the transmission, but also multiplies engine torque at low vehicle speeds and serves as a fluid coupling between the engine and the transmission. Curved vanes inside the housing set up a flow of ATF that drives another vaned wheel called the turbine. The turbine drives a hollow shaft that transmits power to the transmission.

ATF Pump

ATF must be circulating under pressure before the automatic transmission can function. The ATF pump that creates this pressure is located in the extreme left-hand end of the transmission case. A long pump driveshaft, which passes through the center of the hollow turbine shaft, drives the ATF pump. Because the pump driveshaft is splined directly to the torque converter housing, the pump circulates ATF whenever the engine is running, regardless of selector lever position.

Planetary Gear System

A torque converter alone cannot supply the torque multiplication needed for all driving conditions. The output of the torque converter is therefore routed into a planetary gear system. The planetary gear system consists of two clutches, two brakes, and two planetary gearsets—one gearset for forward operation of the vehicle and the other gearset for reverse.

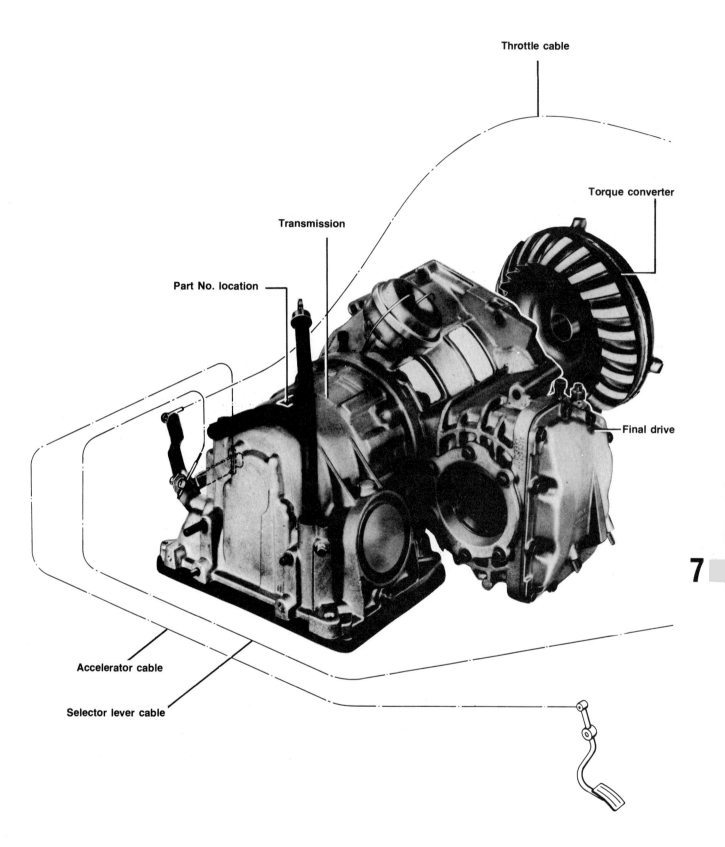

Throttle cable

Torque converter

Transmission

Part No. location

Final drive

Accelerator cable

Selector lever cable

7

Fig. 1-1. Transaxle with automatic transmission.

The two hydraulically operated multiple-disk clutches control the delivery of the torque converter's turbine output to the planetary gearsets. The clutch at the right-hand end of the transmission is called the forward clutch because it transfers power to the planetary gears in all forward gears. The clutch at the left-hand end of the transmission is called the direct and reverse clutch because it transfers power to the planetary gears only when the transmission is in direct (3rd gear) or in reverse. See Fig. 1-2.

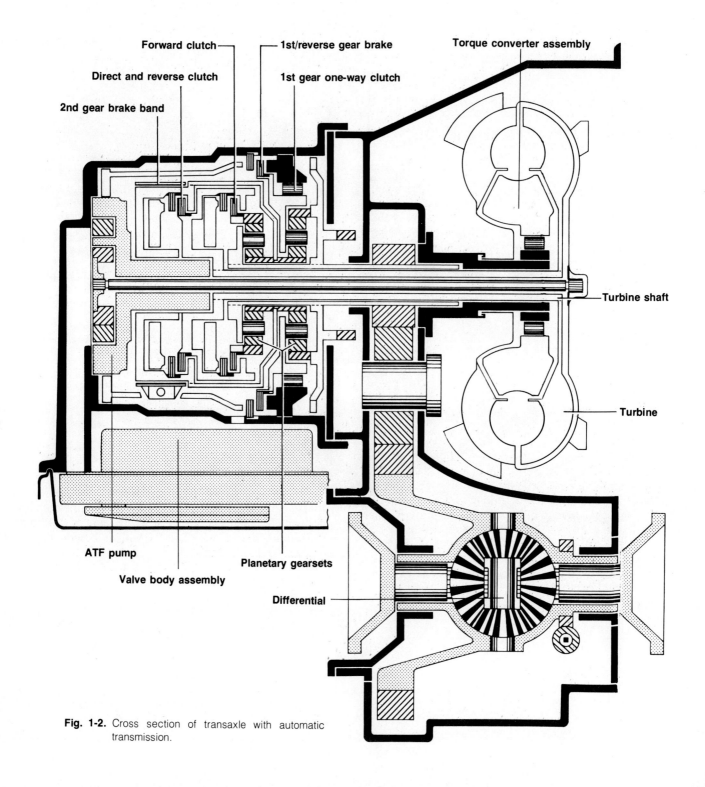

Fig. 1-2. Cross section of transaxle with automatic transmission.

One of the two brakes is a band that contracts around the direct and reverse clutch drum in order to provide 2nd gear. For this reason, it is known as the 2nd gear brake band. The second of the two brakes is a multiple-disk brake that is applied hydraulically in order to obtain reverse operation. This brake is also applied when the selector lever is at **1** in order to lock the 1st gear one-way clutch in both directions of rotation and thus provide additional engine braking. Owing to its two functions, the multiple-disk brake is called the 1st/reverse gear brake.

Hydraulic Controls

The hydraulic control system directs and regulates hydraulic pressure from the ATF pump, thereby controlling shifting of the planetary gear system. Shifts are produced by the piston-type servo for the 2nd gear brake band, the ring-shaped piston for the multiple-disk 1st-reverse brake, and the two ring-shaped clutch pistons.

Three primary control devices regulate the movement of the control valves in the automatic transmission's valve body assembly. One of these is the manual valve, which is connected to the selector lever by a flexible cable. Moving the lever changes the setting of the valve and produces the necessary application of hydraulic pressure for the drive range selected. The second primary control device is the throttle pressure valve, which is operated by the accelerator cable and makes the transmission responsive to variations in engine speed and load. A third primary control device, the governor, controls ATF pressure relative to its rotational speed and makes the transmission responsive to variations in vehicle speeds.

Final Drive

The final drive consists of the drive pinion, which is concentric with the turbine shaft and the ATF pump driveshaft, the intermediate gear, the ring gear, and the differential. The teeth on the ring gear, the intermediate gear, and the drive pinion are helically-cut for silent running. The differential gearset, which consists of the two differential sidegears and the two differential pinions, allows the front wheels to turn at different speeds, as is necessary when making turns (the outside wheel must travel farther than the inside wheel in the same amount of time).

2. MAINTENANCE

The following routine maintenance jobs should be performed at the time or mileage intervals prescribed in **LUBRICATION AND MAINTENANCE**. There, in addition to instructions for carrying out each task, you will find the specifications and the quantities for the lubricants required.

1. Checking ATF level and, if necessary, adding ATF

2. Checking kickdown operation

3. Checking final drive hypoid oil

4. Changing ATF.

3. TROUBLESHOOTING

Before diagnosing automatic transmission troubles, review the history of the unit. This review may offer important clues to present difficulties. The following should be checked before making repairs or adjustments:

1. Be sure that the engine is tuned-up and running right.

2. Inspect the transaxle for external damage, loose or missing screws, and obvious leaks. Check the final drive hypoid oil for ATF contamination caused by faulty seals.

3. Check the ATF level. Rub some ATF between your fingers and sniff it to detect the burned odor that means burned friction linings. If the ATF is dirty, it may be clogging the automatic controls.

4. Check the adjustment and operation of the selector lever cable and throttle cable.

3.1 Road Testing

Drive the car in all drive ranges and under as many road conditions as possible. Note the shift points both up and down. They should take place quickly, without interrupting the power flow. Listen for engine racing between gears, a possible indication of slipping clutches or a slipping 2nd gear brake band. The correct shift points are given in **Table a**.

Table a. Automatic Shift Points

Shift	At full throttle mph (kph)	Kickdown mph (kph)
1st to 2nd gear	20–23 (32–37)	36–39 (58–62)
2nd to 3rd gear	51–55 (82–88)	68–69 (109–110)
3rd to 2nd gear	31–36 (50–58)	64–65 (102–104)
2nd to 1st gear	15–17 (24–27)	32–35 (51–56)

3.2 Troubleshooting Table

Table b may suggest remedies for defects that you observed during road testing. The numbers in bold type in the Remedy column refer to numbered headings in this section of the Manual where the repair or adjustment is described.

When troubleshooting the automatic transmission, try to pin down the main component involved: torque converter, planetary gear system, or hydraulic controls. If **Table b** fails to pinpoint the malfunction adequately, carry out the tests described in **3.3 Stall Speed Testing** and **3.4 Pressure Testing**.

Table b. Automatic Transmission Troubleshooting

Problem	Selector lever position	Probable cause
1. No drive (car will not move)	R. D. 2, 1	a. ATF level low b. Drive plate broken or not bolted to torque converter c. Manual valve not hooked to selector lever cable d. Sticking main pressure valve e. ATF pump or pump drive faulty—no pressure f. Broken gear or shaft—possibly in final drive
2. No drive in forward gears	D, 2, 1	a. Forward clutch plates burned or worn out b. Forward clutch diaphragm spring borken
3. No drive in 1st gear	D, 2	a. 1st gear one-way clutch slipping b. Forward clutch plates burned or worn out c. Forward clutch diaphragm spring broken
4. No drive in 1st gear (engine braking deceleration gear)	1	a. 1st/reverse brake disks burned or worn out
5. No drive in 2nd gear	D, 2	a. 2nd gear brake band incorrectly adjusted b. 2nd gear brake band burned or worn out
6. No drive in 3rd gear	D	a. Direct/reverse clutch plates burned or worn out
7. No drive in reverse	R	a. 1st/reverse brake disks burned or worn out b. Direct/reverse clutch plates burned or worn out c. Forward clutch seized
8. Irregular drive in all forward gears gears	D, 2	a. ATF level low b. ATF pump pickup strainer partially clogged
9. No upshift into 2nd gear	D, 2	a. Faulty governor drive b. Governor dirty c. Governor incorrectly assembled during repair d. Valve body assembly dirty e. Loose accumulator cover plate f. 1st/2nd gear shift valve sticking
10. No upshift into 3rd gear	D	a. Governor dirty b. Valve body assembly dirty c. Ball valves missing from transfer plate d. 2nd/3rd gear shift valve sticking
11. No downshift into 2nd gear	D	a. Governor dirty b. 2nd/3rd gear shift valve sticking
12. No downshift into 1st gear	1	a. Governor dirty b. 1st/2nd gear shift valve sticking

Remedy
a. Check and, if necessary, correct ATF level. **LUBRICATION AND MAINTENANCE** b. Install bolts. If necessary, replace drive plate. **ENGINE AND CLUTCH** c. Connect and adjust selector lever cable. **4.2** d. Remove, disassemble, and clean valve body. **6.1, 6.2** e. Make pressure test **(3.4)**. If no pressure, replace faulty fpump or pump driveshaft.   If driveshaft is broken, check pump gears for free movement. **3.4, 11.2, 11.3** f. Remove, disassemble and inspect transaxle. Make necessary repairs. **9, 11.1, 11.2, 12**
a. Repair forward clutch. **11.5** b. Repair forward clutch. **11.5**
a. Repair or replace 1st gear one-way clutch **11.2, 11.6** b. Repair forward clutch. **11.5** c. Repair forward clutch. **11.5**
a. Replace 1st/reverse brake disks. **11.2**
a. Adjust 2nd gear brake band. **5.1** b. Replace and adjust 2nd gear brake band. **11.2, 5.1**
a. Repair direct/reverse clutch. **11.4**
a. Replace 1st/reverse brake disks. **11.2** b. Repair direct/reverse clutch. **11.4** c. Repair forward clutch. **11.5**
a. Check and, if necessary, correct ATF level. **LUBRICATION AND MAINTENANCE** b. Remove ATF pan. Clean strainer. **6.1**
a. Replace governor shaft and, if necessary, ring and pinion gearset. **7, 12** b. Remove and clean governor. **7** c. Assemble governor correctly. **7.3** d. Remove, disassemble, and clean valve body. **6.1, 6.2** e. Remove valve body assembly. Install accumulator cover plate correctly. **6.1** f. Remove, disassemble, and clean valve body. **6.1, 6.2**
a. Remove and clean governor. **7** b. Remove, disassemble, and clean valve body. **6.1, 6.2** c. Separate transfer plate from valve body. Check ball valves. **6.1** d. Remove, disassemble, and clean valve body. **6.1, 6.2**
a. Remove and clean governor. **7** b. Remove, disassemble, and clean valve body. **6.1, 6.2**
a. Remove and clean governor. **7** b. Remove, disassemble, and clean valve body. **6.1, 6.2**

7 ■

continued on next page

Table b. Automatic Transmission Troubleshooting (continued)

Problem	Selector level position	Probable cause
13. Downshift to 1st gear delayed (jerky engagement)	D, 2	a. 1st gear one-way clutch slipping
14. Shift(s) take place below normal speed given in **Table a**	D, 2	a. Governor dirty b. Valve body assembly dirty
15. Shift(s) take place above normal speed given in **Table a**	D, 2	a. Governor dirty b. Valve body assembly dirty c. Paper gasket for transmission or intermediate plate damaged
16. Gear engagement jerky when selector lever is moved from N to D or R	D, R	a. Engine idle speed too fast b. ATF level low
17. Gear engagement delayed on upshift from 1st to 2nd gear	D, 2	a. ATF level low b. Valve body assembly dirty c. 2nd gear brake band incorrectly adjusted d. 2nd gear brake band burned or worn out e. Incorrect piston installed in 2nd gear brake band servo during repair
18. Gear engagement delayed on upshift from 2nd to 3rd gear	D, 2	a. ATF level low b. Valve body assembly dirty c. 2nd gear brake band incorrectly adjusted d. 2nd gear brake band burned or worn out e. Incorrect piston installed in 2nd gear brake band servo during repair f. Direct/reverse clutch plates burned or worn out g. Incorrect direct/reverse clutch installed during repair
19. Kickdown fails to operate	D, 2	a. Accelerator cable incorrectly adjusted
20. Vehicle does not accelerate as quickly as it should	D, 2, 1, R	a. Engine needs a tune-up b. Throttle cable incorrectly adjusted c. Accelerator cable incorrectly adjusted
21. Vehicle fails to achieve maximum speed	D	a. Engine needs a tune-up b. Throttle cable incorrectly adjusted c. Accelerator cable incorrectly adjusted
22. Parking lock fails to engage	P	a. Parking lock mechanism damaged b. Selector lever cable misadjusted
23. Front wheels locked (car can not be moved by pushing, rear wheels turn freely)	R	a. Parking lock mechanism jammed
24. ATF needs to be added often, no visible leaks	—	a. Governor shaft seal leaking ATF into final drive housing b. O-ring and gaskets between transmission and final drive leaking ATF into final drive housing c. Drive pinion shaft oil seal leaking ATF into final drive housing
25. ATF needs to be added often, leakage visible externally	—	a. ATF filler tube leaking b. Torque converter seal leaking c. Torque converter bushing worn d. O-ring for governor cover leaking e. Nuts for transmission case/final drive housing studs loose f. O-ring and gaskets between transmission and final drive leaking ATF to outside
26. ATF appears very dirty, smells burnt	—	a. 1st/reverse brake disks burned b. 2nd gear brake band burned c. Direct/reverse clutch linings burned d. Forward clutch linings burned

Remedy
a. Repair or replace 1st gear one-way clutch. **11.2, 11.6**
a. Remove and clean governor. **7** b. Remove, disassemble, and clean valve body. **6.1, 6.2**
a. Remove and clean governor. **7** b. Remove, disassemble, and clean valve body. **6.1, 6.2** c. Separate transmission fromfinal drive. Reassemble with new gaskets correctly installed. **11.1**
a. Adjust idle. See **FUEL AND EXHAUST SYSTEMS** b. Check and, if necessary, correct ATF level. **LUBRICATION AND MAINTENANCE**
a. Check and, if necessary, correct ATF level. **LUBRICATION AND MAINTENANCE** b. Remove, disassemble, and clean valve body. **6.1, 6.2** c. Adjust 2nd gear brake band. **5.1** d. Replace and adjust 2nd gear brake band. **11.2, 5.1** e. Replace 2nd gear brake band servo piston with correct piston. **8**
a. Check and, if necessary, correct ATF level. **LUBRICATION AND MAINTENANCE** b. Remove, disassemble, and clean valve body. **6.1, 6.2** c. Adjust 2nd gear brake band. **5.1** d. Replace and adjust 2nd gear brake band. **11.2, 5.1** e. Replace 2nd gear brake band servo piston with correct piston. **8** f. Repair direct/reverse clutch. **11.4** g. Replace direct/reverse clutch. **11.4**
a. Adjust accelerator cable. **FUEL AND EXHAUST SYSTEMS**
a. Tune-up engine. **ENGINE AND CLUTCH, FUEL AND EXHAUST SYSTEMS** b. Adjust throttle cable. **FUEL AND EXHAUST SYSTEMS** c. Adjust accelerator cable. **FUEL AND EXHAUST SYSTEMS**
a. Tune-up engine. **ENGINE AND CLUTCH, FUEL AND EXHAUST SYSTEMS** b. Adjust throttle cable. **FUEL AND EXHAUST SYSTEMS** c. Adjust accelerator cable. **FUEL AND EXHAUST SYSTEMS**
a. Repair parking lock mechanism. **11.8** b. Adjust selector lever cable. **4.3**
a. Repair parking lock mechanism. **11.8**
a. Replace governor shaft seal. **7** b. Replace O-ring and gaskets. **11.1** c. Replace drive pinion shaft oil seal. **12.1**
a. Tighten filler tube union or replace filler tube. **6.1** b. Repalce torque converter seal; check bushing. **10, 12.1** c. Replace torque converter bushing and seal. **10, 12.1** d. Replace O-ring. **11.1** e. Torque nuts to 3.0 mkg (22 ft. lb.). **11.1** f. Replace O-ring and gaskets. **11.1**
a. Replace 1st/reverse brake disks. **11.2** b. Replace and adjust 2nd gear brake band. **11.2, 5.1** c. Repair direct/reverse clutch. **11.4** d. Repair forward clutch. **11.5**

7

3.3 Stall Speed Testing

This test provides a quick check of the torque converter and the planetary gear system. You should only test the stall speed if the car accelerates poorly despite a perfectly-tuned engine. A precision electric tachometer must be used for this test, as dashboard instruments are not calibrated with sufficient accuracy.

> **CAUTION** ——
>
> *Never extend this test beyond the time it takes to read the tachometer—20 seconds maximum. Prolonging the test may overheat the transmission and damage the seals.*

To test:

1. Connect the tachometer according to the instrument manufacturer's instructions. Then start the engine.

2. Set the parking brake and depress the foot brake firmly to hold the car stationary.

3. Place the selector lever in **D** and floor the accelerator pedal. Instead of revving up, the engine should run at a reduced rpm, known as stall speed.

If the rpm at stall is about 400 rpm below the specified 1900 to 2200 rpm stall speed—and the engine is in a proper state of tune—something is wrong with the torque converter. If the rpm at stall is above 2200 rpm, there is slippage in the forward clutch or the 1st gear one-way clutch. The test can also be made with the selector lever at **R.** If the reverse stall speed is too high, it indicates slippage in either the direct and reverse clutch or in the multiple-disk 1st/reverse brake.

> **NOTE** ——
>
> Slippage in the forward clutch—and especially slippage in the 1st/reverse brake—can be caused by inadequate hydraulic pressure as well as by worn clutch or brake components. Indeed, slippage caused by low pressure may lead to clutch or brake wear. This excessive wear will recur if you do not correct the low pressure condition at the same time as you repair the transmission's clutches and brakes. Transmission internal leaks are the usual cause of inadequate hydraulic pressure.

3.4 Pressure Testing

A main pressure test will locate internal leaks and other troubles in the hydraulic controls. Though you can make the full-throttle test while driving the car on a highway, whenever possible this test should be carried out on a dynamometer. The pressure gauge should have a range of 0 to 150 psi or 0 to 10 kg/cm².

> **NOTE** ——
>
> To eliminate noises in the forward clutch, a new valve body is installed in the later 1977 models, beginning with Transmission No. 25 11 6. This new valve body produces higher main pressures than those given in the following test. However, at this printing the Factory had not yet published new main pressure specifications. The new valve body is identified by the code letter L. See **6.1 Removing and Installing Valve Body Assembly.**

To test:

1. Using a long hose so that you can place the gauge inside the car, connect the pressure gauge to the main pressure tap on the transmission (Fig. 3-1). Tie the hose to the car body so that it cannot become entangled with the wheels.

Fig. 3-1. Main pressure tap on transmission case.

2. Start the engine and warm it up to its normal operating temperature. Make sure that the idle speed is adjusted to specifications, as described in **FUEL AND EXHAUST SYSTEMS.**

3. Place the selector lever at **D.** With the car stationary and the engine idling, the main pressure should be between 41 and 42 psi (2.90 and 3.00 kg/cm^2).

4. Place the selector lever at **R.** With the car stationary and the engine idling, the main pressure should be between 104 and 105 psi (7.35 and 7.40 kg/cm^2).

5. With the car's speedometer indicating a speed above 25 mph (40 kph) and the selector lever at **D,** floor the accelerator. During full-throttle acceleration, the main pressure should be between 83 and 84 psi (5.85 and 5.95 kg/cm^2).

6. After disconnecting the test gauge hose, install the plug for the pressure tap to 1.0 mkg (7 ft. lb.). Then run the engine and check the plug for leakage.

Main pressures that are higher or lower than those specified usually mean that the valve body is dirt-clogged or that the valves in the valve body are sticking. This trouble can be remedied by removing and cleaning the valve body. But, while high pressures always indicate sticking valves, low pressures may also indicate a worn ATF pump or internal ATF leaks past seals, gaskets, and metal mating surfaces.

7 ■

4. SELECTOR LEVER AND CABLE

The selector lever shares no parts with the gearshift lever used with the manual transmission. A cable couples the selector lever with the lever on the automatic transmission. This cable is not repairable and must be replaced as a unit if either the cable or its flexible conduit is worn or damaged.

4.1 Removing and Installing Selector Lever

The entire selector lever and cable mechanism is shown in Fig. 4-1. The contact plate designated in the illustration is for the neutral safety switch. The function of the neutral safety switch is to keep the engine's starter from operating except when the selector lever is at **N** or **P**.

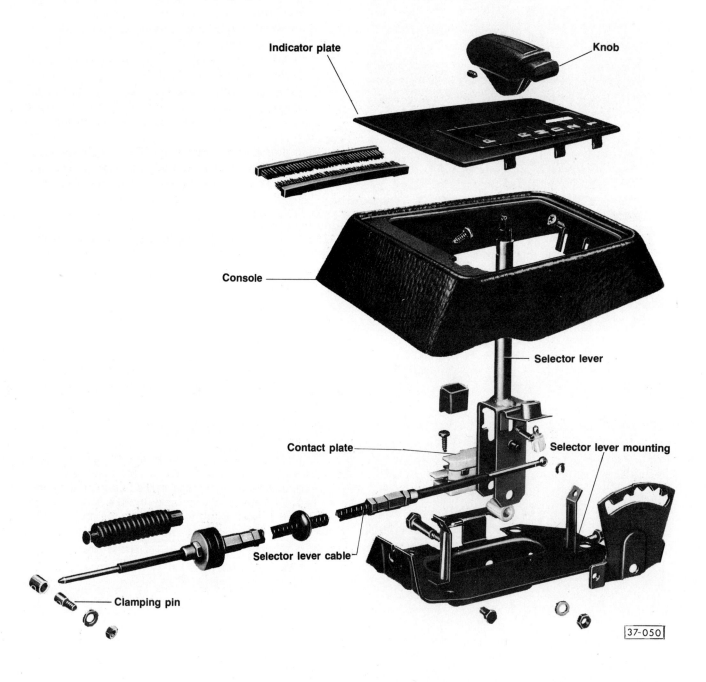

Fig. 4-1. Exploded view of selector lever and cable.

To remove selector lever:

1. Disconnect the battery ground strap.

2. Loosen the setscrew that holds the knob to the top of the selector lever. Then remove the knob assembly.

3. Carefully pry loose and remove the indicator plate. Then remove the screws that hold the selector lever console and remove the console.

4. Remove the four bolts and washers that hold the selector lever assembly to the car's floorboard.

5. Pry off the E-clip. Then detach the cable and its conduit from the selector lever and mounting.

6. Disconnect the wires from the indicator light and the contact plate. Then remove the selector lever assembly as a unit. If further disassembly is necessary, use Fig. 4-1 as your guide.

Installation is the reverse of removal. Before you install the console, adjust the cable as described in **4.3 Adjusting Selector Lever Cable.** Check that the engine's starter operates only with the selector lever at **N** or **P.** If necessary, reposition the contact plate so that the neutral safety switch operates correctly.

4.2 Removing and Installing Selector Lever Cable

Individual cable components, other than the rubber boot, are unavailable as replacement parts. If either the cable or its conduit is damaged, replace the cable as a unit.

To remove selector cable:

1. If the cable is not broken, engage **P.** Loosen the setscrew that holds the knob to the top of the selector lever. Then remove the knob assembly.

2. Carefully pry loose and remove the indicator plate. Then remove the screws that hold the selector lever console and remove the console.

3. Pry off the E-clip. Then detach the cable and its conduit from the selector lever and mounting.

4. Completely free the cable and conduit from the selector lever assembly and the floorboard so that the cable and conduit can be pulled out from the engine compartment.

5. Working inside the engine compartment, loosen the nut for the cable clamping pin so that the cable end is free to be withdrawn from the lever on the transaxle. Loosen the cable conduit nut so that the conduit is free from the bracket.

6. Detach the cable from the lever and the conduit from the bracket. Then pull out the cable and the conduit as a unit.

Installation is the reverse of removal. Following installation, adjust the cable as described in **4.3 Adjusting Selector Lever Cable.**

4.3 Adjusting Selector Lever Cable

Adjust the selector lever cable following installation of the cable—or whenever the correct letter or number on the indicator plate is not illuminated with the selector lever in a particular drive range.

To adjust:

1. Select **P.** If the cable is not attached to the transaxle, as in installing a new cable after the original cable has broken, select **P** by hand-moving the operating lever on the transaxle to the left. Try to push the car forward and backward in order to make sure that the parking pawl has engaged inside the transmission.

2. Loosen the nut for the clamping pin that holds the cable to the operating lever on the transaxle. Make sure that the selector lever inside the car is fully engaged in the **P** position.

3. Make sure that the operating lever on the transaxle is fully engaged in the **P** position by pushing the operating lever to the left. Then tighten the nut for the cable clamping pin.

To check selector lever cable adjustment:

1. Start the engine with the selector lever at **N.** Then, with the car held stationary by the parking brake, keep the engine running at a steady 1000 to 1200 rpm throughout the following tests.

2. Move the selector lever to **R.** The engine speed should drop, indicating that the transmission has engaged reverse gear.

3. Move the lever to **P.** The engine speed should increase, indicating that reverse gear has disengaged. Without depressing the button on the knob, pull the selector lever back toward **R.** The engine speed must not drop, as this would indicate that reverse gear has re-engaged.

4. Depress the button on the knob, then repeat the test described in step 2.

5. Move the selector lever to **N.** The engine speed should increase, indicating that reverse gear has disengaged.

6. Move the selector lever to **D.** The engine speed should drop, indicating that the transmission has engaged 1st gear.

7. Adjust or readjust the cable if the correct response is not obtained in any of the preceding tests.

7

5. AUTOMATIC TRANSMISSION ADJUSTMENTS

Aside from adjusting the selector lever cable, as described under the preceding heading, the automatic transmission has only two adjustments. These are adjusting the accelerator cable and adjusting the 2nd gear brake band. Accelerator and throttle cable adjustments are covered in **FUEL AND EXHAUST SYSTEMS.**

5.1 Adjusting 2nd Gear Brake Band

The 2nd gear brake band can be adjusted either with the transaxle in the car or with the transaxle removed. In either case the axis of the planetary gear system must be in a horizontal plane during adjustment, as it would be with the car on level ground. If this precaution is not observed—especially with the transaxle removed—the 2nd gear brake band may jam during adjustment. This would make necessary at least partial disassembly of the transmission in order to realign the band.

To adjust:

1. Loosen the locknut for the adjusting screw. Then center the 2nd gear brake band by torquing the adjusting screw to about 1.0 mkg (100 cmkg or 87 in. lb.).

2. Loosen the adjusting screw. Then retorque it to 0.5 mkg (50 cmkg or 43 in. lb.).

3. From this setting, back the screw off exactly 2½ turns. Then, while holding the adjusting screw as shown in Fig. 5-1, tighten the locknut. Finally, torque the locknut to 2.0 mkg (14 ft. lb.).

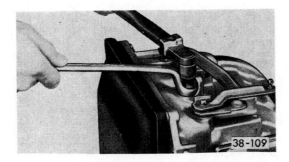

Fig. 5-1. 2nd gear brake band adjusting screw being held stationary while locknut is tightened.

6. SERVICING VALVE BODY AND VALVE BODY ASSEMBLY

Servicing the valve body assembly normally involves only removal and cleaning. However, it may also be necessary to remove the valve body assembly from the transmission before you can replace or repair other transmission components.

6.1 Removing and Installing Valve Body Assembly

The valve body assembly can be removed with the transaxle in the car. The valve body assembly must also be removed for cleaning during more extensive repairs with the transaxle out of the car.

To remove:

1. Drain the ATF (automatic transmission fluid). Remove the ATF pan screws. Then take off the ATF pan and the gasket.

2. Remove the screws that hold the pump pickup's ATF strainer to the valve body assembly. Remove the ATF strainer.

3. Eleven bolts hold the valve body assembly to the transmission case. Remove ten of the bolts, keeping installed the bolt indicated in Fig. 6-1.

4. While supporting the valve body assembly so that it does not fall, remove the eleventh bolt. Then remove the valve body assembly.

5. If you wish to remove the accumulator piston and its spring, remove the three Phillips head screws for the accumulator cover plate. Remove the cover plate, the spring, and the accumulator piston.

> **NOTE** ——
>
> Two kinds of accumulator pistons have been installed. One kind is cast aluminum with a separate sealing ring. If you replace the sealing ring, its lip must point toward the pressure side of the piston (point away from the cover plate). The second kind of piston is stamped from sheet metal with a sealing lip permanently bonded to it. The two kinds of accumulator pistons are readily interchangeable.

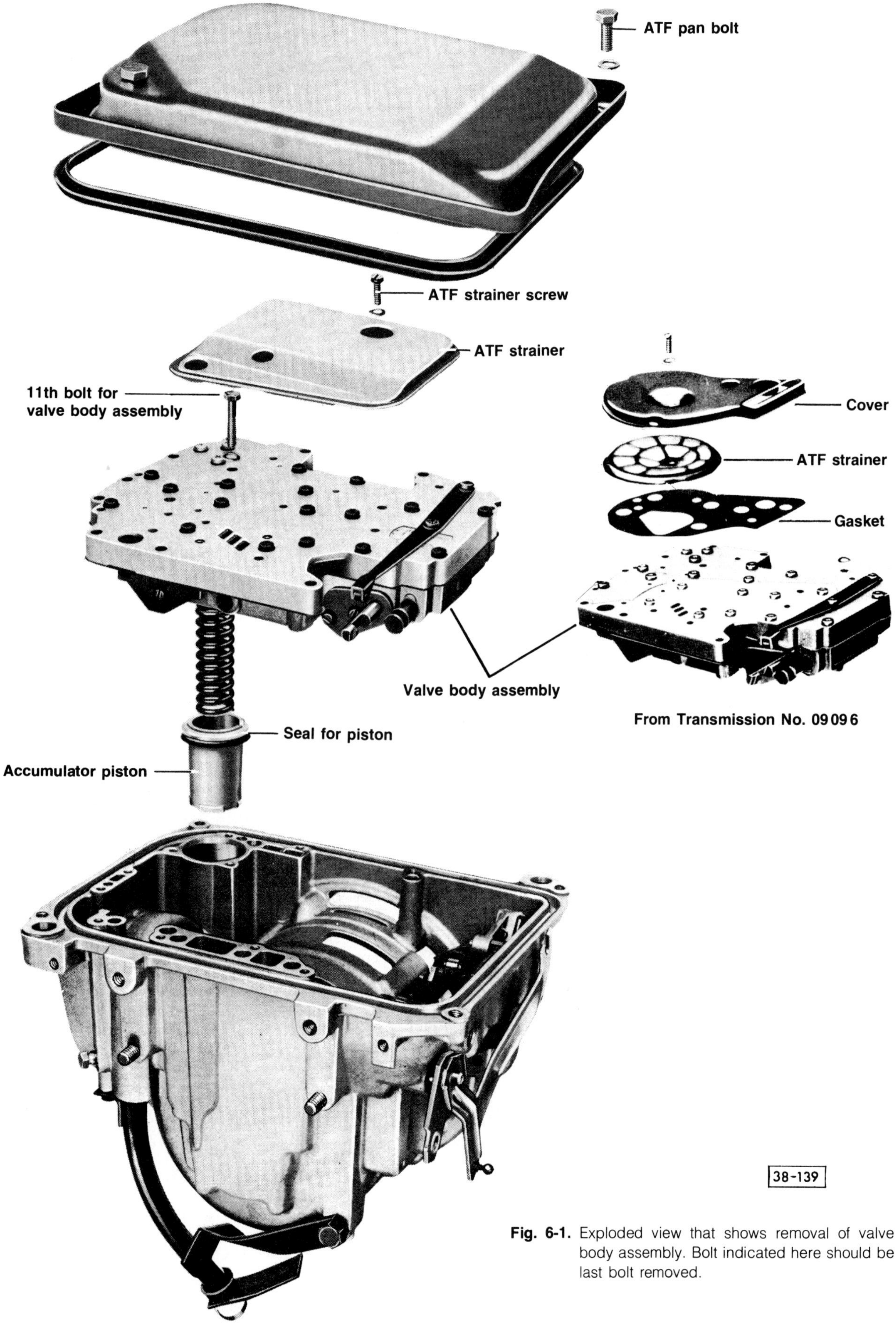

ATF pan bolt

ATF strainer screw

ATF strainer

11th bolt for
valve body assembly

Cover

ATF strainer

Gasket

Valve body assembly

From Transmission No. 09 09 6

Seal for piston

Accumulator piston

7

38-139

Fig. 6-1. Exploded view that shows removal of valve
body assembly. Bolt indicated here should be
last bolt removed.

To disassemble valve body assembly:

1. Place the assembly on a clean workbench with the valve body down. Then remove the 19 Phillips head screws that hold the valve body, the separator plate, and the transfer plate together. See Fig. 6-2.

2. Lift off the separator plate and transfer plate as a

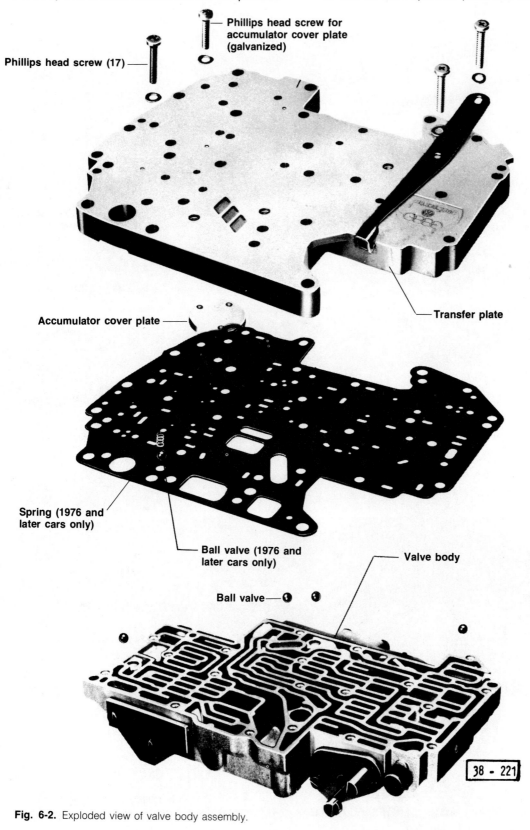

Phillips head screw for accumulator cover plate (galvanized)

Phillips head screw (17)

Transfer plate

Accumulator cover plate

Spring (1976 and later cars only)

Ball valve (1976 and later cars only)

Ball valve

Valve body

38 - 221

Fig. 6-2. Exploded view of valve body assembly.

unit—so that the ball valves in the valve body will remain in the valve body and the ball valve in the transfer plate will be kept in place by the separator plate.

3. Place the transfer plate and separator plate on the workbench with the transfer plate down. Then lift off the separator plate.

If you are replacing either the transfer plate or the separator plate, the new components must be marked as indicated in Fig. 6-3 and Fig. 6-4. Do not install components from an automatic transmission that was not originally used in a car covered by this Manual.

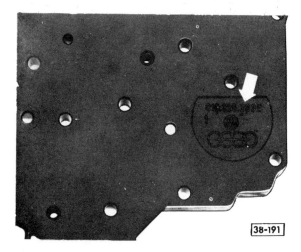

Fig. 6-3. Marking of transfer plate. Number 010 325 283C (1975 cars) or 010 325 283 E (1976 and later cars) should appear at point indicated by arrow.

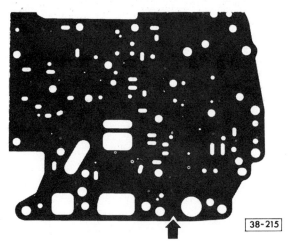

Fig. 6-4. Marking of separator plate. On 1976 and later cars, there should be only one notch at point indicated by arrow. 1975 cars have no notch.

Assembly is the reverse of disassembly. The locations of the ball valves are shown in Fig. 6-5 and Fig. 6-6. All

ball valves are identical, being 6-mm balls. Torque the Phillips head screws to 40 cmkg (35 in. lb.).

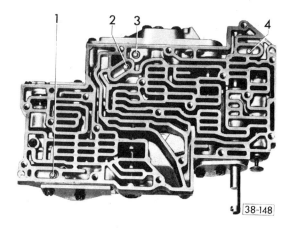

1. Direct and reverse clutch ball valve
2. Reverse gear brake ball valve
3. 1st gear ball valve (selector lever at **1**)
4. 1st gear ball valve (selector lever at **D**)

Fig. 6-5. Locations for ball valves in valve body (arrows).

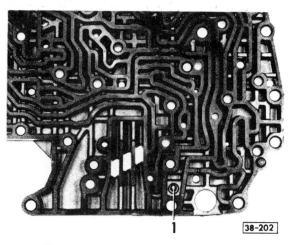

Fig. 6-6. Location for ball valve (**1**) and spring in 1976 and later model transfer plate.

To install valve body assembly:

1. If you have removed the accumulator piston, lubricate its sealing ring with ATF. Then install the piston, the spring, and the cover. Torque the three Phillips head screws to 30 cmkg (26 in. lb.).

   NOTE ——

   The Phillips head screws for the accumulator cover plate are galvanized, whereas the screws that hold the valve body to the separator plate and transfer plate are not. Do not mix up the screws.

2. If you are installing a new valve body assembly, make certain that the correct code letter appears in

7

the location indicated in Fig. 6-7. This letter is the only reliable indication that the valve body is suitable for a car covered by this Manual.

NOTE ——

On 1975 cars, you can replace valve body, code letter A, with valve body, code letter E—if you install the matching-type governor. On 1977 cars, you can replace valve body, code letter H, with valve body, code letter L.

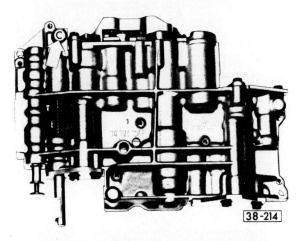

Early 1975 cars: Code letter A (Part No. 010 325 029 E)
Later 1975 cars: Code letter E (Part No. 010 325 029)
1976 cars: Code letter C (Part No. 010 325 029 A)
Early 1977 cars: Code letter H (Part No. 010 325 031 B)
Later 1977 cars: Code letter L (Part No. 010 325 031 C)

Fig. 6-7. Location of code letter (arrow) that is stamped into boss on valve body.

3. Position the valve body assembly on the transmission case so that the manual valve and the kickdown valve are correctly engaged with their operating levers, as shown in Fig. 6-8.

Fig. 6-8. Manual valve (arrow **A**) and kickdown valve (arrow **B**) correctly engaged with operating levers.

4. Attach the valve body assembly to the transmission case with the 11th bolt, indicated previously in Fig. 6-1. Install the 10 remaining bolts. Then, working diagonally, gradually torque all of the bolts to 40 cmkg (35 in. lb.).

5. Install the ATF strainer. Torque the screws to 30 cmkg (26 in. lb.).

NOTE ——

The ATF strainer used prior to Transmission No. 09 09 6 cannot be cleaned, so replace it if the ATF was dirty or contaminated or if the ATF strainer itself is obviously dirty or clogged.

6. Install the ATF pan together with a new gasket. Working diagonally, gradually torque the ATF pan bolts to 2.0 mkg (14 ft. lb.).

CAUTION ——

Do not use sealer on the gasket, as any surplus may find its way into the ATF and cause the control valves to stick. Never tighten the ATF pan bolts to more than 2.0 mkg (14 ft. lb.) in an attempt to cure a leaking gasket. Overtightening will deform the pan and make it impossible to get a good seal. Always install a new gasket to correct leaks.

7. Refill the transmission case with ATF as described in **LUBRICATION AND MAINTENANCE.**

6.2 Disassembling and Assembling Valve Body

As a rule, the valve body is disassembled only for cleaning. Unless the ATF is very dirty or contaminated by large solid particles, it usually is sufficient to immerse the complete assembly in cleaning fluid and dry it with compressed air. However, be careful not to hold the air jet so close that it moves the valves violently. This could damage the springs.

Fig. 6-9 and Fig. 6-10 are exploded views of the valve body. Because many of the parts look alike, it is easy to mix them up. This is especially true of the springs. Unless you keep the springs separated and marked for identification, you will have to measure each spring with a micrometer prior to reassembly in order to find its correct place. See **13. Automatic Transmission Technical Data** for spring dimensions. To avoid the need for such measurements, use a compartmental storage tray (Fig. 6-11). Such a tray will also keep the springs from getting bent or stretched, which would upset their precisely calibrated tensions.

Fig. 6-9. Exploded view of valve body used on 1975 cars.

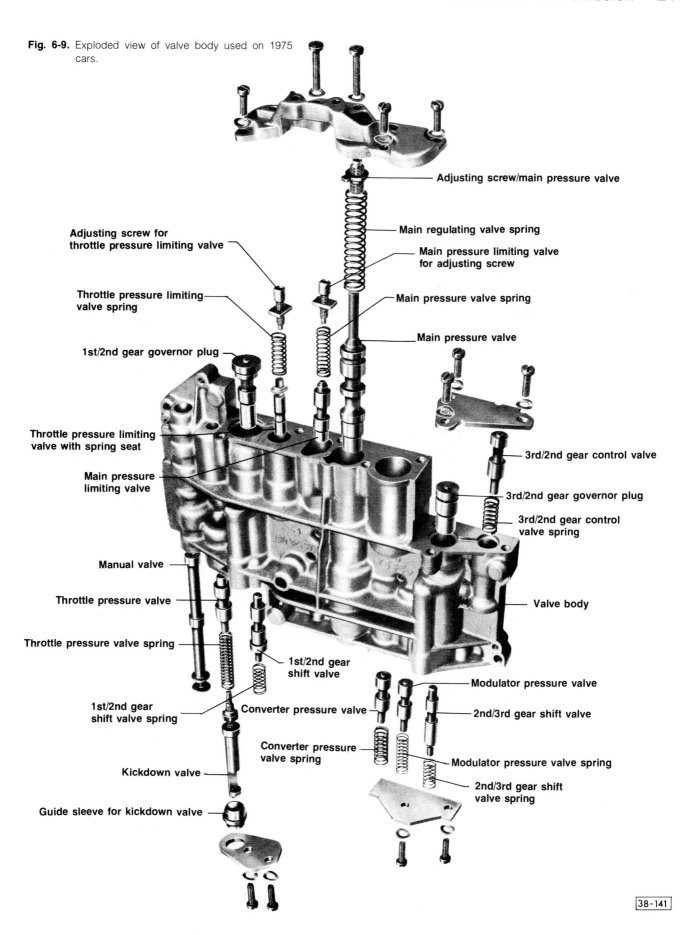

Adjusting screw/main pressure valve

Main regulating valve spring

Main pressure limiting valve for adjusting screw

Main pressure valve spring

Main pressure valve

Adjusting screw for throttle pressure limiting valve

Throttle pressure limiting valve spring

1st/2nd gear governor plug

Throttle pressure limiting valve with spring seat

Main pressure limiting valve

3rd/2nd gear control valve

3rd/2nd gear governor plug

3rd/2nd gear control valve spring

Manual valve

Throttle pressure valve

Throttle pressure valve spring

Valve body

1st/2nd gear shift valve

Modulator pressure valve

1st/2nd gear shift valve spring

Converter pressure valve

2nd/3rd gear shift valve

Converter pressure valve spring

Modulator pressure valve spring

Kickdown valve

2nd/3rd gear shift valve spring

Guide sleeve for kickdown valve

7

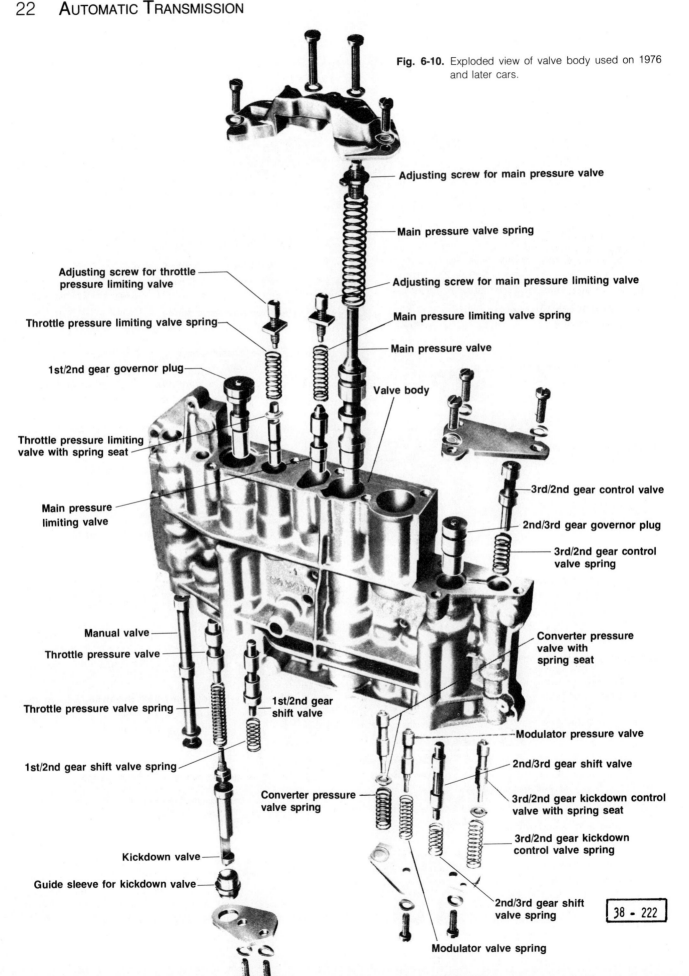

Fig. 6-10. Exploded view of valve body used on 1976 and later cars.

Adjusting screw for main pressure valve

Main pressure valve spring

Adjusting screw for throttle pressure limiting valve

Adjusting screw for main pressure limiting valve

Throttle pressure limiting valve spring

Main pressure limiting valve spring

1st/2nd gear governor plug

Main pressure valve

Valve body

Throttle pressure limiting valve with spring seat

Main pressure limiting valve

3rd/2nd gear control valve

2nd/3rd gear governor plug

3rd/2nd gear control valve spring

Manual valve

Throttle pressure valve

Converter pressure valve with spring seat

Throttle pressure valve spring

1st/2nd gear shift valve

1st/2nd gear shift valve spring

Modulator pressure valve

2nd/3rd gear shift valve

Converter pressure valve spring

3rd/2nd gear kickdown control valve with spring seat

3rd/2nd gear kickdown control valve spring

Kickdown valve

Guide sleeve for kickdown valve

2nd/3rd gear shift valve spring

38 - 222

Modulator valve spring

2008

38-199

Fig. 6-11. Compartmental storage tray for valve body parts.

To disassemble:

1. Remove the valve body assembly from the transmission. Then disassemble it into its three main components as described in **6.1 Removing and Installing Valve Body Assembly.**

2. Remove one of the end plates.

> **CAUTION ——**
>
> *Do not, under any circumstances, alter the settings of any of the adjusting screws located beneath the cast aluminum end plate. These screws can be adjusted properly only at the factory.*

3. One at a time, remove each valve and spring and place it in the storage tray. Carefully use a brass rod to press out sticking or tight-fitting valves.

4. One at a time, remove the other cover plates and repeat the procedure described in the preceding step.

5. Wash all parts in clean kerosene, then dry them with compressed air.

> **CAUTION ——**
>
> *Never use water to clean the valves and valve body—and never dry the parts with fluffy rags or by rubbing them against your clothing. Even a microscopic piece of lint or a small patch of rust can cause a valve to stick in its bore.*

Assembly is basically the reverse of disassembly. Clean the workbench before you start to work. Lubricate each valve with ATF as you reinstall it, then make certain that the valve moves freely of its own weight. Used valves, which will have worn to fit individual bores, must be returned to their original locations. When you install the end plates, be careful not to overtighten the screws. Doing this could easily strip the threads or distort the valve body enough to cause a valve to stick.

7. SERVICING GOVERNOR

The governor for the hydraulic control system is located beneath a round, pressed steel cover atop the final drive housing, just to the right of the transmission case. The cover is held in place by a spring wire clip.

7.1 Removing and Installing Governor

The governor can be removed with the transaxle in the car. The governor is usually removed for cleaning or for replacing worn parts. However, if a new valve body is being installed, a matching governor may be supplied with the new valve body and should be installed whether the old governor is serviceable or not.

To remove:

1. Thoroughly clean the governor housing and the governor cover so that abrasive road dirt cannot accidentally enter the transaxle as the cover is removed.

2. Carefully pry off the spring wire clip that holds the cover to the governor housing. Then remove the cover and its gasket.

3. Withdraw the governor with a clockwise twisting motion that will allow its drive gear to disengage from the helical gear on the transmission's annulus gear flange.

4. Inspect the thrust plate and the drive end of the shaft for wear and scoring.

> **NOTE ——**
>
> Because replacing the entire governor could possibly change the governor pressure, new governor shafts are available separately to replace those that are worn or damaged.

Governor installation is the reverse of removal. Make sure that a new governor is the correct replacement part for the vehicle. Turn the governor as you install it so that the drive gear will engage. If the gasket for the cover is broken or deformed, replace the gasket.

7

7.2 Disassembling and Assembling Governor

Disassemble the governor only if it contains debris from burned clutch or brake linings. Otherwise, just dip it in solvent and dry it with compressed air.

To disassemble the governor, remove the two M 5 X 40 fillister head screws and take off the thrust plate and the housing. Then take out the transfer plate and the balance weight. The weight has been matched to the governor, so do not replace the original weight with a weight from another governor. You can remove the centrifugal weight, the valve, the spring, and the dished washer from the pin by prying off one of the E-clips. See Fig. 7-1 or Fig. 7-2.

Before you assemble the governor, wash all parts in kerosene and dry them with compressed air. Lubricate the parts with ATF as you install them. The transfer plate and, on the late-type governor, the strainer must be installed in the positions shown in the illustrations. Make sure that the angle of the thrust plate is at the center of the housing so that the cover will bear against it.

8. SERVICING 2ND GEAR BRAKE BAND SERVO PISTON

The 2nd gear brake band servo piston can be removed with the transaxle in the car. This job is usually done to replace the piston seals and the cover O-rings. The 2nd gear brake band servo piston must also be removed before the 2nd gear brake band can be removed during disassembly of the transmission's planetary gear system.

To remove the cover and the 2nd gear brake band servo piston, first remove the circlip that retains the cover in the transmission case. Then, using a rubber mallet as shown in Fig. 8-1, tap the cover until the servo piston spring forces the piston and the cover out of the case.

Fig. 7-1. Exploded view of early-type governor used through Transmission No. 27 01.5.

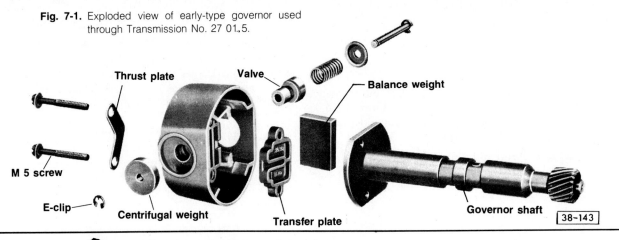

Thrust plate Valve Balance weight M 5 screw E-clip Centrifugal weight Transfer plate Governor shaft 38-143

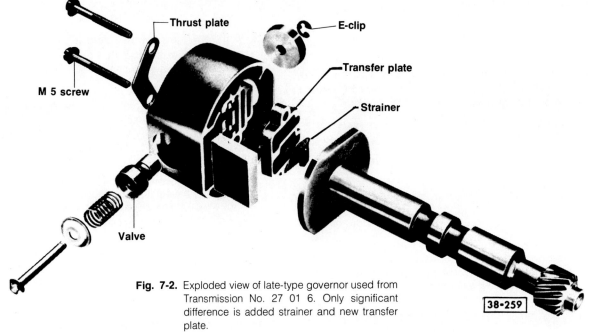

Thrust plate E-clip M 5 screw Transfer plate Strainer Valve 38-259

Fig. 7-2. Exploded view of late-type governor used from Transmission No. 27 01 6. Only significant difference is added strainer and new transfer plate.

Fig. 8-1. Rubber mallet being used to tap cover for 2nd gear brake band servo piston. After a few taps, cover should pop out under pressure from spring.

You can separate the 2nd gear brake band servo piston assembly into its individual components as shown in Fig. 8-2. The piston assembly that is supplied as a replacement part is already correctly assembled and adjusted. The shim, used in adjusting the piston, should never be interchanged with a shim from another piston

assembly nor replaced by an ordinary washer in the event that the shim is lost.

Dip the piston seals and the cover O-rings in ATF before you install them on the piston or the cover. Make sure that the piston seal lips point in the directions indicated in Fig. 8-3.

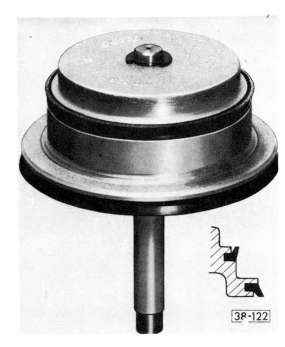

Fig. 8-3. Correct installed positions of piston seals.

7■

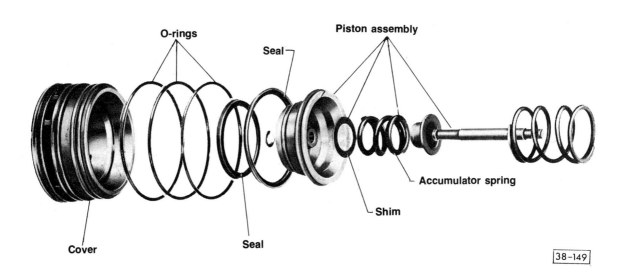

Fig. 8-2. Exploded view of 2nd gear brake band servo piston assembly and cover.

To install the 2nd gear brake band servo piston, first lubricate the piston with ATF and fully insert it into the cover, which should be thoroughly clean and lightly lubricated with ATF. Insert the piston with a twisting motion, being careful that the piston seals are not damaged or forced out of position.

Lubricate the cover O-rings with ATF. Insert the piston assembly and cover into the case, guiding the piston rod into engagement with the 2nd gear brake band. Then, using a suitable lever as shown in Fig. 8-4, press the cover and the piston into the transmission case against spring tension until you can install the circlip. Make certain that the circlip is completely seated in the groove in the transmission case.

Fig. 8-4. Lever being used to press in cover and 2nd gear brake band servo piston assembly.

9. REMOVING AND INSTALLING TRANSAXLE

Some of the necessary disconnecting points for removing the transaxle are indicated by number in Fig. 9-1. We will refer to this illustration throughout the removal procedure.

To remove:

1. Disconnect the battery cables (**1** in Fig. 9-1).

2. Detach the speedometer cable from the speedometer driven gear assembly (**2** in Fig. 9-1).

3. Install the engine support device shown in Fig. 9-2. Then remove the two upper engine-to-transaxle mounting bolts (**3** in Fig. 9-1).

4. Place a transmission jack or a floor jack with a transmission adaptor beneath the transaxle. Raise the jack so that the transaxle is supported. Alternatively, you can attach a hoist to the top of the transaxle, as previously shown in Fig. 9-2.

5. Detach the transaxle side mount from the body (Fig. 9-3).

6. Detach the transaxle rear mount from both the transaxle and the car body by taking off the nuts indicated in Fig. 9-4. Then remove the mount.

7. Detach the driveshaft from the transaxle's drive flanges by taking out the socket-head bolts. Support the detached driveshafts by hanging them from the car body with stiff wire hooks.

Fig. 9-1. Disconnecting points for transaxle with automatic transmission.

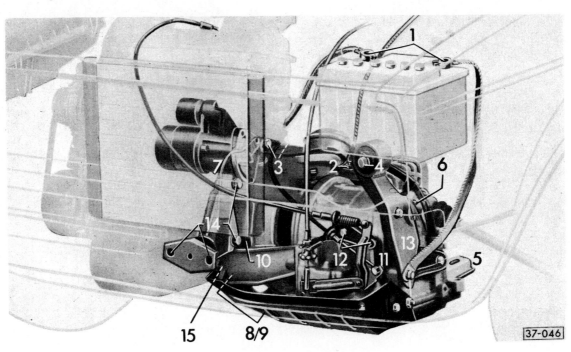

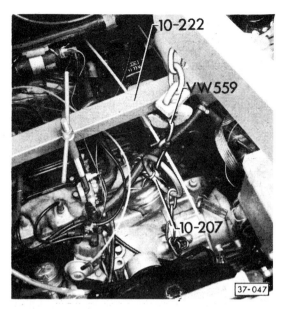

Fig. 9-2. Engine support device installed on engine. Also shown is hoist attached to transaxle for lifting purposes.

Fig. 9-3. Transaxle side mount. During installation, dimension **x** should be equal on both sides.

Fig. 9-4. Nuts that hold transaxle rear mount to transaxle and to car body.

8. Disconnect the wires from the starter. Then take out the three bolts and remove the starter from the car. (The third starter mounting bolt is between the starter and the engine.)

9. Remove the bolts that hold the transaxle protection plate and the torque converter cover plate to the transaxle. Then remove the plates (**8/9**, indicated earlier in Fig. 9-1).

10. Working through the openings in the bellhousing, remove the bolts that hold the torque converter to the engine's drive plate.

11. Move the selector lever to **P.** Then detach the selector lever cable from the operating lever on the transaxle.

12. Detach the accelerator cable/throttle cable bracket from the transaxle. Then disconnect the cables from the lever on the transaxle. Do not alter the cable adjustments by detaching the cable conduits from the bracket.

13. Remove the nuts. Then remove the transaxle side mount from the transaxle.

14. Detach the transaxle front mount from the transaxle only (**14**, given earlier in Fig. 9-1).

15. Remove the remaining bolts and nuts that hold the transaxle to the engine. Then, using the hoist or floor jack, raise the engine/transaxle assembly slightly so that you can swing the left-hand driveshaft upward and out of the way.

16. Carefully pull the transaxle off the hollow dowels that align it with the engine—making sure that the torque converter is separated from the engine's drive plate, not pulled off the transaxle.

17. Lower the transaxle or raise the car. Then remove the transaxle from beneath the car toward the front.

18. Install a bar or wire across the mouth of the bellhousing in order to keep the torque converter from falling out.

To install:

1. Position the transaxle beneath the car. Raise the transaxle until it can be pushed onto the hollow dowels on the engine. Then loosely install two bolts and nuts to hold the transaxle to the engine.

2. Lift the engine/transaxle assembly until the left-hand driveshaft can be slipped into the recess in the drive flange. Then lower the engine/transaxle assembly to its normal position in the car.

3. Install all of the engine-to-transaxle mounting bolts and nuts to a torque of 5.5 mkg (40 ft. lb.).

4. Install the transaxle front mount but do not tighten the nuts and bolts.

7 ■

5. Loosely install the transaxle front mount on both the transaxle and the bracket on the car body.

6. Install the throttle cable, the accelerator cable, and their bracket.

7. Reconnect the selector lever cable to the operating lever on the transaxle—making sure that both the operating lever and the selector lever are at **P.**

8. Install the bolts that hold the torque converter to the engine's drive plate. If necessary, hand-turn the crankshaft with a wrench placed on the bolt that is in the center of the crankshaft pulley. Torque the torque converter mounting bolts to 3.0 mkg (22 ft. lb.).

9. Install the torque converter cover plate and the transaxle protection plate. Torque the cover plate bolts to 1.5 mkg (11 ft. lb.). Torque M 10 protection plate bolts to 2.5 mkg (18 ft. lb.); torque M 8 protection plate bolts to 2.0 mkg (14 ft. lb.).

NOTE ——

On 1976 and later cars, M 10 bolts are used at the points indicated in Fig. 9-5. On earlier cars, M 8 bolts are used. If a new transmission case is installed on a 1975 car, enlarge the holes in the plate to 10.5 mm (or 7/16 in.). If a new plate is installed on a 1975 car, use flat washers together with M 8 bolts.

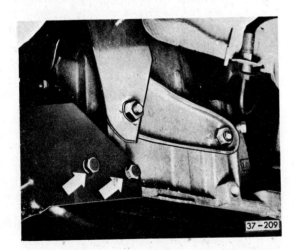

Fig. 9-5. Bolts that hold protection plate to transaxle (arrows).

10. Install the starter. Torque the bolts to 3.0 mkg (22 ft. lb.). Then reconnect the starter wires.

11. Install the socket-head bolts that hold the driveshafts to the drive flanges. Torque the socket-head bolts to 4.5 mkg (32 ft. lb.).

12. Loosely install the transaxle rear mount on both the transaxle and the car body.

13. Reconnect the speedometer cable.

14. Reconnect the battery cables and any other wires that were disconnected during removal of the transaxle.

15. Remove the engine support device. Then, with careful reference to the instructions given in conjunction with engine installation in **ENGINE AND CLUTCH,** align the engine/transaxle mountings. With the mounts aligned and the nuts and bolts torqued, check the selector cable adjustment as described in **4.3 Adjusting Selector Lever Cable.** If the throttle and accelerator cables require adjustment, adjust them as described in **FUEL AND EXHAUST SYSTEMS.**

CAUTION ——

If you have drained either the ATF or the hypoid oil, be sure to refill the transaxle as described in **LUBRICATION AND MAINTENANCE** *before you start the engine or move the car.*

Repairing Engine/Transaxle Mountings

After removing and installing any of the engine/transaxle mountings, you should always align the mountings as described in conjunction with engine installation in **ENGINE AND CLUTCH.** The mountings can be replaced, for the most part, using common hand tools. To replace the rubber bushing of the transaxle left mounting, please follow the instructions given in **MANUAL TRANSMISSION.**

10. TORQUE CONVERTER

Up to this point we have covered repairs that can be carried out with the transaxle in the car—although they may also be carried out with the transaxle removed. Servicing the torque converter, however, demands that the transaxle be removed. The marking shown in Fig. 10-1 identifies replacement torque converters that are suitable for use in the cars covered by this Manual.

Fig. 10-1. Letter **K** on lug, which identifies torque converters suitable for use in cars covered by this Manual.

10.1 Removing and Installing Torque Converter

The torque converter usually requires removal only when you must replace the seal, replace the bushing, or clean the torque converter after a transmission failure has contaminated the ATF. Since the torque converter is a welded assembly, you must replace it as a unit if it is leaky or noisy, if it has loose welds, or if a stall speed test shows the unit to be faulty.

To remove:

1. Remove the transaxle as described in **9. Removing and Installing Transaxle.**

2. Remove the wire or the securing bar that you installed across the mouth of the bellhousing during transaxle removal.

3. Grasp the torque converter with both hands. Remove it by pulling it with a twisting motion off its support tube on the final drive housing.

CAUTION ——

Do not rock or tilt the converter when you remove or install it. This could damage the seal, the stator one-way clutch, or other components in the torque converter hub.

Before you install the torque converter, inspect it thoroughly as described in **10.2 Inspecting and Repairing Torque Converter.** If the seal seat on the hub is rough, worn, or pitted, you should replace the torque converter. Otherwise, the seal will wear out in a very short time.

Installation is the reverse of removal. Make sure that the pump shaft is completely seated in the pump inside the transmission by checking the shoulder indicated in Fig. 10-2. Then install the torque converter, turning it slowly clockwise and counterclockwise so that the turbine and pump shaft splines can engage.

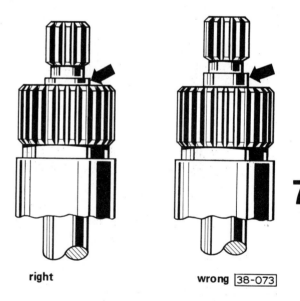

right   wrong [38-073]

Fig. 10-2. Installation of pump shaft being checked prior to installation of torque converter. Shoulder indicated by arrows must not project more than about 2 mm (or $1/16$ in.) above end of turbine shaft.

7

10.2 Inspecting and Repairing Torque Converter

Inspect the torque converter seal that is on the torque converter one-way clutch support tube on the final drive housing. Use a cold chisel, as shown in Fig. 10-3, to drive off faulty seals. Dip the new seal in ATF. Then, using the tool shown in Fig. 10-4, drive the seal on as far as it will go.

CAUTION ——

The seal is soft silicone rubber and easily damaged. Silicone seals must not contact gasoline or similar cleaning solutions. Replace seals that have been torn or exposed to cleaning solvents.

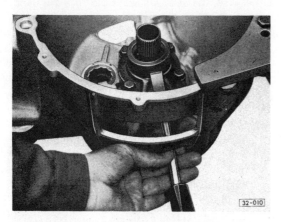

Fig. 10-3. Faulty torque converter seal being removed.

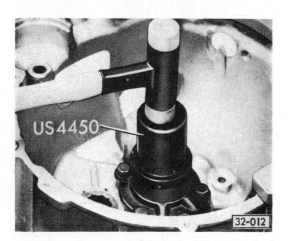

Fig. 10-4. New torque converter seal being driven onto one-way clutch support on final drive housing.

Check the seal seat surface that is indicated in Fig. 10-5. The edge of the seat should be chamfered. If it is not chamfered, round the edge with fine emery cloth so that the edge will not damage the seal as the torque converter is installed. If the seal contact area itself is scored, rough, or pitted, replace the torque converter in order to prevent rapid seal wear. Do not attempt to smooth the seal contact area of the torque converter with emery cloth.

Fig. 10-5. Seal seat (arrow) on torque converter. If you must round edge with emery cloth, cover hub opening to keep out grit.

A leaking torque converter seal is often caused by a worn bushing in the torque converter hub, so check the bushing every time you replace a seal, as shown in Fig. 10-6. Replace the bushing if its inside diameter exceeds 34.25 mm (1.348 in.) or if it is out of round by 0.03 mm (.001 in.) or more.

Fig. 10-6. Torque converter bushing being checked.

To replace the torque converter bushing, remove it with an expansion tool and slide hammer as shown in Fig. 10-7. Press in the new bushing as indicated in Fig. 10-8. Replacement bushings are manufactured to size and require no reaming or honing.

Fig. 10-7. Torque converter bushing being removed. Expansion tool is extractor US 4452.

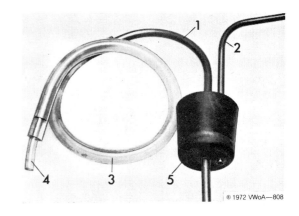

1. Steel or copper tube ³/₁₆ × 8 in. (4 × 200 mm)
2. Steel or copper tube ⅛ × 6 in. (3 × 150 mm)
3. PVC hose ¼ × 14 in. (6 × 350 mm)
4. PVC hose ⅛ × 1¼ in. (3 × 30 mm)
5. Conical rubber plug 1½ in. (35 mm) diam.

Fig. 10-9. Siphon parts available at auto stores.

To drain the torque converter, install the siphon as shown in Fig. 10-10. Push the siphon line pipe through the rubber plug until it contacts the torque converter bottom, then place the siphon hose over the oil receptacle. Blow air into the short tube to start the siphon. Let the torque converter drain overnight or for about eight hours.

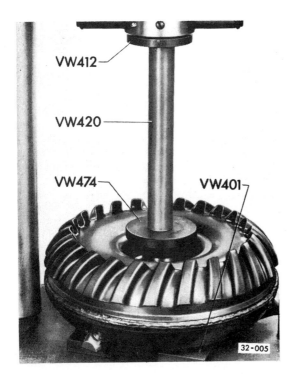

Fig. 10-8. Torque converter bushing being installed.

10.3 Cleaning Torque Converter

When charred material from a burned clutch disk or other pollutants have entered the ATF, remove the residual ATF from the torque converter with the home-made siphon shown in Fig. 10-9.

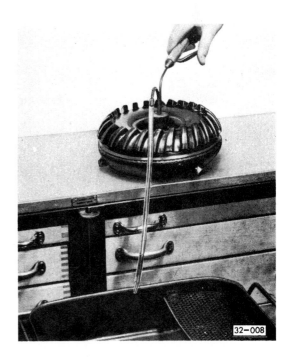

Fig. 10-10. Siphon and oil receptacle in position.

11. REPAIRING AUTOMATIC TRANSMISSION

Thoroughly clean the outside of the transaxle before you disassemble it so that dirt will not enter the hydraulic controls or the mechanical parts. Study the repair procedures on the following pages. If they require equipment that you do not have, the transaxle should be turned over to a specialist before any disassembly.

CAUTION ——

If you lack the skills, the tools, or a suitable workshop for automatic transmission work, we suggest you leave these repairs to an Authorized Dealer or other qualified shop. We especially urge you to consult an Authorized Dealer before attempting repairs on a car still covered by the new-car warranty.

11.1 Separating and Rejoining Automatic Transmission and Final Drive

A transmission stand such as the one shown here is a great help when you must take the transaxle apart. Do not disassemble the transaxle on the shop floor as dirt and debris may get into the working parts. If you need to repair the final drive, install the transaxle on the stand as shown in Fig. 11-1. If you need to repair the automatic transmission, install the transaxle on the stand as shown in Fig. 11-2.

Fig. 11-1. Final drive bolted to repair stand preparatory to transmission removal.

Fig. 11-2. Transmission case held by nuts (arrows) to repair stand preparatory to final drive removal.

To disassemble:

1. After cleaning the outside of the transaxle and draining the ATF, remove the torque converter. Cover the torque converter's hub opening in order to keep out dirt and foreign matter while the converter is removed.

   NOTE ——

   You need not drain the hypoid oil unless you intend to disassemble the final drive.

2. Remove the governor as described in **7.1 Removing and Installing Governor.**

3. Remove the four M 8 nuts from the steel studs that hold the final drive housing to the transmission case. Separate the main parts of the transaxle as shown in Fig. 11-3.

4. Withdraw the pump shaft and the turbine shaft from the transmission. Cover the end of the transmission to keep out dirt while you repair the final drive or cover both ends of the final drive to keep out dirt while you repair the transmission.

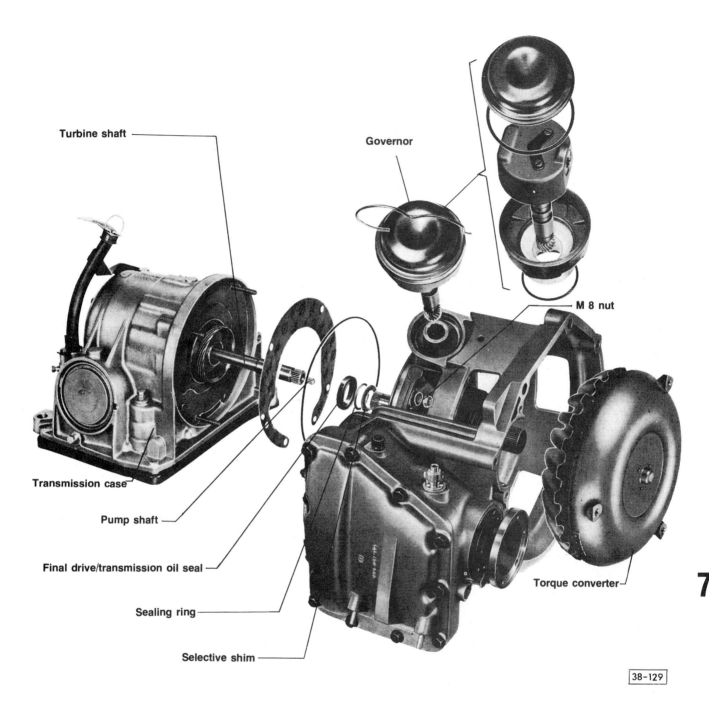

Turbine shaft

Governor

M 8 nut

Transmission case

Pump shaft

Final drive/transmission oil seal

Sealing ring

Selective shim

Torque converter

38-129

7

Fig. 11-3. Main parts of transaxle separated.

To assemble:

1. If you are installing a new transmission, the correct studs must be installed to the correct length. Fig. 11-4 and Fig. 11-5 give the stud length dimensions.

Fig. 11-4. Correct installed lengths for transmission-to-final drive studs. Dimension **a** should be 44.00 mm (1.732 in.) with stud Part No. N 900 028 01.

Fig. 11-5. Correct installed lengths for transmission mounting studs. Dimension **a** should be 14.00 mm (.551 in.) with stud Part No. N 014 517 1. Dimension **b** should be 34.00 mm (1.339 in.) with stud Part No. N 014 692 1.

2. Obtain two new transmission-to-final drive gaskets. The transmission axial play must be adjusted before you assemble the transaxle—whether or not you have replaced any part other than the gaskets. Do not reuse the old gaskets.

3. Pry out the final drive/transmission oil seal as shown in Fig. 11-6. Then remove the sealing ring and the selective shim.

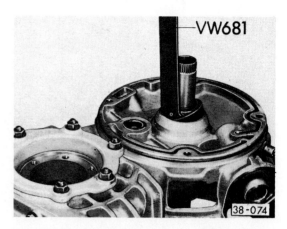

Fig. 11-6. Final drive/transmission oil seal being removed.

4. To adjust the transmission axial play, you must first determine dimensions **a** and **b** as given in Fig. 11-7. From these measurements, you will be able to compute dimension **x** (total axial play with no shim) and the shim thickness required to limit axial play to specifications (dimension **y**). Obtain a straightedge and a vernier depth gauge for making the measurements.

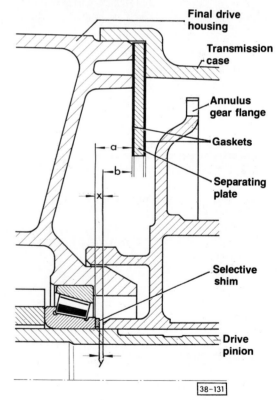

Fig. 11-7. Dimensions used in adjusting transmission axial play. Dimension **a** is distance from drive pinion bearing to edge of final drive housing. Dimension **b** is obtained from two measurements made on the transmission. Dimension **x** is computed from dimensions **a** and **b**. Dimension **y** is correct axial play.

5. To determine dimension **a,** place the straightedge across the final drive housing as shown in Fig. 11-8. Using the vernier depth gauge, measure the distance from the upper surface of the straightedge to the edge of the tapered-roller bearing inner race. Write down the measurement.

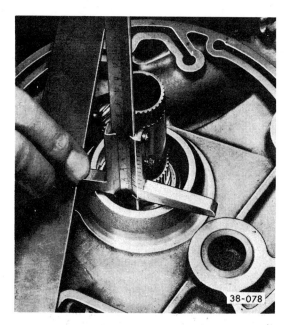

Fig. 11-8. Method of making first measurement used in determining dimension **a**.

6. Make a second measurement from the top of the straightedge to the edge of the final drive housing, as shown in Fig. 11-9. This measurement will accurately determine the thickness of the straightedge you are using. Write down the measurement.

7. Subtract the straightedge thickness, as determined in step 6, from the measurement you made in step 5. The difference is dimension **a,** which should be written down for use in selecting a new shim.

CAUTION ——

Every number in the following examples is imaginary. Using them for actual adjustments could seriously damage the transmission.

Example:

Distance from top of straightedge		
to bearing race	18.70 mm	
Distance from top of straightedge		
to housing −	8.00 mm	
Dimension **a** =	10.70 mm	

Fig. 11-9. Method of determining the exact thickness of the straightedge when it is placed on final drive housing.

8. Install first a new gasket in the transmission case and then the separating plate and its screw. Finally, place a second new gasket atop the separating plate.

9. To determine dimension **b,** place the straightedge across the transmission case as shown in Fig. 11-10. Using the vernier depth gauge, measure the distance from the upper surface of the straightedge to the gasket atop the separating plate. Write down the measurement.

7

Fig. 11-10. Method of making first measurement used in determining dimension **b**.

10. Make a second measurement from the top of the straightedge to the shim surface on the shoulder of the annulus gear flange, as shown in Fig. 11-11. Write down the measurement.

Fig. 11-11. Method of making second measurement used in determining dimension **b**.

11. Subtract the measurement made in step 10 from the distance from the top of the straightedge to the gasket, which you measured in step 9. The difference is dimension **b**, which should be written down for use in selecting a new shim.

Example:

Distance from top of straightedge to gasket atop separating plate	19.20 mm
Distance from top of straightedge to shim shoulder on annulus gear	− 10.00 mm
Dimension **b** =	9.20 mm

12. To compute dimension **x**, subtract dimension **b** from dimension **a**. Use dimension **x** to select the correct shim combination from **Table c.**

Example:

Dimension **a**	10.70 mm
Dimension **b**	− 9.20 mm
Dimension **x**	= 1.50 mm

Table c. Axial Play Selective Shims

Two shim thicknesses are available:	
Part No. 010 323 345 A	0.40 mm thick
Part No. 010 323 346 A	1.20 mm thick

Dimension x (mm)	Number and thicknesses of shims to be installed
0.23–0.84	no shim required
0.85–1.24	1 shim, 0.40 mm thick
1.25–1.64	2 shims, each 0.40 mm thick
1.65–2.04	1 shim 1.20 mm thick
2.05–2.44	1 shim 0.40 mm thick plus 1 shim 1.20 mm thick
2.45–2.84	2 shims 0.40 mm thick plus 1 shim 1.20 mm thick
2.85–3.24	2 shims 1.20 mm thick
3.25–3.64	1 shim 0.40 mm thick plus 2 shims 1.20 mm thick
3.65–3.88	2 shims 0.40 mm thick plus 2 shims 1.20 mm thick

13. Check the clutch piston rings (Fig. 11-12) for radial and axial wear. If necessary, compare them with a new piston ring. Replace worn or damaged rings.

NOTE ———

If you have replaced the turbine shaft, make sure that it is the correct part by measuring its length as indicated in Fig. 11-13.

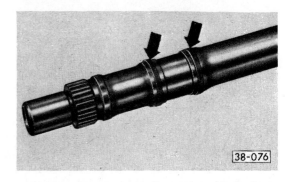

Fig. 11-12. Locations (arrows) of piston rings on turbine shaft.

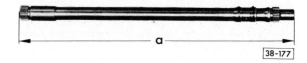

Fig. 11-13. Length of turbine shaft used in cars covered by this Manual. Dimension **a** is 265.1 mm (10 7/16 in.).

14. Check that the piston rings on the turbine shaft are correctly seated. Lubricate the piston rings with ATF. Then install the turbine shaft—piston ring-end first—in the transmission.

15. Install the correct selective shim(s) in the final drive. Install a new sealing ring, then drive in a new final drive/transmission oil seal as shown in Fig. 11-14. The seal lip must be toward the final drive.

Fig. 11-14. Final drive/transmission oil seal being driven in.

16. Install a new large O-ring on the final drive housing and lubricate it with ATF. Then install the final drive on the transmission. Torque the four M 8 nuts to 3.0 mkg (22 ft. lb.).

17. If you are replacing the ATF pump driveshaft, make sure that you have the correct shaft by checking its length, as indicated in Fig. 11-15. Then lubricate the splines with ATF and install the pump shaft through the center of the turbine shaft.

Fig. 11-15. Length of pump shaft used in cars covered by this Manual. Dimension **a** is 316.5 mm (12^{15}/$_{32}$ in.).

18. Make sure that the pump shaft is completely seated in the pump inside the transmission by checking the shoulder indicated in Fig. 11-16. Then install the torque converter, turning it slowly clockwise and counterclockwise so that the turbine and pump shaft splines can engage.

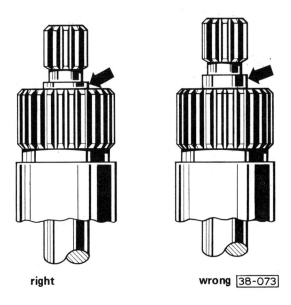

right   wrong 38-073

Fig. 11-16. Installation of pump shaft being checked prior to installation of torque converter. Shoulder indicated by arrows must not project more than about 2 mm (or ^{1}/$_{16}$ in.) above end of turbine shaft.

19. Install the governor. Install the transaxle in the car before you refill the transmission with ATF as described in **LUBRICATION AND MAINTENANCE.**

7

11.2 Disassembling and Assembling Automatic Transmission

Study Fig. 11-17 carefully so that you become familiar with the names of the various parts. These names will be referred to frequently on the following pages. The illustration also shows the positions of the parts inside the transmission case.

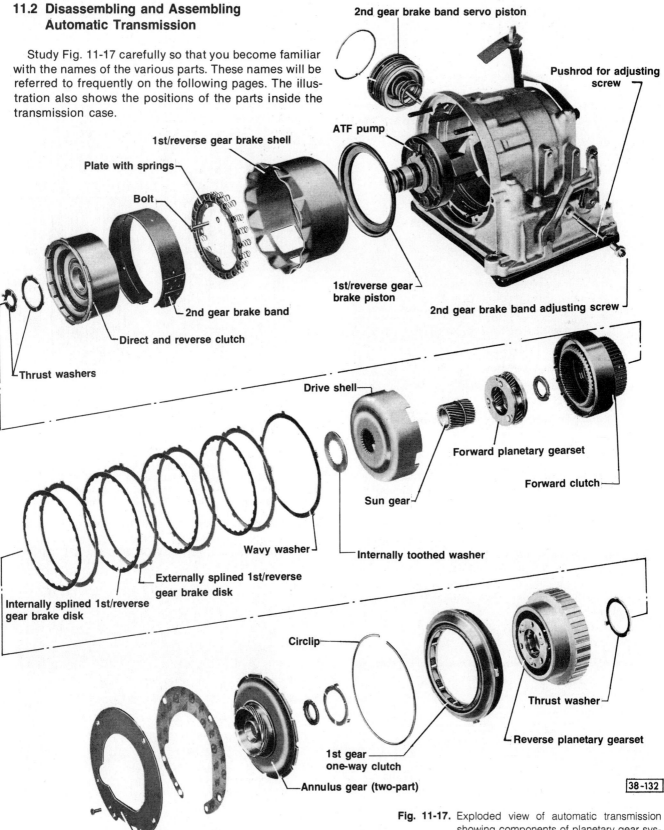

2nd gear brake band servo piston

Pushrod for adjusting screw

1st/reverse gear brake shell

ATF pump

Plate with springs

Bolt

1st/reverse gear brake piston

2nd gear brake band

Direct and reverse clutch

Thrust washers

2nd gear brake band adjusting screw

Drive shell

Forward planetary gearset

Sun gear

Forward clutch

Wavy washer

Internally toothed washer

Externally splined 1st/reverse gear brake disk

Internally splined 1st/reverse gear brake disk

Circlip

Thrust washer

Reverse planetary gearset

1st gear one-way clutch

Annulus gear (two-part)

Separating plate

38-132

Fig. 11-17. Exploded view of automatic transmission showing components of planetary gear system. Many parts used on 1975 cars are not interchangeable with corresponding parts used on 1976 and later cars.

To disassemble:

1. Mount the transmission on a stand or secure it to the workbench.

2. Remove the screw that holds the separating plate. Then remove the separating plate and the gasket.

3. Remove the annulus gear and the two thrust washers that are behind the annulus gear.

4. Using a screwdriver, carefully pry the circlip out of its groove, beginning near the gap in the circlip, as indicated in Fig. 11-18.

Fig. 11-18. Point (arrow) at which you should begin prying circlip out of groove.

5. Make two hooks, similar to those shown in Fig. 11-19, out of $^3/_{16}$-in. welding rod. Then, using the hooks as shown in Fig. 11-20, lift out the one-way clutch, the disks for the 1st/reverse gear brake, and the reverse planetary gearset.

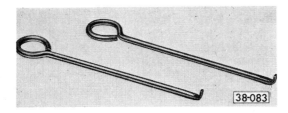

Fig. 11-19. Hooks for lifting out one-way clutch and other transmission internal components.

6. Lift out the thrust washers. Then remove the sun gear, driving shell, forward planetary gearset, and forward clutch as a unit.

7. Remove the circlip for the 2nd gear brake band servo piston cover. Then, using a rubber mallet, tap the cover as shown in Fig. 11-21 until the cover and the piston pop out under spring pressure.

Remove the cover and the piston assembly as a unit.

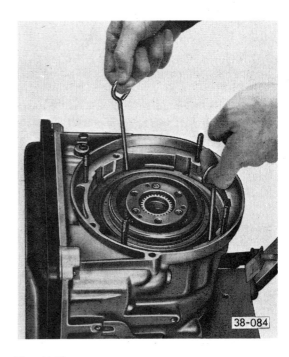

Fig. 11-20. 1st gear one-way clutch being removed.

NOTE ——

For detailed instructions on removing, repairing, and installing the 2nd gear brake band servo piston, please consult **8. Servicing 2nd Gear Brake Band Servo Piston.**

Fig. 11-21. Rubber mallet being used to tap cover for 2nd gear brake band servo piston.

7

8. Loosen the locknut for the 2nd gear brake band adjusting screw. Then remove the screw and locknut and withdraw the pushrod for the adjusting screw.

9. Lift out the remaining planetary gear system components that are housed in the 1st/reverse gear brake shell.

10. Take out the five bolts that hold the plate with springs and the ATF pump to the transmission case. Then lift out the plate with springs, the 1st/reverse brake shell, and the ATF pump and 1st/reverse brake piston.

NOTE ——

If you wish to replace the thrust washer that is on the ATF pump, do so as illustrated in **11.3 Disassembling and Assembling ATF Pump.**

To assemble:

1. Lubricate the 1st/reverse gear brake piston with ATF, then install the piston on the ATF pump.

2. Install the ATF pump and brake piston in the transmission case as a unit. Position the pump so that the lug indicated in Fig. 11-22 is toward the top of the transmission case.

Fig. 11-22. Anti-rotation lug for thrust washer on ATF pump (arrow). Install pump so lug is toward top of transmission case.

3. If you replace the 1st/reverse gear brake shell, measure the new shell in order to determine whether it is the correct replacement part for cars covered by this Manual. See Fig. 11-23. Install the 1st/reverse gear brake shell as shown in Fig. 11-24.

4. Assemble the plate with springs as indicated in Fig. 11-25. Then install the plate so that the springs contact the 1st/reverse gear brake shell and the bolt holes in the plate match those in the ATF pump.

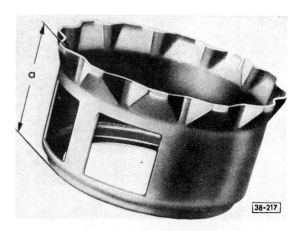

Fig. 11-23. Correct 1st/reverse gear brake shell for cars covered by this Manual. Dimension **a** should be 94.9 mm (3 $\frac{47}{64}$ in.).

Fig. 11-24. 1st/reverse gear brake shell correctly installed. Lug (arrow) goes in groove at top of transmission case.

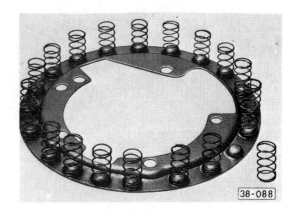

Fig. 11-25. Correct installation of springs on plate. If necessary, you can use vaseline as an adhesive to hold loose-fitting springs in place. 1975 springs are of wire 0.80 mm (.031 in.) thick. 1976 and later springs are of wire 1.00 mm (.039 in.) thick.

5. Loosely install the five bolts that hold the plate with springs and the ATF pump to the transmission case. Working diagonally, gradually tighten the bolts to a final torque of 40 cmkg (35 in. lb.).

CAUTION ——

After you have torqued the bolts, temporarily insert the pump driveshaft so that you can hand-turn the pump gears. If the pump's internal parts are jammed or binding, owing to incorrect installation or overtightened bolts, severe transmission damage could result when the car's engine is started.

6. Install new O-rings on the cover for the 2nd gear brake band servo piston. The piston should be correctly installed inside the cover as described in **8. Servicing 2nd Gear Brake Band Servo Piston.** Lubricate the O-rings with ATF. Then press in the cover and piston against spring tension as shown in Fig. 11-26. Install the circlip.

Fig. 11-26. Lever being used to press in cover and 2nd gear brake band servo piston.

7. Turn the transmission case to a horizontal position, so that the cover for the 2nd gear brake band servo piston points down. Then position the 2nd gear brake band inside the case, correctly engaging it with the servo piston. Loosely install the pushrod for the adjusting screw, the adjusting screw, and the locknut.

8. Keeping the case in its horizontal position, lubricate the direct and reverse clutch with ATF. Then insert the direct and reverse clutch into the trans-

mission case, sliding it onto the neck of the ATF pump and into the 2nd gear brake band. See Fig. 11-27.

Fig. 11-27. Direct and reverse clutch being installed while transmission case is in its horizontal position. 1975 clutch is different from that of 1976 and later cars.

9. Torque the 2nd gear brake band adjusting screw to about 100 cmkg (87 in. lb.) in order to prevent the brake band from shifting its position. Then turn the transmission case so that its open end is uppermost.

10. Using vaseline as an adhesive, stick the thrust washers to the forward clutch. Then install the forward clutch atop the direct and reverse clutch. If necessary, consult Fig. 11-17, given earlier.

7 ■

NOTE ——

The forward clutch, the forward planetary gearset, the sun gear, the drive shell, the internally toothed washer, the reverse planetary gearset, and the annulus gear are all different on 1975 cars from corresponding parts of 1976 and later cars.

11. Install the thrust washer, the forward planetary gearset, the sun gear, the drive shell, and the internally toothed washer. If necessary, consult Fig. 11-17, given earlier.

12. Using vaseline as an adhesive, stick the thrust washer to the reverse planetary gearset. Then install the gearset.

13. Install the wavy washer. Then install four externally splined 1st/reverse gear brake disks and four

internally splined 1st/reverse gear brake disks—alternately, beginning with an externally splined disk. See Fig. 11-28.

Fig. 11-28. Reverse planetary gearset installed preparatory to installation of 1st/reverse gear brake disks. Use tip of screwdriver to align externally splined disks with grooves in case and internally splined disks with splines on reverse planetary gearset.

14. Install the 1st gear one-way clutch. Turn the planetary gearset's planet carrier as indicated in Fig. 11-29 until the one-way clutch slips into place.

Fig. 11-29. 1st gear one-way clutch being installed. Turn planet carrier clockwise, as indicated by arrow.

15. Check the operation of the 1st gear one-way clutch as shown in Fig. 11-30. It should be possible to turn the planet carrier clockwise but, owing to the locking of the one-way clutch, impossible to turn the planet carrier counterclockwise.

Fig. 11-30. 1st gear one-way clutch being checked. Special tool can be used to turn planet carrier.

16. Install the circlip. If all transmission components have been correctly installed, the circlip groove will be uncovered as indicated in Fig. 11-31. Do not attempt to force in the circlip on an incorrectly assembled transmission.

Fig. 11-31. Circlip groove (arrow) uncovered, indicating that transmission is correctly assembled.

17. Using a new gasket, install the separating plate. Torque the screw to 70 cmkg (61 in. lb.).

NOTE ——

You should adjust the transmission end play as described in **11.1 Separating and Rejoining Automatic Transmission and Final Drive**—whether or not you have installed new parts in the transmission.

18. Place the transmission in a horizontal position as shown in Fig. 11-32. Make sure that the 2nd gear brake band adjusting screw is torqued to 100 cmkg (87 in. lb.), then loosen the adjusting screw. Torque the screw to 50 cmkg (43 in. lb.) and, from this position, back off the screw by exactly 2½ turns. Hold the screw stationary while you torque the locknut to 2.0 mkg (14 ft. lb.). For additional information, consult **5.1 Adjusting 2nd Gear Brake Band.**

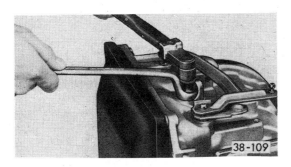

Fig. 11-32. 2nd gear brake band being adjusted. Transmission must be horizontal in order to keep band from slipping or jamming, which could make disassembling the transmission necessary.

11.3 Disassembling and Assembling ATF Pump

Whenever you remove the ATF pump, carefully inspect the housing, both gears, and the cover plate. Replace the pump if these parts are worn or damaged. The drive plate and the piston rings (Fig. 11-33) can be replaced individually, as can the thrust washer.

Fig. 11-33. Exploded view of ATF pump.

To disassemble:

1. Remove the two M 4 screws, then remove the cover plate.

2. Remove the 11-mm (7/16-in.) ball and the ball spring. Remove the inner gear, the outer gear, and the drive plate.

3. Using needle nose pliers as shown in Fig. 11-34, unhook the ring ends and carefully remove first the small and then the large piston rings.

4. Take off the thrust washer.

© 1974 VWoA—1009

Fig. 11-34. Clutch piston rings being removed from ATF pump.

7

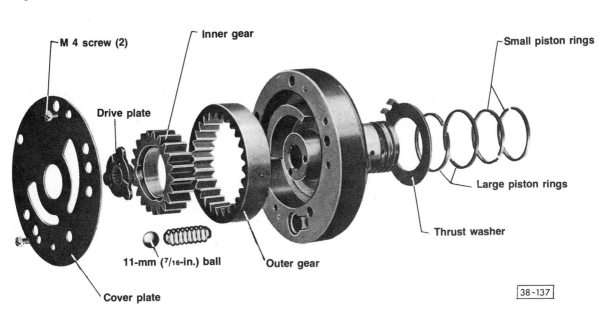

M 4 screw (2)   Inner gear   Small piston rings

Drive plate

Large piston rings

Thrust washer

11-mm (7/16-in.) ball   Outer gear

Cover plate

38-137

To assemble:

1. Thoroughly clean all parts in kerosene. Blow out the ATF passages with compressed air.

2. Install the thrust washer (Fig. 11-35) so that the claws on the washer point away from the piston ring grooves and are engaged on the lug on the pump housing.

38-106

Fig. 11-35. Thrust washer installed on pump housing. Washer must be installed before clutch piston rings are installed.

3. Carefully install first the large and then the small clutch piston rings, making sure that the ring ends hook correctly.

4. After lubricating all parts thoroughly with ATF, install the gears and the drive plate—making sure that the extended hub of the drive plate is inserted into the shaft opening of the pump housing.

5. Insert the ball valve spring and then the 11-mm ($^7/_{16}$-in.) ball.

6. Align the cover plate with the pump housing, then install the two M 4 screws.

> **CAUTION ——**
>
> *Check that the pump gears turn freely by hand-turning them with the pump driveshaft. Check this again after the pump has been installed. If the pump's internal parts are jammed or binding, owing to incorrect assembly or installation, severe transmission damage could result when the car's engine is started.*

11.4 Disassembling, Checking, and Assembling Direct and Reverse Clutch

The direct and reverse clutch has undergone two important modifications during the model years covered by this Manual. The earliest 1975 models have a direct and reverse clutch with five externally splined plates, whereas all later cars have a direct and reverse clutch with three externally splined plates. Owing to the difference in the depth of the circlip grooves (Fig. 11-36), you must always install the original number of plates when repairing either kind of direct and reverse clutch.

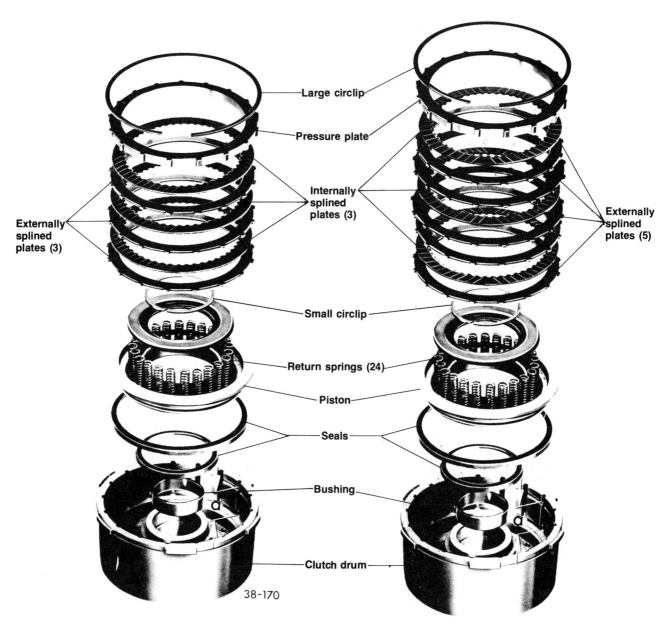

Late-type (from Transmission No. 28 04 5

Early-type (through Transmission No. 28 04 4)

Fig. 11-36. Exploded views of early-type and late-type direct and reverse clutches. Dimension **a** is 31.3 mm (1 15/64 in.) on early clutch, 27.0 mm (1 1/16 in.) on later clutch. Piston and springs have also been changed during model years covered by this Manual.

To disassemble:

1. Using a screwdriver, pry out the large circlip.

2. Remove the pressure plate, the internally splined plates, and the externally splined plates.

3. Put the clutch on a press and force down the spring plate until you can pry out the small circlip (Fig. 11-37). Then raise the press ram and remove the spring plate.

4. With a twisting movement, pull the clutch piston with return springs out of the clutch drum. Remove the piston seals and the springs.

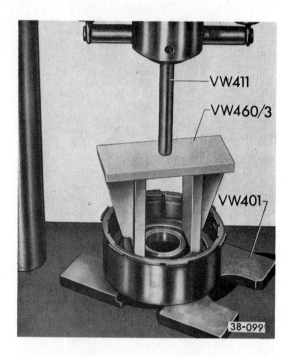

Fig. 11-37. Spring plate being pressed down so that small circlip can be removed or installed.

5. Using an extractor tool and the repair press, press out the clutch drum bushing as shown in Fig. 11-38.

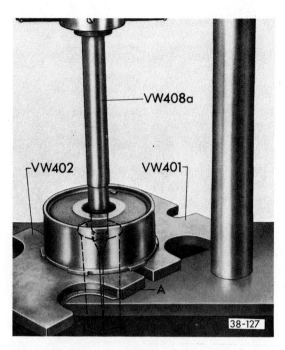

Fig. 11-38. Clutch drum bushing being removed. Phantom drawing (dashed line) shows extractor.

To check clutch:

1. Check for wear or damage on the friction surfaces of the piston and the clutch drum, and in the grooves that the externally splined clutch plates ride in.

> **NOTE** ——
>
> If you replace the clutch drum, make certain that you obtain the correct replacement part by measuring dimension **a** given in Fig. 11-39.

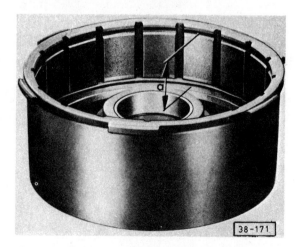

Fig. 11-39. Identification of direct and reverse clutch drum. Through Transmission No. 28 04 4, dimension **a** should be 31.3 mm (1^{15}/$_{64}$ in.); from Transmission No. 28 04 5, dimension **a** should be 27.0 mm (1^{1}/$_{16}$ in.).

2. Check the ball valve in the clutch drum for freedom of movement. Make sure that the drilling is clear.

3. Inspect the externally splined plates. If any plate is scored or has radial grooves, replace the plate. Plates that are merely discolored can be reused.

4. Inspect the internally splined plates. Replace any plate that is worn, damaged, or burned.

5. Inspect the springs. Replace springs that are broken or distorted.

To assemble:

1. If you are installing new internally splined plates, soak them in ATF for at least 15 minutes before you install them. Use only plates with lining markings such as those shown in Fig. 11-40.

Fig. 11-40. Pattern on surface of internally splined direct and reverse clutch plates used on cars covered by this Manual. Do not install plates with a different pattern of markings.

2. Press in a new clutch drum bushing until it is flush with the hub of the drum (Fig. 11-41).

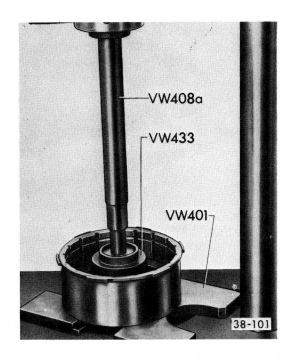

Fig. 11-41. New clutch drum bushing being pressed in.

3. Install new piston seals. The seal lips should point into the drum toward the source of hydraulic pressure.

4. Place a stiff plastic sheet in the clutch drum as shown in Fig. 11-42. Lubricate the seals with ATF, then insert the piston into the drum with a twisitng motion.

© 1974 VWoA—3341

Fig. 11-42. Plastic sheet used to prevent damage to seals during piston installation. Insert piston with twisting motion (arrow). Clutch shown is not for a car covered by this Manual.

5. Insert the 24 return springs and the spring plate. Using the repair press, press down the spring plate until you can snap the small circlip into its groove. See Fig. 11-37 given earlier.

NOTE ——

If you have installed the modified piston, which has been factory-installed beginning with Transmission No. 28 01 6, you must also install the new-type springs (Part No. 010 323 129 A) that are 24 mm long. (The old-type springs, Part No. 010 323 129, are 26 mm long.) The new-type piston can be identified by checking dimension **a**, given in Fig. 11-43.

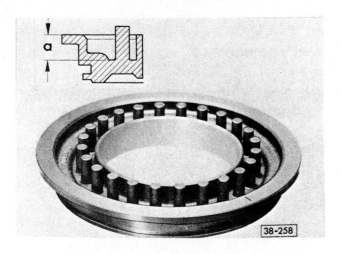

Fig. 11-43. Piston installed beginning with Transmission No. 28 01 6. Dimension **a** is 12 mm. On pistons factory-installed in earlier transmissions, dimension **a** is 14 mm.

6. Install the internally splined and the externally splined plates. The sequence in which you install the plates depends on the depth of the circlip groove. See Fig. 11-36 given earlier.

7. Install the pressure plate and the thinnest-available circlip (Part No. 010 323 157 A). Then, using feeler gauges in various combinations, measure the clearance between the pressure plate and the circlip, as shown in Fig. 11-44. If the clearance is greater or smaller than 2.05 to 2.50 mm (.081 to .098 in.), select a different circlip from **Table d** that will bring the clearance within this range.

8. Install the correct circlip. Then recheck the clearance in order to make certain that no mistake has been made.

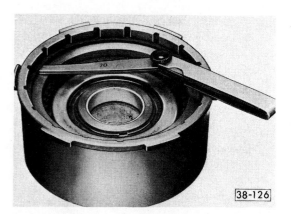

Fig. 11-44. Clearance between circlip and pressure plate being measured with feeler gauges.

Table d. Available Large Circlips for Direct and Reverse Clutch

Large circlip thickness	Part Number
1.50 mm (.059 in.)	010 323 157 A
1.70 mm (.067 in.)	010 323 157 B
2.00 mm (.079 in.)	010 323 157
2.30 mm (.091 in.)	010 323 157 C
2.50 mm (.098 in.)	010 323 157 D

11.5 Disassembling, Checking, and Assembling Forward Clutch

Fig. 11-45 gives an exploded view of the forward clutch. Though there have been modifications to some of the clutch components during the model years covered by this Manual, the number and locations of the parts remain unchanged.

To disassemble:

1. Using a screwdriver, pry out the clutch plate circlip. Then remove the pressure plate, the forward annulus gear, the internally splined and the externally splined clutch plates, and the thrust plate.

2. Carefully pry out the diaphragm spring circlip. Remove the diaphragm spring.

3. Either pull out the piston or expell it by injecting compressed air.

NOTE ——

The forward clutch piston sealing lips are vulcanized to the piston. Replace the entire piston if there is leakage past the sealing lips or if the lips are obviously worn or damaged.

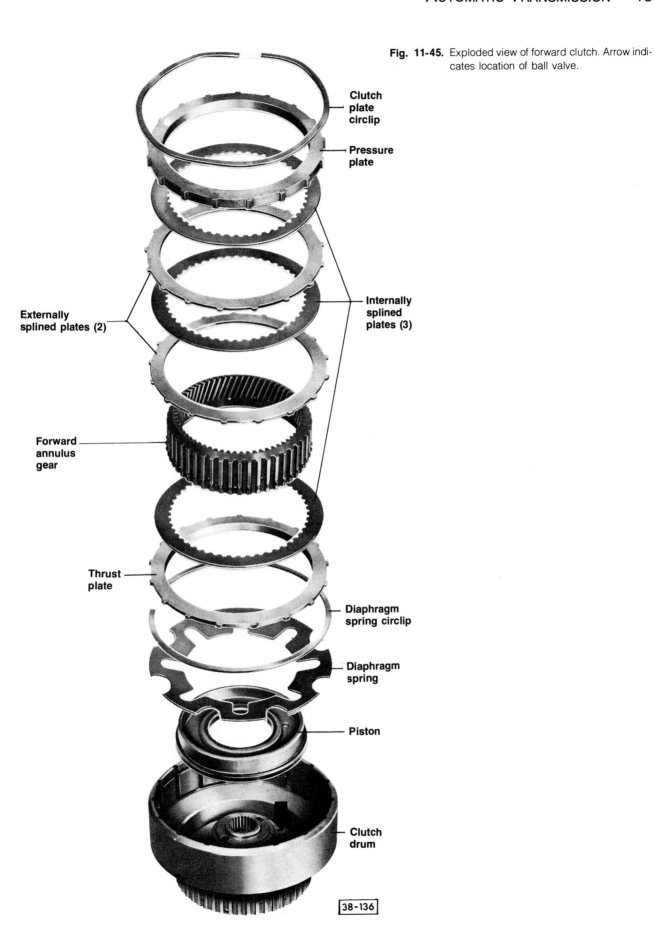

Fig. 11-45. Exploded view of forward clutch. Arrow indicates location of ball valve.

Clutch plate circlip

Pressure plate

Internally splined plates (3)

Externally splined plates (2)

Forward annulus gear

Thrust plate

Diaphragm spring circlip

Diaphragm spring

Piston

Clutch drum

38-136

7

To check clutch:

1. Shake the drum. If the drilling is clear, you should hear the ball valve rattle. If not, clean the drilling. Replace faulty drums (the ball valve is not replace-able separately).

   NOTE ——

   The clutch drum and the diaphragm spring were changed in production, beginning with Transmission No. 21 01 5. The new-type clutch drum is identified by a groove (Fig. 11-46). If you must replace the clutch drum, always use the new-type drum and its match-ing diaphragm spring.

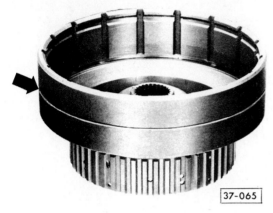

Fig. 11-46. New-type clutch drum identified by groove (arrow).

2. Check the diaphragm spring. When the piston is installed, the spring should reach at least to the lower edge of the circlip groove. Replace faulty springs.

   NOTE ——

   The old-type diaphragm spring, shown in Fig. 11-47, is no longer available as a re-placement part. If you must replace an old-type spring with the new-type spring shown in Fig. 11-48, you must also install the new-type clutch drum shown previously in Fig. 11-46.

Fig. 11-47. Old-type diaphragm spring.

Fig. 11-48. New-type diaphragm spring that will not fit in old-type clutch drum.

3. Inspect the externally splined plates. Replace any plate that is scored or has radial grooves. Plates that are merely discolored can be reused.

4. Inspect the internally splined plates. Replace any plate that is worn, damaged, or burned.

To assemble:

1. If you are installing new internally splined plates, soak them in ATF for at least 15 minutes before you install them. Use only plates with lining markings such as those shown in Fig. 11-49.

Fig. 11-49. Pattern on surface of internally splined for-ward clutch plates used on cars covered by this Manual. Do not install plates with a different pattern of markings.

2. If you are installing a new clutch drum, check dimension **a,** given in Fig. 11-50, to make sure that you have obtained the correct replacement part.

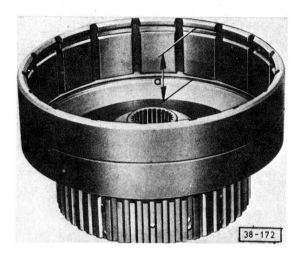

Fig. 11-50. Position of circlip groove on forward clutch drum used on cars covered by this Manual. Dimension **a** should be 26.2 mm (1 $^1/_{32}$ in.).

Fig. 11-51. Forward clutch end play being measured with dial indicator. Move annulus gear up and down as indicated by double arrow.

3. Lubricate the piston's sealing lips with ATF. Install the piston in the clutch drum with a twisting motion—being careful not to damage the sealing lips.

4. Install the diaphragm spring so that the convex side is toward the piston. To retain the diaphragm, use snap ring Part No. 010 323 157 which is 2.03 mm thick.

> **NOTE ——**
>
> The diaphragm spring should be under some tension when the diaphragm spring circlip is installed—and it should not be easy to snap the circlip into its groove. If inserting the circlip does not put the diaphragm spring under tension, replace the diaphragm spring.

5. Install the thrust plate. If one side is chamfered, install the chamfered side toward the diaphragm spring.

6. Install one internally splined plate. Then install the forward annulus gear so that the short splines beneath its retaining ridge are engaged in the installed internally splined plate.

7. Install (1) an externally splined plate, (2) an internally splined plate, (3) another externally splined plate, and (4) an internally splined plate—in that order.

8. Install the pressure plate and the pressure plate circlip (Part No. 010 323 159 B). Then, using the setup shown in Fig. 11-51, measure the forward clutch end play. Move the annulus gear up and down so that the dial indicator will show the play between the pressure plate and the pressure plate circlip.

9. If the end play measured in step 8 is not between 0.50 and 0.90 mm (.020 and .035 in.), select a new pressure plate from **Table e** that will bring the end play within the prescribed range.

Table e. Available Forward Clutch Pressure Plate Thicknesses

Pressure plate thickness	Part Number
6.00 mm (.236 in.)	010 323 253 F
6.40 mm (.252 in.)	010 323 253 A
6.80 mm (.268 in.)	010 323 253 B
7.20 mm (.283 in.)	010 323 253 C
7.60 mm (.299 in.)	010 323 253 D

11.6 Disassembling and Assembling 1st Gear One-way Clutch

The early-type 1st gear one-way clutch used through Rabbit Chassis No. 175 3168 464 and Scirocco Chassis No. 535 2019 464, sometimes caused a hard downshift from 2nd to 1st gear. This can be eliminated by installing the present ten-lug replacement cage in the one-way clutch. The original cage has five lugs.

7

Fig. 11-52 is an exploded view of the 1st gear one-way clutch. To disassemble the one-way clutch, first remove the rollers and their springs. Then remove the circlips. Using a plastic hammer, carefully drive the cage out in the direction indicated by the arrow.

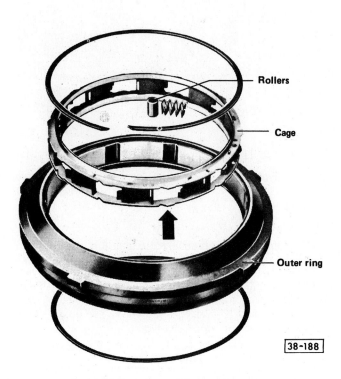

Fig. 11-52. Exploded view of 1st gear one-way clutch.

To assemble:

1. If you replace either the cage or the outer ring, check the markings on the original parts in order to determine the correct replacement part. (Beginning with Transmission No. 03 09 5, the cage seat diameter of the outer ring is decreased.) Fig. 11-53 shows the markings on the late-type parts.

2. Install the lower circlip in the groove of the outer ring (Fig. 11-54).

3. Heat the outer ring to 150° to 200°C (or 300° to 390°F). Use an oven or a hotplate that has an automatic temperature control.

NOTE——

It may not be necessary to heat early-type outer rings, owing to their larger inside diameter.

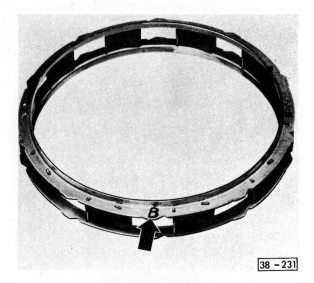

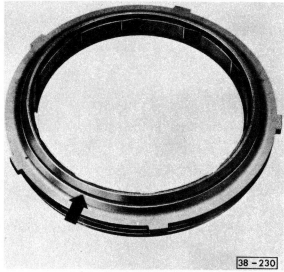

Fig. 11-53. Markings on late-type cage and outer ring. Cage with "B" (top arrow) can be used with both early-type and late-type outer rings. However, clutch will not lock properly if early-type cage (without "B") is installed in late-type outer ring marked with groove (bottom arrow).

Fig. 11-54. Circlip correctly installed in groove of outer ring.

4. Grip the upper shoulder of the cage with two pairs of pliers. Quickly place the cool cage in the heated outer ring, as indicated in Fig. 11-55.

CAUTION —

The heat from the outer ring will quickly transfer to the cage, causing the cage to stick inside the outer ring. If the cage is not correctly located against the lower circlip and inside the outer ring, do not try to press it into position after the cage has stuck. Instead, carefully knock out the cage, allow it to cool down, then start over again.

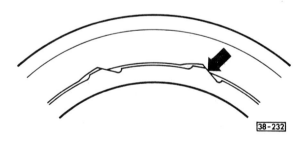

Fig. 11-55. Cage correctly positioned in outer ring. Cage must rest against lower circlip. Short sides of lugs on cage must be firmly against ramps of outer ring, as indicated by arrow.

5. Install the upper circlip.

6. Install the rollers and the springs—making sure that the springs are positioned as shown in Fig. 11-56.

Fig. 11-56. Rollers and springs correctly installed in 1st gear one-way clutch.

11.7 Disassembling and Assembling Annulus Gear (two-part)

Fig. 11-57 is an exploded view of the annulus gear that engages the planet gears of the reverse planetary gearset. The two-part gear should be disassembled only if it is necessary to replace one of the components. If you replace the circlip, be sure to obtain the correct replacement part (Part No. 090 323 369).

Hub with governor drive gear

Annulus gear with flange

Fig. 11-57. Exploded view of annulus gear (two-part). Disassembly and assembly requires only the removal or installation of the circlip.

11.8 Disassembling and Assembling Transmission Internal Linkage

Fig. 11-58 is an exploded view of the transmission's internal linkage. Whenever you disassemble the automatic transmission, check the condition of the parking lock pawl and the detent notches of the selector segment on the manual valve operating lever. Replace worn or damaged parts.

Assembling Parking Lock

Beginning with the 1976 models, the thickness of the parking lock pawl is 8.5 mm (.335 in.) rather than 6.5 mm (.256 in.), as on 1975 cars. The thicker pawl can be installed in a 1975 transmission if you also install the new-type spring for the parking lock pawl.

In assembling the parking lock mechanism, check the rollers on the parking lock operating lever for ease of movement and freedom from wear. The spring for the

parking lock pawl should be installed so that it will retract the parking lock pawl from engagement with the notches in the periphery of the annulus gear flange.

To prevent ATF leaks, the cylindrical end of the pin for the parking lock pawl must be installed flush with the surface of the transmission case. Check the operation of the parking lock mechanism before you install the valve body assembly.

Assembling Operating Lever and Kickdown Lever Linkages

You should install new O-rings during the installation of the levers and shafts. Torque the large nut to 2.0 mkg (14 ft. lb.); torque the small nut to 1.5 mkg (11 ft. lb.). The locking bolt and the M 8 bolt should likewise be torqued to 2.0 mkg (14 ft. lb.). Install the operating lever for the kickdown valve so that it is angled toward the center of the transmission, as shown in Fig. 11-59.

Fig. 11-58. Exploded view of transmission internal linkage. Valve body assembly must be removed for access to these parts.

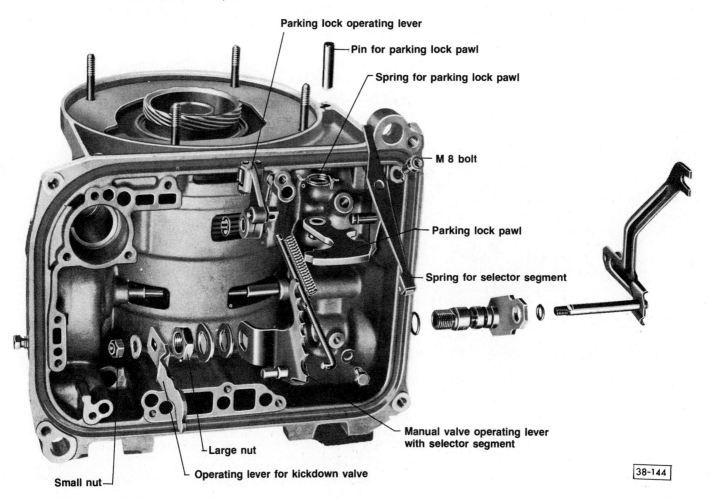

Fig. 11-59. Operating lever for kickdown valve correctly installed.

12. Final Drive

The final drive covered here is the most easily adjustable final drive ever used in a Volkswagen car. For this reason, final drive adjustments are described in conjunction with the actual removal and installation procedures, rather than being covered separately as in **MANUAL TRANSMISSION.**

12.1 Removing, Installing, and Adjusting Differential

Fig. 12-1 illustrates the removal of the differential. Instructions for replacing the drive flange oil seals with the transaxle installed can be found in **12.5 Replacing Drive Flange Oil Seal.**

Fig. 12-1. Exploded view showing differential removal. Disassembly and repair of the speedometer driven gear is covered along with the speedometer in **ELECTRICAL SYSTEM.**

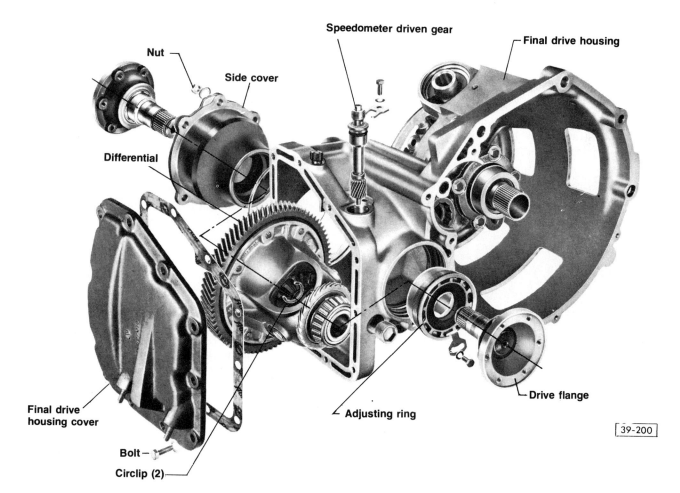

To remove:

1. Mount the final drive housing on the repair stand as shown in Fig. 12-2. Then take out the bolts and remove the final drive housing cover and its gasket. Remove the speedometer driven gear.

Fig. 12-2. Final drive mounted on repair stand. Drain hypoid oil before you begin disassembly.

2. Using two screwdrivers on each circlip, at the points indicated by the arrows in Fig. 12-3, press off the circlips that hold the differential sidegears to the sidegear shafts.

3. Pull the drive flanges out of the final drive housing together with the sidegear shafts. Turn the drive flanges as you pull them out so that the sidegear thrust washers do not catch in the circlip grooves of the sidegear shafts.

Fig. 12-3. Ends of circlips (arrows) where you should press with screwdrivers to remove circlips.

4. Remove the nuts and washers that hold the side cover, then remove the cover.

5. Mark the position of the adjusting ring (Fig. 12-4). Remove the bolt and lock plate, then remove the adjusting ring.

Fig. 12-4. Adjusting ring being removed. Mark ring and final drive housing as indicated by arrow.

6. Remove the differential from the final drive housing.

To install and adjust:

1. If you have replaced the differential housing, either differential tapered-roller bearing, the side cover, or the adjusting ring, you must adjust the differential. If so, install a torque gauge on the drive pinion as shown in Fig. 12-5. Then spin the drive pinion and write down the turning torque indicated by the torque gauge.

> **NOTE ——**
>
> Both the drive pinion and the intermediate gear must be correctly installed and adjusted before you measure the turning torque. The bearings must be lubricated with hypoid oil. If necessary, consult **12.3 Removing, Installing, and Adjusting Drive Pinion and Intermediate Gear.**

Fig. 12-5. Torque gauge installed on drive pinion preparatory to measuring turning torque of drive pinion and intermediate gear.

2. Position the differential inside the final drive housing so that it is meshed with the intermediate gear. Lubricate the differential tapered-roller bearings with hypoid oil.

3. Install a new O-ring on the side cover. Lubricate the O-ring and the oil seal lip with multipurpose grease, then install the side cover. Working diagonally, gradually torque the nuts to 3.0 mkg (22 ft. lb.).

4. Install a new O-ring on the adjusting ring. Then lubricate the O-ring, the oil seal lip, and the threads of the adjusting ring with multipurpose grease.

5. If you do not need to adjust the differential, screw in the adjusting ring until the marks that you made on the ring and the final drive housing prior to removal are correctly aligned.

6. If you must adjust the differential, install the adjusting ring until it just makes contact with the differential bearing. Pry the oil seals out of the adjusting ring and the side cover. Then, using the torque gauge as shown in Fig. 12-6, spin the final drive gears as you gradually tighten the adjusting ring. Tighten the ring until the turning torque is 7 cmkg (6.0 in. lb.) greater than the turning torque you obtained in step 1.

Example:

Turning torque for drive pinion and intermediate gear alone	27 cmkg (23.5 in. lb.)
Turning torque specified for differential (constant number)	+ 7 cmkg (6.0 in. lb.)
Turning torque with differential correctly adjusted	= 34 cmkg (29.5 in. lb.)

Fig. 12-6. Differential being adjusted by measuring total final drive turning torque.

7. Install the lock plate and torque its bolt to 1.0 mkg (7 ft. lb.). If previously removed, drive in new drive flange oil seals with Tool VW 194, after first lubricating the seals' lips with multipurpose grease. If necessary, consult **12.5 Replacing Drive Flange Oil Seal.**

8. Lightly lubricate the machined surfaces of the drive flange/sidegear shaft assemblies with multipurpose grease. Insert the drive flanges, turning them clockwise and counterclockwise so that the splines on the sidegear shafts engage the splines of the differential sidegears.

7

9. Push each sidegear shaft as firmly as possible against the differential pinion shaft. Then install the thickest possible circlip. See Fig. 12-7.

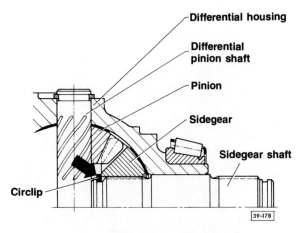

Fig. 12-7. Installed position of sidegear shaft circlip (arrow).

There are two available circlips. One is 2.00 mm thick (Part No. 020 409 299) and the other is 2.30 mm thick (Part No. 020 409 299 A). If the thicker circlip jams sideways when you install it, use the thinner circlip.

10. Install the final drive housing cover together with a new gasket. Working diagonally, gradually torque the bolts to 3.0 mkg (22 ft. lb.).

11. Install the speedometer driven gear.

12.2 Disassembling and Assembling Differential

Fig. 12-8 is an exploded view of the differential. The tapered-roller bearing inner races need only be removed if they require replacement. If you replace the bearings or the differential housing, you must adjust the differential during installation. See **12.1 Removing, Installing, and Adjusting Differential.**

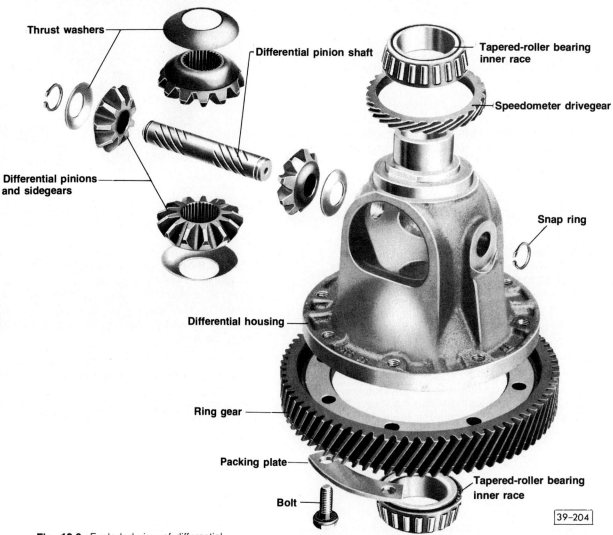

Fig. 12-8. Exploded view of differential.

To replace bearings:

1. Use the setup shown in Fig. 12-9 to remove the tapered-roller bearing inner race from the end of the differential that is opposite the ring gear. Use a puller, as shown in Fig. 12-10, to remove the tapered-roller bearing from the ring gear end of the differential housing.

> **NOTE** ——
>
> You can also use the setup shown in Fig. 12-9 to remove the speedometer drivegear. You can remove and install the speedometer drivegear without first removing the tapered-roller bearing inner race.

> **CAUTION** ——
>
> *If you remove both bearings at the same time, be careful not to mix them up. If the positions of used bearings are reversed, the bearings may make noise and wear rapidly.*

Fig. 12-9. Tapered-roller bearing inner race being removed from end of differential opposite ring gear.

2. Heat each tapered-roller bearing inner race to approximately 100°C (212°F) in a pan of oil placed in a larger pan of boiling water. Alternatively, you can heat the inner race in an oven. Press on the tapered-roller bearing inner race as shown in Fig. 12-11.

> **CAUTION** ——
>
> *If you replace a tapered-roller bearing inner race, you must replace the outer race also, using the matching race from the bearing set. If you install new bearings, you must adjust the differential during installation as described in **12.1 Removing, Installing, and Adjusting Differential.***

Fig. 12-10. Tapered-roller bearing inner race being removed from ring gear end of differential.

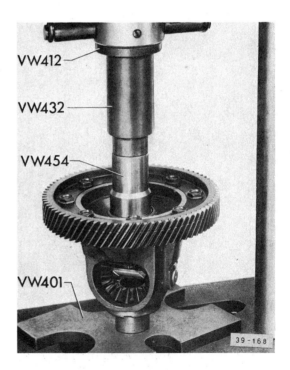

Fig. 12-11. Tapered-roller bearing inner race being installed on differential.

7

3. If you have removed the speedometer drivegear, heat the drivegear to approximately 100°C (212°F) in a pan of oil placed in a larger pan of boiling water, or in an oven. Then press on the speedometer drivegear as shown in Fig. 12-12.

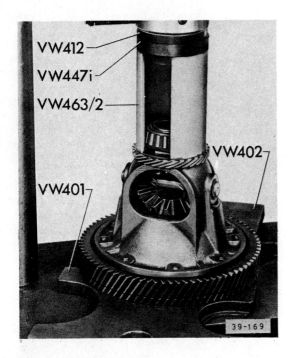

Fig. 12-12. Speedometer drivegear being installed.

4. To replace the tapered-roller bearing outer race in either the adjusting ring or the side cover, first pry out the drive flange oil seal. Then press out the bearing outer race as shown in Fig. 12-13.

> **CAUTION** ——
>
> *If you remove both bearing races at the same time, be careful not to mix them up. If the positions of used bearings are reversed, the bearings may make noise and wear rapidly.*

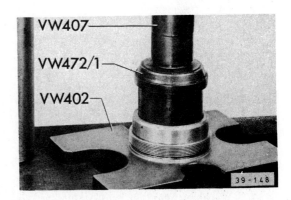

Fig. 12-13. Tapered-roller bearing outer race being removed. Reverse position of tool VW 472/1 in order to press the race back in.

5. Heat the adjusting ring or the side cover to approximately 100°C (212°F) in a pan of oil placed in a larger pan of boiling water, or use an oven. Then, using the same tools you used to remove it, press in each outer race. Use the tool shown in Fig. 12-14 to install a new oil seal, after first lubricating the seal's lip with multipurpose grease.

Fig. 12-14. Drive flange oil seal being installed. Drive in seal until it is flush.

To disassemble differential:

1. Remove the bolts. Then press the differential housing out of the ring gear using the tools shown in Fig. 12-15.

> **CAUTION** ——
>
> *The differential shown in the following illustrations is from a transaxle with manual transmission. In removing or installing a ring gear for a differential used in the transaxle with automatic transmission, use the tools shown—however, the ring gear must be removed in the opposite direction.*

Fig. 12-15. Differential housing being pressed out of ring gear.

Fig. 12-16. Sidegears being installed in differential housing (housing shown is for transaxle with manual transmission). Insert sidegears through opening, then rotate into position as indicated by arrow.

2. Remove both snap rings for the differential pinion shaft. Then, using a brass drift, drive out the differential pinion shaft.

3. Remove the differential pinions, the differential sidegears, and the thrust washers.

To assemble:

1. Insert the pinion thrust washers. Insert the differential pinions. Drive in the differential pinion shaft—being especially careful not to damage the thrust washers.

2. Install the snap rings for the differential pinion shaft.

3. Insert the sidegears and their thrust washers as shown in Fig. 12-16. Position the sidegears so that they are meshed with the pinions and are 180° apart. Then rotate the sidegears and their thrust washers into position inside the housing.

4. Heat the ring gear to approximately 100°C (212°F) in a pan of oil placed in a larger pan of boiling water. Alternatively, you can heat the ring gear in an oven. Install the heated ring gear on the differential housing as shown in Fig. 12-17.

NOTE ——

The guide pins shown in Fig. 12-17 are helpful for installing the ring gear. The pins can be made by grinding the heads off two long bolts that fit the threads in the differential housing.

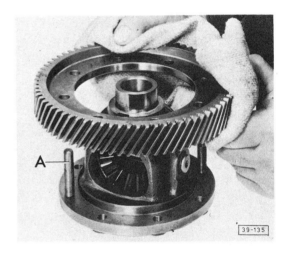

Fig. 12-17. Heated ring gear being installed on differential housing (housing shown is for transaxle with manual transmission). One of two guide pins is at **A**. Protect your hands with gloves or hold the hot ring gear with rags, as shown.

5. Install the bolts that hold the ring gear to a torque of 7.0 mkg (50 ft. lb.).

7

12.3 Removing, Installing, and Adjusting Drive Pinion and Intermediate Gear

Fig. 12-18 illustrates the removal of the drive pinion and the intermediate gear. Instructions for replacing the various oil seals are given in **12.4 Removing and Installing Drive Pinion and Intermediate Gear Bearings and Oil Seals.**

To remove:

1. Remove the differential as described in **12.1 Removing, Installing, and Adjusting Differential.**

2. Remove the lock plate for the intermediate gear shaft. Mark the position of the shaft, then remove the intermediate gear shaft as shown in Fig. 12-19.

3. Remove the intermediate gear, its tapered-roller bearings, and the thrust washer from the final drive housing.

Fig. 12-19. Intermediate gear shaft being removed. Mark shaft and final drive housing as indicated by arrow.

Fig. 12-18. Exploded view that illustrates removal of intermediate gear and drive pinion.

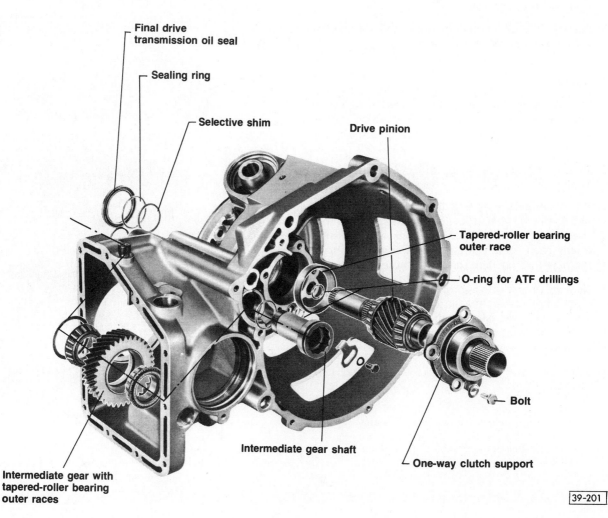

Final drive transmission oil seal

Sealing ring

Selective shim

Drive pinion

Tapered-roller bearing outer race

O-ring for ATF drillings

Bolt

Intermediate gear shaft

One-way clutch support

Intermediate gear with tapered-roller bearing outer races

39-201

4. Take out the bolts. Then remove the torque converter one-way clutch support from the final drive housing.

5. Remove the drive pinion from the final drive housing.

> **CAUTION** —
>
> *If, after removing the drive pinion, you replace the final drive housing, the one-way clutch support, the drive pinion, or either of the drive pinion's tapered-roller bearings, you must adjust the drive pinion as described in the next procedure. If no adjustment is required, install the drive pinion as described later under this heading.*

To adjust drive pinion:

1. Remove the final drive/transmission oil seal and the drive pinion oil seal that is in the one-way clutch support. Then remove the tapered-roller bearing outer race from the one-way clutch support and remove the shim. Reinstall the outer race without the shim. These jobs are described in **12.4 Removing and Installing Drive Pinion and Intermediate Gear Bearings and Oil Seals.**

2. Place the transmission-mounting flange of the final drive housing uppermost.

3. Install the drive pinion in the one-way clutch support. Then lift the drive pinion and one-way clutch support up inside the bellhousing and install them in the final drive housing. Torque the bolts to 2.5 mkg (18 ft. lb.).

> **CAUTION** —
>
> *Do not lubricate the tapered-roller bearings. Also, the tapered-roller bearing outer race must already be installed in the final drive housing. Do not turn the drive pinion as you seat its tapered-rollers against the outer race in the one-way clutch support, nor when you install the drive pinion in the final drive housing. If the bearings are lubricated or turned during installation, the measurement you are about to make will be inaccurate.*

4. Install a metric dial indicator as shown in Fig. 12-20. Zero the dial with no gauge pin preload.

5. Move the drive pinion fully up and down once without turning it, as indicated in Fig. 12-21. Write down the maximum dial indicator reading.

> **CAUTION** —
>
> *Turning the drive pinion will cause the bearings to settle, thus causing an inaccurate reading.*

Fig. 12-20. Dial indicator in position to measure drive pinion axial play with no shim installed in one-way clutch support. Tool VW 385/17 is a magnetic plate that provides a uniform surface for the dial indicator's gauge pin.

7

Fig. 12-21. Drive pinion end play being measured. Lift drive pinion up and down as indicated by double arrow.

6. To determine the ideal thickness for the shim you will install in the one-way clutch support, add 0.20 mm to the dial indicator reading that you obtained in step 5.

CAUTION ——

The dial indicator reading and the ideal shim thickness given in the following example are imaginary. Using these numbers on an actual car could cause transaxle noise or drive pinion bearing failure.

Example:

Maximum dial indicator reading obtained in step 5	1.38 mm
Constant number added to provide specified degree of bearing preload	+0.20 mm
Ideal thickness for shim installed in one-way clutch support	=1.58 mm

7. Using the ideal shim thickness that you have computed, select the correct shim from **Table f.**

NOTE ——

Do not use burred or damaged shims. Check the shim thickness at several points with a micrometer in order to determine the thickness accurately.

Table f. Available Drive Pinion Bearing Shims

Ideal shim thickness in mm	Thickness of shim to be installed	Part Number
0.95 to 1.00	1.00	010 519 141 AA
1.01 to 1.05	1.05	010 519 141 AB
1.06 to 1.10	1.10	010 519 141 AC
1.11 to 1.15	1.15	010 519 141 AD
1.16 to 1.20	1.20	010 519 141 AE
1.21 to 1.25	1.25	010 519 141 AF
1.26 to 1.30	1.30	010 519 141 AG
1.31 to 1.35	1.35	010 519 141 AH
1.36 to 1.40	1.40	010 519 141 AJ
1.41 to 1.45	1.45	010 519 141 AK
1.46 to 1.50	1.50	010 519 141 AL
1.51 to 1.55	1.55	010 519 141 AM
1.56 to 1.60	1.60	010 519 141 AN
1.61 to 1.65	1.65	010 519 141 AP
1.66 to 1.70	1.70	010 519 141 AQ
1.71 to 1.75	1.75	010 519 141 AR
1.76 to 1.80	1.80	010 519 141 AS
1.81 to 1.85	1.85	010 519 141 AT
1.86 to 1.90	1.90	010 519 141 BA
1.91 to 1.95	1.95	010 519 141 BB
1.96 to 2.00	2.00	010 519 141 BC
2.01 to 2.05	2.05	010 519 141 BD
2.06 to 2.10	2.10	010 519 141 BE
2.11 to 2.15	2.15	010 519 141 BF
2.16 to 2.20	2.20	010 519 141 BG

8. Remove the one-way clutch support and the drive pinion. Remove the tapered-roller bearing outer race from the one-way clutch support.

9. Install the correct shim in the one-way clutch support, then press in the tapered-roller bearing outer race.

To install drive pinion and intermediate gear:

1. If you have replaced the final drive housing, the one-way clutch support, the drive pinion, or either of the drive pinion's tapered-roller bearings, adjust the drive pinion as described in the preceding procedure—if you have not already done so.

2. Inspect the bolt hole for the intermediate gear shaft lock plate bolt and the ATF drillings for the one-way clutch support. Select new O-rings and, if necessary, a new bolt using the data given in **Table g.**

3. Lubricate the drive pinion's tapered-roller bearings with hypoid oil only. Install the drive pinion in the final drive housing.

4. Insert a piece of tight-fitting hose into the hole indicated in Fig. 12-22. When you suck on the hose, the ball valve in the one-way clutch support should seal. If not, replace the one-way clutch support.

NOTE ——

The ball valve must seal to prevent ATF from draining out of the torque converter when the engine is not running.

5. Install a new large O-ring on the one-way clutch support. Install the correct new O-rings in the ATF drillings of the final drive housing (Fig. 12-23).

6. Install the one-way clutch support on the final drive housing. Working diagonally, gradually torque the bolts to 2.5 mkg (18 ft. lb.).

7. If you have replaced the final drive housing, the intermediate gear, the intermediate gear shaft, the intermediate gear thrust washer, or either of the intermediate gear tapered-roller bearings, install a torque gauge on the drive pinion as shown in Fig. 12-24. Then measure the turning torque of the drive pinion.

NOTE ——

To measure the drive pinion's turning torque, spin the drive pinion 15 or 20 turns in each direction with the torque gauge. Then, while spinning the drive pinion, read the turning torque off the gauge. Write down the reading, which you will use in adjusting the intermediate gear.

Table g. ATF O-rings and Lock Plate Bolts

Date of change during manufacture	Hole description	Part description	Part Number
Through Jan. 11, 1976 (Trans. No. 11 01 6)	ATF drilling 18.5-mm ($^{47}/_{64}$-in.) in dia.	14 X 2.5-mm O-ring	N 028 201 2
From Jan. 12, 1976 (Trans. No. 12 01 6)	ATF drilling 20.5-mm ($^{13}/_{16}$-in.) in dia.	16 X 2.5-mm O-ring	010 409 563 A
Through Nov. 24, 1975 (Trans. No. 24 11 5)	Drilled-through bolt hole	Lock plate bolt 15-mm ($^{19}/_{32}$-in.) long	Use standard M 8 X 15 bolt
From Nov. 25, 1975 (Trans. No. 25 11 5)	Blind bolt hole	Lock plate bolt 12-mm ($^{15}/_{32}$-in.) long	Use standard M 8 X 12 bolt

Fig. 12-22. Ball valve drilling (arrow) in one-way clutch support.

Fig. 12-23. ATF drilling O-rings (arrows) installed in final drive housing. Correct diameter O-rings must be used.

Fig. 12-24. Torque gauge used to measure drive pinion turning torque.

8. Install new O-rings on the intermediate gear shaft.

NOTE ——

If the intermediate gear does not need to be adjusted, install the gear shaft until the marks you made prior to removal are correctly aligned. If you must adjust the intermediate gear, do so as described in the next step.

7

9. To adjust the intermediate gear, install the gear shaft and gradually tighten it while spinning the drive pinion rapidly with the torque gauge. Tighten the gear shaft until the turning torque is 15 cmkg (13.0 in. lb.) greater than the turning torque that you measured in step 7 for the drive pinion alone. See Fig. 12-25.

Example:

Turning torque for drive
        pinion alone 12 cmkg (10.5 in. lb.)
Turning torque specified
    for intermediate gear
      (constant number) +15 cmkg (13.0 in. lb.)
_____
Turning torque with
    intermediate gear
    correctly adjusted = 27 cmkg (23.5 in. lb.)

Fig. 12-25. Intermediate gear being adjusted. Tighten intermediate gear shaft while spinning drive pinion with torque gauge.

10. Using the correct bolt, install the lock plate for the intermediate gear shaft. Torque the bolt to 1.5 mkg (11 ft. lb.).

11. Install the differential as described in **12.1 Removing, Installing, and Adjusting Differential.**

12.4 Removing and Installing Drive Pinion and Intermediate Gear Bearings and Oil Seals

To remove the final drive/transmission oil seal, pry it out as shown in Fig. 12-26. Drive in the new seal so that its lip points toward the final drive. See Fig. 12-27.

NOTE ——

Do not install the seal until after you have determined the correct thickness for the new selective shim and have installed the new shim in the final drive. Shim selection and installation are described in **11.1 Separating and Rejoining Automatic Transmission and Final Drive.**

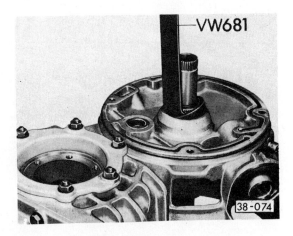

Fig. 12-26. Final drive/transmission oil seal being removed with hook-shaped tool.

Fig. 12-27. Final drive/transmission oil seal being driven in.

With the final drive/transmission oil seal removed, as previously described, you can drive out the tapered-roller bearing outer race that is in the final drive housing. Use a drift to remove the outer race, working all around the outer race so that it is not forced out at an angle. Use a bearing driver with a tapered face to drive in the tapered-roller bearing outer race. See Fig. 12-28.

Fig. 12-28. Drive pinion tapered-roller bearing outer race being driven into final drive housing.

1. Tapered-roller bearing outer race
2. Pinion adjusting shim
3. Oil seal
4. O-ring
5. Torque converter oil seal

Fig. 12-29. Exploded view of one-way clutch support.

Fig. 12-29 is an exploded view of the one-way clutch support. The shim thickness must be determined with the help of precision measurements if you replace the drive pinion, the final drive housing, the one-way clutch support, or either of the drive pinion's tapered-roller bearings. See **12.3 Removing, Installing, and Adjusting Drive Pinion and Intermediate Gear.** The torque converter seal can be removed and installed as described in **10.2 Inspecting and Repairing Torque Converter.**

CAUTION ——

The torque converter seal is soft silicone rubber and easily damaged. Be careful when clamping the one-way clutch support in a vise. Silicone seals must not contact gasoline or similar cleaning solutions. Replace torque converter seals that have been torn or exposed to cleaning solvents.

To remove the oil seal from the one-way clutch support, pry it out as shown in Fig. 12-30—being careful not to scratch the tapered-roller bearing outer race. Drive in a new oil seal so that its lip points toward the final drive. See Fig. 12-31.

Fig. 12-30. Oil seal being pried out of one-way clutch support.

Fig. 12-31. Oil seal being driven into one-way clutch support.

Remove the tapered-roller bearing outer race from the one-way clutch support as shown in Fig. 12-32. If you have removed the tapered-roller bearing outer race from the final drive housing, be careful not to mix up the two outer races. If the positions of used bearings are reversed, the bearings may make noise and wear rapidly.

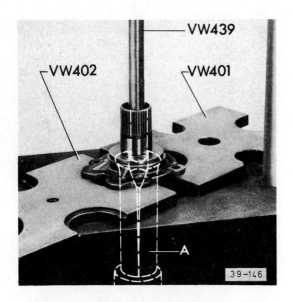

Fig. 12-32. Tapered-roller bearing outer race being removed from one-way clutch support. Expansion mandril is shown by the phantom drawing (dashed lines) at **A**.

To install the tapered-roller bearing outer race in the one-way clutch support, heat the one-way clutch support to approximately 100°C (212°F) in a pan of oil placed in a larger pan of boiling water. Alternatively, you can use an oven. Then press the outer race fully in, as shown in Fig. 12-33.

NOTE ——

If you must adjust the drive pinion, press in the outer race without a pinion adjusting shim. The outer race must be pressed fully in, whether there is a shim installed or not.

Fig. 12-34 is an exploded view of the drive pinion. If you replace either tapered-roller bearing or the drive pinion itself, you must adjust the drive pinion as described in **12.3 Removing, Installing, and Adjusting Drive Pinion and Intermediate Gear.** Though the drive pinion, the intermediate gear, and the ring gear are each available separately, it is recommended that you not replace the drive pinion without also replacing the intermediate gear and the ring gear.

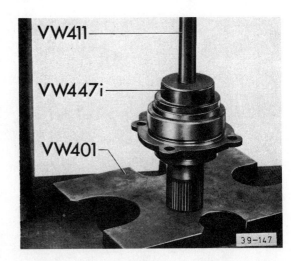

Fig. 12-33. Tapered-roller bearing outer race being pressed into one-way clutch support.

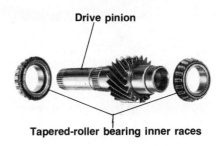

Fig. 12-34. Exploded view of drive pinion.

The same tools are used in removing and installing either of the two drive pinion tapered-roller bearing inner races. Remove the inner race as shown in Fig. 12-35. Once the inner race is removed, the bearing is no longer serviceable and must be replaced with a new bearing.

Fig. 12-35. Tapered-roller bearing inner race being removed from drive pinion.

Heat the new drive pinion tapered-roller bearing inner race to approximately 100°C (212°F) in a pan of oil placed in a larger pan of boiling water. Alternatively, you can use an oven. Then press the inner race fully onto the drive pinion as shown in Fig. 12-36.

To install a tapered-roller bearing outer race in the intermediate gear, heat the intermediate gear to approximately 100°C (212°F) in a pan of oil placed in a larger pan of boiling water. Alternatively, you can use an oven. Then press in the outer race as shown in Fig. 12-38.

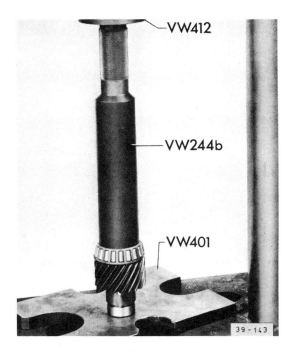

Fig. 12-36. Tapered-roller bearing inner race being pressed onto drive pinion.

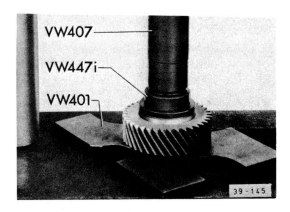

Fig. 12-38. Tapered-roller bearing outer race being pressed into intermediate gear.

12.5 Replacing Drive Flange Oil Seal

Fig. 12-39 is an exploded view of the right-hand drive flange and the adjusting ring, showing the position of the drive flange oil seal. Notice that the drive flange is separate from the sidegear shaft. The sidegear shaft remains installed in the transaxle when you remove the drive flange for seal replacement.

Use an expansion mandril and a repair press to remove the tapered-roller bearing outer races from the hub of the intermediate gear. See Fig. 12-37.

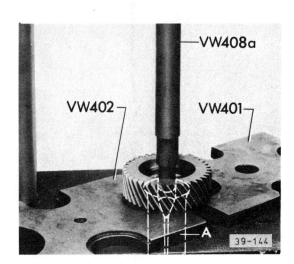

Fig. 12-37. Tapered-roller bearing outer race being removed from intermediate gear. Expansion mandril is shown in phantom drawing (dashed lines) at **A**.

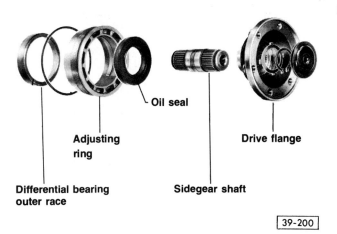

Fig. 12-39. Exploded view of right-hand drive flange and adjusting ring. Left-hand drive flange is identical, but seal is pressed into side cover, there being no adjusting ring.

To replace seal:

1. Detach the front wheel driveshaft from the drive flange by taking out the socket-head bolts. If necessary, consult **MANUAL TRANSMISSION.**

2. Pull the driveshaft away from the drive flange, then suspend the driveshaft from the car body with a stiff wire hook.

> **NOTE ——**
>
> On the left-hand side, you must remove the nut and clamp bolt that hold the suspension ball joint stud in the bottom of the wheel bearing housing, then pull the stud out of the bearing housing so that the control arm hangs down. If necessary, consult **SUSPENSION AND STEERING.**

3. Pry the dust cap out of the center of the drive flange. Remove the circlip and the dished washer, then use a puller such as the one shown in Fig. 12-40 to pull the drive flange off the sidegear shaft.

Fig. 12-40. Left-hand drive flange being removed. Puller shown here mounts on drive flange with M 8 X 20 bolts. If you use another kind of puller, be careful not to damage the threaded hole in the sidegear shaft.

4. Use a hooked tool, or a large screwdriver, to pry the faulty seal out of its recess (Fig. 12-41).

Fig. 12-41. Oil seal being pried out.

5. Pack the open side of the new seal with multipurpose grease. Then drive in the seal as shown in Fig. 12-42.

Fig. 12-42. Drive flange oil seal being driven in.

6. Inspect the drive flange. Replace the flange if it has a groove worn into it at the point where it is contacted by the oil seal.

7. Install the drive flange as shown in Fig. 12-43. The special tool screws into the threads that are in the center of the sidegear shaft.

Fig. 12-43. Drive flange being installed.

8. With the drive flange fully seated in the transaxle, install the dished washer so that its convex side is away from the drive flange. Then, using circlip pliers, install a new circlip over the end of the sidegear shaft—but do not attempt to seat the circlip in its groove.

13. AUTOMATIC TRANSMISSION TECHNICAL DATA

I. Automatic Transmission Test Data

9. Drive the circlip inward against the tension of the dished washer, as shown in Fig. 12-44, until the circlip snaps into its groove. Install a new dust cap.

Fig. 12-44. Tool used to drive circlip in (arrow) against tension of dished washer (transaxle with manual transmission shown).

10. Attach the front wheel driveshaft to the drive flange. Torque the socket-head bolts to 4.5 mkg (32 ft. lb.).

11. If you have replaced the left-hand oil seal, raise the suspension control arm and insert the ball joint stud into the bearing housing. Then install the clamp bolt and its nut to a torque of 3.0 mkg (22 ft. lb.).

Test Conditions	Specifications
Torque converter at stall speed (brakes locked, wide-open throttle)	1900 to 2200 rpm

Automatic shift points
  a. 1st gear to 2nd gear
 	
  b. 2nd gear to 3rd gear
 	
  c. 3rd gear to 2nd gear
 	
  d. 2nd gear to 1st gear
	
	20 to 23 mph (32 to 37 kph) at full throttle
	36 to 39 mph (58 to 62 kph) during kickdown
	51 to 55 mph (82 to 88 kph) at full throttle
	68 to 69 mph (109 to 110 kph) during kickdown
	31 to 36 mph (50 to 58 kph) at full throttle
	64 to 65 mph (102 to 104 kph) during kickdown
	15 to 17 mph (24 to 27 kph) at full throttle
	32 to 35 mph (51 to 56 kph) during kickdown

Main pressures*
  a. At idle: car stationary with selector
      lever at **D**
  b. At idle: car stationary with selector
      lever at **R**
  c. Wide open throttle: car moving at a
      speed above 25 mph (40 kph)
      with selector lever at **D**
	
	41 to 42 psi (2.90 to 3.00 kg/cm²)
	
	104 to 105 psi (7.35 to 7.40 kg/cm²)
	
	83 to 84 psi (5.85 to 5.95 kg/cm²)

*Main pressures will be somewhat higher beginning with Transmission No. 25116, owing to new valve body.

II. Valve Body Springs

Description	Part No.	No. of coils	Wire thickness mm (in.)	Free length (approximate) mm (in.)	Coil inner diameter mm ±0.30 mm (in. ±.012 in.)
Throttle pressure limiting valve spring	003 325 119	14.5	1.10 (.043)	35.30 (1.390)	7.70 (.303)
Main pressure limiting valve spring	003 325 119	14.5	1.10 (.043)	35.30 (1.390)	7.70 (.303)
Main pressure valve spring	003 325 131	16.5	1.50 (.059)	68.50 (2.697)	11.90 (.469)
Throttle pressure valve spring	010 325 175 B	16.0	1.25 (.049)	43.40 (1.709)	7.75 (.305)
Modulator valve spring (1975)	003 325 185	11.5	0.80 (.031)	28.50 (1.122)	7.75 (.305)
Modulator valve spring (1976)	003 325 185	12.0	0.70 (.028)	18.70 (0.736)	5.30 (.209)
1st/2nd gear shift valve spring	010 325 207	6.5	0.90 (.035)	19.90 (0.783)	8.10 (.319)
2nd/3rd gear shift valve spring	010 325 207	6.5	0.90 (.035)	19.90 (0.783)	8.10 (.319)
3rd/2nd control valve spring	003 325 227 A	12.5	1.00 (.039)	32.40 (1.276)	7.70 (.303)
Converter pressure valve spring (1975)	003 325 247	9.5	1.25 (.049)	27.30 (1.075)	8.13 (.320)
Converter pressure valve spring (1976)	003 325 227 A	12.5	1.00 (.039)	32.40 (1.276)	7.70 (.303)
3rd/2nd gear kickdown control valve spring (not used in 1975)	003 325 207 A	11.5	0.90 (.035)	28.40 (1.118)	8.10 (.319)

NOTE ——

Though the throttle pressure limiting valve spring and the main pressure limiting valve spring are identical, used springs should not be interchanged. Nor should 2nd/3rd gear shift valve springs and converter pressure valve springs be interchanged once they have seen service, though they are identical when new.

III. Tightening Torques

Location	Designation	mkg	ft. lb.	cmkg	in. lb.
Main pressure tap plug in transmission case	Threaded plug	1.0	7		
Locknut for 2nd gear brake band adjusting screw	nut	2.0	14		
Valve body to separator plate and transfer plate	Phillips head screw			40	35
Accumulator cover to transmission case	Phillips head screw			30	26
Valve body assembly to transmission case	bolt			40	35
ATF strainer to valve body	Phillips head screw			30	26
ATF pan to transmission case	bolt	2.0	14		
Engine to transaxle	bolt and/or nut	5.5	40		
Torque converter to drive plate	bolt	3.0	22		
Torque converter cover plate to bellhousing	bolt	1.5	11		
Protection plate to transaxle	M 8 bolt	2.0	14		
	M 10 bolt	2.5	18		
Starter to bellhousing	bolt	3.0	22		
Driveshaft constant velocity joint to drive flange	socket-head bolt	4.5	32		
Transmission case to final drive housing	nut	3.0	22		
Plate with springs and ATF pump to transmission case	bolt			40	35
Separating plate to transmission case	fillister head screw			70	61
Spring for selector segment to transmission case	M 8 bolt or fillister head screw	2.0	14		
Locking bolt for operating lever shaft	M 8 bolt	2.0	14		
Operating lever for manual valve to shaft	nut	2.0	14		
Operating lever for kickdown valve to shaft	nut	1.5	11		
Side cover to final drive housing	nut	3.0	22		
Lock plate for differential adjusting ring to final drive housing	bolt	1.0	7		
Final drive housing cover to final drive housing	bolt	3.0	22		
Ring gear to differential housing	bolt	7.0	50		
Torque converter one-way clutch support to final drive housing	bolt	2.5	18		
Intermediate gear shaft lock plate to final drive housing	bolt	1.5	11		
Suspension ball joint stud in front wheel bearing housing	clamp bolt and nut	3.0	22		

BODY AND INTERIOR

Contents

Body and Interior

The Volkswagen Rabbit and Scirocco have unit construction steel bodies that are exceptionally strong and light. Their lightness contributes greatly to the outstanding performance and fuel economy that these cars deliver. Because very few screws and bolts are used in assembling the body, there is little opportunity for annoying rattles to develop. A quiet ride is further ensured by the application of plastic-impregnated sound-dampening material to the floor plates and the body panels.

The floor plate, which is formed by welding together three subassemblies, is the same on both Rabbit and Scirocco models. An equal number of body panels go into the construction of Rabbits and Sciroccos but these panels are shaped differently on each of the two models. During manufacture, the various body panels and subassemblies, plus a number of smaller pressed steel panels and plates, are joined by electric welding into a durable, integrated structure.

The front fenders and the grille are bolted to the main body structure so that they can be easily and economically replaced in the event of damage. The hood, the doors, and the luggage compartment lid are also removable. These bolt-on components can easily be replaced by persons with little or no knowledge of auto body repair.

Though all body panels are available as replacement parts, replacement panels must be butt welded to the undamaged parts of the body after the damaged panels have been cut away. This work should be undertaken only by an experienced body repair technician. If you lack the skills, special equipment, or a suitable workshop for extensive body repairs, we suggest that you leave this work to your Authorized Dealer or other qualified shop. We especially urge you to consult your Authorized Dealer before attempting repairs on a car still covered by the new-car warranty.

Also covered in this section of the Manual is the ventilation and heating system. Repairs related to the gauges and the instrument cluster are covered in **ELECTRICAL SYSTEM.** For information on the care and maintenance of carpeting, seat upholstery, and other interior appointments, we suggest that you refer to **LUBRICATION AND MAINTENANCE,** or to the Owner's Manual that is supplied with the car.

8 ∎

1. GENERAL DESCRIPTION

Because the engine, the transaxle, and the driving wheels are all located at the front of the car (Fig. 1-1), the longitudinal hump in the front floor panel is not used to accommodate a driveshaft. The hump has been designed to serve as a strengthening member and as a housing for the exhaust system, the parking brake cables, and the hydraulic brake lines.

Doors and Windows

The front passenger doors are attached to the front body pillars by concealed hinges. On four-door models, similar hinges are used to attach the rear passenger doors to the center body pillars. Only the front passenger doors are equipped with lock cylinders but all passenger doors have press-down locking buttons. Except for the driver's door, the buttons can be used to lock the doors from outside the car without a key.

Curved glass is used for the side windows as well as for the windshield and the rear window. The windows in the front passenger doors may be raised or lowered. Except on basic models, an electrically heated rear window is installed to prevent fogging.

Hood and Luggage Compartment Lid

Except on basic Rabbit models, the engine hood is equipped with a lock that must be released from inside the car before the hood can be opened. The lock control lever is located beneath the left-hand end of the dashboard. The engine hood opens on hinges mounted beneath the front cowl panel.

The luggage compartment lid is mounted on hidden upward-opening hinges suspended from the roof reinforcing members. A lock is installed on the luggage compartment lid. This lock takes the same key as the ignition/steering column lock.

Fenders and Trim

The front fenders are bolted onto the main body structure so that they can be readily replaced in the event of collision damage. The rear fenders are integral with the body outer side panels. Therefore, replacement of the rear fenders requires cutting and welding.

For maximum corrosion resistance, most of the decorative bright trim pieces are either stainless steel or anodized aluminum. The model-identification markings and emblems are, however, chrome plated.

Seats and Interior

The front seats are individually mounted and can be moved forward or backward. Except on basic models, the angle of the seat backs is also adjustable. Locks built into the seat backs keep them upright even during hard braking. The rear seat backrest is mounted on the body. The rear seat cushion is readily removable for access to the rear seat belt mountings and, on fuel injection models, to the access panel for the fuel gauge sending unit.

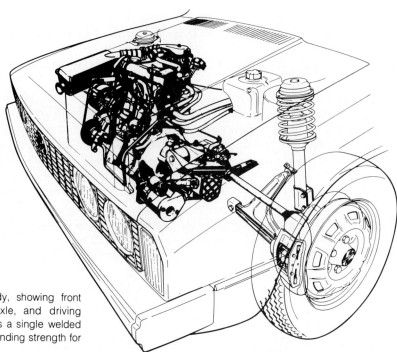

Fig. 1-1. Phantom view of front body, showing front location of engine, transaxle, and driving wheels. Entire nose of car is a single welded subassembly that has outstanding strength for its weight.

The portions of the floor plate that are within the passenger compartment are soundproofed with thermoplastic damping material. This material also acts as an insulator against road heat. Except on basic models, the floor and front side panels are carpeted. The leather-like plastic used in the upholstery is easily cleaned vinyl, perforated for improved ventilation when used on seat areas.

Ventilation and Heating

The flow-through ventilation system admits air to the car interior through a grille in the engine hood. Air from the car's interior is exhausted through vents in the luggage compartment lid. Controlled amounts of incoming air can be admitted to the passenger compartment through four vents in the face of the dashboard, two vents beneath the dashboard, and a full-length slot along the lower inside edge of the windshield.

A fan can be used to create a flow through the ventilation system while the car is moving slowly or standing still. On 1975 and 1976 models, this fan has two speeds. On 1977 and later models, the fan has three speeds. The ventilating air can be heated in order to warm the car's interior. Except for the outboard vents in the face of the dashboard, which are for unheated air only, heated air is available through all of the ventilation vents listed above.

2. MAINTENANCE

Only one maintenance operation, lubrication of the door hinges and the door checks, is required at regular mileage intervals. During routine servicing, the operation of the heater valve should be checked. These procedures are covered in **LUBRICATION AND MAINTENANCE.** Care of the body, trim, upholstery, and windows is also described briefly in **LUBRICATION AND MAINTENANCE.**

3. TOWING AND LIFTING CAR

To prevent body damage, it is important that the car be towed or lifted correctly. For short distance, on-the-wheels towing, towing eyes have been provided, as shown in Fig. 3-1 and Fig. 3-2. You should always observe state laws and municipal ordinances governing towing.

> **WARNING ——**
> *The vacuum powered brake servo works only while the engine is running. To prevent an accident, the driver of a car that is being towed on its wheels must be prepared to apply greater than normal force to the brake pedal. Otherwise, it may not be possible to slow or stop the towed car before it strikes the vehicle that is doing the towing.*

> **CAUTION ——**
> *Automatic transmission fluid does not circulate through an automatic transmission when the engine is not running. Never tow a car with an automatic transmission faster than 30 mph (48 kph) or farther than 30 miles (48 kilometers). Bearings can be damaged by lack of lubrication. If you must tow the car farther, lift the front wheels.*

> **NOTE ——**
> You cannot start the engine of a car with an automatic transmission by towing or pushing the vehicle.

Fig. 3-1. Front towing eye (arrow). There are two of these eyes, one on each front bumper impact damper support.

Fig. 3-2. Rear towing eye (arrow). There are two of these eyes, one on each rear bumper impact damper support.

To lift the car with a floor jack, position the jack as shown in Fig. 3-3 or Fig. 3-4.

CAUTION ——

Never lift the vehicle by placing a jack beneath the engine, the transaxle, the rear axle beam, or the front suspension track control arms. Doing these things can cause serious damage to the car.

Fig. 3-3. Car being lifted at front. Place jack beneath lifting socket under front door hinge pillar.

Fig. 3-4. Car being lifted at rear. Place jack beneath welded flange of side member/floor plate—at point indicated by triangular mark on side member.

3.1 Lifting Rabbit Model on Hoist

In lifting a Rabbit model on a hoist, as shown in Fig. 3-5, place the lifting pads at the points indicated in Fig. 3-6 and Fig. 3-7.

WARNING ——

Place additional weight in the luggage compartment before you remove heavy components from the rear of a car that is on a hoist—such as the rear axle, the fuel tank, the spare wheel, the luggage compartment lid, or the rear bumper. Otherwise, the car may tip forward when the center of gravity changes upon removal of the heavy part.

Fig. 3-5. Rabbit model raised on hoist.

Fig. 3-6. Correct placement of lifting pad at front of body. Position pad beneath lifting socket under front door hinge pillar. Be careful not to damage fuel line in this area.

Fig. 3-7. Correct placement of lifting pad at rear of body. Position pad beneath welded flange of side member/floor plate—at point indicated by triangular mark on side member.

3.2 Lifting Scirocco Model on Hoist

In lifting a Scirocco model on a hoist, as shown in Fig. 3-8, place the lifting pads at the points indicated in Fig. 3-9 and Fig. 3-10.

> **WARNING ——**
>
> *Place additional weight in the luggage compartment before you remove heavy components from the rear of a car that is on a hoist—such as the rear axle, the fuel tank, the spare wheel, the luggage compartment lid, or the rear bumper. Otherwise, the car may tip forward when the center of gravity changes upon removal of the heavy part.*

Fig. 3-8. Scirocco model raised on hoist.

Fig. 3-9. Correct placement of lifting pad at front of body. Position pad beneath lifting socket under front door hinge pillar. Be careful not to damage fuel line in this area.

Fig. 3-10. Correct placement of lifting pad at rear of body. Position pad beneath welded flange of side member/floor plate—at point indicated by triangular mark on side member.

4. REMOVING AND INSTALLING BOLT-ON COMPONENTS

The removal and installation of the bumpers, the front fenders, the doors, the hood, and similar components does not require a thorough knowledge of automobile body repair. For the most part, the work can be done with ordinary hand tools. The shaded parts in Fig. 4-1 are the main bolt-on components of the body.

Fig. 4-1. Bolt-on components (shaded areas) of body.

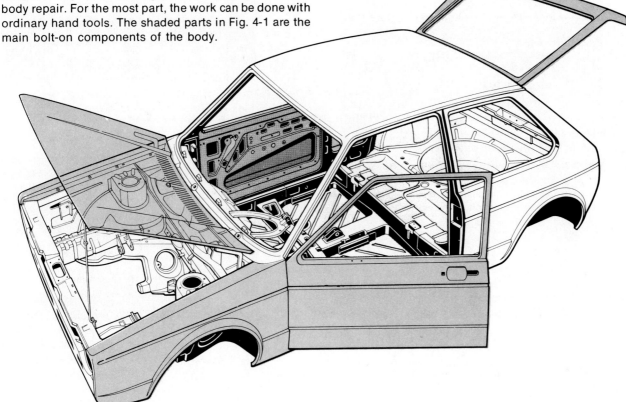

4.1 Removing and Installing Bumpers

The front and the rear bumpers are mounted on spring-loaded damping elements. The damping elements are bolted to reinforced supports on the car body. If only part of the bumper assembly needs to be replaced, it is best first to remove the bumper assembly as a unit and then to disassemble it for repairs.

To remove:

1. In removing a front bumper from a Rabbit model, disconnect the battery ground strap. Then disconnect the wires for the bumper-mounted parking lights.

2. Working under the fenders, remove the bolts that hold the bumper damping elements to the car body.

3. Remove the bumper assembly together with the damping elements.

4. In order to separate the bumper assembly into its individual components, take out the bolts and

screws that are accessible from the rear of the bumper.

Installation is the reverse of removal. Lubricate the threads of the nuts, bolts, and screws before you install them. When installing the bumper assembly on the car, install the mounting bolts but do not tighten them. Then adjust the bumper to a uniform gap with the body before you tighten the mounting bolts.

4.2 Removing and Installing Front Fender

The front fenders are bolted onto the body and can be removed and installed using common hand tools. The rear fenders are welded onto the body and can be replaced only by an experienced body repair technician.

To remove:

1. Disconnect the battery ground strap. Then disconnect the wires for the front sidemarker light.

2. Remove the front bumper as described in **4.1 Removing and Installing Bumpers.**

3. Using a wooden or plastic wedge, carefully pry loose the lower body trim strip from the lower rear part of the front fender.

4. Open the front door. Then remove the bolt that holds the upper rear corner of the front fender to the body.

5. Working under the fender, remove the screws that hold the mud flap and the rear edge of the fender to the body.

6. Where applicable, remove the screws that hold the front of the fender to the body.

7. Raise the hood. Loosen, but do not remove, the bolts and speed nuts that hold the top of the fender to the body. Then, to break away the undercoating, pull out on the lower edge of the fender until it is 13 to 25 mm (½ to 1 in.) away from the body.

CAUTION ——

If the fender does not pull away with a moderate amount of effort, check to see that you have not overlooked one or more of the mounting screws or bolts. Excessive force will damage the fender.

8. After you have broken the undercoating, support the fender so that it does not bend of its own weight as the remaining mounting bolts are removed. Then take out the bolts that hold the top of the fender to the body and take off the fender.

Installation is the reverse of removal. Install new beading at the rear of the fender if the original beading is in poor condition. Torque the mounting bolts to 1.5 mkg (11 ft. lb.). Fully undercoat new fenders. If the original fender is reinstalled, renew the undercoating along the joint between the body and the fender, over the heads of the mounting bolts, and wherever the original undercoating was chipped or scratched during removal.

4.3 Removing and Installing Door

The door hinges are welded to the door. The hinges are held to the body by screws. If it is necessary to remove a door, carefully mark the positions of the hinges on the body so that you can easily align the door during installation.

To remove a door, take out the screws that hold the bracket for the door check strap to the body. Use an impact driver to loosen the screws that hold the door hinges to the body. Support the door, then remove the screws and take off the door.

CAUTION ——

If you fail to support the door as you remove the screws from the first hinge, the second hinge may be bent or broken.

During installation, check the weatherseal. If it is cracked, torn, or otherwise damaged, replace it.

NOTE ——

Before installing a new weatherseal, clean away all the old adhesive with a solvent such as Prepsol®. Install the new seal with trim cement.

Using the marks made prior to removal, install the door on the car body. If a replacement door is being installed, install it so that the door contacts the weatherseal evenly all around and the lock works smoothly. Set the hinge screws firmly with the impact driver.

Removing and Installing Door Handle and Lock Cylinder

Fig. 4-2 illustrates the removal of the lock cylinder and the construction of the door handle. You must remove the handle in order to remove the lock cylinder. On four-door models, only the front doors have lock cylinders.

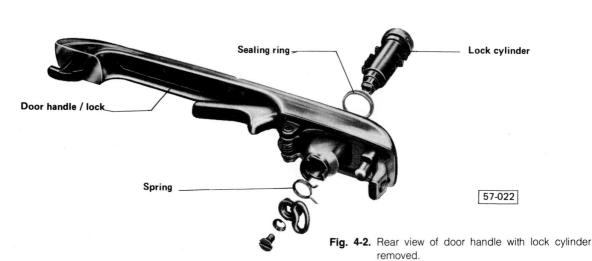

Sealing ring

Lock cylinder

Door handle / lock

Spring

57-022

Fig. 4-2. Rear view of door handle with lock cylinder removed.

To remove the door handle, pry off the plastic cap that is in the edge of the door. Then remove the screw that holds the door handle in the door. Pull the handle free of the door and unhook the handle at its forward edge.

When installing, clean the lock and the door release trigger, then apply door and lock lubricant. Make sure the gaskets are in good condition and that they seat properly when you mount the handle on the door.

If you remove the lock cylinder from the door handle, do so only with the key inserted in the cylinder. Otherwise, the tumblers and the tumbler springs will fall out. During lock cylinder installation, replace the sealing ring if it is hard, cracked, or broken. The hairpin spring that is beneath the lock operating cam must be installed so that it is under tension.

4.4 Removing and Installing Hoods and Lids

When you remove and install the hood or the luggage compartment lid, it is important that the hood or the lid be properly aligned during installation. If misaligned, it may rattle or leak.

To remove hood:

1. Open the hood. If the hood is not being replaced, carefully mark the locations of the hinges on the hood so that you can reinstall the hood in its exact original position.

2. Remove the two hood bolts from one of the hinges.

3. While someone holds the unbolted side, remove the two hood bolts from the other hinge.

4. Working together, lift the hood up and off toward the front of the car.

To install hood:

1. Before you install the hood, check the condition of the rubber weatherstrip that is on the dividing panel at the rear of the engine compartment. If necessary, reglue or replace the weatherstrip.

   NOTE ——
   Before installing a new weatherstrip, clean away all the old adhesive with a solvent such as Prepsol®. Install the new seal with trim cement.

2. Using all four bolts, loosely install the hood on its hinges. Move the hood in the elongated bolt holes until the hinges are in the positions you marked for them prior to removal. If a new hood is being installed, align it with the body so that the gap is even all around and the hood locks engage properly. Then tighten the bolts.

3. Check the lock operation by opening and closing the hood several times. If necessary, adjust the length of the lock pin that is indicated in Fig. 4-3. To do this, loosen the locknut. Then, using a screwdriver, turn the lock pin in or out. When the hood latches solidly—but without being slammed— tighten the locknut.

Fig. 4-3. Lock pin for hood (arrow).

To remove luggage compartment lid:

1. Disconnect the battery ground strap. Open the luggage compartment lid.

2. Disconnect the wires for the electrically heated rear window.

3. Have someone hold the lid while you detach the stay rod or the stay cylinder from the edge of the lid.

4. Keeping the lid steadily supported at all times, use an offset No. 3 Phillips screwdriver to remove the Phillips head screws that hold the lid to the hinges. Then remove the luggage compartment lid from the car.

To install luggage compartment lid:

1. Before you install the luggage compartment lid, check the condition of the rubber weatherstrip. If necessary, reglue or replace the weatherstrip.

   NOTE ——
   Before installing a new weatherstrip, clean away all the old adhesive with a solvent such as Prepsol®. Install the new seal with trim cement.

2. While your helper assists you in positioning the luggage compartment lid, install the four Phillips head screws that hold the lid to the hinges.

NOTE ——

If a new luggage compartment lid is being installed, it may have to be aligned after it is installed on the hinges. To do this, it will be necessary to remove the headliner partially at the rear for access to the bolts that hold the hinges to the car body. Loosen the bolts. Then move the hinges in order to align the lid with the body so that the gap is even all around and the lock engages properly. Tighten the bolts and reinstall the headliner when the adjustment is correct.

3. Check the lock operation by opening and closing the luggage compartment lid several times. If necessary, adjust the position of the lock plate that is on the body using the next procedure under this heading.

4. Reconnect the wires for the electrically heated rear window. Then reconnect the battery ground strap.

To check and adjust striker plate:

1. Close the luggage compartment lid. It should latch solidly—without being slammed. The gap between the lid and the body must be even all around.

2. Slowly press the button of the luggage compartment lid lock. Excessive force should not be required.

3. If the lid cannot be closed without using excessive force, adjust it as follows.

4. Loosen the striker plate. Move the striker plate upward and to the rear in small increments—securing it each time by tightening the screws. Keep checking the latching of the lid as described in the first three steps of this procedure until the lock engages its fully latched position without excessive force being applied to the lid in closing it.

5. If the lid latches fully, but closes too easily and the button is hard to depress, rotate the striker plate counterclockwise around the axis of the lug in order to move the wedge up and to the rear.

6. If the lid does not close easily and the button is too easy to depress, rotate the striker plate clockwise around the axis of the lug in order to move the wedge down and to the front.

4.5 Removing and Installing Window Trim

The window trim (reveal molding) that surrounds the interior of the window is held in place by an adhesive. On some early 1975 models, this molding failed to adhere correctly. Consequently, it was in some cases removed and in others replaced as part of the 1975 Quality Improvements program.

To remove:

1. Remove the lock knob by unscrewing it from the rod.

2. Using a wooden or plastic wedge in order to avoid marring the door, carefully pry off the window trim (reveal molding).

3. Clean the door surface that was beneath the molding with a solvent such as Prepsol®.

NOTE ——

If you wish to remove the molding only, installing no new molding in its place, simply polish the exposed painted area with auto body polish or with an auto body wax that contains a mild abrasive cleaner. Then reinstall the lock knob.

To install:

1. Apply a good trim cement, such as 3-M Weatherstrip Adhesive®, to the new window trim.

2. Position the new trim (molding) on the door, clamping or tying it in place as necessary.

3. When the adhesive has dried adequately to hold the trim (molding), remove the clamps or string. Then install the lock knob.

4.6 Installing Right-hand Outside Mirror on Scirocco

A right-hand outside mirror is available for installation on Scirocco models. This mirror is often installed by dealers as an optional item on new cars. The mirror can also be added to Scirocco models that did not have the mirror installed prior to delivery.

To install:

1. Obtain outside mirror Part No. 171 857 502B, packing seal Part No. 531 857 543, and two socket-head screws Part No. N 33 023.1.

2. Mark the locations for the two screw holes as indicated in Fig. 4-4.

Fig. 4-4. Holes for right-hand mirror being located on Scirocco door. Dimension **a** (measured up from sharp angle in door metal) is 15 mm ($^{19}/_{32}$ in.). Dimension **b** is 418 mm (16 $^{15}/_{32}$ in.) and dimension **c** is 45 mm (1 $^{25}/_{32}$ in.).

8

3. Cautiously drill the holes, using a 3-mm (or ⅛-in.) drill—being careful not to damage the threaded plate that is beneath the door metal.

4. Using a tapered reamer, open up the drilled holes to a diameter of 10 mm (or ⅜ in.), aligning the holes with the threaded plate.

5. Install the mirror. Make sure that the packing seal is correctly fitted between the mirror mounting and the door metal.

5. HEATING AND VENTILATION

Fig. 5-1 and Fig. 5-2 are exploded views of the ventilation and heating system. On 1975 and 1976 cars, the fan motor is accessible after the heater cover and the cutoff flap have been removed. (You remove the cover, the flap, and the motor by working under the engine hood.) If the motor is faulty, the motor and fan should be replaced as a unit.

Close the heater valve before you remove it. In removing the heater valve, it is unnecessary to drain the coolant. Simply disconnect and plug the hoses. If the heater valve is binding or is hard to operate, replace it. If the entire heater must be removed, drain the coolant beforehand as described in **ENGINE AND CLUTCH.** Once the hoses have been disconnected, you can remove the heater by working inside the passenger compartment.

In removing and installing the fan motor and the heat exchanger, you must remove and install a number of metal clips. Remove and install the clips as indicated in Fig. 5-3 and Fig. 5-4.

Fig. 5-1. Exploded view of ventilation and heating system used on 1975 and 1976 cars.

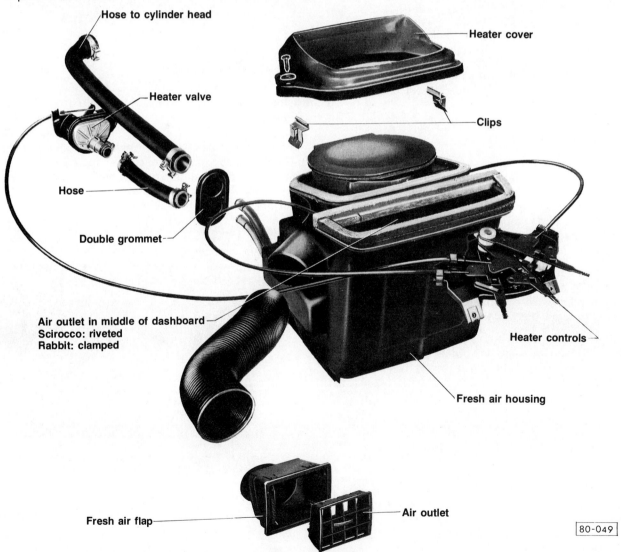

Hose to cylinder head

Heater cover

Heater valve

Clips

Hose

Double grommet

Air outlet in middle of dashboard
Scirocco: riveted
Rabbit: clamped

Heater controls

Fresh air housing

Fresh air flap

Air outlet

80-049

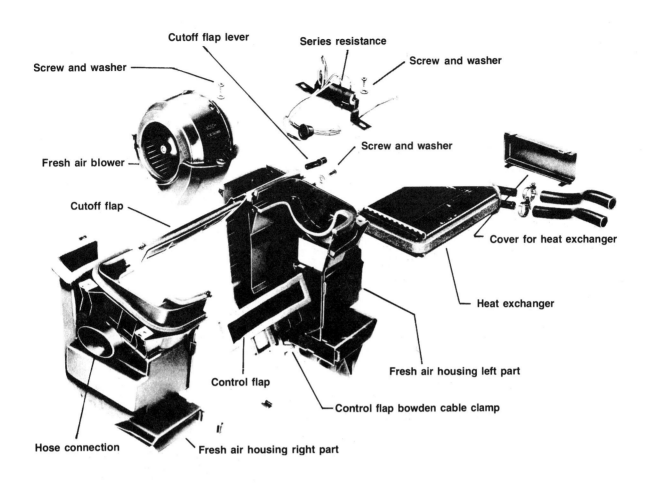

Fig. 5-2. Exploded view of ventilation and heating system used on 1977 and later cars.

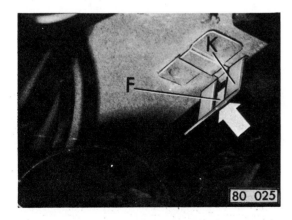

Fig. 5-3. Clip being removed. Using pliers, press retaining spring **F** in direction indicated by arrow. Lift off clip **K**.

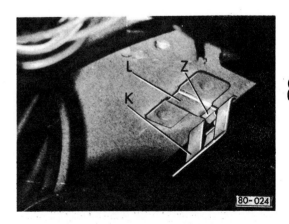

Fig. 5-4. Clip being installed. Insert tab **Z** of clip **K** into retainer **L**. Lift fresh air housing until spring **F**, shown previously in Fig. 5-3, snaps into position.

8

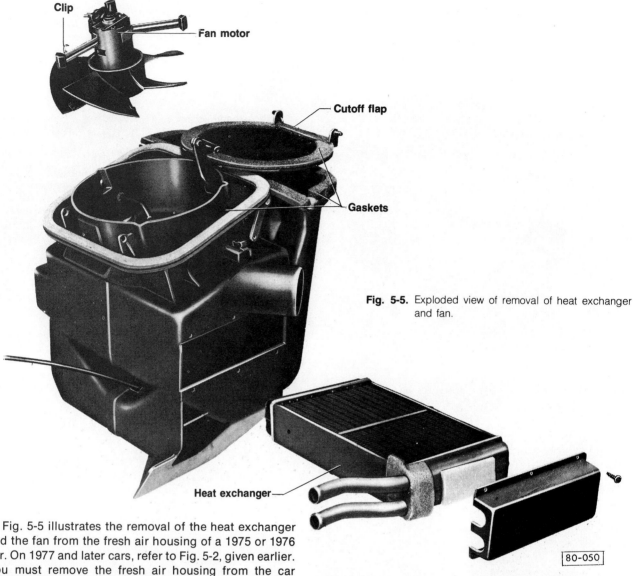

Fig. 5-5. Exploded view of removal of heat exchanger and fan.

Fig. 5-5 illustrates the removal of the heat exchanger and the fan from the fresh air housing of a 1975 or 1976 car. On 1977 and later cars, refer to Fig. 5-2, given earlier. You must remove the fresh air housing from the car before you can remove the heat exchanger. However, the fan and motor can be removed with the heater in the car.

On Rabbit models, the fresh air housing was changed beginning with Chassis No. 175 3210 503. This and subsequent 1975 and 1976 Rabbits do not have connections for the fresh air ducts to the outlets in the dashboard. Instead, fresh air is routed to the outlets from the plenum chamber. Only the new-type housing is available as a spare part.

To install the new-type fresh air housing in Rabbits built prior to Chassis No. 175 3210 503, you must add two connections. Part No. 171 819 741, as described in the procedure that follows.

To add duct connections:

1. Make holes for the ducts by cutting along the ridges in letter **W** in Fig. 5-6.

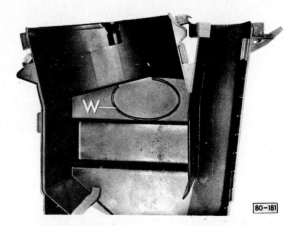

Fig. 5-6. Ridge (**W**) that outlines location of duct connections.

2. Slip the connections in the holes. Then retain the connections in place with the clips.

3. Seal any gaps with liquid rubber or a good sealing compound. See Fig. 5-7.

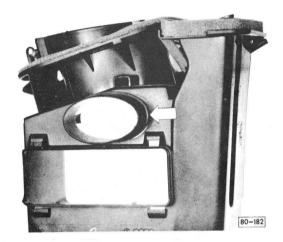

Fig. 5-7. Arrow indicating point where sealing compound may need to be applied.

5.1 Removing, Adjusting, and Installing Ventilation and Heating Controls

The procedure given here can be used to correct incorrect heater control operation. It is also possible to repair heater control levers that have become detached from their pivot.

If you must replace a control cable or a control flap, it is important that the control cable be connected to the control flap lever in the correct way. On 1977 cars, slide the cable eye over the control flap lever pin that is indicated by the numeral **1** in Fig. 5-8. On 1975 and 1976 cars, slide the cable eye over the control flap lever pin that is indicated by the numeral **2** in Fig. 5-8. Then, on 1975 and 1976 cars, cut off the pin at **1**.

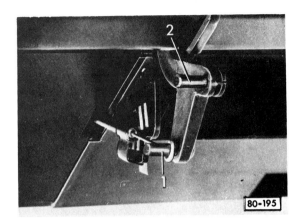

Fig. 5-8. Correct cable installation on replacement flap. Install 1977 cable at **1**; install 1975–1976 cable at **2**.

To remove controls:

1. Disconnect the battery ground strap.

2. Pull the knobs off the heater controls, which are in the center of the dashboard. See Fig. 5-9 or Fig. 5-10.

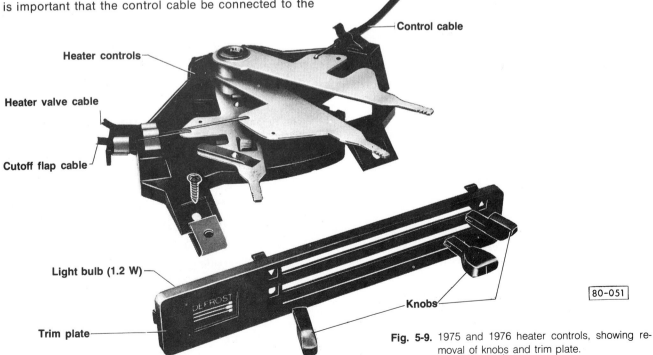

Fig. 5-9. 1975 and 1976 heater controls, showing removal of knobs and trim plate.

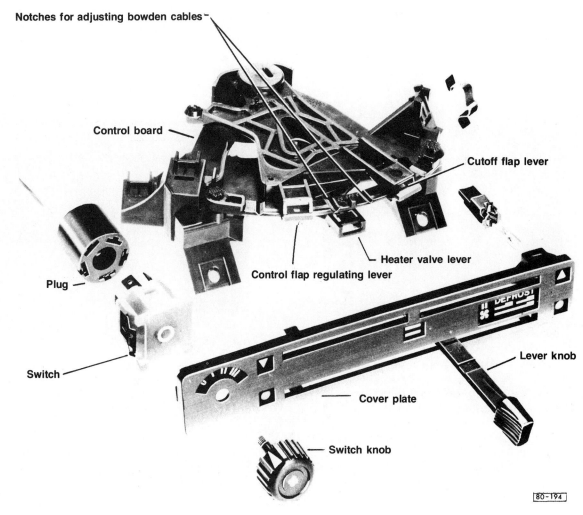

Notches for adjusting bowden cables

Control board

Cutoff flap lever

Plug

Control flap regulating lever

Heater valve lever

Switch

Lever knob

Cover plate

Switch knob

80-194

Fig. 5-10. 1977 and later heater controls, showing removal of knobs and trim plate.

3. Remove the trim plate. Remove the under-dash panels for access to the heater controls.

4. Disconnect the wires for the fan. Disconnect the heater valve cable from the heater controls.

5. Remove the screws that hold the heater controls to the dashboard structure. Then remove the heater controls, detaching them from the flap cables only when absolutely necessary.

> **NOTE** ——
> To remove the switch of a 1977 or later car, press the retaining clips toward the switch, then pull the switch off its support.

To install and adjust:

1. Inspect the cutoff flap cable, the control flap cable, and the heater valve cable. Replace faulty cables.

2. To install and adjust the cutoff flap cable, hand press the cutoff flap into its closed position. Hook the cable onto the correct control lever. Push the lever toward the flap-closed position until it is about 2 mm (.080 in.) from its stop. Then secure the cable conduit to the control quadrant with the clamp.

3. To install and adjust the control flap cable, hook the cable onto the correct control lever. Push the lever fully away from the cable conduit clamp. Then, while holding the lever in this position, pull the cable conduit as far as possible away from the lever and secure it in this position with the clamp.

4. To install and adjust the heater valve cable, open the engine hood and then unclamp the cable conduit from the valve. Move the lever as far as possible toward the conduit clamp location. Then secure the cable conduit with the clamp. Working inside the car, move the cable conduit back and forth on the quadrant until the control is in the off

position. Then secure the cable conduit to the control quadrant with the clamp.

5. The remainder of installation is the reverse of removal. Check that the controls operate correctly before you reinstall the under-dash panels.

NOTE ——

If the heater control levers have come off their pivot spindle, you can repair the controls by installing the new bolt and washers indicated in Fig. 5-11.

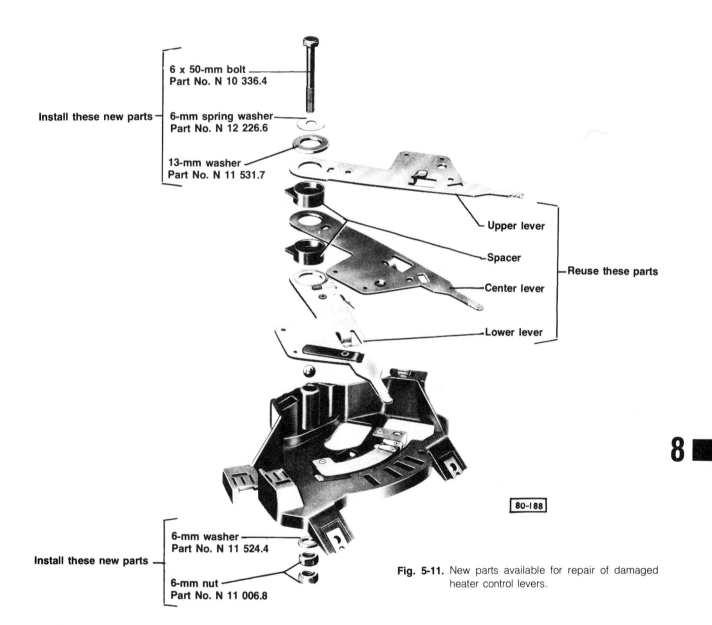

Install these new parts —

6 x 50-mm bolt
Part No. N 10 336.4

6-mm spring washer
Part No. N 12 226.6

13-mm washer
Part No. N 11 531.7

— **Upper lever**

— **Spacer**

— **Center lever**

— **Lower lever**

— **Reuse these parts**

80-188

Install these new parts —

6-mm washer
Part No. N 11 524.4

6-mm nut
Part No. N 11 006.8

Fig. 5-11. New parts available for repair of damaged heater control levers.

8

6. REPAIRING FRONT SUSPENSION MOUNTING

Careless installation of the front suspension system's track control arm can result in stripped threads in the captive nut welded inside the suspension carrier. If the tightening torque of 7.0 mkg (51 ft. lb.) cannot be achieved, the threads are stripped and the captive nut should be replaced.

To replace nut:

1. Using a disk grinder, open the welded seam indicated at **A** in Fig. 6-1. Drill out the spot welds at **B** in Fig. 6-1.

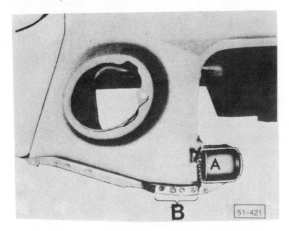

Fig. 6-1. Crossmember being cut open. Open weld **A**; drill out welds **B**.

2. Pry open the suspension carrier plate, as shown in Fig. 6-2. Remove the hardened foam plastic from the area that is to be repaired.

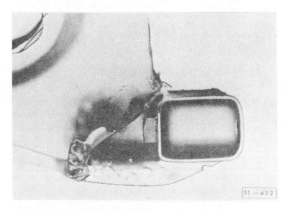

Fig. 6-2. Suspension carrier plate pried open for access to captive nut.

3. Using a cold chisel, as shown in Fig. 6-3, cut the stripped nut off the crossmember. Use a file to remove any burrs that remain following removal of the nut.

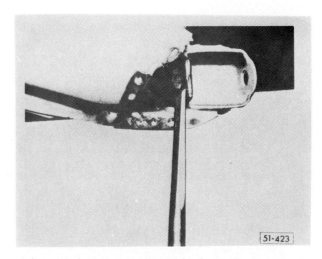

Fig. 6-3. Stripped captive nut being cut off crossmember.

4. Position the replacement nut, Part No. 171 803 190, against the crossmember—aligning it with a bolt as shown in Fig. 6-4. The chamfered end of the nut should be against the crossmember.

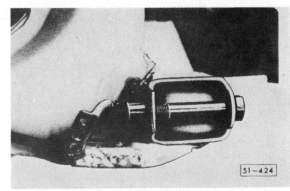

Fig. 6-4. Replacement nut correctly aligned with holes in crossmember.

5. Using MIG (metal inert gas) welding equipment, weld the replacement nut to the crossmember as shown in Fig. 6-5.

Fig. 6-5. Replacement nut correctly welded to crossmember.

6. Bend back the suspension carrier plate, making sure that there are no creases. Then, using the MIG equipment, weld seam **A** and plug-weld holes **B** as given in Fig. 6-6. If necessary, grind smooth the welding areas.

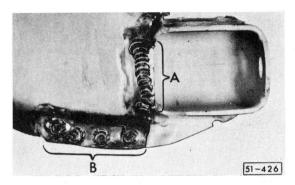

Fig. 6-6. Carrier plate rewelded in areas adjacent to suspension mounting crossmember.

7. Using replacement panel Part No. 171 803 193 or Part No. 171 803 194, cut out a reinforcement plate as indicated in Fig. 6-7.

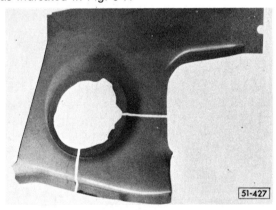

Fig. 6-7. Reinforcement plate (small portion) being cut from replacement panel.

8. Using an 8-mm (or ⁵/₁₆-in.) bit, drill 16 holes in the reinforcement plate, as shown in Fig. 6-8. Align the reinforcement plate with the car body as shown in Fig. 6-9 and secure it with clamps.

Fig. 6-8. Reinforcement plate drilled with 16 holes.

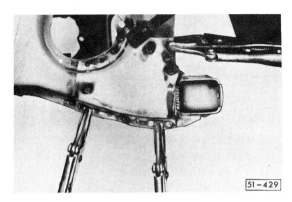

Fig. 6-9. Reinforcement plate aligned with body and held in position by clamps.

9. Using the MIG equipment, weld the seam at **A** in Fig. 6-10. Then plug weld the holes at **B** in Fig. 6-10.

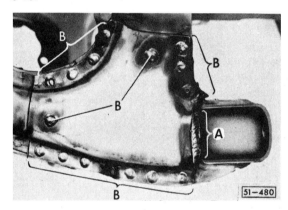

Fig. 6-10. Reinforcement plate welded to body. Seam is at **A**, holes for plug welds are at **B**.

10. Seal the welded seams in order to prevent the entry of moisture. Fill the cavity inside the suspension carrier with fast-hardening liquid plastic foam, then restore the undercoating.

11. In installing the suspension control arm, use a new lock washer Part No. 171 407 239 and a new bolt Part No. N 10 190 4. Install the lock washer so that surface **A**, indicated in Fig. 6-11, is toward the bolt head. Coat the bolt threads with Loctite® or a similar locking compound.

8

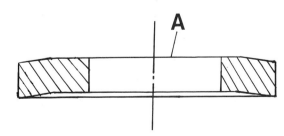

Fig. 6-11. Lockwasher for suspension pivot bolt. Surface **A** goes toward bolt head.

7. REPLACING AND RESHAPING BODY PANELS

Fig. 7-1 shows the panels and subassemblies that are available as replacement parts. A number of smaller plates and panels are also available. These can be determined by consulting the parts department at an Authorized Dealer. All these parts must be welded in place during body repair. Instructions for the removal and installation of the bumpers, the front fenders, the doors, the hood, and the luggage compartment lid are given in **4. Removing and Installing Bolt-on Components.**

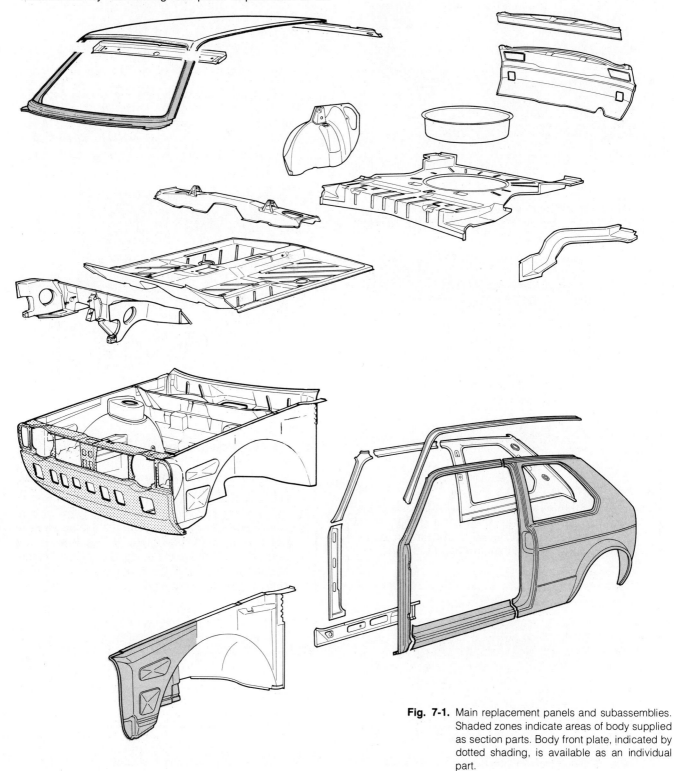

Fig. 7-1. Main replacement panels and subassemblies. Shaded zones indicate areas of body supplied as section parts. Body front plate, indicated by dotted shading, is available as an individual part.

7.1 Floor Plate Dimensions

Rabbit models and Scirocco models both have the same floor plate. The correct dimensions for the floor plate are given in Fig. 7-2. The dimensions should be used in reshaping the floor plate during the repair of collison damage.

Dimension	Location	Length mm ± 2 mm (in. ±1/16 in.)
a	between front subframe (hole centers)	683 (26 7/8)
b	between front and rear subframe mounting points	365 +1 or −3 (14 3/8 +1/32 or −1/8)
c	between subframe mountings (bolt centers)	272 (10 23/32)
d	between rear mounting holes (hole centers)	586 (23 1/16)
e	between front locating holes (hole centers)	1110 (43 11/16)
f	between rear subframe mounting holes and locating holes (hole centers)	204 (8 1/32)
g	between locating hole and subframe mounting hole (hole centers)	192 (7 9/16)
h	between locating holes and holes in rear side member (hole centers)	1478 (58 3/16)
i	between holes in rear side members (hole centers)	1142 (44 31/32)
k	between rear locating holes and holes in rear side members (hole centers)	888 (34 31/32)
l	between rear axle coil spring mountings (buffer mount centers)	1020 ± 4 (40 5/32 ± 5/32)
m	between rear locating holes (hole centers)	1057 (41 5/8)

Fig. 7-2. Floor plate dimensions for Rabbit and Scirocco.

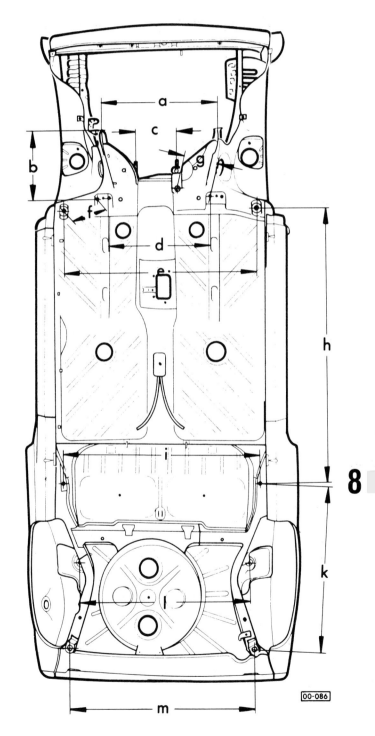

00-086

8

7.2 Body Dimensions

The body dimensions given on the following pages should be used in reshaping the body during the repair of collision damage.

> **NOTE**
>
> If no tolerance is specifically mentioned, all of the dimensions given in the following illustrations are ± 2 mm (or ± $^1/_{16}$ in.).

Rabbit Body Front Section

Fig. 7-3 shows the dimensions that should be measured when checking the Rabbit front body section for damage. If any dimension is not as specified in Fig. 7-4 through Fig. 7-10, the body panels must be replaced or reshaped in order to correct the damage.

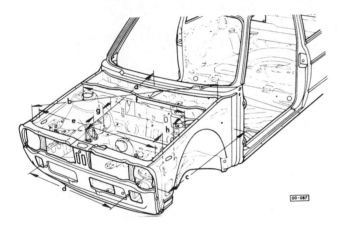

Fig. 7-3. Points at which Rabbit body front section should be measured. Correct dimension for each measurement is given in illustrations that follow.

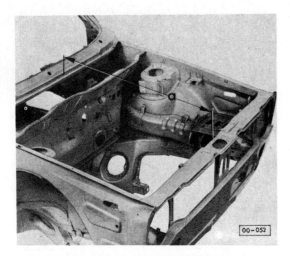

Fig. 7-4. Dimension **a**. Measurement should be 811 mm (or 31$^{15}/_{16}$ in.) from end of cowl panel to folded edge on upper front crossmember.

Fig. 7-5. Dimension **b**. Measurement should be 1500 mm (or 59$^1/_{16}$ in.) diagonally from cowl panel to upper front crossmember.

Fig. 7-6. Dimension **c**. Measurement should be 1039 mm (or 40$^{29}/_{32}$ in.) from hinge pillar center to headlight mounting.

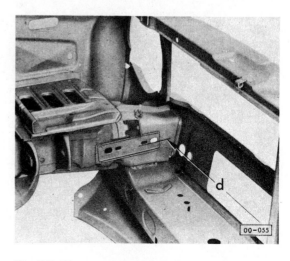

Fig. 7-7. Dimension **d**. Measurement should be 903 mm (or 35$^9/_{16}$ in.) between front sidemembers.

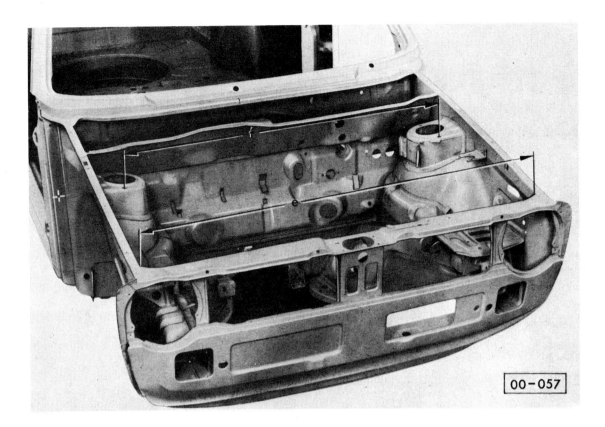

Fig. 7-8. Dimensions **e** and **f**. Measurement at **e** should be 1225 mm (or 48¼ in.) between wheel housing upper front parts. Measurement at **f** should be 1070 mm (or 42⅛ in.) between center of holes in strut mounts.

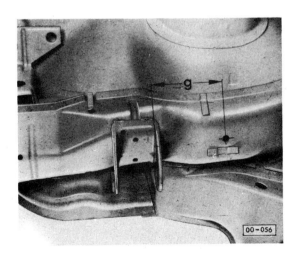

Fig. 7-9. Dimension **g**. Measurement should be 111 mm (or 4⅜ in.) from center of hole in right sidemember to engine mount.

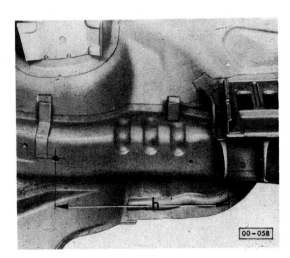

Fig. 7-10. Dimension **h**. Measurement should be 309 mm (12⁵/₃₂ in.) from center of hole in left sidemember to engine mount.

8

Rabbit Body Rear Section

Fig. 7-11 shows the dimensions that should be measured when checking the Rabbit rear body section for damage. If any dimension is not as specified in Fig. 7-12 through Fig. 7-15, the body panels must be replaced or reshaped in order to correct the damage.

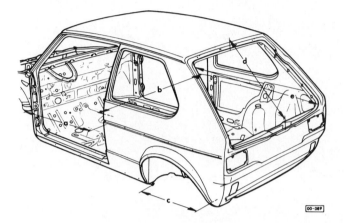

Fig. 7-11. Points at which Rabbit body rear section should be measured. Correct dimension for each measurement is given in illustrations that follow.

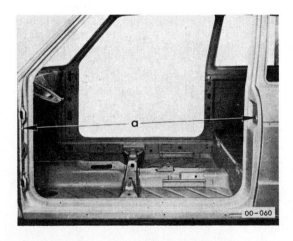

Fig. 7-12. Dimension **a**. Measurement should be 1113 mm (or 43¹³/₁₆ in.) between hinge pillar and side panel.

Fig. 7-13. Dimension **b**. Measurement should be 1302 mm (or 51¼ in.) between both side panel inner surfaces.

Fig. 7-14. Dimension **c**. Measurement should be 717 mm (or 28⁷/₃₂ in.) inside rear wheel housing.

Fig. 7-15. Dimensions **d** and **e**. Measurement at **d** should be 749 mm (29½ in.) between upper and lower flanges for luggage compartment opening. Measurement at **e** should be 1220 mm (or 48¹/₃₂ in.) diagonally from corner to corner of luggage compartment opening.

Scirocco Body Front Section

Fig. 7-16 shows the dimensions that should be measured when checking the Scirocco front body section for damage. If any dimension is not as specified in Fig. 7-17 through Fig. 7-25, the body panels must be replaced or reshaped in order to correct the damage.

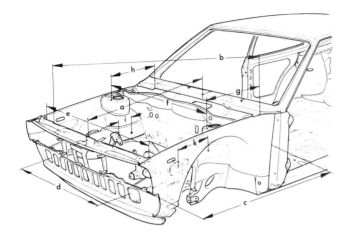

Fig. 7-16. Points at which Scirocco body front section should be measured. Correct dimension for each measurement is given in illustrations that follow.

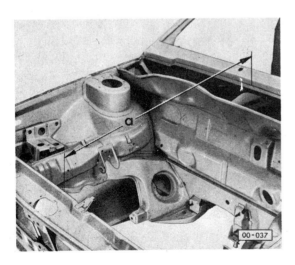

Fig. 7-17. Dimension **a**. Measurement should be 856 mm (or 33 11/16 in.) from end of cowl panel to folded edge on upper front crossmember.

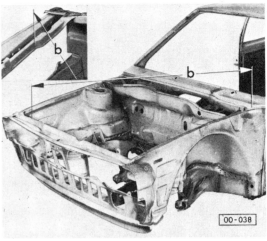

Fig. 7-18. Dimension **b**. Measurement should be 1439 mm (or 56 21/32 in.) diagonally from cowl panel to upper front crossmember.

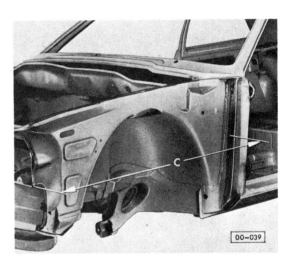

Fig. 7-19. Dimension **c**. Measurement should be 1089 mm (or 42 7/8 in.) from hinge pillar center to headlight mounting.

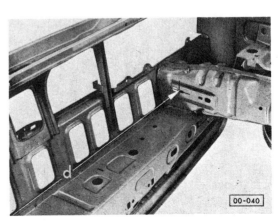

Fig. 7-20. Dimension **d**. Measurement should be 903 mm (or 35 9/16 in.) between front sidemembers.

8

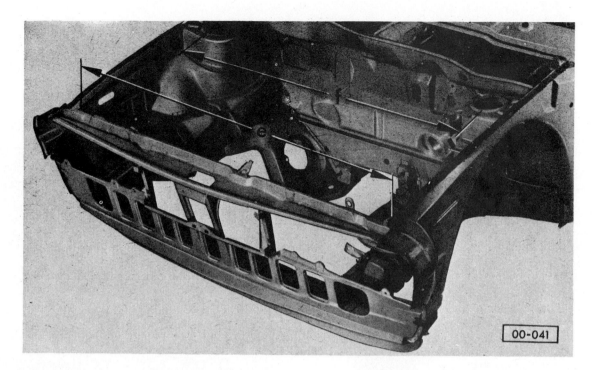

Fig. 7-21. Dimensions **e** and **f**. Measurement at **e** should be 1211 mm (or 47^{11}/$_{16}$ in.) between front wheel housing upper front parts. Measurement at **f** should be 1070 mm (or 42⅛ in.) between centers of holes in strut mounting.

Fig. 7-22. Dimension **g**. Measurement should be 393 mm (or 15^{15}/$_{32}$ in.) from cowl panel to center of hole in strut mounting.

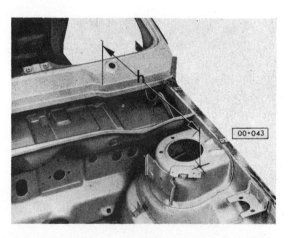

Fig. 7-23. Dimension **h**. Measurement should be 364 mm (or 14^{11}/$_{32}$ in.) from cowl panel to center of hole in strut mounting.

Fig. 7-24. Dimension **i**. Measurement should be 111 mm (or 4⅜ in.) from center of hole in right sidemember to engine mount.

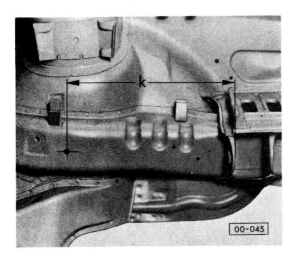

Fig. 7-25. Dimension **k**. Measurement should be 309 mm (or 12⁵/₃₂ in.) from center of hole in left sidemember to engine mount.

Scirocco Body Rear Section

Fig. 7-26 shows the dimensions that should be measured when checking the Scirocco rear body section for damage. If any dimension is not as specified in Fig. 7-27 through Fig. 7-30, the body panels must be replaced or reshaped in order to correct the damage.

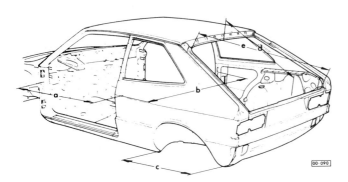

Fig. 7-26. Points at which Scirocco body rear section should be measured. Correct dimension for each measurement is given in illustrations that follow.

Fig. 7-27. Dimension **a**. Measurement should be 1154 mm (or 45 ⁷/₁₆ in.) between hinge pillar and side panel.

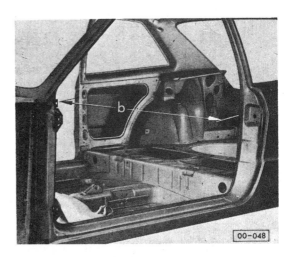

Fig. 7-28. Dimension **b**. Measurement should be 1348 mm (or 53¹/₁₆ in.) between both side panel inner surfaces.

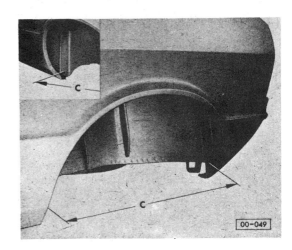

Fig. 7-29. Dimension **c**. Measurement should be 717 mm (or 28⁷/₃₂ in.) inside rear wheel housing.

8

Fig. 7-30. Dimensions **d** and **e**. Measurement at **d** should be 818 mm (or 32$^7/_{32}$ in.) between upper and lower flanges for luggage compartment opening. Measurement at **e** should be 1306 mm (or 51$^{13}/_{32}$ in.) diagonally from corner to corner of luggage compartment opening.

The new-type taillight assembly can be installed in the new-type body panel without modification. However, if you must install the new-type taillight assembly on a car with the old-type rear panel, use self-tapping screw N 43 885.1/B 4.8 X 19. See Fig. 7-32.

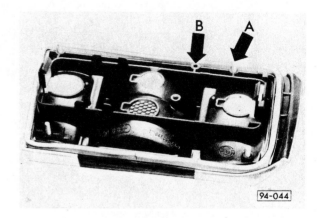

Fig. 7-32. Lug (arrow **A**) for locating taillight assembly in new-type rear panel. To install an old-type panel, drive self-tapping screw into hole at arrow **B**.

7.3 Modifying New-type Taillight for Installation on Old-type Rear Panel

During the 1976 model year, a new taillight assembly was introduced. Consequently, the rear panel of the body was modified as indicated in Fig. 7-31.

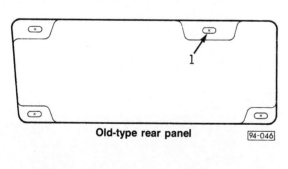

Old-type rear panel   94-046

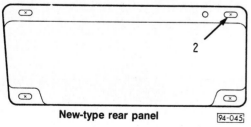

New-type rear panel   94-045

Fig. 7-31. Change in rear panel. Hole at **2** is further outward than hole at **1**.

LUBRICATION AND MAINTENANCE

Contents

9

Lubrication and Maintenance

The service life of your VW depends on the kind of maintenance it receives. The Owner's Manual originally supplied with the car contains valuable information concerning correct car maintenance, which should be used in conjunction with this Manual. Because several model years are covered in this Manual, some of the procedures described may not apply to your car. If you are in doubt, always take the Owner's Manual and the Maintenance Record booklet as your guides.

Some maintenance procedures, such as oil change service, require no special tools and can be carried out by almost all car owners, regardless of their mechanical experience. However, certain other diagnosis and maintenance operations require tools and equipment specifically designed for those operations. Wheel alignment checks, ignition timing, and emission control checks are a few examples. If you lack the skills, tools, or a suitable workshop for performing any of the service steps described, we suggest you leave this work to an Authorized Dealer or other qualified shop. We especially urge you to consult your Authorized Dealer before attempting any repairs on a car still covered by the new-car warranty.

The cars covered by this Manual are equipped with a system of sensors and test wiring that terminates in a central control socket located in the engine compartment. This socket is designed to receive a plug from the cable of the Computer Analysis system. Once the car is connected to the computer, many items can be checked electronically by comparing actual measurements and test data from the car with factory specifications stored in the computer.

The comprehensive test report that is printed as the outcome of the computer analysis tests can tell quite a bit about your car. By taking advantage of this service at an Authorized Dealer, you can save considerable time and effort in determining which parts or systems of your car need to be serviced and which are in satisfactory working order. Never connect any device other than the test plug of the Computer Analysis system to the test network central socket in the engine compartment. Incorrect equipment may damage the plug connections, the test sensors, or the vehicle components that contain sensors.

9

1. LUBRICANTS

Because of the recent improvements in the quality of commercially available lubricating oils, completely new oil recommendations for VW cars became effective in 1975. These new oil recommendations, given below, should be applied to all the cars covered by this Manual.

The lubricants used in your VW have a vital influence on its operation. Use only name brand oils labeled "For Service SD" (or "For Service SE" or both) in the engine. Oils used in 1975 and later cars must be labeled "For Service API/SE". Automatic transmission fluid (ATF) must be labeled DEXRON® with a five-digit number preceded by the letter B. The hypoid oil used in the manual transmission must meet specification MIL-L 2105 API/GL4. Use a hypoid oil that meets specification MIL-L 2105 B API/GL5 for the final drive of the automatic transmission. No additives should be used in the engine oil, hypoid oil, or ATF. Experience has shown that name brand lubricants of the correct specification and viscosity meet all operating needs of the engine and transmission.

Oil viscosity must be suitable to climatic conditions. Viscosity is a term used to describe how readily a liquid flows. High viscosity oils seem thicker and pour more slowly at room temperature than do low viscosity (thinner) oils. When heated, however, oil loses some of its viscosity. A high viscosity oil heated to 93°C (200°F) may pour as readily as a low viscosity oil at room temperature. If an oil has too low a viscosity, it will not maintain an adequate lubricating film between moving parts. A thin, low viscosity oil may maintain this film at low temperatures but become so much thinner after it has warmed up that it leaves the engine parts unprotected.

It might seem that a high viscosity oil is all that is necessary to lubricate an engine properly. Unfortunately, this is not true. If a high viscosity oil is used during cold weather, it will become so thick and resistant to flow that it cannot properly circulate and reach the parts of the engine requiring lubrication. A thick, high viscosity oil will also become so gummy in cold weather that the starter cannot turn the engine fast enough to start it. The proper viscosity oil will remain fluid enough after the engine has cooled to permit easy starting, yet, after the engine has reached operating temperature, will retain sufficient viscosity to maintain an adequate lubricating film.

Single-grade engine oils, such as SAE 30, were formerly recommended for high-temperature use because of the unreliable quality of the then available multi-grade engine oils. The new high standard for engine oils that conform to the API (American Petroleum Institute) service rating API/SE has made these multi-grade oils suitable for use at all temperatures. Car owners will find that these high-quality multi-grade oils offer many advantages in convenience, performance, and economy.

For example, a single-grade oil may have to be discarded after a short period of service owing to the early arrival of winter temperatures. A multi-grade oil, suitable for both summer and winter temperatures, can be left in the engine until the normal oil change mileage has been reached. This feature of multi-grade oils can save the expense of oil changes necessitated by climatic conditions.

By becoming familiar with the oil recommendations, you can be sure that the oil you buy is the correct kind for your car. Inferior lubricants, no matter how attractively priced, are not a good investment; using the wrong oil will greatly shorten the service life of your VW.

Oil Viscosities

The viscosity grade of oil is designated by an SAE (Society of Automotive Engineers) standard number. An oil designated SAE 40 has a higher viscosity (greater resistance to flow) than an oil designated SAE 30. Multi-grade oils have an extended viscosity range and can be used in place of a number of single-grade oils. For example, an SAE 20W-40 oil is suitable for use within a range of temperatures that would require three different single-grade oils in order to cover it (SAE 40, SAE 30, and SAE 20W-20). **Table a** lists the proper oil viscosity for VW engines under specific climatic conditions.

Table a. Engine Oil Viscosity Specifications

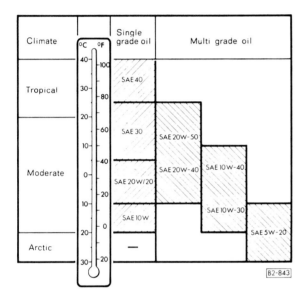

CAUTION ——

Avoid high-speed, long distance driving when using SAE 5W or SAE 10W oil— especially if the outside temperature rises above the limits given for these lubricants. If you anticipate continuous operation that will impose maximum loads on the engine, or if you expect to drive at sustained speeds above 60 mph (100 kph), use the next higher viscosity oil. Under these conditions, SAE 5W or SAE 10W oil may be inadequate to maintain a proper lubricating film between the moving parts of the engine.

The viscosity of transmission oil is also designated by SAE numbers. Use SAE 80W or SAE 80W/90 for general year-round service in the manual transmission. Always use SAE 90 hypoid oil in the final drive of the automatic transmission. ATF is not graded for viscosity and requires no seasonal change.

Greases

Two types of grease are used for lubrication of chassis and driveline parts. Multipurpose grease (lithium grease) has a wider temperature tolerance range than ordinary grease and should be used for most lubrication purposes. The additives in multipurpose grease give it increased pressure resistance and anticorrosion capabilities. It is suitable for use both in plain bearings and in roller bearings. Molybdenum grease is lithium grease with a friction-reducing molybdenum disulfide additive. It is used in the constant velocity joints of the front axle. Use dry stick lubricant in the hood locks and on the sliding surfaces of the door striker plates. The battery terminals should be coated with either silicone spray or petroleum jelly.

2. MAINTENANCE SCHEDULES

The maintenance schedules given in **Table b** should be followed carefully even if your VW is not being serviced by an Authorized Dealer. The right-hand column on page 6 tells where each maintenance job is covered in this Manual. For example, the first operation listed in the table, changing the engine oil, is covered in Section 9 (Lubrication and Maintenance) under heading 3.1 (Changing Engine Oil). The sixth operation listed in the table, checking the valve clearances, is covered in Section 4 (Engine and Clutch) under heading 5.2.

9

Table b. Scheduled Maintenance Services

Maintenance operations	Where operation is covered in Manual
Changing engine oil and checking oil level	SECTION 9 HEADING 3.1
Replacing oil filter	SECTION 9 HEADING 3
Servicing and replacing spark plugs	SECTION 4 HEADING 3.5
Replacing ignition points and, if necessary, distributor cap, distributor rotor, and secondary cables	SECTION 4 HEADINGS 3.2 & 3.4
Checking ignition point gap or dwell, checking ignition timing	SECTION 4 HEADINGS 3.2 & 3.3
Checking cylinder head bolt torque and then checking valve clearance and replacing cyl. head cover gasket	SECTION 4 HEADING 5.2
Checking cylinder compression	SECTION 9 HEADING 4.3
Cleaning and inspecting air cleaner filter element	SECTION 9 HEADING 4.2
Replacing air cleaner filter element	SECTION 9 HEADING 4.2
Checking exhaust system	SECTION 9 HEADING 5.1
Checking clutch pedal freeplay	SECTION 4 HEADING 9.2
Checking V-belt adjustment and belt condition	SECTION 4 HEADING 5.1
Checking and adjusting idle	SECTION 3 HEADING 5
Checking cooling system	SECTION 4 HEADING 4
Replacing fuel filter	SECTION 3 HEADING 3.2
Checking operation and condition of emission controls	SECTION 3 HEADINGS 5 & 9
Replacing EGR filter and checking EGR system visually	SECTION 3 HEADING 9
Checking and, if necessary, cleaning air injection pump filter; checking air injection hoses and valves visually	SECTION 9 HEADING 4.5
Replacing air injection pump filter	SECTION 9 HEADING 4.5
Replacing catalytic converter	SECTION 3 HEADING 10
Replacing activated charcoal filter canister	SECTION 9 HEADING 4.4
Checking PCV system	SECTION 9 HEADING 4.1
Visually checking fuel tank, EEC hoses, and charcoal filter canister	SECTION 3 HEADING 3
Checking operation of lights and switches	SECTION 9 HEADING 6.4
Checking headlight aim	SECTION 5 HEADING 8.1
Checking windshield wipers and washers	SECTION 5 HEADING 7
Checking battery	SECTION 5 HEADING 3.1
Testing charging and starting systems	SECTION 5 HEADINGS 4 & 5.2
Checking constant velocity joint screws and boots	SECTION 9 HEADING 5.4
Checking and correcting transmission hypoid oil level (manual and automatic transmissions)	SECTION 9 HEADING 5.3
Changing manual or automatic transmission hypoid oil and cleaning magnetic drain plug	SECTION 9 HEADING 5.3
Checking automatic transmission ATF level	SECTION 9 HEADING 5.2
Checking automatic transmission ATF pan bolts	SECTION 9 HEADING 5.2
Changing ATF: draining and filling automatic transmission, cleaning ATF pan and replacing strainer	SECTION 9 HEADING 5.2
Checking automatic transmission kickdown operation	SECTION 9 HEADING 6.4
Checking brake fluid level	SECTION 1 HEADING 9.1
Changing brake fluid and checking brake warning light operation	SECTION 1 HEADING 9.1
Checking brake pressure regulator pressures (except Scirocco and basic Rabbit models with automatic trans.)	SECTION 1 HEADING 4.4
Visually checking brake pressure regulator (except Scirocco and basic Rabbit models with manual trans.)	SECTION 1 HEADING 4.4
Checking remaining thickness of brake pads and linings	SECTION 1 HEADINGS 7.1 & 8.1
Checking for brake adjustment (pedal height)	SECTION 9 HEADING 6.4
Checking brake lines and hoses for leaks and damage	SECTION 1 HEADING 6
Checking brake lights	SECTION 1 HEADING 4.1
Checking tires for wear, damage, and correct inflation pressures	SECTION 1 HEADING 11
Checking ball joint dust seals and tie rod end dust seals	SECTION 9 HEADING 5.6
Checking steering play	SECTION 9 HEADING 6.4
Checking steering gearbox boots for leaks, tears, or other damage	SECTION 9 HEADING 5.5
Checking front wheel camber and toe	SECTION 2 HEADING 3
Lubricating door hinges and door checks	SECTION 9 HEADING 6.1
Lubricating hood and trunk lid hinges and locks	SECTION 9 HEADING 6.1
Lubricating oil can points (throttle linkage, clutch linkage, etc.)	SECTION 9 HEADING 6.2

Service intervals (given in thousands of miles/thousands of km)	
1975 models	1976-1977 models
5/8	7.5/12
15/24	15/24
15/24	15/24
15/24	15/24
15/24	15/24
15/24	15/24
15/24	15/24
15/24	15/24
30/48	30/48
15/24	15/24
15/24	15/24
15/24	15/24
15/24	15/24
5/8	7.5/12
15/24	15/24
15/24	15/24
15/24	replace when EGR light comes on
15/24	N/A
30/48	N/A
30/48	replace when CAT light comes on
when inspection shows need	when inspection shows need
15/24	15/24
15/24	15/24
15/24	15/24
15/24	15/24
15/24	15/24
15/24	15/24
15/24	15/24
15/24	15/24
unnecessary except after repair	unnecessary except after repair
15/24	15/24
30/48	30/48
30/48	30/48
15/24	15/24
15/24	15/24
every 2 years	every 2 years
every 2 years	every 2 years
15/24	15/24
15/24	15/24
15/24	15/24
15/24	15/24
15/24	15/24
15/24	15/24
15/24	15/24
15/24	15/24
15/24	15/24
15/24	15/24
15/24	15/24
15/24	15/24

3. OIL CHANGE SERVICE

In addition to the operations described under **3.1 Changing Engine Oil,** you should check the coolant level in the radiator at each oil change. Do not remove the radiator cap until the engine has had an opportunity to cool. Otherwise, the radiator may overflow and some coolant will be lost. The coolant level should reach the full mark, as indicated in Fig. 3-1. If it is necessary to add coolant, follow the instructions given in **ENGINE AND CLUTCH.**

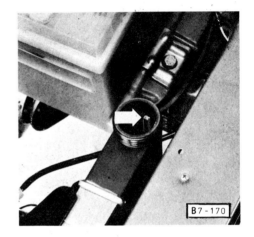

Fig. 3-1. Radiator full mark (arrow).

While you are changing the oil, it is wise to check the battery electrolyte as described in **ELECTRICAL SYSTEM.** First test the specific gravity of the electrolyte with a hydrometer. Then, if necessary, add distilled water in order to bring the electrolyte level above the cell separators or to the bottom of the filler tubes on batteries that are so equipped.

3.1 Changing Engine Oil

The oil should be drained from the engine while it is hot. Drive the car to a level place and stop the engine. Drain the oil by placing a pan of at least 6-liter (or 6-quart) capacity beneath the engine. Then remove the oil drain plug from the engine's oil pan and allow the oil to drain into the collecting pan. If you are going to change the oil filter, as described under the next heading, you can do this job while the oil is draining.

When the flow has diminished to one drop per minute, reinstall the drain plug. Torque the plug to 3.0 mkg (22 ft. lb.). Then, if you have changed the oil filter, refill the crankcase with 3.7 U.S. quarts (3.2 Imperial quarts, 3.5 liters) of oil labeled ''For Service SE''. If you have not changed the oil filter, you will need only 3.2 U.S. quarts (2.6 Imperial quarts, 3.0 liters) of this oil.

9

Always make a final check of the oil level after the engine has been run long enough to fill the filter and has been stopped long enough for oil to drain down off internal engine parts. Check the dipstick to make sure that the level is correct before you drive the car. See Fig. 3-2.

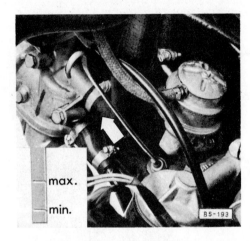

Fig. 3-2. Engine oil dipstick (arrow). The oil should be between the min. and max. marks on the dipstick. The difference between the marks is about 1 U.S. quart (.85 Imperial quart or 1 liter).

Replacing Oil Filter

The oil filter is located on a flange on the front side of the engine. To change the filter, place a drip pan beneath the filter location. Then, using an oil filter wrench, turn the filter counterclockwise until it is off the flange. Wipe clean the gasket surface of the flange. Coat the gasket of the new filter with engine oil, then screw on the filter as tightly as you can using your bare hand only.

After you have refilled the engine with oil, run the engine until the new filter is filled and under pressure. Check visually for leaks around the filter. Stop the engine and, after waiting for the oil to drain down off the engine's internal parts, recheck the oil level.

4. ENGINE COMPARTMENT MAINTENANCE OPERATIONS

Because the automatic transmission fluid dipstick is located in the engine compartment, you should check the ATF level before you raise the car on a hoist. Instructions for checking the ATF level are given in **5.2 Checking and Correcting ATF Level.**

4.1 Checking PCV (Positive Crankcase Ventilation) System

The engine has no PCV valve that requires periodic cleaning or replacing. The PCV system consists of a hose that connects the cylinder head cover with the air intake elbow. You can quick-check the system by disconnecting the hose from the cylinder head cover and blowing through it.

At the prescribed service interval, remove the PCV hose. Soak the hose in a low-volatility petroleum-base solvent. Scrub out the inside of the hose with a suitable brush. Then blow the hose dry with compressed air.

4.2 Servicing Air Cleaner

The air cleaner used on fuel injection engines is different from the air cleaners used on engines with carburetors. All the dust that is present in the air drawn into the engine is trapped and retained by the pleated paper filter element in the air cleaner.

To service carburetor air cleaner on Rabbit:

1. Release the clips that hold the cover to the air cleaner housing. Then lift the cover off as shown in Fig. 4-1.

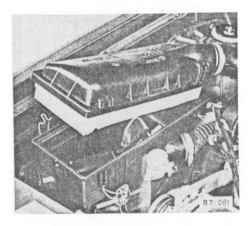

Fig. 4-1. Carburetor air cleaner for Rabbit model. Cover has been lifted for access to filter, which is shown in the cover.

2. Lift out the pleated paper filter element.

3. If you have removed the filter element for inspection purposes only, first tap the element lightly on a hard surface in order to knock off all loose dust. Never wash the filter element in solvent or blow it off with a powerful blast of compressed air. This can ruin the filter. After knocking off the dust, hold

the filter up to a bright light and check for cracks in the pleats. If any crack or hole is found, replace the filter element.

4. Before installing either a new or a used filter element, wipe clean the air cleaner housing using a lightly oiled, lint-free cloth.

5. Install the filter element and the cover.

> *CAUTION* ——
>
> *In installing either a new or a used filter, the word UP, which is printed in large letters on one side of the filter element, must be on top. This is especially important when you install a used filter because, with the filter reversed, previous accumulations of dirt will be drawn into the engine.*

To service carburetor air cleaner on Scirocco:

1. Release the clips that hold the front part of the air cleaner to the rear part. Then pull off the front part as indicated in Fig. 4-2.

Fig. 4-2. Carburetor air cleaner for Scirocco model. Remove front part as indicated by arrow.

2. Lift out the pleated paper filter element.

3. If you have removed the filter element for inspection purposes only, first tap the element lightly on a hard surface in order to knock off all loose dust. Never wash the filter element in solvent or blow it off with a powerful blast of compressed air. This can ruin the filter. After knocking off the dust, hold the filter up to a bright light and check for cracks in the pleats. If any crack or hole is found, replace the filter element.

4. Before installing either a new or a used filter

element, wipe clean the air cleaner housing using a lightly oiled, lint-free cloth.

5. Install the filter element and the front part of the air cleaner.

> *CAUTION* ——
>
> *In installing either a new or a used filter, the word UP, which is printed in large letters on one side of the filter element, must be away from the carburetor. This is especially important when you install a used filter because, with the filter reversed, previous accumulations of dirt will be drawn into the engine.*

To service fuel injection air cleaner:

1. Release the clips that hold the mixture control unit on to the air cleaner housing. Then lift up the mixture control unit as indicated by the white arrow in Fig. 4-3.

2. Lift out the pleated paper filter element.

Fig. 4-3. Air filter being removed (black arrow) after mixture control unit has been lifted up (white arrow).

3. If you have removed the filter element for inspection purposes only, first tap the element lightly on a hard surface in order to knock off all loose dust. Never wash the filter element in solvent or blow it off with a powerful blast of compressed air. This can ruin the filter. After knocking off the dust, hold the filter up to a bright light and check for cracks in the pleats. If any crack or hole is found, replace the filter element.

4. Before installing either a new or a used filter element, wipe clean the air cleaner housing using a lightly oiled, lint-free cloth.

5. Install the filter element in the air cleaner housing.

9 ∎

Then hand-press the mixture control unit onto the housing and retain it in place with the clips.

> **CAUTION** ——
>
> *In installing either a new or a used filter, the word UP, which is printed in large letters on one side of the filter element, must be toward the mixture control unit. This is especially important when you install a used filter because, with the filter reversed, previous accumulations of dirt will be drawn into the engine.*

4.3 Testing Engine Compressions

To check the cylinder compression, remove the spark plugs. Then install a compression testing gauge in one of the spark plug holes. Crank the engine with the starter for a few moments while the accelerator is pressed to the floor or while the throttle valves are held wide open. Normal compression pressure is 142 to 184 psi (10 to 13 atu). If the pressure for any cylinder is below 107 psi (7.5 atu)—or if the pressure differential between any two cylinders exceeds 42 psi (3.0 atu)—the valves may need to be ground, the piston rings replaced, or the cylinders bored to accept new oversize pistons.

To determine whether it is the piston rings or the valves that are causing low compression, squirt a small quantity of SAE 40 oil into the low-reading cylinder(s) through the spark plug hole(s). Then repeat the compression test. If the readings are significantly higher, the piston rings, pistons, or cylinders are at fault. If the compression pressure readings are still low, suspect faulty valves.

Before assuming that the problem is in the valves, however, check the valve adjustment to make sure that there is at least a small amount of clearance between the camshaft lobes and the adjusting disks. If there is no measurable gap, adjust the valves as described in **ENGINE AND CLUTCH,** then repeat the compression test. If the pressure is still low, the valves need grinding.

4.4 Replacing Activated Charcoal Filter Canister

The activated charcoal filter canister is located in the engine compartment. It is connected by a hose to the air cleaner.

To replace the canister, remove the hoses that are connected to it, then take out the Phillips head screw in the canister mounting bracket. Note the positions of the hose installations so that the hoses can be installed on the new canister in their correct positions. Installation is the reverse of removal.

4.5 Cleaning and Replacing Air Injection Pump Air Filter

The air cleaner for the air pump has a pleated paper filter element. Remove the hose clamp that holds the air cleaner to the pump. Then remove the air cleaner and disassemble it as shown in Fig. 4-4. To clean the filter element, tap it against a hard surface in order to knock off all loose dirt. Replace torn or damaged filters. Assemble and install the air cleaner using either a cleaned or a new filter, as specified in **2. Maintenance Schedules.**

> **WARNING** ——
>
> *Never wash the filter element in solvent. This will ruin the filter and could cause a fire or explosion.*

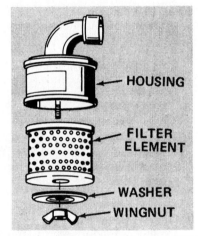

© 1974 VWoA—3725

Fig. 4-4. Components of air pump air cleaner.

5. UNDER-CAR MAINTENANCE OPERATIONS

Except for checking the level of the automatic transmission fluid (ATF), which should be done with the car on the ground, the maintenance operations described under the next six numbered headings should be done with the car raised on a hoist. Alternatively, you can support the car on jack stands.

> **WARNING** ——
>
> *Never work beneath a car that is supported solely by a jack. There is a very real danger that the jack may fail or accidently release, allowing the car to fall.*

5.1 Checking Exhaust System

Momentarily cover the tailpipe opening with a pad of rags while the engine is running. Hissing sounds coming from underneath the car signal leakage. Darker or lighter areas around joints in the system may indicate escaping gases. Check that the exhaust pipe and muffler mountings are secure and that the rubber parts of the mountings are in good condition.

5.2 Checking and Correcting ATF Level

(automatic transmission only)

The dipstick for the ATF in the automatic transmission is inserted into the ATF filler tube on the left-hand side of the engine (Fig. 5-1). The dipstick is attached to the cap for the ATF filler tube. The level should be checked with the ATF warm and the engine idling. The transmission selector lever must be in neutral and the parking brake set. Correct ATF level is very important for the proper functioning of the automatic transmission.

Pull out the dipstick and wipe it clean. The ring-shaped handle should be in a vertical position when you reinsert the dipstick to measure the fluid level.

Fig. 5-1. ATF dipstick handle (arrow), located above transaxle, near battery.

The ATF level is correct only if it falls between the two marks on the dipstick. Add ATF, if necessary, but only as much as is needed. Keep in mind that the difference between the lower and the upper marks is only 13.5 U.S. oz. (11.25 Imperial oz.; 398 cm³). Use a clean funnel for adding ATF. The ATF added must be labeled DEXRON® with a five-digit number preceded by the letter B.

Changing ATF, Cleaning ATF Pan, and Replacing ATF Strainer

The task of changing the ATF, cleaning the ATF pan, and replacing the ATF strainer should normally be done at the mileage specified in **2. Maintenance Schedules.** Do the work twice as frequently as specified if the car is used under severe conditions, such as trailer towing, stop-and-go driving, or extended mountain driving.

Remove the drain plug from the transmission ATF pan and allow as much ATF as possible to drain. Remove the transaxle protection plate, then remove the screws that hold the ATF pan. Pry the pan loose from the bottom of the transmission case and lower it carefully. Pour out the remaining ATF.

> **CAUTION ——**
>
> *Do not tow the car or run the engine while there is no ATF in the transmission. This could ruin the bearings in the transmission.*

Wash the ATF pan in solvent and dry it with compressed air. Never use fluffy rags when cleaning the automatic transmission. Lint from them could cause the control valves in the transmission to jam.

Inspect the filter-type ATF strainer. If it is obviously dirty or clogged with debris from burned clutch or brake linings, replace it. The filter-type strainer used in the automatic transmission covered by this Manual cannot be cleaned. During installation of the filter-type strainer, torque the screws to 30 cmkg (26 in. lb.).

Using a new gasket without sealer, install the ATF pan. Working diagonally, tighten the pan bolts to 2.0 mkg (14 ft. lb.). Install the drain plug. Install the transaxle protection plate. Torque protection plate M 10 bolts to 2.5 mkg (18 ft. lb.); torque protection plate M 8 bolts to 2.0 mkg (14 ft. lb.).

Refill the transmission with 3.2 U.S. quarts (2.6 Imperial quarts, 3.0 liters) of ATF. Do not fill above the top mark on the dipstick, as checked with the ATF warm, the engine idling in neutral, and the parking brake set. The ATF used must be labeled DEXRON® with a five-digit number preceded by the letter B. With the engine running and the ATF at the correct level, check visually for leaks around the ATF pan gasket.

9 ■

> **CAUTION ——**
>
> *Never tighten the pan bolts over 2.0 mkg (14 ft. lb.) in an attempt to cure a leaking gasket. Overtightening will deform the pan and make it impossible to get a good seal. Always install a new gasket to correct leaks.*

5.3 Checking and Changing Hypoid Oil

The hypoid oil level in both the manual transmission and the final drive of the automatic transmission should be kept at the lower edge of the filler hole in the side of the transmission case or the final drive housing. The level is correct if hypoid oil just barely drips from the hole with the plug removed. The level may be considered satisfactory if you can feel the oil with your fingertip just below the edge of the filler hole. Hypoid oil is added, if necessary, through the oil filler hole (Fig. 5-2).

Fig. 5-2. Filler hole (**A**) and drain hole (**B**) of manual transmission. Locations are similar on automatic transmissions.

The drain plug in the bottom of the manual transmission contains a magnet that traps metallic particles as they settle in the oil. The accumulation can be cleaned from the magnet periodically by removing the plug. Have a cork of appropriate size ready to plunge into the transmission drain hole as soon as the magnetic plug is removed. Very little hypoid oil will be lost if the filler plug is left installed so that air cannot enter readily. After cleaning the magnetic plug and reinstalling it, correct the hypoid oil level to make up for any that was lost.

Changing Hypoid Oil

It is unnecessary to change the hypoid oil of the transaxle with automatic transmission—unless the oil has become contaminated or a temperature change makes it necessary to use an oil of a different viscosity. However, the hypoid oil in either the automatic transmission transaxle or the manual transmission transaxle should always be changed 600 mi. (1000 km) after rebuilding the manual transmission or the final drive of the automatic transmission transaxle.

The oil will drain faster if it is warm. Remove both the filler plug and the drain plug. Install the drain plug after drips have slowed to one every 20 seconds.

Refill with hypoid oil of the correct specification and viscosity. See **1. Lubricants.** If you attempt to put the oil in too rapidly, it may overflow and give the impression that the case is already full even though only a small amount has been put in. See **Table c** for the correct refilling quantity.

Table c. Hypoid Oil Refill Quantities

Final drive of automatic transmission transaxle	25 oz. (1.3 Imperial pints, 0.75 liters)
Manual transmission transaxle	2.6 pints (2.2 Imperial pints, 1.25 liters)

5.4 Checking Constant Velocity Joint Screws and Boots

The rubber boots over the constant velocity joints should not be cracked or torn. Instructions for removing the driveshafts and replacing the boots can be found in **MANUAL TRANSMISSION.**

The socket-head screws that hold the constant velocity joints to the flanges should be torqued to 4.5 mkg (32 ft. lb.).

5.5 Checking Steering Gearbox Boots

The rubber boots of the steering gearbox should not be cracked or torn. If dirt has entered the steering through a tear in a boot, the steering gearbox should be removed, disassembled, and cleaned before you install a new boot. See **SUSPENSION AND STEERING.**

5.6 Checking Ball Joint and Tie Rod Seals

The rubber seals on the suspension ball joints and the tie rod ends should be checked to make certain that none is torn or cracked. To replace seals, use the procedures given in **SUSPENSION AND STEERING.**

6. BODY AND INSIDE-VEHICLE MAINTENANCE OPERATIONS

There are only a few routine maintenance steps for the body and interior of your car, but they are important steps. Especially make sure that the driving controls are in good working order before you take the car on a road test following servicing.

6.1 Body Lubrication

Lubricate the door locks and the lock cylinders with lock lubricant. The body hinges, the hood latch, the auxiliary hood catch, and the door check straps should be lubricated with SAE 30 or SAE 40 engine oil or with polyethylene grease. Lubricate the door hinges with engine oil. Use polyethylene or multipurpose grease on the seat runners, the seat back pivots, and the trunk latch.

6.2 Oil Can Points

In addition to such things as the hood latches, already mentioned, you should check for other parts that require lubrication with an oil can. The clutch linkage and the carburetor linkage are two examples. However, under no circumstances should you ever apply oil to rubber parts. Squeaking suspension bushings and similar rubber components should be lubricated with brake fluid or glycerine.

6.3 Seat Belt Inspection

The seat belts should be kept clean. If cleaning is necessary, wash the belts with a mild soap solution without removing them from the car. Do not bleach or dye the seat belts or use any other cleaning agents. They may weaken the webbing.

Carefully check the condition of the webbing while you are cleaning the belts or the interior of the car. Frayed or damaged belts should be replaced. Also check that the belts operate properly and are correctly installed.

6.4 Checking Controls

During inside-vehicle maintenance, be sure to check the headlight switch positions, to see whether all tail lights, headlights, parking lights, instrument panel lights, and interior lights are in proper working order. Check the headlight high beams and low beams, the turn signals and, where applicable, the back-up lights.

Depress the foot brake pedal, making sure that there is good pedal height. If not, adjust the brakes as described in **BRAKES AND WHEELS**. Also check the operation of the parking brake. Turn the steering wheel from side to side with the car stationary. There should be no play. If there is excessive play, check the steering linkage for worn tie rod ends, worn suspension parts, or a worn or misadjusted steering gearbox. See **SUSPENSION AND STEERING**.

On cars with automatic transmissions, check the automatic transmission kickdown operation during a road test. If the kickdown fails to operate, or if the kickdown produces a forced downshift before the accelerator pedal reaches its full-throttle position, adjust the accelerator pedal and cable as described in **FUEL AND EXHAUST SYSTEMS**.

6.5 Body Preventive Maintenance

Clean debris from the body drain holes, including any holes in the bottoms of the doors. Make sure that the seat back latches hold the seat backs securely. If necessary, lubricate the latches with polyethylene or multipurpose grease.

Door weatherstrips should be lubricated with silicone spray or with talcum powder. If any weatherstrip is loose, clean away the old cement. Then reglue the weatherstrip with trim cement (available from automotive supply stores).

7. BASIC CAR CARE

The following brief guide will help you keep your car looking as good as it runs.

7.1 Care of Car Finish

The longer dirt is left on the paint, the greater the risk of damaging the glossy finish, either by scratching or simply by the chemical effect dirt particles have on the painted surface.

Washing

Never wash the car in direct sunlight. Beads of water not only leave spots when dried rapidly by the sun's heat, but act as tiny magnifying glasses that burn spots into the finish. Use plenty of water, a car-wash soap, and a soft sponge.

Begin by spraying water over the dry car to remove all loose dirt. Then apply lukewarm soapy water. Rinse the car after sponging off the soapy water, using plenty of clear water under as little pressure as possible. Wipe the car dry with a chamois or soft terrycloth towel to prevent water-spotting.

Waxing

For a long-lasting, protective, and glossy wax finsih, apply a hard wax, such as Classic Car Wax, after the car has been washed and dried. Waxing is not needed after every washing, and a more effortless shine can be obtained by using a car-wash liquid containing wax. You can tell when waxing is required by looking at the finish while it is wet. If the water coats the paint in smooth sheets instead of forming beads that roll off, waxing is in order.

9 ■

Polishing

Use paint polish only if the finish assumes a dull look after long service. You can use polish on the car's brightwork to remove tar spots and tarnish, but afterwards apply a coat of wax to protect the clean plating.

Washing Chassis

The best time to wash the underside of the car is just after it has been driven in the rain. Spray the chassis with a powerful jet of water to remove dirt and deicing salt that may have accumulated there.

Special Cleaning

Tar spots can be removed with tar remover. Never use gasoline, kerosene, nail polish remover, or other unsuitable solvents. Insect spots also respond to tar remover. A bit of baking soda dissolved in the wash water will facilitate their removal. This method can also be used to remove spotting from tree sap.

The windshield wiper blades can be removed periodically and scrubbed with a hard bristle brush and alcohol or a strong detergent solution to remove debris. The windows themselves can be cleaned with a sponge and warm water, then dried with a chamois or soft towel. If you use commercial window washing preparations, make certain they are not damaging to automotive finishes.

7.2 Care of Interior

Clean the carpet with a vacuum cleaner or whisk broom. Dirt spots can usually be removed with lukewarm soapy water. Use spot remover for grease and oil spots. Do not pour the liquid directly on the carpet, but dampen a clean cloth and rub carefully, starting at the edge of the spot and working inward. Do not use gasoline, naptha, or other flammable substances to clean the carpeting.

Leatherette Upholstery and Trim

Use a dry foam cleaner. Grease or paint spots can be removed by wiping with a cloth soaked with this cleaner. Use the same cleaner, applied with a soft cloth or brush, on the headliner and side trim panels. For cloth covered seat areas, use the techniques described previously for cleaning the carpeting.

7.3 Tires and Accessories

Never use tar remover, gasoline, or any other petroleum-based substance for cleaning tires. These liquids damage rubber. Whitewall tires can be cleaned with tire sidewall cleaner. Rubber paints, commonly sold as tire dressing, are largely cosmetic.

Accessories

Most chrome-plated accessories can be polished and waxed along with the rest of the car's bright trim. The radio antenna should be lubricated only if hardened grease and collected dirt are interfering with raising or lowering the antenna. Do not use abrasive polish or cleaners on aluminum trim or accessories. They will destroy the mirror-like shine of anodized surfaces.